DATE DUE

JUN 9 1992		
SEP 8 1992		
MAY 3 1 1995		
JUL 2 6 1995		
SEP 1 1 1995		
MAR 8 0 1997		
FEB 1 7 1998		

DEMCO 38-297

FUNDAMENTALS OF
LEARNING
AND
MEMORY

Fourth Edition

FUNDAMENTALS OF

LEARNING

AND

MEMORY

Fourth Edition

JOHN P. HOUSTON

University of California, Los Angeles

HBJ

Harcourt Brace Jovanovich, Publishers

San Diego   New York   Chicago   Austin   Washington, D.C.

London   Sydney   Tokyo   Toronto

23191418

1-92

PREFACE

The success of the first three editions of *Fundamentals of Learning and Memory* has directly led to this edition. Each of the previous editions contained up-to-date information about learning and memory, using both animal and human data as the basis for analysis. This edition will be even more effective in presenting, clearly and concisely, the major issues and controversies that compose the field of learning and memory.

1. *Organization.* The basic organization of the book, which is built around the concepts of acquisition, transfer, and retention, has not changed. Because users of the third edition were pleased with the tight flow of the organization, I did not make any major changes in the structure of the text. I have, however, provided a number of boxes that cover particularly exciting current developments within the field. These boxes provide in-depth coverage of interesting topics selected from the book that serve to illuminate the issues under consideration and to make the concepts easier to grasp.

2. *Length.* Based on reviewers' comments, I have tried to keep the length of the fourth edition about the same as the third. I have tried to move the entire edition forward—tightening the coverage of some less important topics, eliminating information of little value, and incorporating issues that have gained in importance since the appearance of the last edition. If anything, the breadth of the text has been expanded through concise selection and elaboration of the crucial issues in learning and memory.

3. *References.* As was true of the earlier editions, the references in the fourth edition of *Fundamentals of Learning and Memory* have been completely updated. Older, less-crucial sources have been deleted and new references added, including several hundred that postdate the third edition. These changes give the book a fresh feel and ensure that it will continue to be one of the most up-to-date textbooks in the field of learning and memory.

4. *Emphasis on Human and Animal Learning.* This book continues to be written for those who believe a course in learning should attempt to identify the principles of learning and memory, regardless of the species under study. Thus data from both human and animal research have been included.

5. *Writing Style.* In each edition of *Fundamentals*, I have attempted to create a book that is not only stimulating and engaging but easy to read and comprehend. Part of the success of this attempt stems from my effort to deal with issues rather than simply listing an endless series of empirical facts. While this edition, like the earlier ones, is geared to upper-division students, lower-division and graduate students should also find it helpful.

6. *Ancillaries.* An Instructor's Manual, written by Alvin Y. Wang, accompanies the fourth edition. Each chapter has a detailed outline and an extensive overview. The manual also features helpful learning objectives and teaching tips, additional resource materials, and essay and multiple-choice test questions for each chapter.

7. *Acknowledgments.* Many people have provided me with invaluable assistance in completing this edition. In particular, I would like to thank the following reviewers for their suggestions and guidance: Kevin Joseph Kennelly, University of North Texas; Terry Libkuman, Central Michigan University; Elizabeth Pemberton, University of Iowa; and Alvin Y. Wang, University of Central Florida.

I would also like to thank the capable staff at Harcourt Brace Jovanovich: Marcus Boggs, acquisitions editor; Cynthia Sheridan, associate editor; Cheryl Hauser, manuscript editor; Stephanie McCullough, production editor; Cathy Reynolds, designer; Karen DeLeo, art editor; and Diane Southworth, production manager.

CONTENTS

4

Biological Constraints on Learning   87

PART 2

ACQUISITION   121

5

The Roles of Contiguity and Rehearsal in Learning   125

11

Improving Memory through Organization, Elaboration, and Imagery   317

PART 5

SELECTED COGNITIVE PROCESSES   347

12

Concepts and Problems   351

13

Language   383

INTRODUCTION

This section introduces you to the language of the field of learning and to many of the basic conditions and variables that psychologists in the field consider. In addition, it examines differences among the many ways of learning, or learning tasks. Finally, it discusses the constraints that natural selection places on learning processes.

Chapter 1 brings the field of learning into focus in two ways. The first way is to define learning. Although such a definition is helpful, it is probably impossible to encompass all that is meant by *learning* in a single sentence. Accordingly, the second attempt to circumscribe the field of learning involves briefly looking at a number of the different learning tasks employed and investigated by psychologists. These tasks range from basic conditioning paradigms to more complex verbal processes, including problem solving, concept formation, and language.

Chapter 2 examines *classical* and *instrumental conditioning* in detail. These two types of learning tasks have been extremely important and influential in all aspects of the field of learning. The wide variety of learning tasks outlined in Chapter 1 and the selected tasks dealt with in greater detail in Chapter 2 lead to an important question in Chapter 3: Do these various tasks represent fundamentally different learning processes, or are they merely different expressions of some common, underlying learning process? On the one hand, if these tasks do represent fundamentally different types of learning, we will be forced to develop theories and models that encompass each of the distinct learning processes. On the other hand, if some common process accounts for all of these tasks, a single model should suffice. Chapter 3 examines representative learning tasks in relation to one another. Both the similarities and differences among them are considered in detail, leading to the conclusion that we cannot affirm with any certainty that these tasks represent fundamentally different learning processes. The similarities among the tasks are strong enough to suggest that some unitary process may account for them all.

Recent research has suggested that not all species are ready to learn all responses equally easily. Certain species seem *prepared* to learn certain responses but not others. In Chapter 4 we examine the biological constraints on learning and deal with the fact that each animal brings to every learning situation certain capabilities and predispositions to act and learn in certain ways. These predispositions may be formed by the pressures of natural selection.

CHAPTER

1

WHAT IS LEARNING?
A DEFINITION AND
SOME EXAMPLES

A DEFINITION OF LEARNING

What do we mean by the word *learning*? It is a commonly used word, and as a student you are involved with the learning process. But how would you define it? Stop for a moment and try to frame a definition.

As you probably found, this task is not easy. Psychologists have the same problem. They, too, are unsure how to define it. *Learning* is one of those words people use and seem to understand but are hard pressed to define. As a result many different definitions are currently used in the field of psychology. Some are very specific and concrete; others are diffuse and general. Here is one good one.

Gregory Kimble (1967) has developed a definition of learning that seems to encompass many of the elements of other definitions. Essentially the same definition has been proposed by others (for instance, Logan, 1970). Hence, it makes a good example. According to Kimble's definition, *learning is a relatively permanent change in behavior potentiality that occurs as a result of reinforced practice*. Let us look at some of the terms in this definition. Why does Kimble include the term *permanent* in his definition? What kinds of behavior change would he like to exclude by using *permanent*? Among others, he might want to exclude temporary changes in behavior resulting from shifts in motivation. When we are tired, for example, we sleep. The shift from the waking state to the sleeping state represents an enormous change in our behavior. But it does not represent new learning. It can be argued that changes in behavior resulting from fatigue should not be considered learned changes. Many other motivational factors, such as hunger, thirst, and sex drive, can affect, or change, our behavior without involving new learning. If we are hungry, for example, and a steak, a knife, and a fork are placed in front of us, we will probably eat the steak using the utensils. Our behavior changes. But does the change from not eating to eating represent new learning? Probably not. We utilize old, established habits (that is, the fundamentals of using a knife and fork), but we are not learning anything new. When we have finished eating and our hunger is reduced, we will revert to our former mode of behavior (not eating). Hence, *temporary* changes in behavior, resulting from fluctuations in motivational states, tend to be excluded from the category of learned changes.

What about the term *practice*? Why does Kimble include it in his definition? He seems to be arguing that only changes occurring as a result of practice are learned changes and that unpracticed changes can occur, which we would not want to call learned changes. Among these are, for example, the effects of aging or maturation. An enormous range of unlearned changes can be attributed to aging. As we grow older, for instance, our short-term memory may deteriorate. That is, we may have increasing difficulty remembering new material for short periods of time. That is a big change. But such a change does not represent learning. We did not *learn* to be more forgetful. In addition, various physiological factors can produce unpracticed changes in behavior that are not considered learned changes. For example, disease and accidents can yield strong, permanent, unlearned changes in our behavior.

Why does Kimble consider learning to involve changes in "behavior potentiality" rather than in behavior? Why complicate the situation? An example may clear up the issue. At this moment, residing within you, somewhere, somehow, is the knowledge, or the learning, necessary to brush your teeth. But you are not brushing your teeth at this moment. We can say the capacity to brush is latent. It is in there somewhere, but it is not being expressed as overt behavior at this moment.

We have acquired the capacity to brush, but that capacity is not always apparent, or expressed overtly.

Psychologists distinguish between *learning* and *performance*. *Performance* refers to *the translation of learning into behavior, usually through the involvement of motivation*. For example, if your mouth felt very unpleasant, you would probably drop what you were doing and brush your teeth. You would be *motivated* to brush, and it would be the thrust of this motivation that would impel you to brush, or to translate the brushing potentiality into observable, overt behavior. Learning is "invisible." It lies within us as a potentiality and can only be observed when it interacts with motivation and is translated into, or expressed as, overt behavior.

The distinction between learning and performance is crucial, and we will return to it many times in future sections. Performance cannot always be taken as a measure of how much learning has occurred. For example, if one child spells every word in a spelling test correctly and another child spells none correctly, we cannot conclude that the first child has learned more than the second. The second child may *know* all the words, but for any number of reasons she may refuse to reveal her learning. When we try to infer how much learning has occurred by looking at performance, we must be aware of the fact that motivation as well as learning determines performance.

Finally, consider the term *reinforced practice*, which Kimble includes in his definition. The concept of reinforcement is extremely complicated. For the moment, think of reinforcement as reward. According to Kimble's definition, an animal will not learn to do something unless the action leads to, or is followed by, a reward. Children will not learn to pick up their toys unless the behavior is followed by a reward. The reward may come in the form of parental praise and approval, or it may be something the children like or enjoy, such as candy or a trip to the zoo. The avoidance of punishment may also be rewarding. Children may even be able to reward themselves by congratulating themselves.

The question whether reinforcement is *necessary* for learning to occur is very controversial and has been so for many years. Many psychologists feel that reinforcement is essential, whereas others maintain with equal conviction that it is not. Whether rewards will *facilitate* performance does not seem to be the question. If a child tells a joke and adults laugh, they may end up hearing that same joke to the point of tedium. Most psychologists would argue that reinforcements help to strengthen behaviors in one way or another. But some of them would add that reinforcement is not *absolutely essential* for learning to occur. They feel that learning can occur in the absence of reinforcement. For example, as we drive down the highway, caught up in our latest set of concerns, we pay very little attention to the passing scenery. Yet at the end of our journey, if someone asks what we saw along the road, we may well be able to remember many events and objects. Where or what was the reinforcement for this incidental learning?

Examine the issue a little more closely. Consider the possibility of a situation in which everyone would agree that learning occurs but that involves no reward. Does our ability to remember the name of a stranger we met only briefly at a crowded party constitute learning without reward? Some argue that we have rewarded ourselves in this case. We might pride ourselves on being able to remember names. Remember that rewards do not have to be food pellets or trips to Bermuda. They can be very subtle and covert. What about the incidental highway learning just described? Is that learning without reinforcement? Some have contended that the very acts of perceiving and processing information are reinforcing. Many studies seem to suggest that we *will* learn responses that are rewarded by the opportunity to process information. For example, monkeys will learn to open little windows for nothing more than the opportunity for visual exploration (Butler, 1953). Thus go argument and counterargument, and we begin to see the dilemma. Each time a new, reward-free learning situation is proposed, the reinforcement theorist is able to find some possible reinforcing event in it. For example, Harlow, Harlow, and Meyer (1950) have proposed that the mere manipulation of objects is rewarding, and Hill (1965) has argued that any kind of activity can be rewarding. The final step in the argument seems to come when it is proposed that the act of learning rewards itself. If we accept this, then it becomes impossible to conceive of a situation that involves learning without reward. Hence, the issue, as interesting as it is, must be laid aside. We shall return to the concept of reinforcement many times, for even though it may not be fully understood, it is one of the most powerful variables in any learning situation.

So much for Kimble's definition of learning. Psychologists have many different ideas about what would be an adequate definition. Kimble's definition merely represents one viewpoint. For example, Staddon and Ettinger (1989) define learning as "a specific and relatively permanent change in an animal's potential produced by the environment" (p. 151). Hall (1989), on the other hand, defines it as a "neurological process that arises from experience and is inferred from changes in the organism's behavior" (p. 14). And finally, Crider, Goethals, Kavanaugh, and Solomon (1989) characterize learning as "a relatively permanent change in immediate or potential behavior that results from experience" (p. 209). As you can see, each of these alternative definitions has something in common with Kimble's definition, and yet each has its own emphasis and flavor as well. For our purposes Kimble's definition is the most useful and complete one available.

EXAMPLES OF LEARNING TASKS

Another way to bring the field of learning into focus is to describe some of the learning tasks psychologists have used and studied in the laboratory. Obviously, there are many different learning situations. We can learn to stay out of trouble, we can learn to throw a ball, we can learn to be a lawyer at night school, and we can learn the birds native to the western United States. These different learning situations may or may not represent fundamentally different types of learning. They may or may not require different theories to account for them. No one is quite sure how many truly different ways we can learn things. As you read about the different learning tasks described in what follows, keep in mind that, although they may seem quite distinct, they do not necessarily represent different underlying learning processes.

Because we sometimes use the term *learning* and sometimes *conditioning*, it is necessary to distinguish between these two labels. On the one hand, *conditioning* generally refers to classical conditioning and instrumental conditioning, which are discussed below. *Learning*, on the other hand, is a much broader term. It usually refers to conditioning and also to more complex situations. In other words, all conditioning situations are forms of learning, but some learning tasks involve more than conditioning.

Figure 1.1 Pavlov posed with his assistants and one of the dogs from his classical conditioning experiments.

Classical Conditioning

Many people have heard of Pavlov's experiments in which dogs were conditioned to salivate at the sound of a tone. These experiments represent something called *classical conditioning*. Although trained as a physiologist, Pavlov has had a tremendous impact on the field of psychology with his classical conditioning studies (see Figure 1.1). The experimental paradigm was as follows. Before the conditioning experiment (Anrep, 1920) the dog's salivary duct was surgically treated so that saliva flowed through a small opening to outside the dog's cheek, where it could be collected and measured accurately. The dog was then trained to stand in a harness, as depicted in Figure 1.2a. A tuning fork was sounded. Several seconds later a small amount of dry meat powder was moved close to the dog's mouth, and the dog was allowed to eat it. On the first trial (or pairing of the sound with the meat powder) the sound stimulated no salivation, but the food did. The procedure was to continue pairing the sound and the meat powder over a series of trials. After a number of pairings the tuning fork was sounded alone. No meat powder was presented afterward. It was found that the sound alone elicited a salivary response. The salivary response had become conditioned to the sound of the tuning fork.

As we shall see, many different responses can be classically conditioned (see, for example, Figure 1.2b). But the Pavlovian situation allows us to identify the basic elements of all classical conditioning situations. (Incidentally, classical conditioning is sometimes referred to as *Pavlovian conditioning* and sometimes as *respondent conditioning*; these labels can be used interchangeably.)

THE UNCONDITIONED STIMULUS.   The unconditioned stimulus (UCS) in the Pavlovian situation is the meat powder. It is a stimulus that, before the conditioning experiment, consistently and regularly elicits a response. *Every time* we present

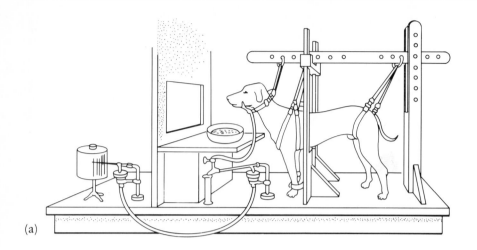

(a)

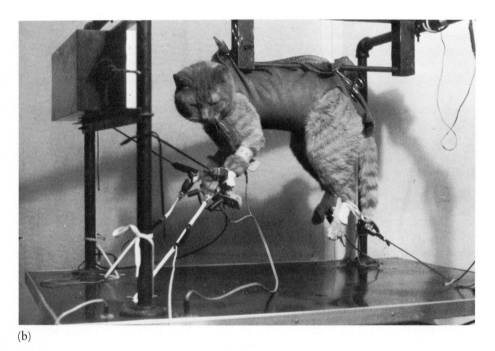

(b)

Figure 1.2 Two classical conditioning situations. (a) Pavlov's salivary conditioning apparatus. (b) A modern conditioning situation. After repeated pairings of a tone and light shock to the forepaw, the tone alone will begin to elicit forepaw withdrawal. [(a) Adapted from Yerkes, R. M., and Morgulis, S. The method of Pavlov in animal psychology. *Psychology Bulletin*, 1909, 6, 257–73. Fig. 2, p. 264. Copyright 1909 by the American Psychological Association. (b) From Wickens, C., Tuber, D. S., and Wickens, D. D. Memory for the conditioned response: The proactive effect of preexposure to potential conditioning stimuli and context change. *Journal of Experimental Psychology: General*, 1983, 112, 41–57. Fig. 1, p. 43. Copyright 1983 by the American Psychological Association. Reprinted by permission. (Photo courtesy of Delos Wickens.)]

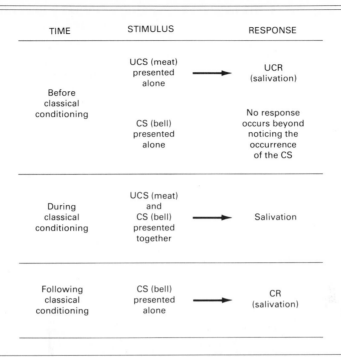

TIME	STIMULUS	RESPONSE
Before classical conditioning	UCS (meat) presented alone →	UCR (salivation)
	CS (bell) presented alone	No response occurs beyond noticing the occurrence of the CS
During classical conditioning	UCS (meat) and CS (bell) presented together →	Salivation
Following classical conditioning	CS (bell) presented alone →	CR (salivation)

Figure 1.3 The stages of classical conditioning. A UCS will elicit a UCR before conditioning, whereas a CS will not elicit a response. During conditioning the CS and UCS are presented together, and the CS acquires the capacity to elicit a CR that is similar to the UCR.

the meat powder, the dog salivates. The capacity of the UCS to elicit a regular response can be innate or learned. It does not matter, so long as it elicits a response consistently before the conditioning experiment begins.

THE UNCONDITIONED RESPONSE.   The unconditioned response (UCR) is the consistent response to the UCS. In the Pavlovian situation the salivation in response to the meat powder is the UCR.

THE CONDITIONED STIMULUS.   The conditioned stimulus (CS) is the sound of the tuning fork. The CS is a stimulus that does not initially elicit salivation. We pair the CS (sound) with the UCS (meat powder) over and over. With repeated pairings the CS will begin to elicit a salivary response when it is presented by itself.

THE CONDITIONED RESPONSE.   The conditioned response (CR) is the learned response elicited by the CS. That is, if we sound the tuning fork alone and the dog salivates, then that salivary response is called the CR. If the dog salivates to the UCS alone, that response is a UCR, not a CR. Students often ask if the CR and the UCR are the same thing. Saliva is saliva. A good point; but, strange as it may sound, the CR and the UCR may well differ in important ways. This problem will be considered later in more detail. Figure 1.3 shows the steps involved in classical conditioning.

CLASSICAL CONDITIONING IN EVERYDAY LIFE.   Classical conditioning occurs every day. You may have had an experience such as this: You meet someone you think is very attractive. You approach, saying, "Why don't you stay awhile? Watch TV or something?" Very gentle. Very casual. The person gives you a flat, irritable look and says, "What in the world for?" You are humiliated, angry, and hurt, but you manage to live through it. A couple of days later one of your friends happens to mention the person in passing. You immediately feel a warm flush crawling up the back of your neck. That cringing is probably a CR. Many of our emotional reactions are probably classically conditioned. If we consistently experience strong emotions, either positive or negative, in a given situation, then anything that reminds us of the situation in the future may well trigger a conditioned emotional reaction. We cannot avoid it. It seems to be automatic.

Suppose your instructor should march into class one day, raise a pistol loaded with blanks above his head, shoot "Boo!" and fire. The next day all your instructor need do is walk in, raise the pistol, and yell "Boo!" *without* firing. Almost everyone will experience a good CR.

Instrumental Conditioning

Imagine this situation: You are in a large, white, empty room. You do not know how you got there, but you do know you are very hungry. Extremely hungry. There is a metal bar protruding from one of the walls of the room, and there is a little hole in the wall near the bar. There is a ventilation grate in the ceiling but no windows and no doors. What would you do in this situation? You might explore, try to escape, sit down and cry, pound the walls, pace back and forth, or call for help. You might also investigate the metal bar and the small hole. Let's say that at some point in your explorations you press the bar with your hand. As you do so, it makes a clicking sound and you jump back, startled. As the click sounds, a small cracker rolls out of the hole beneath the bar. You eat the cracker. As you are still hungry, you give it another try and eat the resulting food. You have discovered that pressing the bar and the delivery of food are related. You settle down, press the bar, and eat until your hunger is satisfied.

The situation just described, in which the probability of a particular response (the bar press) has been increased through the immediate delivery of a reinforcer (the food), is *instrumental conditioning*. (It is also called *operant conditioning*.) The response was instrumental in obtaining something wanted and needed.

B. F. Skinner, a former Harvard professor and author, has contributed heavily to the importance of instrumental conditioning in the field of learning. His work with rats and pigeons and his development of the famous Skinner box (see Figure 1.4) form the basis for much of what we presently know about instrumental conditioning. In its simplest form a Skinner box contains a lever and a food tray. The apparatus is set up so that, each time the lever is pressed, a small piece of food will be delivered to the tray. A hungry rat placed in this box will explore, discover the bar, and eventually learn to press the bar regularly in order to obtain the food. Figure 1.5 shows a more elaborate Skinner box of the type used in modern laboratory research.

Although this learning situation appears very simple, many psychologists feel that we can learn a great deal about human behavior by observing rats and other animals in this sort of apparatus. Psychologists choose rats as subjects because, in

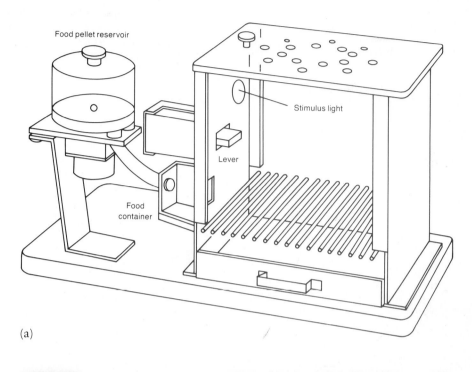

(a)

(b)

Figure 1.4 Examples of Skinner boxes: (a) drawing of uninhabited box and (b) photo of inhabited box.

Operant Conditioning Demonstration Units

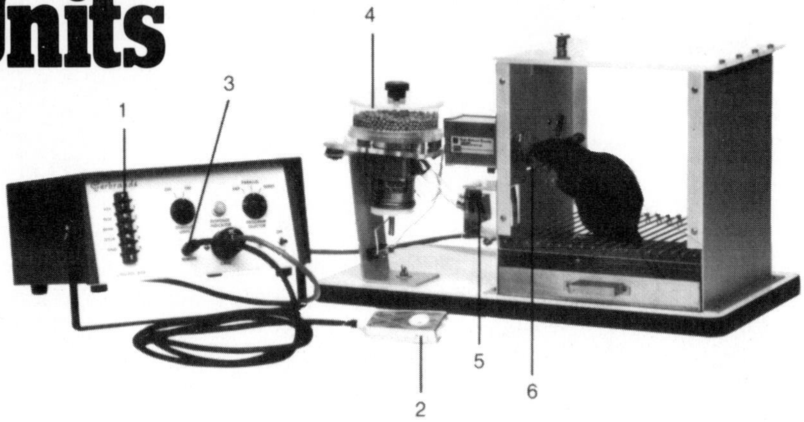

Gerbrands Operant Conditioning Demonstration Units and accessories offer the professional and student researcher a reliable, convenient, and economical means of demonstrating and studying the effects of the schedules of reinforcement. Feeders, cages, and other components are the same Gerbrands high quality instruments furnished separately to research laboratories throughout the world. These quality features will insure years of reliable, trouble-free service:

1. Solid state control unit with combination handle/stand. Functional, easy-to-read front panel assures **ease of operation. Students can operate unit with a minimum of instruction.** D.C. output: 28 volts at 3 amps. Output connectors for recording or counting responses, reinforcements, and other events.
2. Experimenter's **remote hand-switch** provides complete control of all basic schedules of reinforcement.
3. Input connector permits **automatic programming** of all basic schedules of reinforcement.
4. **Low current**, fast acting pellet dispenser. Dipper feeder and pigeon feeder models also available.
5. **External pellet tray** with removable clear plexiglas cover. Animal eating and nosing behavior visible to entire class. Does not get fouled with animal feces.
6. **Quality stainless steel rat lever** mounted in a rigid casting. Maintains pellet force adjustment.

Five different models available.
Write for complete details.

GERBRANDS CORPORATION

8 Beck Road, Arlington, MA 02174 (617) 648-6415
Quality instrumentation since 1930.

Figure 1.5 Skinner boxes become big business. (Used by permission of Gerbrands Corporation, Arlington, MA.)

addition to being small, inexpensive, curious, and ready to learn, they are often handled in ways that would be inappropriate for other subjects, such as human undergraduates. Nevertheless, researchers using animals are required to conform to strict standards of health, comfort, space, and feeding. At present, animal experimentation is extremely controversial. Many people feel that research involving pain should not be done at all. Others feel differently. We must each evaluate for ourselves the risk-benefit ratio involved in animal research (Cohen, 1986; Miller, 1986).

Instrumental conditioning must be one of the most common forms of learning we encounter in our everyday life. Children learn to play games because those activities are rewarding. Our pets learn to respond to our calls because of rewards. Students learn course materials for grades, recognition, and advancement. Adults learn the requirements of their jobs for pay, promotions, and the pleasure of doing their work. In fact, people who have been in a coma for 6 months can learn to move their head, eyes, or fingers when rewarded with their favorite music (Boyle & Greer, 1983).

There is no end to the instances of instrumental conditioning in our life, and yet there remains considerable confusion over the relationships among instrumental conditioning and the other forms of learning that we shall consider. In Chapter 3 we shall discuss important differences and similarities among a number of learning tasks.

Discrimination Learning

Another learning task that psychologists use and study is called *discrimination learning*. This task can be illustrated by placing a hungry pigeon in a Skinner box with two illuminated disks—a blue one on the right and a yellow one on the left—attached to the wall of the box. It is characteristic of hungry pigeons to engage in a good deal of pecking behavior. They peck the walls, the floor, and the disks. The experimenter sets up the situation so that, each time the pigeon pecks the blue disk, it is rewarded with a kernel of corn. Each time it pecks the yellow disk, it receives no reward. The blue disk is called the *positive stimulus*, and the yellow, the *negative stimulus*. At first the pigeon pecks the two disks about equally. But as time goes on, it responds more and more often to the blue disk, the one that yields food. The pigeon discriminates between the colors. Or does it? Can we conclude on the basis of the situation described that the animal has learned a blue-yellow discrimination? No we cannot, for it may have been learning a position discrimination. That is, it may have been ignoring the colors and attending to the positions of the positive and negative stimuli. If it pecks the one on the right, it is rewarded. If it pecks the left disk, nothing happens. We cannot be sure whether the animal is discriminating color or position. How can we avoid this confusion and ensure that the pigeon is learning a color discrimination? One way is to switch the positions of the colors on successive trials. Put the blue one on the left part of the time, and put it on the right part of the time. Then the animal will be forced to utilize the color cues.

Figure 1.6 depicts a Lashley jumping stand, which is another piece of apparatus used in discrimination learning. The rat must learn how to gain access to the food table behind the stimuli and how to avoid falling into the net. If it leaps against the incorrect, or negative, stimulus, it bumps its nose and falls. If it jumps against the correct, or positive, stimulus, the card tips over easily, allowing the animal to reach the table.

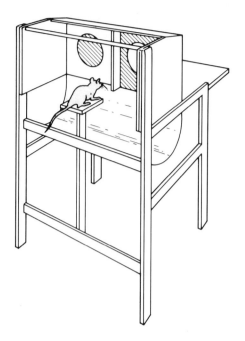

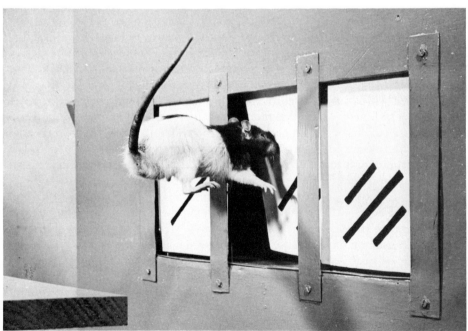

Figure 1.6 The Lashley jumping stand. If the animal leaps against the positive stimulus, the card falls over easily, enabling the animal to reach the safety of the table. If the animal jumps against the negative card, it bumps its nose and falls to the net below.

It is reasonable to ask if discrimination learning is not just another kind of instrumental conditioning. Often it is, but it is a special kind of conditioning in which the *emphasis* is on the formation of a discrimination between two extremely salient cues. All conditioning involves discrimination learning. For example, a rat in a Skinner box must discriminate the bar from the rest of the box. It must learn that pressing the wall or its own foot will not do any good. It is just that in discrimination learning the *focus* of the study is on the discrimination process.

The discrimination-learning paradigm has definite counterparts in the real world. Discrimination learning is an essential part of everyday life. Imagine for a moment that you have lost the ability to discriminate. What would life be like if you could not discriminate? Most likely, it would be short. If you failed to discriminate red circles from green circles, you would find it difficult to drive an automobile in the city. If you failed to discriminate female bodies from male bodies, all sorts of peculiar things might happen to you. If you suddenly lost the ability to discriminate, you would respond the same way to widely varying and sometimes inappropriate stimuli. We all learn to restrict our responses to stimuli that will yield rewards and to inhibit our responses to stimuli that yield no reward or, worse yet, yield punishment.

Finally, it should be pointed out that discrimination learning is involved in classical as well as instrumental situations. For example, if a dog is given two potential CSs (two tones) but only one of them is followed by a UCS, the dog must discriminate between the two before the appropriate CS–CR connection will be established.

Serial Learning

In a typical human *serial learning* situation the subject is brought into the laboratory and is seated in front of a microcomputer monitor. Before the experiment begins, the subject is told that a word or some other type of verbal material will appear on the screen. A few seconds later this word will disappear, and a second word will take its place. This pattern will be repeated until the subject has seen the entire list of, say, 15 words. The subject's task is to remember these words and to remember the order in which they occur. After the subject has seen the list once all the way through, he or she is signaled that the list has ended and that the computer is about to present the words again in exactly the same order. The subject's task is to anticipate which word will next appear on the screen. Each time a word appears, the subject tries to recall and say aloud the word that will next appear. This is called serial anticipation learning.

Serial, or sequential, learning, in which items are learned in a specific order, seems to be an integral part of our everyday life. Some examples include the memorization of phone numbers, the alphabet, poetry, and historical information. Language behavior, in general, possesses a strong sequential component. The hope is that our simple serial task will help us understand these more complicated serial behaviors. The serial learning task allows us to control, in a strict sense, any number of variables that we suspect might be important in determining serial learning.

It should be pointed out that serial, or sequential, learning is not limited to verbal tasks or to humans. For instance, animals such as rats are engaging in a form of serial learning when they learn to run through a maze. Their everyday life is also probably full of serial learning tasks (for example, finding their way along rafters and through walls). One popular way to study sequential animal learning is to use the *serial-pattern* design (Self & Gaffan, 1983). Rats run down an alley for food pellets. On successive runs the number of pellets might be 14, 7, 3, 1, 0. Through repeated exposure to this specific pattern of rewards the rats eventually learn to run faster when big rewards are upcoming and slower when smaller rewards await them. We will consider exactly what it is that the rats learn in Chapter 10. For now it is enough to realize that some kind of serial learning is occurring.

Paired-Associate Learning

Paired-associate (PA) learning is another of the many types of tasks available to the learning psychologist. In this task subjects must learn to associate, or pair, two items. In a typical human experiment the subjects will again be seated in front of a monitor. A stimulus item (for example, a word or nonsense syllable) will appear on the left of the screen for a couple of seconds. Then on the right a response item will appear. These two words will be paired throughout the experiment. Then the screen will be cleared, and a second pair composed of two different words will be displayed, first the stimulus word on the left and then the response word on the right. The subjects' task is to recall and say aloud the correct response word each time they see a stimulus word. Typically they have about 2 seconds to try to recall each response word before it is displayed by the computer. Lists vary in length, and an average one contains 8 or 10 pairs. Table 1.1 contains a typical paired-associate list. The subjects are usually asked to respond to the list until they have mastered it completely (that is, until they can recall correctly each response item given the stimulus items). Sometimes, depending on the experimenter's purpose, all subjects are given a set number of trials rather than asked to master the list completely.

The pairs in a PA list are almost always rearranged from trial to trial, for a very simple reason. If the order of the items were kept constant, the subject could learn the responses in a serial fashion and totally ignore the stimulus components. The experimenter would not know whether the subject was learning a serial list composed of the response units or a PA list composed of both stimulus and response units.

Our life is filled with learning situations that have something in common with PA learning. Associating names with faces, telephone numbers with people, and Spanish words with English equivalents all seem to approximate PA learning. The entire process of giving verbal meaning to the world through labeling seems to be related to the laboratory paradigm. And animals, too, must learn to associate specific responses with specific stimuli.

Free Recall

Another interesting task has been used for many years. In a *free recall* task subjects are given a list of verbal items and are then asked to recall the items in any order. Since the subjects are free to recall the items in any order, this task enables us to learn about what they do with, or how they organize, the materials that they are trying to learn. From a long list of randomly presented nouns, for example, a subject might first recall all the nouns that had something to do with people, then move on to all the nouns that had something to do with animals, and so on. The subjects cluster responses according to categories. It seems that recalling the nouns by category makes the job easier. Not surprisingly, this method suggests that some complicated organizational processes are going on inside the subjects. The mate-

Table 1.1   A Typical Paired-Associate List Involving Syllables as Stimuli and Words as Responses

STIMULI		RESPONSES
TUM	⟶	SINCERE
JAK	⟶	POTENT
BAV	⟶	FURTHER
GOG	⟶	BASHFUL
WIF	⟶	MIGRANT
DEX	⟶	IMMENSE
LOH	⟶	ACUTE
PEC	⟶	GALLANT

rials are not spit out in the same order in which they were fed. The subjects actively process the materials, seeking ways to make the task easier.

If someone asks us to recall all our known blood relatives, we may search through some hierarchical scheme. We might start with our maternal grandparents and trace down through the generations. Or we might try to recall all cousins first, then uncles, and so on. But we would probably not recall the materials randomly; we would utilize some scheme, structure, or outline to make the search and retrieval processes easier and more efficient. Free recall is one of the tasks that enables us to peek into these enormously complicated and individualized organizational activities.

Lexical Priming

A great deal of attention has been given recently to the study of lexical memory. A lexicon is an ordered set of words (such as a dictionary). Thus, roughly speaking, your lexicon is your vocabulary. When psychologists study lexical memory, they are interested in how we store, organize, and utilize the words in our vocabulary. One of the techniques widely used to study lexical memory is called *priming in lexical decisions* (Gardiner, 1988; Mitchell & Brown, 1988; Ratcliff & McKoon, 1988). The basic procedure is this: Subjects are shown, for a split second, an item such as *canary* and asked to make a rapid decision about it, such as whether it is a word or what the word is. But *before* they are shown *canary*, they are shown a "prime," or a "probe." This prime can be related to *canary* (such as *bird*), or it can be unrelated to *canary* (such as *tar*). It has been found repeatedly that decisions about the target *canary* are made faster and more accurately if the prime is closely related to the target. It is as though the prime activates or sensitizes the target such that it is more readily processed. As we shall see in later chapters, priming in lexical-decision situations is currently one of the most basic tools used to study the structure of our memory stores.

Priming differs from the tasks we have been discussing in an interesting and important way. Specifically, priming measures or reflects learning that occurred *before* the experiment began (that is, your learned vocabulary), whereas the other tasks usually involve new learning that occurs within the experimental session. More will be said about this distinction later.

Generation Effects

An enormous amount of attention has also been given to *generation effects* in the recent literature (Gardiner, 1988; Gardiner, Gregg, & Hampton, 1988; Hirshman & Bjork, 1988; Nairne, 1988; Nairne & Widner, 1988). Generation refers to the fact that items an individual generates will be better remembered than items that individual merely reads.

Generation tasks have taken several forms. For example, in one experiment a generate group might be asked to fill in the following blank: *Cold is the opposite of* _____, while subjects in a read group would merely be asked to read, *Cold is the opposite of hot.* The experimenters would then conclude that a generation effect was demonstrated if the generate subjects were able to remember hot better than the read group. Other generation tasks use rhyme. In this type of task the generate subjects might be asked to think of a word that rhymes with *glove* (e.g., *love*), while read subjects would be asked merely to read, *love* rhymes with *glove.* The data have shown that words generated by subjects are remembered more consistently than words merely presented to the individual. Similar tasks have produced similar results. At the present time the focus of attention is on why these effects occur at all. Currently, researchers have at least three hypotheses about the nature of generation effects (see Gardner, Griggs, & Hampton, 1989). We will return to a detailed analysis of these hypotheses and their attendant data in a later chapter.

Generation effects, although different in many other ways, are similar to priming effects in that they involve materials that the subject learned before the experiment began (e.g., that *glove* and *love* rhyme and that *hot* is the opposite of *cold*).

Concept Formation

A *concept* is a symbol that stands for a class of objects or events that have common properties (Houston, Hammen, Padilla, & Bee, 1989). Thus, *cow* is a concept because it stands for a large number of different objects, each of which possesses some characteristics in common with all the others. *Boat, towel,* and *ant* are concepts because they stand for large numbers of individual objects that, although differing in some ways, possess certain identifiable common characteristics. In fact, with a few exceptions all nouns are concepts, because nouns stand for large groups of objects or events that have something in common. Proper nouns are among the words that do not appear to be concepts, because they refer only to a single thing (for example, Mars, George Washington).

Although most words are concepts, not all concepts are words. Concepts can be nonverbal. For example, infants can possess a concept of *dog* or *adult* long before they have acquired any language at all. Similarly, animals, which are essentially nonverbal, can learn concepts too. In Chapter 12 we shall compare animal and human concept formation (see Blough, 1989; Roberts & Mazmanian, 1989).

Concepts are enormously important in our thinking. They can simplify our thought processes. For example, they free us from the task of having to label each and every new object or event we encounter. We can normally fit new objects and events into existing categories. When we see a new house, for example, we do not have to give that specific object its own unique name or label; we just think, "Oh, that's one more house."

Concepts are related to one another in complicated ways. For example, they can encompass one another. *Flower* is a concept. But flower is also an instance of the

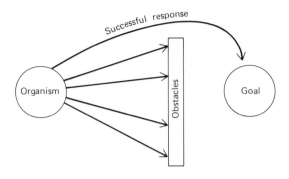

Figure 1.7 Problem solving. The problem is to overcome, or outflank, the obstacles by making the correct response.

concept *plant*, which, in turn, is an example of the concept *living thing*. And living thing is an instance of the concept *object*. In other words, concepts are related in complex ways that seem to help us think about and understand the world around us.

Because concepts are so important in thinking, psychologists have been interested in studying them. They have devised sophisticated experimental methods that help us understand how concepts are formed, or learned, and how they are used (Rosch, 1989). Psychologists, as we shall see in Chapter 12, have also developed a number of theories about how concept formation progresses. For now, it is sufficient to understand that concept formation is one of the important and complex forms of learning that will be explored in this text.

Problem Solving

Problems refer to situations in which the organism is motivated to reach some goal but is blocked from attaining it by some obstacle or obstacles (see Figure 1.7). Problems come in all shapes and sizes. Some are complex, long-term issues, such as the problem of trying to become an attorney; whereas others are short term and simple, such as the problem of trying to open the refrigerator door. The obstacles may be physical, social, or emotional; they may be real or imagined; they may be many or few.

Box 1.1 contains some sample problems, the answers to which are given on page 22. Give them a try. Once you have tried to solve these problems, you will be able to reflect on the complexity of the mental activities associated with their solution. One of the learning situations concerning us most in the real world (problem solving) is also one of the most complicated and difficult to study. Undoubtedly we would rather understand problem solving than paired-associate learning. Yet the PA task seems to receive more attention in the field of learning than does the more complicated, relevant problem-solving situation. It is as though psychologists hoped that an eventual understanding of the problem-solving situation would follow, or evolve, from a thorough understanding of more limited, simplified learning situations. As we shall learn, however, problem solving remains poorly understood.

Box 1.1 Sample Problems (Answers in Box 1.2)

1. By moving only two matches make four boxes out of these five boxes (using all matches in the solution).

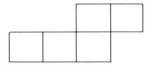

2. Complete this meaningful sequence.

    O T T F F S S __ N

3. You are on the way to the city and you meet a man at a fork in the road. You do not know which fork to take. You know that the man is one of two brothers who live in the area. One of these brothers always tells the truth, whereas the other never tells the truth. You don't know which one you are facing. You can ask him one question, which he can answer with a yes or no, which will assure you of taking the correct fork. What is that question?

4. Nine steel balls all look alike. Eight of the balls weigh the same amount, whereas one is heavier than the rest. You are given a pan balance and allowed two weighings of any combination or number of these balls to discover which one is the heavy one.

5. Without lifting your pencil from the paper, draw four straight lines through all nine points.

    •   •   •

    •   •   •

    •   •   •

6. What is the longest word you can think of that spells the same thing forward and backward?

7. What is the longest piece of *prose* you can think of that spells the same thing forward and backward? (By the way, these are called palindromes.)

8. Vacuum is an English word containing a double U sequence. Can you think of another one?

Syllables, Words, and Prose

Psychologists use a variety of materials in the human learning tasks that we have been discussing. Although words are often employed, they are not the only verbal unit utilized. As we have seen, nonsense syllables are often employed. Typically, a nonsense syllable is a three-letter sequence, such as ZXB or JAX, which is presumed to possess little meaning. (CCCs are consonant-consonant-consonant sequences, and CVCs are consonant-vowel-consonant sequences.) The idea behind their development was that, if we could utilize verbal units that were relatively free from preexperimentally established meaning, then we would be in a better position to study pure, new learning unencumbered by previously established habits. Unfortunately, nonsense syllables are never really devoid of meaning. For

Table 1.2   The Involvement of Learning in Psychology

AREA OF PSYCHOLOGY	SAMPLE CONCERNS INVOLVING LEARNING
Physiological	What chemical changes in the brain account for learning and memory? What drugs will affect memory?
Perception	Do we learn to perceive depth, or is our depth perception innate? How does inaccurate perception affect learning?
Developmental	How do children learn sex roles? Are there certain times, or stages, when a child is ready to learn certain things such as reading?
Measurement and testing	Can we teach children to do better on intelligence tests? Do intelligence tests measure how much one has learned, how bright one is, or both?
Motivation	Will the urge to satisfy our curiosity help us learn? How do we acquire the need to achieve?
Emotion	Are emotions learned? Will strong emotions such as fear and anger help us learn, or hinder our learning?
Personality	Can our personality traits be modified by learning? Is personality learned?
Abnormal and clinical	Is an abnormal fear of horses explainable in terms of learning? Is schizophrenia a learned reaction? How can the principles of learning help reduce suffering due to mental illness?
Social	Are attitudes learned? Can we learn to be independent of group pressure? Will an audience help or hinder learning?
Community	How do we teach families and friends to be more supportive of people in trouble? Can people having difficulties learn to seek support from the community?
Environmental	Can learning be improved by varying the environment? What is the relationship between crowding and learning?
Industrial	Can employees and employers learn to get along with one another? How do we best teach people to operate machinery in an efficient manner?

Adapted from Houston, J. P., Hammen, C., Padilla, A., and Bee, H. *Invitation to psychology* (3rd ed.). San Diego: Harcourt Brace Jovanovich, 1989. Table 5-1, p. 195. Copyright © 1989. Reprinted by permission.

instance, VUL, NAP, and even REZ probably elicit some kind of responses as you read over them. It may be impossible to come up with a truly nonsensical syllable. Partially as a result of this realization, psychologists have recently displayed a turn away from nonsense material. In fact, it is fair to say that recent years have seen a move toward the study of more meaningful rather than less meaningful materials. Thus, as we shall see, the literature is now filled with studies of memory for sentences, prose, connected discourse, and language in general.

THE IMPORTANCE OF LEARNING STUDIES

As a fitting close to this chapter it is appropriate to underscore the fact that learning appears to be crucial in most, if not all, areas of psychology. As you can see in Table 1.2, psychologists working in all the major fields of the science are concerned with problems involving learning. Without a firm understanding of learning these intriguing questions could not be answered.

SUMMARY

Learning can be defined in many ways. According to our sample definition, learning refers to a relatively permanent change in behavior potentiality that occurs as a result of reinforced practice. In this definition, changes in behavior resulting from

Box 1.2 Solutions to the Problems in Box 1.1

1.

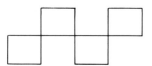

2. O T T F F S S E N
   These are the first letters of the numbers one through nine.
3. Point to either fork and ask the man if his brother would say this was the correct fork. If he says "No," then it is the correct fork. If he says "Yes," it is the wrong fork.
4. Weigh any three against any other three. If one group of three is heavier than the other, then it contains the heavy ball. If not, then the remaining unweighed group of three contains the heavy ball. To determine which of three balls is the heavy one, weigh any one against any other one.
5.

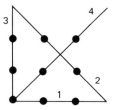

6. POP (so so)
   OTTO (not bad)
   MADAM (very good)
   RADAR (also very good)
   REDIVIDER (excellent)
7. Madam, I'm Adam.
   Step on no pets.
   Sit on a potato pan, Otis.
   Anna: "Did Otto peep?" Otto: "Did Anna?" (Each word is also a palindrome.)
8. Continuum

motivational fluctuations, maturation, and various physical and physiological factors are excluded from consideration. Learning must be distinguished from performance, which is the translation of learning into behavior. Reinforcement, under this definition, is necessary for learning to occur.

A second effort to bring the field of learning into focus involves examining examples of learning tasks employed by psychologists in their laboratories. These tasks include classical conditioning, instrumental conditioning, discrimination learning, serial learning, paired-associate learning, free recall, priming in lexical decisions, generation, concept formation, and problem solving. Two points should be kept firmly in mind. First, these are only a few of the many learning paradigms employed by psychologists. Second, psychologists are uncertain about whether these tasks represent many different, distinct types of learning or merely different varieties of some common underlying process.

CHAPTER

2

CLASSICAL AND INSTRUMENTAL CONDITIONING

INTRODUCTION

This chapter is devoted to a more detailed consideration of classical and instrumental conditioning. These topics deserve special consideration because more has been done with these two learning situations than most of the others. Classical conditioning will be considered first, and examples, procedures, and basic phenomena will be presented. The same kind of consideration then will be given to instrumental conditioning.

Students are sometimes confused by the terms *operant conditioning* and *respondent conditioning*. For our purposes, *operant conditioning is the same as instrumental conditioning*, and *respondent conditioning is identical to classical conditioning*. The terms *operant* and *respondent* were developed by B. F. Skinner and are used by a large number of psychologists. Although some investigators attempt to distinguish between operant and instrumental conditioning and between respondent and classical conditioning (Hall, 1989), this text does not.

CLASSICAL CONDITIONING
Examples

Classical conditioning is not limited to situations in which dogs salivate and bells ring. If it were, we would not give it a second thought. The phenomenon is, in fact, widespread. It occurs across a large number of animals, responses, and situations. Let us look at a few selected examples, which should provide some idea of the diversity of classical conditioning situations.

EYE BLINK AND THE NMR.   In one of the most widely used classical conditioning situations a human eye blink is conditioned to some neutral stimulus, such as a sound or a light, that does not initially elicit a response (Kehoe, 1983). In these situations a puff of air (the UCS) is directed toward the subject's eyeball. As one would imagine, the air puff causes the subject to blink (the UCR). At or very nearly at the time the air hits the eyeball, a CS, such as a bell, tone, or light, is presented. Successive pairings of the UCS (air) and the CS (bell, tone, or light) eventually lead to the situation in which the CS alone is capable of eliciting a blink (the CR) (Figure 2.1).

One problem that has concerned investigators in this area is the fact that the conditioned eye blink at least partially blocks the receipt of the air puff. Thus the eye-blink situation resembles an instrumental conditioning situation in which a response (the CR) is rewarded by the avoidance of the somewhat noxious air puff. Two things have been done to remedy this situation. First, some investigators have used mild shock to the paraorbital area of the eye as the UCS. The idea is that this particular UCS cannot be avoided by the blink, as can the air puff.

The second response to this difficulty has been to condition the nictitating membrane response (NMR) in the rabbit rather than the eye blink in the human. The nictitating membrane is a thin membrane located under the eyelid of the rabbit. In a sense it is a second eyelid. When the animal blinks both the eyelid and the nictitating membrane close over the eye. But the nictitating membrane seldom completely covers the cornea. With the eyelid held open by a suture and an air puff used as the UCS, the NMR cannot completely eliminate the aversive quality of the UCS.

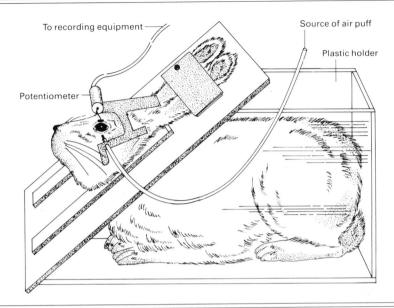

To recording equipment

Source of air puff

Plastic holder

Potentiometer

Figure 2.1 Diagram of the rabbit eye-blink conditioning preparation. A puff of air directed at the eye or a mild shock to the skin below the eye serves as the UCS. Eye blinks are detected by a potentiometer. (From Domjan, M., and Burkhard, B. *The principles of learning and behavior*. Copyright © 1982 by Wadsworth Inc. Reprinted by permission of the publisher, Brooks/Cole Publishing Company, Monterey, California.)

Thus conditioning of the NMR has become the response of choice; it is free from the confusion which surrounds the use of the human eye blink (see Figure 2.1) (Gormezano, Prokasy, & Marshall, 1987).

THE ELECTRODERMAL RESPONSE.   The electrodermal response (EDR) measures the ease with which electric current will pass across the surface of the skin. Shock may be used as a UCS. Perspiration in response to the shock (the EDR) is the UCR. When a suitable CS is paired with the shock a number of times, the CS alone will begin to elicit a reduction in skin resistance. As we shall see in Chapter 3, the EDR is useful in lie detection because lying tends to make us perspire. The EDR was formerly called the galvanic skin response (GSR).

CONDITIONING USING SICKNESS AS THE UCR: TASTE AVERSION.   In another interesting example Garcia, McGowan, and Green (1972) describe conditions in which the drinking of a saccharin solution (CS) was paired with X-irradiation (UCS), which makes rats sick. Later the subject rats showed a definite aversion to the taste of saccharin. The notion here is that the taste of saccharin (CS) produced a CR composed of an unpleasant sensation similar to the original UCR (sickness). If you have been thoroughly inebriated, you know that the sight of a liquor bottle can make you feel ill all over again.

More will be said in Chapter 4 about taste-aversion learning, as this form of conditioning is often called. Clearly taste-aversion learning is one of the most widely and intensely studied kinds of conditioning (Klunder & O'Boyle, 1979; Kurz & Levitsky, 1983; Monroe & Barker, 1979; Peters, 1983).

SEMANTIC CONDITIONING.   Words and language can be involved in classical conditioning as well as the more physiological responses that we have been discussing. For example, much has been written about *semantic classical conditioning* (Maltzman, 1977). In a typical semantic conditioning situation, a series of words might be presented to the subject. Some of these words are paired with a mild shock, and some are not. Then in the second phase of the experiment words that are similar to the words in the original list are presented without shock. Words similar to the original shock-associated words elicit the same kind of fear and nervousness that the shock elicits. Second-phase words similar to the nonshock original words elicit no fear and no anxiety. In other words, verbal elements can take on meaning through a classical conditioning process. Whatever it is that our real mother elicits in us can be conditioned to the word *mother*. Whatever it is that large, threatening dogs elicit in us can be classically conditioned to the words *mad dog*. Words can "take on" emotional meaning through classical conditioning.

MASOCHISM.   Masochism refers to a pattern of behavior in which pleasure appears to be derived from pain. Although there are many psychodynamic interpretations of masochism, the phenomenon can also be interpreted as an instance of classical conditioning.

Pavlov (1927) first used a very mild shock as a CS in a salivary conditioning situation. Because the shock was so minimal, the dogs had no fear of it, nor did they hesitate to jump eagerly into the conditioning harness. The shock merely served as a cue, or sign, that meat powder was to follow. Gradually over a series of days Pavlov increased the intensity of the CS shock. Ultimately he was able to use a fairly powerful shock as the CS. Yet the dogs acted as though they did not mind the shock at all. They continued to be eager to get on with the experiment. The painful shock had become a cue for pleasure (meat powder presentation). Had the dogs received the strong shock on their first trial, they would have howled. Through this training procedure, however, pain somehow had become a sign for pleasure.

Human masochistic behavior may be similar. Through the masochist's history pain may become pleasant in the sense that it becomes associated with, or predicts the occurrence of, pleasure. For example, a young boy may need the companionship of his father, but the only way he can get it is to engage in painful roughhousing with him. Therefore, the boy suffers the pain to gain the social contact he needs. Over time the pain itself might become mildly pleasant because of its association with intense social gratification.

PHOBIAS.   Phobias are powerful but irrational fears that affect our life adversely. For example, one individual might be terrified of heights, germs, or being outdoors. Another might be terrified by being *indoors*. Table 2.1 contains some common phobias and their names. Many of these debilitating fears may involve classical conditioning. If a boy saw his family being burned to death, for example,

Table 2.1   Phobias

NAME OF PHOBIA	FEARED STIMULUS
Acrophobia	Height
Agoraphobia	Open spaces
Ailurophobia	Cats
Anthophobia	Flowers
Anthropophobia	People
Aquaphobia	Water
Astraphobia	Lightning
Brontophobia	Thunder
Claustrophobia	Closed spaces
Cynophobia	Dogs
Equinophobia	Horses
Herpetophobia	Reptiles
Mysophobia	Contamination, dirt
Nycotophobia	Darkness, night
Ophidiophobia	Snakes
Pyrophobia	Fire

he might develop a powerful fear of fire through classical conditioning. The UCS would be the death of the family. The UCR would be terror. The CS would be fire, and the CR would be the fear response connected to and elicited by the fire. In Chapter 3 we will learn how many of these phobias can be eliminated through a process called *systematic desensitization*.

CONDITIONING OF THE IMMUNE SYSTEM.   The human immune system protects the body against germs and other disease-causing materials. Recent research has shown that even this delicate system can be modified through the use of classical conditioning. Ader (1985) demonstrated this principle by using cyclophospha-mide, a substance that has been found to suppress the immune system. He first fed rats a flavor they had not previously encountered and then injected them with cyclophosphamide. Later, after the cyclophosphamide was cleared from them, the rats were treated in one of two ways. Half the rats were injected with germs. In this case the immune system reacted normally and attacked the germs. The other half of the rats were injected with germs and also reexposed to the novel flavor. In this case the immune response to the germs was lessened; conditioned suppression appeared. The cyclophosphamide was the UCS, the novel flavor served as the CS, suppression in response to the cyclophosphamide was the UCR, and suppression in response to the novel flavor was the CR.

ADDITIONAL EXAMPLES.   Scores of animals and responses have been involved in classical conditioning. Chick embryos (Hunt, 1949), *planaria* (Thompson & McConnell, 1955), and human fetuses (Spelt, 1948) have undergone condition-ing. Heart rates (Hall, 1976) and pupillary dilation (Goldwater, 1972) have been classically conditioned. And Bitterman, Menzel, Fietz, and Schafer (1983) have successfully conditioned proboscis extension in honeybees (*Apis mellifera*). The point here is that classical conditioning is not restricted to the Pavlovian situation. It is pervasive in the animal kingdom, and it is pervasive in human life.

Temporal Spacing of CS and UCS

We already know that classical conditioning will occur when CS onset precedes UCS onset. But what about when the CS *follows* the UCS? Will classical conditioning occur then? If your instructor walked into your classroom, fired a pistol, and then shouted "Boo!" would conditioning occur? If it did at all, the conditioned response to the CS would be very weak. Thus, we can see that the *temporal spacing* of the CS and the UCS is critical in classical conditioning. Names have been given to the various temporal patterns.

DELAYED CLASSICAL CONDITIONING.   In delayed procedures the onset of the CS always precedes the onset of the UCS. The CS is then left on *at least until the beginning* of the UCS. It may then be terminated or continued into, and even beyond the duration of, the UCS.

SIMULTANEOUS CLASSICAL CONDITIONING.   In simultaneous conditioning, the onset of the CS occurs at the same time as the onset of the UCS. In addition, the two stimuli are usually terminated together.

TRACE CLASSICAL CONDITIONING.   In trace conditioning the CS is presented and *terminated* before UCS onset.

BACKWARD CLASSICAL CONDITIONING.   In backward conditioning the CS follows the UCS. Generally speaking, very poor conditioning occurs with this pattern.

   Figure 2.2 is a graphic representation of these four types of classical conditioning. The delayed procedures are best. Typically, the simultaneous and backward procedures produce little if any conditioning. Trace procedures may, under certain specific conditions, yield some conditioning.

TEMPORAL CLASSICAL CONDITIONING.   One final form of classical conditioning must be mentioned. In temporal conditioning the UCS is presented at absolutely regular intervals; no obvious CS is used. Conditioning still occurs, however, because the regular time interval becomes the CS. It is the end of this regular interval (say, 10 seconds) that is consistently paired with the UCS and becomes the effective CS.

How Does One Observe a CR? Test Trials and Inhibition of Delay

Let us assume that your instructor has given you several delayed classical conditioning trials using a pistol and shouting "Boo!" Of course, the class is startled and alarmed each time the stimuli are presented. But is the startle response a CR or a UCR? Because both the CS and UCS are presented, we cannot be sure. The observed startle response may be a mixed response, possessing both learned and unlearned components. One way to differentiate a CR from a UCR is to leave out

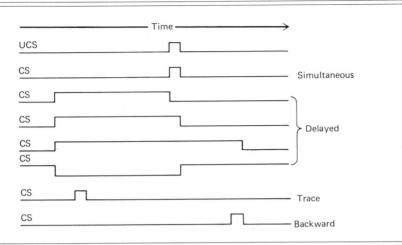

Figure 2.2 Temporal arrangements of the CS and the UCS used in four conditioning procedures. The upward movement of a line represents the onset of a stimulus, and the downward movement of a line represents the offset of a stimulus.

the UCS on a given trial. Any response that then occurs on such a test trial must be a CR.

There is a problem with this procedure for observing a CR. If we leave out the UCS on a given trial, we have instituted what is called an *extinction* trial. In classical conditioning, extinction refers to the fact that presentation of the CS alone, without the UCS, will lead to a cessation of the response. That is, your instructor cannot put the pistol away, say "Boo!" every day for the rest of the semester, and expect you to respond each time. You would extinguish, or stop responding, after a time. If we try to observe a CR by occasionally leaving out the UCS, we are slipping extinction trials into the learning situation. We are diluting the learning situation and will obtain a distorted picture of the increasing strength of the CR. It is a dilemma. We want to know if CRs are occurring, but we do not want to leave out the UCS for fear of partially extinguishing or weakening whatever CR strength we already have. The more we leave out the UCS, the more checks we have on the developing CR. But an increase in the number of such checks also increases the number of unwanted extinction trials.

Fortunately, nature comes to the rescue. As it turns out, after delayed training has progressed for a while, the CR begins to *precede* the onset of the UCS. That is, the CR will occur, or begin, *after* the onset of the CS but before the onset of the UCS. In our example the instructor would call out "Boo!" Then, *before* the gun went off, the class's conditioned startle response would begin. The CR occurs *in anticipation* of the UCS. Thus, in delayed procedures there is no need to leave out the UCS, because the CR begins in that little delay between the CS and the UCS. If the experimenters observe a response occurring before the onset of the UCS, they call it a CR. It could not be a UCR because, by definition, a UCR is a response to the UCS. The fact that the CR eventually just precedes UCS onset is sometimes called *inhibition of delay*.

Is the CR the Same as the UCR?

An eye blink is an eye blink, right? Perhaps not. Classical conditioning has some-times been thought of as the simple *transfer* of a given response from one stimulus (UCS) to another (CS), but additional research has revealed that the CR may not be identical to the UCR (Kimble, 1961; Mackintosh, 1983). For example, the UCR tends to be a more potent, "larger" response than the CR. Thus, an unconditioned eye blink will tend to involve a bigger movement of the eyelid than a conditioned eye blink and will last longer. In addition, UCRs tend to occur faster than CRs in response to their initiating stimuli. Specifically, the UCS–UCR interval tends to be shorter than the CS–CR interval.

THE CR AS A COMPONENT OF THE UCR.   There are at least two views of the nature of the CR. One view holds that the CR is a *component* of the UCR. In the salivary conditioning situation, for example, the UCS (meat powder) elicits a very compli-cated pattern of reactions, including salivation, tongue smacking, licking, and the like, but the CS (tone) elicits only some of these. The same effect appears in other conditioning situations. When your instructor shouts "Boo!" without firing the pistol, for example, you will experience a startle reaction, but it may not be as complete or dramatic as the one that follows the actual firing of the gun.

THE CR AS A PREPARATORY RESPONSE.   A second view holds that the CR is a re-sponse that prepares the animal for the UCS. In delayed eye-blink conditioning the CR may begin after the onset of the CS but before UCS onset. It is as though the CR is preparing the animal for the UCS (air puff). One way to think about it is that the CR may actually allow the animal partially to avoid the noxious air puff.

These two views, the preparatory and the component positions, are not mutu-ally exclusive. *The CR may well be a partial response and, at the same time, pre-pare the animal for the UCS.*

Responses beyond the CR and UCR

Another interesting discovery is that in delayed eye-blink situations many different kinds of blinks are occurring, not just CRs and UCRs. For example, *random* blinks often occur, and they are a potential source of confusion in conditioning experi-ments. If the subject happens to blink randomly just before the onset of the UCS, there is a danger that the experimenter will call that blink a CR. In addition, some subjects are more than helpful in conditioning situations; they blink voluntarily. The experimenter does not want to count these *voluntary responses* as true CRs. Fortunately, voluntary responses tend to begin earlier in the CS–UCS interval than true CRs and to last longer. But they are a problem. Finally, there is the *alpha response*, a small blink that occurs immediately after the onset of the CS. It can easily be confused with a true CR even though it occurs earlier in the CS–UCS interval and is smaller than the typical CR. The alpha response is a UCR to the CS, or a small startle response. The bell alone occasionally causes the subject to blink a little. The alpha response is not a learned response but is a reflex response to the CS.

We can begin to see that classical conditioning is quite complicated (see Holland & Rescorla, 1975). What began as a simple situation, in which one response was supposed to be transferred from one stimulus to another, turns out to involve many different responses. (For deeper excursions into the nature of classical conditioning you are referred to Wickens, 1984, and Gormezano, Prokasy, & Thompson, 1987.)

Some Selected Phenomena and Areas of Research in Classical Conditioning

PSEUDOCONDITIONING.   Pseudoconditioning is an interesting phenomenon in which the UCS is first presented alone for a series of trials. Then the CS is presented alone. On this very first presentation of the CS, which has never been paired with the UCS, something resembling a CR is elicited. For example, 50 successive solitary puffs of air may be directed toward the subject's eye. Then a bell may be sounded by itself. The subject will blink. The effect is called pseudoconditioning because the CS and the UCS have never been paired. The argument is that there has been no opportunity for learning to occur. Pseudoconditioning has been observed in humans (Prokasy, Hall, & Fawcett, 1962), cats (Harlow & Toltzein, 1940), goldfish (Harlow, 1939), and many other species (see Razran, 1971; Balsam, 1985).

Pseudoconditioning can be demonstrated in the classroom. Suppose that your instructor fires a blank pistol on 20 successive mornings without ever saying "Boo!" Then on the 21st day the instructor says "Boo!" instead of firing the gun. Pseudoconditioning would be demonstrated if you, as a subject, reacted to the verbalization in a manner similar to your response to the report of the gun.

Researchers have several different interpretations of pseudoconditioning. One interpretation is that the response to the CS is a result of generalized excitement. The implication is that after a series of UCS presentations we are so excited and ready to respond that we will respond to anything, even a neutral stimulus such as a tone. Another interpretation is that pseudoconditioning may actually be true classical conditioning and not "pseudo" at all. How could that be? Where is the pairing of a CS and a UCS that is essential to the classical conditioning paradigm? The trick is to find the CS. We are looking for something common to the presentation of the UCS alone (air puff) and to the presentation of the CS alone (bell). One possibility is *a change from nothing to something*, or *a change from no stimulation to stimulation*. This change is common to the presentation of the air puff and the bell. During the series of trials when the UCS is being presented, our newly discovered CS (change from no stimulation to stimulation) is present. It is "paired" with the air puff. Then when the bell alone is presented, our subtle CS (change from no stimulation to stimulation) is also present (see Wickens & Wickens, 1942). Thus, pseudoconditioning may actually be true classical conditioning in which the CS is a subtle energy change.

THE CS–UCS INTERVAL.   The amount of time between CS onset and the UCS onset has long been one of the major concerns in the field of classical conditioning. Generally speaking, a CS–UCS interval of about .5 of a second has proved optimal in some situations. Although the data suggest that this is true, the reasons for it are not at all clear. Studies that have varied the CS–UCS interval sometimes suggest that either longer or shorter intervals are less effective in the development of conditioned responses (see Figure 2.3) (Kimble & Reynolds, 1967; Spooner & Kellogg, 1947; Wolfle, 1930, 1931). However, the relationship between conditioning and

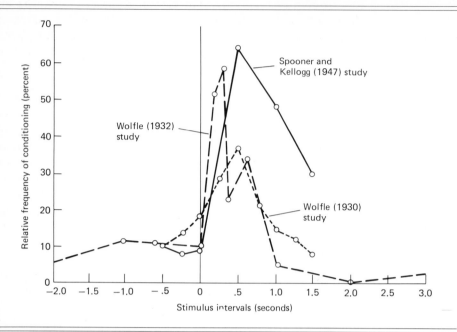

Figure 2.3 Relationship between conditioning and the CS–UCS interval. Note that the maximum frequency of conditioned responses occurs when the CS–UCS interval is approximately .5 second. Keep in mind that longer and shorter intervals can also be effective. (Adapted from Spooner, A., and Kellogg, W. N. The backward conditioning curve. *American Journal of Psychology*, 1947, 60, 321–34. Fig. 2, p. 327. © 1947, 1975 by the Board of Trustees of the University of Illinois. Reprinted by permission of the University of Illinois Press.)

the CS–UCS interval is not a simple one. In some cases this .5 second rule does not hold. For example, Ross and Ross (1972) present data suggesting that at least in some situations the optimal interval is strongly affected by the complexity of the CS. In some of their studies longer CS–UCS intervals were needed for optimal conditioning when a complex CS was being used. In additional cases classical conditioning appears to occur over very long CS–UCS intervals. For example, Kehoe, Gibbs, Garcia, and Gormezano (1979) used what is called a *serial compound* CS. What this means is that two CSs (such as a bell and a buzzer), rather than just one, were presented before the UCS was presented. In one condition the first CS (CS1) was presented. Then, approximately 18 seconds later, the second CS (CS2) was presented. Then CS2 was followed by the UCS. In this serial pattern it was found that CS1 came to elicit a CR, something that would not have occurred had CS1 been presented alone without the introduction of CS2 just before UCS onset. Conditioning to CS1 alone would not have occurred because the CS1–UCS interval was too long (18 seconds). Exactly why the introduction of CS2 helped conditioning over this relatively long interval is not known, but an upcoming section will have something to say about two possible explanations. The point here is that classical conditioning did occur over a long (approximately 18-second) CS–UCS interval.

Surprisingly, classical conditioning can be obtained over even longer CS–UCS intervals. In the *bait-shyness* effect, discussed in detail in Chapter 4, conditioning appears to be demonstrable even when the interval is one of *hours* rather than minutes or seconds (see Dickinson & Mackintosh, 1978). The relationship between conditioning and the CS–UCS interval is far from simple and is not completely understood at the present time.

CS AND UCS INTENSITY.   The intensity of the CS and of the UCS also seems to be important in classical conditioning. In general, more intense CSs and UCSs will lead to faster conditioning and to a higher degree of final conditioning (see Kamin & Brimer, 1963; Kehoe, 1983). This relationship seems to hold true over quite a broad range of stimulus intensities. If CS or UCS intensity is too high, however, conditioning may be impaired. This disruption may occur because very intense stimuli probably elicit strong unwanted unconditioned responses that mask the occurrence of the conditioned responses that the experimenter is trying to observe (see also Grice & Hunter, 1964).

MULTIPLE–RESPONSE MEASURES.   One trend in the study of classical conditioning focuses on the fact that classical conditioning involves many different, and perhaps related, changes within the organism (Black & Prokasy, 1972). In eye-blink experiments, for example, the experimenter has traditionally considered the blink to be a specific CR to a specific CS. As it turns out, the blink is not the only response that can be elicited by the CS. There may be important concurrent changes in, for example, heart rate and skeletal activity. The trend in the field is to examine the relationships among these various response systems, to look at the actions of the whole organism in response to the CS, and to avoid looking at a simple CR, such as the eye blink in isolation. The questions being asked are: How are the different response systems related? Can changes in one be predicted from changes in the others? The goal is to understand the overall pattern of behaviors involved in classical conditioning.

The situation is complicated further by the fact that different CSs tend to elicit different constellations of responses that make up the overall CR. A light used as a CS, for example, will tend to elicit a set of CR components that is slightly different from the set of responses elicited by a bell or a buzzer (Holland, 1977). Holland (1979), for instance, has shown that an auditory CS may be associated more strongly with a startle response and head jerks, whereas a visual CS may be associated with rearing (standing) behavior in the rat. In summary, the nature of the CR that we obtain in classical situations is, at least in part, dependent on the nature of the CS.

CS PREEXPOSURE EFFECT: LATENT INHIBITION.   Repeated presentation of the CS before presentation of the paired CS and UCS will sometimes lead to poorer conditioning than if the CS is paired with the UCS from the outset. If a tone is sounded alone for 150 trials and is then paired with an air puff, the resulting eye blink conditioning will be slower than if the tone had not been presented alone. The phenomenon is called *latent inhibition, or the CS preexposure effect.* Some workers have felt that the preconditioning exposure to the CS reduces the subject's attention, or orientation, to the CS. In other words, if someone rings a bell endlessly, we will adapt to it, or pay less attention to it, and its effectiveness as a cue in learning will be reduced accordingly. Much of the work on latent inhibition has been done in the Soviet Union, but its appeal has been spreading in the United States and Europe (Best, Gemberling, & Johnson, 1979; Channell & Hall, 1983; Dawley, 1979; Hall & Pearce, 1979; Pearce & Hall, 1979).

One line of recent research has asked whether latent inhibition effects will be the same in very young animals as they are in adults (Kramer, Hoffman, & Spear, 1988). Somewhat surprisingly, differences have been found. For example, Hoffman and Spear (1989) have actually found that preexposure to the CS will help subsequent learning rather than hinder it when the subjects are 10-day-old preweanling rats. This kind of finding suggests that we may eventually have to develop rules and principles of learning that vary depending on the age of the organisms involved.

UCS PREEXPOSURE EFFECT.   The *UCS preexposure effect* (sometimes called *habituation*) refers to the situation in which the UCS, rather than the CS, is presented alone for a series of trials before the CS and UCS are paired. When this is done, conditioning is again slowed (see Batson, 1983; Randich & Haggard, 1983; Matzel, Schactman, & Miller, 1988).

At this point one might ask about the relationship between UCS preexposure and pseudoconditioning. Both procedures involve the same manipulation. The UCS is presented alone for a series of trials. Yet in pseudoconditioning, something like a CR is obtained on the very first presentation of the CS, whereas in habituation, conditioning is slowed over a series of CS–UCS pairings. It seems that the difference between the two phenomena may lie in the fact that the pseudoconditioning effect appears on the very first presentation of the CS and is a transitory effect. That is, its impact will not be observed over a long series of CS–UCS pairings. Habituation, in contrast, refers to a decrement that occurs over a long series of CS–UCS pairings. Pseudoconditioning may actually occur in habituation experiments on the first trial or two, but it is neither strong enough nor lasting enough to affect, or counteract, the decrement in conditioning that appears over a long series of CS–UCS pairings.

COMPOUND STIMULUS EFFECTS.   Rescorla and Wagner (1972), and others, have argued that classical conditioning involves competition for associative strength among all the stimuli present in the environment. Although the experimenter focuses on and manipulates a CS such as a bell, other stimuli in the situation (for example, the background stimuli) might potentially serve as functional CSs. Thus, it becomes the task of the investigator to tease out and isolate those stimuli that actually function as the CS in any given situation.

Many recent studies have employed *compound stimuli* in these efforts to isolate and understand effective CSs. A compound stimulus is a stimulus composed of two or more discrete components. Thus, a compound CS might be composed of a bell and a buzzer or of a light, a bell, and a shock. The question becomes one of determining which components will become effective CSs and under what conditions. The following compounding phenomena represent some of the results that have already been obtained in this intriguing search.

Table 2.2   The Steps Used to Demonstrate Sensory Preconditioning and Higher-Order Conditioning

	SENSORY PRECONDITIONING	HIGHER–ORDER CONDITIONING
Step 1	Pair bell and light	Pair bell with UCS, such as meat powder
Step 2	Pair bell with UCS, such as air puff	Pair bell with light
Step 3	Test for eyeblink with light alone	Test for salivary response with light alone

1. *Sensory preconditioning.* Assume that we are dealing with two discrete stimulus elements—say, a bell and a light. Call the bell *A* and the light *X*. The first step in demonstrating sensory preconditioning is to pair *A* and *X* together repeatedly; then pair *A* with a UCS such as an air puff to the eyeball until *A* begins to elicit a conditioned blink; and finally, present *X* alone. If *X* elicits a blink, even though it has never been paired with the air puff, then sensory preconditioning has been demonstrated (Fudim, 1978; Pfautz, Donegan, & Wagner, 1978) (see Table 2.2).

2. *Higher-order conditioning.* Also known as second-order conditioning, higher-order conditioning refers to the situation in which the CS from one learning task is used as the UCS in a subsequent task (Cheafle & Rudy, 1978; Szakmary, 1979). For example, a bell might be paired first with meat powder in a salivary conditioning situation. Once the bell was eliciting a conditioned salivary response, the meat powder could be removed entirely, and the bell could be paired with a light. Higher-order conditioning is demonstrated if the light begins to elicit a conditioned response (see Table 2.2). In effect the bell is now the UCS, and the light is the CS. Interestingly, some responses, such as fear, seem to be much easier to second-order condition than others, such as the eye blink (Popik, Stern, & Frey, 1979).

3. *Overshadowing.* First, pair *AX* with a UCS. Then test for the effectiveness of *A* and *X* alone in eliciting the CR. If the more salient element displays greater control over the CR than the other, we say that overshadowing has been demonstrated (Odling-Smee, 1978). The fact that the CS component manipulated by the experimenter usually displays greater control than the background stimuli in the environment is a form of overshadowing (see Jackson & Fritsche, 1989; Kraemer, Lariviere, & Spear, 1989).

4. *Compounding.* Pair *AX* with a UCS. Then test with *A*, with *X*, and with *AX*. If a CR is elicited by the *AX* compound but by neither *A* nor *X* alone, then we say that compounding has occurred.

5. *Kamin's blocking effect.* Pair *A* with a UCS. Then pair *AX* with the same UCS. Then test for the effectiveness of *X* in eliciting a CR. In this case *X* will often be less effective in eliciting the CR than it would be if *A* had not initially been paired with the UCS. In other words, the fact that *A* already elicits the CR somehow blocks the establishment of a strong *X*–CR connection during the *AX*–UCS pairing (Cheafle & Rudy, 1978; Haggbloom, 1983; Kamin, 1969b; Kohler & Ayres, 1979; Rescorla & Colwill, 1983; Stickney & Donahoe, 1983).

6. *Conditioned inhibition.* Also known as conditioned suppression, conditioned inhibition refers to the following effect. On some trials *A* is paired with the

UCS. On other trials *AX* is paired with the UCS. Conditioned inhibition is demonstrated when it is found that *A* elicits a CR, whereas *AX* is less likely to do so (Memmott & Reberg, 1977; Rescorla & Holland, 1977).

7. *Serial compounding.* We have already seen in connection with our discussion of the CS–UCS interval that conditioning over long intervals can occur when two successive CSs are presented before the UCS in a CS1–CS2–UCS sequence. This stimulus compounding effect is particularly instructive, because it points out how many of the stimulus compounding effects that we have discussed may be interrelated. Specifically, it has been suggested that the serial compound effect might be explainable in terms of some of the other compounding effects (Kehoe et al., 1979). The long CS–UCS interval might be bridged by either higher-order conditioning or by a sensory preconditioning effect. In terms of the sensory preconditioning effect it would be argued that CS1 and CS2 are paired, that CS2 is then paired with the UCS, and that CS1, because of its pairing with CS2, would then be capable of eliciting a CR. The higher-order conditioning explanation would hold that CS2, initially paired with the UCS, becomes the effective UCS when it is paired with CS1. Whether these explanations will hold up remains to be seen. But they, and all the stimulus compounding effects, do indicate the complexity and, yet, the predictability of stimulus control effects in classical conditioning.

Cognitive Theory

Recent thinking about classical conditioning has led many investigators to the conclusion that conditioning is most effective when the CS *predicts* the occurrence of the upcoming UCS for the subject (Dickinson & Mackintosh, 1978; Frey & Sears, 1978; Mackintosh, 1975; Rescorla & Wagner, 1972; Rescorla, 1985, 1988). Conditioning is most effective when the CS *signals* the fact that the UCS is impending or when it provides the subject with *information* about the very near future.

The argument is that subjects will start blinking (CR) in response to a bell only when that bell (CS) lets the subjects know that an air puff (UCS) is about to hit their eye. If the bell does not help the subjects know when the air puff is about to occur—that is, if the air puff is as likely to occur in the absence of the bell as in its presence—then little or no conditioning will occur. It makes sense, doesn't it? In fact, Rescorla and Wagner (1972) have found that, when the UCS is to occur equally with or without the CS, the CS will not begin to elicit a CR. But when the UCS is more likely to follow CS presentation than it is to occur in the absence of the CS, the CS has informational value. It *tells* the subject that the UCS is about to occur and the subject blinks. This approach, termed the *informational theory*, is also known as the *expectancy* approach. The CS must predict the impending occurrence of the UCS, or conditioning will be minimal.

BLOCKING AND THE RESCORLA–WAGNER MODEL.   The Rescorla-Wagner idea is that, if a stimulus doesn't tell the subject anything new or additional about the upcoming occurrence of the UCS, the stimulus will not become an effective CS. This hypothesis can be used to explain, among many other things, the blocking effect. Remember that in blocking, a stimulus *A* is first paired with a UCS. Thus, through this pairing *A* already signals the upcoming occurrence of the UCS. Then

X is paired with A and followed by the same UCS. But X doesn't convey any additional information, so it doesn't become an effective CS. It is redundant in the sense that any information it might convey is already being conveyed by A.

Practical Uses of Classical Conditioning

Before moving on to consider instrumental conditioning, it should be made clear that classical conditioning has been put to good use outside the laboratory. Box 2.1 contains two good examples of the usefulness of classical conditioning. Many more practical uses of classical conditioning will be mentioned throughout this text.

SELECTED EXAMPLES OF INSTRUMENTAL CONDITIONING
Instrumental Reward Training

A rat's learning to press a bar for food in a Skinner box is a straightforward example of *reward training*. The animal is *rewarded when it makes a particular response*. As is true of classical conditioning, reward training is pervasive in our life as well. Children learning to tie their shoes for parental approval, adolescents learning a paper route for spending money, college students absorbing course materials for a grade, athletes mastering a sport for money and recognition, and college professors learning to publish experiments for promotions all represent reward training. The essential characteristic of the situation is that the animal, or human, must first make a particular response before it receives something it wants or needs.

Female *Rhesus* monkeys will learn to press levers when lever pressing is rewarded by access to male monkeys. (Incidentally, when given a choice between males, females will lever-press for the males that groom the most and ejaculate the most [Michael, Bonsall, & Zumpe, 1978].) Even garter snakes will learn for rewards. Kubie and Halpern (1979) have found that they will learn to follow trails through mazes that have been scented with earthworm extract when they are fed at the end of the maze. The literature is filled with hundreds of studies of reward training, some of which we examine below.

SHAPING.   *Shaping* is an important concept developed in connection with reward training. It refers to the reinforcement of successive approximations to a desired response. The best way to train a rat to press a bar is first to reinforce approximations to the full-blown bar press, then to reinforce closer approximation, and finally to reinforce only an actual bar press. Initially, we reinforce the hungry animal each time it turns toward the bar. After this response is firmly established, we reinforce the animal only if it moves toward the bar. Finally, we reinforce the animal only if it actually presses the bar. In other words, we guide the animal slowly toward the response in which we are interested. If we were to wait for the full bar press to occur "spontaneously" before we reinforced anything, we might never bring the response under our control.

This same sort of shaping technique can be used in many human situations. For example, it is often used in attempts to teach autistic children to speak. In attempting to establish verbal repertoires psychologists may deprive these disturbed children of one meal and then reinforce them with food (for example, bits of

---

Box 2.1 Bed-Wetting and Lie Detecting

Bed-Wetting

Bed-wetting, or **enuresis**, has been analyzed in terms of classical conditioning. Normally, a wet bed (the UCS) evokes a waking response (the UCR). In time, the wet bed is paired with bladder tension (the CS). Through repeated pairings, the bladder tension (CS) normally acquires the capacity to elicit the waking response (the CR). But some children do not learn this CS–CR connection, probably because wetting the bed does not awaken them. Therefore, these children sleep through the bladder tension and wet the bed.

As far back as 1938 psychologists were attempting to control enuresis through classical conditioning. They reasoned that since the CS (bladder tension)–CR (waking) connection has not been learned, it may be established by pairing the CS (bladder tension) with an alternative UCS that will elicit the desired waking response. If, each time the child's bladder is full, a bell rings loud enough to waken the child, then the waking response should become classically conditioned to the bladder tension.

How can the situation be arranged so that a bell rings only when the bladder is full? The answer is actually rather simple. Develop a special sheet containing fine electrical wires. As soon as the child begins to wet the bed, the urine (which fortunately is a fine conductor of electricity) closes an electrical circuit and causes a bell located near the child's head to ring. The bell wakes the child, thereby completing a "learning trial." Such an apparatus has, in fact, been developed and successfully marketed. After a period of learning, the child begins to wake up in anticipation of the bell. The CS (bladder tension)–CR (waking response) connection has been established. Of course the apparatus uses low-voltage batteries so there is no danger of shock. While controversial, this apparatus has been successful in many cases. It is a clear example of how basic research can provide a solution to a practical problem.

The Polygraph or "Lie Detector"

Another way in which the principles of classical conditioning have been put to work outside the laboratory involves *polygraph machines* or "lie detectors." These devices are supposed to be able to detect when a person is lying by recording changes in blood pressure, pulse rate, breathing, and the amount of perspiration produced by the skin. But strictly speaking, they are not lie detectors at all. They are emotion detectors. By recording changes in the four variables mentioned, we can detect strong, classically conditioned emotional reactions. As you know from experience, strong emotions, such as fear or anxiety, can cause an increase in sweating and heart rate, as well as a change in breathing.

Suppose as a young child you managed to crawl under your house and stumbled into a nest of large, fat, brown spiders. You suffered a number of bites, to say nothing of the scrapes and bumps acquired during your spectacular exit. In later
(continued on page 39)

---

sugar-coated cereal) each time they make any sound at all. At first, any sound is reinforced. Grunts, snorts, syllables, and squeaks are all reinforced. Then, as training progresses and the rate of sound production goes up, the teacher becomes more selective in reinforcing. He or she refrains from reinforcing just any sound and will

(continued from page 38)
years the mere mention of spiders, particularly fat, brown ones, might be enough to trigger a strong sense of disgust and fear. This reaction could be detected by the polygraph machine, even if you tried to conceal it. The situation involves classical conditioning. The UCS is the experience with the spiders in childhood, the CS is the verbal label "spider," and the CR is the fear and revulsion triggered by the mention of spiders.

The most familiar use of polygraph machines has been in police work. The notion is that criminals will lie to conceal their guilt, but they cannot control their emotional reactions, and so the lie detector will pick up these "signs of guilt." However, serious questions have been raised about this use of the polygraph. For example, suppose four big police officers escorted you to a police station, attached you to a strange machine with wires, looked at each other significantly, and asked, "Did you murder Elizabeth K. Stone?" Even an innocent person might have a strong emotional reaction to such a question asked under these circumstances. The polygraph cannot distinguish between *types* of reactions, such as guilt or alarm. It can measure only the *amount* of reaction. Therefore, direct questions such as "Did you murder Elizabeth K. Stone?" are unsuitable for detecting lies—or truth either.

One way to avoid emotional responses from innocent people in answer to such direct, general questions is to consider minute details of the crime or to focus on elements of the crime that could be known only by the guilty party. Suppose a victim has been murdered with the leg of a chair. The police might show all suspects a series of pictures of common objects, including the actual murder weapon. In this case, the murderer might reveal his guilt by reacting strongly to the murder weapon but not to the remaining objects. Innocent parties, on the other hand, would be unlikely to react strongly to the leg of a chair.

Even with these refinements, the use of polygraph records has been extremely controversial and their reliability often has been questioned. Some types of psychopathic individuals appear to be able to "beat the lie detector" because they have no strong feelings about their crimes. Similarly, drugs of various sorts will affect polygraph records.

In addition to police work, the polygraph has been used in psychotherapy situations. Suppose that a therapist is attempting to determine what is bothering a new patient. She asks the patient if he is in any way disturbed by, or concerned about, his sex life. He responds with a knowing look and a little chuckle. "No. No. Everything is just fine there. Just fine." But if, at the same time that the patient is speaking with such outward calm, the recording needles of the polygraph machine are jumping wildly, the therapist might suspect that the controlled verbal report is concealing strong inner reactions to the topic of sex. The word "sex" might be a CS for all sorts of emotional reactions, and the polygraph could be useful in detecting this area of concern.

begin to reward only those sounds that begin to approximate some desired verbal response (for example, a word). Gradually the child's sounds are *shaped* to conform to the desired pattern. This shaping technique appears to be quite successful in teaching previously mute children to produce distinct verbal behaviors (Hewett,

1965; Kerr, Myerson, & Michael, 1965; Lovaas, 1967; Lovaas, Berberich, Perdoff, & Schaeffer, 1966). Sometimes children who would otherwise remain nonverbal can be taught sign language instead of speech behavior (Carr & Kologinsky, 1983). And finally the siblings of autistic children can be taught how to use reward training. Not only do they help their autistic brothers and sisters, but they end up liking them better, too (Schreibman, O'Neill, & Koegel, 1983).

TOKEN ECONOMIES.   Reward training, as we just saw, is not limited to laboratory exercises. It has often been applied successfully in dealing with practical problems. *Token economies* represent a very good example of the usefulness of reward training. In a token economy desirable behaviors are immediately reinforced or rewarded with tokens, which may later be exchanged for primary reinforcers such as food, beverages, and privileges. For example, the staff of a mental hospital may reinforce desirable behaviors (positive speech, cooperation, completion of chores, neat appearance) with poker chips, gold stars, or check marks, which may later be turned in for any number of more basic rewards (clothing, personal items, games, tools, snacks, television time, recreational privileges).

Tokens have been used in a number of settings, including hospitals, schools, outpatient clinics, and homes. For example, Atthowe and Krasner (1968) successfully used a token economy on a closed ward of chronic psychiatric patients in a Veterans Administration hospital. Tokens were awarded when the patients cared for their personal needs, attended their scheduled activities, helped on the ward, or showed increased responsibility in any way. Similarly, Schaefer and Martin (1966) report success in overcoming "apathetic" behaviors displayed by hospitalized schizophrenics through the use of token reinforcement procedures. Tokens that could be exchanged for cereal, candy, or small toys have also been shown to be effective in training retarded children to use sentences (Lutzker & Sherman, 1974). Tokens have been used in large-scale educational systems (see Klein, 1979) as well as in hospitals. One need only look in a recent issue of the *Journal of Applied Behavior Analysis* or some similar journal to discover the widespread use of the technique.

PSYCHOGENIC POLYDIPSIA.   Another interesting use of reward training involves the treatment of psychogenic polydipsia. This condition, usually occurring in schizophrenics, involves the intake of enormous amounts of water. In some cases intake exceeds the individual's capacity for excretion, resulting in vomiting, agitation, seizures, coma, and even death. Calamari, Hansen, and Kaliher (1988) report a case in which water refusal was rewarded with foods that the schizophrenic patient particularly liked, resulting in the normalization of water intake.

OTHER REWARDS.   Experimenters have been very creative in devising and using additional types of rewards. For example, Pierce and Risley (1974) have demonstrated that the opportunity for recreational activities can serve as an effective reinforcer. They set up a situation in which the young members of an urban recreational center could obtain additional recreation time if they recruited new members for the center. If a youngster brought in one new member, he or she was allowed to enter the center an hour earlier than the other members. The technique appeared to be fairly successful in a series of recruitment drives.

Powell, Felce, Jenkins, and Lunt (1979) point out that one of the chronic problems found in homes for the elderly is that the guests often spend excessive amounts of time just sitting about doing nothing. They engage in very little physical activity or social interaction. These authors report that they were able to increase healthy social and physical activities by rewarding these activities with the opportunity to engage in a little indoor gardening. The chance to garden, in itself enjoyable, was an effective reinforcer when it was made contingent on the occurrence of other sorts of engagement.

Knight and McKenzie (1974) have reported that bedtime thumb sucking can be eliminated through the manipulation of story reading. Several young girls, all dedicated thumb suckers, were reinforced for not thumb sucking by being read a bedtime story. The authors report that this method was extremely successful. (There are those who would probably argue that the behavior need not have been eliminated under any circumstances.) (See also Friman, 1988.)

Social rewards are probably used more widely than any other type of reward. Factors such as praise, attention, flattery, and support are powerful reinforcers for most people. For example, Rekers and Lovaas (1974) report a case in which a young boy had taken on many female characteristics. He preferred feminine clothes and activities, his voice had distinctive feminine qualities, and he enjoyed feminine cosmetic articles. In attempting to change this behavior pattern (some might want to argue that it should not have been changed), the mother of the child was taught to socially reinforce masculine behaviors. She was taught to praise, encourage, and support masculine activities and interests and to ignore (extinguish) feminine behaviors. Although social reinforcers were not the only ones used in this study, they did form an important part of the situation and did appear to have a significant impact on the child's behavior. The authors report that three years later the boy displayed most of the characteristics of traditional masculine behavior.

ADDITIONAL BEHAVIORS.   Just as a wide variety of reinforcers have been used in practical situations, so, too, have many different behaviors been altered through the use of reward training. Everything from tics (Finney, Rapoff, Hall, & Christophersen, 1983) to dog bites (Tortora, 1983) have been altered. For example, a potentially dangerous form of self-starvation has been treated using reward training. Anorexia nervosa often affects intelligent young people. They simply stop eating and, on occasion, have been known to die from this condition. It has often been assumed that the condition is a physiological one, and medical doctors sometimes recommend tube feeding to keep the patients from starving.

Garfinkel, Kline, and Stancer (1973) decided to treat the condition as if it were a learned rather than a physiological condition. This was a bold decision, because so little research had been done on the condition. They treated five women who were hospitalized with the condition. Basically, they rewarded weight gains and ignored losses. The reinforcers were weekend passes and opportunities to engage in social activities. Within 12 weeks almost all of the patients' original weight had been regained.

Care should be taken in concluding that positive reinforcement techniques are the cure for anorexia nervosa. Other investigators (for example, Van Buskirk, 1977) point out that the situation can often be quite complex and that neither behavior modification nor psychotherapeutic techniques are perfect cures.

Many other behaviors, including overeating (Wilson, 1979), energy conserva-tion (Seaver & Patterson, 1976), and grief (Ramsay, 1979) have been altered through reward training. The point here is that psychology is doing some good beyond the confines of the laboratory by using the principles of conditioning.

Avoidance Training

EXAMPLE.   In *avoidance training* the animal *receives unpleasant stimulation when it fails to make a particular response.* The apparatus depicted in Figure 2.4 can be used to demonstrate avoidance training. One side of the box is painted black. The other side, painted white, has a metal grid floor. Electric current can be passed through this grid. A hurdle, or fence, separates the black side from the white side. When a rat is placed in the white side, it engages in normal rat behavior, nosing about and exploring the box. The apparatus is set up such that the current will be turned on in, say, 15 seconds. If by that time the animal has not climbed over the barrier, removing itself from the white box, it will be shocked. If it does move into the black box before the 15 seconds have elapsed, it will not be shocked. When the rat is first placed in the box, it will typically wander about. When it receives the first shock, it squeaks, leaps about, and soon scrambles into the black box. The experimenter begins another trial, picking up the rat and placing it back in the white box. The rat again has 15 seconds to jump the fence or be shocked. You can easily imagine what will happen in this situation. Over a series of trials the rat learns to jump the fence promptly when placed in the white box. No question about it. It is leaving, thank you very much. After a series of trials the rat no longer receives any shock at all. It has learned to avoid the shock.

EXTINGUISHING THE AVOIDANCE RESPONSE: FLOODING.   In a reward training situ-ation it is easy to imagine what will happen if the reinforcement is removed. If a rat is no longer given food for pressing a bar, it will stop pressing quite quickly. This is called *extinction* of the response. Similarly, if a high hurdler practices 10 hours a day and never makes the team, he or she will probably stop practicing. But what about the avoidance situation? What do you think the rat will do if the shock is permanently removed from the situation? No more shock. Just a white box and a black box. Interestingly enough, it keeps right on jumping even though there is no need for it. It never waits long enough to find out that it will not be shocked. If left to its own devices, the rat will maintain its avoidance response for a very long time.

There are ways to ensure extinction of avoidance responses. For example, one way is to make the barrier so high that the rat cannot jump over it. It is forced to stay in the white box and discover it will no longer be shocked. The rat is rather unhappy for a while, but sooner or later the response drops out. This technique for extinguishing the response is called *flooding* (Mineka & Gino, 1979). Another way to eliminate the avoidance response is to present the aversive stimulus no matter what action is taken.

THE TWO–FACTOR THEORY OF AVOIDANCE CONDITIONING.   One particular the-ory of avoidance conditioning has been very influential (Mowrer & Lamoreaux, 1942, 1946). According to this interpretation, avoidance conditioning involves both instrumental conditioning *and* classical conditioning (see Mineka, 1979).

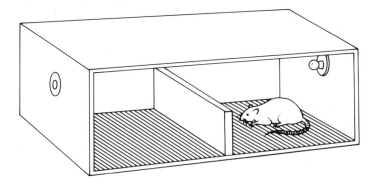

Figure 2.4 Apparatus in which rat can be conditioned to avoid a shock.

When a rat is placed in the white box and shocked, a kind of classical conditioning occurs. The rat's reaction to the shock becomes classically conditioned to the white box. Mowrer and others have called this conditioned reaction fear. One can think of the rat's reaction to the shock as something else if one wishes, but fear is close enough for our purposes. The white box is the CS. The shock is the UCS. The fear elicited by the shock is the UCR. The fear elicited by the white box is the CR. Thus, the first factor in the two-factor theory is the classical conditioning of a fear reaction. The second factor refers to the notion that the rat will learn to escape from the fear-producing situation in an *instrumental* fashion. When the rat finds itself in the white box, it experiences conditioned fear. It then leaps the barrier. The termination of the fear-producing stimuli, and consequently the fear itself, is the reward, or reinforcement, for the escape behavior.

In summary, the two-factor theory holds that a negative emotional reaction becomes classically conditioned to a particular set of stimuli. The animal then instrumentally learns to escape from these circumstances and is reinforced by the reduction in the conditioned emotional reaction. You are referred to Bolles (1970), Rescorla and Solomon (1967), and Wahlsten and Cole (1972) for discussions of the two-factor theory.

LEARNED HELPLESSNESS.   One interesting development in the field of avoidance conditioning has been the discovery of the *learned helplessness* phenomenon (Jackson & Minor, 1988; Lee & Maier, 1988; Maier & Warren, 1988; Maier, Seligman, & Solomon, 1969). If, before normal avoidance training, a dog has experienced *inescapable* shock, it will sometimes fail to learn the avoidance response. For example, if a dog is shocked repeatedly in a Pavlovian harness, without any opportunity for escape, and is then placed in an avoidance situation where shock can be avoided by leaping a barrier, the dog will sometimes remain relatively silent and motionless during the shock periods. It will fail to learn the escape response. After unavoidable shock the dog somehow operates as though action would be fruitless. It is without "hope."

Similar reactions have been observed in humans (Miller & Norman, 1979). Sometimes prisoners of war adopt an aggressive stance and attempt to subvert the purposes of their captors. Others become apathetic, listless, and without the will to escape or resist (Strassman, Thaler, & Schein, 1956). The difference between the two types of prisoners seems to lie in their attitude about the effectiveness of their own actions. The active, resisting prisoners believe that they can improve the situation through action, whereas the "helpless" prisoners believe that there is no hope. They feel that any action on their part would be futile or perhaps dangerous. Similarly, Rowland (1977) has found that particularly unnerving environmental events, such as the death of a significant other, relocation, or retirement, can lead to a sense of helplessness, and even to death, in elderly people.

Susceptibility to learned helplessness may be, in part, inherited. Anisman, Grimmer, Irwin, Remington, and Sklar (1979) report that they were able to breed rats selectively such that some lines were more susceptible to the phenomenon than others.

There are at least five ways of looking at, or theorizing about, learned helplessness:

1. *Seligman's interpretation.* The original Seligman approach stressed the idea that the animal, during inescapable shock, learns that its own responses are independent of shock offset; they will not do any good. This interpretation emphasizes the notion of "hopelessness." Seligman (1975) proposed that learned helplessness can serve as a model for *human depression*. Specifically, he felt that depression brought on by unpleasant uncontrollable events in our environment can best be thought of in terms of learned helplessness.

Seligman's idea was a bold and good one, but it proved to be too simpleminded to account for all instances of human depression. Specifically, it failed to account for *cognitive* events, which can influence and determine the nature of depression. The nature of depression depends on how a person *thinks* about the causes, nature, and consequences of that depression. For example, suppose two people fail an exam. One of them attributes the failure to personal inadequacy, whereas the second person decides that the test was so difficult and unfair that no one could have passed it. The first person's self-esteem may suffer, whereas the second person's won't. In other words, the same event (failure) can lead to different feelings, depending on how each person interprets the causes of that event.

Abramson, Seligman, and Teasdale (1978) presented a sweeping reformulation of the model of depression to account for the role of cognition in depression. They proposed three important dimensions. The first of these, *personal versus universal attributions*, we have just considered. If you attribute failure to your own shortcomings, you will feel worse than if you attribute that failure to some external cause.

Seligman's second dimension, *specific versus global attributions*, was introduced to account for the fact that depression and helplessness sometimes seem quite specific (I only fail at school) and sometimes quite general (I can't do anything right). The earlier formulation, which argued that depression was similar to what happens to dogs when they are unavoidably shocked, could not account for these subtle but substantial differences in depression.

Finally, Seligman's third dimension, *stable versus unstable attributions*, was developed to account for the fact that some depressions seem to last forever, whereas others go away. If you flunk an exam and conclude that you did so because you are dumb, then you may be depressed for quite a while. But if you conclude that you flunked because you momentarily panicked, then you may get over your depression soon.

Seligman's interpretation is interesting because it was first developed in connection with basic animal research but was then expanded to account for variations in human depression that are the result of our *thinking* about who we are and what has happened to us.

2. *Competing-response interpretation.* While Seligman and his colleagues have moved toward a consideration of how cognitive events affect depression, others have formulated alternative theories of the basic helplessness phenomenon. For example, some have argued that it is not the inescapability of shock that is critical to the phenomenon. They propose that the shock results in the development of motor responses that are incompatible with later escape. These competing responses, learned during shock, later compete with the animal's efforts to learn the escape response. During shock, for example, the animal may find crouching to be at least partially rewarding. Then during the subsequent nonshock phase, when escape is possible, this learned crouching behavior will compete with, or interfere with, the active motor responses that are necessary for escape. According to this view, the animal is feeling neither helpless nor hopeless. It is merely continuing to do what has been rewarding in the past—that is, crouch (Anderson, Crowell, Cunningham, & Lupo, 1979; Anisman, de Catanzaro, & Remington, 1978; Bracewell & Black, 1974).

3. *Neurochemical interpretation.* Anisman (1978) and others have stressed the biochemical events that occur during inescapable shock. Specifically, Anisman argues that shock (stress) depletes brain norepinephrine and perhaps causes other neurochemical changes as well. These chemical changes result in deficits in motor activity, which could account for the lack of escape learning.

4. *Dual-process model.* Glazer and Weiss (1976) are sympathetic with the neurochemical interpretation. But they point out that the proposed chemical changes are only temporary. Such changes could account for learning deficits only over a period of a few hours, whereas the learned helplessness phenomenon has appeared when escape learning has been separated from inescapable shock by several months. For instance, Fenton, Calof, and Katzev (1979) shocked guinea pigs within 24 hours of their birth and found that the escape learning deficit still appeared when the animals were full grown. To account for these facts Glazer and Weiss (1976) have constructed a dual-process model. According to this interpretation, chemical changes are presumed to account for deficits in escape learning that occur over short periods of time, whereas long-term deficits are attributed to the effects of competing motor responses that have been learned during inescapable shock.

5. *Egotism.* Another cognitively based theory proposes that egotism plays a part in the human learned helplessness phenomenon (Frankel & Snyder, 1978; Mikulincer, 1988). The idea is that humans have a fragile sense of self-esteem that they wish to protect. If a person fails miserably in an effort to solve unsolvable problems, his or her sense of self-worth will be threatened. So the person will quit trying. The person can then rationalize the failure by claiming that it is due to a lack of effort rather than due to any lack of ability.

OPOIDS AND LEARNED HELPLESSNESS. Recent work has led to the intriguing discovery that the brain itself produces opiatelike pain-suppressing substances (Leibeskind, Lewis, Shavit, Terman, & Melnechuk, 1983; Lewis & Leibeskind, 1983). Apparently the brain has built-in pain suppressing systems. The guess is that, when pain becomes too great, these systems begin producing opiatelike substances that temper the pain.

Opiates (morphine, heroin, and the like) are drugs derived from plants. Opoids, in contrast, are these more recently discovered analgesics produced by the brain itself. The opoids include, among others, the endorphins, which have received considerable attention.

The emerging picture is that these pain-suppressing systems do not come into action too soon; if they responded to the mildest pain, the organism would never be warned of any danger. If pain is so great that it becomes maladaptive, however, it is to the animal's advantage to produce opoids. Under conditions of stress one would expect opoids to be produced.

What has all this to do with learned helplessness? Maier, Sherman, Lewis, Terman, and Leibeskind (1983) reasoned that, if helplessness is stressful, it should lead to opoid production. That is exactly what they found; learned helplessness is followed by opoid production.

This is not a theory of helplessness. Rather, it is one more piece in the overall puzzle presented by the helplessness phenomenon.

Escape Training

Another variety of instrumental conditioning is called *escape training*. In this situation *inevitable unpleasant stimulation is continued unless the subject makes a particular response.* Imagine the avoidance-learning situation just described, but with one slight change. In escape training the current is *always* on in the white box. The rat is dropped into the white box and is, obviously, shocked when it lands on the grid. It quickly learns to escape by leaping the barrier. The difference between avoidance and escape training is that in escape training the animal can never completely avoid the shock. No matter how hard it tries, it is always shocked at the beginning of every trial.

Many laboratory examples of escape training are available. Leeming and Little (1977) enclosed houseflies (*Musca domestica*) in a Plexiglas tube. One half of the tube was lighted, hot, and, presumably, very uncomfortable. The other half was relatively dark and cool. The houseflies quickly learned to escape from the uncomfortable side and to spend their time in the shady portion.

Of course, escape training is not limited to "lower" animals and the laboratory. When an enthusiastic father tosses his screaming, 4-year-old nonswimmer into the family pool, the child is undergoing escape training. Swim or sink. The child hits that unpleasant water every time, just as the rat hits the electrified grid on every trial. (It is true that the child's dislike of the water may lessen with exposure, but those first few tosses into the water surely represent escape training.)

THE RELATIONSHIP BETWEEN ESCAPE AND AVOIDANCE TRAINING. If you think back to the discussion of avoidance training, you can see that avoidance training really involves classical conditioning of the fear reaction and instrumental *escape* training. In other words, the animal learns to escape the unavoidable fear that has been classically conditioned to the white box. It can learn to avoid the shock completely, but it cannot avoid the fear completely. It can only escape that unpleasant emotion, because fear is elicited every time it is placed in the white box, no matter how quickly it jumps the barrier.

Punishment Training

In *punishment training* the animal *receives unpleasant stimulation when it makes a particular response.* Suppose that a cat has been trained to run from a start box, through a maze, and into a goal box, where it is rewarded with food. If the situation is suddenly changed to one in which the animal is shocked in both the maze and the goal box, the animal will stop running and will spend most of its time in the safe starting box. If children have had a lot of rowdy fun in the first grade but are routinely punished for such disruptive behavior by their new second-grade teacher, they will probably drop the offensive action. Punishment training can also involve the withholding of anticipated positive stimuli as a means of teaching the subject what not to do, such as withholding dessert when a child misbehaves at dinner. Solomon (1964) argues that the essence of punishment training is that the animal is being taught what *not* to do, whereas in escape and avoidance training the animal is being taught what to do.

The effects of punishment are complicated and tricky. For example, some responses are much more susceptible to punishment than others. Shettleworth (1978) found that three different responses of golden hamsters were unequally affected by punishment. Face washing, standing and rearing on the hind legs, and scrabbling (standing against a wall and moving the forelegs) were differentially affected. A second complexity in the punishment situation is the fact that certain responses will be affected by certain kinds of punishment but not by others. Klunder and O'Boyle (1979) investigated the effects of punishment on the tendency of mice to attack and eat crickets. They found that when shock was used as the punisher, both attacking and eating could be reduced. But when the punisher was an injection of lithium chloride, which makes the mouse ill, the tendency to eat crickets was reduced by a much larger degree than was the tendency to attack the insects. Finally, Dunham (1978) points out that unpunished responses of various sorts can undergo changes during the punishment of some other response.

Schwartz (1989) outlines the following principles of punishment:

1. To obtain maximum punishment effects the punishing stimulus should be as intense as possible. Obviously this principle, although true, causes difficulties when we consider, say, the punishment of children. We have to ask at what point punishment becomes cruel.
2. The delay between the occurrence of the unwanted response and the punishment should be as short as possible. Again this principle, although true, can cause problems in life outside the laboratory. Sometimes it is not possible to introduce punishment immediately. Parents often find themselves saying to their children, "Just wait until I get you home! Then you will be sorry!" Unfortunately, the delayed punishment may prove to be less effective than immediate punishment would be.

3. The strength of punishment should not be increased gradually. Maximum punishment should be used from the outset. Again this principle causes problems in everyday life. Often parents will try some minimal or moderate level of punishment initially, only to increase the level of punishment as it becomes apparent that the lowest levels do no good. Parents don't want to hurt their children so they begin with low levels of punishment. Unfortunately, this technique is not the most effective; if possible it is better to use maximum punishment from the beginning, something many parents are not willing to do.

It is important to note that in spite of these principles, the application of punishment may not always work out as planned. If, for example, you wish to stop your dog from escaping through a hole in the backyard fence, you may wait patiently by the hole until the dog attempts to go through. As it passes through the opening, you may swat it with a newspaper. That is punishing a particular response, or is it? Maybe not. Your dog may well avoid you for two weeks and continue to use the hole in the fence.

AVERSION THERAPY.   Punishment has been used successfully in eliminating many human responses. In *aversion therapy*, which is essentially a punishment technique, unpleasant stimuli are associated with unwanted behaviors. Aversion therapy is often used to try to break "bad habits."

In one interesting study Morosko and Baer (1970) attempted to treat alcoholics by using a punishment procedure. Subjects were presented with six cups of liquid. Four of them contained nonalcoholic beverages, and the other two contained alcoholic beverages. Initially, the subjects were required to drink the contents of all six cups. They were shocked as they drank the two alcoholic beverages. On subsequent trials the subjects were allowed to omit the alcoholic beverages and thereby avoid the concomitant shock. Consumption of alcohol dropped markedly. The avoidance effect persisted beyond the laboratory situation. Follow-up work indicated that many of the subjects decreased their everyday drinking (see also Wilson, Leaf, & Nathan, 1975).

Nocturnal bruxism is the grinding of the teeth during sleep. If left untended this condition can lead to unnecessary tooth wear, periodontal problems, and face and head pain. Vasta and Wortman (1988) treated this condition using a form of punishment. Specifically, following an episode of bruxing the patient was required to engage in a specified period of voluntary teeth clenching. Apparently the voluntary bruxing served as a punishment because these investigators report a rapid and substantial reduction in nocturnal bruxing. They point out that this system, compared to other methods, including drug treatment, is rapid, convenient, and inexpensive.

Friman (1988) provides yet another interesting variation of applied punishment training. He begins by noting that unwanted childhood behaviors such as excessive thumb sucking are often accompanied by other behaviors such as holding dolls. In this study thumb sucking was punished by the removal of the desired doll. Figure 2.5 shows clearly that this manipulation was successful. During a baseline period, when the doll was present, thumb sucking was high. During treatment periods, when the doll was removed, thumb sucking dropped rapidly. Follow-up measures

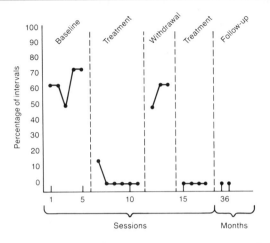

Figure 2.5 The percentage of intervals in which doll holding and thumb sucking occurred across baseline, intervention, withdrawal, and follow-up sessions. From Friman, P. C. Eliminating chronic thumb sucking by preventing a covarying response. *Journal of Behavior Therapy and Experimental Psychiatry*, 1988, *19*, 301–304. Figure 1 on p. 301.

taken three and six months later revealed that the reduction in thumb sucking showed some permanence. Parenthetically, it should be noted that some thumb sucking is normal and adaptive in very young children. So we need not worry unless the behavior is chronic after the age of four or five.

Goldiamond (1965) reduced stuttering by following it with delayed feedback of the subject's own voice. (Delayed feedback is highly aversive to most people.) In addition, Pierce and Risley (1974) effectively reduced certain unwanted behaviors in an urban recreational center by following them with punishing stimuli. Each time individuals engaged in such acts as leaving trash about, leaving pool cues out, crowding in line, arguing, or breaking things, they were punished by restrictions on their recreation time. Depending on the severity of the offense, from 1 to 15 minutes of recreation time were canceled. Many additional instances of aversion therapy are available. For example, Singh (1979) reduced breath holding in a 15-month-old boy by administering the smell of ammonia (see also Doke, Wolery, & Sumberg, 1983). Gray (1979) reports a case in which a child who constantly pulled out her own hair (a condition known as *trichotillomania*) was slapped four times on the hand each time she pulled her hair. She stopped. Aversion therapy can also be used to reduce obesity, overeating, and smoking. Clearly, aversion therapy should be used with great caution. The administration of pain must be carefully considered (see Lundin, 1974). Techniques such as the use of electric shock or ammonia fumes are very controversial (Dixon, Helsel, Rojahn, Cripollone, & Lubetsky, 1989).

STOP THOUGHT.   An interesting variation on the punishment theme involves *stop thought* (Turner, Holzman, & Jacob, 1983; Tyron, 1979; Tyron & Palladino, 1979). Stop thought, although controversial, is often taken as an effective way of eliminating obsessive thoughts, which we cannot seem to get out of our mind. They can be mild (Did I leave the lights on?) or very severe (I want to hurt someone). In all cases, they recur and become disruptive in our life.

In the stop-thought technique subjects are trained to shout "Stop!" either aloud or to themselves, each time the obsessive thought begins. The sharp command "Stop!" is thought of as a mild punishment. In some cases the subject is asked to imagine a therapist or other authoritarian figure shouting "Stop!" The technique appears to be at least partially successful in reducing obsessive thoughts.

TIME OUT.   Sometimes undesirable behaviors can be eliminated by what has come to be known as the *time-out technique*. Basically, time out is a form of temporary social isolation. Several hundred studies have been published that describe the elimination of various kinds of preadolescent misbehaviors using time out. In a typical study, disruptive classroom behaviors might be eliminated by requiring the problem child to sit in a semi-isolated chair for a specified period of time.

Although many successes have been reported, the technique is not completely problem-free. For example, Roberts (1988) points out that putting a child in a time-out chair does not necessarily guarantee that the child will stay in that chair; some problem children will simply not stay put. In his study, Roberts used two forms of punishment to ensure that the misbehaving children stayed in the time-out chair. In one condition, escaping children were spanked while in another condition the escapees were confined for a brief time in a "barrier-enforced time-out room." Both methods were successful. In essence, Roberts used additional punishment to ensure that the children would experience the original time-out punishment.

THE RELATIONSHIP BETWEEN AVOIDANCE AND PUNISHMENT TRAINING.   Mowrer (1960) has argued that punishment training is not that different from avoidance training. He writes that in both cases fear is classically conditioned and then instrumentally escaped. As we already know, in avoidance conditioning a rat's fear is classically conditioned to the white box. The rat then learns instrumentally to escape from that situation. In punishment training the fear is classically conditioned to the *punished response itself*. The response itself is then avoided. It is as though the *thought* of making the punished response makes us afraid to do it.

Keep in mind that, although distinctions have been made between reward, avoidance, escape, and punishment training, these distinctions are operational and descriptive. A little thinking has led us to the position that the four types have a good deal in common.

Positive versus Negative Reinforcement

Positive reinforcement usually refers to anything that, if presented to the organism following a response, will increase the probability of that response's occurring. For example, if a hungry rat presses a bar and is then given food, that reinforcement is called a positive one. Things such as food, water, sex, and the opportunity to explore are usually considered to be positive reinforcers.

Negative reinforcement usually refers to something aversive that, if *taken away* from the animal, will increase the probability of a response's occurring. For example, if an animal leaps a barrier and shock is *removed*, then the probability of the escape response will have been strengthened. Generally speaking, noxious stimuli, such as shock, are considered to be negative reinforcers. They must be removed to obtain the reinforcing effect.

Now, having made this neat distinction between positive and negative reinforcers, can we argue that it might be a superficial one? Consider the rat pressing the bar for food. Does this situation involve a positive or a negative reinforcer? We are tempted to say positive, because we are presenting something to the animal following its response. Is it possible, though, that the reinforcing factor in this situation is the *removal of hunger pangs* and not the mere presentation of the food? Is it possible that this situation involves a negative reinforcer? It is as though psychologists have distinguished between positive and negative reinforcers not on the basis of what is important to the animal but on the basis of what they do in the experimental situation. Positive and negative reinforcers may be opposite sides of the same coin. As far as the animal is concerned, the presentation of food may normally be the same as taking away hunger pains. The removal of shock may be the same as presenting the state of not being shocked.

If we entertain the possibility that positive and negative reinforcers may be opposite sides of the same coin, then we must consider the possibility that reward training and escape training are identical. In reward training the rat may merely be learning to escape from the unpleasant state of being hungry or otherwise deprived. In escape training the rat may be reinforced by the presentation of the state of nonshock. The two processes may well coincide. When we are hungry and seek food, we may well be reinforced by the presentation of food *and* the removal of hunger pangs. It is difficult to separate the presentation of pleasant factors and the removal of unpleasant ones.

Some interesting experiments bear on this issue. They suggest that both the presentation of food *and* the removal of hunger reinforce behavior. A discussion of these studies will be delayed until a later section.

Responding versus Not Responding

If an animal is punished for making a particular response and ceases to make that response, it is customary to say that we have taught the animal what not to do. A response has been eliminated. But is that the case? Is it not possible to think of the act of not responding as an actual response in some cases? When we try not to be rude to others, because we know it will lead to punishment, are we not actually engaging in some kind of response? If we think of the act of not responding, or inhibiting a response, as an active response, then punishment training and reward training become closely related. Punishment training can be thought of as reward training in which the response of not responding is rewarded by the absence of punishment. Before we accept the psychologists' distinction, we should think carefully about the meaning of their terms. These definitions are not as clean and crisp as we would like them to be.

Behavior Modification and Cognitive Behavior Modification

In exploring the various classical and instrumental types of learning, we have seen many examples of the ways in which practical human problems can sometimes be solved. Many of these examples involve behavior modification. *Behavior modification* is a very general term referring to any effort to alter human behavior through the application of the basic principles of conditioning. Traditionally, behavior modification has focused on changing overt, observable, noncognitive behavior (Peniston, 1988). It has been thought of as an alternative to the psychotherapies that essentially try to change the way people think and act by engaging them in conversation. Behavior modification techniques, for the most part, have tried to avoid "what goes on in the mind" and tried to emphasize the impact of reinforcement techniques on observable behaviors such as temper tantrums, drinking, smoking, and so on. Although behavior modification has addressed some cognitive problems (for example, phobias), the orientation has been to treat the human as though he or she were a laboratory animal whose physical behavior could be altered in much the same manner that we alter the behavior of the white rat—physically, nonverbally, and noncognitively.

Beginning in the mid-1970s a new orientation began to take hold within the ranks of behavior modifiers. The term *cognitive behavior modification* began to appear more and more often. Proponents of cognitive behavior modification, or CBM, argue that, if we can change the way people think, then we can assist them in their efforts to adjust. If we can alter the ways in which people describe themselves, if we can alter their beliefs, and if we can train them in a variety of coping skills, such as seeking information, anticipating problems, and achieving relaxation, then we may be able to improve their lot (Manning, 1988; Watson-Perczel, Latzker, Green, & McGimpsey, 1988).

A study by Neumann, Critelli, Tang, and Schneider (1988) represents a good example of cognitive behavior modification. Their concern was with male-dating anxiety; apparently such anxiety is a widespread problem among college males. In describing their successful cognitive behavior modification method they state:

> Subjects . . . were asked to identify negative self-statements occurring before, during, and after . . . past interactions with females. The irrational, self-defeating, and self-fulfilling nature of these self-statements was stressed, and group discussions focused on more appropriate, positive self-statements they might make during these situations. In addition, subjects were also given problem examples on cassette, with the tapes being stopped at key points to elicit group discussion of subjects' own self-statements or of those presented on tape. . . . Homework assignments included nightly relaxation practice, and the monitoring and recording of self-statements throughout the week. These self-statements were then discussed in group during the next session (p. 137).

Clearly, this form of therapy is of the cognitive variety. It involves altering how people feel about themselves.

A number of criticisms have been leveled against CBM. Aside from the fact that it is difficult to define, Ledwidge (1978, 1979) argues that CBM is a step in the wrong direction. He asserts that CBM is taking us back to mentalistic concepts such as thoughts and cognitions, which are next to impossible to define or measure. In a sense, CBM is turning back toward psychotherapeutic methods, where words and talk are the elements involved in changing behavior. Thus, CBM represents a turn toward just what behavior modification theorists first wanted to avoid—having to deal with elusive, unobservable elements such as thoughts, ideas, and images.

Criticism of CBM has not gone unanswered (see Locke, 1979; Mahoney & Kazdin, 1979; Meichenbaum, 1979b). Essentially, the CBM position is that a thought is as much a behavior as a bodily movement and, as such, should be subject to ordinary principles of learning. A thought, or a cognition, is not something mysterious and qualitatively different from a physical act. Even though it may be more difficult to measure, it is, nonetheless, a behavior. The CBM position holds that, although thoughts, beliefs, and cognitions might have been too difficult for us to study at one time, the time has now arrived for us to recognize their importance in our efforts to alter the human condition.

The crux of their argument is that we can no longer deny the importance of thought in determining behavior. Thoughts and physical actions interact with each other and affect each other. To ignore the power of thought in determining behavior is shortsighted and an obvious and enormous oversimplification.

Whatever the final outcome—which is hoped would be a softening and a blending of these two viewpoints—CBM seems to be firmly established (see Barrios & Shigetomi, 1979; Hollandsworth, Glazeski, Kirkland, Jones, & Van Norman, 1979; Mahoney, 1979; Meichenbaum, 1979a; Moon & Eisler, 1983).

MIXED METHODS: ASSERTION TRAINING.   Are behavior modification efforts *either* cognitive or noncognitive? Quite often the answer is no. Sometimes cognitive and noncognitive elements seem to be intertwined and intermingled within the same treatment.

Assertion training provides a good example of the way in which cognitive and noncognitive factors may be involved in a given treatment technique. Many of us are not assertive enough. We tend to become frustrated because we feel that we are being used or pushed around by others. When an unreasonable request is made of us ("Lend me $20, will you?"), we tend to say yes instead of politely but firmly saying no. We have not developed the technique of saying no. Assertion training (see Derry & Stone, 1979) is a technique designed to help us say no. We can learn to refuse to do what we should not be expected to do, and we can learn to ask for what we deserve.

Some steps in a sample assertion training program are given in Table 2.3. As you read through these steps, notice the blend, or mixture, of cognitive and noncognitive steps. Sometimes you are asked to change your ways of thinking, whereas at other points you are encouraged to change your behaviors. In other words, it may eventually prove to be impossible to separate, in any concrete way, cognitive and noncognitive behavior modification techniques. The distinction between cognitive and noncognitive behavior modification, which is receiving so much attention, may eventually fall by the wayside.

SELF–DIRECTED INTERVENTION.   Traditionally, behavior modification efforts have involved external control in the sense that rewards and punishments have been manipulated by someone *other than the subjects*. Thus, the experimenter has been in charge of deciding which of the subjects' actions should be rewarded or punished. But this is expensive in terms of time and effort. If it would work, a much

Table 2.3 Steps in Assertion Training

1. Examine your interactions. Are there situations that you need to handle more assertively? Do you at times hold opinions and feelings within you for fear of what would happen if you expressed them? Do you occasionally blow your cool and lash out angrily at others? Studying your interactions is easier if you keep a diary for a week or longer, recording the situations in which you acted timidly, those in which you were aggressive, and those that you handled assertively.

2. Select those interactions in which it would be to your benefit to be more assertive. They may include situations in which you were overly polite, overly apologetic, timid, and allowed others to take advantage of you, at the same time harboring feelings of resentment, anger, embarrassment, fear of others, or self-criticism for not having the courage to express yourself. Overly aggressive interactions in which you exploded in anger or walked over others also need to be dealt with. For *each* set of nonassertive or aggressive interactions, you can become more assertive, as shown in the next steps.

3. Concentrate on a specific incident in the past. Close your eyes for a few minutes and vividly imagine the details, including what you and the other person said and how you felt at the time and afterward.

4. Write down and review your responses. Ask yourself the following questions to determine how you presented yourself:

    a. Eye contact—did you look directly at the other person, in a relaxed, steady gaze? Looking down or away suggests a lack of self-confidence. Glaring is an aggressive response.
    b. Gestures—were your gestures appropriate, free flowing, relaxed, and used effectively to emphasize your messages? Awkward stiffness suggests nervousness; other gestures (such as an angry fist) signal an aggressive reaction.
    c. Body posture—did you show the importance of your message by directly facing the other person, by leaning toward that person, by holding your head erect, and by sitting or standing appropriately close?
    d. Facial expression—did your facial expression show a stern, firm pose consistent with an assertive response?
    e. Voice tone and volume—was your response stated in a firm, conversational tone? Shouting may suggest anger. Speaking softly suggests shyness, and a cracking voice suggests nervousness. Tape recording and listening to one's voice is a way to practice increasing or decreasing the volume.
    f. Speech fluency—did your speech flow smoothly, clearly, and slowly? Rapid speech or hesitation in speaking suggests nervousness. Tape assertive responses before you try them out in problem situations, so you can practice and improve your fluency.
    g. Timing—were your verbal reactions to a problem situation stated at a time closest to the incident that would appropriately permit you and the other person time to review the

(continued on page 55)

more practical procedure would be to have the subjects themselves monitor their own behavior and decide for themselves when they do and do not deserve a reward. This process of *self-direction* does away with the impractical necessity of having someone else constantly watch the subjects.

Recent years have seen many efforts to establish such self-directed interventions. For example, Black and Friesen (1983) had obese subjects make a monetary deposit. They could "win back" this deposit only if they lost weight. Traditionally, the subjects would have had to come in and be weighed by someone else to see if they had lost weight. But in their minimal intervention program Black and Friesen let the subjects make all the decisions about how much weight had been lost and how much of the deposit they deserved to have returned. The self-directed program resulted in significant weight loss (see also Burgio, Whitman, & Reid, 1983).

O'Brien, Riner, and Budd (1983) found that with a little initial help children were able to reward themselves for doing what their mother wanted them to do in

Table 2.3   *(continued from page 54)*

incident? Generally, spontaneous expressions are the best, but certain situations should be handled at a later time—for example, challenging some of your boss's erroneous statements in private rather than in front of a group that he or she is making a presentation to.

h. Message content—for a problem situation, which of your responses were nonassertive or aggressive, and which were assertive? Study the content and consider why you responded in a nonassertive or aggressive style.

5. Observe one or more effective models. Watch the verbal and nonverbal approaches that are assertively used to handle the types of interactions with which you have been having problems. Compare the consequences between their approach and yours. If possible, discuss their approach and their feelings about using it.

6. Make a list of various alternative approaches for being more assertive.

7. Close your eyes and visualize yourself using each of the above alternative approaches. For each approach, think through what the full set of interactions would be, along with the consequences. Select an approach or combination of approaches that you believe will be most effective for you to use. Through imagery, practice this approach until you feel comfortable that it will work for you.

8. Role-play the approach with someone else, perhaps a friend or counselor. If certain segments of your approach appear clumsy, awkward, timid, or aggressive, practice modifications until you become comfortable with the approach. Obtain feedback from the other person about the strengths and shortcomings of your approach. Compare your interactions with the guidelines for verbal and nonverbal assertive behavior to Step 4. It may be useful for the other person to role-play one or more assertive strategies, which you would then practice by reversing roles.

9. Repeat Steps 7 and 8 until you develop an assertive approach that you are comfortable with and believe will work best for you.

10. Use your approach in a real-life situation. The previous steps are designed to prepare you for the real event. Expect to be somewhat anxious when you first try to be assertive. If you are still too fearful of attempting to be assertive, repeat Steps 5–8. For those few individuals who fail to develop the needed confidence to try out being assertive, professional counseling is advised—expressing yourself and effective interactions with others are essential for personal happiness.

11. Reflect on the effectiveness of your effort. Did you "keep your cool"? Consider the nonverbal and verbal guidelines for assertive behavior discussed in Step 4; what components of your responses were assertive, aggressive, and nonassertive? What were the consequences of your effort? How did you feel after trying out this new set of interactions?

12. Expect some success with your early efforts but not complete personal satisfaction. Personal growth and interacting more effectively with others is a continual learning process.

Adapted from Zastrow, C. How to become more assertive. In C. Zastrow and D. H. Chang (Eds.), *The personal problem solver.* Englewood Cliffs, N.J.: Prentice-Hall, 1977, pp. 238–240. Reprinted by permission of Prentice-Hall, Inc.

the home. Mother didn't control the rewards; the children did. The children monitored their own behavior and gave themselves a token each time they did something that was desired. Tokens could later be exchanged for more tangible rewards.

Posobiec and Renfrew (1988) have taken the concept of self-directed intervention a step further; they had their subject not only self-administer the program but design it as well. They were concerned with *bulimia*, which is a condition involving binge eating usually followed by self-induced vomiting. Their subject, a 20-year-old undergraduate, had a nine-year history of bulimic behavior, including fasting for several days followed by binge eating and vomiting several times a day. Her weight fluctuated dramatically; during one six-month period her weight went from 198 lb to 87 lb.

The investigators first taught her some of the basic principles of conditioning. She then assumed responsibility for designing a workable treatment program. She decided which reinforcers would be used. She decided which behaviors would be

Box 2.2 Computers and Obsessive Compulsive Behavior: A Case Study

Ms A, a 58-year-old single female with a 37-year history of obsessive compulsive disorder, was self-referred to our clinic and had no prior psychotherapy of any kind. Her obsessive thoughts included fears of hurting other people, especially small children and of saying or writing obscenities without her awareness. Her checking rituals included locks on doors, windows, and automobiles, electrical switches and appliances, faucets, emergency brake in automobile, poisonous substances, sharp objects, the position of her hands and feet, and anything she had written, including checks and letters. At the time of the initial behavioral assessment, she reported 33 objects which were checked daily at home, and another 24 objects which were checked outside the home and at work. Ms A was highly motivated to change her rituals, but reported that the majority of her checking rituals occurred when she was alone, and she was reluctant to ask her sister, with whom she lived, for help in behavioral treatment.

To facilitate the learning process two portable computers were used in sequence. The first, a laptop-size computer . . . was used initially in the home to familiarize the patient with the procedure. The second, a calculator-size computer . . . was substituted after the patient was familiar with the technique, and was carried outside the home.

A computer program (OC-CHECK) was developed to closely follow the behavioral procedures used with patients seen in our obsessive compulsive disorder clinic. Patients are instructed to consult the program (requiring 2–5 minutes) each time an urge occurs to engage in checking rituals, or each time some object is actually checked; with the computer modifying its instructions and feedback in each case. In the former case, OC-CHECK instructs the patient to resist the urge to check for a period of 3 minutes, which is counted off by the computer; the patient is then reminded that no negative consequences will result from continuing to resist the urge to check. In the latter case, OC-CHECK reminds the patient that it is desirable to consult the computer before checking. The program stores the date, time, intensity, and frequency of all urges to check and checking rituals, and feedback is given regarding the number of checks performed each day.

To permit patients to use the computer program more conveniently outside the home, a shortened version of OC-CHECK was developed to run on the calculator-size computer. The elements of the original program were maintained, but data were totaled each week.

On beginning use of the laptop computer (see Figure 1a) Ms A's records indicated an immediate reduction in frequency of checking rituals carried out at home. She reported improved ability to comply with behavioral instructions of exposure and response prevention, and after 17 weeks of using the laptop computer, Ms A reported that her checking rituals at home were reduced to their (continued on page 57)

reinforced and which would be extinguished. By carefully self-administering her self-designed program she was able to completely eliminate bulimic behavior for as long as nine months.

Further advances in the process of self-administered behavior modification have involved the use of portable computers as the case study in Box 2.2 indicates.

(continued from page 56)

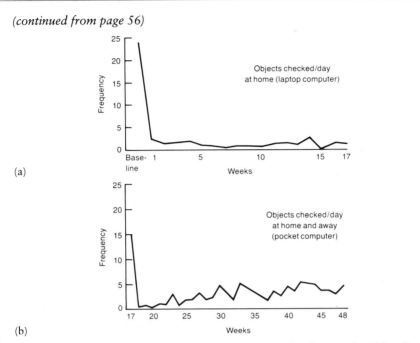

Figure 1 Frequency of objects checked per day over 48 weeks of case study. (a) Baseline indicates frequency of checking rituals at home following 36 months of standard behavioral treatment and pharmacotherapy. Dependent measure is objects checked/day at home, where laptop computer was used. (b) Week 17 represents beginning of pocket computer use to generalize reductions outside the home. Dependent measure is objects checked/day outside the home.

lowest level in 30 years, and she listed 20 objects in her home she no longer checked.

After Ms A substituted the pocket computer for use both at home and at work, her records indicated an immediate decline in total checking rituals (see Figure 1b). Ms A's checking remained at low levels over the following 31 weeks of using the pocket computer, although moderate fluctuations continue with changing life and job stresses and mood fluctuations. When Ms A did not use the computer on several days, she reported an increase in checking rituals. After 49 weeks of using the program, Ms A's computer records indicate that the intensity of her urges to check have begun slowly to decrease concordant with her decreased checking rituals.

Reprinted from Baer, L., Minichiello, W. E., Jenike, M. A., & Holland, A. Use of a portable computer to assist behavioral treatment in a case of compulsive disorder. *Journal of Behavior Therapy and Experimental Psychiatry*, 1988, 3, 237–240. Reprinted by permission of Pergamon Press.

Although self-directed experiments look hopeful and allow for the tailoring of individual programs (Straw & Terre, 1983), they may not be appropriate for all problems. For example, Holden, O'Brien, Barlow, and Stetson (1983) report that self-directed programs are relatively ineffective in helping agoraphobics (those who fear open spaces).

SUMMARY

1. Classical conditioning is a widespread phenomenon. Examples include *nictitating membrane* and *eye-blink conditioning, conditioning of the EDR, aversive conditioning using sickness as the UCR, semantic conditioning, masochism, phobias,* and *immune system conditioning.*

2. The temporal spacing of the CS and the UCS is an important variable in the study of classical conditioning. Typical CS–UCS patterns include *delayed, simultaneous, trace,* and *backward procedures.*

3. A CR may be observed by leaving out the UCS occasionally or, in the case of delayed and trace procedures, by observing the development of the CR before the onset of the UCS.

4. The CR is not the same as the UCR. The CR has been viewed as a component of the UCR and as a response that prepares the organism for the UCS.

5. Responses within the typical conditioning situation are not limited to CRs and UCRs. For example, random blinks, voluntary responses, and UCRs to the CS (alpha responses) have been identified in eye-blink conditioning.

6. Pseudoconditioning refers to the fact that a CS, when presented alone following a long series of solitary UCS presentations, will often elicit a response resembling a CR. Pseudoconditioning has been interpreted in terms of generalized excitement and as a case of true classical conditioning.

7. The length of the CS–UCS interval is a critical variable in classical conditioning. In many cases an interval of about .5 of a second seems to be optimal, but this optimal interval interacts with other variables, such as CS complexity.

8. CS and UCS intensity is positively related to strength of conditioning.

9. A recent trend in the field, multiple-response measurement, has focused on the fact that classical conditioning involves many different, and perhaps related, changes within the organism.

10. Latent inhibition (the CS preexposure effect) refers to the fact that repeated presentations of the CS alone, before paired presentation of the CS and UCS, will sometimes lead to poor conditioning.

11. The UCS preexposure effect refers to the finding that repeated presentations of the UCS, before paired presentation of the CS and UCS, will also lead to poor conditioning.

12. A compound CS is a CS composed of two or more discrete components.

13. Compound stimulus effects include *sensory preconditioning, higher-order conditioning, overshadowing, compounding, blocking, conditioned inhibition,* and *serial compounding.*

14. Recent informational theories of classical conditioning argue that conditioning occurs only when the CS predicts, or carries information about, the upcoming UCS.

15. Bed-wetting, or enuresis, can be eliminated with classical conditioning.

16. The polygraph is based on classical conditioning procedures.

17. Instrumental reward training refers to a situation in which the animal is rewarded when it makes a particular response.

18. Shaping refers to the reinforcement of closer and closer approximations to a desired response.

19. Tokens, money, social rewards, and many other reinforcers have been used to reward many human behaviors, including polydipsia.

20. In avoidance training the animal is punished when it fails to make a particular response.
21. Relative to reward-trained responses, avoidance-trained responses are extremely durable under conditions of extinction, but flooding can eliminate them.
22. The two-factor theory of avoidance conditioning argues that "fear" is classically conditioned to the punishment situation and that the animal then learns, in an instrumental fashion, to escape from this fear. The reduction in fear is the reinforcer.
23. Learned helplessness refers to the fact that avoidance learning following inescapable shock will sometimes be very poor.
24. Five theories of learned helplessness include the Seligman formulation, the competing-response interpretation, the neurochemical interpretation, the dual-process model, and the egotism interpretation. Opoids may be produced by the brain during learned helplessness.
25. In escape training, inevitable punishment is continued unless the animal makes a particular response.
26. In punishment training the animal is punished when it makes a particular response.
27. Maximum punishment effects occur when the punishment is as intense as possible, when the delay between response and punishment is short, and when maximum punishment is used from the outset. Aversion therapy involves punishment.
28. Mowrer argues that punishment and avoidance training are essentially the same thing. In avoidance training "fear" is classically conditioned to the external situation, whereas in punishment training "fear" is somehow classically conditioned to the punished response itself.
29. Positive reinforcement usually refers to anything that, if presented to the animal, will increase the probability of a response's occurring. Negative reinforcement usually refers to anything that, if taken away from the animal, will increase the probability of a response's occurring.
30. The distinction between positive and negative reinforcers may be a superficial one. The presentation of something positive may not be different from the removal of something negative.
31. It is possible that the act of not responding is, in some situations, an actual response. If this position is taken, then many of the distinctions among the different types of conditioning become blurred.
32. Traditional behavior modification is currently being influenced by cognitive behavior modification.
33. Assertion training involves both forms of behavior modification.
34. Self-directed minimal intervention procedures are being used more and more often.

CHAPTER

3

LEARNING TASKS: SOME SIMILARITIES AND DIFFERENCES

INTRODUCTION

In this chapter we shall examine some of the important similarities and differences among the various learning and memory tasks commonly used in research. These tasks (for example, classical and instrumental conditioning, verbal learning tasks, and cognitive tasks) appear to be quite distinct on a procedural level. Are we sure, however, that these different tasks reflect different underlying learning processes, or is it possible that they are encompassed within some common learning process? Do we have the ability to learn in more than one way?

Several representative situations will be examined. They include instrumental conditioning, classical conditioning, paired-associate (PA) learning, language learning, and priming in lexical decisions. First, PA learning will be examined in relation to other types: Is it more like instrumental conditioning, or is it more closely related to classical conditioning? Does it clearly represent a totally separate kind of learning? Next, we shall briefly consider the possibility that language learning and lexical-decision situations are closely related to the other situations under consideration. Finally, differences between classical and instrumental conditioning will be examined. Are the traditional differences between these two types of learning substantial, or might they be superficial ones that do little to uphold the position that classical and instrumental conditioning are fundamentally different?

This exercise is limited in that it considers only selected learning tasks. If it can be shown that these types are closely related, there is no guarantee that all other types of learning (for example, problem solving, sequential learning, and generation effects) will also be closely tied together. But the weight of the evidence would suggest that such a possibility should be taken seriously.

The implications of these questions are far reaching. *If, on the one hand, it is found that humans possess the capacity to learn in several different ways, perhaps utilizing different levels or aspects of the nervous system, then theories, laws, rules, models, and generalizations governing each of these learning capacities will have to be developed. If, on the other hand, it is eventually determined that some underlying process can account for all the disparate types of learning situations, then some single, fundamental explanatory system may suffice.*

We should be aware of a danger here. A lack of precision in our thinking about learning tasks may lead us to "find" similarities among tasks when they do not really exist. Thus, we must be careful not to overemphasize similarities when those similarities may be superficial. We seek neither to accept unwarranted similarities nor to dismiss legitimate ones. Rather, we wish to grasp all the possible interpretations of some fairly complicated situations.

PAIRED–ASSOCIATE LEARNING

Paired-associate learning, essentially a human task, requires the subject to associate pairs of verbal units. Does this learning task definitely represent some unique form of learning, or is it possible that it may be included in some other category, such as classical or instrumental conditioning?

It can be argued that PA learning is an instance of instrumental reward training. Suppose that a subject is required to associate the nonsense syllable BEV with the nonsense syllable JAX. When the computer exposes JAX, the subject's task is to recall and say aloud "BEV." The reward, or reinforcement, for making the correct response comes in the form of response confirmation. The computer, by exposing

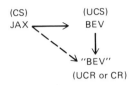

Figure 3.1 Schematic representation of paired-associate learning as an instance of classical conditioning.

BEV, informs the subject that he or she was correct in saying "BEV." Making correct responses is definitely rewarding for the average subject in this situation. Thus, the PA situation contains many of the elements of the typical Skinner box situation. The human sees the stimulus word, makes a response, and is rewarded. The rat sees the bar, presses it, and is rewarded.

This does not mean we have *proved* that paired associates are learned in exactly the same way that the rat learns to press a bar. Our mental activities (organizing, testing hypotheses) are quite a bit more complicated than the rat's mental operations. But it does suggest that the essential observable qualities of the two situations (*stimulus, response,* and *reinforcement*) are duplicated. In other words, it would seem premature to conclude that instrumental conditioning and PA learning represent clearly different types of learning.

The situation is complicated by the fact that PA learning can be thought of as an instance of classical rather than instrumental learning (Figure 3.1). Consider the JAX–BEV pair. Assume, for the sake of argument, that JAX is a CS and that the printed syllable BEV is a UCS. In the PA learning situation JAX (the CS) is presented just before BEV (the UCS). This corresponds to a delayed classical conditioning procedure. When the printed syllable BEV is presented, the subject reacts to it. That is, the subject thinks, or perhaps even says, "BEV." The saying or thinking of BEV may be considered the UCR. It happens every time the printed syllable BEV is presented. At first JAX (the CS) does not elicit the thought or the verbalization BEV. As JAX (CS) and BEV (UCS) are paired over and over, JAX (CS) begins to elicit the thought or verbalization BEV. When JAX (CS) elicits BEV, we call *that* BEV a CR. Note that, as conditioning progresses, BEV (CR) begins to occur in *anticipation* of the UCS (BEV). It corresponds to the pattern obtained in classical conditioning, where the CR follows the CS and precedes the UCS.

Interpretations of PA learning have not been limited to classical and instrumental learning. Many investigators have begun to think of human learning and retention in terms of information processing, with an emphasis on storage and retrieval mechanisms (Bourne, Dominowski, & Loftus, 1979; Lindsay & Norman, 1972). A detailed consideration of the information-processing approach will be discussed in later sections.

In summary, PA learning cannot clearly be distinguished from classical and instrumental conditioning. It may or may not represent a distinct learning process. Probably the most scholarly stance to assume is one based on an awareness of the many alternative ways of thinking about PA learning—and about human learning in general.

LANGUAGE LEARNING

Without doubt, language is a powerful tool, and our ability to learn and use this tool sets us apart from most of the rest of the animal kingdom. As we shall see, language acquisition involves complex processes that are not as yet fully understood. But it is instructive at this juncture to point out that our now familiar friends, classical and instrumental conditioning, as well as paired-associated learning, have much in common with at least some aspects of language learning.

For example, PA learning, at least on some level, resembles what we do when we attach verbal meaning to words. When we learn that *ocho* in Spanish means *eight* in English, we are forming a paired associate. When we learn definitions, we are engaging in a rough form of PA learning. The whole process of associating verbal meanings with verbal units resembles PA learning. Of course, there are alternative interpretations of language acquisition, but at the same time it is difficult to deny that at least some aspects of language learning resemble PA learning.

Similarly, some aspects of language acquisition can be thought of in terms of classical conditioning. For example, the word *dad* may acquire some of its emotional meaning through classical conditioning. The real father is the UCS. The spoken word *dad* is the CS. The real father (UCS) elicits some complex emotional response (UCR) in the child. This emotional response becomes conditioned to the word *dad* (CS), such that when the word *dad* occurs in the absence of the actual father, a CR (resembling the UCR) will occur.

Finally, language acquisition can be thought of as resembling instrumental conditioning. It is like reward training; each time a child says the word *mama*, he or she receives love, attention, and praise. Using words is instrumental in getting what we want.

But do not be misled by these parallels between language learning and the other forms of learning. Language learning is complex and may involve many different processes.

PRIMING

The priming procedure in experiments involving lexical decisions is, relative to tasks such as classical and instrumental conditioning, a newcomer in the field of learning and memory (see Donnelly, 1988; Law & Tulving, 1988). As you will recall from Chapter 1, a lexical-decision task requires subjects to make some decision about a briefly exposed item, such as deciding if the item is a true word or if it has an *H* in it. The priming effect refers to the fact that these decisions are made more quickly and accurately if, before the subjects see the briefly exposed target item, they see a word that is related to that target. For example, people more quickly recognize that *canary* is a true word if they are first shown *bird* rather than first being shown *rock*. The argument is that *bird* somehow activates *canary* and makes it more easily processed. This priming technique is useful in studying how words are organized in our vocabulary (see Mitchell & Brown, 1988; Ratcliff & McKoon, 1988).

This task seems quite different from classical and instrumental conditioning, doesn't it? But if we think about it for a moment, some of these differences disappear. Specifically, priming is really only testing learning that occurred *before* the experiment began. It is testing a person's vocabulary, and that vocabulary was certainly well established before the subject walked in and began the priming experiment. And there is every reason to assume, as we learned in the preceding section, that classical and instrumental learning may be involved in language learning, including vocabulary learning. Thus, *priming may be nothing more than a way to test the strength of learning that was accomplished through classical or instrumental events long before the priming experiment began.*

COMPARING CLASSICAL AND INSTRUMENTAL CONDITIONING

After suggesting that any number of different human verbal tasks can be thought of as being closely related to classical and instrumental conditioning, the relationship between these two learning tasks can be addressed directly. Are they related forms of some underlying process? The answer to this question has been shifting slowly. Years ago it was assumed that instrumental and classical conditioning represented two distinct learning systems. More recent research has suggested that this traditional distinction may have to be abandoned or, at least, modified.

Our discussion will proceed in three stages. First, we will look at some of the problems inherent in trying to compare the two types of conditioning. Second, we will examine in detail some of the attempts to condition the same response both classically and instrumentally. Finally, we will explore the ways in which the traditional distinction, so firmly held for so many years, is beginning to be questioned.

Instrumental Conditioning in Classical Conditioning

It may well be that we never have a case of pure classical conditioning or a case of pure instrumental conditioning. Instrumental conditioning may always involve classical conditioning, and classical conditioning may always possess attributes of the instrumental paradigm. In classical eye-blink conditioning, the CR may reduce the impact of the noxious UCS. By blinking, the subject partially avoids the air puff. To the extent that the CR does avoid the air puff, it becomes instrumental in the animal's life. It affects its future well-being. Hence, this classical situation possesses attributes of the instrumental paradigm.

Even the use of a rabbit's nictitating membrane response (NMR) does not eliminate the possibility that the CR reduces the noxious quality of the UCS. Although the NMR seldom sweeps past the midline of the pupil, it does appear to block at least some of the aversive air puff (see Gormezano, Prokasy, & Thompson, 1987).

Other types of classical conditioning also involve reinforced instrumental learning. In the salivary conditioning situation meat powder (UCS) eaten after salivation may promote digestion or may be more pleasant than dry meat powder eaten without preliminary salivation. Hence, the conditioned salivary response may be reinforced. It is difficult to be certain about these things, but the idea that classical conditioning may involve instrumental conditioning has been discussed by a number of authors (Coleman, 1975; Gormezano, Kehoe, & Marshall, 1983; Dickinson & Mackintosh, 1978). The issue lives on. For example, Miller, Greco, Vigorite, and Marlin (1983) reported evidence for the idea that a CS warns the rat of upcoming tail shock. The rat then prepares for that unpleasant shock experience, either by bracing against it or perhaps even by releasing opiatelike endorphins in the brain. On the other side of the issue we have Domjan and Burkhard (1982) arguing just as strongly that classical conditioning can occur in the absence of this kind of reinforcing event.

Classical Conditioning in Instrumental Conditioning

HOPE AND FEAR.   Just as classical conditioning never seems to be quite pure, so instrumental conditioning never seems to be completely free of classical conditioning elements. The case of instrumental avoidance learning has already been examined; "fear" may be classically conditioned followed by instrumental escape from that fear. Even more interesting is the fact that classical conditioning has been implicated in simple reward training (Trapold & Overmeir, 1972). If a rat is trained to press a bar in a Skinner box and is reinforced for doing so, then it experiences the pairing of the Skinner box (CS) with the food (UCS). The positive reaction to the food, whatever you want to call it, becomes conditioned to the situation such that, when the rat is placed in the Skinner box in the future, it will experience a CR. This CR has been called, among other things, hope, conditioned excitement, and incentive motivation. A rough counterpart of this kind of CR would be what you might experience when you are very, very hungry and approach your favorite restaurant. You can almost taste the food. The closer you get, the more excited you become. The conditioned excitement seems to pull you toward your goal. It somehow interacts with your instrumental behaviors.

The upshot is the current emphasis on the idea that classical conditioning is always present in instrumental situations. Classical conditioning, furthermore, is assumed to provide some of the motivation for the instrumental behavior. Whether it is classically conditioned fear or hope, these conditioned responses are such that they provide some of the push behind the instrumental response (Lovibond, 1983).

AUTOSHAPING.   Autoshaping (Brown & Jenkins, 1968; Gamzu & Schwam, 1974; Pisacreta, Redwood, & Witt, 1983; Wasserman & Molina, 1975) refers to what happens when reinforcement is presented, regardless of whether the animal responds. (For related work see Skinner's [1948] early, classic analysis of so-called *superstitious behavior*.) In a typical autoshaping experiment the illumination of a key is always followed by delivery of food. Thus, a hungry pigeon need not respond at all in this situation. It need only wait until the key lights up and then eat the food, which always follows the light. And yet it has been observed that the pigeon does peck the key. The key-pecking response develops even though it is not necessary for the receipt of a reward.

This effect calls into question the very nature of what is normally called instrumental conditioning. It suggests that a strong element of classical conditioning is present in the typical instrumental-conditioning situation. The UCS is the food. The food (UCS) automatically elicits a pecking response (the UCR). The UCS (food) is paired with a CS (the light). After a series of such pairings, the CS (light) comes to elicit a CR (pecking in response to the light), which resembles the UCR (pecking in response to the food).

In summary, even if classical and instrumental conditioning are different, they are linked so inextricably that for all practical purposes, attempts to separate them may finally prove to be futile.

Conditioning the Same Response Two Ways

Early experimenters assumed that the way to separate classical and instrumental conditioning would be to isolate one response and then condition that response both classically and instrumentally. If one or the other conditioning procedure yielded better conditioning of that given response, then it could be argued that the two procedures do differ and that one is superior to the other. Although the approach makes sense, the results have been equivocal. Sometimes instrumental conditioning leads to faster conditioning (Brogden, Lipman, & Culler, 1938), and sometimes classical conditioning is superior (Logan, 1951).

In the former study guinea pigs were shocked (the UCS) in a revolving exercise wheel. The shock produced running (the UCR). A buzzer (CS) was paired with the shock. In the classical, or nonavoidance, condition the animal was shocked whether it ran or not. In the instrumental, or avoidance, condition the animal was not shocked if it ran but was shocked if it failed to run. The group that could avoid the shock (instrumental conditioning) did a lot more running over a series of trials than did the group that received the shock no matter what it did. This study seems to suggest that instrumental conditioning is superior to classical conditioning.

In contrast, in the Logan (1951) study an eye blink (CR) either avoided an air puff (instrumental conditioning) or did not avoid an air puff (classical conditioning). The nonavoidance, or classical, group yielded faster conditioning than did the avoidance, or instrumental, group. Thus, one study suggests that classical conditioning is superior, whereas the other suggests that instrumental conditioning is superior. Numerous problems arise from this type of comparison experiment, and they have occupied psychologists for many years. Hellige and Grant (1974a, 1974b) provide a treatment of this approach.

Three Differences between Instrumental and Classical Conditioning

If you had taken this course a number of years ago, you might have read that instrumental and classical conditioning were clearly distinct with several obvious differences between the two types of conditioning. Things were relatively simple then. But matters have become a bit more complicated, and psychologists have begun to question the validity of these traditional differences.

DISTINCTION 1: CONTIGUITY AND REINFORCEMENT.   Many psychologists believe that instrumental conditioning involves reinforcement, whereas classical conditioning does not. According to this position, all instrumental responses, such as bar pressing, are laid down, or acquired, through the application of reinforcement. Unless the animal is reinforced, the response will not be acquired. In contrast, classically conditioned responses are presumed to be acquired without the aid of reinforcement. If a response (such as an eye blink) occurs in the presence of a stimulus (such as a buzzer), that response will be connected to that stimulus automatically and without reinforcement. According to this position, temporal *contiguity* of the stimulus and response is supposed to be *necessary* and *sufficient* for classical conditioning to occur. (Two things are temporally contiguous if they occur close together in time.) Temporal contiguity is assumed to be necessary for instrumental conditioning but not sufficient. For instrumental conditioning to occur both contiguity and reinforcement are required.

We already know where this distinction begins to break down. Classical conditioning may well involve subtle types of reinforcement. A conditioned eye blink, for example, may be reinforced in that it partially avoids the noxious air puff. Although it has not been clearly established that classical conditioning always involves reinforcement, it is a possibility. To the extent we feel that this interpretation is valid, we shall want to reject the notion that classical conditioning does not involve reinforcement. On this basis classical and instrumental conditioning cannot be distinguished with any certainty, for reinforcing qualities can be identified in both situations. Kimmel (1965) has considered this argument in detail.

Furthermore, studies (see Rescorla & Wagner, 1972) have indicated that temporal contiguity may be necessary but not, after all, *sufficient* for classical conditioning to occur. You will recall from Chapter 2 that an experiment can be conducted to demonstrate that, if a UCS is equally likely to occur or not to occur with a CS, then that CS will not begin to elicit a CR even though it occurs in temporal proximity to the UCS and the UCR. In other words, the CS and the UCS do occur together in a contiguous relationship, at least part of the time, but no conditioning occurs. Thus, reinforcing events can be identified in classical situations, and, further, contiguity is not sufficient for classical conditioning to occur.

DISTINCTION 2: THE EFFECT OF RESPONSES ON THE ANIMAL'S FUTURE.   What happens to an animal in an instrumental conditioning situation is strongly affected by whether it responds. If it responds, it receives a reinforcement. If it fails to respond, it gets nothing. Events in the classical conditioning situation, by contrast, are often presumed to be independent of the animal's actions. If the animal fails to respond to the CS, it receives the UCS. If it responds to the CS, it *still* receives the UCS. The CS and UCS are delivered in the same manner each time, regardless of the animal's actions. Hence, many psychologists have concluded that in classical conditioning the animal's future is unaffected by its actions, whereas in instrumental conditioning the animal's actions strongly affect its future.

This argument is specious. As we have seen, the animal's future is indeed affected by its conditioned response in a classical situation. Receiving an air puff against a partially closed eye is probably not the same as receiving one against a fully opened eye.

This so-called distinction is closely tied to the previous one. To the extent that an animal's conditioned response is followed by a reinforcer (air-puff avoidance), then that conditioned response is clearly affecting the animal's future (Estes, 1969; Wahlsten & Cole, 1972).

DISTINCTION 3: VOLUNTARY VERSUS INVOLUNTARY RESPONDING.   Of all the distinctions between instrumental and classical conditioning, the one most commonly cited involves the notion that classical conditioning is a simpler type of learning and that only *involuntary* responses can be modified by it. Because instrumental conditioning is presumed to be a more complicated type of learning, it is argued that only *voluntary* responses can be modified by this technique.

The distinction seems to make sense, in some intuitive way, when one surveys the responses discussed in previous sections. Involuntary responses, such as eye blinks, heart rate, and salivation, have been modified by classical procedures. Complicated voluntary responses, such as bar pressing and leaping over barriers, have been modified by the instrumental procedures. The assumption behind this distinction is that the two types of conditioning involve different levels, or aspects, of the total nervous system, with the classical procedures involving involuntary response systems and the instrumental procedures modifying more advanced voluntary responses. As we shall see, there is doubt among psychologists about the validity of this distinction.

Can Involuntary Responses Be Instrumentally Conditioned?

Against all traditional thought, Neal Miller has asked the intriguing question: Can involuntary responses be conditioned instrumentally? In other words, can the strength of an involuntary response be increased if it is followed by a reinforcement? Over a number of years Miller (1973, 1978) and his colleagues have conducted a series of experiments that seem to suggest that involuntary responses can actually be conditioned instrumentally.

Miller concentrated on visceral responses (for example, heart rate and intestinal contraction), which are mediated by the autonomic nervous system. The basic design of his experiments is as follows: The skeletal muscles of a rat are paralyzed with curare. (As these muscles are voluntarily controlled by the animal, paralysis removes them as a source of possible contamination in the experiment.) Paralysis with curare does not affect the involuntary responses under consideration. Next, the visceral response (say, heart rate) is recorded accurately. A rat's heart rate is not constant. Sometimes it increases a little; sometimes it decreases. Each time the experimenters observe one of those little, spontaneous increases, they reward the animal. One problem Miller had to face was how to reward a paralyzed rat. He solved the problem by using escape from mild shock to the tail as one reinforcement. The animal had to increase its heart rate to escape shock. Miller found that rats will increase their heart rate from 5% to 20% in order to escape shock. He has also used brain stimulation as a reinforcer.

It is possible that in the situation Miller used (the animal in paralysis and being shocked) the heart rate would go up due to fear, excitement, tension, or general arousal. Recognizing this possibility, Miller rewarded some animals when they showed a decrease in heart rate. These animals decreased their heart rate over a series of sessions. Hence, the effect cannot be attributed to excitement or arousal.

Figure 3.2 indicates that, when animals are rewarded for increases or decreases in heart rate, they will show increases and decreases, respectively. But animals rewarded for intestinal contraction or relaxation will not alter their heart rate (even though they will alter their intestinal activities). This *specificity* of the learning is further evidence for the notion that the experiment is not just increasing the general arousal level of the animal.

In addition to his work with heart rate and intestinal contraction Miller has been able to condition urine formation. He has also reported being able to train a rat to blush in one ear but not the other. Keep in mind that the instrumental training of so-called involuntary responses argues against the position that instrumental and classical conditioning can be distinguished on the voluntary-involuntary basis.

TWO TYPES OF MEDIATION: MUSCULAR AND COGNITIVE.   Some investigators have suggested that such experiments do not clearly demonstrate instrumental conditioning of involuntary responses. They argue that the effect on the involuntary system is mediated, or affected by, voluntary responses. For example, if you were

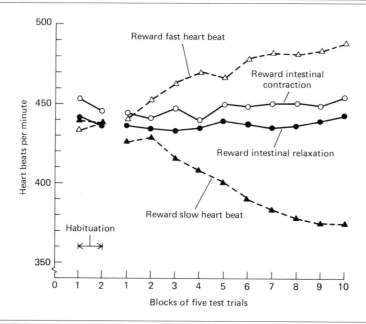

Figure 3.2 Heart rate changes in rats rewarded for increases and decreases in heart rate, and heart rates of rats rewarded for intestinal contraction and relaxation. (After Miller, N. E., and Banuazizi, A. Instrumental learning by curarized rats of a specific visceral response, intestinal or cardiac. *Journal of Comparative and Physiological Psychology*, 1968, 65, 1–17. Fig. 4., p. 5. Copyright 1968 by the American Psychological Association. Reprinted by permission.)

offered $5 for every increase you could produce in your pulse rate, you would quickly earn a lot of money by running around the block. The *voluntary* running response would cause the increase in the involuntary pulse rate.

Mediation can be either muscular or cognitive. Let us begin with the fact that many of our so-called involuntary behaviors can be affected when we engage in certain voluntary *muscular* actions. Running around the block in order to increase one's pulse rate is an example of this sort of muscular mediation. It has been demonstrated in the laboratory, too. For instance, Levenson (1976) reports that heart rate can be altered by changing breathing patterns and by engaging in certain forms of muscle tension. This represents a case in which we are not *directly* affecting or controlling the heart rate. The effect is mediated by voluntary muscular activity.

Voluntary muscular mediation of changes in involuntary systems remains a serious problem in this field. But some evidence suggests that more direct, non-mediated effects can be obtained. The first example is Miller's work with curare and rats described above. Some human data are also available. Miller (1978) and Bracker (1977) report and describe experiments that indicate that *paralyzed* humans can learn to control their blood pressure. In these cases, sad as they are, voluntary muscular mediation is impossible.

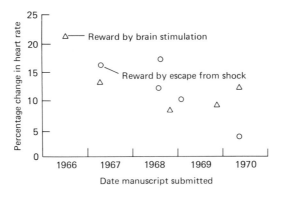

Figure 3.3 Progressive decline in amount of learned change in heart rate obtained in 10 experiments over a five-year period. (Adapted from Miller, N. E. Interactions between learned and physical factors in mental illness. *Seminars in Psychiatry*, 1972, 4, 239–254. Fig. 8., p. 247. Reprinted by permission of Grune & Stratton, Inc., New York, N.Y.)

The second form of mediation can be called *cognitive mediation*. In brief, we can affect certain involuntary responses by *thinking* certain thoughts. Miller (1978) describes two paralyzed human patients who were able to increase their blood pressure by thinking about either sex or horse races. Thinking about exciting, dangerous, or highly emotional things can affect our so-called involuntary responses. To the extent that we assume that thinking is voluntary, we have another case, in addition to muscular mediation, in which involuntary activity is mediated by voluntary behavior. Even in those cases where muscular mediation is eliminated through paralysis, mental mediation can be operating. Thus, the case of a pure, incontestable instance of direct, unmediated control of involuntary activity still eludes us.

Apparently we are very clever about mediating control of involuntary responses. Hatch and Gatchel (1979) report that subjects sometimes begin their control of heart rate by thinking arousing thoughts. But when these arousing thoughts begin to lose their edge and go flat, the subjects will switch to some form of muscular activity to continue the heart rate control (see also Goldstein, 1979).

THE PROBLEM OF REPLICATION.   Another problem in this area of research has been the progressive decline in curare results obtained by Miller over several years (see Figure 3.3). Miller acknowledges this decline, describes it as a vexing phenomenon, and speculates about its causes. He wonders if it results from some subtle form of contamination in our environment or from changes in the rats themselves due to extensive breeding practices or antibiotic treatment. He himself is skeptical of these results (Miller, 1978). In fact, he (Dworkin & Miller, 1986) has recently analyzed six experiments involving over 2,500 rats and has concluded that the instrumental control of involuntary responses is currently an open question: He does not know whether it is possible or not.

Whatever the final outcome, Miller has suggested that so-called involuntary responses may well be affected by the procedures we normally describe as instrumental. This argument undermines the voluntary-involuntary distinction between instrumental and classical conditioning.

Summary of the Comparison

The three distinctions between classical and instrumental conditioning mentioned in the preceding pages are not the only ones that have been proposed. But they are perhaps the most important ones. The clarity of these distinctions has begun to fade, and with new thinking and research it seems that at the very least one must conclude that instrumental and classical conditioning are very closely related. Some thinkers (Bindra, 1972) have gone as far as to assert that classical and instrumental conditioning are the outcomes of some fundamental underlying process.

PROCEDURAL COMPARISONS.   To make sense of the array of learning tasks it is useful to distinguish three ways in which learning tasks can be compared. If we merely look at the *procedures* involved in the various learning tasks, it is clear that they do differ. No one would deny that classical procedures differ from instrumental procedures. In instrumental conditioning a reward is given only when the animal responds, whereas in classical conditioning the experimenter presents the CS and UCS whether the animal responds or not. But we have already seen that what the experimenter thinks is important may or may not be important to the animal. Despite the insistence that events in classical conditioning are independent of the animal's response, we have seen that they are not. Thus, if we are to discover true differences among the various learning situations, we must look beyond these superficial procedural differences.

COMPARISONS AT THE NEUROLOGICAL LEVEL.   Learning tasks can be compared in terms of their location in the nervous system. If one task involves, or is associated with, action in one part of the nervous system, then it can be distinguished from other types of learning that are to be found in other levels of the nervous system. Yet it has proved difficult to separate learning tasks on this basis. The traditional distinction between involuntary classical conditioning and voluntary instrumental conditioning has broken down. Instrumental conditioning has been at least implicated in those aspects of the nervous system (for example, the autonomic nervous system) that were once presumed to be the domain of classical conditioning alone.

BEHAVIORAL COMPARISONS.   In view of the fact that procedural distinctions may be superficial and neurological distinctions difficult to maintain, we must look for other ways to try to compare various learning tasks. For example, we can determine whether the tasks react in similar ways to the same manipulations. Say, for example, that we are faced with two children and want to find out how similar they are. We might begin by taking something from each of them. If they both scream and yell, look hurt, or react with scorn, then we have some evidence for the idea that, at least in some ways, the children are similar. The more similarities we can find, the more common responses the two children have in similar situations, the more likely we are to believe that they are similar in some fundamental ways.

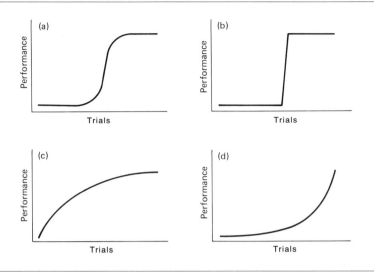

Figure 3.4 Performance curves, real and fanciful.

The same kind of comparison technique can be applied to learning tasks in an effort to answer the following types of questions: How are various tasks affected by the same important variables (for example, amount of practice and external distractions)? Do they show similar increases, or decreases, in performance? Or are they totally different in their responses to a given variable? To the extent that they react similarly to a wide range of variables, we have some evidence for the conclusion that they are similar, or operate according to the same behavioral laws.

COMMON PHENOMENA: SIMILARITIES AMONG TASKS
Acquisition

What happens to performance as practice continues? The simplest answer is that performance increases as practice increases. But further questions can be asked. For example, what is the specific form of the relationship between practice and performance? Does performance increase slowly at first and then more rapidly as practice increases? Or does performance start out rapidly and then level off? Figure 3.4 suggests some of the relationships, both reasonable and fanciful, that might exist between practice and performance. Without some advance knowledge it is difficult to decide which of these curves represents the general relationship between performance and practice.

One might also wonder whether the relationship might differ for various types of learning tasks. For example, are word-list recall, classical conditioning, and instrumental conditioning represented by similar curves? Figure 3.4c represents the curve most often obtained with all three of these tasks. As practice, or the pairing of the CS and the UCS, increases in classical conditioning, the probability of the CR increases quite rapidly and then levels off (see Figure 3.5a). Similarly, the most common finding in instrumental learning is that the response builds up rapidly and

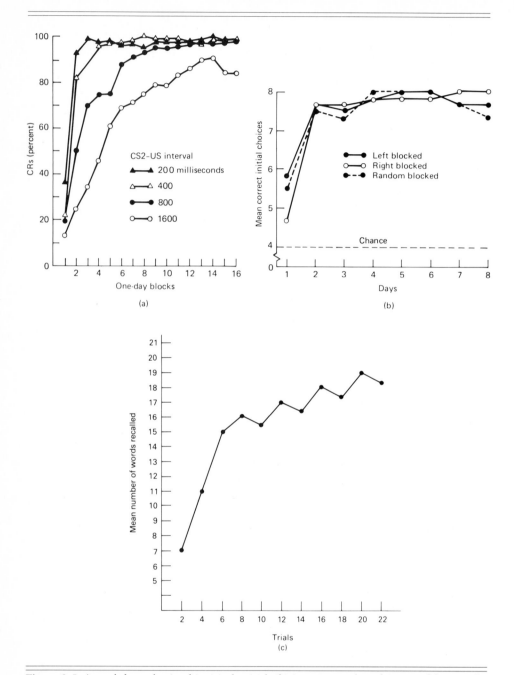

Figure 3.5 Actual data obtained in (a) classical, (b) instrumental, and (c) word-list recall situations. Notice that all curves are negatively accelerated and resemble the hypothetical curve in Figure 3.4c. [(a) Adapted from Kehoe, E. J. The role of CS–UCS contiguity in classical conditioning of the rabbit's nictitating membrane response to serial stimuli. *Learning and Motivation*, 1979, *10*, 23–28. Fig. 1, p. 28; (b) adapted from Roberts, W. A. Spatial memory in the rat in a hierarchical maze. *Learning and Motivation*, 1979, *10*, 117–140. Fig. 7, p. 128; (c) unpublished data gathered by author.]

then levels off (see Figure 3.5b). And finally, if subjects are shown a list of words 20 times and asked to recall as many of them as they can after each exposure, their performance also shows an initial spurt and then a leveling off (see Figure 3.5c).

This characteristic form is termed a *negatively accelerated performance curve*, which means that increases in performance start out rapidly and then level off. The fact that the negatively accelerated performance curve is characteristic of many learning tasks is a tiny bit of evidence for the conclusion that the tasks are similar. That they yield similar curves in response to the same variable (practice) suggests that they might possibly operate according to the same behavioral laws.

Three points should be kept in mind. First, the negatively accelerated curve is only characteristic of these tasks—it does not always appear. It is the most commonly observed curve but not the only one that can be obtained. On the one hand, a PA list can be constructed that is so easy it will be learned on the first trial (composed, for example, of pairs such as heigh-ho, one-two, and black-white). On the other hand, PA lists can be developed that are next to impossible to master (composed, for example, of such pairs as XZKQZZKXO–QKQXQXZKX, QZKXKZXQX–QXKKZQZKX, and XZKZQKZXQ–XKKQXZQKQ). Second, keep in mind that these are not learning curves. They are performance curves. If you recall, performance refers to the translation of learning into behavior through the involvement of motivation. All we can observe is performance, or behavior, which is affected by motivation as well as learning. Third, remember that we have been selective in comparing only a few learning tasks. If it is found that they react in similar ways to a wide range of variables, we must still be careful about wanting to conclude that all types of learning tasks are similar.

Extinction

Extinction refers to *a decrease in response strength with repeated nonreinforcements*. If food is no longer given to a rat after the animal presses a bar, it will gradually cease to press. A similar effect will also appear in classical conditioning. One of the most common findings in classical conditioning is that, if the UCS is removed from the situation, the CR will fade. If a bell (CS) is presented over and over again without an air puff (UCS), the blink (CR) will lessen and finally cease altogether. Extinction appears in various verbal and cognitive tasks, too. For example, we will learn in Chapter 8 how paired-associate learning can be extinguished. We will find that, if a subject has first connected BAV to JAX and is then no longer reinforced for giving BAV as the response, the probability of JAX's eliciting BAV will decrease.

Thus, extinctionlike effects appear in many tasks. Again, in hindsight, this result is far from astounding. But things might have turned out differently. Classically conditioned responses might have been permanent. Instrumentally conditioned responses might have been obliterated by the mere passage of time rather than through this active extinction process. While any number of things might have been true, the fact that they show similar extinction effects adds to the argument that they are all operating according to the same laws.

Extinction is an interesting and controversial phenomenon. In a sense, it means that things are not forgotten passively. If the bar-pressing rat is left alone in its home cage, away from the bar, it will retain the bar-pressing behavior for long periods. The mere passage of time does little to reduce the response; for it to be erased the animal must make the response over and over again and not be rein-forced. This view is difficult to reconcile with our subjective feelings about how we forget things. Though our memories just seem to fade with time, the literature on extinction suggests that humans may not forget things passively. When something is forgotten, it may undergo an active extinction process in which the responses are made but not reinforced. Although this proposition is extremely controversial, evidence suggests that much of our forgetting is not passive. A good deal of corre-spondence exists between experimental extinction, as observed in the Skinner box, and normal human forgetting. The relationship between human forgetting and animal extinction will be discussed in a later chapter, where alternative views of human memory will be presented.

EXTINCTION AS ACQUISITION.   Extinction can be thought of as nothing more than an acquisition process. For example, when the rat's bar-pressing response is extin-guished, this situation may be envisioned as one in which the animal actually learns not to respond or acquires the response of not responding. Human subjects may have to learn not to say "BAV" when they see JAX. According to this interpreta-tion, the organism's response is not just dropped out owing to nonreinforcement. The animal is actually learning something new. It is learning not to make the response.

INSTRUMENTAL SITUATIONS: TANTRUMS.   The principle of extinction has often been used in behavior-modification situations to eliminate undesirable instrumen-tally conditioned responses. For example, Williams (1959) made the assumption that the temper-tantrum behavior of a 21-month-old boy was a learned behavior that the parents were unknowingly rewarding. Each time the boy threw a tantrum at bedtime, the parents became greatly concerned; this concern was rewarding to the child, because it delayed bedtime and gained attention from the parents. If we assume that the behavior is maintained because it is rewarded, we go about elim-inating it in the same way we extinguish bar pressing in a Skinner box. We remove the reinforcement. We put the individual on an extinction schedule. We assume that the boy's tantrum is being reinforced by "getting his own way" or by his receiving attention from his parents when tantrum behaviors are shown. Eliminate these rewards, and the behavior should subside. Williams demonstrated this rela-tionship. The behavior was terminated by gently putting the child to bed, leaving the room, and closing the door. The first night the screaming and raging lasted 45 minutes before the child finally dropped off to sleep. (That amount of storming would cause all but the most carefully instructed parent to break down and enter the room.) As can be seen in Figure 3.6, the length of the tantrums dropped dra-matically on successive nights. The curve labeled "First extinction" represents the initial series of nights without social reinforcement or attention. After this first extinction, the child's aunt began taking care of the child in the absence of the parents. The tantrums started again, and the aunt fell into the trap of staying in the room until the child fell asleep. The tantrum behavior had to be extinguished all over again (see "Second extinction" in Figure 3.6). According to the author, fol-lowing the second extinction no further tantrums were reported during a two-year follow-up.

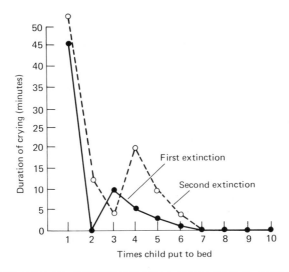

Figure 3.6 Duration of crying as a function of the number of times the child was put to bed. (Adapted from Williams, C. D. The elimination of tantrum behavior by extinction procedures. *Journal of Abnormal and Social Psychology*, 1959, 59, 269. Fig. 1, p. 269. Copyright 1959 by the American Psychological Association. Reprinted by permission.)

CLASSICAL SITUATIONS: SYSTEMATIC DESENSITIZATION.   We have already learned in Chapter 2 that phobias, or strong irrational fears, may be the result of classical conditioning. If they are, then we should be able to extinguish them. One of the best-known forms of extinction therapy is that of *systematic desensitization* (Wolpe, 1958, 1969). Some individuals find themselves inordinately frightened by certain types of stimuli and situations (death, illness, social contacts, being alone, injections, fear of losing their mind, pregnancy, medicines, fainting). These anxieties, fears, or phobias can be quite incapacitating. That is, the critical stimuli elicit such a strong fear reaction that the subject is unable to function as well as he or she might in everyday life.

Systematic desensitization involves two steps. In the first phase the subject is taught to relax. *Relaxation responses* can be encouraged in a number of ways. In one technique the therapist asks the subject to alternately tighten and relax specific muscles. For instance, "Tighten or clench the muscles in your right arm. Now relax them." Through this process the subject learns what it feels like to relax and can learn to recognize, and establish, a relaxed condition (see Holland & Tarlow, 1980).

Having trained the subject to relax, the therapist moves on to the second phase of systematic desensitization, which deals directly with the fears, or the phobic reactions. The object of desensitization will be to eliminate these fears. The fear-producing stimuli are thought to be conditioned stimuli (CSs). They have, in the past, been paired with a UCS, which elicits a fear reaction (UCR). The fear the subject experiences in response to the CS is a conditioned response (CR), or a conditioned fear. We extinguish a CR by presenting the CS alone, over and over again, without the UCS. With one major variation this same extinction procedure forms the basis of desensitization. In initial interviews the therapist asks the subject to list fear-producing stimuli and to rank them in terms of the strength of the fear they produce. Thus, a *hierarchy* of fear-producing stimuli and situations is produced by the subject. The therapist then asks the subject to think about, to dwell on, and to imagine the *weakest* of these stimuli or situations. The subject is instructed to relax and to imagine this weak fear-producing situation until it no longer elicits any fear at all. Essentially this is an extinction procedure. The CS is present without the UCS.

At the same time, it is a little more than a simple, pure extinction procedure, because the subject is encouraged to relax in the presence of the CS. In a sense, the relaxation response is assumed to become conditioned to the CS while the fear response is extinguished. This process, in which one CR is extinguished while another is established, is called *counterconditioning*. The fear response is replaced by the relaxation response (see Capaldi, Viveiros, & Campbell, 1983).

Once the fear of the weakest stimulus has subsided and the subject has become able to relax in its presence, the subject goes on to the next most potent stimulus in the hierarchy. By gradually moving up the hierarchy and by extinguishing fear at each step and replacing it with relaxation, the subject is able to overcome fear of even the most frightening stimuli. Sample hierarchies for claustrophobia, death, and illness are given in Table 3.1. Hierarchies, of course, differ from individual to individual.

Although phobias and anxiety have often been combated with the systematic desensitization procedure (see Donovan & Gershman, 1979), it should be noted that many additional procedures have also been used in trying to deal with these thorny problems (see Emmelkamp, 1979; Ohman, 1979).

It should also be noted that extinction procedures have been applied to more than just tantrums and phobias. Similar extinction procedures have been effective with, among others, deviant sex-role behaviors (Rekers & Lovaas, 1974), passivity (Johnston, Kelley, Harris, & Wolf, 1966), aggressive behavior (Allen, Henke, Harris, Baer, & Reynolds, 1967), vomiting (Munford & Pally, 1979), stomach pain (Miller & Kratochwill, 1979), hair pulling (Sanchez, 1979), and excessive television viewing (Wolfe, Mendes, & Factor, 1984).

Spontaneous Recovery

Spontaneous recovery refers to the fact that *an extinguished response will, with rest, recover some of its strength*. The general procedure for demonstrating spontaneous recovery involves four steps (Figure 3.7). First, the animal learns a particular response. Second, that response is extinguished through nonreinforcement. Third, the animal is allowed to rest. Fourth, the strength of the response is tested following the rest interval. If the response is stronger at the end of the rest phase than it was at the end of the extinction phase, then spontaneous recovery is said to have occurred. After the response has recovered, it may be brought back to full strength through further reinforcement, or it may be reextinguished through nonreinforcement.

This phenomenon appears in verbal, classical, and instrumental conditioning situations. Pavlov (1927) reports experiments of the following sort. Dogs were classically conditioned to salivate. Then the CS was presented alone for a series of extinction trials. These extinction trials reduced the number of drops of saliva

Table 3.1   Anxiety Hierarchies

A. Claustrophobic Series
   1. being stuck in an elevator (the longer the time, the more disturbing)
   2. being locked in a room (the smaller the room and the longer the time, the more disturbing)
   3. passing through a tunnel in a railway train (the longer the tunnel, the more disturbing)
   4. traveling in an elevator alone (the greater the distance, the more disturbing)
   5. traveling in an elevator with an operator (the longer the distance, the more disturbing)
   6. on a journey by train (the longer the journey, the more disturbing)
   7. being caught in a dress with a stuck zipper
   8. having a tight ring on her finger
   9. visiting and unable to leave at will (for example, if engaged in a card game)
   10. being told of somebody in jail
   11. having polish on her fingernails and no access to remover
   12. reading of miners trapped underground

B. Death Series
   1. being at a burial
   2. being at a house of mourning
   3. the word *death*
   4. seeing a funeral procession (the nearer, the more disturbing)
   5. the sight of a dead animal (for example, a cat)
   6. driving past a cemetery (the nearer, the more disturbing)

C. Illness Series
   1. hearing that an acquaintance has cancer
   2. the word *cancer*
   3. witnessing a convulsive seizure
   4. discussions of operations (the more prolonged the discussion, the more disturbing)
   5. seeing a person receive an injection
   6. seeing someone faint
   7. the word *operation*
   8. considerable bleeding from another person
   9. a friend points to a stranger, saying, "This man has tuberculosis."
   10. the sight of a blood-stained bandage
   11. the smell of ether
   12. the sight of a friend sick in bed (the more sick looking, the more disturbing)
   13. the smell of methylated spirits
   14. driving past a hospital

Adapted from Wolpe, J. The systematic desensitization treatment of neuroses. *Journal of Nervous and Mental Disease*, 1961, 132, 189–203. P. 197. Copyright 1961 by The Williams & Wilkins Co., Baltimore. Reprinted by permission.

secreted in response to the CS from 10 to 3. The animal was then allowed to rest for approximately half an hour. At the end of the rest interval the CS was presented alone, and 6 drops of saliva were secreted. The salivary response had spontaneously recovered some of its strength. Characteristically, recovery is not complete. The response does not usually return to the highest level obtained during the acquisition phase.

Lewis (1956) has demonstrated spontaneous recovery of an instrumentally conditioned response. He first trained rats to run down a straight alley to food. He extinguished the response and then allowed the rats to rest. At the end of the rest interval Lewis observed that the extinguished running response had spontaneously recovered some of its strength.

Spontaneous recovery of verbal material has been shown, too (Houston, 1966b; Slamecka, 1966). The general procedure has been to extinguish a learned list and then to observe whether the extinguished, or forgotten, list will recover some of its strength with time (Postman, Stark, & Fraser, 1968). The details of this procedure will be considered in a later section. For now, it is sufficient to say that the "forgotten" associations do seem to recover some of their strength with rest.

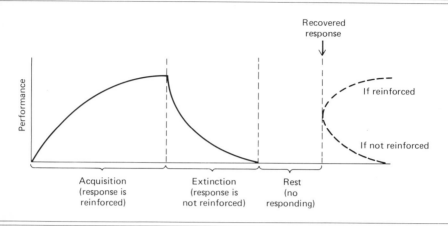

Figure 3.7 Schematic representation of the course of acquisition, extinction, and spontaneous recovery.

In summary, acquisition, extinction, and spontaneous recovery all seem to be common to many learning tasks. This suggests that, at least on a behavioral level, the tasks are closely related.

External Inhibition

External inhibition refers to the fact that a new stimulus introduced during acquisition, along with the CS, will slow the acquisition process. If a buzzer is suddenly sounded along with the CS in eye-blink conditioning, the conditioning will be slowed. The same kind of effect can be obtained in instrumental conditioning. For example, Winnick and Hunt (1951) trained rats to run down an alley to obtain food at the end. A buzzing sound introduced at the beginning of a trial slowed the rat's performance dramatically.

Few verbal or cognitive tasks deal directly with external inhibition, but imagine what would happen if you were trying to learn a list of Greek words and someone sounded a buzzer out of the blue. You would be externally inhibited, to say the least.

SHADOWING.   Some studies in cognitive psychology resemble, if they don't actually duplicate, the external inhibition effect. For example, Treisman (1960) put earphones on her subjects and delivered different messages to each ear. Subjects were told to attend only to, say, the right ear and to ignore what was coming into the left ear (see Figure 3.8). Furthermore, they were asked to say out loud what they had heard in the right ear; that is, they were asked to "shadow" the right-ear message. Treisman found that, although subjects were pretty good at ignoring the left-ear message (an external inhibitor?), they occasionally became distracted and repeated what they had heard through the left ear rather than what they had heard on the right side, as Figure 3.8 illustrates. Performance was disrupted by an external stimulus.

External inhibition can be thought of as a distraction effect. Any change in the conditioning situation that distracts the subject from the task will reduce performance accordingly.

Figure 3.8 The shadowing effect. (From *Cognition* by Margaret Matlin. Copyright © 1983 by Holt, Rinehart and Winston, Inc. Reprinted by permission of the publisher.)

Subjects tend to adapt to external inhibitors. The disruptive quality of an external inhibitor is temporary. After a number of trials in which the buzzer is presented along with the CS, performance returns to its original level.

Stimulus Generalization

Stimulus generalization refers to the fact that *a response conditioned to one stimulus will tend to be elicited by other similar stimuli.* The greater the difference between the conditioned stimulus and the test stimulus, the less is the tendency for the test stimulus to elicit the response.

For example, we have all learned to stop our car when we see round, red lights. Suppose that we were faced with a red light that was not quite so bright and not quite so red as the ones we were used to. We would probably stop anyway. What if the light were very dim or square? Our stopping response might not be so salient. Or if the light were pink and oblong? Or if it were purple and one foot off the ground? We can see that, *as the similarity between the new, test stimuli and the original, round, red stimulus decreases, our generalized tendency to stop will decrease.*

Stimulus generalization has been one of the main concerns in the field of learning, and thousands of studies have been published concerning it. The importance of stimulus generalization in our own life is undeniable. Suppose for the moment that you cannot generalize. If you connect a response to a given stimulus, then *only* that stimulus will elicit the response. Similar stimuli will not elicit the response. Your life will probably be dangerous and confusing. We need to generalize in order to get along in the world. Otherwise we would run red lights in strange towns and have trouble identifying strangers as people.

Stimulus generalization has often been demonstrated in classical conditioning (Moore, 1972). In general, a two-step experimental procedure is used. First, a CR is connected to a particular CS (for example, a given tone). Second, after learning is completed, similar stimuli (varying tones) are presented. It is usually found that the probability of the response to the varying test stimuli increases as the similarity between the test stimuli and the original stimulus is increased.

Guttman and Kalish (1956) have demonstrated stimulus generalization in instrumental conditioning. Their general procedure has been to train pigeons to peck a colored disk. The pecking response is rewarded with food. After the response is well established, the pigeons are tested with other colors. As the similarity between the training and the test stimuli increases, the response to the test stimuli increases. This effect is summarized by the *stimulus generalization gradient* depicted in Figure 3.9.

Morosko and Baer (1970) describe an interesting case of stimulus generalization. Alcoholic subjects were shocked while ingesting small cups of alcoholic beverages. They learned to avoid the shock by refraining from drinking the beverages. Follow-up work indicated that the avoidance behavior generalized across alcoholic beverages. When subjects were shocked for drinking vodka, they showed a decreased interest in drinking other forms of liquor as well. But as we would expect from our knowledge of stimulus generalization gradients, the effect was only partial; that is, the trained variety was the most aversive. The subject shocked for drinking vodka continued to drink such beverages as beer, but in reduced amounts.

As we have seen, another interesting experiment suggests that stimulus generalization operates in connection with verbal materials. In *semantic conditioning* a response is connected to a verbal item (for example, a word). Varying test words are then presented to the subject. It is usually noted that the response is elicited by similar test stimuli (Maltzman, 1977). In one experiment Lang, Geer, and Hnatiow (1963) presented 12 very hostile words (such as *annihilation*) along with some neutral ones (*abstract*). Each time a hostile word was presented, the subject was shocked. The shock yielded a change in the *galvanic skin response* (GSR). (The GSR is an index of the electrical conductivity of the surface of the skin. In other words, when we are shocked, we perspire a little. The perspiration conducts electricity. The GSR is now often called the electrodermal response or EDR.) After the training period, subjects were presented *new* test words that were highly hostile, hostile, slightly hostile, or neutral. The authors found that, the higher the hostility of the test words, the greater was the change in the GSR. The GSR had generalized from the hostile training words to the similar hostile test words.

We will return to stimulus generalization in Chapter 7. For now, realize that this phenomenon occurs in many learning tasks. It is one more piece of evidence for the conclusion that learning tasks are behaviorally related.

Discrimination

One of the situations illustrating discrimination learning that was described earlier involved a hungry pigeon and two disks of different colors. One disk was called the negative stimulus, and the other, the positive stimulus. If the pigeon pecked the positive stimulus, it received a reward. If it pecked the negative stimulus, it received no reward. The bird gradually discriminated between the colors and restricted its response to the positive stimulus. These events constitute an instance of discrimination learning in an instrumental conditioning situation. The same kind of discrimination formation occurs in classical conditioning. If one stimulus (for example, a buzzer) is consistently paired with a UCS while another stimulus (a light) is presented but not accompanied by the UCS, then a CR gradually develops in con-

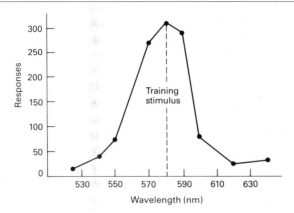

Figure 3.9 Stimulus-generalization gradient for pigeons that were trained to peck in the presence of a colored light of 580 nm wavelength and then tested in the presence of other colors. (From Guttman, N., and Kalish, H. I. Discriminability and stimulus generalization. *Journal of Experimental Psychology*, 1956, *51*, 79–88. Copyright 1956 by the American Psychological Association.)

nection with the buzzer but not the light. The animal discriminates between the two potential CSs and only responds to the one that is paired with the UCS.

Of course, cognitive and verbal tasks also involve discrimination formation. For example, many discriminations are required before a PA list can be mastered. Suppose that the stimuli in a PA list are very similar to one another (for example, QZKL, KLZQ, QZLK, KLQZ, KZQL, and QLZK). Before subjects can connect the proper responses to these stimuli, they must distinguish one from another. They all look pretty much alike at first, but continued exposure allows the subjects to discriminate among them. Thus, just as in classical and instrumental conditioning, discrimination formation is an integral part of verbal and cognitive learning processes.

Summation

Assume that a given response is separately connected to two different stimuli. If the two different stimuli are then presented together, the strength of the response is often greater than it is to either of the stimuli alone. This effect is called *summation*, and it can be demonstrated in many learning situations. Pavlov conducted experiments in which a salivary response was first connected to a given CS. The salivary response was then conditioned to a second, different CS. When the two CSs were presented together, the amount of saliva produced was greater than that produced by either CS alone. The same kind of effect can be obtained in instrumental conditioning. For example, one might run an experiment in which a rat is trained in a T maze. The rat might first be required to run right for food if a buzzer is sounded and left if no buzzer is sounded. It might then be trained to turn right if a light is turned on and left if the light is not turned on. In the final step both the light and the buzzer would be presented. If the tendency to turn right in response to both the stimuli is greater than it was to either stimulus alone, then we would conclude that summation has been demonstrated.

Hill and Wickens (1962) ran an experiment that demonstrated summation in PA learning. In part of their study, subjects first learned PA lists in which the stimuli were nonsense syllables and the responses were words. They then learned a second list in which the responses were the *same words* but the stimuli had been changed to colors. In the final phase the colors and the nonsense syllables were presented together. The authors noted that a definite advantage had been gained by having been trained with each of the different stimuli alone.

CONCLUSION

All of this discussion of similarities and differences has not conclusively demonstrated that these and other types of learning tasks represent fundamentally distinct learning processes. It is premature to conclude either that they do or do not represent truly different kinds of learning.

Eventually it may be possible to develop a unitary model that will account for all these task variations. Obviously, the problem is that the different learning situations are so varied that it is extremely difficult to imagine a single model that would encompass them all. In addition, the similarities we have discussed may be more apparent than real—they may be the result of a lack of precision in our language rather than any identity of basic process. But it was not the intent of this chapter to prove that the many learning tasks definitely represent different forms of some unitary, underlying process. Rather, the intent was to suggest that such a unitary process is a possibility and that this possibility should be given serious consideration before we expend considerable amounts of energy building new and distinct models for every new task we invent (see Tarpy, 1975).

SUMMARY

1. It is important to consider whether our various learning tasks reflect truly different learning processes. If they do, then theories and models governing each learning capacity must be developed. If it is determined that some common, underlying process accounts for all the various learning tasks, then a single model should suffice.
2. Paired-associate learning can be thought of as either classical or instrumental conditioning. Language learning also has much in common with other forms of learning.
3. The priming task may test the strength of learning that was accomplished preexperimentally through classical and instrumental conditioning.
4. A comparison of classical and instrumental conditioning is hampered by the fact that classical conditioning seems to possess reinforcement characteristics of the instrumental paradigm. Similarly, instrumental conditioning situations may never be free of classical conditioning elements as demonstrated by the autoshaping effect.
5. Attempts to distinguish between classical and instrumental conditioning by instrumentally and classically conditioning the same responses have been relatively unfruitful.
6. The notion that instrumental conditioning involves reinforcement whereas classical does not is challenged by the fact that potentially reinforcing events can be identified in all classical paradigms and that contiguity is not sufficient for classical conditioning to occur.

7. The notion that an animal's future is affected by its response in instrumental conditioning but not in classical conditioning also seems to be untrue. Classically conditioned responses do appear to affect the animal's future.

8. The idea that involuntary responses can only be classically conditioned is challenged by the apparent instrumental conditioning of so-called involuntary visceral responses. But this area of research is not free from problems. Replication is often difficult. In addition, some involuntary responses may be mediated by muscular and mental voluntary responses.

9. Comparisons of learning tasks at a procedural level yield distinct, but superficial, differences.

10. Distinctions among the various learning tasks at a neurological level have proved difficult to maintain.

11. Behavioral comparisons of the various learning tasks reveal a wide range of similarities. The various tasks respond in similar ways to many sorts of manipulation. Similar *acquisition* and *extinction* curves appear in many different tasks. *Spontaneous recovery, external inhibition, stimulus generalization, discrimination*, and *summation* also appear in the various tasks.

12. At present, it would seem premature to draw definite conclusions about the existence of multiple learning processes. Although a good number of similarities appear among a number of learning tasks, the final significance of these similarities remains to be seen.

CHAPTER

4

BIOLOGICAL

CONSTRAINTS

ON LEARNING

THE "INTERCHANGEABLE–PARTS" CONCEPTION OF LEARNING

American psychologists have spent the better part of this century developing what can be termed the "interchangeable-parts" conception of learning. According to this model, certain laws and generalizations govern the development of associations between all stimuli and all responses. The nature of the stimuli, the nature of the responses, and the nature of the animal doing the learning are not considered to be particularly important. In this chapter we will examine and challenge that view. Specifically, we will explore the predispositions that animals have to learn in certain ways.

Stimulus and Response Interchangeability

According to the interchangeable-parts conception, the specific nature of the stimulus is relatively unimportant in determining the course of learning. As long as the animal can perceive the cue, it can use it. For example, if we are training a dog to respond to a signal, it does not make much difference whether the cue is a light, a bell, or a mild shock. The notion is that, as long as we reinforce the animal when it responds to the stimulus, learning will occur in pretty much the same fashion, regardless of the nature of the stimulus. Curiously, this American belief in the equivalence of stimuli can be traced back to Pavlov (1928), who stated that *any stimulus* that is selected—a visual stimulus, a sound, an odor, or a touch—can become a conditioned stimulus.

The same thinking has been applied to responses. Suppose that a dog is confined within a box and wants to escape. In one condition it must bark to gain release. In another condition it must roll over to escape. According to this line of thinking, it should not make much difference which of these two responses is required. Learning should progress at about the same rate in either case. The responses should be interchangeable.

"Unequal" Stimuli and Responses

Unfortunately, this simple, elegant model does not really fit the facts of nature. A growing body of literature suggests that such a conception vastly oversimplifies reality. For example, Garcia and Koelling (1966) showed that, when a specific flavor, a certain sound, and a particular light are all paired with an aversive stimulus, rats will associate the flavor but not the sound or the light with the aversive stimulus. In other words, the three stimuli are differentially effective as stimuli; they are not interchangeable. Similarly, chemically induced illness is easily associated with taste but not so easily associated with odor (Garcia & Rusiniak, 1979; Hankins, Rusiniak, & Garcia, 1976). One stimulus works much better than the other.

Just as some stimuli are more easily involved in a given association than others, certain responses seem to be conditioned more readily than others (Morgan & Nicholas, 1979). It is a simple matter to teach a rat to press a bar or leap a barrier for food. But if you try to teach a rat to *scratch* for the same reinforcement, you will be in for a hard time. The animal just does not seem ready to learn this particular response when food is the reinforcement, even though it already knows how to scratch and presumably learned to do so in order to gain relief from itching. In a similar vein, Charlton (1983) has shown that it is very difficult to get hamsters to groom for food even though they are readily able to learn other tricks for the same reinforcement.

Interacting Stimuli and Responses

To complicate things further, it should be noted that certain responses are readily associated with particular stimuli but not with others, whereas other responses are readily associated with the opposite stimuli. In the rat, for example, shock-produced fear is easily linked to odor but not so easily to taste. Conversely, illness is readily associated with the opposite stimulus (taste) and not so easily with odor (Garcia & Rusiniak, 1979).

We are faced with the notion that each animal brings to every learning task certain capabilities and predispositions to act in certain ways. These distinct capabilities may well be the result of natural selection as well as of the individual animal's past life experiences (Domjan & Galef, 1983).

THE CONTINUUM OF PREPAREDNESS

Seligman (1970) has defined a continuum of preparedness, which may help us grasp the significance of these facts. According to Seligman, animals are differentially *prepared* to associate certain responses with certain stimuli. Preparedness can exist in any degree, from completely prepared to completely unprepared. The relative preparedness of an animal to connect a given response to a given stimulus is operationally defined by Seligman in terms of *the number of pairings of the stimulus and response required for learning to occur.*

This is a somewhat circular definition. On the one hand, preparedness is defined in terms of the number of pairings required for learning to occur. Ease of learning, on the other hand, is indexed by degree of preparedness. An independent measure of preparedness would be needed to overcome this circularity. But the concept of preparedness *does* have some heuristic value. (That is, it serves to promote and encourage discovery and investigation.)

Preparedness in Instrumental Conditioning

Although few would argue with the fact that many diverse responses and stimuli can be associated in roughly comparable ways, a wide array of data suggests that the notion of equivalent associability must be tempered by a consideration of genetically and evolutionarily determined factors and predispositions that animals, including humans, bring to the learning situation.

Let us begin with some examples of *unprepared instrumental conditioning*. Konorski (1967) attempted to reinforce yawning in dogs with food. Konorski reports that, whereas other responses are easily trained, it is extremely difficult, if not impossible, to train a dog to yawn for food. The animal is unprepared to associate these events. Using monkeys, Bolles and Seelbach (1964) reinforced various responses with noise offset and punished others with noise onset. Some responses, such as exploratory behavior, could be strongly affected by both noise onset and offset, but grooming behavior was relatively unaffected by either event (see also Charlton, 1983).

As a final example of *unprepared instrumental conditioning* consider avoidance conditioning. You will recall from Chapter 2 that in this type of conditioning the organism is subjected to a noxious stimulus if it fails to respond within a certain time interval. In our initial discussion of this form of learning we made it clear that a hurdle-jumping response will be easily and rapidly learned when reinforced by the removal of the noxious stimulus. But other responses, such as that old standby, the bar press, are acquired very poorly if at all. Rats just don't seem to be wired to press a bar in order to escape and avoid aversive stimulation, even over thousands of trials (Modaresi, 1989). As you can see in Figure 4.1 even after a hundred trials, bar pressing in an avoidance situation remains near zero while hurdle jumping is easily mastered.

As an example of *prepared instrumental conditioning* we may refer to autoshaping which was introduced in Chapter 3 (Brown & Jenkins, 1968). Pigeons were exposed to a lighted key. Grain was presented each time the key was lit, regardless of what the bird did. The pigeon was not required to do anything. It was free to stand there and receive and eat the grain as it was delivered. But the pigeon began to peck the light despite the fact that no response was required for the delivery of food. The key-pecking behavior was maintained even though it had no effect on food delivery. Autoshaping will be discussed in some detail in Chapter 6. For now, think of it as an example of extreme preparedness in an instrumental situation (see also Brandon & Bitterman, 1979; Durlach, 1983; Pisacreta, Redwood, & Witt, 1983).

Preparedness in Discrimination Learning

Discrimination learning involves the presentation of two stimuli, one positive and one negative. If the animal responds to the positive stimulus, it is reinforced. If it responds to the negative stimulus, it is not reinforced. Several investigators (Dobrzecka & Konorski, 1967, 1968; Lawicka, 1964; Szwejkowska, 1967) have found dogs quite ready to discriminate among certain types of stimuli in certain situations, but not others. For example, they attempted to teach dogs either to go and receive food or to stay, based on verbal commands. One voice tone from the experimenter was the positive stimulus, whereas a *different* voice tone from the same experimenter was the negative stimulus. The animals mastered this discrimination easily, going in response to one tone and staying in response to the other. But when the positive and negative stimuli were changed, quite different results were obtained. If a given voice tone came from *above* the dog, it represented the positive stimulus. If the same voice tone, from the same experimenter, came from *below* the dog, it represented the negative stimulus. In this case the dogs had a great deal of trouble learning the discrimination. These and other results showed that the animals were not prepared at all to use the *location* of the voice as a cue in deciding whether to go or stay.

Humans Are Prepared—Sometimes

Are humans prepared to associate certain events and unprepared to associate others? Even though much of the "evidence" is speculative and anecdotal, it does seem that humans are more ready to learn certain things than they are others.

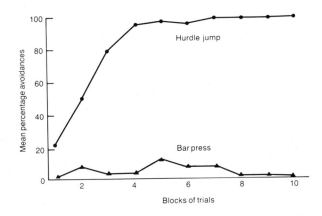

Figure 4.1 Mean percentage of avoidance responses of bar-press and hurdle-jump groups in blocks of 10 trials. Notice that the bar press has not been learned even after 10 blocks. From Modaresi, H. A. Reinforced versus species-specific defense reactions as determinants of avoidance bar pressing. *Journal of Experimental Psychology: Animal Behavior Processes*, 1989, *15*, 65–74. Fig. 1, p. 67.

Let us begin with some behaviors that seem to be acquired easily, almost automatically. Lenneberg (1967) has argued that we are very much prepared to learn an important class of materials—language. As we shall see in Chapter 13, we seem to learn language without a great deal of elaborate training. Human children acquire language with ease, and they seem to do it in all cultures in roughly the same manner. Adult humans do not have to set up elaborate training procedures to ensure that their children will acquire language. It is accomplished efficiently. The child seems prepared to acquire language. We use language almost incessantly and in an almost effortless stream.

There are other examples of human preparedness. For example, humans learn to walk with a minimum of effort and training. Walking seems almost automatic and innate. Some investigators, in fact, classify walking as an innate behavior, or one that requires no learning at all. Whether walking turns out to be purely innate is still open to question. The fact that some feral children have been found to walk on all fours suggests that upright walking is not purely innate. But we can be sure that upright walking is at the very least an extremely prepared sort of behavior. As shown in Figure 4.2, even newborn infants will engage in many of the complex movements associated with walking. Even though they cannot hold themselves upright, these infants are *ready* to move in this manner.

Infants tend to grasp with their hands. This behavior, too, is often described as innate. Whatever it is, it is an extremely prepared activity, and one that needs little, if any, practice to be established very firmly (see Figure 4.3).

Sucking, smiling, laughing, and crying are additional examples of highly prepared human behaviors. Eibl-Eibesfeldt (1972) reports that all people, regardless

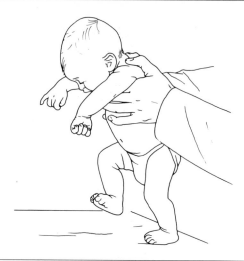

Figure 4.2 Newborn infants will, when held erect, engage in many of the complicated movements associated with walking.

of the culture they live in, momentarily flick their eyebrows upward when they recognize someone (see Figure 4.4). This eyebrow-flick response is so pervasive and so widespread that we are led to believe or at least strongly suspect that it is an innate, extremely prepared response.

Eibl-Eibesfeldt's observations of deaf and blind individuals lend further support to the idea that many human behaviors are highly prepared and that their occurrence is not dependent on extensive training. For example, Figure 4.5 shows that a deaf and blind girl has many of the same facial expressions that hearing and sighted individuals do even though she has never had the opportunity to learn these expressions through the use of hearing and vision.

Proceeding to the other end of the preparedness continuum, we find negative constraints on human behavior, just as on animal behavior. In other words, some

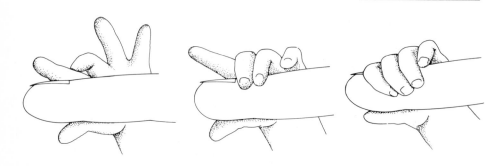

Figure 4.3 The infant's hand-grasping behavior is extremely prepared, perhaps requiring no learning at all. Note that the middle fingers are closed first, and the thumb, last.

Figure 4.4 The possibly innate eyebrow flick in, from top to bottom, the Waika Indian, Balinese, and Papuan cultures. In each case the right-hand expression occurs after recognition, and the left-hand expression occurs before recognition. (From *Love and Hate* by Irenaus Eibl-Eibesfeldt. English translation copyright © 1971, 1972 by Methuen and Co. Ltd. and Holt, Rinehart and Winston, Inc. Originally published in Germany under the title *Liebe und Hass: Zur Naturgeschishte Elementarer Verhaltensweisen* by R. Piper and Co. Verlag, Munich 1970. © R. Piper & Co. Verlag, Munich 1970. Reprinted by permission of Henry Holt and Company, Inc.)

behaviors seem difficult for humans to learn. Every parent knows only too well, for example, how difficult it is to teach children to be polite and to brush their teeth. Nursery school teachers are often struck by the difficulties involved in establishing "sharing" behavior (McCarthy & Houston, 1980). Youngsters learn to run, jump, quarrel, talk, and the like long before they even grasp the rudiments of sharing. In fact, many teachers of young children assume that, if they can encourage even a "readiness" to share, they are doing well. Somehow, sharing is just not one of our most highly prepared behaviors. Even when reinforced regularly, it is difficult to establish and maintain.

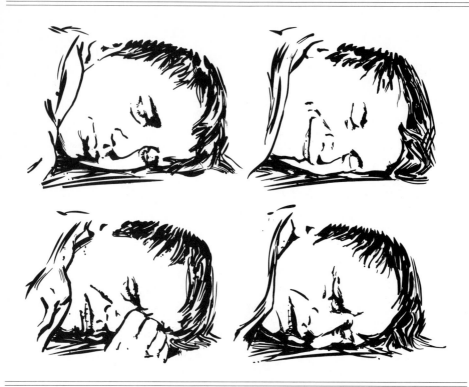

Figure 4.5 Possibly innate facial expressions in a deaf and blind female, including relaxation, smiling, and crying. (From *Love and Hate* by Irenaus Eibl-Eibesfeldt. English translation copyright © 1971, 1972 by Methuen and Co. Ltd. and Holt, Rinehart and Winston, Inc. Originally published in Germany under the title *Liebe und Hass: Zur Naturgeschishte Elementarer Verhaltensweisen* by R. Piper and Co. Verlag, Munich 1970. © R. Piper & Co. Verlag, Munich 1970. Reprinted by permission of Henry Holt and Company, Inc.)

Caution . . . Pigeon Crossing

Care must be taken before we make general statements about preparedness. For example, consider the radial maze (Olton, 1978). This piece of equipment looks something like a wagon wheel with the rim removed. A piece of food is placed at the outer end of each arm or spoke. The animal being tested must move to the end of the arm, eat the food, and then return to the hub of the wheel where it can select another baited arm in which to move. The maze is used to test spatial memory. When the animal returns to the hub, will it remember which arms it has already been in, or will it waste time and energy going down an arm it has already visited and emptied of food? Rats and other rodent species are very good at this task; they refrain from entering a previously visited spoke or arm. But pigeons show very poor performance on this task; they can't seem to remember which arms have been visited and which have not.

Does this mean that the pigeon is unprepared to master spatial memory tasks? Perhaps not. Specifically, pigeons may have quite good spatial memory, perhaps as good as the rat. But it might not show up in this particular apparatus. As Spetch and Honig (1988) point out, pigeons are not used to operating in confined alleyways that the rat adores. They are used to feeding in open areas. Furthermore, they are not used to having to return to a hub before they can make their next choice; they normally walk or fly directly to their next choice.

Accordingly, Spetch and Honig set up an open-field analog of the radial maze. Food was placed at appropriate spots on the floor without any barriers or alleyways. The pigeons were free to walk directly to their next-choice spot. In this situation, the pigeons performed very well. They went from one spot to the next without repeating. In other words, pigeons have good spatial memory when the stimulus situation or context is such that this ability is free to emerge.

TASTE AVERSION: BAIT SHYNESS

Exterminators, or those who poison animals for commercial purposes, are familiar with the fact that, when an animal eats poisoned bait and survives, it develops an aversion for the flavor of that particular bait. The flavor becomes in some way a danger signal, similar to what is experienced by people who become wary of a particular delicacy that has made them ill.

Psychologists have brought this phenomenon into the laboratory and have discovered some interesting things about it. They have shown that animals learn quickly to avoid distinctively flavored solutions when ingestion of these solutions is followed by gastrointestinal distress or some other type of malaise. Although this avoidance is not limited to flavors (odors can become aversive as well), journals in the field are filled with articles concerned with this so-called *taste-aversion* effect (Domjan, 1980; Garcia, Ervin, Yorke, & Koelling, 1967; Garcia & Rusiniak, 1979; Garcia, Rusiniak, & Brett, 1977; Mitchell, Kirschbaum, & Perry, 1975; Monroe & Barker, 1979; Riley, Jacobs, & Mastropaolo, 1983). In a typical experiment, rats are given saccharin-flavored water and simultaneously exposed to X rays. X-irradiation makes rats sick after an hour or so. After drinking and becoming ill, the rats subsequently show a distinct aversion for the saccharin flavor. They somehow associate the flavor with the illness. The aversion can persist through many weeks of preference testing.

A great deal of work has been done with these kinds of taste aversion. Garcia and Rusiniak (1979), and Garcia, Rusiniak, and Brett (1977) point out that similar effects have been obtained with rats, mice, cats, monkeys, ferrets, coyotes, birds, fish, and reptiles. Flavors have included sweet, sour, bitter, salty, coffee, fruit juice, and milk. Malaise has been caused by ingested toxins, injected drugs, X rays, gamma rays, neutron bombardment, transfusion of blood from irradiated donor animals, and motion sickness. Garcia, Hankins, and Rusiniak (1974) also report some unpublished data indicating that humans find foods distasteful that are coincidentally followed by sickness. Bernstein (1968) reports that children undergoing chemotherapy can develop a learned taste aversion for ice cream. Furthermore, as we shall see, learned aversions for particular odors and sights can be established under certain circumstances.

Aversion for more than just external stimuli can be established. Peters (1983) has shown that an aversion to copulatory behavior in male rats can be established by pairing such activity with the injection of lithium chloride, a chemical that makes the animal ill. And finally, the true complexity of the situation is underscored by

Pelchat, Grill, Rozin, and Jacobs (1983), who point out that the *nature* of the aversive response depends on the nature of the discomfort. Suppose that two people eat shrimp and that one gets food poisoning, whereas the other develops hives. The poisoned individual, on the one hand, may not only avoid shrimp but also come to dislike them intensely. The hives sufferer, on the other hand, may avoid shrimp but still like the flavor. Thus we can see that *bait shyness* is a widespread and complex phenomenon. Many different stimuli, responses, animals, and noxious elements have been utilized.

Garcia, Hankins, and Rusiniak (1974) summarized some of the general principles that have emerged from all this research. They report that other things being equal the stronger the flavor, the greater the aversion. In addition, the more severe the illness, the stronger the aversion. Finally, the strength of the aversion decreases as the time between ingestion and illness is increased. We might expect these correlations. Strongly flavored foods followed by immediate, severe illness will yield the greatest aversion.

The Relationship between Bait Shyness and Avoidance Conditioning

We can see that the bait-shyness phenomenon possesses many, but perhaps not all, of the qualities of the avoidance-conditioning paradigm. You will recall that Mowrer conceived of avoidance conditioning as a two-step process. Fear, or some other emotional response, is first classically conditioned and then instrumentally avoided. In the bait-shyness situation the flavor can be considered a CS, and the noxious agent, the UCS. The UCR is the illness caused by the UCS. We pair the flavor (CS) with the noxious agent (UCS). Through this pairing the CS (flavor) comes to elicit a CR that in some sense approximates the UCR (illness). The presentation of the flavor (CS) elicits a "conditioned illness." The animal then avoids, or escapes from, the CS and its associated unpleasantness. In a sense, the bait-shyness effect is similar to the rat's jumping a barrier to escape from a distinctive compartment that has been associated with shock.

Bait shyness differs from the typical avoidance-conditioning situation in at least one important way. In the bait-shyness learning situation often a long delay (sometimes hours) occurs between presentation of the CS (flavor) and occurrence of the illness. Most of the conditioning situations described to this point involve CS–UCR intervals of no more than a few seconds. And CS–UCR intervals of more than a few seconds usually result in very poor conditioning. No one knows for sure why conditioning can be obtained in the bait-shyness situation with these long delays. Some feel that bait shyness represents a different kind of learning altogether. Others feel that some trace of the CS (flavor) is brought forward in time such that it does occur, or exist, at the time the illness occurs. This latter position holds that bait shyness involves ordinary trace classical conditioning and does not represent a new or different variety (see also Logue, 1979). A detailed consideration of this interesting issue will be presented in the next chapter in our discussion of the general issue of stimulus-response contiguity (see also Domjan, 1980).

Preparedness and Bait Shyness

Garcia and Koelling (1966) ran an experiment in which several things happened to rats all at once. While the animals were drinking saccharin-flavored water, they were X-irradiated; in addition, lights flashed and a noise sounded at the same time.

The question was which of the CS elements (flavor, sound, or light) would become aversive. Interestingly, only the flavor became aversive. The animals showed no aversion at all to the flashing light or sound. The argument is that the rats were *unprepared* to associate lights and noise with illness but were prepared to associate flavor with illness. The investigators ran another experiment, in which flavor, noise, and flashing lights were paired with foot shock rather than X-irradiation. In this case the light and noise became aversive, but the flavor did not.

These results seem to fit some kind of logical schema, probably because they are adaptive. Natural selection would favor animals prepared to associate illness with taste and not with other external environmental events. It would favor animals predisposed to associate foot pain with external events rather than with what they had eaten. The reverse is ridiculous and maladaptive from an evolutionary standpoint. Animals predisposed to avoid the flavors that they experienced when their feet hurt probably would not last very long.

The ability to learn these aversion responses seems to be at least partially determined by genetic mechanisms. This idea is supported by the fact that strains of rats can be selectively bred for strong and weak acquisition of bait-shyness responses (Hobbs & Elkins, 1983; Maggio & Harder, 1983).

This kind of experimentation has led to the generalization that some animals, such as the rat, are phylogenetically *prepared* to associate internal events (such as illness) with internal cues (such as taste sensations) but not with external cues (such as noises). All of this is part and parcel of the notion that biology places complex constraints on learning. What we have learned in this section is not only that different stimuli and responses are unequally learnable but also that different sensory systems in different species are unequally capable of handling and encoding different forms of information.

Novelty and Taste Aversion: Preexposure Effects

Suppose that a rat drinks a flavored solution and is injected with lithium chloride. Then, an hour later, the rat drinks another, differently flavored solution. Finally, two hours after the initial injection, the animal becomes ill. To which of the two flavors will the aversion be developed? Even though the lithium chloride was injected when the animal drank the first solution, what will keep the animal from associating the illness with the more recent flavor? Although this situation is complicated, it appears that the more *novel*, or new, a flavor, the more likely it is to be picked up by the animal as the culprit. If the animal has never tasted the first flavor, whereas the second flavor is familiar, then that first flavor tends to become aversive. But if the second flavor is more novel than the first, then the animal may avoid it rather than the first flavor, which was, in fact, the one that occurred during lithium chloride poisoning. The animal could "make an error" here by avoiding the wrong flavor. If you went to a party and were poisoned by turkey just before you ate some harmless snake meat, the next day you might suspect the snake meat because it was novel.

Dawley (1979) presents some evidence that supports this novelty interpretation. He found that, when rats were repeatedly given a particular flavor before the flavor was paired with lithium chloride, an aversion toward that flavor developed slowly. In other words, *preexposure* to the flavor reduced its novelty value. Similar results have been reported by Riley, Jacobs, and Mastropaolo (1983). The importance of novelty in aversion learning has been extended by Kurz and Levitsky (1983), who have shown that rats will avoid a novel *place* as well as a novel taste when they are injected with lithium chloride. If you get sick after eating a meal on your first submarine ride, you may in the future avoid submarines as well as the type of food you ate.

Bait Shyness and the Control of Predation

Aside from its theoretical implications bait shyness has some practical relevance. As is widely known, there is a continuing conflict between conservationists and ranchers over the coyote and its undeniable tendency to eat little lambs. Naturalists argue that the coyote, which occupies an important niche in the ecology of our lands, should be preserved. Ranchers think of the coyote as a pest and a killer that should be eliminated. The ranchers' view is that the coyote must go so that the sheep may remain. As a result coyotes are hunted and poisoned in enormous numbers.

The bait-shyness phenomenon may offer a solution that will allow both the prey and the predator to survive. Gustavson, Garcia, Hankins, and Rusiniak (1974) tested the effectiveness of predation control through bait shyness under quite natural conditions. They fed coyotes lamb flesh dosed with lithium chloride, causing the coyotes to become extremely ill. After several such meals and subsequent illnesses the coyotes were offered the opportunity to attack live lambs and live rabbits. The coyotes refused to attack the lambs. The coyotes, in fact, ran from them. Their predatory habit had been effectively curbed. But they were more than willing to attack rabbits after having eaten treated lamb flesh. The aversion was specific to lamb flesh. Further experimentation indicated that the consumption of treated rabbit flesh would inhibit attacks on rabbits but not on lambs.

Garcia, Hankins, and Rusiniak (1974) note that this kind of research could easily lead to reasonable predation-control programs. Bait that smells and tastes like lamb and has been treated with lithium chloride could be scattered about the countryside. Coyotes and wolves would consume the bait, experience the illness, and refrain from attacking lambs. They would restrict their attacks to rabbits and other natural prey, thereby protecting both ranchers' stock and the balance of the ecosystem. This kind of predation-control program seems especially promising when one considers that it may well be applicable to many different types of prey and predators.

Bait Shyness and Aversion Therapy

As we learned in Chapter 2, a treatment used with humans resembles the bait-shyness effect (see Fantino, 1973). In aversion therapy humans are stimulated with some strong noxious event while they are engaging in the behavior to be controlled (smoking, drinking, eating). The most widely used noxious events are electric shock and drugs that induce illness (Sherman, 1973). The "bad habit," or the object of the habit, when paired with a noxious event, becomes aversive in much the same way that the flavor of a particular food becomes aversive in the bait-shyness effect. Wolpe and Lazarus (1966) describe typical procedures using electric shock. Electrodes are attached to the subjects' arms. The level of shock employed as a noxious stimulus is often just beyond the point at which the subjects describe it as being distinctly unpleasant. The shock is presented either while they are actually engaged in the unwanted behavior or when they are *imagining* that they are engaged in it.

The technique in which the subject imagines rather than engages in the behavior appears particularly useful when the target behavior cannot easily, or practically, be brought into the treatment situation. For example, Lazarus (1960) reports a case in which a 10-year-old boy had developed the habit of waking in the middle of the night and going to his mother's bed. Needless to say, this behavior, which occurred regularly each night, began to put some strain on the family relationships. No amount of parental bribery, punishment, or reward seemed to help. Aversion therapy finally terminated the behavior. Electrodes were attached to the boy's arm, and he was asked to imagine that he was in his mother's bed. When he felt that he had a good strong image of the requested situation, he was to say "mother's bed." At that moment the experimenter turned on the current. When the patient could no longer tolerate the shock (typically after a few seconds) he was to say "my bed." At that point the shock was terminated. The treatment appears to have been very successful. The child regularly slept in his own bed thereafter. The point is that the child did not actually have to be shocked in his mother's bed. An image of the situation was sufficient.

It should be noted, however, that aversive control is not always so successful. For example, it has been only mildly successful with alcoholism. In other words, although aversion therapy can be helpful in many situations, it is far from a "miracle" technique.

SPECIES–SPECIFIC DEFENSE REACTIONS

In this chapter we have spoken of a continuum of preparedness but have said little about why certain events are associated more easily than others. In general the pressures of natural selection probably contribute to the existence of the continuum. But Bolles (1970) has gone further in attempting to explain at least some differences in preparedness. He has presented a persuasive argument concerning the nature of avoidance conditioning. He addressed the problem that some avoidance responses are easily learned by certain species, whereas others are not. As we have seen, rats will learn to jump or run to avoid shock, but they have a difficult time learning to press levers to avoid shock. Pigeons will learn to fly away to avoid something unpleasant (Bedford & Anger, 1968), but it is difficult to train them to peck a key to avoid negative stimuli (Rachlin & Hineline, 1967). Why do these differences exist? Bolles (1970) argues that animals have *species-specific defense reactions (SSDRs)*, such as running, flying, freezing, or fighting. These are innate, automatic behaviors that occur in response to any novel or sudden stimulus event. He argues that these innate defense reactions are those that are established easily in avoidance-conditioning experiments. Arbitrary responses, such as the bar press, which have been selected for the psychologist's convenience, are not acquired easily. Bolles maintains that, if a particular avoidance response is acquired easily, then it *must necessarily* be an SSDR.

He illustrates his case with a little fable. A furry little animal ran about the forest eating and copulating as much as possible. One day it was attacked by a large predator. Luckily, it escaped. It was hurt and frightened, but nothing more. Some time later, while running through the forest again, it perceived a conditioned stimulus. That is, it heard, saw, or smelled something that had preceded the first attack. It was frightened by this sign, or cue, and ran for safety. From that day on the little animal successfully avoided attack by the bad predator. The fable fits the ordinary conception of avoidance learning. Based on Mowrer's two-factor theory, one would argue that fear had been classically conditioned to the cues preceding the first attack. Later these cues produced fear, which was instrumentally avoided. Fear reduction reinforced the escape response.

Bolles argues that this reasoning is "utter nonsense." First, predators do not present cues just before they attack. Owls do not hoot 2.5 seconds before they hit their prey. Coyotes do not consistently give recognizable signs before they pounce. The whole idea, we must assume, is for predators to minimize such telltale signs. They might occasionally slip up, but Bolles points out that *predators do not allow their prey enough trials for ordinary avoidance conditioning to occur.* Mice do not generally escape from owls dozens of times. Bolles suggests that the little animals stay alive not because of laboratory-type avoidance conditioning but because of innate SSDRs. Whenever the animal is faced with novel or sudden stimuli, it flies, freezes, or runs *innately* and automatically. It has not learned these responses through narrow escapes. They are automatic responses to novel or sudden stimulus situations. As Bolles points out, gazelles do not run from lions because they have been bitten by lions. They automatically run from any large object that approaches them (see Blanchard, Mast, & Blanchard, 1975). Prey will react with an SSDR to the sudden presentation of a harmless stimulus as well as to the sudden appearance of a truly dangerous predator.

One can see how Bolles's hypothesis might account for our laboratory data. Rats may well come into our experiments neurally wired, or prepared, to run in response to danger or any other sudden stimulus change. Bar pressing, however, is not one of their SSDRs and is therefore difficult to establish.

Obviously, Bolles's hypothesis does not answer all our questions (see Modaresi, 1989). It is one interpretation of the limited avoidance-conditioning situation and does not account for other types of preparedness. But it is provocative and does suggest that we must consider the innate survival mechanisms that the animal brings to our mechanized, arbitrary, laboratory learning situations.

INSTINCTIVE DRIFT

Instinctive drift is an interesting concept developed by Breland and Breland (1961, 1966). It is relevant to our consideration of preparedness, and an example or two should clarify its meaning. The Brelands attempted to train a raccoon to pick up coins and place them in a 5-inch metal box. Raccoons have the reputation of being tractable, eager, and quite intelligent. Hence, the Brelands expected little difficulty in establishing this particular response sequence. At first things proceeded fairly well. Each time the raccoon dropped the coin in the box, it was reinforced with food. But after a while, instead of promptly dropping the coins in the box, the raccoon spent seconds, and sometimes minutes, rubbing the coins together and dipping them in the box. All it had to do was let go to be reinforced. But it seemed to have difficulty in letting go at all. As time went on, the rubbing and dipping behavior became still stronger even though it resulted in fewer and fewer reinforcements. It seemed as though the raccoon's innate "washing behavior" had crept into the conditioning situation. Parenthetically, the Brelands suggest that the so-called washing behavior may help raccoons break away the exoskeleton of their natural prey, the crayfish.

In another situation Breland and Breland attempted to train pigs to pick up large wooden coins and place them in a bank. At first the pigs eagerly performed the correct responses, picking up, carrying, and depositing the coins without hesitation. But over a period of weeks the reinforced behavior deteriorated. The pigs began to drop the coins, root them, pick them up, drop them again, and root them again. In some instances the pigs finally required ten minutes to carry four coins a distance of six feet. The pigs' natural food-gathering responses appeared to intrude into the learning situation. These "disruptive" behaviors seemed to violate what is typically thought to be true of learning situations. That is, they used more energy than the simple, required responses. In addition, they resulted in fewer reinforcements (see Figure 4.6).

In attempting to account for this type of "misbehavior" Breland and Breland (1961) write:

> It seems obvious that these animals are trapped by strongly instinctive behaviors, and clearly we have here a demonstration of the prepotency of such behavior patterns over those which have been conditioned.
>
> We have termed this phenomenon "instinctive drift." The general principle seems to be that whenever an animal has strong instinctive behaviors in the area of the conditioned response, after continued running the organism will drift toward the instinctive behavior to the detriment of the conditioned behavior and even to the delay or preclusion of the reinforcement. In a very boiled-down, simplified form, it might be stated as "learned behavior drifts toward instinctive behavior." (p. 69)

The Brelands indicate that these conclusions are not to disparage the use of learning principles. They merely suggest that the assumptions underlying what we have termed the interchangeable-parts conception of learning must be tempered by a consideration of the animal's instinctive apparatus. The Brelands assert that the animal does not come to the laboratory as a *tabula rasa*, that species differences are important, and that all responses are not equally conditionable to all stimuli.

FORAGING

Consider a rat in a Skinner box learning to press a bar for food. Admittedly, this apparatus has been an influential and important tool in the study of learning. But how realistic is it? Does it contain elements found in the animal's natural habitat? The recent ethological influence in the field of learning has led to the conclusion that, in fact, the Skinner box is a very artificial situation and that learning might be better studied and understood in situations more closely resembling the animal's natural habitat.

This realization has led to what have commonly been called studies of *foraging* (Commons, Kacelnik, & Shettleworth, 1987; Kamil, Krebs, & Pulliam, 1987; Shettleworth, 1989). In these studies efforts are made to provide more naturalistic

(a)

(b)

Figure 4.6 Bears, monkeys, and other species can be taught a wide range of behaviors, but, as time passes, the behaviors will "drift" toward more instinctive, less-conditioned, responses. [From (a) E. K. Degginger/Animals Animals, (b) Zig Leszczynski/Animals Animals.]

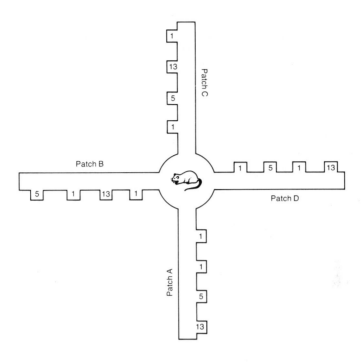

Figure 4.7 Each arm of a four-arm radial maze is called a patch. Each patch contains four feeding stations. Twenty food pellets are distributed among the stations within each patch as shown. (From Ibersich, T. J., Mazmanian, D. S., and Roberts, W. A. Foraging for covered and uncovered food in a radial maze. *Animal Learning and Behavior*, 1988, 16, 388–394. Reprinted by permission of Psychonomic Society, Inc.)

settings within which learning and innate responding can interact. According to Collier (1983) the elements which make up the overall foraging event include

(1) searching for food;
(2) recognizing or identifying food;
(3) actually procuring food, such as catching or picking it;
(4) handling food, such as peeling or crushing; and
(5) eating the food.

Some but not all of these elements exist in a typical Skinner box. By adding in elements drawn from natural habitats the psychologist attempts to understand the strategies the animal uses to maximize net energy gain relative to the time and energy required to feed.

The journals are currently filled with articles about foraging; one good example should suffice for our purposes. Ibersich, Mazmanian, and Roberts (1988) used the four-arm radial maze depicted in Figure 4.7. This maze is similar to the radial maze described earlier in that the rat must return to the center hub before moving into a new arm. It differs from the standard radial maze in that each arm, called a *patch*, has four *feeding stations*. Twenty food pellets are distributed in each arm as depicted. Of the two groups of rats in the experiment, one group was tested with the feeding stations open and readily accessible. The second group could see the food but had to open a little lid to get at the food.

What is the optimal strategy here? What would you do? The authors found that in the accessible or open condition the rats merely visited the stations in the order they encountered them, from the hub to the end of the arm. But in the covered condition, where extra time and effort were required to get at the food, the rats became more selective, visiting the stations containing 5 or 13 pellets first and the stations containing a single pellet last. The extra time and effort involved in getting at the food in the covered condition produced selective foraging in the rats.

At present there is considerable controversy concerning the ultimate value of foraging experiments (see Shettleworth, 1989), but at the very least these experiments seem to suggest that we can discover a great deal about learning if we focus on naturally occurring feeding strategies. They also suggest that animals are highly prepared to alter their feeding strategies in the face of variable environmental demands.

ETHOLOGY: INNATE BEHAVIOR

Concepts such as SSDRs and instinctive drift underscore the fact that animals are extremely well prepared to display certain behaviors. It seems as though certain response systems are built into the organism. These responses are not dependent on learning; they will occur automatically when the appropriate environmental stimuli are perceived. A gazelle does not have to learn to run when it sees a lion; the running response occurs automatically when the lion is seen. A mouse, even though it has never seen a cricket before, will attack and kill these insects (Timberlake & Washburn, 1989). Rat pups, when pinched on the nape of the neck, will draw up their legs involuntarily (Wilson, 1988). This *transport response* produces a compact package for the mother to carry (see Figure 4.8). Such released responses are called *innate* responses; they represent the most prepared of all behaviors.

Most psychologists would agree that some behaviors are clearly innate, some learned, and some probably represent a complex mixture of learned and innate components (see Haig, Rawlins, Olton, Mead, & Taylor, 1983). Exactly how innate and learned behavior interact and affect each other remains an intriguing question.

Within *ethology*, a subdivision of biology concerned with behavior in relation to the environment, many of these issues about innate behavior are addressed. Hence, we shall spend a little time learning about this field. Ethologists, represented by illustrious Europeans such as Konrad Lorenz, Nikolaas Tinbergen, and Karl von Frisch, believe that a true understanding of behavior must include a consideration of innate factors as well as the role of learning. They reject the interchangeable-parts conception of behavior; to the contrary, they believe that much of behavior is predetermined and precisely defined by genetic and biological factors.

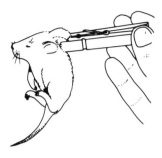

Figure 4.8 The transport response in a 15-day-old rat pup. Notice that the pup draws up its legs and becomes a compact package for easy carrying. (From Wilson, C. The effects of sensory stimulation in inducing or intensifying the "transport response" in white rats. *Animal Learning and Behavior*, 1988, *16*, 83–88. Reprinted by Psychonomic Society, Inc.)

Six Concepts

REACTION–SPECIFIC ENERGY.   Tinbergen (1952) has observed that the male stickleback fish will attack and drive off other males intruding into its territory but will not attack females. We can use this interesting bit of behavior to introduce the main concepts developed by the ethologists to account for innate behavior. The term *reaction-specific energy* refers to the idea that a pool, or source, of energy exists only for the occurrence of a particular behavior (for example, the stickleback's attack behavior).

INNATE RELEASING MECHANISM.   We know that the stickleback doesn't attack constantly. It attacks only under certain conditions. To account for this fact the ethologists speak of an *innate releasing mechanism*. Think of this factor as a plug in a basin. It stops up and contains the energy that would otherwise flow and would be expressed as attack behavior.

SIGN STIMULUS.   A *sign stimulus* is the stimulus that, through being perceived by the organism, pulls the plug and releases the reaction-specific energy. Sign stimuli tend to be fairly simple, but they have an enormous impact on the animal. For example, the sign stimulus that releases stickleback attack behavior is the red belly of the intruding male. Nothing but that red belly will do the job. Perfect replicas of male intruders without red bellies are ignored. But very unrealistic replicas *with* red bellies are attacked fiercely (see Figure 4.9). Sign stimuli are assumed to open innately the flood gates without being dependent on learning (see Domjan, Greene, & North, 1989).

FIXED ACTION PATTERN.   The rigid, stereotyped attack behavior released by the sign stimulus is called a *fixed action pattern*. When the stickleback sees a red belly, it attacks and drives the intruder away regardless of what else is going on in the environment.

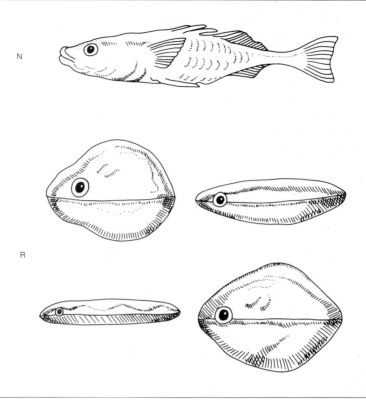

Figure 4.9 Fighting behavior in the male stickleback can be elicited to varying degrees by these models. The N model, while an accurate model of the fish, lacks a red throat and belly. The four R models have the correct coloration but are otherwise very crude reproductions. (Adapted from Tinbergen, N. *The study of instinct.* Oxford, England: Oxford University Press, 1951.)

VACUUM REACTIONS.   Sometimes, when the male has not aggressed for a long period (because it has not seen a red belly), it will attack anyway. It may attack a stimulus that only remotely resembles the normal sign stimulus (for example, a pink belly). In fact, given a long enough time without the appearance of a sign stimulus the fish may attack just about anything. This behavior, called a *vacuum reaction*, is explained by the idea that reaction-specific energy builds up to the point at which it blows out the cork by itself without the cork's having been removed by a sign stimulus.

SUPERNORMAL STIMULI.   Given a choice between its own egg and a larger egg some birds, such as the oyster catcher, will incubate the larger egg (see Figure 4.10). Given a choice between its own brown spotted egg and a black spotted egg some birds, such as plovers, will choose the *supernormal stimulus*. In other words, these behaviors seem to be strictly controlled by the nature of the sign stimuli.

Figure 4.10 An oyster catcher attempts to incubate a supernormal egg. (From Mazur, J. E. *Learning and behavior*. Oxford, England: Oxford University Press, 1986.)

The Hydraulic Model

Tinbergen (1951) has proposed a hydraulic model of innate behavior, depicted in Figure 4.11. Reaction-specific energy builds up like water collecting behind a dam. The innate releasing mechanism holds in the water. A sign stimulus, depicted by the weight in the pan, will pull the stopper and release the accumulated energy. Thus, two factors can release the energy. First, a sign stimulus can pull the plug. Second, the building pressure within the reservoir can lead to a "blowout" (and thus the occurrence of a vacuum reaction). Once released, the energy or water flows into a sloped container. The more water or energy, the more different holes in the pan it will flow through. Tinbergen used this sloped-pan mechanism to account for the fact that released behavior sometimes seems more complete than it does at other times. The stickleback is assumed to attack more fully and completely when the energy flows through more holes in the pan; the overall attack response is more complete.

The most complete response will occur (1) when the sign stimulus is most appropriate, thereby exerting a greater pull on the plug, and (2) when a great deal of energy has accumulated, thereby exerting a greater push on the plug and a greater flow into the sloped pan.

Although ethology is quite popular, its methods and concepts have not escaped criticism. Ethologists have not been able to disentangle learned and innate components of behavior. But they have been able to demonstrate and clarify for us the fact that innate influences do, in fact, exist and that they probably interact with modifications due to learning. Lorenz (1969) uses the example of the jackdaw to emphasize his belief that innate and learned elements interact to produce behavior. The jackdaw knows, innately, that it must collect twigs and push them together to form a nest. But it *doesn't* know, innately, which twigs are most suitable. This it must learn through a process of trial and error. Thus the ethologists, while not having all the answers, consistently show that any full and final understanding of behavior will have to include a consideration of innate factors.

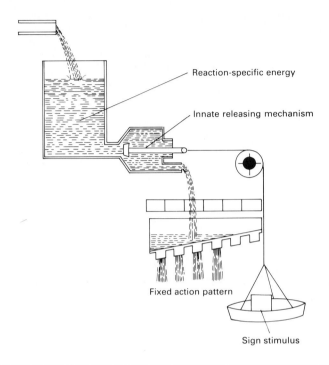

Reaction-specific energy

Innate releasing mechanism

Fixed action pattern

Sign stimulus

Figure 4.11 The hydraulic model of instinctive behavior. (Adapted from Lorenz, K. The comparative method of studying innate behavior patterns. *Symposia of the Society of Experimental Biology*. Cambridge, England: Cambridge University Press, 1950.)

IMPRINTING

We now turn to *imprinting*, which is important for two reasons. First, it is a substantial and intriguing area of investigation on its own. Second, it exemplifies the current problem we all have in trying to disentangle learned and innate elements in behavior.

In its simplest form imprinting includes the fact that a newly hatched bird will approach, and form a social attachment to, the first moving object it encounters, whether it be the real parent or some parent surrogate. The longer the bird is exposed to the target object, the stronger the filial tendency becomes. Lorenz (1937) noticed that, if the first object a gosling encounters is a human, the gosling will approach that human. In the future the gosling will approach the human in preference to its real mother. After the egg cracks and the bird struggles out, it straightens up, dries out, takes a little time to get organized, and looks around. It approaches the first moving object it encounters and becomes imprinted on it (see Figure 4.12).

Many different kinds of stimuli will serve as a "mother." Objects that have been successfully used as parent surrogates include balloons and electric trains (Fabri-

Figure 4.12 These geese became imprinted on Konrad Lorenz, because he was the first moving object they observed. (From Nina Leen/*Life Magazine*, © Time Inc.)

cius, 1955; Fabricius & Boyd, 1954), footballs (Ramsay, 1951), moving lines (Smith & Hoyes, 1961), animals of a different species (Baer & Gray, 1960), and colored boxes (Salzen & Sluckin, 1959) to mention a few. Most of the experimental work has been done with various birds, but some authors argue that imprinting occurs to one degree or another in animals such as dogs, primates, and even humans (Hoffman & Ratner, 1973). We shall return to the question of imprinting in humans in a later section.

We can see how this phenomenon might be adaptive. Those birds that wander off rather than staying close to their parent would probably be less likely to survive. But is imprinting learned, or is it innate and unlearned behavior? Does it represent some combination of learned and innate behaviors? No one quite knows, but these are the questions the psychologist and ethologist address.

Sample Apparatus and Procedures

Hess (1964, 1972) has done a good deal of influential experimental work on imprinting. A description of his procedures should provide a good example of the kind of experimental rigor obtainable in connection with the imprinting process. Hess's (1959) apparatus is depicted in Figure 4.13. It consists of a circular walkway enclosed with Plexiglas walls. The decoy, or object on which the duckling will be imprinted, is a model of a male mallard duck equipped with a loudspeaker, which

Figure 4.13 The imprinting apparatus. (Adapted from Hess, E. H. Imprinting. *Science*, 1959, *130*, 133–141. Fig. 1, p. 134. Copyright 1959 by the American Association for the Advancement of Science.)

will emit a human voice saying "gock, gock, gock, gock." The decoy also contains a heating unit. Mallard ducklings are hatched in incubators and immediately placed in small cardboard boxes until they are used in the experiments. The notion here is that they will not become imprinted on anything in their dark little compartments. In the imprinting procedure the ducklings are released into the apparatus by remote control. The decoy begins to move and emit the "gock" sound. The little duck follows, round and round, presumably being imprinted on the decoy. When the experimenter wishes to terminate the imprinting procedure, the duckling is tumbled through a little trap door.

As a test of the strength of the imprinting the experimenter then places two decoys in the apparatus. One is the male decoy they were imprinted on; the other might be a model of a female mallard emitting the recorded sounds of a real female duck. The duckling is reintroduced into the apparatus, and the experimenter observes which decoy attracts it. During these kinds of tests most ducklings respond to the male decoy, thereby demonstrating the imprinting effect. Small blocks, or barriers, placed between the ducklings and the male model do not deter the little ducklings. They clamber over these obstacles to be near their "mother."

Experimenters can vary any number of factors in this apparatus. For instance, they can vary the nature of the decoy and the sound it emits. They can vary the time spent in the apparatus and the speed of the decoy. In one set of experiments Hess wanted to know if it was the *time* the duckling spent with the decoy or the *distance* it traveled following the decoy that was important in determining the imprinting effect. Accordingly, in one condition Hess kept the time spent in the apparatus constant while varying the speed of the decoy. This enabled him to vary the dis-

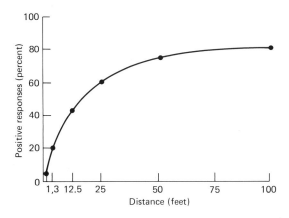

Figure 4.14 Strength of imprinting as a function of the distance traveled, with exposure time held constant. (Adapted from Hess, E. H. Imprinting. *Science*, 1959, *130*, 133–141. Fig. 6, p. 137. Copyright 1959 by the American Association for the Advancement of Science.)

tance traveled by the ducks in a given period. The results of this experiment are shown in Figure 4.14. Imprinting clearly increased in strength as the distance the duckling followed the decoy increased. In a companion experiment Hess varied the time the duckling spent in the presence of the decoy while keeping the distance traveled constant. In this case imprinting did not vary as a function of time. Thus, Hess concluded that the distance traveled is more important than the time of exposure in determining the strength of the imprinting effect.

Natural versus Laboratory Imprinting

We have already learned that psychologists are becoming more and more convinced that to understand complex behavioral phenomena, such as foraging, we must study them in situations resembling the animal's natural habitat (Ilersich, Mazmanian, & Roberts, 1988; Shettleworth, 1989; Spetch & Honig, 1988). Hess (1973) has come to the same conclusion with respect to imprinting. He has argued that to understand imprinting completely, we must study it as it occurs in *natural settings*, as well as in the laboratory. He feels that there are important differences between imprinting in the laboratory and in nature. He points out, for example, that imprinting occurring in natural settings seems much less reversible than imprinting obtained in the laboratory. Furthermore, he argues that the whole imprinting experience, from the little bird's viewpoint, must be very different in the natural and laboratory settings. In the normal course of a laboratory study, eggs hatched in an incubator do not all hatch at once. Eggs hatched by the mother in the field all hatch *within a few hours of one another*. Although this seems a small difference to us, it may represent an enormous difference to a tiny duckling peeking out of its eggshell.

Because he feels it is important to study imprinting under as natural conditions as possible, Hess (1973) has developed an apparatus that combines, or integrates,

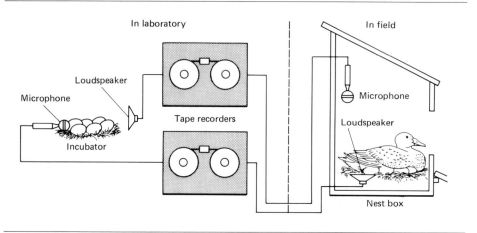

Figure 4.15 Hess' apparatus used to measure and control vocal interactions between unhatched ducklings in laboratory incubator and female mallard on nest in field. (Adapted from Hess, E. H. "Imprinting" in a natural laboratory. *Scientific American,* 1972, 227, 24–31. Copyright © 1972 by Scientific American, Inc. All rights reserved.)

natural qualities with laboratory control. Though not completely natural, this system contains many elements missing in most laboratory experiments, as shown in Figure 4.15. Specifically, even though the ducklings are hatched in an incubator in this apparatus, they are subjected to the clucking sounds made by a female mallard as it sits out in the field. The unhatched ducklings not only hear the female, but can also return vocalizations to it as well—all the while enclosed in the shell. As we shall soon learn, these *prehatching vocal interactions* are critical in the overall imprinting process.

Nonvisual Imprinting

Traditionally, imprinting based on vision has been the subject of most research. The emphasis has been on birds hatching and *looking* around. But it now turns out that imprinting may involve other sensory channels as well. Sounds, for example, may be as important as sight in the overall imprinting event. Hess (1973) believes that vocal interaction between the female duck and its unhatched ducklings is part of, and strengthens, the overall imprinting event. In a sense, imprinting has already begun before the eggs are hatched. The female's vocalization appears to increase as hatching approaches. The discovery of this form of interaction is important because it suggests that imprinting is more complicated than was first thought. Specifically, it suggests that imprinting involves *multiple sensory channels*. That is, imprinting involves sound as well as sight, and other forms of sensory stimulation as well.

Imprinting can occur on the basis of scent. Fantino and Logan (1979) point out that goats and European shrews will imprint on odor. Baby shrews, for example, will imprint on the first piece of cloth soaked in a distinctive odor that is presented to them. (Shrews, by the way, are small mouselike mammals with a voracious appetite.) Thus, imprinting appears to be a complex event (see also Brown & Hamilton, 1977). We now turn to a detailed consideration of whether imprinting is innate, learned, or some combination of the two.

Imprinted Behavior as Innate Behavior

ETHOLOGICAL INTERPRETATIONS.   It is not difficult to grasp the primary controversy surrounding the nature of imprinting. Although ethologists sometimes disagree (see Hess, 1970), they have argued that imprinted behavior is *genetically determined*. That is, when the appropriate moving stimulus is perceived, the young bird automatically and in a predetermined fashion approaches and follows that object. It seems as if the behavior pattern is already there, waiting to be released by the appropriate stimulus.

As we have seen, ethologists speak of sign stimuli and fixed action patterns. Sign stimuli are a certain limited range of critical stimuli that, when perceived, automatically release a fixed action pattern (for example, approach and follow). Imprinting, according to this view, is a built-in mechanism. Whenever one of the critical sign stimuli is perceived, the fixed action pattern is triggered, or unblocked. In this interpretation there is no learning. Practice is unnecessary, and reinforcement is unnecessary.

Rajecki (1973) has argued against this interpretation on two grounds. First, he challenges the concept of a limited range of sign stimuli. According to the ethologists themselves, not all stimuli are releasers. Only a certain set of stimuli is supposed to be effective in unblocking the fixed action pattern. But Rajecki points out that an enormous number of stimuli have been found to be effective sign stimuli—for example, blinking lights (James, 1959, 1960) and live hawks (Melvin, Cloar, & Massingill, 1967). It may be that all of these varied stimuli are included in some range, but the range is so wide and so diverse that the concept of a *limited* set of releasers is of little value. It does not help us understand what is going on. Second, Rajecki (1973) questions the notion that the fixed action pattern is really all that fixed. It seems that the ethologists wish to conclude that the pattern consists of a limited set of prescribed behaviors (for example, approach and follow and nothing more). But Rajecki notes a case in which a domestic chick not only became imprinted on a swan goose but copied its feeding habits and some of its calls as well. The fixed action pattern seems to be less fixed than the ethologists would have us believe.

Thus, although the sign stimulus–fixed action pattern sequence is appealing and does account for a good deal of the data, it seems that there is more to imprinting than this simple concept would imply. The concept of a limited set of sign stimuli and fixed behaviors cannot easily account for the variability in both imprinting stimuli and imprinted responses.

THE CRITICAL PERIOD.   Because the sign stimulus–fixed action pattern is unsatisfactory, we need to find something else that would suggest that the imprinting process is different from ordinary learning. Very early observations (Heinroth, 1911; James, 1890; Lorenz, 1935, 1937; Spalding, 1873) led to the conclusion that birds will form social attachments with moving objects but that such attachments will be formed only during a very brief period soon after hatching. It seems that it takes a little time before imprinting can occur, presumably because the very young bird is still a little shaky and disorganized. Then there ensues a brief period during which imprinting readily occurs. Following this "critical period" there seems to be a lessening of the tendency to imprint and an increase in the tendency to flee from any novel stimulus.

These early field observations have been substantiated in the laboratory. Hess (1959) and Hess and Schaefer (1959) varied the ages of ducklings to be imprinted. That is, the ducklings were kept safely in their cardboard containers for varying amounts of time before they were exposed to the male mallard decoy. The results, depicted in Figure 4.16, indicate that from 13 to 16 hours old seems to be the best age to obtain the imprinting phenomenon. The point Hess wishes to make is that ordinary learning is not restricted to a critical period. It can occur more or less readily at any age level. Hess (1964) argues that the critical period is one of several characteristics that set imprinting apart from most learned behavior (see also Gallagher, 1977).

Unfortunately, the notion of a critical period does not set imprinting apart from ordinary learning. Hess himself (Hess, 1959) sets the stage for a rejection of the notion. He argues that the rise and fall in the effectiveness of the imprinting procedures result from two interacting factors. First, the initial rise in imprinting may stem from the duck's growing locomotor capacity after hatching. That is, the very young duck may *want* to imprint, but its little legs are so wobbly that it cannot get up on them and get the job done. Second, the decrease in imprinting after age 13–16 hours seems to result from the duck's growing capacity to experience fear and its resulting unwillingness to follow novel stimuli. Thus, the duck may possess the *capacity* to imprint beyond the critical period, but it does not normally do so because it has gradually developed the capacity to fear novel objects and does not follow them after a certain age.

Several experiments suggest that fear does, in fact, block imprinting beyond the critical period (Bateson, 1964, 1969; Hoffman, Ratner, & Eisener, 1972; Sluckin & Salzen, 1961). Basically, all these studies exposed the bird to the harmless but fear-producing novel stimulus for a prolonged period of time. They did not allow the bird to flee. As time went on, the bird discovered that the stimulus would do no harm. Once fear was reduced, these older birds began to form social attachments to the stimuli. In a nutshell, imprinting may not be limited to a critical period. It may merely be blocked by a normal pattern of developing fear reactions. If the fear is removed, imprinting occurs beyond the so-called critical period.

OTHER DIFFERENCES?   Hess and his associates have suggested a number of other important differences between imprinting and ordinary learning. Unfortunately, none of these potential differences seems to have been established to everyone's satisfaction.

For example, Kovach and Hess (1963) have argued that in ordinary learning situations noxious stimulation presented in the presence of a particular object will lead to avoidance of that object. But in their experiments, noxious stimulation (shock) applied to birds in an imprinting situation led to an increase in *approach* rather than avoidance behavior. However, other more carefully controlled experiments have failed to support this distinction between imprinting and learning (Bar-

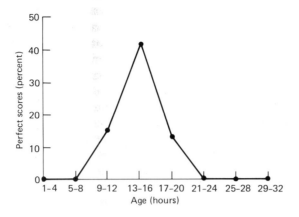

Figure 4.16 Imprinting as a function of age. (Adapted from Hess, E. H. Imprinting. *Science*, 1959, *130*, 133–141. Fig. 2, p. 135. Copyright 1959 by the American Association for the Advancement of Science.)

rett, Hoffman, Stratton, & Newby, 1971; Hoffman & Ratner, 1973). Noxious stimulation can lead to avoidance during imprinting, just as it does in ordinary learning situations.

Hess (1973) has also argued that imprinting differs from ordinary learning in that it is more long lasting and more irreversible. But these proposed distinctions have fallen on hard times, too. Life is filled with examples of long-lasting learning. (Will you ever forget your name or the alphabet?) And it has also been shown that imprinting can be reversed (Gaioni, Hoffman, De Paulo, & Stratton, 1978).

Interaction Models

Although there have been some attempts to characterize imprinting as nothing more or less than ordinary learning (see Fabricius, 1962; James, 1959; Moltz, 1960, 1963), these efforts have been no more successful than the attempts to argue that imprinting is completely different from ordinary learning.

Still others, in what may prove to be the best approach, have proposed that imprinting involves the interaction of *both* learning and innate elements. For example, Hoffman and Ratner (1973) suggest that imprinted behavior is partly innate and partly learned. The first assumption they make is that certain classes of stimuli (for example, moving objects) *innately* elicit filial responses. If a stimulus drawn from this critical class is presented to an immature bird, the bird will approach the stimulus in an innate fashion, with no learning necessary. If the authors left their model at this point, we would have to predict that the bird would run about following *any* moving stimulus. But we know that this is not the case. The bird does not become imprinted on the whole class of stimuli but rather on one particular stimulus drawn from that class. This is where the authors bring in the notion of classical conditioning. Assume that the decoy is a moving, green football. The critical aspect of the decoy (the fact that it is a moving object) is the UCS. This

UCS innately elicits a UCR (approach and follow). The CS is composed of those *initially neutral* aspects of the decoy that distinguish it from other moving objects (for example, green color, small size). Initially, it is only the moving quality of the object that elicits filial responses. The other attributes of the decoy (greenness, smallness) are, at first, neutral or ineffective in eliciting filial responses. But when the ball is presented to the duck, the *filial responses are classically conditioned to those initially neutral attributes*. Thus, in the future, the presentation of the ball will elicit filial behavior because of both the innate UCS (moving object)–UCR (approach) relationship, and because of the conditioned CS (green, small)–CR (approach) connection. When the duck was presented a choice between a man and the football, the combination of the innate and conditioned filial tendencies would ensure a preference for the football.

The final fate of their model remains to be seen, but Hoffman and Ratner (1973) have attempted to clarify the ambiguous status of the imprinting concept by accounting for both innate and learned elements within the process, and their interpretation has received some support (see Gaioni et al., 1978). But their model is not free of difficulties. For instance, it depends on the assumption of a *limited* set of releasers. We have seen that this concept may be difficult to justify.

Imprinting and the Preparedness Continuum

Let us return to the main thread of the chapter. Not all responses are connected to all stimuli equally easily. How does imprinting relate to this theme? We have seen that it is difficult, if not impossible, to resolve the question of whether imprinted responses are innate, learned, or both. After reviewing the status of imprinting, many students, to say nothing of researchers in the field, are left with a certain sense of dissatisfaction. One way to lessen this uneasy feeling, or to gain a perspective on the issue, is to think about imprinting in relation to other behaviors on the preparedness continuum. We can think of the preparedness continuum presented in Figure 4.17 as a dimension of survival mechanisms. All of the behaviors encompassed by the dimension are designed, or somehow function, to ensure the survival of the species. Some are more fixed, or predetermined, than others. Figure 4.17 contains a few sample behaviors. You may consider where additional behaviors might fall on the dimension.

Purely innate behavior represents one extreme end of the dimension. Present a stimulus to the animal, and the response will occur automatically. Neither practice nor reinforcement is necessary to establish this association. It seems as if the connection is already there, or built into the animal's nervous system.

At the other end of the continuum we find events that just do not seem to be learnable, no matter how much practice or reinforcement is involved. As noted, for instance, it is almost impossible to teach a dog to yawn for food (Konorski, 1967).

Imprinting can be considered an instance of highly prepared learning. It does not require much practice at all, nor is much, if any, reinforcement necessary for it to be established. The little duckling is *ready* to associate its filial responses with certain stimuli. The very fact that imprinting is so prepared actually leads to the confusion about whether it is innate or learned. By thinking of it as prepared behavior one can avoid some of this confusion. Rather than worrying about whether it is or is not learned behavior, we can merely think of it as very prepared behavior.

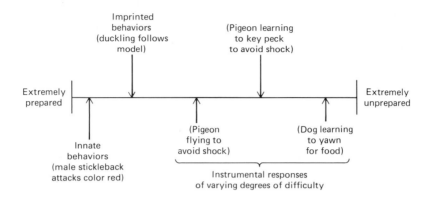

Figure 4.17 The preparedness continuum as a dimension of survival mechanisms, with some selected behaviors included.

Ethologists have traditionally examined behavior near the prepared end of the dimension, whereas learning psychologists have looked at less prepared behaviors. The controversy over innate versus learned behaviors may be a matter of degree rather than kind.

It should be kept in mind that the preparedness continuum does not really explain anything. It is merely a frame of reference that enables us to put certain behaviors in perspective, to consider them in relation to one another, and to sort out our thoughts about how they might or might not differ.

Humans and Imprinting

Do humans imprint, or is the concept one that makes sense only in reference to "lower" organisms? Certainly, tiny children do not pad along in single file behind their parents. But very young children obviously do form strong social attachments to their parents or caretakers. They do tend to straggle after a moving parent, they sometimes react with fear when a strange adult approaches, and they approach their parents when offered a choice between a parent and a stranger.

We tend to think of ourselves as possessing survival mechanisms that, when compared with those of the so-called lower animals, fall somewhere near the unprepared end of the dimension. That is, we tend to think of ourselves as more adaptive, more flexible, and less in the grip of rigid behavior patterns. But some authors have argued that we do possess characteristics reminiscent of imprinted, or at least highly prepared, behaviors. For example, our early socialization has been assumed by some to possess attributes of the imprinting process. Bowlby (1969) argues that human infants develop attachment behavior in a manner that is quite similar to the imprinting process observed in other mammals and in birds (see also Ainsworth, 1973).

Unfortunately, we really have little more than speculation and opinion concerning the existence of imprinting in humans. But the question is exciting, and it should generate a good deal of interesting research in the years to come.

IMPLICATIONS FOR GENERAL LEARNING THEORY

This chapter began with a discussion of the interchangeable-parts conception of learning, which has evolved gradually in American psychology. We then traced a number of areas of research that contradict this model of learning. These findings call into question the very notion that we may be able to arrive at a unified general theory of learning. The questions we might ask are these: Do different degrees of preparedness require different laws, or different principles of learning? Does learning occur in a different manner at different points on the preparedness continuum?

Seligman (1970) speculates that the laws of learning may very well vary with the continuum of preparedness. He writes: "Detailed studies which compare directly the delay of reinforcement gradients, extinction functions, etc., for prepared versus unprepared associations are needed. It would be interesting to find that the extinction and inhibition functions for prepared associations were different than for unprepared associations" (p. 416).

We are on a frontier of sorts. We have taken the issue of learning into the laboratory and have established, with some rigor, a set of general principles that seem to govern the establishment of associations in that setting. Now we are challenged by the notion that our rules and laws, developed under restricted laboratory conditions, may not apply to, or completely account for, learning accomplished by varied animals in the world outside the laboratory. New rules and laws may have to be developed for more diverse species, behaviors, and environmental settings (see Papini, Mustaca, & Bitterman, 1988).

SUMMARY

1. For the better part of this century many American psychologists have adopted a concept of learning that holds that all responses are about equally conditionable to all stimuli.
2. This position is challenged by a growing body of literature, which indicates that the rule of equivalent associability is inadequate.
3. Seligman has proposed a continuum of preparedness, which suggests that animals may be differentially prepared to associate certain events.
4. Animal studies supporting the notion of a preparedness continuum come from the fields of instrumental conditioning, discrimination learning, and avoidance conditioning, among others.
5. Humans, as well as other animals, are prepared to associate some events and unprepared to associate others.
6. A given species may seem unprepared to learn a response in one particular setting but quite prepared to learn the same response in another situation, particularly when the second setting more closely resembles the animal's natural feeding habitat.
7. Bait shyness refers to the fact that, if an animal eats poisoned bait and survives, it will develop an aversion to the flavor of that bait.
8. Although bait shyness possesses many of the characteristics of avoidance conditioning, one apparent difference is that the bait-shyness effect can be established with extremely long intervals (hours) between consumption and illness.
9. Bait shyness supports the notion of a preparedness continuum, because it has been found that an aversive reaction will be associated only with certain aspects of the bait (for example, flavor). The animal is unprepared to associate

illness with other aspects of the bait situation (such as visual aspects). Preparedness differences may well be related to the pressures of natural selection.

10. The "novelty," or newness, of a stimulus will determine whether it becomes the functional CS in aversive-taste conditioning.

11. In a practical sense bait shyness may be useful in the control of predation.

12. Use of the bait-shyness effect resembles aversion therapy in humans. In aversion therapy the human is stimulated with a noxious agent while engaging in or imagining the unwanted behavior (for example, smoking or overeating).

13. Species-specific defense reactions (SSDRs) are innate reactions that animals automatically produce in response to sudden or novel stimuli. Bolles argues that, if an avoidance response is easily acquired in the laboratory, it must necessarily be an SSDR.

14. Instinctive drift refers to the fact that after continuous conditioning innate behaviors sometimes begin to intrude into conditioning situations.

15. Forging experiments attempt to illuminate how animals go about searching for, recognizing, procuring, handling, and eating food in situations that resemble their natural habitats.

16. Ethologists have proposed the concepts of reaction-specific energy, innate releasing mechanisms, sign stimuli, fixed action patterns, vacuum reactions, and supernormal stimuli in their study of innate behavior.

17. Tinbergen presents a hydraulic model of innate behavior.

18. Imprinting refers to the fact that a newly hatched bird will approach and follow the first moving object it encounters. The distance the bird follows the object seems to be more important than the time of exposure in determining the strength of imprinting.

19. Imprinting should be studied in natural settings as well as in the laboratory, because there are important differences between these two situations.

20. Auditory imprinting and olfactory imprinting, as well as visual imprinting, have been observed.

21. Imprinting may be a multiple-channel event.

22. Some authors have argued, without total success, that imprinted behavior is completely innate.

23. The concept of a critical period refers to the idea that imprinted social attachments will be formed only during a very brief period in the bird's life soon after hatching.

24. Additional experimentation has shown this assumption to be false. Once fear is removed, older birds form social attachments. Imprinting is not limited to a critical period and on this basis cannot be distinguished from learning.

25. Some authors have argued that imprinting and learning call forth different responses to the presentation of a noxious stimulus. Analysis of the experimental work indicates that this distinction between imprinting and learning is also difficult to maintain.

26. Although some have argued that imprinting differs from learning in that it produces behaviors that are long lasting and irreversible, many learned behaviors also have these characteristics.

27. Some authors have taken the opposite view, asserting that imprinted behavior is learned. Currently no conditioning model of imprinting is entirely satisfactory.

28. If innate behavior and learned behavior are thought of as continuous rather than dichotomous, much of the confusion concerning the nature of imprinting evaporates. Imprinting can be thought of as highly prepared behavior falling somewhere near the innate end of the preparedness continuum.
29. Some authors have speculated that the process of early socialization in humans is similar to imprinting.
30. Psychologists have taken learning into the laboratory and have established with some rigor a set of laws and principles that seem to govern behavior in that limited setting. The areas of research described in this chapter represent a challenge to that set of laws. Whether our laboratory-based laws will be sufficient to account for the diverse behaviors of various species in different environmental settings remains to be seen.

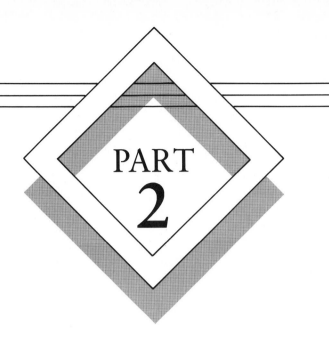

PART 2

ACQUISITION

There are several ways to approach the field of learning. One way is to consider, in a sequential fashion, the works of influential theoreticians in the field. Good examples of this reasonable strategy are provided by Bower and Hilgard (1981) and Hill (1971). We shall take an alternative tack in which issues and problems, rather than theories, are considered sequentially. We shall trace the issues that have been of concern to all major thinkers in the field and refer to their works when relevant. Other examples of this approach include books by Schwartz (1989), Gordon (1989), and Hale (1989).

The next three parts of the text are labeled Acquisition, Transfer, and Retention. A few comments concerning this breakdown of the field are in order. When first faced with the field of learning, students are often perplexed by the mass of data and interrelated issues. They have difficulty in grasping the limits of the field and making it in some way comprehensible and manageable. One way to ensure some grasp of the field is to think of it as reducible to these three subprocesses. Almost any learning study, whether reporting animal or human learning, can be included in one of these categories. The major thrust of the investigation is usually with one or the other of these processes.

Acquisition refers to those processes that occur during the establishment of an association. When we deal with acquisition, we are concerned with events relating to the building of associations, presumably through practice and reinforcement. If we study how a rat increases its lever-pressing behavior for food, we are focusing on the acquisition process. If we study the relationship between a child's increasing ability to read and the amount of praise given for each success, we are primarily concerned with acquisition.

Transfer refers to the effects of one learned task on subsequent attempts to learn or perform additional tasks. Positive transfer refers to the situation in which the learning of one task facilitates the learning of additional tasks. If we observe that children's ability to memorize one set of vocabulary words is facilitated by their having previously learned another set of words, we have demonstrated positive transfer. Negative transfer refers to the situation in which prior learning hinders present performance. We can see how important the concept of transfer is in the field of education. Educators want to be able to arrange classroom materials and procedures so that positive transfer is obtained.

Retention refers to what happens to associations or learning after practice has ceased. After associations have been acquired and are no longer being rehearsed, what happens to them? Do they "remain with us" forever? Do they fade away? How quickly? What factors determine the rate at which things are forgotten? As we ask these kinds of questions and focus our attention on the fate of learned associations, we are primarily concerned with the retention process.

Two notes of caution should be sounded about our approach. First, some studies are obviously, and legitimately, concerned with more than one of these processes. For instance, a given study may easily be concerned with the establishment of associations and with their eventual fate once practice has ceased. Second, and more importantly, the distinctions among acquisition, transfer, and retention are in fact somewhat arbitrary and superficial. They should be taken as convenient, but not necessarily crystal-clear, distinctions. For instance, acquisition is probably never free of retention effects. Consider a paired-associate learning situation, such as the learning of a list of Spanish-English equivalents. The subjects acquire the list by repeatedly rehearsing it. Although the emphasis is on the acquisition process, the situation is obviously not free from retention effects. The subject must remember the materials from trial to trial. To the extent that she utilizes what she learned on the last trial, the retention process is intertwined with the acquisition process.

Similarly, transfer experiments always involve the retention process. For one task to affect performance on a second task, either positively or negatively, it must be remembered. Furthermore, retention experiments involve transfer processes. In fact, retention experiments may represent a special case of transfer—the one in which the two successive tasks are identical. The subjects learn a list of word pairs on Day 1. On Day 2 they are given the stimulus words and asked to recall the response words. We are looking at the effect of one list on the subsequent performance of the very same list, or, in other words, a transfer situation in which the two successive tasks are as identical as we can make them.

Without reviewing all the possibilities we can see that the processes of acquisition, transfer, and retention are all interconnected. You might take a moment to pursue some of the combinations. In what way do acquisition experiments almost always involve transfer effects? How is acquisition involved in retention? How is retention involved in transfer?

In Part Two some of the major issues in the area of *acquisition* are considered. Traditionally, the issues of *contiguity, practice,* and *reinforcement* have maintained central positions in this arena. In fact, major theoreticians most often disagree about these three issues, or variables. Their roles in the acquisition process are controversial. We shall see what is known about each by drawing on both animal and human research.

The contiguity issue is taken up in the first part of Chapter 5. Must a response occur in the presence of a stimulus for learning to occur? Or can an association be established if the stimulus occurs at Time 1 and the response does not occur until Time 2? Is stimulus-response contiguity necessary and sufficient for learning to occur?

In the latter part of Chapter 5 we deal with the role of *practice* in learning. Is practice, or *rehearsal*, necessary for learning to occur? What is the relationship between rehearsal and strength of learning? The answer seems obvious. The more we practice, the more we learn; but it is not quite so simple as it might appear. For instance, some argue that increasing practice does not increase the strength of learning. They argue, and quite persuasively, that learning occurs in an all-or-none fashion. According to this controversial position, learning is either complete or does not occur at all in a given trial.

In Chapter 6 we deal with the role of *reinforcement* in acquisition. Is reinforcement necessary for learning to occur? What happens to learning when we vary such factors as the amount and kind of reinforcement that we deliver to the animal? What are some of the current models, or conceptions, of reinforcement? The answers to these and other questions will introduce the reader to the complexity and importance of reinforcement in the overall learning process.

CHAPTER

THE ROLES
OF CONTIGUITY
AND REHEARSAL
IN LEARNING

HOW IMPORTANT IS CONTIGUITY IN LEARNING?

One of the oldest assumptions in the field of learning is that temporal contiguity of the stimulus and response is necessary for learning to occur. Psychologists have generally assumed that *the response must occur in the presence of or very soon after the stimulus for an association to be established*. In other words, only events that occur together in time can be associated.

Intuitively, it seems extremely unlikely that two events will be associated if they are separated by any considerable length of time unless, of course, the subject somehow brings them together, either mentally or physically (see Rescorla & Cunningham, 1979). For example, there is no intuitive reason to assume that an event experienced today (for example, the sound of a hand clap) will in any way be associated with a particular response made tomorrow (speaking the word *table*). The fact that noncontiguous learning seems so unlikely may account for the contiguity principle's being accepted so universally and uncritically. Few seem to doubt it. But believing something to be true is not the same as knowing it to be true, and so we shall revisit this issue. We shall challenge the law of contiguity by attempting to discover instances of noncontiguous learning in the experimental literature. If we can find some examples of noncontiguous learning, then the notion that contiguity is *necessary* for learning to occur must be modified.

We can also ask whether stimulus-response contiguity (S-R) is *sufficient* for learning to occur. If a response occurs in the presence of a perceived stimulus, will learning always take place, without any other conditions (such as reinforcements) being met? Is contiguity *all* that is necessary?

If experiments can be found that demonstrate the *presence of learning in the absence of contiguity*, then we will have some reason to believe contiguity is not *necessary* for learning to occur. But to answer the question of the *sufficiency* of S-R contiguity we have to conduct a different search. We have to turn things around to look for an *absence of learning in the presence of contiguity*. If we can find such situations, we shall have some evidence for the notion that S-R contiguity is not all it takes for learning to occur. Thus, two searches must be undertaken, one for noncontiguous learning (relevant to the necessity of contiguity) and another for the absence of learning in the presence of S-R contiguity (relevant to the sufficiency of contiguity).

WHAT ARE STIMULI AND RESPONSES?

Before we begin our dual search, we should consider the nature of stimuli and responses a little more closely. The text has adopted what is usually referred to as an S-R, or behaviorist, language. According to this particular way of speaking and thinking, learning refers to an increase in the tendency to behave, or respond, in a particular fashion when confronted with a particular stimulus situation. We refer to this *increasing tendency to respond as the building, or strengthening, of an association* between that particular response and that particular stimulus situation. The S-R language is not the only way to speak of learning. But it is convenient, and it has been widely adopted. Like any language it has its limitations, and its use must be kept in perspective.

Stimuli

Logan (1970) defines a *stimulus* as *"any adequate change in energy falling upon an appropriate sensory receptor"* (p. 8). In other words, any detected energy change can serve as a stimulus. For example, lights, sounds, tastes, odors, and shock can serve as stimuli. The offset of any of these can be as effective as their onset. Relationships can serve as stimuli. An animal can learn to respond to the brighter of two stimuli, regardless of their absolute values. Even responses can sometimes function as stimuli. When we speak and hear ourselves, for instance, the sounds can serve as stimuli for further responses. If we detect that we are speaking too loudly, we may respond by speaking more softly. In addition, we use the sound of our own voice to keep track of where we are in our sentences.

Presumably, other types of action are equally affected by the stimulus qualities of our responses. For instance, if gymnasts did not receive sensory input, or feedback, from the body as they went through their complicated routines, they would probably lose track of what they were doing. Visual cues and the like would help, but they would not be sufficient. We would hardly expect a top-notch performance from athletes who were dependent on seeing their legs go over the bar without also feeling it happen.

Thinking probably represents another case in which responses serve as stimuli. One "thought" leads to another. One cognitive action, or response, serves as a cue for the next.

Any detected event that is distinguishable from other events can serve as a stimulus. Keep in mind, however, that not all energy changes are equally effective as stimuli. For instance, a pigeon will readily associate illness with visual stimuli, but not so readily with taste. Rats, on the other hand, readily associate illness with taste but not with visual stimuli. An effective stimulus for one species may not be so for another (Garcia & Koelling, 1966).

In addition, if we are not *paying attention* to a particular energy change, it tends not to be used as a stimulus. Attention is an important, but poorly defined, concept in psychology (see Bourne, Dominowski, & Loftus, 1979). At any given moment our sensory receptors are being bombarded by a large number of energy changes, each of which has the potential to be a stimulus. But somehow we are not aware of all of them at any given moment. We channel our attention, focusing on only a few of these many potential stimuli. As you read these words, for instance, you are attending to the print. You are probably not attending to your hands, even though they are part of the total stimulating pattern. You can attend to them if you wish. Without moving your eyes away from the printed words you can be aware of their position, their shape, and their movement. If an energy change is to be effective as a stimulus, our attention must be directed toward it.

And finally, the *continuation* of a stimulus is not dependent on the continued stimulation of sensory receptors by some outside energy source. Once an external stimulus has activated sensory receptors, the message is "taken into" the organism and maintained therein. *Traces* of external stimuli, or the neural remainders of external stimuli, can take various forms and can persist for varying amounts of time.

The term *stimulus trace* has been used in several ways. On the one hand, it has been used to refer to essentially sensory phenomena. For instance, we are all familiar with afterimages. As children we discovered that if we stared at a lightbulb for some time and then looked away, we could still see something that resembled the bulb. This afterimage, or trace, fades rather quickly. It represents one instance in which a terminated external stimulus "lives on" within the organism.

The afterimage represents a stimulus trace that decays rather rapidly, but some traces may persist indefinitely. Consider what you might do if an attractive person gave you a phone number in a crowded, noisy situation. You might desperately rehearse it, hoping to preserve the trace until you could write it down or until it became part of your permanent memory. The entire field of memory and retention is, in a sense, concerned with stimulus traces. When we remember something, we are often dealing with the trace of a long-gone external stimulus.

Critics of the S-R approach have argued that it is impossible to identify the effective stimulus in a learning situation. What, for example, is the stimulus for laughing at a joke? What is the stimulus for reaching a creative solution to a problem? What is the stimulus for learning to swim? Some feel that the S-R conception, with its emphasis on discrete, identifiable stimuli, is simpleminded. It may well be. The criticism is just, and we cannot brush it aside easily.

Yet several points can be made in defense of the S-R position. First, just because we cannot *always* identify the functional stimulus does not mean that we *never* can. In many situations the most important stimuli can be identified easily. Second, just because we cannot always observe the effective stimuli directly does not necessarily mean that such stimuli do not exist. It may merely be beyond our technical ability to measure or observe them at the present time. Third, the S-R language, although imperfect, does provide a structure within which to think of the complicated world of learned events.

Responses

It is as difficult to define a *response* as it is to define a stimulus in our S-R language. Let us say a college student, wanting to get acquainted with one of his classmates, asks her if she will join him for a cup of coffee. To his inquiry the woman responds with a flat no. That no is undoubtedly a "response," but it is more difficult to determine where the response began and where it ended. As she listened to the man's question, she apparently experienced some kind of emotional reaction. Her emotional reaction was then somehow translated into a verbal response. But the response does not even end there. Presumably neither she nor he would immediately return to a state of nonresponding. In all likelihood some sort of uncomfortable disengagement process would ensue. Even after they had gotten away from each other, the chain of behaviors would not end. They both would probably think about the encounter for some time. The situation obviously involves a chain, or series, of complex actions and reactions.

We must now try to handle this enormously complicated situation with our S-R conception of behavior. We must do two things in order to isolate a distinct response from this "behavior chain." First, we acknowledge the fact that behavior is *continuous*. We are always doing something; we never stop behaving. We may be more or less active, but we are always behaving. For example, we behave even when we are asleep: We breathe, we produce antibodies, we jump at the tiny suspicious sound of a window being rattled, but we remain undisturbed when a truck goes by. Many of us keep track of time, so that we awaken more or less at the time we wish to awaken.

Second, having acknowledged that behavior never ceases, we can define a *response as any identifiable segment of this continuous behavior process*. As Logan (1970) puts it, "a response is any glandular secretion, muscular action, or other objectively identifiable aspect of the behavior of an organism" (p. 25). A response can be anything from a muscle fiber twitch to the complex, goal-oriented behavior of the whole organism. The key here is that the segment must be *objectively identifiable*. Scientists must be able to agree that a given segment of behavior has occurred. If they cannot, they have gotten nowhere. For example, psychologists might not agree that our female friend had rejected the male. They could agree that she had responded with a verbal rejection, but they might not agree whether she meant it or not. Further observations would have to be made before agreement could be reached.

In summary, we accept the notion that behavior is not discrete. It is a continuing process from which we select segments to study. They may be short segments (for example, pronouncing the letter *T*, eye blinks) or long segments (success in college, the development of political attitudes). We then attempt to devise methods of measurement that will ensure that we can all agree whether or not our chosen behavior segment has occurred. The psychology of learning is the study of how these behavior segments become more and more likely to occur in the presence of particular stimuli.

IS CONTIGUITY NECESSARY? IS IT SUFFICIENT?

To return to the main thread of this chapter, we now begin our search for experiments that will disprove, or at least require modification of, the contiguity principle. We begin by looking for learning that occurs in the absence of S-R contiguity. (Later we shall seek situations in which learning does not occur even though S-R contiguity is established.) If we can convince ourselves that we have some clear examples of noncontiguous learning, then we may want to reevaluate the contiguity principle.

Subjective Organization and Contiguity

The first of several areas that we will review has to do with the concept of subjective organization (SO) (Tulving, 1962, 1964, 1966). In the simplest kind of SO experiment a randomly arranged list of unrelated words is presented, one word at a time, to the subjects. The subjects then attempt to recall as many of the words as they can, *in any order* they wish. The list then is presented to the subjects again, but this time in a *new random order*. The subjects again attempt to recall the words. The experiment involves a series of these successive phases of presentation and recall.

Tulving noticed that the subjects began to recall certain items next to each other, or sequentially, even though the items were scattered throughout the random presentation orders. The number of pairs the subjects began to recall sequentially increased as the experiment progressed. Each subject began to develop his or her own unique sets of items that were consistently recalled together. It seemed that the subjects somehow organized the materials "inside their head."

The fact that items are consistently recalled together in the absence of temporal contiguity during the input phase suggests that we may have found an instance of noncontiguous learning. Two items do not occur together in time during the presentation phase, yet they are consistently recalled together. Some kind of association has developed between them. Where is the temporal S-R contiguity?

At least two answers are possible to this question. One answer may be that the subjects merely bring items together "in their own minds." That is, even though the items are never presented together externally, nothing prevents the subjects from carrying traces of the items for long periods. Such an argument is certainly reasonable, but few hard data support it. This hypothesis may well be correct, but we would not want to accept it without some objective demonstration of its validity.

Another analysis suggesting that S-R contiguity occurs in SO experiments has to do with the output, or recall, phase of the experiment (Wallace, 1970). In many SO experiments the subjects are asked to write down all the words they can remember on a sheet of paper. In addition, they are typically given several minutes to attempt recall on each trial. Suppose that one subject randomly recalls and writes down *barn* and *fiction* together on the very first trial. Let us assume that he has no association between them at this time. There they are, right in front of him. He knows he is going to have to try to recall the list again. He rapidly rehearses the items he has already recalled, hoping to preserve them for the next trial. By looking at *barn* and *fiction* together he is, in effect, experiencing S-R contiguity. They occur together in time after all. We can see how SO might build up over trials. Two items randomly recalled together on the first recall trial would be rehearsed as a pair. The resultant association between them would lead to a greater likelihood that they would be recalled together on future trials, and so on.

Wallace (1970) presents data that support this *output-rehearsal hypothesis*. He found that amount of SO decreased when he set up experiments so that rehearsal during the output phase was reduced. For instance, he found that SO decreased when he substituted oral recall for written recall. In oral recall S-R contiguity is much more fleeting and less stable than in written recall. He found that SO decreased when the subjects were required to write down successively recalled items in noncontiguous positions on the recall sheet. The scattered positions of successively recalled items presumably reduced the probability that they would be rehearsed in a contiguous manner.

In summary, what appeared to be noncontiguous learning may be the result of either "mentally" established contiguity, or S-R contiguity established during the recall phase of the experiments. Subjective-organization experiments do not, after all, provide us with a clear instance of noncontiguous learning.

Paired-Associate Learning and Contiguity

In paired-associate (PA) experiments temporal S-R contiguity is the rule rather than the exception. The experimenter generally ensures that the response will occur in the presence of the stimulus. Each time through the list, the stimulus term is normally presented alone for 2 seconds. The stimulus and the response terms are then presented together for 2 seconds. Hence, PA research is not an ideal place to look for learning in the absence of S-R contiguity.

In a few studies, however, the *time* between the PA stimulus and the PA response has been varied. In these studies the stimulus is first presented alone. Then there ensues an empty time interval, which is varied in length. Finally, the response term is presented alone. The question is whether learning will occur when the stimulus and the response are separated in time. Guthrie (1933) and Martin and Schultz (1963) employed intervals ranging from 2 to 6 seconds. Interestingly, they found *better* learning with *longer* intervals. These results would seem to be in conflict with the contiguity principle. The greater the separation of the stimulus and the response in time, the better is the learning. The reason for this seeming contradiction soon became apparent. Martin (1966) attempted the same type of experiment, but with one major modification. He had the subjects count backward by threes during the intervals. Under these conditions the effect reported by Martin and Schultz (1963) could not be replicated. In other words, the increase in learning with increases in the interval in the earlier experiments must have had something to do with what the subjects *did* during that interval. In the earlier experiments subjects were left free to rehearse or to carry the stimulus trace forward in time, and their performance improved as the interval increased. In Martin's (1966) experiment the subjects were prevented from rehearsing or carrying the stimulus trace forward, and their performance did not improve as the interval increased. Counting backward by threes presumably distracted the subjects from the task at hand and prevented them from utilizing the time in rehearsal or maintaining a stimulus trace.

The ideal experiment investigating S–R contiguity in the PA situation would involve not only temporal separation of the stimulus and the response but also control of the subject's activities during the interval. Nodine (1969) ran an experiment with these qualities in mind. The subjects learned PA lists with intervals ranging from 0 to 6 seconds. In addition, Nodine varied the interval activities of the subjects. In some conditions subjects named numbers in an attempt to *minimize* rehearsal and the carrying forward of the stimulus. In other conditions subjects were asked to pronounce the stimuli over and over again during the interval, thereby *maximizing* mediated S–R contiguity. In a final set of conditions the subjects were free to do as they wished during unfilled intervals. Nodine's analyses suggest that *both* S–R contiguity and rehearsal within the interval are important. The two factors appear to operate against each other. On the one hand, as the interval increases, the tendency for an association to be formed between the stimulus and the response *decreases*. This is the contiguity principle in action. On the other hand, if the subject is not prevented from rehearsing or carrying the stimulus trace forward, then the tendency for an association to be formed increases as the interval increases.

In summary, these studies suggest that, unless the stimulus is closely followed by the response or unless the subject can carry the stimulus trace forward in time, there is little chance that learning will occur. Once again the necessity of contiguity is upheld.

The CS–UCR Interval and Contiguity

In Chapter 2 we saw that a CS–UCS interval of about .5 of a second is often optimal for classical conditioning. Longer and shorter intervals result in poorer conditioning. Generally speaking, these facts tend to support the contiguity principle: For learning to occur, a *response* (the UCR elicited by the UCS) must occur at the same time, or very soon after, the stimulus (the CS). But if there are any exceptions to this rule, then we may be able to think about them in terms of noncontiguous learning.

Revusky (1968) ran an interesting bait-shyness experiment in which a sweet solution (the CS) was ingested at a given time. *Seven hours later* the rats were X-irradiated and became ill (the UCS–UCR sequence). Despite this exceedingly long CS–UCR, or stimulus-response, interval, an aversion to the sweet flavor developed. Many investigators have obtained similar results (Garcia, Ervin, & Koelling, 1966; Smith & Roll, 1967).

This result does seem to come closer than the other types of experimentation we have discussed to demonstrating noncontiguous learning. But some have argued persuasively that learning over long CS–UCR intervals does not represent noncontiguous learning. In presenting their argument they evoke the idea of trace conditioning. Some kind of lingering trace of the CS (sweet flavor) might bridge the long CS–UCR interval (see Kehoe, Gibbs, Garcia, & Gormezano, 1979).

Two types of trace might be operating here. First, we might consider actual *physical* traces of the stimulus, such as chemicals lingering in the mouth or other parts of the system. Although such physical traces might bridge the time gap, Garcia, McGowan, and Green (1972) argue against such a possibility. They report that extremely transient tastes were as effective in ensuring conditioning as stronger, more lingering tastes. If a physical trace had mediated the learning, we would have expected the more durable physical traces to be more effective, but they were not.

A more likely trace interpretation is based on the mechanisms of memory. That is, the memory of the CS, or the neurological trace of the physical stimulus, is much more likely to mediate the time gap than is an actual physical trace of the stimulus. As mentioned earlier, the more novel a CS, the more likely it is to become an effective stimulus (see Dawley, 1979; Garcia & Rusiniak, 1979). This novelty effect seems to support the memory interpretation, because a novel CS is probably more likely to be remembered than a less novel one. Although some investigators (Garcia, McGowan, & Green, 1972) feel that mediators cannot account for the full effect, these kinds of potential "mental" mediators have not been eliminated from the methodology of these experiments. In conclusion, noncontiguous learning has not been demonstrated conclusively. The most reasonable conclusion to draw at present is that S-R contiguity is extremely important, if not actually necessary, for the establishment of associations.

Contiguity and CS "Blocking"

So much for the question of the necessity of contiguity in learning. We now turn to our second major search—that having to do with whether S-R contiguity is *sufficient* for learning to occur. If a response occurs in the presence of a stimulus, will an association be formed between the two, or must other conditions be met for learning to take place? The simplest sort of search is to look for experiments that fail to show any learning occurring even though S-R contiguity exists.

We have already visited Kamin's blocking effect in Chapter 2 (see Cheafle & Rudy, 1978; Haggbloom, 1983; Kamin, 1969b; Kohler & Ayres, 1979; Rescorla & Colwill, 1983). But the effect is relevant to the issue of the sufficiency of contiguity. As you will recall, a blocking experiment often involves two groups. One group is presented with a compound stimulus (designated AX) paired with a UCS. A second group, before receiving identical treatment, is given pretraining, during which the A component of the compound stimulus is paired with the UCS. Then, following AX–UCS training, X is tested alone. It is found that X is more likely to elicit a CR when the subject did not have prior training with the A component alone. But when you think about it for a moment, it becomes apparent that X was paired with the UCS (and therefore with the UCR) the same number of times in both groups. Stimulus-response contiguity was established equally in both groups, and yet learning was not equal. This effect suggests that there must be something more to learning than S-R contiguity. If S-R contiguity was a sufficient condition for learning to occur, then X should have become an equally effective CS in both groups.

Informational Theory

In Chapter 2 we also described briefly some informational theories of classical conditioning (see Mackintosh, 1975; Rescorla & Wagner, 1972). According to these theories, a stimulus becomes an effective CS only when it provides the subject with information about the occurrence of a forthcoming UCS. What is the relevance of this for the question of the sufficiency of S-R contiguity? These theories argue that, although S-R contiguity may be necessary, it is certainly not sufficient for learning to occur.

Consider the kind of experiment that these investigators have reported. In one condition a CS is paired with a UCS a given number of times. In another condition the same CS is paired with the same UCS the same number of times. (S-R contiguity is identical in both conditions.) But in the second condition the UCS is also presented equally often *without* the CS. That is, the UCS is as likely to occur without the CS as with it. In other words, the occurrence of the CS in the second condition tells the subject nothing about the occurrence of the UCS.

If S-R contiguity were sufficient for learning, then the CS in *both* conditions should become effective, because S-R contiguity is identical. But that is not at all what happens. The CS only becomes effective (starts eliciting a CR) in the first condition, where it predicts the occurrence of the UCS.

Simultaneous and Backward Conditioning

In Chapter 2 we outlined some of the temporal relationships between the CS and the UCS. As you will recall, delayed and trace procedures yield favorable conditioning while simultaneous and backward procedures do not. As Matzel, Held, and Miller (1988) point out, the lack of conditioning in the simultaneous and backward situations has been a persistent problem for those who argue that contiguity is sufficient for learning to occur. It would seem intuitively that the best conditioning should occur in the simultaneous condition because S-R contiguity is perfect in this situation. And yet no conditioning tends to appear in this situation.

The informational approach to the understanding of conditioning seems much more able to explain these findings than does a strict contiguity position. According to the informational theories, a CS must predict an upcoming UCS for it to become a functional CS. While such a prediction can occur in the trace and delayed conditions, it cannot occur in the simultaneous and backward conditions. In backward conditioning the onset of the UCS has come and gone before the CS even occurs. In simultaneous conditioning the CS cannot predict the onset of the UCS either because they occur at exactly the same time. In conclusion, it seems that a lack of conditioning in the simultaneous and backward situations argues against the idea that contiguity is sufficient for conditioning to occur; the informational theories seem to be better able to account for these failures.

Contiguity and Short-Term Memory

Glenberg and associates (Glenberg & Adams, 1978; Glenberg & Bradley, 1979; Glenberg, Smith, & Green, 1977) have reported data from short-term memory situations that bear directly on the question of the sufficiency of S-R contiguity. Basically, their experimental situation involves the following: Subjects are first given a four-digit number and instructed to remember it. Pairs of words are then presented, and the subjects are asked to repeat the pairs a prescribed number of times. The subjects are then asked to recall the four-digit number. They are led to believe that the word pairs are simply "fillers" and that they will not be asked to recall these words. Repeating the word pairs is merely supposed to prevent the subjects from rehearsing the critical four-digit number. In other words, the subjects believe that they are not supposed to try to learn the word pairs. But then, following the test for recall of the four-digit numbers, the subjects are given a surprise test for the word pairs. If S-R contiguity is sufficient for learning, these word pairs should be learned. But they are not. In one experiment the subjects were given one member of each pair and asked for the second member. Only 2 correct responses were obtained in 1080 tries. In other words, virtually nothing had been learned even though S-R contiguity had been established. We know that the subjects attended to the word pairs, because they vocalized them. But still no learning occurred. In short, S-R contiguity was not sufficient for learning to occur.

A review of the available literature leads us to conclude that S-R contiguity is extremely important, if not actually *necessary*, for learning to occur. But S-R contiguity does not appear to be *sufficient* for learning to occur. Other factors, such as reinforcement, intent, motivation, and information, which we will explore in upcoming chapters, appear to be essential to the learning event.

THE ROLE OF REHEARSAL IN LEARNING

Having completed our review of the role of contiguity in learning we now turn to the second major topic of this chapter—that of the role of *practice*, or rehearsal, in learning. Does rehearsal enhance learning? If so, how? What happens to the strength of the association as we increase the frequency with which the response occurs in the presence of the stimulus? Intuitively, the answer seems simple: The more we practice, the more we learn. The more that athletes practice their particular sport, the better they will be at it. The more we study, or rehearse, materials for an exam, the better we know them—up to a point, of course. Once we have completely mastered the materials, further rehearsal will lead to little additional gain.

Our intuitive sense of the world argues that the relationship between rehearsal and learning is positive, with continued practice leading to continued gains until the task is mastered. But psychological research and thinking have suggested that the relationship between learning and rehearsal may not be so simple. There is some question about the role of rehearsal in the learning process. Some psychologists argue that our intuitive sense is correct, and that learning is gradual, *like stage lights coming up slowly in a theater*. Other psychologists have argued that learning occurs in an all-or-none position, *like a kitchen light being snapped on abruptly*. According to the all-or-none position, learning occurs completely in one trial, or it does not occur at all.

At first glance the all-or-none interpretation does not seem to make sense. The data from classical conditioning, instrumental conditioning, discrimination learning, free-recall learning, and just about any other type of learning situation suggest that increases are gradual, cumulative events. There are few dramatic rises from zero performance to complete performance in one trial. How does the all-or-none position explain these kinds of data? For now, think of it like this: When you sit down to study for the examination in this class, it will appear that your mastery of the material is gradual. Your overall grasp of the content of the class will increase slowly through the agonizing hours. And yet, even though it appears that your grasp of the material is slowly becoming stronger, any given bit of learning may occur in an all-or-none fashion. You may all of a sudden hook up, or associate, the name Garcia with bait shyness. You may in an all-or-none fashion connect the label *backward conditioning* with the notion of the UCS coming before the CS. Similarly, a golfer's game might gradually improve over the years, but this improvement might be the result of lots of little bits of learning that occur in an all-or-none fashion. One day the golfer might abruptly learn to keep her head down. The next week she might abruptly learn to follow through properly, and so on. The appearance of gradual improvement might be the summed result of many little, discrete bits of learning that occur in an all-or-none fashion. This issue is an interesting one, and we will return to it in later sections of this chapter.

LEARNING CURVES

A learning curve is a visual representation of performance over a series of trials, or time intervals. In Chapter 3 we saw that the relationship between performance and practice is typically summarized by a negatively accelerated learning curve (see Figure 3.4). That is, as practice progresses, performance increases rapidly at first and then levels off. This negatively accelerated curve is a widespread phenomenon appearing in many diverse areas of investigation. But it is not the only curve that appears in our research. Even though the negatively accelerated curve is very characteristic, we do not want to fall into the trap of thinking of it as "the" learning curve that represents some irrefutable mathematical law of nature.

Learning Curves Are Not Learning Curves

Learning curves are not really learning curves at all; they are performance curves. That is, they are the result of how much the organism has learned *and* how motivated it is. If you recall, performance refers to the activation of learning through the involvement of motivation. To infer the amount of learning that has occurred we must be able to measure performance *and* estimate the organism's level of motivation.

If we observe one rat rapidly running down a straight alley to food, for example, and a second rat walking rather aimlessly along in the same apparatus, we cannot immediately conclude that the first rat has learned more than the second rat. It may just be more motivated. We can see how errors could be made in estimating the amount of learning. If we were not aware that the first rat was hungrier than the second, we might incorrectly conclude that the first rat had learned more. Some experimental designs help us to decide whether performance differences result from learned or motivational factors. These designs will be discussed in the section of Chapter 6 concerned with amount of reinforcement.

Performance Measures

Given that the amount of learning is inferred from some index of performance, what measures of performance are available? For example, how do we measure the performance of a rat running down a straight alley for food? We could do it in any number of ways. We could measure its running speed; the faster it runs, the more we assume it has learned. We could measure the latency of its response; that is, we could measure how long it remains in the starting box before it starts off down the alley. The quicker it leaves the box, or the shorter the latency, the more learning we would infer. We could use resistance to extinction by removing food from the situation. The longer the rat persists in running down the alley to an empty goal box, the more learning we would want to infer.

If we consider something like paired-associate learning, we run into a number of different performance measures. For example, the amount of PA learning is often estimated by counting the number of correct responses that the subject produces in a given number of trials. The parameter *trials to criterion* is also used as a measure of performance. The experimenter counts the number of times the subjects must go through the list before they meet some predetermined criterion (such as once, or perhaps twice, through the list without an error). The availability of all these performance measures creates problems. We will now examine a few of them.

RELIABILITY OF THE MEASURE.   Suppose that psychologists wish to study the effects of smoking on driving an automobile. They have their subjects puff away and then observe their ability to drive through a carefully constructed driving course. The psychologists find, relative to some appropriate control, that the subjects show poor driving ability. Though tempted to conclude that smoking hurts driving ability, the experimenters must first ask themselves several questions. One of these has to do with the reliability of their performance measure. The measure must yield *similar results on different occasions*. If the experimenters ran the same subject through the same test on several different occasions, they should obtain similar results. If they do, then they are using a reliable measure. If they do not, then their measure is unreliable, and their conclusions are invalid.

SENSITIVITY OF THE MEASURE.   The top half of Figure 5.1 contains some hypothetical data produced by two rats in a straight runway situation. In each case the rats were fed when they reached the goal box at the end of the runway. Rat 1 was given 30 trials and then taken out of the testing situation. At that time it was running at a constant speed. Its performance had leveled off. After 30 trials Rat 2 was running at the same constant speed as was Rat 1. But instead of being removed from the situation Rat 2 was given an additional 10 trials. During these additional trials (Trials 31–40) Rat 2 showed no improvement whatsoever. Thus, after 40 trials Rat 2 was performing at the same level Rat 1 had reached after 30 trials. The question is this: How much have the two rats learned? If we use running speed as an index of how much was learned, then we conclude that the two rats had learned the same amount and that Rat 2 had learned nothing during Trials 31–40.

There is a problem with this conclusion. A rat can run just so fast. Once it has reached its top speed, it can go no faster, *but it might still be learning*. Rat 2 may be learning during Trials 31–40, but the increase in learning would not show up in running speed because a ceiling had been reached. If we assume that some learning

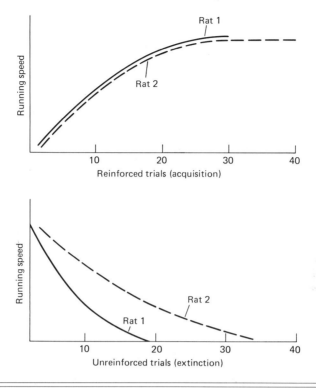

Figure 5.1 Hypothetical acquisition and extinction curves for two rats given different numbers of acquisition trials.

might occur during Trials 31–40, it would be a mistake to use running speed as our performance measure, because it would not be sensitive at all levels, especially the higher levels.

One way of resolving this issue would be to utilize some other, more sensitive, performance measure, such as resistance to extinction. If we removed food from the situation and allowed Rat 1 and Rat 2 to extinguish, we might find that Rat 2 would run for no food longer and faster than Rat 1 (see the bottom half of Figure 5.1). We would then conclude that Rat 2 actually had learned more than Rat 1, even though the difference did not appear when we used running speed as our measure.

The point is that, whenever we choose a performance measure, we must assure ourselves that it will accurately reflect learning at all levels, or at least at those levels likely to be involved in our study. If we do not, then we may be led to incorrect conclusions.

Averaging Data

GROUP VERSUS INDIVIDUAL DATA.   In a typical learning curve trials are plotted on the abscissa, and the units in which the behavior is measured are plotted on the ordinate. Given such a system it would be helpful if we could plot a *single*

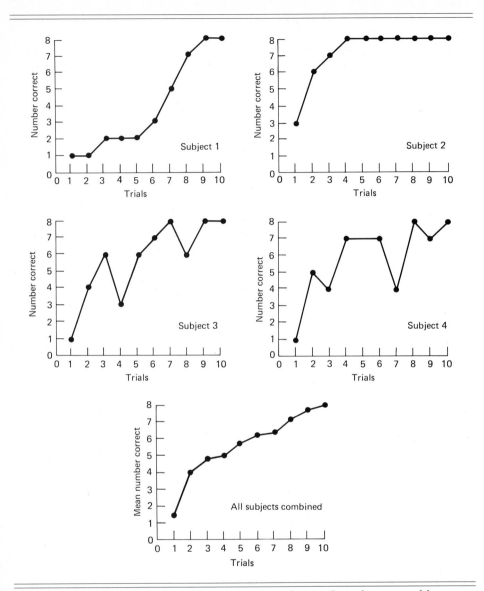

Figure 5.2 Some hypothetical paired-associate data, showing how the scores of four subjects are averaged.

individual's performance across trials and then make some sense of it, but most of the time we cannot. Individuals are variable in their behavior and follow a unique course through the learning process, and so we are often forced to average the scores from several individuals to obtain a clear picture of the stable and consistent trends underlying the variable individual behaviors.

For example, the top four panels in Figure 5.2 contain hypothetical data from four different subjects as they learned a list of words. As you can see, their progress through the trials was extremely variable. Subject 1 began slowly and finished with

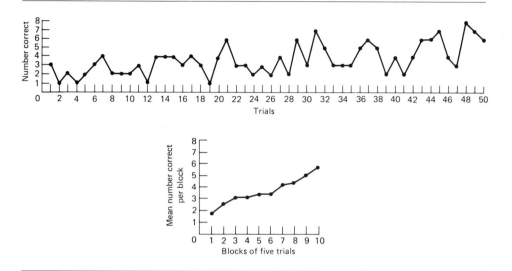

Figure 5.3 Blocking of data. The data from the upper graph are blocked and replotted in the graph below. The data points in the lower graph are average numbers correct across five adjacent trials in the upper graph. Notice how much easier it is to grasp the gradual growth of the learning function in the blocked graph below, even though some detail is lost. (These are hypothetical data.)

a bang. Subject 2 began rapidly but leveled off. Subjects 3 and 4 provided equally unique records. If we were left with these four unique records, we would not know what to say about how the learning of the list progressed. So we combine the four records in an attempt to obtain a clearer picture. The averages of the scores of the four individuals on each trial are depicted at the bottom of Figure 5.2. Here we see something that begins to approximate the familiar negatively accelerated learning curve. This trend, or function, was obscured by the variability of the individual records. The assumption we must make is that, if we could control all the unknown factors that yield high individual variability, each individual curve would approximate the average curve. We are, in a sense, assuming that the averaged data reveal the "real" learning curve. Without averaging we might miss these stable trends, or relationships. We would not see the forest for the trees.

TYPES OF AVERAGING.   Among the number of methods to average data, each has its advantages and disadvantages. Experimenters choose the one that best suits their needs and purposes. We have just discussed one of the most popular methods, wherein curves are smoothed by combining the scores from a number of individuals on each trial. In another method, scores obtained from a single individual over a series of runs through the task are combined. In still another technique, scores from adjacent trials are combined. For example, one might plot average performance in *successive blocks* of five trials, rather than performance on each trial. This technique loses detail, but it does make it easier to see general trends by eliminating minor peculiarities in the data (see Figure 5.3).

Cumulative response curves are also popular. They are curves in which the units of behavior, or scores, are allowed to *accumulate* over trials, or periods of observation. For example, Figure 5.4 contains data obtained from a pigeon pecking a key for food over a series of four-minute intervals. Figure 5.4a contains a cumulative record of the responses. The same data are presented in Figure 5.4b, but in this case the *average numbers of responses per minute* are plotted against successive time intervals.

At any given point on the cumulative curve we can read the *total* number of responses made from the beginning of the experiment. If the bird stops pecking, the cumulative record levels off and remains horizontal until the bird begins pecking again. It can never go down. When the bird begins to respond again, the curve goes up as we add on new responses. The advantage of the cumulative curve is that we can quickly and easily observe changes in the bird's rate of responding. The steeper the slope of the curve, the faster the bird is responding. The flatter the slope, the more slowly it is responding.

The noncumulative method employed in Figure 5.4b also has its advantages. For example, we can quickly determine how many responses the bird produced during any given time interval. It is not so easy to obtain this information from the cumulative curve. Many experimenters try to use both methods of plotting their data, for each yields quick and convenient information about the subject's performance.

These methods and others are all available to the psychologist. Psychologists as a whole, however, have never been able to decide which method is best. Some psychologists have, in fact, gone so far as to say that group curves are next to worthless in attempting to understand individual behavior (Sidman, 1952). Perhaps the best we can do at present is to be extremely careful in interpreting averaged data and to be aware of the differences among the alternative methods. We should be careful about putting too much weight on one method and should attempt to look at our data from several different angles. With this cautionary note in mind we now turn to a consideration of the two opposing theories of the role of rehearsal in learning.

GRADUAL VERSUS ALL–OR–NONE LEARNING
Hull's Approach

Clark L. Hull's system provides a good example of the *incremental* approach to the role of rehearsal in learning. Hull believed that *learning increases gradually, or incrementally, as a result of reinforced practice* (1943, 1951, 1952). Hull developed an equation for behavior, which can be expressed as

$$\text{Response probability} = (D \times H \times K \times V) - (I)$$

The equation implies that the probability of a response's occurring is a function of the interaction of at least five major variables. The elaboration of the system is complicated, but the underlying ideas are not. If you give it a moment's thought, you will probably be able to identify most, if not all, of Hull's major variables. Imagine a rat faced with a lever in a Skinner box. Imagine a child in the kitchen faced with a refrigerator. The question is this: What factors will determine whether the rat presses the lever and whether the child opens the refrigerator door? In both

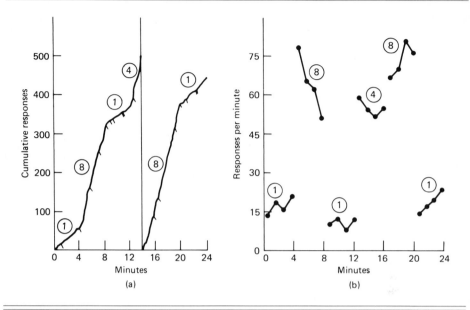

Figure 5.4 Comparison between two procedures for presenting results. Panel (a) contains a segment of a record obtained from a cumulative recorder. The paper is fed through the recorder at a constant speed; each response moves the pen a fixed distance across the paper. Thus, the rate of response is shown by the *slope* of the curve. The pen automatically resets to the baseline at some preselected point (in this case, after 500 responses). The same responses were also indicated on electromechanical counters, and those counts are plotted in the panel on the right. The results show the effects of training a pigeon with different amounts of food per reinforcement. The bird was reinforced occasionally (on the average, once per minute) for pecking an illuminated key. The color of the key indicated which reinforcement condition was in effect. Reinforcements consisted of delivery of either one, four, or eight hemp seeds. The reinforcement condition changed every four minutes. Delivery of reinforcements is shown by a slight oblique mark on the record. Among the advantages of the cumulative record are instant information concerning the progress of the experiment and an indication of the sequential changes in the behavior. The plot of responses trial-by-trial (or minute-by-minute, in this case) allows the dependent variable to be read with greater ease. In the first minute of this experiment, for example, it is clear from panel (b) that the average response rate was approximately 14 pecks per minute, but it would be difficult to determine this from the cumulative record. In practice, both cumulative recorders and digital counters are usually used, since each form of recording has its own advantages. (Adapted from *Experimental Psychology*, Third Edition, edited by J. W. King and Lorrin A. Riggs. Copyright 1938, 1954, © 1971 by Holt, Rinehart and Winston, Inc. Reprinted by permission of Holt, Rinehart and Winston.)

these situations the reward for making the response in question (pressing the lever or opening the door) is food. So the hungrier the organism, the more motivated each will be to perform the required behavior. The first of Hull's variables, *D*, or *drive*, is designed to encompass the influence of how motivated the subject is to perform. Drive level is measured in terms of time of deprivation or amount of noxious stimulation. The more deprived or the more noxiously stimulated the animal, the greater is its drive state and, hence, the greater is the tendency to act so as to reduce that drive state. Drive instigates action, and action seeks to reduce drive. Hull went through several steps in his thinking about drive, but for our purposes we can think of it as a motivational construct tied to, or measured in terms of, time of deprivation or amount of noxious stimulation.

Another factor that might contribute to the rat's or the child's tendency to respond is how many times each has responded in the past and been reinforced for doing so. Experience in a given situation clearly affects the probability of a response's occurring. That is what H, or *habit*, in Hull's system is all about. Habit reflects how much the organism has already *learned*. If the child has opened the refrigerator door in the past and been reinforced for doing so, then he will be more likely to open it in the future. Hull measured H in terms of the number of reinforced responses. The more times the rat presses the bar and is reinforced, the greater is the habit strength.

Two points should be made here. First, in Hull's system reinforcement is produced by a rapid diminution of D. A response is reinforced if it is quickly followed by a reduction in drive. For Hull, learning, or an increase in H, is the *result* of a response's being followed by drive reduction. The rat learns to press the bar because it is reinforced for doing so. If it is not fed and D is not reduced, learning will not occur. Hull's drive-reduction interpretation of reinforcement is not the only way to think of reinforcement, as we shall see later, but it has been an influential conception. The second point is that D activates H; D multiplied by H yields a response probability. This conception corresponds to our earlier distinction between learning and performance. Performance (response probability) refers to the activation of learning *(H)* through the involvement of motivation *(D)*.

To return to the topic of the discussion, we should ask what else might determine behavior, and the contents of the refrigerator seem likely to have some bearing. A chocolate cake might induce the child to respond, whereas something less palatable might be less likely to stimulate a response. Hull acknowledged the importance of these factors with his K construct. Hull's K, or *incentive motivation*, is measured in terms of the *quantity* of the goal (the more the better) and in terms of the *quality* of the goal (cake might be better than turnips). The greater K is, the greater is the probability of the response's occurring. K is a "pull" factor; the child is pulled toward the cake. Drive, or D, on the other hand, is a "push" factor; the child is driven toward the refrigerator by hunger.

Thus, *total* motivation includes both D and K; D pushes while K pulls. The child is driven toward the refrigerator by hunger and simultaneously attracted by the knowledge that the cake is inside. H is Hull's learning factor, and both D and K are motivational terms.

The clarity of the stimulus situation might also help determine the behavior of our organisms. If the rat can barely see the lever, it will be less likely to respond to it. If the lever is bright, distinct, and intense, then the rat will be more likely to respond to it. Apparently, Hull was trying to account for this aspect when he postulated V, or *stimulus intensity dynamism*. Hull's V refers to the probability that a response will increase as the intensity of the stimulus increases. In other words, we are more likely to respond to intense stimuli than to less intense ones.

You will note that all four of Hull's variables that we have discussed thus far contribute positively to the probability of a response's occurring and that their relationship is multiplicative. Thus, if *any one* of them is zero, then response probability is zero. The fifth, and last, variable subtracts from response probability. Hull called this last factor *I*, or *inhibition*. In a very rough sense *I* is a fatigue factor. It is measured in terms of the amount of work involved in making a response and in terms of the number of times the response has been made. The harder it is for the child to open the refrigerator door and the more times in a row he has done it, the less likely he is to do it again.

Thus, there is nothing esoteric about Hull's model. It is based on a series of intuitively obvious assumptions about what might contribute to behavior. It is a survival model in which *contiguity, practice*, and *reinforcement* are all important. Learning occurs when a response is quickly followed by a drop in drive level. Learning occurs in a gradual, incremental fashion and not in an all-or-none manner. Another interesting aspect of Hull's conception of *H* is that, once reinforced practice ceases, *H* does not dissipate, or fade away. It remains constant for the life of the organism. Such a conception suggests that learning is permanent. Once we learn something, it is "in storage" forever, even though we may not always be able to retrieve it. Does this conception seem accurate? (See Box 5.1.)

Guthrie's and Estes' Approaches

We now turn to a consideration of the all-or-none approach. Although there have been many variations of the basic all-or-none position, we shall limit our discussion to two of the more influential systems. First, Guthrie's original interpretation of learning laid the groundwork for later, more formal, expressions of the all-or-none position. Second, Estes' *stimulus-sampling model* represents one of the more mathematical statements of Guthrie's earlier ideas.

The very simplicity of Guthrie's theory is intriguing. It can be summed up in one sentence: *A combination of stimuli that has accompanied a movement will on its recurrence tend to be followed by that movement* (Guthrie, 1935, 1952). If a response occurs in the presence of a stimulus, learning will be complete and automatic. No further practice is necessary, and no reinforcement is necessary.

On the surface Guthrie's statement seems contrary to the real world. It implies that learning occurs completely in one pairing of the stimulus and the response. Yet we know that in most situations (for example, a rat pressing a bar for food), the strength of a response seems to grow gradually as practice continues. We have already seen that S-R contiguity, though perhaps necessary, does not appear to be sufficient for learning to occur. To resolve this apparent contradiction Guthrie distinguishes between *acts* and *movements*. Acts are the complex responses that we observe and study. Riding a bicycle, discovering a concept, saying a word, and typing a letter are acts. Each of these total acts is made up of *many different movements*. For example, a movement in bicycle riding might be pushing down with the left foot or grasping with the right hand. Each individual movement is learned in one trial, although mastery of the total set of movements may require many trials. To master the total complex act, many different responses must be connected to many different stimulus configurations. *The gradual improvement with practice that we observe is the result of a growing number of learned movements, each of which is acquired in all-or-none fashion.*

Box 5.1 Are Memories "Forever"?

Much information is stored within us that we cannot retrieve at a particular moment. We have all had the experience, while taking an exam, of realizing that we know the answer to a question but being unable to come up with it. Many of us have had the embarrassing experience at a social gathering of stumbling over a familiar person's name. But do these common experiences mean that *all* information is stored *permanently*, even if it is occasionally beyond our ability to retrieve it? At least two areas of research bear on this issue.

ELECTRICAL BRAIN STIMULATION.   Penfield (1969) reports work done with patients undergoing brain surgery. While under local anesthesia the patients were conscious and able to report their experiences. As part of the surgical procedures the patients' exposed brains were lightly stimulated with an electrical current. As the electrode was touched to the surface of the cortex, some patients reported vivid memories of past events. As long as the electrode was held in place, the memory persisted. As soon as the electrode was removed, the memory ceased. Some of the memories appear to have been accurate and to have represented events from the distant past. Many of the memories were of events that the patients had completely "forgotten" or at least had not thought of for long periods. The implication here is that memories are somehow stored in the brain permanently even though we cannot normally retrieve them. It took the electrical current to activate these long-dormant memories.

Although Penfield's work certainly suggests that many memories are stored and inaccessible, it does not prove that *all* memories are stored permanently. Much information may still be encoded but eventually lost. And some researchers question whether Penfield's patients retrieved accurate memories of true events or merely experienced new sensations that resembled old events (see Squire, 1987). In addition, less than 10% of Penfield's patients reported these memorylike experiences.

HYPNOTIC AGE REGRESSION.   Under hypnosis some patients can be encouraged to "go back" in their life, or to "become" younger and younger (McConnell, 1974). Obliging subjects begin to act so as to suggest that they are becoming younger; they use baby talk and physically act like children. In addition, they appear to have memories of their childhood that are attainable only under the hypnotic trance. You can see that these results might be used to bolster the argument that memories are permanent.

But the age-regression phenomenon has received a great deal of criticism. First, many investigators (Barber, 1970; Orne, 1970) argue that hypnosis itself is overrated. They argue that many subjects are "role playing," or acting the way they think the hypnotist wants them to act. Nonhypnotized subjects can do many, if not all, of the highly publicized hypnotic tricks, such as suspending oneself between two chairs by the head and the heels. These investigators feel that subjects want to oblige the hypnotist and so go along with her or his suggestions. Second, many of the memories recalled by hypnotized subjects are no more accurate than the memories of nonhypnotized subjects (O'Connell, Shore, & Orne, 1970). In other words, enough controversy surrounds the age-regression phenomenon to suggest that we take it with a grain of salt.

Neither age regression nor Penfield's work conclusively proves that memories are lifelong. Although Hull postulated that they were, his position has yet to be verified experimentally.

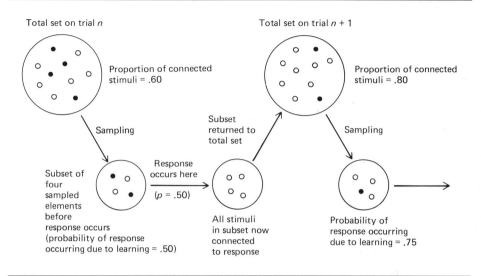

Figure 5.5 The stimulus-sampling model: (○) stimulus connected to response (●) stimulus not connected to response.

Estes (1959) attempted to translate Guthrie's basic notions into a more formal, mathematical expression. We present his stimulus-sampling model here in simplified form. We can restate Guthrie's original proposition in the following form:

1. If R_1 occurs in the presence of S_1, then R_1 will be connected to S_1 completely and automatically.
2. If a different response (R_2) occurs in the presence of S_1, then R_2 will be completely and automatically connected to S_1, and R_1 will be completely disconnected from S_1. In other words, a stimulus can be connected to only one response at a time, and it will be connected to the most recently occurring response.
3. The probability of a response's occurring equals the proportion of presented stimuli to which it is connected.

Let us try to understand these statements. The critical point is that the probability of a response's occurring equals the proportion of the presented, or sampled, stimuli to which it is connected. This statement implies that any given situation in which a response can occur probably consists of many stimuli, each of which may or may not be connected to the response. Imagine the total set of stimuli that can impinge on an animal in a learning situation (say, in a bar-press paradigm). This imaginary set is not just the stimuli that are actually impinging on it at any given moment, but all the various stimuli that might possibly impinge on it at different times. These stimuli include all the sights, sounds, smells, odors, tastes, and so on that can act on the animal. No one really knows how many there are or, for that matter, exactly what they are. This total set of stimuli that must exist but cannot be measured is represented at the upper left of Figure 5.5. Imagine further that some of these many stimuli are already connected to the bar press. Next imagine a subset of stimuli that actually act on the animal at a given moment. This subset represents a sample drawn from the larger total set. That is, at any given moment the animal is facing in a particular direction, it is hearing certain sounds, smelling certain odors, and so on. The animal cannot experience the total set at any given moment, but it does experience a subset of the total set.

Figure 5.5 contains a very stylized example of the way in which learning progresses in the stimulus-sampling model. Focus on the first subset of four stimuli drawn from the total set. Two of these stimuli have already been connected to the response, and two have not. At this point the probability of a response's occurring *due to learning* is .50. (The italics are important here, for the response may actually occur with a much higher probability. For instance, in classical conditioning the occurrence of the response is ensured on every trial by the presence of the UCS. Thus, the .50 probability refers to the probability of the response's occurring *due to learning* and does not encompass the fact that the UCS evokes the response on each trial.) If the response does occur, then the two previously unconnected stimuli become completely connected. The four stimuli, now all connected to the response, are returned to the total set. The proportion of conditioned elements in the total set has now increased to .80. On the next trial a second subset is sampled. Because all stimuli are equally likely to be sampled, the proportion of connected stimuli in this second subset is likely to be higher than in the preceding subset. Thus, the probability of the response's occurring *due to learning* is higher the second time around (.75 in Figure 5.5), and so on. On each successive trial a subset of stimuli is sampled from the total set. If the response occurs, then all the unconnected elements of the subset are connected to the response, and the entire subset is returned to the total set. The proportion of connected stimuli grows gradually on successive trials. The model, although it considers learning to be an all-or-none event, predicts the incremental result that we obtain in the real world. In fact, it predicts a negatively accelerated performance curve, because the proportion of connections that can be established on successive trials must eventually decrease as the supply of unconnected stimuli is gradually exhausted.

What, Actually, Is One Trial?

Researchers have made a number of attempts to pit the all-or-none and the gradual-growth positions against each other experimentally (Estes, 1960; Rock, 1957; Voeks, 1954). Unfortunately, these clever and interesting attempts failed to provide conclusive support for either position. The all-or-none position has probably fared worse than the gradual-growth hypothesis (Battig, 1968; Jones, 1962; Postman, 1962a; Underwood & Keppel, 1962), but neither hypothesis has scored a clear victory.

One of the problems inherent in many of these comparative experiments has to do with the nature of "the trial." What is one trial? Is it one presentation of the stimulus and the response by the experimenter? Is it one subvocal rehearsal by the subject? Is it one, but only one, firing of some complex, unknown sequence of neural activities? These questions are seldom addressed in all-or-none research. For example, implicit in some comparison experiments is the assumption that one presentation of the materials represents, or corresponds to, a single occurrence of the response in the presence of the stimulus. And yet, if we look a little closer, it

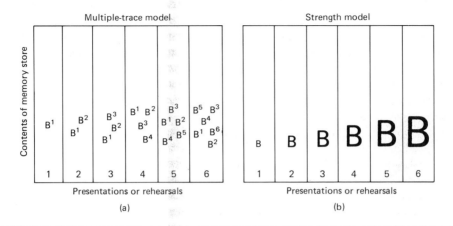

Figure 5.6 Symbolic representations of the multiple-trace (a) and strength (b) models of learning and memory. The multiple-trace model argues that each presentation of an item is encoded in memory as a discrete, unique event. The strength hypothesis proposed that, each time an item is presented, the strength, or potency, of a single trace is increased.

seems that these experiments must involve multiple repetitions, or rehearsals. If we present a stimulus and a response to a subject for two seconds, more than likely she rehearses the pair as many times and in as many ways as she can before the next pair appears. Humans are certainly capable of several such mental rehearsals in two seconds. So far, no one has been able to control the number of rehearsals perfectly.

Multiple-Trace versus Strength Models

A number of investigators have wondered whether the relationship between practice and learning is better thought of in terms of a *multiple-trace* conception or a simple *strength* interpretation (see Ghatala, Levin, Bell, Truman, & Lodico, 1978; Hintzman & Stern, 1978; Whitlow & Skaar, 1979). Basically, both approaches are concerned with the relationships between practice and learning. They differ in terms of the postulated effects of rehearsal. The multiple-trace position argues that each presentation of a stimulus is stored as a separate, distinct representation of that stimulus. Strength theory, on the other hand, maintains that each presentation of an item adds to the strength of one single representation of that item.

Consider Figure 5.6. Assume for the moment that you are not familiar with the letter *B* and are trying to learn it. It is presented to you for rehearsal in a series of trials by the experimenter. According to the multiple-trace theory, each time you perceive *B*, it is somehow stored as a discrete representation. As trials progress, you add to your growing store of little, internal *B*s. According to the simple strength theory, something quite different happens each time you perceive and rehearse *B*. Here the argument is that you have only one single internal representation of *B* but that this single *B* grows in strength as trials progress.

Clearly, neither of these theories argues that we actually have physical *B*s stored somewhere within us. The business with all the little *B*s or the one growing *B* is merely a convenient way to think about how our memory system operates. By adopting one or the other of these positions we are merely assuming that the memory system operates *as if* we had little *B*s or one big *B* stored within us.

Exactly how the distinction between multiple-trace and strength theories relates to the issue of one-trial versus incremental learning, just discussed, is not entirely clear. In one sense it can be argued that the strength position resembles the incremental position more than it does the one-trial position, whereas the multiple-trace theory resembles the one-trial position more than it does the incremental position.

Specifically, the strength model argues that a single internal representation of the external object *grows in strength* with repeated exposures to that stimulus. The multiple-trace model, in contrast, contends that discrete, distinct representations are added on each practice trial and that the overall strength of storage is, in some sense, reflected by the sum total of all these discrete representational elements. The more times an item is presented, the more traces of that item there will be in memory, and the more traces are stored, the more likely the item is to be found when we search our memory for it.

The way to choose between these two interpretations is to find predictions in which they differ. Although the issue is far from resolved, multiple-trace theories have been fairly accurate (see Whitlow & Estes, 1979). Whatever the final outcome of the controversy concerning the multiple-trace versus strength models, you should realize that this distinction represents the concern psychologists have for the relationship between learning and practice.

MASSED VERSUS DISTRIBUTED PRACTICE

The study of massed practice (MP) versus distributed practice (DP) has a long history, not only in connection with humans but in connection with animals as well (see Fanselow & Tighe, 1988). In its simplest form, the MP–DP controversy is this: If our practice trials are spaced, or separated in time, is learning more or less efficient than if the trials are bunched together? If we have six hours to study for three exams, should we give each topic two consecutive hours, or should we give each topic eight fifteen-minute segments separated by intervals during which we study one of the alternative topics? The most common hypothesis has been that distributed practice will be superior to massed practice. Early experimental data bearing on this issue were extremely complicated and often contradictory (see Archer, 1954; Jung & Bailey, 1966; Kimble, 1949; Underwood, 1961). But late investigations began to yield consistent MP–DP effects. Melton (1970) points out that these new and significant effects began to appear as new verbal tasks were developed. For example, significant MP–DP effects have appeared in free-recall learning situations (Madigan, 1969; Underwood, 1970; Waugh, 1970). You will recall that items in this type of experiment are presented randomly, and the subject is asked to recall them in any order. Although there have been exceptions (Waugh, 1967), the general finding is that recall of items presented twice is better if the two presentations are separated by one or more intervening items. Distributed practice seems to be superior to massed practice. In general, spaced presentation seems to lead to superior retention in free-recall situations (Hintzman, Block, & Summers, 1973; Shaughnessy, 1976).

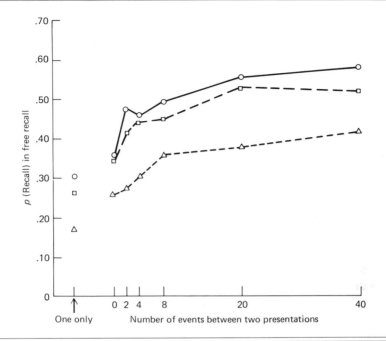

Figure 5.7 Probability or recall of words that occur once or twice, with varying numbers of other words occurring between the two presentations of a given word. Presentation rates: (○) 4.3 seconds; (□) 2.3 seconds; (△) 1.3 seconds. (Adapted from Melton, A. W. The situation with respect to the spacing of repetitions and memory. *Journal of Verbal Learning and Verbal Behavior*, 1970, 9, 596–606. Fig. 1, p. 602.)

Melton (1970) has labeled this phenomenon the *lag effect*. As can be seen in Figure 5.7, the effect refers to the fact that in free recall the probability of recalling a repeated item is positively related to the number of intervening items. The farther apart the two presentations of the repeated item, the better is the recall of that item. In other words, distributed practice is better than massed practice.

Contextual Interpretation

Although there have been other interpretations of the MP–DP lag effect (for example, Elms, Dye, & Herdian, 1983; Glenberg, 1977, 1979; Greeno, 1970), one of the more popular has to do with subjects' ability to code an item in a context of other items (D'Agostino & DeRemer, 1973; Elmes, Greener, & Wilkinson, 1972; Gartman & Johnson, 1972). If the two presentations of the critical item are separated by other items, then each presentation of the critical item occurs in a unique verbal context and is surrounded by a variety of different items. The subjects can associate the critical item with these different contexts, thereby enriching their coding of the critical item. Massed presentations, in contrast, represent a reduction in the richness and variety of the context in which the critical item is to be learned. Both presentations occur in roughly the same context.

Encoding-Variability Interpretation

Encoding variability (see Martin, 1971) refers to the idea that any given stimulus is composed of many different attributes, or components. Thus, the stimulus *dog* is made up of three different letters, a sound, three letter positions, and so on. At any given time a response may be connected to part of the overall stimulus but not necessarily to the entire stimulus. If you wanted to associate *doll* with *dog*, you might pay attention to the letter *d* in *dog* and not to the *o* or the *g*. *Doll* could also be associated with *dog* in any number of other ways, however. That is, the encoding can be variable. The next point to consider is that the more diverse and rich the encoding, the stronger the association will be. If *doll* can be connected with *dog* in a number of different ways (for example, using one letter at a time and using the whole word *dog*), then the association between *dog* and *doll* will be strong. The richer and more elaborate the coding—that is, the more different ways *doll* is associated with *dog*—the better is the association.

What has all this to do with massed and distributed practice? The argument is that distributed practice leads to richer and more diverse, more variable, coding. When a given item (say, two paired nouns) is presented twice close together in time, the subject is likely to use the same code each time (for example, "*doll* goes with *d*"). But if the item is distributed in time, the subject is more likely to use two different codes on the two presentations ("*doll* goes with *d*" on the first presentation and "*doll* goes with the word ending in *g*" the second time the pair is presented).

In other words, encoding is likely to be more variable under distributed conditions than under massed conditions and thus is likely to be stronger. The encoding-variability interpretation of the superiority of distributed practice is similar to the contextual interpretation just discussed. The difference between the two is that the contextual interpretation focuses on the variability of the contextual stimuli (what surrounds the item), whereas the encoding-variability hypothesis emphasizes variability *within* the item itself. Both factors may well contribute to overall MP–DP effects.

LEVELS OF PROCESSING

Thus far we have discussed the controversy over one-trial versus incremental learning and several issues relating to patterns of practice. In all these areas we have been concerned with the *quantity* of rehearsal and the patterning of that rehearsal. But psychologists are also interested in the *quality*, or type, of rehearsal. They are interested not only in how much we rehearse but also in what kind of practice we engage in. As we shall see, both the durability of learning and its ultimate usefulness depend heavily on the *kind* of rehearsing we do.

The emphasis on the quality rather than the quantity of rehearsal began with, among other things, the introduction of the concept of *levels of processing*, developed by Craik and Lockhart (1972). Essentially, the phrase refers to the idea that the durability of learning depends on *how* we rehearse. More specifically, the "deeper" our rehearsal, the better and more durable is the learning. Craik and Lockhart suggest that we can rehearse materials (for example, a list of words) merely by attending to the physical nature of the stimulus (for example, what it looks like). This processing is considered to be relatively "shallow" and results in relatively weak learning. Or we can rehearse materials by attending to their sound (a little deeper form of processing). Finally, we can process or rehearse words on a

Table 5.1   Levels of Processing Tasks

LEVEL OF PROCESSING		
SHALLOW (STRUCTURAL)	INTERMEDIATE (ACOUSTIC)	DEEP (SEMANTIC)
Does this word begin with a capital?	Does this word have an "r" sound in it?	Can you hold this in your hand?
Do these two words begin with the same letter?	Does this word rhyme with this other word?	How familiar is this?
How many syllables does this word have?	Where does the accent fall in this word?	Is this a word?
Is this word typed in lower case letters?	Does this word end in an "est" sound?	How pleasant is this?

Table from Houston, J. P., Bee, H., and Rimm, D. C. *Invitation to psychology*. New York: Academic Press, 1983. Fig. 6, p. 236. Copyright ©1983 by Harcourt Brace Jovanovich, Inc. Reprinted by permission.

semantic level (that is, having to do with the meaning of the word). Semantic processing represents "deep" processing and results in durable traces, or durable learning. The deeper the level of processing, the more durable is the trace.

Support for the Concept

An experiment by Craik and Tulving (1975) will serve as a good example of the type of experimental design most often used in the study of levels of processing. Subjects were shown a long series of words for very brief periods. These words were flashed on a screen, one at a time, for less than one second each. In some instances subjects had to judge whether the word flashed on the screen was typed in capitals. In this form of shallow processing, the subject's attention is drawn to the physical, structural properties of the stimulus. In a second kind of condition the subjects had to judge whether the flashed stimulus word rhymed with another designated word. This kind of phonemic, acoustical processing represents an intermediate level of processing. Finally, in the condition involving the deepest level of processing the subjects had to decide whether the flashed word fit into an empty space in a sentence. This semantic level of processing involves the meaning of the word. Then, in a surprise test the subjects were asked to recall all the words. As expected, in agreement with the levels-of-processing hypothesis that deeper processing will lead to more durable learning, items in the semantic condition were recalled more accurately than items in the phonemic condition, which, in turn, were recalled more accurately than the items in the structural condition. Recall increased as depth of processing increased.

This experimental design is widely used. It really involves *incidental* learning, because the subjects are never actually instructed to learn the words, only to orient toward them and to make some judgment about them. The recall test is always a surprise. The fact that level of processing relates to durability of trace in many populations of humans has been well documented (Bellezza, Cheesman, & Reddy, 1977; Cermak & Reale, 1978; Craik & Tulving, 1975; McDowall, 1979; Moeser, 1983).

Some of the types of tasks that have been used to produce different levels of processing are contained in Table 5.1. Notice in the last column of the table that

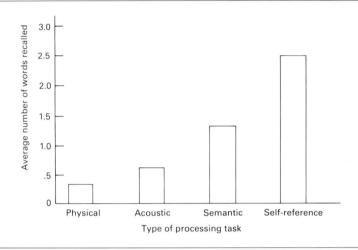

Figure 5.8 Number of words recalled as a function of level of processing. (From *Cognition* by Margaret Matlin. Copyright © 1983 by CBS College Publishing. Reprinted by permission of Holt, Rinehart and Winston.)

rating the pleasantness of a word is categorized as an instance of deep processing. Packman and Battig (1978) and others have found that rehearsing or processing words by rating them in terms of pleasantness actually does seem to be a good way to ensure recall of those words. They gave subjects lists of words and asked them to rate the words on various dimensions. Some words were rated in terms of how pleasant they were, whereas others were rated in terms of such factors as familiarity, meaningfulness, imagery, concreteness, and number of attributes. Uniformly, the words rated in terms of pleasantness appeared to be recalled best at a later time, whereas the remaining modes of processing did not appear to differ in terms of how well words were recalled.

Level of processing has been related to many other areas of investigation. For example, Smith, Theodor, and Franklin (1983) showed that the *priming effect* can be influenced by depth of processing. You will recall from Chapter 1 that the priming effect refers to the fact that, if one word is shown for a split second and then the subject is asked to make some decision about a second word, the decisions about that second word will be faster and more accurate if the first word (the prime) is related to the second word. Smith, Theodor, and Franklin took the investigation one step further and varied the depth of processing of the prime. They found that, the deeper the prime was processed, the faster and more accurately decisions were made about the second word. In order of increasing depth, the levels of processing they used were these:

1. Respond if a star is next to the prime.
2. Respond if a certain letter is in the prime.
3. Respond if the prime has more than one syllable.
4. Read the prime.
5. Respond if the prime is a living thing.

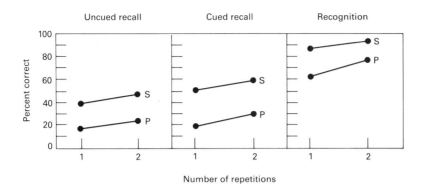

Figure 5.9 Percentage correct on three memory tests as joint function of number of repetitions (one versus two) and depth of processing (semantic versus phonemic). (Adapted from Nelson, T. O. Repetition and depth of processing. *Journal of Verbal Learning and Verbal Behavior*, 1977, *16*, 151–171.)

In another interesting study Rogers, Kuiper, and Kirker (1977) propose a level of processing that may even be deeper than semantic processing. They call this deepest of all processing tasks *self-reference*. In this kind of task the subject is asked things such as "Does this word describe you?" and "Have you ever done this?" As you can see in Figure 5.8, when it was compared with the usual processing procedures, self-reference was the most effective. Apparently, if we relate something to our own wonderful selves, we really remember it well.

Criticism of the Concept

The levels-of-processing approach has been heavily criticized on a number of grounds. First, it has been characterized as being too vague and ill-defined to be accepted as a substantial, testable theory. Second, the definition of depth of processing is somewhat circular (Baddeley, 1978). It is said that deeply processed words are the ones that are remembered and that remembered words must have been deeply processed. The problem is that there is no *independent* measure of depth of processing currently available (Nelson, 1977). Third, there are important exceptions to the rule that deeper processing leads to more durable traces. For example, the levels-of-processing approach argues that mere rote repetition of material at a given level will not help us to remember it; we must process at a deeper level if we wish to improve the durability of the trace. But Nelson (1977) reports data suggesting that rote rehearsal does, after all, help us remember things and that it is not absolutely essential to increase the depth of processing. He had subjects process at a phonemic level ("Does the word contain an 'r' sound?") or a semantic level ("Does the item represent a living thing?"). In addition, subjects were given either one or two repetitions of the entire list of 30 words. Finally, they were tested for retention with uncued (unprompted) recall, cued (prompted) recall, or recognition. As you can see in Figure 5.9, regardless of the type of recall test or level of processing, repetition *did* help retention. These results contradict the levels-of-processing approach that argues that mere repetition will not increase retention provided the depth of processing remains constant. Similarly, Kolers (1976) had subjects read some material upside down. One year later they were still able to recall some of this material. The argument—which you may disagree with—is that the processing that goes on when you read something upside down is relatively shallow. (You are just trying to figure out what those inverted words and letters are, much less what they relate to.) And yet this information, processed on such a shallow level, was recalled a year later. In other words, these data suggest to some that deep processing is not necessary for the formation of durable traces.

On the basis of this sort of evidence, Baddeley (1978) concludes that deeper processing can lead to more lasting learning but that it is not always essential. Still, even though it may not always be necessary, learning often appears to become more durable as the level of processing becomes richer and deeper.

Two Hypotheses: Elaboration and Distinctiveness

Walker and Jones (1983) and others have tried to explain exactly *why* it is that deeper processing leads to better retention. Two hypotheses have been proposed. The first of these, the *elaboration hypothesis*, maintains that semantic processing leads to richer, more varied encoding. When you process the word *cat* semantically (in terms of its meaning), you are more likely to store more information and more elaborate information than you are if you try to process it structurally (in terms of what the word looks like). The idea is that complex, varied, substantial information stimulated and stored by semantic processing will lead to better retention than will the skimpy information stimulated by shallower processing.

The second hypothesis, called the *distinctiveness hypothesis*, holds that deep, or semantic, processing leads to better retention because it tends to help make the stimulus more distinct from other information in storage. *Cat* is more likely to become distinct from other stimulus words if it is processed in terms of its meaning rather than in terms of its simple physical structure. Perhaps deeper processing will eventually be shown to increase both elaboration and distinctiveness.

These and other conceptual advances are helping to overcome some of the difficulties faced by the levels-of-processing approach. However, skepticism remains high concerning its eventual fate. We shall look at this approach in more detail in Chapter 11 when we address and contrast current models of memory. Whatever the final outcome with respect to the levels-of-processing analysis, Craik and his associates have done the field a service by underscoring the fact that *how* we rehearse is as important as *how much* we rehearse. Still other areas of research and thought make this same point, as we shall now see.

TYPE I AND TYPE II REHEARSAL

In the context of this concern for levels of processing a number of authors have proposed two categories of rehearsal activity (Craik & Lockhart, 1972; Glenberg, Smith, & Green, 1977; Rundus, 1977; Woodward, Bjork, & Jongeward, 1973). Type I rehearsal, or *maintenance rehearsal*, is designed to hold information in mind, to keep it ready, but not to process it so deeply that it becomes part of our permanent store of information. Here we are concerned with shallow rehearsal, such as the verbal practice of a telephone number so that we do not forget it while we search for a pencil and paper. Type II rehearsal, or *elaborative rehearsal*, is a deeper process in which we try to prepare materials for future use. Here we might try to practice the telephone number in such a way that we can forget about it now and yet still be able to recall it later. To do this we might have to process at a deeper level. We might make up a story using the numbers involved or scan the number for associations such as dates or ages that are meaningful to us. In a sense, Type II rehearsal is whatever we do to transfer memories from temporary to permanent storage.

Although intriguing, the distinction between Type I and Type II rehearsal is not entirely clear cut. For example, Naire (1983) found that, contrary to expectations, Type I rehearsal *does* sometimes lead to more permanent memory. He presented digits to subjects and told them that they would be tested on them at the end of a retention interval. The subjects were told that the filler task (rehearsing paired associates) was unimportant and was merely required to prevent them from re-hearsing the digits, which were supposed to be the critical items. Then, in a sur-prise, Naire tested for recall of the paired associates. He found that the subjects could recall some of them. This wasn't supposed to happen; Type I rehearsal is not supposed to lead to permanent storage. So we must be cautious about the Type I–Type II distinction (see Naveh-Benjamin & Jonides, 1984a, 1984b).

CONTROLLED VERSUS AUTOMATIC PROCESSING

Another interesting distinction being made in the literature is between *controlled* and *automatic* processing, or between processing that requires mental effort and processing that requires no conscious effort (Posner & Snyder, 1975; Schneider & Shiffrin, 1977).

Controlled processes are seen as requiring mental effort, being done one at a time, and being limited by our available mental capacity. Automatic processing, in contrast, requires no effort, can involve parallel processing of more than one thing at a time, and is not limited in terms of capacity. Controlled processing is seen as being slower than automatic processing.

Generally speaking, anything we do consciously of our own free will involves controlled processing, and anything we do without being aware of it involves auto-matic processing. An example should help make clear the distinction between these two kinds of processing. You can get a feel for the difference by first labeling the objects shown in Figure 5.10a. That's easy, isn't it? Now label the objects presented in Figure 5.10b. You will probably have trouble here, because it is difficult to ignore the incorrect words printed on the pictures (Rosinski, Golinkoff, & Kukish, 1975). The idea here is that the verbal label "looks up" its visual representation automat-ically whether you want it to or not (Wood, 1983). Controlled processing (naming the drawings) is pitted against automatic processing (thinking of the representa-tion of the word) (see also Reiner & Morrison, 1983). The verbal label is more likely to interfere with the naming of the visual object than vice versa, because we can read words faster than we can label pictures. You can demonstrate this by reading the words in Figure 5.10b. You shouldn't have much trouble. We shall return to the distinction between controlled and automatic processing several times, especially in our discussion of memory.

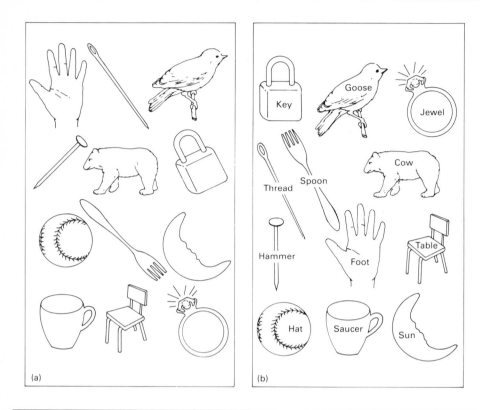

Figure 5.10 The task is to label the pictures as quickly as you can. (Adapted from Rosinski, R. R., Golinkoff, R. M., and Kukish, K. S. Automatic semantic processing in a picture-word interference task. *Child Development*, 1975, 46, 247–253.)

ELABORATIVE REHEARSAL

Our discussion of rehearsal has led us to the inescapable fact that, when we rehearse, we don't merely repeat a response over and over. Although we can, if we wish, simply repeat an item, we are much more likely to organize, interpret, relate, catalog, and generally elaborate when we rehearse. We are active, creative rehearsers; we try to enhance learning by tailoring our rehearsal methods to suit the task at hand.

Elaborative rehearsal is such an important process and covers so many topics that an entire chapter (Chapter 11) is devoted to it. For now, two examples of the many kinds of elaborative rehearsal that have been identified should suffice.

Let's begin with an example of elaborative rehearsal in paired-associate learning. It is logically possible that we learn a paired associate such as *doctor-stone* merely by repeating the elements over and over. But that isn't what actually happens. To the contrary, we usually learn paired associates through the use of many different elaborative strategies. We can relate the stimulus to the response, we can make up

Table 5.2   An Example of Each Elaborator Type Reported for the Paired Associate
Doctor–Stone

ELABORATOR TYPE	ELABORATORS
Related to both	gallstone
Stimulus related	Mr.
Response related	Flintstones
Idiosyncratic	movie

Adapted from Wang, A. Y. Individual differences in learning speed. *Journal of Experimental Psychology: Learning, Memory, and Cognition*, 1983, 9, 300–311. Table 1, p. 302. Copyright 1983 by the American Psychological Association. Reprinted by permission.

an image, or a "mental picture," involving the two units, and we can make up a sentence, story, or rhyme using the two elements.

Wang (1983) had subjects learn paired associates and then asked them how they had learned the items. Table 5.2 contains some of the types of elaboration actually used by the subjects. As you can see, they sometimes produced elaborators that helped them learn the item *doctor-stone* by linking the stimulus and the response (*gallstone*). Sometimes they elaborated on the stimulus alone (*Mr.*), sometimes on the response (*Flintstones*), and sometimes in an idiosyncratic, or uniquely individual, fashion (*movie*).

Wang found that learning was best accomplished when the elaboration involved both the stimulus and the response. He also found that fast learners do more elaborating than slow learners. And finally, he found that, if he took the elaborations developed by fast and slow learners and gave them to new subjects, the new subjects receiving the fast learners' elaborations did better than subjects receiving elaborations from slow learners. In other words, rehearsal involving more elaboration and more complex elaboration seems best.

The above example indicates one way in which we can elaborate within a single to-be-learned unit. But elaboration can help us when we are trying to learn an entire list as well. Rabinowitz and Mandler (1983) gave two groups of subjects the same list of items but organized the items differently in each condition. As you can see in Table 5.3, half the time the phrases were put into what the authors call a taxonomic organization, and half the time the exact same phrases were presented to the subjects in a schematic organization. Which organization do you feel would lead to better learning? Their results indicate that the schematic organization led to significantly better learning of the phrases. The authors speculate that this superiority may be due to the fact that items presented schematically are more easily used in making up a single mental image, or scene, than those presented taxonomically.

As we shall see, these two examples of elaborative rehearsal do nothing more than scratch the surface of the kinds of elaboration that will be discussed in Chapter 11. The point to remember here is that rehearsal is turning out to be a multifaceted concept; it involves much more than simply repeating a response over and over. When we rehearse, we often systematize, relate, order, select, and transform information in our effort to learn. We are active rather than passive rehearsers. And there are many different ways to rehearse (see Peterson, Thomas, & Johnson, 1977).

Table 5.3 Arrangement of Stimulus Materials into Two Organizational Structures

TAXONOMIC ORGANIZATION	SCHEMATIC ORGANIZATION
Food	Going skiing
eat pineapple	go to mountains
eat peanuts	put on down jacket
eat birthday cake	buy lift ticket
drink hot chocolate	ski down slopes
drink champagne	drink hot chocolate
Clothing	Going to a ballet
put on evening dress	buy opera glasses
put on team cap	put on evening clothes
put on paper hat	go to theater
put on bathing suit	watch ballet
put on down jacket	drink champagne
Places	Going to a party
go to mountains	buy present
go to Hawaii	go to party
go to theater	put on paper hat
go to party	eat birthday cake
go to stadium	play charades
Activities	Going to a baseball game
play charades	put on team cap
watch ballet	go to stadium
ski down slopes	buy admission ticket
watch baseball game	watch baseball game
swim in ocean	eat peanuts
Things one would buy	Going to Hawaii
buy admission ticket	buy plane ticket
buy lift ticket	go to Hawaii
buy plane ticket	eat pineapple
buy opera glasses	put on bathing suit
buy present	swim in ocean

Adapted from Rabinowitz, M., and Mandler, J. M. Organization and information retrieval. *Journal of Experimental Psychology: Learning, Memory, and Cognition,* 1983, 9, 430–439. Table 1, p. 432. Copyright 1983 by the American Psychological Association. Reprinted by permission.

SUMMARY

1. One of the oldest and most widely held assumptions in the field of learning is that temporal *contiguity* of the stimulus and the response is *necessary* for learning to occur.

2. Some psychologists feel that S-R contiguity is *sufficient* for learning to occur, whereas others think it is necessary but not sufficient. Although the contiguity principle is an assumption of most existing theories of learning, its validity has not been well documented.

3. The strength of an S-R association is revealed by the likelihood of a particular response's occurring in the presence of a particular stimulus situation.

4. A stimulus can be defined as any detectable energy change. Offset and onset of such things as lights, sounds, odors, and tastes can serve as stimuli. Relationships and responses can serve as stimuli. Some energy changes are more effective as stimuli than others, particularly across species. An energy change must be attended to before it can function as an effective stimulus.

5. The notion of a stimulus trace refers to the fact that the continuation of a stimulus is not dependent on continued stimulation of sensory receptors. Once an external stimulus has activated sensory receptors, the message is "taken

into" the organism and maintained. Afterimages represent stimulus traces of an essentially sensory nature. Memories represent traces of a more complicated, "cognitive" nature.

6. A response is defined as any objectively identifiable segment of the continuous behavior process.

7. In subjective organization experiments subjects are presented with a list of randomly arranged, unrelated words and asked to recall them in any order they wish. The list is presented again, but in a new random order. The subjects again try to recall them, and so on. Subjective organization refers to the fact that, as the experiment progresses, the subjects begin to recall the words in the same order, even though the words are presented in a new random order on each trial. This would seem to suggest noncontiguous learning. But additional research has revealed that the subjects may either (1) bring the elements together "in their own minds" or (2) rehearse them contiguously during the recall phase.

8. Studies in the area of paired-associate learning also support the contiguity principle. If the time between the stimulus and response items is increased *and* the subjects are prevented from rehearsing or carrying a trace of the stimulus forward in time, then learning decreases.

9. Research reported in an earlier chapter indicated that one of the best CS–UCS intervals in classical conditioning is often .5 of a second, and this supports the contiguity principle. Yet bait-shyness studies reveal that conditioning can occur with CS–UCS intervals of several hours. Rats that have been X-irradiated several hours after ingesting distinctly flavored solutions will still develop an aversion to that flavor. Some feel that this demonstrates noncontiguous learning. Others evoke the trace-conditioning notion to explain away the challenge. At present it must be admitted that the possibility of stimulus traces being carried forward in these experiments has not been effectively eliminated.

10. Although the bait-shyness effect is provocative, noncontiguous learning has not been demonstrated clearly and conclusively. The constant possibility of confounding through the action of stimulus traces has thus far impeded our quest for learning in the absence of S-R contiguity.

11. The literature on the sufficiency of S-R contiguity was also reviewed. Kamin's blocking effect in classical conditioning suggests that simple S-R contiguity is not sufficient for learning to occur.

12. Informational interpretations of classical conditioning and their supporting experiments also argue against the sufficiency of S-R contiguity.

13. The absence of conditioning in the simultaneous paradigm is better accounted for by informational theory than by contiguity theory.

14. Studies of short-term memory indicate that materials presented contiguously but incidentally (without the subject's intending to learn them) will not be learned.

15. Our conclusion is that S-R contiguity may well be necessary but that it is not a sufficient condition for learning.

16. The *negatively accelerated learning curve* is common, but it is not the only curve that appears in our research.

17. So-called learning curves are actually performance curves, and their form is determined by both learning and motivation.

18. We try to infer the amount of learning from a wide range of *performance measures*, including such factors as running speed, response latency, resistance to extinction, number of correct responses, and trials to criterion.

19. When choosing a performance measure we must be sure it is (a) reliable and (b) appropriately sensitive.

20. Because individual performance data are often so variable, we are forced to *average the scores* to obtain a clear picture of the stable trends underlying variable individual behaviors.

21. Depending on our purposes, we can "smooth" out our curves by combining scores from a number of individuals on each trial, by combining scores from adjacent trials, or by combining scores obtained from a single individual run through the task several times. *Cumulative learning curves* are popular ways of displaying data.

22. Although learning curves present data in a clear, simple fashion, no one curve can tell the whole story. A given curve merely represents one vantage point from which we can view our data. Averaging techniques can distort our data.

23. The *incremental* and *all-or-none* conceptions are two theories of learning.

24. Hull's incremental system assumes behavior to be a function of at least five major variables. *Drive*, a motivational factor, is measured in terms of time of deprivation or extent of noxious stimulation. *Habit* refers to how much the organism has learned about a particular situation through reinforced responding. *Incentive motivation* is measured in terms of the quantity and quality of the reward. As *stimulus intensity* increases, the probability of the response increases. *Inhibition*, which detracts from the tendency to respond, is measured in terms of how much work is involved in making the response and how many times the animal has made the response.

25. Reinforcement, in Hull's system, refers to the rapid diminution of drive. Habit is a negatively accelerated function of the number of reinforced responses.

26. Hull's theory suggests that learning, or *H*, is permanent and stays with the organism until death. Studies of electrical brain stimulation and hypnotic age regression suggest that many memories normally unavailable to us are still stored within us. Neither form of investigation proves conclusively that *all* memories are stored permanently, however.

27. The *all-or-none position* is illustrated by Guthrie's theory and Estes' stimulus-sampling model. Guthrie's theory can be summed up by saying, "A combination of stimuli that has accompanied a movement will on its recurrence tend to be followed by that movement." Acts, or the total behaviors that we observe and study, are made up of many movements. The gradual improvement in an act is the result of an increase in the number of these small movements, which are each learned in an all-or-none fashion.

28. Estes' *stimulus-sampling model* represents an attempt to translate Guthrie's basic notions into a more formal, mathematical form. According to Estes, response probability equals the proportion of stimuli to which it is connected. "Learning" refers to the gradual growth in the proportion of stimuli connected to the response over successive trials.

29. Several investigators have unsuccessfully attempted to find conclusive experimental support for the all-or-none position.

30. *Multiple-trace models* argue that, each time an item is presented, the item is represented in memory as a unique, discrete event. *Strength theory* maintains that, each time an item is presented, the strength of a single memory representation is increased.

31. Multiple-trace theory may be closer to the all-or-none position, whereas strength theory may be closer to the incremental position.

32. Much current research centers not so much on whether practice helps learning but on how learning varies as the conditions of practice vary.

33. *Distributed*, or spaced, *practice* has been shown to produce better learning than *massed practice*.

34. Melton's *lag effect* refers to the finding that the probability of recall of a repeated item in free recall is positively related to the number of intervening items.

35. The superiority of distributed practice and the lag effect can be interpreted in terms of a *contextual effect* or in terms of *encoding variability*.

36. Recent studies have been concerned with the quality as well as the quantity of rehearsal.

37. *Level of processing* refers to the idea that, the deeper we process information, the better we will remember it. Shallow processing occurs when we attend to such things as the way a word looks. Deeper processing occurs when we attend to such things as the sound and, at the deepest level, the meaning of the word.

38. Criticism of the levels-of-processing approach has been extensive. For example, some information that is processed on a shallow level can be learned well and remembered over long periods.

39. The elaboration and distinctiveness hypotheses may account for depth-of-processing effects.

40. *Type I rehearsal* is shallow practice designed to maintain information without transferring it to permanent memory. *Type II rehearsal* is deeper and renders information recallable in the future.

41. Processing can occur in either an automatic or controlled fashion.

42. Rehearsal is more likely to involve some type of elaboration than it is to involve simple rote rehearsal of the material. This holds for lists or groups of material as well as for single items.

CHAPTER

6

REINFORCEMENT: FACTS AND THEORY

DEFINITIONS AND PARAMETERS OF REINFORCEMENT

There is very little disagreement about the nature of reinforcers on an operational level. Reinforcers are defined in terms of their effects. Any stimulus is a reinforcer if it increases the strength of a response. You will recall that we distinguished between positive and negative reinforcers in Chapter 2. A positive reinforcer is anything that, when presented to the animal, will increase the probability of the response's occurring (for example, food). A negative reinforcer is anything that, when taken away from the animal, increases the probability of the response (for example, shock). Reinforcers, both positive and negative, increase response probability.

These definitions seem to be the limit of common agreement; at this point opinions concerning the nature of reinforcement begin to diverge. As soon as we ask *why* reinforcers reinforce, we lose any semblance of unanimity. We have already seen, for example, that Hull (1943) thought of reinforcement in terms of the rapid diminution of drive level. But Thorndike (1913) earlier defined reinforcement and punishment in terms of "satisfying" and "annoying" states of affairs. According to Thorndike, S-R connections are strengthened if the occurrence of the response is followed by a satisfying state of affairs and weakened if it is followed by an annoying state of affairs.

With these brief examples we can begin to see the extent of the controversy surrounding the theoretical nature of reinforcement. We shall return to the question of theory later in this chapter. For now, let us direct our attention to some empirical questions that do not require the adoption of one or the other of these various theoretical positions. We shall first look at an outline of the more important parameters of reinforcement.

Imagine a hungry rat in a Skinner box. Imagine a student in a college course. Each organism can be induced to acquire more or less complicated responses through the application of certain reinforcers. The rat will work for food, whereas grades, praise, or satisfaction may be sufficient to reinforce the student. We can vary many attributes, or characteristics, of reinforcing situations. One of the most obvious factors is the *amount of reward* presented immediately following the occurrence of a response. The rat might receive one, two, three, or more pellets following a correct response. The student might be heartily praised for a correct response, or she might receive nothing more than a curt nod from the instructor. It is not unreasonable to suspect that these variations would be important in learning. A second major factor has to do with the time between the occurrence of the response and the receipt of the reward, or the *delay of reinforcement*. The rat might receive its reinforcement immediately after making the response, or it might be forced to wait 10 seconds, 20 seconds, or even longer before receiving the reward. Similarly, the student might be praised immediately, or the teacher might wait until after class to deliver the praise. Finally, we can reinforce every response our subject makes, but we need not. We can *partially* reinforce the subject, or reinforce something less than every response. For example, we might want to set up a *schedule of reinforcement*, in which we only reinforce every second, third, fourth, or *n*th response, leaving the remainder of the responses unreinforced. Intuitively, one would expect learning to be strongly affected by manipulations involving the schedule of reinforcement.

These three factors (schedule, delay, and amount) have emerged as critical parameters of reinforcement. We shall consider each of them individually.

SCHEDULES OF REINFORCEMENT

Continuous reinforcement (CRF) refers to situations in which every response is reinforced. As we have noted, we need not reinforce every response our laboratory subject makes. We are free to present reinforcements in any pattern we wish and can reinforce any portion of the occurring responses. In the real world continuous reinforcement is probably the exception rather than the rule. When kittens are learning to pounce on moving objects, they are far from completely successful in their early attempts. As youngsters learn to play basketball, they miss more baskets than they make. And yet these behaviors are learned. Continuous reinforcement is not necessary for learning to occur (even though it is often used in the laboratory). The study of schedules of reinforcement is concerned with the impact of these patterns of partial reinforcement on the acquisition of behaviors and represents the formalized investigation of everyday patterns of reinforcement and their effects on behavior.

THE MAJOR TYPES OF SCHEDULES

FIXED–INTERVAL SCHEDULE.   In a fixed-interval (FI) schedule the animal is reinforced for the first response that occurs after the end of a given time interval. For example, in an FI 10 schedule the animal is reinforced for the first response that it makes after 10 seconds have elapsed since its last reinforced response. It must then wait another 10 seconds before it can obtain another reinforcement. It is free to respond during the 10-second interval, but it will not be reinforced for these responses. The very first response following the end of the interval is the only one that is reinforced.

An FI schedule of reinforcement leads to a very specific kind of responding. The animal develops a response strategy to fit the reinforcement schedule. A reasonable strategy for an FI schedule would be to pause after the receipt of the reinforcement, as there is no need to respond continuously, and then, as the end of the interval approaches, respond more and more frequently. This kind of responding is exactly what we observe in laboratory animals. Long pauses follow reinforcements. The rate of responding accelerates as the end of the interval approaches. As can be seen in Figure 6.1, a characteristic "scalloping" effect is observed in the cumulative records of FI schedules.

In a very rough way the studying behavior of students sometimes follows this pattern. Suppose that a given class has a midterm exam and a final exam. These exams are reinforcing events (positive or negative, depending on how you look at them). Many students do very little studying as the semester begins. As the midterm approaches, studying behavior picks up until it reaches a high rate just before the exam. After the exam it drops to zero and remains there, only to accelerate again as the final exam approaches. Obviously, not all students study in this manner, and obviously, not all materials are handled in this fashion (see Figure 6.2). But an interesting, and quite striking, correspondence exists between the effects of FI schedules and the effects of our traditional examination patterns.

It might be argued that "mail-checking behavior" also resembles behavior under the control of an FI schedule. If we know that the mail arrives promptly at noon, we do not begin to look for it at 8 A.M. As noon approaches, we begin to look, listen, and check the mailbox. After the delivery arrives, there is very little chance that we will check again until the next day.

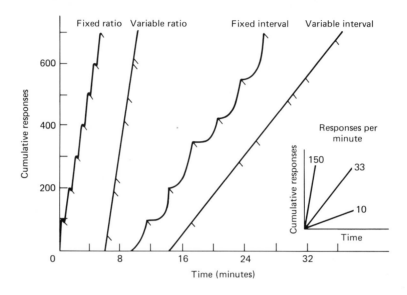

Figure 6.1 Stylized cumulative-response records obtained under four common schedules of reinforcement. Slash marks in the records indicate presentations of reinforcements. (Adapted from *Operant Learning, Procedures for Changing Behavior* by J. L. Williams. Copyright © 1973 by Wadsworth, Inc. Reprinted by permission of the publisher, Brooks/Cole Publishing Company, Monterey, California.)

As a final example, Weisberg and Waldrop (1972) have presented an amusing analysis of the bill-passing behavior of the U.S. Congress. As can be seen in Figure 6.3, Congress passes very few bills during the first few months of a given session. As the time for adjournment approaches, the rate of bill passage accelerates—in a pattern just like that of a rat in a Skinner box, scalloping and all. Actually, the similarity between the two situations may be more fanciful than real, for we know very little about the pressures on Congress that produce this pattern of behavior. As Lundin (1974) suggests, the scalloping could result from the increasing demands of various lobbies, special-interest groups, and powerful constituents.

THE VARIABLE–INTERVAL SCHEDULE.   In a variable-interval (VI) schedule the animal is again forced to wait before it can obtain a reinforcement, but the time interval is variable. After the animal has responded and been reinforced, it might have to wait for 5 seconds before being able to receive a reward. Then it might have to wait for 3 seconds, and then 30 seconds, and so on. A VI 2 schedule is one in which the *average* time interval between reinforcement is 2 seconds.

It seems that steady responding is most efficient in this case (see Figure 6.1). Because the animal is unable to judge the length of the time intervals, it cannot pause as it does in the FI situation. It must constantly "check in" with a steady stream of responses. As one would expect, the response rate is high when a short

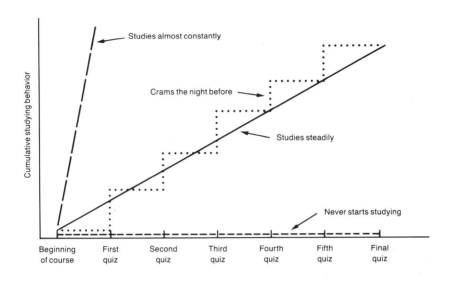

Figure 6.2 Hypothetical studying patterns. Although examination patterns often resemble a fixed-interval schedule, and the text argues that scalloping often appears in students' studying behavior, we have all met exceptions to the rule. Some people rarely stop studying, some only turn to the books just before the exam, some keep up a steady rate throughout the semester, and some never study at all. In these cases the individual is probably responding to some alternative set of reinforcers and some other, more powerful, schedule. For example, the person who does not study at all may be rewarded for doing so by his peers. The crammer may have had great success with this technique in the past. The continuous studier may find relief from anxiety by constantly studying.

average interval is employed and lower when a longer average interval is utilized. The studying behavior of students taking a class in which the instructor gives pop quizzes or surprise exams will show these characteristics.

THE FIXED–RATIO SCHEDULE.   In a fixed-ratio (FR) schedule a certain number of responses must be made before the reward is delivered. In an FR 10 schedule a pigeon must peck a key 10 times before being reinforced. This schedule yields extremely high rates of responding (see Figure 6.1). The animal responds rapidly until it receives its reinforcement. Interestingly, the FR schedule often produces a mild *postreinforcement pause*. It is not nearly so pronounced as the scalloping effect obtained with FI schedules, but it is a definite characteristic of the FR schedule. The higher the ratio, the longer is the postreinforcement pause.

This postreinforcement pause has sometimes been called a *procrastination effect* (Domjan & Burkhard, 1982). For example, if you are writing a term paper composed of several sections, you may work rapidly until you have completed one section. Then you may heave a sigh of relief, take a break, and procrastinate for a while before you begin the next section.

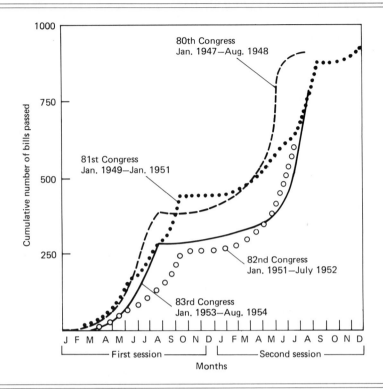

Figure 6.3 Fixed-interval work habits of Congress. (Adapted from Weisberg, P., and Waldrop, P. B. Fixed-interval work habits of Congress. *Journal of Applied Behavior Analysis*, 1972, *5*, 93–97. Fig. 1, p. 94.)

Employees working on the assembly line in a factory find themselves required to process large numbers of units for a certain amount of pay. They are working under an FR schedule. In the case of a "speedup," unscrupulous employers require a certain number of units for a certain amount of pay. Once that level of responding is obtained, they run the assembly line faster, forcing the workers to produce more and more for the same amount of pay.

Extremely high fixed ratios can be established by gradually increasing the number of responses required for a reward, but this cannot be done all in one step. Findley and Brady (1965) describe an experiment in which 120,000 responses were required before a chimpanzee received food. This example is extreme, of course, and most situations both inside and outside the laboratory involve much smaller ratios.

THE VARIABLE–RATIO SCHEDULE.   In the variable-ratio (VR) schedule the number of responses required of the subject varies. A rat may first be required to press a lever 10 times for a reward. Then 3 responses may be required, then 7, then 4, and so on. In a VR 20 schedule the *average* number of required responses is 20. This schedule also produces high rates of responding (see Figure 6.1). The principal difference between this schedule and the FR schedule is the absence of the postreinforcement pause in the VR situation. Variable-ratio responding is strong and steady.

The most striking example of VR scheduling outside the laboratory comes from the world of gambling. When the vacationing schoolteacher stands in front of a slot machine in Las Vegas punching in nickels for hours on end, he is in the grip of a VR schedule. The machine is programmed to pay off after irregular numbers of responses. Jackpots obtained all over the casino are announced over a loudspeaker in order to create the impression of a more favorable ratio. Slot machines located in spots where the customer is unlikely to return (for example, airports, bus terminals) may be programmed to pay off only rarely.

Every year, the Girl Scouts come around with their boxes of cookies. Every year, eager little Cub Scouts show up at the door with tickets to the annual Scout-O-Rama. These children may be under the spell of a VR schedule. They must ring door bells to sell, but they do not know how many they will have to ring before they make a sale. Nor will sitting at home waiting for the end of an interval make a sale. They have to make variable numbers of responses to sell. What makes it worse is that they know that every other member of their organization is out there doing the same thing, raising the ratio minute by minute, in a highly competitive situation.

CONTINUOUS VERSUS PARTIAL REINFORCEMENT.   It seems strange in a way, but partial-reinforcement schedules sometimes produce higher rates of responding than does continuous reinforcement. For example, Stephens, Pear, Wray, and Jackson (1975) rewarded mentally retarded children for learning the names of pictures. They told the children "good" and gave them candies as reinforcers. Part of the time the children were reinforced for every correct response they made (CRF), and part of the time they were placed on an FR schedule. As is shown in Figure 6.4, four out of five children definitely responded more often under the FR schedule, with the fifth child responding so seldom as to make a schedule comparison difficult.

Although this study was done with mentally retarded children, partial schedules often seem to produce greater response rates in other humans and animals as well. (It should be noted that it may be best to *begin* learning under continuous reinforcement and then shift to partial reinforcement to attain maximum response rate. Continuous reinforcement is better to "get the organism started," but once responding has begun, shifting to a partial schedule may yield the highest rate.)

MULTIPLE SCHEDULES.   Multiple schedules consist of two or more simple schedules presented one after the other (see Norborg, Osborne, & Fanting, 1983). In addition, distinctive cues, such as colored lights, are associated with or presented during each of the simple phases. For example, suppose that a pigeon is pecking a key for food under a *mult* FI 3 VR 10 schedule. What this means is that it is first trained under an FI schedule. Some cue, such as a red light, is present while the bird is undergoing training. When the schedule is shifted to VR 10, the red light is replaced by, say, a green light. Each time the schedule is changed, the cue is changed.

As might be expected, the animal shifts its pattern of responding as the schedule shifts. But it is not a simple situation. The animal's responding under any given schedule is often affected by the nature of the preceding schedule. Multiple schedules involve complicated interaction effects. The nature of these complex interactions has recently come under rather intense investigation (see Pittenger, Pavlik, Flora, & Kontos, 1988).

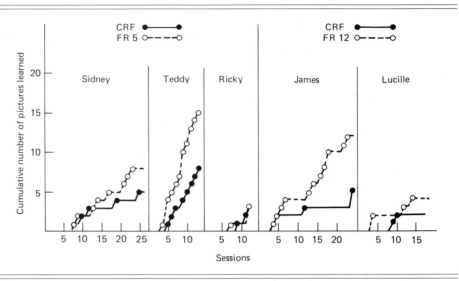

Figure 6.4 Partial reinforcement yields higher correct response rates than continuous reinforcement. Retarded children were reinforced with candy and a verbal "good" either continuously (CRF) or partially (FR 5 and FR 12) for naming pictures. The FR schedules produced higher correct response rates. (Adapted from Stephens, C. E., Pear, J. J., Wray, L. D., and Jackson, G. C. Some effects of reinforcement schedules in teaching picture names to retarded children. *Journal of Applied Behavior Analysis*, 1975, 8, 435–447. Fig. 1, p. 439.)

The *mixed schedule* is a variation of the multiple schedule in which no external cues (such as colors) are associated with the schedules. The shift from one schedule to another can be detected only from the changed patterns of reinforcement. As expected, this often reduces the ease or efficiency with which the animal shifts from one form of responding to the next.

CHAINED SCHEDULES.   In chained schedules two or more successive schedules must be completed before a reinforcement can be obtained. For example, in an FI 5 FR 10 chained schedule the animal must first respond after 5 seconds have elapsed and must then give 10 responses, regardless of their timing, before it will be reinforced.

In chained schedules external stimuli (such as colors) are associated with each successive phase in the chain. *Tandem schedules* are the same as chained schedules, except that there are no such changes in external stimuli when the successive phases are completed. Thus, in tandem schedules the animal is not provided with information concerning the completion of successive phases.

Concurrent Schedules and the Matching Law

Concurrent schedules are those in which the animal is faced with two or more levers or keys. Each key operates according to its own schedule. The animal is free to press any key. Thus, in a *concurrent* FI 2 FI 8 schedule, responses to one key are reinforced every 2 seconds, and responses to a second key are reinforced every 8 seconds.

The *matching law* (Herrnstein, 1970) refers to the fact that the relative frequency of responding on a key matches the relative frequency of reinforcement for responses on that alternative. In other words, the animal responds most often to the key, or lever, that delivers a reinforcement most often, and the responses are made in direct proportion to the frequency of that reinforcement.

Matching behavior has been demonstrated many times with animals (see Real & Hobson, 1983). But we humans display matching behavior, too. For example, Conger and Killeen (1974) told subjects that they would be talking with three other people. Actually, these three people were confederates of the experimenter who had been told to reinforce the subject according to different schedules. Reinforcement consisted of making positive remarks and so on. The matching law was supported by the fact that the relative amounts of time the subjects spent freely choosing to talk to each of the three confederates matched the relative rates of reinforcement delivered by the confederates.

Why do animals, and humans, display matching behavior in choice situations? What is behind this intriguing piece of behavior? At present the answer is not clear, and the issue is being hotly debated (see Williams & Royalty, 1989, and Hinson & Studdon, 1983, for opposing theoretical views).

Schedule-Induced Behavior

Partial-reinforcement schedules not only increase the strength of the responses that are being reinforced but also stimulate so-called *schedule-induced* behavior (Beck, Huh, Mumby, & Fundytus, 1989). This means that during those intervals when no reinforcement is possible, both animals and humans will begin to develop certain behaviors such as pacing back and forth, clenching the jaw, and (in the case of some animals, at least) attacking pictures of members of one's own species. Other schedule-induced behaviors include biting, eating, drinking, running, and licking. None of this behavior is reinforced by the schedule in effect, and yet it does develop, and quite strongly. Muller, Crow, and Cheney (1979) find that these behaviors are "not readily explained by current principles of learning."

But the situation may not be that mysterious. It may be that these schedule-induced behaviors are merely being reinforced by factors beyond the control of the experimenter. For example, if you were on an FI 10 schedule when the reward was 50¢, you might well develop some pacing or jaw-clenching behaviors during the interval to (1) ward off boredom, (2) reduce tension and frustration, and (3) receive some kind of stimulation. In other words, these behaviors may be nothing more than responses reinforced by subtle but strong reinforcers.

Cohen and Campagnoni (1989) observed the behavior of pigeons during intervals between the presentation of grain. They found the birds moved to the back of the cage and refused to locate themselves near the food dispenser. Why? The authors have two hypotheses. First, the birds may be avoiding the food dispenser because it is in a frustrating location, given that grain was only occasionally available. Second, the birds may be retreating to the rear of the cage in order to obtain some pleasant sensory change. A little stimulus variety helps pass the time. This second hypothesis was supported by the fact that, while in retreat, the animals will readily learn to press a bar for a change in the color and intensity of the cage lighting.

One thing can be said with certainty about schedule-induced behavior: It varies as a function of the length of time between reinforcements. As you can see in Figure 6.5, these "extra" behaviors first increase and then decrease as the time between reinforcements increases. Exactly why this relationship exists is not known.

Autoshaping

An interesting variation on the theme of schedules of reinforcement may turn out to be extremely important. Autoshaping (Brown & Jenkins, 1968; Gamzu & Schwam, 1974; Jenkins & Moore, 1973; Pisacreta, Redwood, & Witt, 1983) refers to what happens when reinforcement is presented, regardless of whether the animal responds. (For related work see Skinner's [1948] early, classic analysis of so-called *superstitious behavior*.) In a typical autoshaping experiment the illumination of a key is always followed by delivery of food. Thus, a hungry pigeon need not respond at all in this situation. It need only wait until the key lights up and then eat the food, which always follows the light. And yet it has been observed that the pigeon does peck the key. The key-pecking response develops even though it is not necessary for the receipt of a reward.

This effect, although quite controversial, calls into question the very nature of what is normally called instrumental conditioning. What it suggests is that a strong element of classical conditioning exists in the typical instrumental-conditioning situation. The UCS is the food. The food (UCS) will automatically elicit a pecking response (the UCR). The UCS (food) is paired with a CS (the light). After a series of such pairings, the CS (light) comes to elicit a CR (pecking in response to the light), which resembles the UCR (pecking in response to the food).

This problem goes back to one that was outlined in an earlier chapter. The distinction between classical and instrumental conditioning is difficult to maintain. The autoshaping effect suggests that classical conditioning is so intertwined with even the simplest instrumental-conditioning situation that it is impossible to conclude that we ever have a pure case of classical or instrumental conditioning (see also Durlach, 1983; Rescorla, 1979; Robbins, 1988).

Extinction: The "Partial-Reinforcement Effect"

Thus far we have been speaking of the relationship between schedules of reinforcement and the *acquisition* process. We now shall look at how *extinction* is related to partial reinforcement. One of the most widely noted phenomena in the field of learning is the fact that resistance to extinction following partial reinforcement is greater than resistance to extinction following continuous reinforcement (Pittenger, Pavlik, Flora, & Kontos, 1988; Platt & Day, 1979; Seybert, Baer, Harvey, Ludwig, & Gerard, 1979). All four of the simple schedules (VI, FI, VR, FR) produce greater resistance to extinction than does continuous reinforcement (CRF). Although we will not deal with these points in detail, it should be noted that each of the four simple schedules produces its own characteristic pattern of responding during extinction (see Williams, 1973). What we are primarily concerned with here is the fact that *all* partial schedules yield greater resistance to extinction than does CRF—that is, *the partial-reinforcement extinction effect (PREE)*.

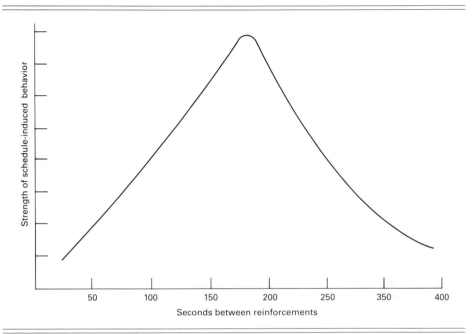

Figure 6.5 Hypothetical data relating time between reinforcements to schedule-induced behavior.

If you reinforce a rat only part of the time and then remove reinforcement all together, the rat will go on responding during this extinction phase longer than it would if it had been reinforced 100% of the time. Humans display the same effect in everyday life. For example, suppose a child asks his mother for a piece of candy and she says no. Then he asks again and again. Finally, in exasperation, she gives in and reinforces him with candy. What may happen if this pattern persists is that the child will become something of a demanding brat. He never seems to give up. He has been partially reinforced and is thus less likely to give up his begging, nagging behavior than is a child who is refused candy after having been given candy each and every time he asked for it.

THE DISCRIMINATION HYPOTHESIS.   There are at least three interpretations of the PREE. According to the first of these, the discrimination hypothesis (Mowrer & Jones, 1945), subjects on a partial reinforcement schedule may be less likely to notice that anything has changed at all when they are put on an extinction schedule. They are used to a lot of trials without reinforcement and may, at least temporarily, fail to discriminate between partial reinforcement and extinction. Continuously reinforced subjects, by contrast, may much more easily notice the differences between CRF and extinction and may thus stop responding sooner.

Although intuitively appealing, the discrimination hypothesis has not been well supported experimentally (Gibbs, Latham, & Gormezano, 1978; Theios, 1962). The next two interpretations have met with more success.

FRUSTRATION THEORY.   Amsel (1958) has proposed another interpretation of the PREE. According to this position, partially reinforced animals experience frustration when they make a response and are not reinforced. This emotion becomes classically conditioned to the learning situation (for example, a runway and goal box). But because they are reinforced part of the time, they do learn the response and, more importantly, learn to make the response in the presence of this conditioned emotional frustration. They are "used to" feeling frustrated and so continue to respond during extinction. Now consider the continuously reinforced animal that is suddenly put on extinction. It has never been frustrated during acquisition; therefore, it has not learned to respond in the presence of frustration. The frustration it feels during extinction is disruptive and facilitates extinction.

SEQUENTIAL THEORY.   The final interpretation of the PREE is called the sequential theory. Capaldi (1971) proposed that animals can remember whether they were reinforced on the preceding trial and that it is this memory of not having been rewarded recently that motivates them to respond on the present trial. If you were in the rat's place you might say to yourself, "I know my responses are rewarded some of the time, and I haven't been rewarded recently, so it's probably time for a reward. I guess I'll respond now."

Both the sequential theory and the frustration theory have stimulated a good deal of supportive research. Both mechanisms may contribute to the PREE.

Schedules: Humans and Animals

Most of the schedules and data we have discussed have been developed using "lower" animals. It may legitimately be asked if the same effects will always be obtained with humans. The answer varies, depending on the psychologist whom you consult and the task involved. We take the position in this text that a quite good, though not perfect, correspondence exists between the patterns obtained with animals and humans. For example, Yukl, Wexley, and Seymore (1972) reinforced the scoring of IBM answer cards with either continuous reinforcement or a VR 2 schedule. The pattern of their results tended to agree with the data obtained in animal experiments. Using mentally deficient children, candy as reinforcement, and a variety of schedules, Orlando and Bijou (1960) found the behaviors generated by their selected schedules were quite similar to those obtained with experimental animals. Verplanck (1956) presents data suggesting that normal college students act very much like experimental animals when subjected to various scheduling manipulations (see also Davidson & Grayson Osborne, 1974; Karen, 1974). Thus, there is substantial evidence for the notion that we are learning something about humans when we manipulate schedules of reinforcement with animals. Of course, there are exceptions to this tidy correspondence between animal and human behavior. In investigating human choice behavior, for example, Schmitt (1974) has been led to suggest that humans and animals differ quite markedly in terms of their responses to variations in rate of reinforcement.

Does the partial-reinforcement extinction effect appear with humans as well as with experimental animals? The answer is that the available results are inconclusive. On the positive side, we have reports that resistance to extinction is greater following partial reinforcement when the subjects are children and the responses are such things as pressing down the nose of a clown and placing rubber balls in holes (Bijou, 1957a, 1957b). Furthermore, Brackbill (1958) found learned smiling responses in infants to be more resistant to extinction following partial reinforcement (see also Nation & Massad, 1978). But others (see Keppel, Zavortink, & Shiff, 1967) have failed to find PREE in human situations. In addition, Pittenger and Pavlik (1989) argue that PREE may be limited to certain specific experimental designs when humans serve as subjects.

In summary, it can be argued that the similarities between human and animal responses to schedule manipulations outweigh the differences. In view of the complex unpredictability on the part of humans it is not surprising that our animal and human data do not always look alike. Failures to find similarities between animal and human behavior may not result from any basic differences in the underlying mechanisms of learning. They may stem from our ignorance of the multiple interests and purposes of the complex human.

DELAY OF REINFORCEMENT

The investigation of *delay of reinforcement* began decades ago (see Skinner, 1938; Wolfe, 1934) and continues today (see Thomas, Lieberman, McIntosh, & Ronaldson, 1983; Urcuioli & Kasprow, 1988). If the time between a response and the subsequent delivery of the reinforcement is increased, learning tends to be inhibited. If a rat is forced to wait for its reward after each lever press, for example, it will learn the response much less quickly than if it were reinforced immediately after each response. If children are rewarded immediately after picking up their toys, they will be more likely to learn than if they were forced to wait until the end of the week for their reward. If the reward is delayed too long, learning may not occur at all.

The relationship between delay of reinforcement and learning tends to assume a characteristic form. Figure 6.6 contains several stylized *delay-of-reinforcement gradients*. Two things should be noted about these gradients. First, performance drops off rapidly as the delay increases. Second, even though it does drop off, *some* performance gains do occur even under conditions of delayed reinforcement. Most of the experimental work has involved delays from several seconds to several minutes. Under some conditions delays of a few seconds can eliminate learning, whereas under other conditions long delays have little effect on performance. Let us now consider why these differential effects appear.

The Role of Secondary Reinforcers

Over the years a little story has developed concerning delay-of-reinforcement effects. In a very early experiment Watson (1917) trained rats to dig down through sawdust to reach a cup containing food. Half of the animals were permitted to consume the reward immediately. The other half were required to wait for 30 seconds before eating the food. Surprisingly, Watson found no differences between the two groups in terms of their digging performance. Delaying the reinforcement for 30 seconds did not hinder learning in the slightest. One obvious reason for this result has to do with the fact that the delayed animals waited in the vicinity of the food cup. They could smell the food and see the cup, which they associated with the reward. In other words, the presentation of the cues that the animal associated with food (smell, sight) probably reinforced the digging response immediately.

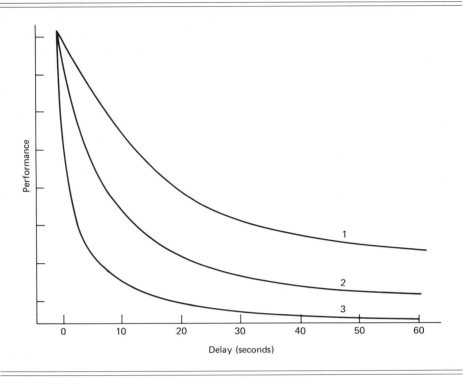

Figure 6.6 Some hypothetical delay-of-reinforcement gradients.

These cues (smell, sight of cup) that the animal associated with the primary reinforcer (food) are called *secondary reinforcers*. A secondary reinforcer is *a neutral stimulus that, through constant association with primary reinforcers, acquires reinforcing properties itself.* For example, money is a secondary reinforcer. Green rectangles of paper are, in and of themselves, of little value to us. And yet many of us will work madly to obtain them. The green paper has acquired reinforcing properties because it has been associated or paired with more primary reinforcers (food, warmth, drink, comfort, and the like).

We will consider secondary reinforcers in detail in a later section. For now it is sufficient to understand that secondary reinforcers have been heavily implicated in delay-of-reinforcement effects. Over the years a hypothesis concerning delays and secondary reinforcers has emerged. Some psychologists argue that immediate reinforcement is necessary for learning to occur. If an experiment demonstrates a performance increase when primary reinforcers are delayed, then that performance increase must result from the immediate, and not delayed, delivery of secondary reinforcers.

This hypothesis is an interesting one, and to test it we could try to eliminate potential secondary reinforcers from our experiments with delaying reinforcement. Performance under conditions of delay should then be reduced. With successive eliminations of additional secondary reinforcers we should note a continuing drop in our gradient, such as the shift from gradient 1 to 3 in Figure 6.6.

Just such an experimental strategy has developed in the literature. A well-known group of studies (for example, Grice, 1948; Perin, 1943; Perkins, 1947) was concerned with the removal of contaminating secondary reinforcers in delay-of-reinforcement experiments. An example of their strategy will suffice. Wolfe (1934) trained rats to choose one arm (left or right) in a T maze. Once the rats were released from the starting box, they were allowed to proceed to the choice point and to turn and move in the direction of the goal box. But before reaching the goal box the animals were held in a delay chamber for varying amounts of time. Then they were released and allowed to proceed to the end of the arm. Wolfe found that rats could be delayed as long as 20 minutes and still learn the response. Perkins (1947) called attention to a very important aspect of this situation. When the rat turns in the correct direction, it is always held in a very distinctive delay box. The box might not seem distinctive to us, but to a confined rat the environment must surely be so. It might contain a paint smudge here, a unique crack there, or perhaps slight variations in texture. It is this distinctive delay box that is always followed by reward. Hence, the delay box must become a secondary reinforcer. Every time the animal chooses the correct arm and is held in the distinctive delay box, it is reinforced immediately by the presence of the box. If it chooses the incorrect arm, it is confined in another distinctive delay box (different paint smudges, smell, and so on). This chamber is never associated with or followed by a reward. Hence, it does not become a secondary reinforcer.

To remove the distinctive delay box as a source of secondary reinforcement Perkins (1947) merely switched delay boxes on successive trials. Thus, neither box was consistently associated with either reward or absence of reward. Under these conditions the gradient fell. Less learning was observed under conditions of delay when the secondary reinforcer was removed.

Additional sources of secondary reinforcement (for example, proprioceptive cues, or "feelings," associated with making a left or a right turn) were eliminated in subsequent experiments. As each successive source of secondary reinforcement was removed, the gradient fell an additional step. Hence, for many (see Spence, 1947) it has been assumed that learning might not occur at all in the absence of some kind of immediate reinforcement. According to this position, either primary or secondary reinforcement must occur immediately after the occurrence of the response. But the issue has yet to be resolved to everyone's satisfaction. More recent experimentation has suggested that some learning may, after all, occur in the absence of any immediate reinforcement (Lett, 1973; Lieberman, McIntosh, & Thomas, 1979; Urcuioli & Kasprow, 1988). These results have been obtained in both aversive-conditioning and T-maze situations.

Thus, it is really too early to tell where this story will end. The most reasonable position to take is that secondary reinforcers are often involved in delay-of-reinforcement experiments and that their removal does reduce learning under conditions of delayed primary reinforcement. Nevertheless, there may well be situations in which learning can occur when reinforcement is truly delayed.

Humans and Delay of Reinforcement

Given that the situation is confusing with respect to animal studies, what can we possibly hope to say about human learning and delay of reinforcement? One thing can be said with some certainty: If secondary reinforcers are involved in animal experiments, they are enormously involved in human delay situations. Humans are capable of performing very well under conditions of extreme delay. Presumably many of the readers of this text are plowing on without the hope of anything remotely resembling a primary reward in the foreseeable future. And yet they keep after it, slogging away, presumably being maintained by the presence of all sorts of secondary reinforcers (such as congratulating themselves on having beaten down one more chapter). Any sort of long-range human learning endeavor (for example, pursuit of career goals) is probably maintained through the involvement of secondary reinforcers.

Experimental work supports the notion that reinforcement delays (for example, delaying feedback on performance) are not particularly effective in reducing human learning (Bilodeau, 1966; Brackbill, Adams, & Reaney, 1967). Many studies show that humans are capable of learning in spite of long delays.

What it may come down to is that humans are generally better able to bridge time gaps than animals. For example, language allows us to reinforce ourselves on the completion of any given response even though the primary reward may be delayed. We can think ahead, see the relationship between our current action and our ultimate goal, and thereby reinforce ourselves "ahead of time."

AMOUNT OF REINFORCEMENT

What is the relationship between *amount* of reinforcement and performance level? Will a rat's running speed vary as a function of the amount of food it is given at the end of the runway? Will children do better in school if they receive more praise from the teacher? These are the kinds of questions that prompt a consideration of the relationship between amount of reward and performance.

The answers we have been able to obtain in the laboratory are not as clear cut as we would like them to be. Studying the effects of variations in the amount of reward has been difficult over the years. In a very general, oversimplified way we can suggest that performance increases as the amount of reward increases (see Gallistel, 1978; Osborne, 1978). The greater the amount of reward, the better is the performance. Beyond a certain point further increases in the magnitude of the goal may fail to result in further increases in performance.

Components of the Situation

Two early and widely quoted studies relating performance to amount of reward were done by Crespi (1942) and Zeaman (1949). Zeaman had rats run down a 3-foot runway to a goal box. Different groups of rats received different amounts of cheese (.05, .2, .4, .6, .8, 1.6, or 2.4 grams) once they reached the goal box. Zeaman found that the latency of the running response (time required to leave the start box) decreased as the magnitude of the reward increased. These and similar studies led to the general notion that performance increases as the amount of reward increases (see Wielkiewicz, 1979). But as psychologists continued their examination of the amount-of-reward variable, they began to realize that it is quite a complicated problem and that there are at least three and perhaps four distinct components to the amount-of-reward situation.

First, one must consider the *mass* or *volume of the reinforcer* (for example, grams of food ingested or volume of water consumed). Second, the *amount of consuming activity* the animal engages in may be important (number of licks, pecks, or swallows). Third, one must consider the *quality* as well as the quantity of the reward (for example, sweet versus neutral flavor). Two or more of these factors are often confounded in a given experimental situation. If we merely vary the number of pieces of corn that we give to pigeons, for example, we have confounded volume of food with amount of consuming activity (one peck per kernel).

Much of the work in this area has been designed to tease out the independent effects of these various components. For example, one way to separate the consuming component from the ingested-volume component is to sever surgically the animal's esophagus. In this way liquids can be introduced directly into the animal's stomach, thereby eliminating the potentially confounding effects of consuming activities. Similarly, liquids can be consumed only to emerge from the opening in the esophagus, thereby allowing the measurement of the effects of consuming activity independent of the effects of ingested volume (Mook, 1963). Another way to study the independent effects of consuming behavior is to divide a given amount of reward into varying numbers of parts. Thus, consuming activity (number of pecks or licks) can vary even though the total volume of ingested material is constant (Hall & Kling, 1960; Hulse, 1960). The quality-versus-quantity issue can be examined by simultaneously varying the volume of the reward (small, medium, large) and the quality of the reward (citric, basic, saccharin) (Collier, 1962). Some researchers have attempted to explore the complicated effects of variations in quantity and quality of reward in human subjects (for example, Weiner, 1966).

In general, it can be said that all three components (quantity, quality, and consuming activity) appear to contribute to the reinforcing effect in a positive fashion. At present it is not possible to determine which of the three components is the most influential. In fact, a *fourth* component may be involved. In this component, the *number of food units* differs in the reward presented to the animal. Capaldi, Miller, and Alptekin (1989) rewarded rats with either a single 300-mg pellet or with four 75-mg pellets. They found that rats developed a preference for the four 75-mg alternative, in spite of the fact that the total amount of reward was the same in both conditions (300 mg). At first glance this multiple-unit factor might seem the same as the amount-of-consumatory-activity factor described above. But the two are not identical, simply because the amount of consumatory behavior might be the same, or roughly so, in the four-unit and the one-unit conditions.

Insects and Amount of Reward

We now know that magnitude of reward is important for vertebrate species such as rats, pigeons, and humans. But what about invertebrates such as insects? Do they respond to variations in amount of reward the same way we do, or is their nature so different from ours that the relationship between their performance and amount of reward is unique? Buchanan and Bitterman (1988) present evidence that suggests that humans are not so different from the insects in this respect. They trained honeybees to come to a target that was either an orange spot covered with a drop of strong sucrose solution or a blue spot covered with a drop of weak sucrose solution. After 32 training trials with each target the sucrose was removed from the water even though the colors remained. In other words, the bees were put on an extinction schedule. As you can see in Figure 6.7 the tendency to continue responding

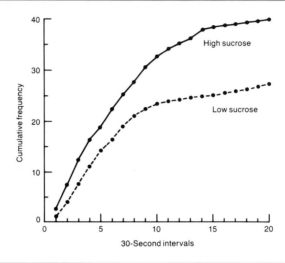

Figure 6.7 Mean cumulative responses during extinction to the high-sucrose target and the low-sucrose target after equal training with each target. (From Buchanan, G. M., and Bitterman, M. E. Learning in honeybees as a function of amount and frequency of reward. *Animal Learning and Behavior*, 1988, 16, 247–288. Fig. 1, p. 249. Reprinted by permission of Psychonomic Society, Inc.)

to the strong-solution target was more persistent than the tendency to respond to the weak-solution target. Bees, just like humans, will work harder and respond longer for larger amounts of reward.

Reinforcement Contrast

An interesting phenomenon has been discovered within the context of studying amount of reward. Suppose that you have a summer job picking fruit. You are paid 25¢ for each basket you fill. For three weeks you work furiously. Then the boss informs you that the pay rate has been reduced to 12.5¢ a basket. You may well be tempted to place your basket gracefully over his head and walk off the job. At the very least your performance will go down. The reinforcement contrast effect refers to the fact that it may drop *below* the level at which you would have performed if you had been receiving 12.5¢ right from the beginning. This is a negative contrast effect, and it reflects your "depression." Temporarily, you do not even pick at the rate you would have maintained had you been receiving the lower pay rate all along. A positive contrast effect might be demonstrated if your pay rate were suddenly shifted upward, say, to 37.5¢ a basket. You would be elated, and your performance might temporarily jump *beyond* the level at which it would have been if you had been receiving 37.5¢ all along (Figure 6.8).

These effects have been demonstrated in the laboratory. They were originally observed and described by Crespi (1942) and Zeaman (1949). Zeaman trained rats to move down runways for either small or large rewards. The amounts were then suddenly shifted. His data appeared to reveal both positive and negative contrast effects. Later, Collier and Marx (1959) first reinforced rats with one of three con-

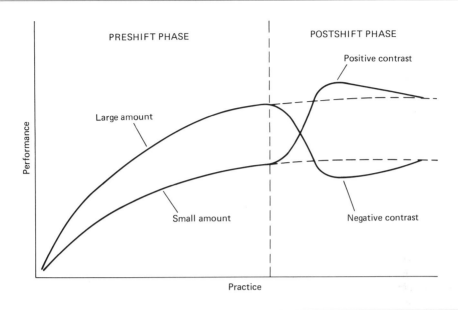

Figure 6.8 Idealized positive and negative reinforcement contrast effects. During the preshift phase, one group receives a large amount of reinforcement, whereas the other receives a small amount. The amounts given to the two groups are then reversed during the postshift phase, yielding the contrast effects.

centrations of sucrose solution. All three groups were then trained to lever-press for the middle concentration. Rats that were initially reinforced with the lower concentration and then shifted to the middle concentration produced higher response rates than did the rats trained throughout on the middle concentration (positive contrast). Rats initially trained on the high concentration and shifted to the middle concentration displayed lever-pressing rates *below* those displayed by the rats trained on the middle concentration throughout (negative contrast).

Although the negative-reinforcement contrast effect stands as a viable concept in the field (Papini, Mustaca, & Bitterman, 1988), researchers have questioned the validity of the positive contrast effect. Beginning with Spence (1956) and continuing into later years (Dunham & Kilps, 1969; Hulse, 1973), a number of investigators failed to obtain a positive effect or have discredited apparent positive effects. For example, Hulse (1973) first rewarded rats using a random arrangement of 1 and 10 pellets. Half of the rats then learned to lever-press for 1 pellet, whereas the remaining half learned the same response for 10 pellets. When rats learned to lever-press for 1 pellet following the mixed condition, they learned more slowly than if they had received initial learning with just 1 pellet. But in contrast to earlier reports the corresponding positive effect was not obtained. That is, rats that were shifted to 10 pellets did not exceed the performance level that they would have attained had they been trained on 10 pellets throughout. Whether this and similar failures to find the positive contrast effect result from a true lack of the effect or to methodological difficulties remains to be seen (see also Rabiner, Kling, & Spraguer, 1988).

Impulsive Behavior

We have considered in depth two of the important parameters of reinforcement, namely amount and delay of reinforcement. Although we have discussed them separately, they are not necessarily unrelated. An interesting example of the inter-action of these two factors has to do with *impulsive behavior*. We have all behaved impulsively at one time or another. If a child is told she can either have one piece of candy now or two later the child may opt for the smaller but more immediate gain. Such situations involve the interaction of delay and amount of reward. In the choice between larger but more delayed and smaller but more immediately re-ceived reward, we sometimes appear to be impulsive rather than self-controlled.

Logue, Chavarro, Rachlin, and Reeder (1988) have taken the issue of impulsivity into the laboratory. They gave pigeons multiple choices between large delayed and small immediate rewards. The pigeons consistently acted in an impulsive manner; they chose the smaller, less delayed, rewards just as we often do. Thus, in at least these experimental conditions, the delay factor seems to be more important than the amount factor.

SECONDARY REINFORCEMENT

As we have noted, a *secondary reinforcer* is a neutral stimulus that has, through repeated associations with a primary reinforcer, acquired reinforcing properties. In a typical animal experiment rats might first be trained to run down a straight alley to a black goal box containing food. Once the running response was well estab-lished, the animals would be removed from the alley and placed in a T maze. One arm of the T maze would be black, and the other would be white. No food would ever be presented in the T maze. The rat would be allowed to run from the starting box and choose one of the arms. In this situation rats typically learn to choose the black arm even though food is never presented. Through association with the food the black color has become a secondary reinforcer, and it reinforces the turning response in the T maze.

Psychologists have devised a number of procedures for detecting the existence and strength of secondary reinforcers. The method just described is called a *choice test*. The animal is allowed to choose between the secondary reinforcer and some neutral stimulus configuration. In a typical *extinction test*, the animal may first be trained to obtain food by bar pressing. Each time the bar is pressed, the releasing mechanism yields a distinctive clicking sound. This sound becomes a secondary reinforcer. Following initial training, extinction is carried out under two condi-tions. In one, the mechanism is adjusted so that the bar press yields the clicking sound but no food. In the other, a bar press produces neither the click nor the food. In this situation resistance to extinction tends to be greater when the bar press pro-duces the click, demonstrating that the click does, in fact, maintain the response.

Parameters

Intuitively, it seems possible that a neutral stimulus will become a stronger second-ary reinforcer if it is paired with a larger *amount of primary reward*. A $5 bill is of greater value than a $1 bill, presumably because it is associated with more food, comfort, excitement, and so on. The experimental data indicate that, if a subject learns to associate one particular stimulus with a large amount of reward and another distinct stimulus with a smaller amount, then the stimulus associated with the larger amount will become a stronger reinforcer (Fantino & Logan, 1979; Reynolds, Pavlik, & Goldstein, 1964). This finding supports our intuitive notion.

It also seems reasonable to assume that the strength of a secondary reinforcer will increase as the *number of times it is paired with the primary reinforcer* increases. The available data (for example, Bersh, 1951; Fantino & Herrnstein, 1968; Miles, 1956) suggest that this is the case, although the effect seems to be less than overwhelming. The strength of a secondary reinforcer increases only slightly as the number of pairings with the primary reinforcer increases.

A number of investigators have been concerned with the relationship between *duration of deprivation*, or *drive level*, and the strength of secondary reinforcers. Interestingly, the conclusion we can draw from the results of a sizable amount of experimentation is that this variable is not particularly important in determining the strength of a secondary reinforcer. Secondary reinforcers acquired under conditions of high drive are no stronger than secondary reinforcers acquired under conditions of low drive (see Brown, 1956; Hall, 1951).

Finally, the influences of *schedules of reinforcement* on the strength and durability of secondary reinforcers have been examined. Two conclusions can be reached. First, *intermittent* pairing of the primary reinforcer with the secondary reinforcer seems to result in a stronger secondary-reinforcement effect (Armus & Garlich, 1961; Kendall, 1974). It is as if a $5 bill will become more valuable, and a stronger secondary reinforcer, if it is not always associated with primary rewards. Second, secondary reinforcers become even stronger if the intermittent presentation of a primary reward described above is *variable* (Davison, 1972; Hursh & Fantino, 1973). That is, if a primary reward is presented in a fixed manner, the strength of a secondary reinforcer will be less than that obtained if the primary reward is presented in a variable manner. A $5 bill will become more valuable if it is associated with a primary reward in some variable, intermittent pattern.

Some Theoretical Issues

IS CLASSICAL CONDITIONING INVOLVED?   Many psychologists feel that secondary reinforcers are established through a process of classical conditioning. If a neutral stimulus is repeatedly paired with a primary reward(s), then the animal's reaction to the primary reward becomes classically conditioned to the neutral stimulus.

This mechanism may not be all there is to the establishment of secondary reinforcers; there are other theories (see Fantino, 1977; Rachlin, 1976). And yet the classical-conditioning interpretation does receive some support in the literature. Bersh (1951) gave rats a pellet of food 0, .5, 2, 4, or 10 seconds after the onset of a light (see Figure 6.9). Following this phase all rats bar-pressed for the light alone. Bersh found that the strength of the secondary reinforcer was strongest when the CS–UCS interval (time between light and pellet) was approximately .5 of a second. Longer and shorter intervals resulted in weaker secondary reinforcers. The superiority of the .5-second interval corresponds with the general effectiveness of the .5-second CS–UCS interval in many classical-conditioning situations.

SECONDARY REINFORCERS AS CARRIERS OF INFORMATION.   Egger and Miller (1962, 1963) came up with the interesting notion that merely pairing a neutral stimulus with a primary reward is not sufficient for the neutral stimulus to become a powerful secondary reinforcer. To become powerful the neutral stimulus must

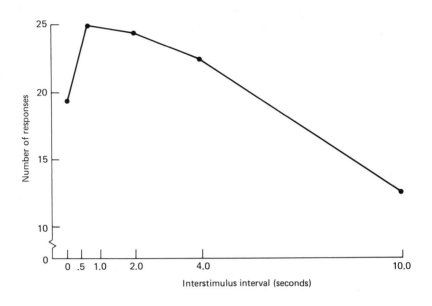

Figure 6.9 Secondary reinforcer strength as a function of the CS–UCS interval. (Adapted from Bersh, P. J. The influence of two variables upon the establishment of a secondary reinforcer for operant responses. *Journal of Experimental Psychology*, 1951, *41*, 62–73. Fig. 1, p. 66. Copyright 1951 by the American Psychological Association. Reprinted by permission.)

convey information about the forthcoming appearance of the primary reinforcer. If the neutral stimulus provides the animal with no additional information about the upcoming primary reward, then it will be a less effective secondary reinforcer. This hypothesis is an extention of an earlier one, sometimes called the discrimination hypothesis (Marx & Knarr, 1963; Schoenfeld, Antonitis, & Bersh, 1950).

In one condition of their 1962 experiment Egger and Miller presented two neutral stimuli (light and tone) before the presentation of food. One of the stimuli (say, the light) was switched on first. One-half second later the tone began. Both stimuli would then remain on for 1.5 seconds, at which time the food was presented. In this situation the light informed the animal that food was forthcoming. The subsequent beginning of the tone, .5 of a second later, provided the animal with little or no new information (it already knew that the food was coming). In agreement with the hypothesis the light became a much stronger secondary reinforcer than the tone.

The notion that the mere pairing of a neutral stimulus and a primary reward will result in the development of a secondary reinforcer is further weakened by the recent information interpretations of classical conditioning. You will recall from Chapter 2 that Rescorla and Wagner (1972) have shown that classical conditioning will not occur if the UCS is as likely to occur in the *absence* of the CS as it is to occur in the presence of the CS. Mere pairing provides only a weak source of conditioning, not only in typical classical-conditioning situations but also in those involving the establishment of a secondary reinforcer (Rose & Fantino, 1978; Squires, Norborg, & Fantino, 1975). The CS must provide information about the probability of the forthcoming UCS if that CS is to become effective.

DO SECONDARY REINFORCERS HAVE MOTIVATING PROPERTIES?   In addition to their reinforcing properties secondary reinforcers may have motivating properties. For example, a $5 bill may not only be a reward; it may also activate us, motivate us, or urge us toward action. If you were walking calmly down the street and suddenly spied a $5 bill on the sidewalk, your behavior would probably change rapidly, taking on an extremely motivated quality; the sight of the bill would urge you to action. Although this is an old issue (see Dinsmoor, 1950), Williams (1970) has provided some evidence that supports the notion that secondary reinforcers motivate as well as reinforce. Rats were trained to run down an alley for food. Presentation of the food was accompanied by a tone (the secondary reinforcer). During testing all animals were confined in the starting box for 20 seconds. During this delay the tone was either not sounded or was sounded for an interval of .5, 5, or 15 seconds. The tone was terminated by the opening of the door. Williams found that, the longer the animals were subjected to the tone in the starting box, the faster they left the box once the door was open. The tone seemed to have energized, or motivated, the animals.

SECONDARY REINFORCERS AS UNDETECTED PRIMARY REINFORCERS.   A sneaking suspicion that creeps into secondary-reinforcement experiments is that some supposedly neutral stimuli may actually be primary reinforcers and, hence, not neutral at all. An enormous body of literature documents the fact that humans and other animals will respond to and seek out novel and changing stimuli. For example, animals will easily respond for nothing more than a change in illumination (Glow & Winefield, 1978; McCall, 1966). Human infants as young as three months can be trained to make a variety of responses when rewarded with various visual and auditory stimuli (Sisqueland, 1970). Such "neutral" stimuli as light and sound onset and offset, changed visual patterns, novel odors, and the opportunity to explore visually the surrounding environment can be shown to have reinforcing properties (Berlyne, 1969; Butler, 1965; Fowler, 1965). Many of these secondary-reinforcement experiments employ such "neutral" stimuli. Adequate controls are needed to ensure that they are, in fact, neutral and not reinforcing in and of themselves. In choosing neutral stimuli experimenters must be aware of this type of possible confounding.

Tokens

It almost goes without saying that secondary reinforcers operate in the human realm. They may be very concrete or quite abstract. As we learned in Chapter 2, tokens can serve as secondary reinforcers. Nelson and Cone (1979) provide a good example of the power of tokens as secondary reinforcers in the treatment of psychiatric inpatients. They isolated eight behaviors and first observed the frequency with which these behaviors occurred without any special attention given to them. The results of these initial observations are the baseline data in Figure 6.10. Then

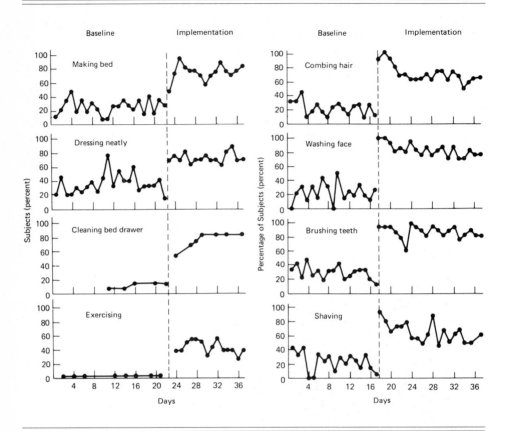

Figure 6.10 Tokens serve as secondary reinforcers in a token economy for psychiatric inpatients. During baseline periods no tokens were distributed. During implementation periods the desired behaviors earned tokens. (Adapted from Nelson, G. L., and Cone, J. D. Multiple-baseline analysis of a token economy for psychiatric inpatients. *Journal of Applied Behavior Analysis*, 1979, 12, 255–271. Figs. 1 and 2, pp. 264–265.)

they began to reward these behaviors with tokens. Each time one of the behaviors was observed, the patient received a token that could later be exchanged for goods and supplies at the hospital store. As the implementation data in Figure 6.10 indicate, token, or secondary, reinforcement was effective in increasing all eight desired behaviors in this group of patients.

Tokens can be used effectively with animals, too. In some very early work Wolfe (1936) and others first trained chimpanzees to deposit tokens in order to receive grapes as rewards (see Figure 6.11). They then observed that the chimps would learn *new* responses when they were reinforced with nothing more than a token. The tokens had become "chimp money." As long as they were eventually allowed to trade in the tokens for food the chimps would quickly learn new responses for token rewards. When housed with other chimps, the animals would sometimes hoard, beg for, and even steal tokens.

Figure 6.11 Token Reinforcement. A chimp is being trained to deposit tokens to produce food reinforcement. Following this training the chimp will then learn new responses when rewarded with a token. The tokens will have become secondary reinforcers. (Courtesy of Yerkes Regional Primate Research Center, Emory University.)

Social Reinforcers

On a less physical level Skinner (1953) has suggested that *social reinforcers* such as attention, approval, and affection may actually be secondary reinforcers. For example, such verbal gestures as "fine," "good," "excellent," and so on may represent

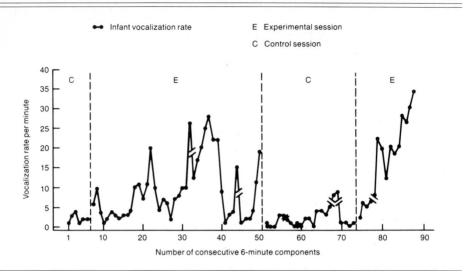

Figure 6.12 Vocalization rate as a function of social reward in a Down syndrome child. Note that the vocalization rate was higher during experimental sessions. (From Poulson, C. L. Operant conditioning of vocalization rate of infants with Down syndrome. *American Journal on Mental Retardation*, 1988, *93*, 57–63. Fig. 3, p. 60.)

secondary reinforcers. Poulson (1988) has provided a good example of the power of social rewards. Her subjects were infants with Down syndrome, a form of mental retardation in which up to 95% of the individuals suffer from some degree of speech disorder. Poulson had the parents of Down syndrome infants reward articulations with various forms of social reinforcement, such as making eye contact, touching, and encouraging the infant to vocalize. There were two conditions in the study. In the experimental sessions parents socially rewarded the infant only when it made verbalizations. In the control sessions the same amount of social reward was presented but *not* after vocalizations. As you can see in Figure 6.12 vocalization was significantly higher in the experimental periods than in the control periods.

THEORIES OF REINFORCEMENT

Thus far we have been concerned with observable reinforcement effects resulting from the manipulation of a number of critical independent variables. We now turn to a consideration of some of the analytical thinking that psychologists have done with respect to the reinforcement issue. Why do reinforcers reinforce? What are some of the major theoretical interpretations of reinforcement? We shall review a few of the more important conceptions, drawing on a taxonomy suggested by Tapp (1969).

Drive-Reduction Theory

Drive-reduction theory, as exemplified by Hull's system, has already been discussed. According to this approach, reinforcement is equivalent to drive reduction. An animal is in a high drive state if it is experiencing some homeostatic imbalance, some internal physiological need, or some type of strong unpleasant stimulation. If the animal makes a response that reduces the noxious stimulation caused by these sorts of factors, then that response is strengthened. Reinforcement refers to the diminution of noxious drive stimuli. Animals will acquire responses that have been instrumental in reducing drive stimuli (see Houston, 1985).

The drive-reduction conception appears to be adequate when one considers learning related to basic biological drives such as hunger and thirst. When deprived of food or liquid, the animal experiences a state of tension. Responses that reduce these tension states are learned. If the basic biological drives were all that we had to consider, then the drive-reduction conception would seem to be a comprehensive theory. The difficulty lies in the fact that in the past 40 years we have seen an increase in research concerned with rewards that do not reduce any known, or apparent, tissue need. Hundreds of studies have shown that humans and other animals will seek novel, changing, and complex stimuli and that the receipt of these stimuli will be reinforcing. For example, Butler (1953) has shown that monkeys will learn visual discriminations for nothing more than the opportunity to look about a typical laboratory for a few moments. What noxious biological drive state is reduced by looking about a laboratory? Opponents of the drive conception contend that all sorts of curiosity and exploratory behaviors cannot be related to any *known* drive state.

The drive-reduction theoreticians respond bravely by postulating *new* drives to account for these sensory-seeking behaviors. For example, Montgomery (1955) and others have spoken of an exploratory drive that parallels the more basic drives. Fowler (1965) and others have proposed a boredom drive to account for certain sensory-seeking behaviors. Harlow (1953) has postulated a manipulation drive. An activity drive has been suggested by several authors (see Cofer & Appley, 1964). These are but some of the new drives proposed; the list grows longer.

It is too early to determine whether the postulation of these drives is justified. But strong criticism has been directed toward the business of inventing new drives every time a new stimulus is found to be reinforcing. Critics of the drive-reduction position stipulate that there must be a simpler way to account for these diverse behaviors. To fit them all into the drive-reduction mold requires, for some, too much bending and tailoring. They feel that the drive reductionists are stretching their point. The drive-reduction notion might account for a good deal of behavior, but why must it account for all reinforcing events? Perhaps there are other reinforcement mechanisms that can supplement, and not necessarily replace, the drive-reduction conception.

Optimal-Arousal-Level Theories

One alternative to the drive-reduction approach can be labeled the optimal-arousal-level conception. A number of psychologists (for example, Berlyne, 1969; Fiske & Maddi, 1961; Routtenberg, 1968) have noted that reinforcement does not always seem to involve a *reduction* in stimulation, as drive-reduction position implies. Instead, it would appear that *increases* in tension, arousal, or stimulation sometimes seem to be reinforcing. Accordingly, optimal-arousal-level theoreticians argue that the animal has some *preferred level* of arousal it seeks to maintain. On the one hand, when arousal becomes too great, any response that reduces arousal will be reinforced. When we are hungry, responses that are instrumental in reducing the hunger will be reinforced. When we have had enough of a noisy party, escape from that party will be a reinforcing event. On the other hand, if arousal falls *below* a certain level, then any response that *increases* the arousal level will be reinforced. For instance, if you had been sitting around your apartment for days with nothing to do, you would probably engage in behavior that would increase your level of arousal or stimulation. Any movement toward the optimal level, whether an increase or decrease, would be reinforcing.

This type of theory is appealing, because it fits the fact that animals sometimes seek to increase, and sometimes to decrease, stimulation. Its principal shortcoming lies in the fact that it is difficult to quantify, or define, exactly what is meant by arousal. The arousal concept seems similar to the drive concept in that each refers to a state of tension. The principal difference between them is that drive reductionism argues that the animal strives to attain a zero drive level, whereas the optimal-level theory argues that the animal attempts to maintain some preferred level of arousal greater than zero.

Stimulus Theories

The drive-reduction and optimal-arousal-level theories emphasize some internal state that the animal attempts to change or maintain. A number of theories differ from these two in that they focus on the impact of *external stimuli* rather than on the internal state of the organism. There are several varieties. Some of them are quite distinct, whereas others overlap with one another or with the conceptions just outlined. Here are three examples.

STIMULUS–CHANGE THEORIES.   McCall (1966) has argued that *changes in level of stimulation* will be reinforcing. Up to a point, the greater the change, the greater is the reinforcing effect. McCall has been able to demonstrate that rats will work to obtain changes in level of illumination. The emphasis here is on a change in *quantity* rather than in *quality*. Although perhaps somewhat limited, the theory does have heuristic value. It is easy for us to imagine ourselves acting in a manner that will bring about stimulus change. Rats may appreciate a little social change too. Davis and Perusse (1988) claim to have successfully rewarded them by saying "Good girl" and "Way to go" while handling the animals for five seconds.

PREFERRED–LEVEL THEORIES.   In contrast to McCall's theory, Lockhard (1966) suggests that the animal seeks a *preferred level of stimulation* rather than a simple change in stimulation. Any change that is in the direction of the preferred level will be reinforcing. Any change that is away from the preferred level will be punishing. The similarity between this theory and the optimal-arousal-level theories is obvious. The primary difference between them is that one focuses on internal states, whereas the other attends to external stimulation.

STIMULUS–QUALITY THEORIES.   Whereas the stimulus-change and the preferred-level theories focus on the *amount* of stimulation, Pfaffmann (1969), P. T. Young (1966), Sheffield (1966), and others have directed their attention toward the *quality* of the stimulus. In general, their theories are concerned with the fact that certain stimuli (for example, sweet ones) are genetically preferred. The presentation of these stimuli is assumed to be reinforcing in some predetermined fashion, regardless of the arousal state of the animal. Thus, an animal will work to obtain a saccharin solution, even though the solution has no nutritional value. The animal merely likes the flavor and will work for it (see Mehiel & Bolles, 1988).

Response Theories

THE PREMACK PRINCIPLE.   Response theories of reinforcement emphasize the fact that most reinforcing events involve some associated consummatory response (for example, chewing, manipulating, drinking, swallowing, copulating). The making of the response itself may be an important part of the reinforcing event. The emphasis in these theories is on the rewarding properties of consummatory responses. For example, we all like to chew food and to swallow it. These acts can be reinforcing. Consummatory theories do not focus on any tension-reducing events.

Although consummatory theories have taken several forms (for example, Glickman & Schiff, 1967; Sheffield, 1966), one of the more interesting variations is that proposed by Premack (1965, 1971). According to Premack, one response can be used to reinforce another. Given two responses, one of which is more likely to occur than the other, the more likely one can reinforce the occurrence of the less likely one. For example, Premack (1959) found that, if children would rather eat candy than play a game, it is possible to increase their game playing by reinforcing it with candy eating. Similarly, if children prefer to play a game, their candy-eating behavior can be increased by reinforcing it with game playing. Parents often hear their children saying things like "I'll play checkers with you if you'll play cards with me." (What appears to be a marvelous example of cooperation may then, of course, be scuttled by the impossible question: Which game is to be played first?)

RESPONSE–DEPRIVATION HYPOTHESIS.   Timberlake and Allison (1974) have outlined another related interpretation of reinforcement (see also Timberlake, 1980). Quite simply, if we deprive an organism of the opportunity to make a response as often as it normally does, that response will become a reinforcer. Suppose a young child spends a lot of time riding his bike. One day his mother says, "Jimmy if you pick up your toys, I'll let you ride your bike." Jimmy may think, "No. I get to ride all the time anyway." Bike riding will not be reinforcing. But suppose that before making her offer the mother first deprives Jimmy of the opportunity to ride for two days. Then, when she says he can ride if he picks up his toys, he will jump to the task. The response of bike riding has become reinforcing because Jimmy has been deprived of the activity.

Which Theory Is Correct?

A number of investigators have discovered that a rat, given the choice between eating free, available food or pressing a bar to receive food, will often choose to "work" for its food (see Osborne [1977] for a review). The rat will press the bar even though it does not need to because "free food" is always available.

Although the effect itself is intriguing, it is also an instructive example. It can help us see how the many theories of reinforcement that we have been discussing can all interpret the same set of data. For example, when using stimulus theories one has no trouble interpreting the free-food effect. One merely argues that the rat presses the bar because it is seeking stimulus change, or some preferred level of stimulation, or some specific quality of stimulation. In optimal-arousal-level terms it would be argued that bar pressing is maintained because it stirs things up a bit and moves the animal into its preferred level of arousal. Response theorists would argue that the "consumption" of bar-press responses is reinforcing. And drive theorists would suggest that bar pressing reduces an activity drive.

The problem is evident. If all the theories can predict the same events, it is difficult to choose among them. What we must await are a number of accurate predictions that can be made only on the basis of one of the theories. Then we shall know that we have the most accurate theory.

SUMMARY

1. Beyond simple operational notations there is very little agreement among psychologists concerning the nature of reinforcers. It is clear that the important parameters of reinforcement include *schedules, amount,* and *delay* of reinforcement.

2. *Continuous reinforcement* (CRF) refers to situations in which every response is reinforced.

3. In a *fixed-interval* schedule the animal is reinforced for the first response that occurs after the end of a given time interval. Long pauses that follow reinforcement in the FI schedule produce a characteristic "scalloping" effect in cumulative response records.

4. In *variable-interval* (VI) schedules the animal is forced to wait for varying amounts of time before receiving reinforcement. The VI schedule produces steady responding. The longer the average interval, the slower the responding.

5. In the *fixed-ratio* (FR) schedule the animal must make a certain number of responses before it is rewarded. The FR schedule yields high rates of responding and a mild postreinforcement pause. The higher the ratio, the longer is the postreinforcement pause.

6. In the *variable-ratio* (VR) schedule the number of required responses varies. This schedule also produces high response rates but normally does not yield postreinforcement pauses.

7. Partial reinforcement schedules sometimes lead to higher response rates than does CRF.

8. *Multiple schedules* consist of two or more simple schedules presented one after the other. Distinctive cues are associated with each simple phase. Performance on any given phase may be affected by previous phases. In *mixed schedules*, a variation of the multiple pattern, the distinctive cues are not present.

9. In *chained schedules* two or more successive simple schedules must be *completed* before a reinforcement can be obtained. Distinctive cues are associated with each simple phase. *Tandem schedules* are like chained schedules except that the distinctive cues are not present.

10. In *concurrent* schedules the animal is faced with two levers, each of which is associated with its own schedule.

11. In concurrent situations the frequency of responding on an alternative key matches the relative frequency of reinforcement for responses on that alternative. This is the *matching* effect.

12. Matching may *maximize* the number of reinforcements we receive.

13. *Schedule-induced* behavior, such as attack, pacing, and jaw clenching, occurs during intervals between reinforcements and may be reinforced because it reduces tension or increases stimulation.

14. Avoidance of frustration and interest in sensory change may also be involved in the appearance of schedule-induced behavior.

15. Schedule-induced behavior first increases and then decreases as the time between reinforcements increases.

16. Autoshaping refers to the fact that animals will sometimes develop a response to a cue even though that cue is *always* followed by reinforcement. Autoshaping suggests that classical conditioning is intertwined with what is normally called instrumental conditioning.

17. The *partial reinforcement extinction effect* (PREE) refers to the fact that resistance to extinction following partial reinforcement is greater than resistance to extinction following CRF.

18. Frustration theory, sequential theory, and the discrimination hypothesis have all been proposed as explanations of the PREE.

19. Humans respond to many schedule manipulations in roughly the same manner as do "lower" animals.

20. If a reward is *delayed* following the occurrence of a response, then performance drops off. If the reward is delayed too long, then learning will not occur at all. And yet long delays sometimes appear not to hinder learning in the slightest. Successful learning under these conditions has been attributed to the presence of undetected *secondary reinforcers* immediately following the response. (A secondary reinforcer is any neutral stimulus that, through repeated pairings with a primary reward, has acquired reinforcing properties of its own.)

21. If confounding secondary reinforcers are removed from the delay-of-reinforcement experiments, then learning under conditions of delayed primary reinforcement drops off dramatically. Some psychologists feel that learning cannot occur at all unless some type of reinforcement (primary or secondary) is immediate.

22. Delays in the receipt of primary reinforcement are not particularly effective in reducing human performance. Humans are better able to bridge time gaps than are other animals.

23. Performance tends to increase as the *amount* of reinforcement is increased, up to a point.

24. Three components of amount of reward have been identified. They include the volume or mass of the reward, the amount of consuming activity, and the quality of the reward. All three have been found to be important in determining reinforcement effects.

25. A fourth component, number of food units, also seems to be important. Invertebrates, such as honeybees, also display amount of reinforcement effects.

26. *Negative-reinforcement contrast* refers to the fact that if an animal has been working for a high level of reward and is suddenly shifted to a lower level, its performance will temporarily drop *below* the level that it would have maintained had it been experiencing *only* the lower level all along. Although the negative-reinforcement contrast effect is fairly well established, the corresponding *positive-reinforcement contrast effect* has been difficult to obtain.

27. Impulsive behavior, wherein smaller but more immediate rewards are preferred, has been demonstrated experimentally.
28. The existence and strength of secondary reinforcers are detected by various means, including choice tests and extinction tests.
29. Secondary reinforcers can become stronger if they are paired with larger amounts of primary reward.
30. The strength of a secondary reinforcer increases slightly as the number of times it is paired with the primary reward is increased.
31. Duration of deprivation, or drive level, seems to be relatively unimportant in determining the strength of secondary reinforcers.
32. Schedules of reinforcement appear to have a significant impact on the strength of secondary reinforcers. In general, intermittency leads to an increase in the durability of secondary reinforcers, as does variability.
33. Secondary reinforcers may be established through a process of classical conditioning.
34. To become powerful secondary reinforcers, stimuli may have to carry nonredundant information about the forthcoming occurrence of the primary reward.
35. Secondary reinforcers may have motivating properties.
36. Some so-called secondary reinforcers may be nothing more than undetected primary reinforcers, in that some so-called neutral stimuli may satisfy the animal's requirements for novel, changing, and complex stimulation.
37. Human performance is strongly affected by secondary reinforcers such as tokens and praise.
38. Returning to the theoretical controversy, we find that *drive-reduction theory* has difficulty explaining certain sensory-seeking behaviors such as exploration. Many psychologists are unwilling to believe that all reinforcing events involve the reduction of noxious stimulation. They also object to the endless invention of new drives to account for newly discovered reinforcing stimuli. The drive-reduction theory is a good one, but it may not be comprehensive.
39. Alternative theories include the *optimal-arousal-level* conceptions, which assume that the animal seeks to maintain some preferred level of arousal.
40. There are several *stimulus theories* of reinforcement. The stimulus-change theorists argue that changes in level of stimulation are reinforcing. The preferred-level theorists argue that any change away from a preferred level of stimulation will be punishing, whereas any change toward the preferred level will be reinforcing.
41. Stimulus-quality theorists contend that certain stimuli (such as sweet ones) are innately preferred and that their presentation will be reinforcing. The emphasis here is on quality rather than quantity.
42. *Response theories* of reinforcement argue that consummatory responses are reinforcing. Premack's variation on this theme holds that, if one of two responses is more likely to occur, the occurrence of the less likely one can be increased by reinforcing it with the opportunity to perform the more likely one.
43. The *response deprivation hypothesis* is another example of response theory.
44. At present, none of these theories is any more valid than the others. Each probably has something to contribute to the overall picture of reinforcement, and each can account for many of the data, such as the free-food effect.

PART
3

TRANSFER

It is clear that we rarely, if ever, learn anything entirely new. No matter how novel a new learning situation appears, past experiences and habits will be brought into play. We now turn to a consideration of *transfer*, or the effects of our prior learning on subsequent learning. Transfer is a part of the entire learning process, which also includes acquisition and retention.

It is almost unnecessary to point out the tremendous importance of transfer in our daily life. We never truly learn anything in a vacuum. For example, the mere fact that we have acquired language guarantees that many new learning situations will be, in effect, transfer tasks. To the extent that the new learning task involves language, we are involved in a transfer situation.

Our study of transfer will begin by considering the complementary processes of generalization and discrimination. *Generalization* refers to the fact that, if a response is connected to one particular stimulus, the subsequent presentation of similar stimuli will tend to elicit that same response. Generalization is a type of transfer effect in that training with one stimulus affects future performance. *Discrimination* is the opposite side of the same coin. It refers to the reducing of generalization through a process of differential reinforcement. The range of stimuli that will elicit a particular response is decreased. The issues of generalization and discrimination will be discussed in terms of both animal and human action.

We shall also consider *transfer of training*. In studies on this process subjects often learn two successive verbal tasks, which may vary in similarity to each other. Under some circumstances, learning of the second task is facilitated by the prior learning. Under other circumstances, it is hindered. Both empirically determined and theoretically envisioned principles of transfer will be outlined.

In addition, an attempt will be made to point out the ways in which generalization and transfer of training are intimately related to each other. Both involve the impact of prior learning on subsequent performance.

CHAPTER

7

GENERALIZATION

AND

DISCRIMINATION

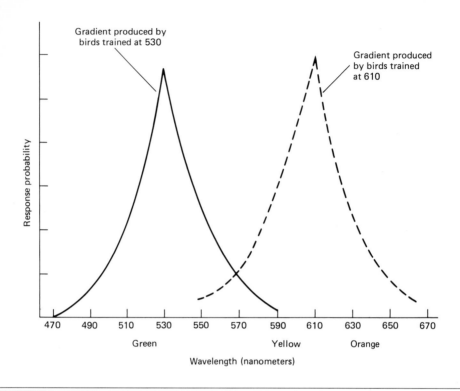

Figure 7.1 Idealized stimulus generalization gradients that might be obtained from groups of birds trained at different points along a wavelength continuum.

GENERALIZATION

Stimulus generalization refers to the fact that, if a response is learned to one particular stimulus, similar stimuli will tend to elicit that response. The greater the similarity, the greater is the tendency. For example, babies may say "Dada" to any approaching man, even though they have been reinforced for saying "Dada" only in the presence of their father. The more the stranger looks like the father, the more likely the baby is to say "Dada."

On a more experimental level we should note the widely quoted results obtained by Guttman and Kalish (1956). These researchers trained pigeons to peck an illuminated key of a certain color. Following the training the birds were presented with a random sequence of colored keys that varied in their similarity to the original training stimulus. Each group produced what is known as a *stimulus generalization gradient*. That is, the greatest numbers of responses occurred during the presentation of the *original* training stimuli. As the various test stimuli became less similar to the original stimulus, the numbers of evoked responses decreased. The birds, originally trained at different points along the color continuum, produced relatively symmetrical generalization gradients around their particular training stimulus value. Figure 7.1 contains some idealized gradients that might be obtained

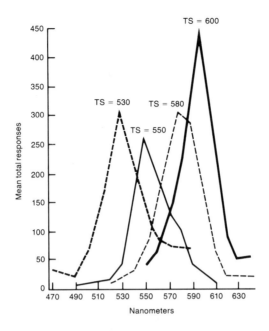

Figure 7.2 Mean total responses on the generalization test as a function of the wavelength of the stimuli for four groups for whom the original training stimulus (TS) was either 530, 550, 580, or 600 nm. (Adapted from Guttman, N., and Kalish, H. I. Discriminability and stimulus generalization. *Journal of Experimental Psychology*, 1956, *51*, 79–88. Copyright © 1956 by the American Psychological Association. Reprinted by permission.)

in this sort of experiment. Figure 7.2 contains some of the original data reported by Guttman and Kalish (1956).

Guttman and Kalish's results are an example of the generalization of an instrumentally conditioned response. But classically conditioned responses generalize, too. For example, Moore (1972) classically conditioned the rabbit's nictitating membrane using a 1,200-hertz tone as the CS. The UCS was a shock delivered to the skin near the eye. After conditioning, wherein the 1,200-Hz tone came to elicit an eye blink, Moore tested for extinction of the conditioned response. He tested for resistance to extinction by presenting not only the 1,200-Hz tone but by presenting higher and lower tonal frequencies as well. As you can see in Figure 7.3, the nictitating-membrane response generalized to the new test frequencies. The closer the test stimulus was to the original 1,200-Hz training tone, the greater the relative number of conditioned eye blinks made during extinction.

Clearly, the ability to generalize can be either adaptive or maladaptive. On the one hand, it would be inconvenient, to say the least, if we failed to recognize or respond to strangers as humans. On the other hand, it would not be particularly adaptive if we generalized too much (for example, if we "recognized" approaching animals as humans).

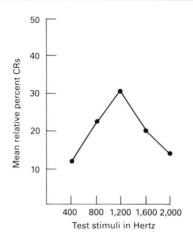

Figure 7.3 Generalization of classically conditioned nictitating-membrane response in the rabbit. [Adapted from Moore, J. W. Stimulus control: Studies of auditory generalization in rabbits. *Classical Conditioning II: Current Theory and Research*, Black/Prokasy (Eds.), © 1972, p. 215. Reprinted by permission of Prentice-Hall, Inc., Englewood Cliffs, New Jersey.]

Variables Affecting Generalization

As is true of many learning phenomena, many variables may affect the shape and form of the stimulus generalization gradient. We shall discuss a few of them.

EXTENDED TRAINING.   What will happen to stimulus generalization as reinforced responding to the training stimulus is increased? For example, what will happen to the baby's tendency to say "Dada" to strangers as the number of times she is reinforced for saying "Dada" to her father is increased? On an intuitive level we might expect an initial increase in stimulus generalization. When the baby first receives reinforcement for saying "Dada," the father might not be all that distinct to her. Hence, we might find an initial failure to distinguish between the father and strangers. But as training continues, the baby gains experience. The father becomes more distinct to her. After considerable training she might be much less likely to confuse strangers with her father. Generalization might decrease.

The experimental data pertaining to this issue are equivocal. On the one hand, Hearst and Koresko (1968) gave groups of pigeons different numbers of training trials on a task where the pecking of a vertical line was reinforced. They then tested for generalization by presenting lines placed at various angles away from the vertical position. They found that the generalization gradients became steeper as the number of training trials increased (see also Razran, 1949). But some investigators have found that extended reinforcement on the original training stimulus leads either to no change or to an actual flattening of the gradient (McCain & Garrett, 1964). The situation appears to be a very complex one, and it is not yet fully understood. The interested reader is referred to Blough and Blough (1977), Mackintosh (1974, 1977), and Steinhauer, Davol, and Lee (1977) for more information.

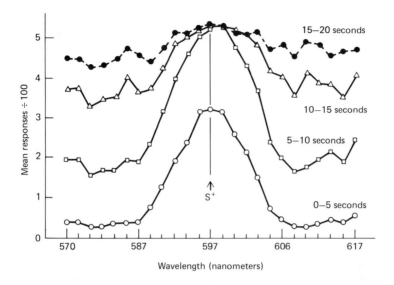

Figure 7.4 The effects of partial reinforcement on stimulus generalization as influenced by time of testing during an FI interval. The birds were tested for generalization either early or later in a 20-second FI interval. Generalization was extreme (flat gradients) when tests occurred later and minimal (steep gradients) when testing occurred early. (Adapted from Blough, D. S. Steady state data and a quantitative model of operant generalization and discrimination. *Journal of Experimental Psychology: Animal Behavior Processes*, 1975, *104*, 3–21. Copyright 1975 by the American Psychological Association. Reprinted by permission.)

THE EFFECTS OF PARTIAL REINFORCEMENT.   Suppose, when referring to her father as "Dada," our baby is sometimes rewarded ("Gooood baby!") and sometimes not (silence). What effect might this partial reinforcement have on the extent to which the response will generalize to other men?

Much of the experimental evidence suggests that generalization will be *more* extensive following partial reinforcement. For example, Hearst, Koresko, and Poppen (1964) trained pigeons to peck a key on four different VI schedules. They found that, as the intervals increased, the generalization gradients became flatter. In other words, generalization increased as the reinforcement became more intermittent.

However, just as a simple answer eluded us in trying to understand the relationship between extended training and generalization, things become pretty complicated here, too. For example, Blough (1975) trained pigeons to peck a light of a certain wavelength. He used an FI 20 schedule. That is, the pigeons had to wait 20 seconds between reinforcements. Blough tested for generalization at different points during the 20-second interval (see Figure 7.4). Some of the time he presented a new test light toward the beginning of the interval, just after a reward had been received for pecking the training light, and sometimes he presented a new test light later in the interval, after the bird had been waiting for a while. Notice in Figure 7.4

that, if he tested early in the interval, the gradients were steep; the birds tended not to peck similarly colored lights if they had just been reinforced for pecking the training light. But when the test lights were presented later in the interval, the gradients became very flat; the pigeon would peck a light at just about any wavelength if it had been waiting.

The Role of Experience in Generalization

Suppose that a baby is kept at home most of the time. He sees very few strangers. The only man he knows is his father, and he calls him "Dada." He has had no experience with a dimension of men. Suppose that we now expose the baby to a variety of men. What kind of generalization will occur? Will he generalize more or less than a baby who has been exposed to many different men all along? Researchers have taken two general positions concerning this issue. Lashley and Wade (1946), on the one hand, argue that the inexperienced baby will respond equally to all men. The stimulus generalization gradient will be flat. They argue that the stimulus dimension (for example, a dimension of men varying in similarity to one another) does not "exist" for the baby until he has had experience with it. Until the baby has had a chance to distinguish among, or compare, men, all men will be equivalent. All men, including the father, will be perceived as the same and will be responded to identically. On the other hand, Hull (1943) and Spence (1937) would argue that the baby will be less likely to respond to less similar men even though he has never had the opportunity to experience various points along the dimension. They would argue that the gradient generated by our inexperienced baby would be steep, and not flat.

Some evidence supports the Lashley-Wade position. Peterson (1962) raised ducks in yellow light (589 nanometers). They never had the opportunity to distinguish one wavelength from another. A control group was raised in normal light. Both groups then were trained to peck a key illuminated by the 589-nm light. Stimulus generalization was then tested by illuminating the key with eight different wavelengths, ranging from 490 nm to 650 nm. The results of the experiment are shown in Figure 7.5. The ducks raised in yellow light generalized perfectly, or failed to discriminate among the various test stimuli. But the controls sharply curtailed their responses as the similarity between the training and the test stimuli decreased. This result supports the Lashley-Wade notion that experience with the stimulus dimension is important in producing generalization decrements. Ganz and Riesen (1962) obtained similar results with infant monkeys raised in total darkness.

Walk and Walters (1973) raised one group of rats in the dark (for up to 60 days) and a control group in normal light. The visually deprived rats showed deficiencies in the ability to discriminate depths. They tended to respond to cliffs of varying depths (4, 6, and 8 inches) as though they were not really there. That is, they tended to tumble over the cliff more often than rats raised in normal light.

However, some data indicate that steep rather than flat gradients may be obtained in the absence of any prior exposure to the many points along the stimulus dimension (Jenkins & Harrison, 1960; Thomas, Mariner, & Sherry, 1969). These investigators have shown that under certain rather specific conditions steep gradients may be obtained when the animal has experienced only a single value along a stimulus dimension (Rudolph & Honig, 1972; Tracy, 1970). For example, Riley

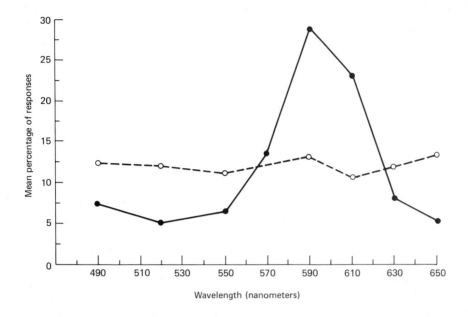

Figure 7.5 Generalization gradients obtained from birds raised in monochromatic environment (dotted line) and from birds raised in normal light (solid line). (Adapted from Peterson, N. Effect of monochromatic rearing on the control of responding by wavelength. *Science*, 1962, *136*, 774–775. Fig. 2, p. 774. Copyright 1962 by the American Association for the Advancement of Science.)

and Levin (1971) raised newly hatched white leghorn chicks in 589-nm light. The chicks were trained to peck a key that was also illuminated with 589-nm light. Then in one condition the chicks were tested for their tendency to peck keys illuminated by either 589-nm, 569-nm, or 550-nm light. As you can see in Figure 7.6, the obtained gradient is not flat as predicted by the Lashley-Wade position.

The conclusion we can draw is that prior experience with many points along the dimension may not be absolutely *essential* for the appearance of a steep rather than a flat gradient, but it *helps*. Our stay-at-home baby might be less likely to call strangers "Dada" than he would his real father, but in all likelihood the tendency to restrict his response to his father would be even stronger had he had prior experience with a variety of strangers.

Primary and Secondary Generalization

Hull (1943) describes primary generalization as that involving some innate or predetermined stimulus dimension. Secondary generalization refers to generalization in which the dimension of similarity is acquired, or learned. For instance, the words *house* and *home* are similar, but that similarity is not innate. It is learned. Generalization across these two stimuli would be considered secondary generalization.

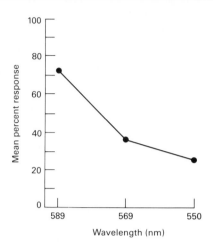

Figure 7.6 Mean relative generalization gradient for chicks tested with all three wavelength values. (Adapted from Riley, D. A., and Levin, T. C. Stimulus-generalization gradients in chickens reared in monochromatic light and tested with a single wavelength value. *Journal of Comparative and Physiological Psychology*, 1971, 75, 399–402. Copyright 1971 by the American Psychological Association. Reprinted by permission.)

SEMANTIC CONDITIONING.   The semantic conditioning effect (see Chapter 2) can be used to illustrate the concept of secondary generalization. In a semantic conditioning study, a response is conditioned to one verbal unit, such as a word. The subject is then presented with additional words, which vary in their similarity to the original training word. The greater the similarity, the greater is the tendency for the test word to elicit the response (Maltzman, 1977). For example, Lacey and his associates (Lacey & Smith, 1954; Lacey, Smith, & Green, 1955) ran a series of studies in which subjects free-associated to long lists of words. The lists contained, among others, several words pertaining to rural life (*cow, corn, plow, tractor*). One of these words was selected by the experimenter as the training word. After each presentation of this critical training word the subjects were shocked and their heart rate monitored. The results indicated that the mere presentation of a word that had been previously followed by shock would yield an increase in heart rate. In addition, and more to our point, the heart-rate response was elicited by the other related rural words. If the presentation of *plow* was followed by a shock, then the presentation of *corn* would produce an increase in heart rate even though *corn* had never been followed by shock. This result demonstrates generalization along a dimension of learned meaning similarity. Parenthetically, it also demonstrates the complexity of generalization effects in human activity.

ACQUIRED EQUIVALENCE OF CUES.   Another early area of research involves the acquired equivalence of cues. In a typical experiment (Jeffrey, 1953) children were taught to move a lever in one direction when a white stimulus was presented and in another direction when a black stimulus was presented. Half the subjects were then taught to call a gray stimulus white, whereas the other half learned to label the same gray stimulus black. All subjects then were presented with a random sequence of white, black, and gray stimuli and were required to move the lever in response to each stimulus. When the gray stimulus was presented to children who had learned to call it white, they moved the lever in the direction appropriate for white. Similarly, children who had learned to call the gray stimulus black moved the lever in the direction appropriate for black. Through learning, gray and white (or gray and black) had been "made similar." Through stimulus generalization the lever responses originally connected to the white or black stimuli were elicited by the gray stimulus.

Semantic generalization, or semantic conditioning, and acquired equivalence of cues are quite closely related. One difference between the two is that in semantic-generalization studies the learned similarity between the stimuli is usually established before the subject enters the test situation. In the acquired-equivalence paradigm the learned equivalence is actually established within the experimental situation (see also Ellis, 1973; Malloy & Ellis, 1970; Saltz, 1971).

Generalization of Extinction

Thus far we have been speaking as though only positive tendencies to make responses generalize. This is not so. Tendencies *not* to make particular responses can generalize, too. If a child has learned not to talk in one particular classroom, then that tendency not to talk can generalize to other similar situations.

In a three-step laboratory demonstration an organism is first trained to respond equally strongly to a number of different stimuli selected from a dimension of stimuli. For example, a pigeon might be reinforced for pecking 10 different circle sizes, so that it would be very likely to peck each and every one of them with a very high probability. Then in the second step one of the circle sizes is randomly selected for extinction. The pigeon is exposed to this one stimulus repeatedly and not reinforced for responding to it. Obviously, the animal stops responding to this particular stimulus; it extinguishes. Then in the third phase of the demonstration the pigeon is tested on the remaining nine stimuli, which it has not seen since the first step in the experiment, when it learned to peck all of them. What is found in this final test phase is that the tendency *not* to peck the stimulus value selected for extinction generalizes, or spreads to these other stimuli. The pigeon will show a reduced probability of responding to circles whose sizes are similar to the one circle selected for extinction (see Figure 7.7).

Behavior Modification and Generalization

Generalization is an important issue in applied psychological work. For example, a critical issue in the field of behavior modification is whether behavior trained in the laboratory will generalize to everyday life. If we put an alcoholic through avoidance conditioning, will he, as soon as we release him from the experimental situation, head for the nearest bar? Will a mute child, trained to speak in a tightly controlled situation, fall mute again once she is removed from that situation?

Some studies report fairly good generalization, whereas others do not (see Geller, 1983). For example, Tracey, Briddell, and Wilson (1974) awarded tokens each time psychiatric patients said positive things about other people or about hospital activities such as dances and the like. In the training condition positive statements

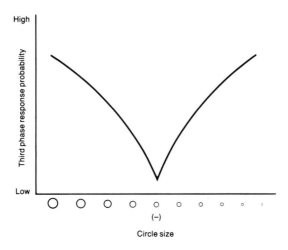

Figure 7.7 Generalization of extinction. These are hypothetical data obtained in the third phase of the experiment. In the first phase, pigeons are reinforced for responding to all circles. In the second phase, pigeons are extinguished at (−) stimulus. In the third phase, pigeons are tested for response strength at all ten circle sizes.

about both people and activities increased substantially. But the important question was whether these increases would carry over into other activities. Some of them did, and some did not. On the one hand, an increase in positive statements about hospital activities actually led to increased attendance at activities. In other words, if patients were rewarded for saying positive things about the hospital dances, they tended to go to the actual dances more often. That response is a pretty strong indication of the generalization of a learned response system. On the other hand, rewarding patients for making positive statements about people in the training situation did not appear to lead to more positive statements about people outside the training situation. This equivocal pattern of results is indicative of the problems facing investigators in this area.

Stevens-Long and Rasmussen (1974) report that autistic children trained in the use of simple and compound sentences sometimes produce novel sentences on their own. In other words, language training may generalize in some complex manner, allowing the children to use the acquired rules and information in the construction of new sentences.

And finally, Kleitsch, Whitman, and Santos (1983) report that increased verbal interaction among elderly retarded patients showed very good generalization. The patients talked more and in many different situations. In addition, nonsubject patients began to talk more, too!

In summary, many behavior-modification studies show good generalization beyond the experimental setting, but in other studies generalization fails to materialize. The importance of generalization and its elusiveness suggest that it should be

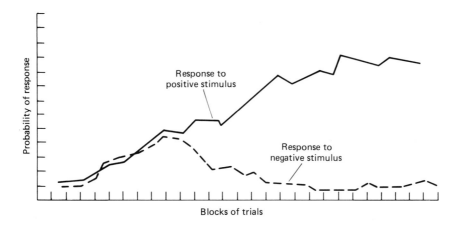

Figure 7.8 The course of discrimination learning. After an initial period, during which the probability of a response to *both* the positive and negative stimulus increases, the response to the negative stimulus drops out while the response to the positive stimulus continues to strengthen. (These are hypothetical data.)

made one of the critical concerns in any behavior-modification study. If a behavior change is limited to the experimental setting, then in a practical sense it is of little interest or value.

DISCRIMINATION AND STIMULUS CONTROL

Generalization and discrimination may well be opposite sides of the same coin. They may bear an inverse relationship to each other. A decrease in stimulus generalization refers to a decrease in the tendency to give the same response to similar stimuli. An increase in discrimination refers to the same thing—the tendency to restrict responses to one stimulus value chosen from a set of similar stimuli. Discrimination refers to a breakdown in the tendency to generalize. It is difficult, if not impossible, to untangle the two processes. Although their exact relationship has never been defined to everyone's satisfaction, some experimental work supports the idea that they are closely related.

Many researchers like to think of both generalization and discrimination in terms of *stimulus control*, or the tendency for stimuli to elicit responses. Generally speaking, generalization refers to relatively imprecise stimulus control, whereas discrimination refers to those processes reflecting the tightening, or sharpening, of stimulus control.

Discrimination Formation

When presented with two stimuli—say, two lights of different color—and rewarded for responding to one but not the other, the animal will most often behave in the manner depicted in Figure 7.8. Notice that initially the animal makes few responses at all. But then, as it discovers that there is something good about the situation (the animal is receiving reinforcement), it begins to respond to *both* stimuli about equally frequently. It is only with a little additional experience that the animal begins to realize that one stimulus is associated with reward and the other is not. After the initial tendency to respond to either stimulus the animal begins to drop the response to the negative stimulus and increase its responses to the positive stimulus.

On the one hand, the environment sometimes demands, or reinforces, generalization. For example, to function successfully and maximize reinforcement one must be able to generalize along such dimensions as red lights. On the other hand, the world sometimes rewards discrimination rather than generalization. For example, the successful wine taster is not one who says, "Hey, all this stuff tastes the same." He is the one who can make finer and finer discriminations among very similar stimuli. (Amateur wine tasters often unknowingly discriminate among labels and colors rather than actual taste differences. Blindfold your local wine expert, and you may well find that he or she has trouble distinguishing one wine from another.) The successful animal is one that can, depending on the demands of the environment, both generalize and discriminate. We must be able to distinguish between those occasions that require generalization and those that demand discrimination. Too much of either process will lead to less than maximum reinforcement.

The mechanism whereby generalization is reduced, or discrimination is increased, involves the reinforcement of responses made to one particular stimulus and the nonreinforcement of responses made to similar stimuli. This mechanism is what we mean by *differential reinforcement*. For example, the baby comes to distinguish her father from other men through a process of differential reinforcement. Her initial tendency to generalize, or to say "Dada" to all men, is reduced by reinforcing "Dada" in response to her father and not reinforcing it when it occurs in response to other men.

Simultaneous versus Successive Methods

Two of the more common methods used in the investigation of discrimination learning have been labeled the *simultaneous* and the *successive* presentation techniques. In the simultaneous method two stimuli are presented together. A pigeon might be presented with two different illuminated keys. A response to one (the positive stimulus) would be reinforced. A response to the other (the negative stimulus) would not be reinforced. With repeated differential reinforcement the pigeon will come to restrict its pecking response to the positive stimulus.

The successive method involves the sequential presentation of the positive and negative stimuli. The two stimuli are presented one at a time in some random order. The animal is free to respond or not respond to each stimulus as it appears. This situation would be comparable to one in which the baby saw either her father or her uncle but never both at the same time.

The Algebraic Summation Interpretation

Hull (1943) and Spence (1936, 1937) developed what has come to be known as the absolute, or the *algebraic summation*, interpretation of discrimination learning. Imagine a dimension of circle size (see Figure 7.9). Choose from this dimension two particular circle sizes. Call one the positive stimulus and the other the negative stimulus. Present these two circles, and *only* these two, to a pigeon. Reinforce the

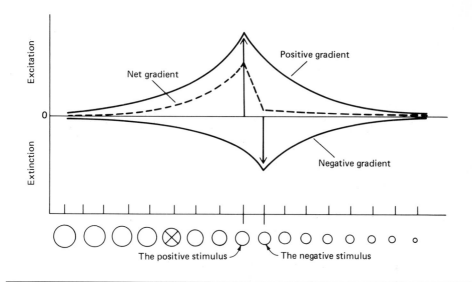

Figure 7.9 An example of the Hullian interpretation of discrimination learning.

pigeon when it pecks the positive stimulus. Do nothing when it pecks the negative stimulus. According to Hull and Spence, each time the pigeon responds to the positive stimulus and is reinforced for doing so, there results an increase in the tendency to respond to that stimulus (see the upward arrow in Figure 7.9). Each time the pigeon pecks the negative stimulus and is not reinforced for doing so, the tendency not to respond to that particular stimulus value increases (see the downward arrow). The positive tendency to respond to the reinforced stimulus generalizes (see the positive gradient in Figure 7.9) along the stimulus dimension. Similarly, the negative tendency also generalizes (see the negative gradient). These two gradients, the positive and the negative, sum algebraically. The resulting *net gradient* in Figure 7.9 is the result of the algebraic interaction of the positive and negative gradients. The probability of a response's occurring at any point along the dimension is determined by the strength of the competing positive and negative tendencies at that point. For example, consider stimulus X in Figure 7.9. At this point the generalized strength of the negative tendency is considerable, but it is not as great as the generalized positive tendency. Hence, if we present circle X to our pigeon, it will probably peck it. The positive tendency outweighs the value of the negative tendency at that point. The net gradient summarizes the resolution of the opposing positive and negative tendencies pulling on the animal.

It is an interesting model, and it leads to many testable hypotheses. For example, what will happen to the probability of the response to the positive stimulus as we increase the number of unreinforced responses that the animal makes to the negative stimulus? What will happen to a baby's tendency to say "Dada" to her father as we increase the number of times she says "Dada" to her uncle and is not reinforced for doing so? On an intuitive basis we might suspect that such training might sharpen the baby's perception of the differences between her father and her uncle and lead to a stronger tendency to respond to the father. But notice carefully what the Hullian model suggests. If we increase the number of unreinforced responses to the negative stimulus, the negative gradient increases. This increase detracts from the tendency to respond to the positive stimulus. Through repeated nonreinforced responding to the uncle we would expect the baby's tendency to say "Dada" to her father to decrease rather than increase. This curious and somewhat unexpected result has received support in the laboratory (see Gynther, 1957; Purtle, 1973).

A Cognitive Approach: Relational Theory

The Hullian theory just described has been challenged by what is called the *relational* theory of discrimination learning (Köhler, 1955). According to this position, the animal in forming a discrimination learns a *relation* between the positive and negative stimuli. When discriminating between two circle sizes the pigeon may well be attending to the fact that one stimulus is larger than the other. In a sense it may be learning that "bigness is goodness." The emphasis here is on the cognitive, somewhat fuzzy, concept of relationship learning rather than the summation of independently established positive and negative gradients. The relational position emphasizes a comparison process and suggests that the animal's response to the stimuli is based on a perceived relation between them. Although somewhat ambiguous, the relational theory may well yield predictions that differ from those generated by the Hullian scheme.

The first differential prediction has to do with a comparison of the simultaneous and the successive methods just outlined. If the relational position is correct, we might expect that the simultaneous method would produce better discrimination learning than the successive method, simply because the relationship between the two stimuli might be more easily perceived. If they were presented together, the perception of the relation would not be dependent on a "memory" of one of the stimuli, as would be the case in the successive presentation method. The experimental data, however, contain all possible results with respect to this question. Neither method seems to be superior under all conditions (see Blough & Lipsitt, 1971; Kimble, 1961). Thus, although the theory seems to generate a distinctive hypothesis, nature and our experiments have not been particularly cooperative in yielding a definitive answer to the question.

Transposition

The *transposition* effect is another phenomenon that bears on the relational-versus-absolute issue. Suppose that an animal has been trained to discriminate between a dark stimulus (the positive stimulus) and a light stimulus (the negative stimulus). Now suppose that we remove the light stimulus from the situation and pair the dark positive stimulus with a new, heretofore unseen, *darker* stimulus. The animal's choice is now between the old positive stimulus, which has been consistently reinforced, and the new darker stimulus, which has never even been seen before. Common sense would argue that the animal would continue to respond to the old positive stimulus. But the relational position would argue that, if the animal has, in fact, learned the relation between the light (negative) and the dark (positive) stimuli and responds on the basis of that relation, then it should respond to the new darker stimulus rather than the old positive stimulus when given a choice between

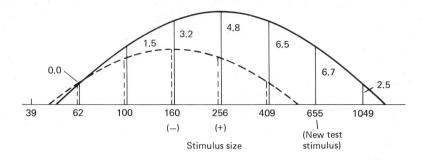

Figure 7.10 Spence's analysis of transposition. During training, responses to stimulus 256 are reinforced and responses to stimulus 160 are extinguished. (Adapted from Spence, K. W. The differential response in animals to stimuli varying within a single dimension. *Psychological Review*, 1937, 44, 430–444. Fig. 1. Copyright 1937 by the American Psychological Association.)

these two. It should have learned that "darkness is goodness." This is exactly what happens. The animal responds to the new, darker stimulus rather than the old, positive one. This transposition effect has been observed with all sorts of animals under many different conditions (see Reese, 1968; Riley, 1968).

At first glance the transposition effect seems to support the relational position. It suggests that the animal is responding on the basis of a perceived relationship rather than discrete stimulus-response connections. And yet Spence (1937), in a classic analysis, argues that simple S-R relationships can, after all, account for transposition effects.

According to his model (see Figure 7.10), a positive excitatory gradient is built up around the positive stimulus (value 256). A negative gradient (dotted line) is built up in connection with the negative stimulus (value 160). The probability of re- sponding to any point along the stimulus dimension depends on the *difference between the positive and negative gradients*. If you will spend a moment with this model, you will realize that it predicts transposition effects very nicely. For exam- ple, suppose that the old positive stimulus (256) was paired with a new test stim- ulus (say, of value 655). According to the model, the probability of responding to stimulus 655 would be greater than the probability of responding to the old positive stimulus (256). This would be a transposition effect, and it is predicted on the basis of discrete S-R connections without any reference to the learning of relationships.

Spence's analysis still stands as one of the more ingenious interpretations of transposition. In effect, it broke the strong grip that the relational theorists had had on the transposition effect since the beginning of the century. This is not to say that Spence's model is perfect, either. For example, it is dependent on *how* one draws the hypothetical gradients. If one wishes, one can redraw the gradients so that transposition is *not* predicted. In addition, his model does not seem to explain certain facts (see Honig, 1965).

Further Cognitive Factors: Noncontinuity Theory

In addition to the relational theory there has been a second challenge of the Hull-Spence interpretation of discrimination formation. This approach is usually labeled *noncontinuity theory* (Krechevsky, 1932). According to this position, which has never been as precisely stated as the Hullian theory, the organism solves a discrimination problem by trying out and abandoning successive hypotheses until the correct one is discovered, perhaps all at once. For example, a rat faced with two doors, one of which leads to food, might first hypothesize that the left door was the correct one. If this failed, the rat would drop that hypothesis and try another, such as "the black door is correct," and so on, until the solution to the problem was found.

In other words, Hull and Spence emphasized the gradual, *continuous* accumulation of habit strengths, whereas Krechevsky emphasized the idea that a discrimination problem may be solved all at once through a process of hypothesis testing.

Tests of these opposing views have usually used a *stimulus reversal procedure*. Specifically, a rat will be given several trials on a black-white discrimination problem where black is correct. During this *presolution period* the animal is given some experience with the problem but not enough to actually solve it. Then the experimenter reverses the cues, or makes the white stimulus the positive stimulus and the black the negative stimulus.

What would the two theories predict here? Continuity theory (Hullian) predicts that the reversed problem would be difficult, because during the presolution period the animal was slowly and continuously learning that black was correct but now black is incorrect. Noncontinuity theory, in contrast, predicts that the presolution experience should have no impact on learning of the reversed problem. The rat will have learned nothing that will affect its ability to learn the reversal.

Most of the experiments using the reversal procedure seem to support the continuity position; reversing cues does seem to retard learning (Mackintosh, 1974; Sutherland & Mackintosh, 1971).

Continuity theory is not "home free," however, because of what is called the *overlearning reversal effect*. Let's suppose that in the experiment described above we give the rat many, many trials before reversing the cues, instead of just a few trials during a presolution period. In effect, we allow the animal to *overlearn* the fact that black is positive before reversing the situation. Hullian continuity theory predicts that the animal will have a great deal of trouble learning the reversal. But in fact, the data indicate that overlearning *speeds up* the learning of the reversal (Mackintosh, 1974).

The upshot is the current suspicion that discrimination learning may involve, under certain conditions, both continuous and noncontinuous subprocesses. It would be an oversimplification to say that either gradually increasing habit strengths or hypothesis testing can completely account for discrimination learning.

Behavioral Contrast

Having spent some time considering major theories of discrimination we now turn to a discussion of some additional issues relating to the discrimination process. The *behavioral contrast effect* is an interesting one. It has been investigated by Reynolds (1961a, 1961b) and others (for example, Keller, 1974; Redford & Perkins, 1974; Williams, 1977). The work done by Reynolds provides a good example of

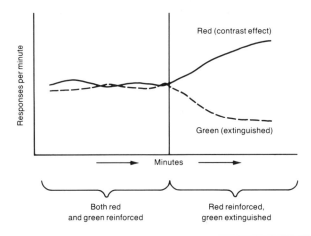

Figure 7.11 Positive behavioral contrast. A pigeon is first reinforced for pecking either a red or a green key. Then when responses to the green key are no longer reinforced, responses to the red key increase. (Hypothetical data.)

the effect. Pigeons were trained to peck a key. Sometimes the key was red, and sometimes it was green. At first the color made no difference, for the pigeon was reinforced regardless of the color of the key. In this phase of the experiment the pigeon pecked the two colors equally frequently. In the second phase of the study the red stimulus became the positive, or reinforced, stimulus, and the green cue became the negative, or unreinforced, stimulus. As one might expect, the response rate to the green key dropped. Responses to this key went unreinforced, and hence they extinguished. But what about the rate of response to the red key? Remember that a response to this key was treated identically in the two phases—it was always reinforced. The shift from the first to the second phase did not involve a change with respect to the red key. In spite of this constant treatment the rate of response to the red stimulus went up during the second phase (see Figure 7.11). This is the positive behavioral contrast effect (see Blough, 1988; Williams, 1988).

How might one explain this effect? Why did the pigeon *increase* its response to the red key even though the size and frequency of the reinforcements stayed the same? Let us first look at what the Hull-Spence model would state about the issue. It seems that their model would predict a decrease in the rate of response to the red key rather than an increase. With the shift to phase two a negative, or inhibitory, tendency would be assumed to build up in association with the unreinforced green key. This negative tendency should generalize and detract from the positive tendency to respond to the red key. Thus, this aspect of the Hull-Spence model does not seem to account for the behavioral contrast effect.

What other ways are there to think about the contrast effect? Williams (1973) and others suggest that *frustration* may be involved. They argue that the animal experiences frustration when it pecks the green key and receives no reinforcement in phase two. (We really have no idea of the nature of the pigeon's subjective experience. We call it frustration for convenience and assume that it is similar to what we experience when we put a quarter in the coffee machine and coffee, but no cup, is returned.) Call it what you like, it is assumed to act as a drive, or motivating, agent. Frustration activates and motivates the pigeon so that it increases its behavior in the presence of the red stimulus.

Clearly, behavioral contrast effect does occur. *Why* it occurs is another question. The following discussion lends some support to the frustration hypothesis.

Errorless Discrimination Learning

Terrace (1961, 1963a, 1963b, 1972) devised a method for discrimination learning in which the animal never actually responds to the negative stimulus. In simple terms, Terrace first establishes a strong response to the positive stimulus alone, and then he very gradually introduces the negative stimulus into the situation. He brings the negative stimulus in so slowly, in such small steps, that the pigeon never responds to it. For example, pigeons can be trained to discriminate between a red key and a green key (negative stimulus) without making an unreinforced response to the green key. The pigeon is trained to peck the red key alone. Then during the presentation of the illuminated red key, the light in the key is momentarily turned off. During these brief dark intervals the pigeon typically draws away from the key. The dark intervals may gradually be lengthened without the pigeon's responding. Then a very dim green light is presented instead of the totally dark key. The pigeon still does not respond to it, even though it is pecking resourcefully at the key when it is red. Very gradually, the intensity and the length of the green light can be increased. Eventually, the key may be green half the time and red half the time. Birds trained in this manner will produce few, if any, responses to the green stimulus. The complete discrimination is formed without errors (see also Doran & Holland, 1979; Fields, 1979). (It should be kept in mind that, although the effect has been obtained many times, it is difficult to establish. Terrace, in fact, describes some situations in which it seems impossible to establish errorless discrimination learning.)

The frustration interpretation of the behavioral contrast effect and errorless discrimination learning are interconnected. If an animal forms a discrimination without ever experiencing the "disappointment" that follows an unreinforced response, it will not experience frustration. If an animal is trained under the errorless method, it never makes unreinforced responses to the negative stimulus. If it never experiences nonreinforcement, it is never frustrated. Thus, if we look for the behavioral contrast effect in an errorless-trained pigeon, we should not expect to find it. If the errorless-trained pigeon does not experience frustration, there will be no frustration to motivate it, or to goad it into responding more frequently to the positive stimulus. Terrace (1964) obtained just this result. He compared contrast effects obtained with errorless-trained birds and normally trained birds. A greater contrast effect appeared under normal (frustrating) conditions. This result lends some support to the frustration interpretation of the behavioral contrast effect. However, there have been some failures to find this effect (Rilling & Caplan, 1975).

Insoluble Discrimination Problems

Thus far we have been speaking of discrimination problems that the animal can solve. Through experience it can maximize reinforcement by responding to one particular stimulus and not responding to another. What happens to its behavior if

Figure 7.12 Rat performing in a Lashley jumping stand. This example is a bit different from the one described in the text. In this photo reinforcement is attained only if the rat jumps at the "odd" card, the one that differs from the other two. (Photo by Frank Lotz Miller from Black Star.)

the problem is too difficult, or even impossible, for the animal to solve? For instance, beyond a certain point we cannot detect differences between the brightness of two lights. What happens to our behavior if we are forced to respond in such an impossible situation, receiving reward for correct responses and perhaps punishment for incorrect ones?

Two experimental techniques have been used for observing behavior in insoluble discrimination situations. In the first method the animal can perceive the differences between the two stimuli, but reward is randomly associated with them (Maier, Glazer, & Klee, 1940; Maier & Klee, 1945). The animal can never be sure to which stimulus to respond. For example, Maier and his associates used a Lashley jumping stand, which, if you will recall, requires the animal to leap across an open space and through one of two little doors (see Figure 7.12). Typically, one door is white and the other black. In a normal, soluble discrimination situation one color will be the correct choice and the other will be incorrect. If the animal jumps toward the correct door, the door opens, and the rat leaps through to safety. If the rat jumps at the incorrect door, the door remains closed; the animal bumps into it and drops down into a net. (As you know, the typical procedure is to switch the color cues from left to right to ensure that the animal learns a color rather than a position discrimination.) In this soluble situation the animal easily learns the discrimination.

Things are not so simple in the insoluble situation. In this condition the experimenter may reinforce the animal (allow safe passage through the door) half the time, regardless of whether the animal jumps to the right or to the left. There is no way that the animal can solve the problem. The animal tries, but it is impossible to obtain reinforcement all the time. Maier found that rats will develop some very peculiar behaviors in this situation. Typically they begin to respond to one side or the other. One rat might jump to the left no matter what the color. Another might fixate on the right-hand door. (You might ask why the rat jumps at all. Simple. The experimenter applies shock until the rat leaps.) Maier describes this fixated jumping as "perseverative responding." We might ask: "So what? As long as there is no way to solve the problem, why not jump to one side? Jumping to one side results in as much reinforcement as switching from side to side." The interesting aspect of the situation develops when suddenly the problem becomes soluble. That is, we may begin reinforcing every response to the black and punishing every response to the white. A naive rat would learn this discrimination quickly. But a fixated rat does not readjust its behavior even though the cues necessary for such a readjustment are there. This fixated behavior will persist through hundreds of trials.

The second paradigm that involves insoluble discrimination problems has been labeled the "experimental neurosis" situation. In the Maier situation just described, reinforcement is randomly associated with distinct stimuli. In the experimental neurosis paradigm, reinforcement is consistently associated with one of two stimuli, but the stimuli become so similar the animal cannot tell them apart. For example, Brown (1942) trained rats to distinguish between lights of two degrees of brightness. An approach to the light one, or a retreat from the dimmer one, was reinforced with food. Incorrect responses were punished with shock. After the discrimination had been established, Brown began to make the two stimuli more and more similar. It became increasingly difficult for the animals to distinguish between the two stimuli. The animals became excited; they trembled, defecated, urinated, and leaped about. Some animals even displayed convulsive behavior. Pavlov (1927) demonstrated similar behaviors using dogs and salivary responses. The dogs were forced to discriminate between a circle and an ellipse. The ellipse was then made progressively more like the circle. As the two stimuli became very similar, the dogs began to salivate at the sight of the apparatus. They whined, barked, and tried to leap free of the restraining apparatus. These so-called neurotic behaviors persisted beyond the confines of the experimental situation.

Clearly, this type of experimentation would be much less likely done today. Current researchers have become much more concerned about animal welfare, and many of them would be unwilling to conduct such experiments under any conditions.

The parallel between these experimental effects and human experiences is pretty straightforward. For example, if overly ambitious parents push a child in his schoolwork, they may exceed his abilities. Behavior problems may result, and the child may become disruptive and unhappy. If he is pressed to respond differentially to stimuli that are beyond his ability to discriminate or that seem to him to be the same thing, then he may break down. For example, if parents consistently demand that a normal seven-year-old distinguish between such words as *laziness* and *idleness*, they may be exceeding his capacities, and they may force him into a state of agitation and discomfort.

DISCRIMINATION IN HUMANS
Human Processes: Verbal and Nonverbal

We have discussed many discrimination experiments, and most of them have involved animals as subjects. But because our primary concern is with humans, rather than rats or pigeons, we should spend a little time considering the role of discrimination processes in human verbal learning tasks. We are not suggesting that all research concerning human discrimination learning has to do with verbal tasks. Quite to the contrary, researchers have investigated the human's ability to discriminate along nonverbal dimensions (see Hansen, Tomie, Thomas, & Thomas, 1974; Hebert, Bullock, Levitt, Woodward, & McGuirk, 1974; Thomas, Svinicki, & Vogt, 1973). These and other investigators have been concerned with the human's ability to discriminate points along such dimensions as weight, brightness, size, and area. In addition, a sizable literature has been built up around the question of our ability to discriminate among pictures. For example, research has revealed that subjects discriminate among pictures more easily than among verbal labels of those pictures (Levin, Ghatala, & Wilder, 1974; Rowe, 1972; Wilder & Levin, 1973). In a later chapter we will devote considerable attention to the overall issue of visual versus verbal memory and humans' abilities to process and code visually presented materials. But for now we shall concentrate on *verbal* discrimination.

The importance of discrimination in human verbal learning is emphasized by the classic *stage analysis* of associative learning (Underwood & Schulz, 1960). According to this analysis, simple verbal learning involves at least three subprocesses, each of which is essentially a discrimination process. As an example, consider subjects trying to master a paired-associate list. First, they must discriminate the stimuli, one from the other. This task is easy if the stimuli are something like common words. But if the stimuli are QZKX, QKXZ, XQZK, KZXQ, and so on, the subjects have a problem. In order to hook responses to these stimuli the subjects must sort them out and distinguish one from the other. This is called *stimulus learning*.

Second, the subjects must make similar discriminations among the responses. If the responses are QZK, KZQ, and ZKQ, they must get them clear in their minds before paired-associate learning can be completed. This is called *response learning* and obviously involves making discriminations.

Finally, in *associative learning* the subjects must make the discriminations necessary to join together the correct stimuli and responses.

Clearly, the stage analysis illustrates the fact that even relatively simple verbal tasks involve many complex and interrelated discriminations.

Verbal-Discrimination Learning

The verbal discrimination (VD) paradigm (Ekstrand, Wallace, & Underwood, 1966; Kausler & Yadrick, 1977; Underwood, Jesse, & Ekstrand, 1964) represents a direct extension of the discrimination paradigm into the field of verbal learning.

LABORATORY EXPERIMENTS.   In a typical VD experiment the subjects are presented with a long series of pairs of verbal items (for example, words). One member of each pair has been arbitrarily designated as the "correct" item by the experimenter. The subjects' task is to identify the correct items. They do not have to recall the items, nor do they have to associate them with any other item. Their sole task is to identify which of the two items within each pair is the "correct" item. They guess at first, and if they are correct, an experimenter so informs them; they are also made aware of their errors. At first, not knowing which of the two items is correct, the subjects will respond to them somewhat randomly. As trials progress and the subjects are "reinforced" through response confirmation, they come to restrict their choice to the correct items. It seems quite similar to the pigeon pecking colored lights for food.

One difference between the VD procedure and typical animal discrimination techniques is that the humans are faced with the task of forming multiple, and almost simultaneous, discriminations. The pigeons are faced with only two stimuli. The humans are presented with a long list of pairs, each of which contains a correct and an incorrect stimulus. If presented with a single pair, the humans would solve the problem in one trial. In order to study the gradual formation of a discrimination in humans, the experimenter must make the task more difficult than that used with animals. This does not necessarily mean that the human solves discrimination problems in a manner fundamentally different from that of the pigeon. It may merely mean that the human is far superior at forming the same sorts of discrimination.

FREQUENCY THEORY.   Aside from parametric investigations, much of the work done with VD has centered on the "frequency theory" interpretation of VD effects (Hasher & Chromiak, 1977; Underwood & Freund, 1970; Underwood, Jesse, & Ekstrand, 1964). According to frequency theory, the discrimination between right and wrong items is made on the basis of the relative frequencies of the members of each pair. Basic to this theory is the idea that items acquire *frequency units* each time the subjects respond to them. The more frequency units an item has acquired, the more likely the subjects are to label that item as the correct one. Ekstrand, Wallace, and Underwood (1966) have clarified what is meant by frequency units. A number of different types of responses can add frequency units to an item. First, *perceiving* an item is one type of response that is presumed to add frequency units to that item. Because the subjects probably perceive both the right and the wrong items on each trial, it is presumed that this type of response adds frequency units to both right and wrong items. Second, *pronouncing* an item adds frequency units. Each time the subjects say the correct item, an additional frequency unit is added to that item. The third, and perhaps most important, type of response that adds frequency units is the *rehearsal* response. These responses presumably occur during the feedback interval when the correct item is clearly identified for the subjects. The subjects rehearse the correct item at this point, adding frequency units. They therefore increase the probability of identifying that item as the correct item in the future. Presumably the right item will be rehearsed much more than the wrong item. Hence, a differential number of frequency units begins to build up in connection with the right and wrong items.

RESPONSE DIFFERENTIATION

Discrimination, as we have seen, refers to the situation wherein the subject limits a given response to one of many similar stimuli. *Response differentiation*, in contrast, refers to the situation in which the subject comes to give one of several similar responses to a specific stimulus situation. For example, when a pigeon is first reinforced for pecking a key, its pecking behavior may be somewhat varied and haphazard. It pecks here and there; some pecks are weak, and others are strong. As training progresses, the responses become more consistent. The pecking behavior is shaped to the point at which it maximizes reinforcement. The pigeon differentiates between more and less successful responses and restricts itself to those that are maximally efficient. When babies first begin to speak, their words are poorly framed. Parents praise them when their responses are accurate and withhold reinforcement when they are not. The responses gradually become differentiated. Poorly vocalized instances drop out. The probability of clearly enunciated sounds, or those that will most likely result in reinforcement, increases.

By and large, more experimental work has been done with discrimination than with response differentiation. But some examples of response differentiation are available in the literature. The concept of shaping, wherein the experimenter gradually induces the subject to emit a particular response by reinforcing successive approximations to that response, has already been discussed. *Verbal conditioning* represents another area of research that encompasses the concept of response differentiation. In a typical verbal-conditioning experiment (Greenspoon, 1955) the subjects are asked to say words as they come to mind. As the subjects respond, the experimenter murmurs "mm-hmm" (or some other subtle form of reinforcement) each time they say a plural word. Control subjects do not receive this form of social reinforcement. Greenspoon found evidence for an increase in the rate of plural word production in the experimental group. In other words, the subjects were able to differentiate between responses that were effective in producing a reinforcement (plural) and those that were not effective (singular). Other varieties of verbal conditioning (for example, Taffel, 1955) have required the subjects to make up sentences using one of six pronouns. The experimenter reinforced the choice of one arbitrarily designated pronoun and did not respond when one of the remaining pronouns was used. Taffel found that the use of the reinforced pronoun increased during the experiment.

The controversy that swirled about the verbal-conditioning effect had to do with the subjects' awareness of what is going on in the experiment. Some authors (Spielberger, 1965) suggested that subjects who exhibit the verbal-conditioning effect are usually aware of the conditions of the experiment. They know, or have discovered, that the experimenter is reinforcing a particular kind of response. These authors also suggested that subjects who are unaware of the reinforcement contingency usually fail to condition. Other investigators, however, appear to have demonstrated verbal conditioning in the absence of awareness (see Kennedy, 1971). Rosenfeld and Baer (1969) ran an experiment in which the experimenter was really the subject and the subject was really the experimenter. One individual was informed that he was to be an experimenter. During an interview with a subject he was to reinforce the subject's chin-rubbing response by nodding his head each time it occurred. In reality, this experimenter was the subject and the subject was the experimenter. The presumed subject (the true experimenter) was in league with Rosenfeld and Baer. During the interview the true experimenter was actually trying to condition the true subject. Each time the true subject said "yeah," the true experimenter reinforced him by rubbing his chin. The results indicated that the true subject increased the rate at which he said "yeah" even though he thought he was the "experimenter" and in control of the situation. The true subject apparently had no idea that he was being conditioned, and yet his response rate went up.

With this classic example of devious psychological experimentation we come to the end of our discussion of stimulus generalization, discrimination, and the related process of response differentiation. In the next section we shall move on to another related topic—*transfer of training*. We shall concentrate on the impact that a given instance of learning may have on subsequent instances of learning. The overlap between transfer effects and generalization should become apparent as we trace through positive and negative transfer phenomena.

TRANSFER OF TRAINING

The effects of prior training on present training may be either positive or negative. For example, bad study habits acquired during high school may have a negative influence on attempts to establish better study habits in college. Learning one language may facilitate the acquisition of subsequent languages. Learning to drive a car certainly aids in learning to drive a truck. Learning to respond fearfully in one social setting may hinder attempts to adjust comfortably in a new set of social circumstances. Such *transfer of training* is discussed here because, as we shall see, it is closely related to stimulus generalization. Specifically, *both transfer of training and stimulus generalization are concerned with the effects of prior learning on subsequent performance.*

An enormous body of literature has grown up around the concept of transfer of training. The basic transfer experiment involves two stages. The subject first learns one task (quite often a paired-associate list) and then attempts to master a second somewhat similar task. Within this simple, convenient framework any number of variables can be manipulated. Historically, the most important variable has been that of the *similarity between the successive tasks*. One of the primary concerns of this section will be to outline the complex relationship between similarity and transfer.

Specific and Nonspecific Transfer

Suppose that we are interested in what effects the learning of one paired-associate list has on the subsequent learning of a second list. Furthermore, suppose that the two lists compose what is commonly known as the A–B, A–D paradigm. What this means is that the *stimuli* in the two successive lists (the A units) are identical, but the *responses* in the two successive lists (the B and D units) are different. One item from the first list might be *valiant–rotten*, and the corresponding pair in the second list might be *valiant–complex*. The subjects are required to associate *rotten* with *valiant* in the first list and then to associate *complex* with the same stimulus term during second-list learning. We want to know if A–D learning will be helped or hindered by the A–B experience. On an intuitive basis we might suspect that the A–B learning would interfere with, or compete with, the subjects' attempts to connect D to A. Each time the subjects try to come up with *complex* during A–D learning, they are hampered by the fact that *rotten*, so recently acquired, continues to pop into their minds.

Intuitive notions aside, we have to find a way to measure the impact of A–B learning on A–D learning. We need a control group that learns the A–D but not the A–B list. This pattern is designated as Design 1 in Table 7.1. We can compare

Table 7.1   Transfer Designs

	FIRST TASK	SECOND TASK
Design 1		
Experimental condition	A–B	A–D
Control condition	None	A–D
Design 2		
Experimental condition	A–B	A–D
Control condition	B–C	A–D

the ease with which the experimental and control groups master the A–D list. Typically, the experimental groups have a more difficult time of it in this particular situation, confirming our intuitive suspicion that the A–B, A–D paradigm is a highly negative transfer paradigm, or a paradigm in which the learning of the second task is hindered by the learning of the first task. It is difficult to connect Ds to As after Bs have already been associated with As.

At this juncture the first of many complications arises. At least two transfer factors contribute to the experimental subjects' ability to master the A–D list. The first, as we have noted, has to do with the fact that the B responses probably compete with the D responses during A–D learning. This influence is termed *specific transfer*. It refers to the impact of *specific* first-list associations on attempts to establish *specific* second-list associations. In this particular paradigm the specific transfer effect is a negative, or disruptive, one. (In other situations, as we shall see, specific transfer effects may be positive.) But another type of transfer factor contributes to the experimental subjects' ability to acquire the A–D list. It is referred to as *nonspecific transfer* and is, in this particular paradigm, a positive influence. What is it about this Design 1 that would give the experimental subjects an *advantage* over the control subjects in learning the A–D list?

LEARNING TO LEARN.   Two nonspecific transfer factors give the experimental subjects an advantage over the control subjects during A–D learning. The experimental subjects have an advantage in that they have already learned one paired-associate list, whereas the control subjects have not. The experimental subjects have undoubtedly already learned something about how to master a paired-associate list. They already know what to look for, what strategies to use, and how to hook up items in efficient ways.

The importance and power of learning to learn have been known for a long time. In a very early study, for example, Ward (1937) had subjects learn 16 lists, one on each of 16 successive days. As you can see in Figure 7.13, the subjects showed an enormous improvement in their ability to learn the successive lists. Whereas it took them almost 40 trials to learn the first list, they were able to learn the last, or 16th, list in fewer than 20 trials. Now that is learning to learn (see also Keppel, Postman, & Zavortink, 1968).

Psychological research has many good examples of learning to learn. In an early and now classic study, Harlow (1949) had monkeys learn 344 successive object

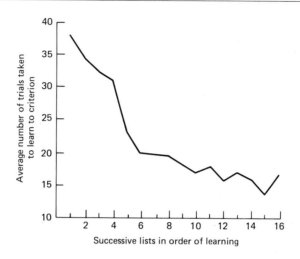

Figure 7.13 The learning-to-learn effect. Subjects learned sixteen successive lists, one per day. Notice that the last list was learned in about half as many trials as the first list. (Adapted from Ward, L. B. Reminiscence and learning rate. *Psychological Monographs*, 1937, 49, 220. Copyright 1937 by the American Psychological Association.)

discriminations. As is evident in Figure 7.14, the monkeys' ability to solve these problems increased sharply as the number of previously solved discriminations increased. By the time the monkeys had solved several hundred of these problems they were solving each new problem quickly, usually within the first few trials. In summary, learning to learn is a widespread and powerful nonspecific transfer effect that occurs, not only with animals (see Oden, Thompson, & Premack, 1988), but with humans as well (see Brown & Kane, 1988).

WARM–UP.   The second nonspecific transfer effect is called *warm-up*. At the time that experimental subjects in Design 1 of Table 7.1 begin A–D learning, they are already "warmed up" when compared with the control subjects.

At the beginning of A–D learning the experimental subjects will not be as distracted as the control subjects. They have already established sensory, postural, and attitudinal sets to learn paired-associate lists. They are ready, whereas the control subjects must settle in.

Learning to learn can be distinguished from warm-up in terms of its *temporal persistence*. Warm-up effects are presumed to be *transitory*. Once practice ceases, the advantage gained by having warmed up dissipates rapidly. The effects of learning to learn are, in contrast, assumed to be more permanent. Once subjects have developed efficient strategies and methods for mastering a particular learning task, regardless of the specific content of the task, these strategies and methods may be maintained, or remembered, over time.

ELIMINATING NONSPECIFIC TRANSFER.   To return to our consideration of the A–B, A–D paradigm, it is clear that two transfer influences operate in the experimental

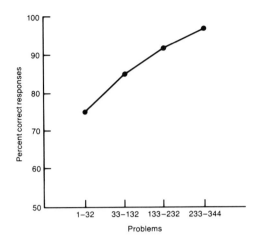

Figure 7.14 Discrimination learning set curve based on responses for Trials 2–6. (Adapted from Harlow, H. F. The formation of learning sets. *Psychological Review*, 1949, *56*, 51–65. Copyright © 1949 by the American Psychological Association. Reprinted by permission.)

condition. One is negative specific transfer, associated with competition between the A–B and A–D associations. The other is positive nonspecific transfer, identified with warm-up and learning to learn. Overall transfer in Design 1 will be determined by both types of transfer.

But suppose that we are interested *only* in specific transfer. We want to estimate it accurately, and we want our estimate to be free of nonspecific transfer effects. If we were to use Design 1, we would underestimate the amount of negative specific transfer. The negative specific transfer effect would be partially mitigated by the advantage that the experimental group gains over the control group through positive nonspecific transfer. Hence, we need an alternative design in which the control subjects are given an *equal* opportunity to warm up and learn to learn. Design 2 in Table 7.1 represents such a design. The control group first learns a list that is *entirely unrelated* to the A–D list. Hence, the control condition in this design is free from any specific transfer. But it does involve nonspecific transfer. The control subjects are allowed the opportunity to warm up and learn to learn. In Design 2 the control and experimental conditions are equated in terms of nonspecific transfer. They differ only in terms of specific transfer. Thus, any difference in the ease with which the experimental and control subjects learn the A–D list must result from specific transfer alone. The design is free from contamination by unwanted nonspecific factors (see Postman, 1969, 1971).

Specific Transfer: Similarity Effects

Having outlined the manner in which psychologists isolate specific from nonspecific transfer, we now turn to a more detailed consideration of some of the more important specific transfer phenomena. The A–B, A–D paradigm just discussed is

Table 7.2   Sample Items Representing Four Basic Two-List Transfer Paradigms

FIRST LIST (A–B)	SECOND, OR TRANSFER, LIST			
	C–D	A–D	A–B'	C–B
LOH–tranquil	GOZ–royal	LOH–royal	LOH–calm	GOZ–tranquil
TUN–afraid	WIF–barren	TUN–barren	TUN–fearful	WIF–afraid
BAV–insane	DEX–spoken	BAV–spoken	BAV–crazy	DEX–insane
JAX–complete	PEC–double	JAX–double	JAX–total	PEC–complete

only one of many possible transfer patterns. For example, we can construct successive lists so that they conform to an A–B, A–B' pattern. In this paradigm the
stimuli in successive lists are identical, and the responses are similar (B' is a unit
that is similar or related to B). A pair from the first list might be *valiant–scared*,
whereas the corresponding A–B' pair would be *valiant–frightened*. If the similarity between the first-list and second-list responses is strong enough, this paradigm tends to yield positive transfer. When subjects are attempting to connect
frightened to *valiant*, the stimulus term *valiant* might cue off the already learned
scared response, which, in turn, might stimulate *frightened*.

We can also construct an A–B, A'–B paradigm in which the responses in the
successive lists are identical and the stimuli are similar. This also tends to be a
positive transfer paradigm. Then there is the A–B, C–B paradigm, in which the
responses are identical and the stimuli are unrelated. The more patterns we devise
and test, the more confusing the situation becomes, and the more difficult it becomes to keep them all straight in one's mind (see Table 7.2).

OSGOOD'S TRANSFER SURFACE.   Fortunately, Osgood (1949) has developed a
mnemonic device that summarizes the transfer effects expected in many paradigms. The device is neither perfect nor comprehensive. But it is convenient, and it
does provide us with a simple method for keeping the welter of transfer paradigms
and similarity relationships somewhat organized. A modified version of the original Osgood surface is shown in Figure 7.15. Consider the plane depicted in the left
side of the figure. Degrees of similarity between first-list and second-list stimuli,
ranging from identity to neutrality (unrelated), are arranged along the width of the
plane. Degrees of response similarity, ranging from identity to neutrality, are
spread along the length of the plane. (Actually, the Osgood surface extended the
response dimension to include opposed and antagonistic responses, but neither
extension has proved to be of much value.) The plane contains points that represent all possible combinations of stimulus and response similarity. The location of
a few of the more important paradigms are indicated on the plane. For example,
the A–B, C–B paradigm is located in the far left corner, where response similarity
is at a maximum (identity), and stimulus similarity is minimal. The A–B, A–B
paradigm (identical lists) is located in the near left corner, and so on.

Now, having located all possible combinations of stimulus and response similarity on a plane, we may ask the next question: How much and what kind of
transfer (positive or negative) do we expect in each of these paradigms? To answer
this question we turn to the right side of Figure 7.15. Here we find a flexed surface

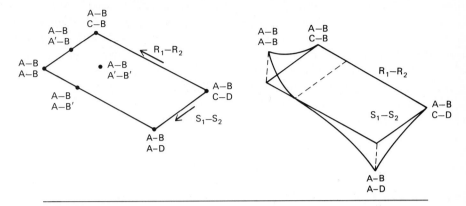

Left side: As stimulus similarity increases with identical responses, transfer increases from zero to maximum positive.

Right side: As stimulus similarity increases with unrelated responses, transfer shifts from zero to maximum negative.

Back side: As response similarity increases with unrelated stimuli, transfer remains at zero.

Front side: As response similarity increases with identical stimuli, transfer shifts from maximum negative to maximum positive.

Figure 7.15 A modified version of the Osgood transfer and retroaction surface. (After Osgood, C. E. The similarity paradox in human learning: A resolution. *Psychological Review*, 1949, *56*, 132–143. Fig. 5, p. 140. Copyright 1949 by the American Psychological Association.)

that is superimposed on and that cuts through our plane at the dotted line. This surface will indicate the kind of transfer that we expect in any given paradigm. Notice that the surface is above the plane at its left end and below the plane at its right end. The vertical dimension represents the direction and amount of expected transfer. If the surface is *above* the plane, we expect *positive* transfer in those paradigms lying under the surface. If the surface is *below* the plane, we expect *negative* transfer.

Suppose that we wish to predict transfer in the A–B, A–D paradigm. First, we locate the A–B, A–D paradigm on the plane. Second, we draw a line, perpendicular to the plane, from the plane to the surface. The *direction* of the line represents the *direction* of the expected transfer. A line drawn upward represents positive transfer; a line drawn downward represents negative transfer. The *length* of the line represents *amount* of transfer. The longer the line, the stronger is the transfer effect. Thus, we expect a large amount of negative transfer in the A–B, A–D paradigm. We must draw a long line downward to reach the surface from the plane at point A–B, A–D. Try predicting transfer in the A–B, A'–B paradigm. First locate the paradigm on the plane. Then draw a line from the plane to the surface at the point. The surface predicts moderate positive transfer in this paradigm.

This model is interesting and important. Once one grasps it, it serves as a convenient summary device. In words it says that when responses are identical and stimulus similarity increases, then transfer will increase from zero to maximum positive (this function is represented by the left edge of the surface). When responses are unrelated and stimulus similarity increases, then transfer will increase from zero to maximum negative (the right edge of the surface). When stimuli are unrelated and response similarity increases, transfer remains at zero (the back edge). When stimuli are identical and response similarity increases, transfer shifts from maximum negative to maximum positive (the front edge).

The overall surface has received some experimental support. Dallett (1962) chose twelve points on the surface representing three degrees of response similarity and four degrees of stimulus similarity. He constructed lists corresponding to these twelve paradigms and tested for transfer. His results support the overall shape and nature of the hypothetical surface.

Serious objections to the surface have been raised, however. The most important of them has to do with the impact of meaningfulness on transfer. It seems that the surface is most suitable as a summary statement of the transfer effects expected when highly meaningful materials are employed. It does not accurately predict the amounts of transfer that will be obtained under conditions of low meaningfulness (Dean & Kausler, 1964; Jung, 1963). Thus, our use of the Osgood surface must be tempered by an awareness of its limitations.

Generalization and Transfer of Training

We have repeatedly noted that transfer and generalization are related in that both are concerned with the effects of prior learning on subsequent performance. In spite of the fact that the two fields have developed somewhat independently (for example, different variables, designs, methods, vocabularies, and investigators), psychologists have taken note of the basic correspondence between the two phenomena.

Consider stimulus generalization. We train a response to a given stimulus. We then present similar stimuli and observe whether the response occurs. The A–B, A′–B transfer paradigm, in which stimulus similarity is varied, seems to be related to stimulus generalization. We connect B to A and then present a similar stimulus (A′). The more similar A′ is to A, the more likely A′ is to elicit B. We can label this effect either stimulus generalization or positive transfer. Variations in interlist stimulus similarity correspond to variations in the similarity between the training and the test stimuli in a typical stimulus generalization study. An awareness of this basic continuity formed the basis for Gibson's (1940) classic analysis of verbal transfer effects in terms of the principles of stimulus generalization.

But a consideration of stimulus generalization is not enough to account for all our observed transfer-of-training phenomena. For example, what about the A–B, A–B′ paradigm? This does not seem to involve stimulus generalization, but it does involve another type of generalization, which we can term *response generalization*. It was left to Osgood (1946, 1949, 1953) to mesh, or integrate, the concepts of stimulus generalization and response generalization in this analysis of transfer effects. Very simply, response generalization refers to the fact that, if a given response is connected to a given stimulus, that stimulus will also tend to elicit similar responses. The less similar the response, the less likely it will be to occur. For example, if a girl's name is Melodie, then there will be a tendency for people to call her Melanie but not much of a tendency to call her Joan. If we connect the word *house* to a given stimulus in the laboratory, then that stimulus will, in one way or another, also tend to elicit *home*. To return to the thread of the analysis, the A–B, A–B′ transfer paradigm seems to involve varying degrees of response similarity. If we connect *house* to a given stimulus and then require subjects to associate *home* with the same stimulus, we will observe a positive transfer effect brought about by response generalization.

Osgood's surface represents an integrated estimation of the effects of both stimulus and response generalization in transfer-of-training paradigms. Largely through his efforts, the concepts of stimulus and response generalization were extended into the field of verbal learning, where they contributed to the theoretical analysis of transfer-of-training effects.

You should not be misled by the fact that generalization and transfer of training are often treated as separate topics within the field of psychology. Their intimate relationship is discussed in more detail by Postman (1971).

SUMMARY

1. *Generalization* refers to the fact that, if a given response is connected to a particular stimulus, similar stimuli will tend to elicit that same response. The greater the similarity, the greater is the generalization.
2. Generalization occurs in both classical and instrumental situations.
3. Some studies show that the generalization gradient will become more peaked as the number of reinforced responses to the training stimulus is increased; others show no change or actual flattening of the gradient.
4. Generalization tends to be greater following partial reinforcement than after continuous reinforcement. However, this effect becomes less clear when one tests for generalization during the intervals between reinforcements.
5. Increased drive level may lead to less generalization in a simple task and more generalization in a complex task.
6. Prior experience with the stimulus dimension tends to result in steeper generalization gradients.
7. *Primary generalization* involves some innate stimulus dimension. *Secondary generalization* involves an acquired, or learned, stimulus dimension.
8. In *semantic conditioning* a response is first connected to a given word. It is then found that similar words tend to elicit that same response.
9. In the *acquired equivalence of cues* paradigm two distinct stimuli are paired. A response is connected to one of the two. It is then found that the remaining stimulus will tend to elicit that same response.
10. Extinction tendencies can generalize too.
11. Generalization is important in applied fields such as behavior modification.
12. *Discrimination* refers to an increase in the tendency to restrict a response to one stimulus value along a stimulus dimension. It is brought about by differential reinforcement. Stimulus generalization and discrimination may well be opposite sides of the same coin.
13. Many think of generalization as imprecise *stimulus control*, whereas discrimination refers to precise stimulus control.
14. In discrimination learning, responses to both the positive and negative stimuli initially increase. Then the response to the negative stimulus drops out, and the response to the positive stimulus increases.

15. In the *simultaneous presentation* technique both the positive and the negative stimuli are presented together. The *successive presentation* technique involves the sequential presentation of the positive and negative stimuli.

16. According to the *Hull-Spence theory* of discrimination learning, the net probability of responding to any point along a dimension is reflected by the algebraic sum of the values of the generalized positive and negative tendencies at that point.

17. The *relational interpretation* argues that in solving a discrimination problem subjects are learning a relation between the stimuli and that subjects respond on the basis of that perceived relationship.

18. *Transposition* refers to the fact that, if subjects learn to discriminate between, say, a large positive stimulus and a smaller negative stimulus and are then presented the large positive stimulus and a still larger new test stimulus, they will tend to respond to that new stimulus rather than to the old positive one.

19. The relational theoreticians argued that the transposition effect proved that subjects learn a relation between the positive and negative stimuli. But Spence was able to predict the same transposition effect using the Hull-Spence model.

20. Noncontinuity theory argues that discrimination is the result of hypothesis testing.

21. If a pigeon is first reinforced for pecking either of two keys and then one key is made the positive stimulus (reinforcement is continued) while the other key becomes the negative stimulus (reinforcement is discontinued), the response to the positive stimulus increases even though its treatment is constant across the two phases of the experiment. This is called *behavioral contrast*. It may result from a motivating frustration factor.

22. In *errorless discrimination learning* a firm response to the positive stimulus alone is established. The negative stimulus is then introduced into the situation so gradually that the animal never responds to it.

23. This form of discrimination formation lends some support to the frustration interpretation of behavioral contrast effects.

24. In *insoluble discrimination situations* the stimuli are made so similar or the reinforcement is presented so randomly that the subject cannot solve the problem. Behavior disturbances, which have been likened to human neurotic and psychotic behaviors, have been observed in animals in these situations.

25. Current concerns for animal welfare make it unlikely that these experiments would be conducted today.

26. Although in this chapter we concentrate on human verbal discrimination processes, humans' ability to discriminate and process visual material is also refined, and it will be discussed in a later chapter.

27. The *stage analysis* of verbal learning suggests that a simple S-R association involves at least three distinct subprocesses, or stages—stimulus learning, response learning, and associative learning. Each stage appears to involve discrimination processes.

28. In *verbal-discrimination learning* (VD) subjects are presented long series of pairs of items over and over. The subject's task is to identify which member of each pair is the "correct" item (as arbitrarily chosen by the experimenter). This paradigm represents a direct extension of the discrimination paradigm into the field of verbal training.

29. The *frequency theory* of VD learning argues that the discrimination between "right" and "wrong" items is made on the basis of the relative frequency of the members of each pair. The more frequency units an item has acquired, the more likely it is to be labeled as the correct item. Perceiving responses, pronouncing responses, and rehearsing responses all add frequency units to an item.

30. Frequency theory accounts for many of the data in VD learning.

31. *Response differentiation* refers to the process wherein subjects refine their response down to the point at which it yields reinforcement with a minimum of effort.

32. *Verbal conditioning* represents an example of response differentiation. Subjects are asked to say words as they come to mind. The experimenter may increase the occurrence of certain types of words (for example, plural nouns) by reinforcing such words with a murmured "mm-hmm."

33. A controversy exists over whether such verbal conditioning can occur when the subjects are unaware of the reinforcement and its relationship to the critical response class.

34. The study of *transfer of training* focuses on the positive and negative effects of prior training on subsequent training.

35. Two general classes of transfer event are referred to as *specific* and *nonspecific transfer*. Specific transfer refers to the impact of specific first-list associations on attempts to establish specific second-list associations. Nonspecific transfer refers to transfer resulting from such factors as *learning to learn* and *warm-up*. These factors are independent of the specific contents of the lists. Warm-up effects are presumed to be transitory, whereas learning-to-learn phenomena are more permanent.

36. The similarity between successive lists has proved to be one of the more powerful transfer variables. The relationship between transfer and interlist similarity is not simple.

37. Osgood has developed a *transfer surface* that summarizes the direction and amount of transfer expected in transfer situations.

38. The surface predicts that, when responses are identical and stimulus similarity increases, then transfer will increase from zero to maximum positive. When responses are unrelated and stimulus similarity increases, transfer will shift from zero to maximum negative. When stimuli are unrelated and response similarity increases, then transfer remains at zero. When stimuli are identical and response similarity increases, then transfer will shift from maximum negative to maximum positive.

39. With a few exceptions the surface summarizes transfer effects obtained with highly meaningful, or familiar, materials. But when materials of a low level of meaningfulness are employed, the surface is not accurate.

40. The relationship between transfer of training and generalization is a close one. Transfer-of-training paradigms involve both stimulus and response generalization. For example, the A–B, A'–B paradigm involves interlist stimulus generalization, whereas the A–B, A–B' paradigm involves response generalization.

PART 4

RETENTION

In this part we focus on retention processes. Once again it should be remembered that it is impossible to separate completely *acquisition, transfer*, and *retention*. A concern for one of these three is a matter of emphasis rather than of clear and distinct differences among them. In Part Four we concentrate on what happens to memory traces after learning has been accomplished. Important points of contact between the study of human and animal memory are stressed toward the end of this part.

In Chapters 8 and 9 we cover six major interpretations of memory. Chapter 8 begins with a discussion of interference. The basic assumption behind interference theory is that retention losses can be traced to the interfering effects of previous or subsequent learning. For example, if we learn a phone number such as 872-6314, we will have little trouble remembering it over time. But if after processing this number we go on to learn 843-1762, 782-6413, 287-1463, and 378-2614, we may then have trouble recalling the original number. In other words, the subsequent learning somehow interferes with our ability to recall the original number. In the latter part of Chapter 8 we move on to a discussion of decay theory and close with a consideration of the consolidation hypothesis.

Chapter 9 begins with a look at separate-store models. This approach draws heavily on information-measurement concepts and the language of digital computers. The individual is seen as an information-processing system. Memory is thought of in terms of the encoding, storage, and retrieval of information. In contrast to the single theory associated with the interference approach, many information-processing models of memory are available. We examine several of them. We then consider the concept of levels of processing and a number of recent semantic-network models.

Chapter 10 begins by noting that psychologists have distinguished among many types of memory. We ask whether these distinctions are valid and whether distinct models will be necessary for the proposed types of memory. Several important distinctions are discussed: short-term versus long-term memory, recall versus recognition, verbal versus visual processing, the processing of alternative forms of information, and animal versus human memory. By drawing on available experimental data we attempt to assess the validity of these various distinctions.

Chapter 11 considers the role of organization and elaboration in improving memory. Organization in memory refers not so much to a particular model as to an orientation toward the study of memory. The basic assumption behind organization research is that we remember materials by relating them to one another, by building "mental structures," and by ordering materials in many different ways. In a sense the organizational approach represents a return to an awareness of the complexity of cognitive events. New methods of assessing organization have stimulated this return to some very interesting problems. We also discuss several lines of research (for example, encoding, mnemonics, and imagery) and attempt to relate them to issues of general concern in the field of memory.

CHAPTER

8

MEMORY MODELS I: INTERFERENCE, DECAY, AND CONSOLIDATION

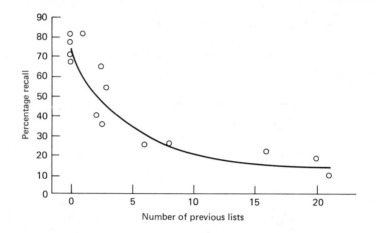

Figure 8.1 Proactive inhibition as a function of the number of previously learned lists. Each point represents the results of a different experimental study. (Adapted from Underwood, B. J. Interference and forgetting. *Psychological Review*, 1957, 64, 49–60. Fig. 3, p. 53. Copyright 1957 by the American Psychological Association. Reprinted by permission.)

MULTIPLE MODELS

Efforts to understand memory have been sprightly and active for many years. Although no single model or theory has proven to be completely adequate, great strides have been made. In this chapter and the next we shall examine six major approaches to the understanding of memory. *Interference, decay,* and *consolidation* theories are discussed in this chapter, and *separate-store models, levels of processing,* and *semantic-network models* are considered in Chapter 9. We begin now with some of the aspects of interference.

PROACTIVE INHIBITION
The Effect

Suppose that you are invited to learn an ordinary ten-item paired-associate list. After mastering the list completely you are dismissed with instructions to return at the same time the next day. When you return, the experimenter presents the stimuli one at a time with instructions to recall the correct responses. You find that you can remember only eight of the ten responses.

You have forgotten 20% of the material in 24 hours. Where did it go? What happened to that material that you knew so well so recently? These questions form the basis of the investigation of memory. We want to know what happened to the other two items and why they were forgotten.

One of the powerful interpretations of forgetting is best introduced by extending the experiment described above. Suppose that on Day 2, after you have recalled the list you learned on Day 1, the experimenter gives you *another* paired-associate list to learn. After you master this second list, she dismisses you with instructions to

Table 8.1   Proactive Inhibition Experimental Design

GROUP	TASK 1	TASK 2	TASK 3*
Experimental	Learns A	Learns B	Retention of B
Control	—	Learns B	Retention of B

*Task 3 measures PI.

return the next day. On Day 3 you attempt to retrieve the second list. You then learn a third list, and so on. Let us say that you learn 20 somewhat similar paired-associate lists on 20 successive days. On each day you are required to recall only the list you learned the previous day. In other words, the retention interval for any given list is 24 hours. The question is this: How much of the 20th list will you be able to recall 24 hours after it is learned?

Some students suspect that recall of that final list will be almost perfect. You have, after all, had all sorts of practice in learning and recalling paired-associate lists. And we have already seen in the last chapter that *learning to learn* can be a powerful aid to performance on successive, similar tasks (see Figure 7.13). But that is not what happens at all. Recall of that final list is extremely poor. In fact, you probably will not be able to recall more than two or three of the items you learned just 24 hours ago. You have forgotten, or are unable to produce, 80% of the correct responses. This is a large effect, and we shall want to find out what causes it. Obviously, it must have something to do with all those prior lists you learned. The language usually used here suggests that the first 19 lists somehow *interfere* with, or compete with, attempts to recall the 20th list. The materials from all those other lists keep popping into your mind as you try to recall the 20th list. The old materials block the correct responses, or confuse you when you try to recall them.

This effect is called *proactive inhibition*. It refers to a disruption in our ability to retrieve a given set of materials owing to the interfering effects of previously learned materials. The more previous lists we have learned, the greater the loss of retention. Figure 8.1 clearly indicates that recall of a given list over 24 hours declines as a function of the number of prior lists learned in the same experiment (Underwood, 1957).

The PI Design

Table 8.1 contains the basic experimental design used to demonstrate proactive inhibition (PI). The critical comparison is between the experimental and control recall of Task 2. If the experimental subjects display poorer Task 2 recall, we say that PI has occurred. The recall of a given list (Task 2) has been disrupted by prior learning (Task 1).

Proactive inhibition is not a theory or an explanation. It is a fact, an important one. It refers to the enormous amount of forgetting that can be attributed to the interfering effects of prior learning. The more we learn, or store, the more susceptible we are to this type of interference. The more organic chemistry we commit to memory, the greater is the possibility of confusion. The more names and faces a professor attempts to match in her lecture section, the greater are the chances that she will have difficulty remembering additional name–face pairings. This is not to say that adding to our storage invariably leads to poorer retrieval of newly acquired materials (see Postman & Gray, 1977). To the contrary, it is possible to overcome potential PI effects by ordering and choosing our materials so that they do not fall into an interfering pattern. In addition, we can build on, or structure, our knowledge so that we actually find *proactive facilitation*, or improved retention, rather than PI. And yet PI has to be considered a major factor in many observed retention losses. Prior learning constitutes a powerful source of interference (see Underwood, 1983).

PI and Negative Transfer

Is proactive inhibition the same thing as negative transfer? No, but students often (and understandably) confuse the two. As you will recall from the last chapter, negative transfer refers to what happens when the subject is *learning* the second list. PI refers to what happens during the *recall* of that second list at a later time, after some retention interval has elapsed. Negative transfer appears during Task 2 in Table 8.1; PI appears during Task 3 in the same table. Negative transfer refers to the inhibiting effects that the learning of A has on the subsequent new *learning* of B. Proactive inhibition refers to the inhibiting effect that the learning of A has on the *recall* of B after some time has elapsed since the learning of B.

Negative transfer can occur *during* a PI experiment (during the performance of Task 2 in Table 8.1), but the effects are different. Proactive inhibition involves three stages and recall of previously learned material, whereas negative transfer involves only two stages and involves new learning.

RETROACTIVE INHIBITION
The RI Design

Retroactive inhibition (RI) is another type of interference. Retroactive inhibition refers to interference resulting from *subsequent* learning. The basic RI design is depicted in Table 8.2. The experimental subjects learn two successive tasks. Then, at the end of some retention interval (typically ranging from zero to several weeks) their ability to retrieve the Task 1 materials is tested. If their retention is poorer than that of the controls, we say that RI has been demonstrated. If a ten-year-old learns numerous baseball statistics connected with the National League and then proceeds to do the same with American League statistics, then his ability to recall the National League statistics may well be less than if he had not acquired the American League materials. In situations like this retroactive-inhibition effects can be large. That is, a great percentage of our responses can be made unavailable through the manipulation of subsequent learning.

Filler Tasks

Note that Table 8.2 suggests that the controls are resting, or doing nothing, while the experimental subjects are learning the second task. Control subjects are not actually allowed to rest during this interval. If they were, they would spend the time rehearsing Task 1, which would give them an advantage over the experimental subjects. During this interval, control subjects typically engage in some *unrelated*

Table 8.2   Retroactive Inhibition Experimental Design

GROUP	TASK 1	TASK 2	TASK 3*
Experimental	Learns A	Learns B	Retention of A
Control	Learns A	—	Retention of A

*Task 3 measures RI.

filler task, which is designed to *prevent them from rehearsing Task 1*. These filler tasks include such things as working perceptual-motor puzzles, counting backward, solving simple mathematical problems, and crossing out designated digits on sheets of endless digits.

Just as proactive facilitation can sometimes be observed in proactive experiments, *retroactive facilitation* sometimes occurs in retroactive experiments. This term refers to the situation in which the materials are structured so that the learning of that second task helps the subjects remember the first task. Although retroactive-facilitation effects are easily demonstrated, our focus will be on interference effects because we are, after all, primarily interested in memory losses in this chapter.

In summary, it seems that our ability to remember a given set of materials is strongly affected by both prior and subsequent learning. Ironically, the very act of learning itself constitutes a source of forgetting. Learning can, under various circumstances, reduce our ability to remember what we have already learned, and it has the potential to disrupt our ability to remember what we will learn in the future. The exact nature of these disruptive processes will be the subject of an upcoming section concerning interference theory.

INTERTASK SIMILARITY

In the last chapter we discussed variations in stimulus and response similarity in two-list transfer situations. Osgood's (1949) transfer surface summarized the various transfer paradigms. Exactly the same similarity variations can be investigated in three-step RI and PI situations. For example, we can devise an RI paradigm corresponding to the A–B, A–D pattern. The subjects learn two successive lists (possessing identical stimuli and unrelated responses). They are then tested for retention of the first, or A–B, list. Similarly, we might want to investigate an A–B, A–B' proactive-inhibition situation in which the subjects are tested for retention of the *second* list (A–B') after they have learned two lists that possess identical stimuli and similar responses. We can vary the similarity of the stimuli or the responses in any manner we wish. We can then test for either first-list retention (RI) or second-list retention (PI).

The close relationship between transfer paradigms and RI and PI designs should now be apparent. In transfer paradigms we focus on, or test, *second-list learning*, whereas in RI and PI paradigms we focus on, or test, *retention of the materials* over time. The PI and RI paradigms add a third step (the retention test) to the two-step transfer paradigms. Thus, transfer is involved in every PI and RI design. It is just that in PI and RI designs we do not focus on second-list *learning*. Rather, we are interested in what happens to the strengths of the materials after learning has been completed. For example, in an A–B, A–D transfer paradigm we look at the subject's performance during learning of the second list. In an A–B, A–D proactive-inhibition paradigm we test for A–D strength not while the subject is first learning A–D but after learning has been completed and some retention interval has elapsed.

We can devise PI and RI paradigms that correspond to every point on the Osgood surface. For example, we can develop RI and PI paradigms that correspond to the A–B, C–D; A–B, C–B; and A–B, A'–B paradigms. Osgood (1949) developed his surface with the idea that it would predict retroactive-inhibition effects as well as transfer effects. It is, in fact, called the transfer and retroaction surface. Thus, the A–B, A–D paradigm is expected to yield both high negative transfer and strong retroactive inhibition (which it does). Similarly, the A–B, A'–D paradigm is expected to yield moderate negative transfer and moderate retroactive inhibition, and so on.

The predictions made from the surface with respect to RI have received some support (Bugelski & Cadwallader, 1956; Gibson, 1941; Hamilton, 1943; Kanungo, 1967). But, as is true of the transfer predictions of the surface, the RI predictions have proved to be less than perfect. The student should thus consider the surface not as a perfect predictor but as a convenient mnemonic device. When one becomes lost in the maze of RI and PI paradigms, the Osgood surface provides a handy mechanism for sorting them all out and for perceiving their relationships to one another.

THE GENERALITY OF INTERFERENCE
Interference and Prose Material

Before we move to a consideration of interference theory, one final point should be made. Interference effects can be quite general and operate in the world outside the laboratory. Even though most of the research seems to be cast in paired-associate, serial, and free-recall situations, we should keep in mind that interference effects are pervasive and are not limited to these somewhat artificial tasks.

For example, interference effects can be observed in what psychologists call connected discourse (see Dempster, 1988; Slamecka, 1960, 1961). Connected discourses include such things as meaningful sentences, paragraphs, and prose in general.

Interference and Spatial Learning

Elmes (1988) has demonstrated that interference theory can account for effects observed in spatial learning. He had human subjects learn to enter and then relearn to enter four specific arms of a twelve-arm radial maze while blindfolded. But between learning and relearning he had subjects in his experimental condition learn a *different* subset of four arms in the same maze. Subjects in the control condition performed an unrelated task between learning and relearning of the original set of four arms. In agreement with the idea that retroactive inhibition can occur in spatial learning, the control subjects had less trouble relearning the original subset of four arms than did the experimental subjects.

Other Areas of Interference

Interference effects have been found in other situations too. For example, interference effects can also be obtained using two languages (López, Hicks, & Young, 1974). That is, if one task is in one language and the second task is in a different language, interference effects can be observed. RI and PI can show up in classical conditioning (Dess & Overmier, 1989), in priming experiments (Neely, Schmidt, & Roediger, 1983), in eyewitness situations (Bekerian & Bowers, 1983), and, as we shall see, in Chapter 10 in many animal activities (Edhouse & White, 1988a, 1988b; Jitsumori, Wright, & Cook, 1988; Roitblat & Harley, 1988; Roitblat & Scopatz, 1983). Interference effects can be obtained with visual stimuli as well as the verbal stimuli that we have been emphasizing (Mendell, 1977) and in free-recall situations (Roediger, Stellon, & Tulving, 1977). The point is that, even though the interference interpretation "grew up" in a "paired-associate neighborhood," its principles and rules seem to guide behavior in many different situations.

THE TWO–FACTOR THEORY OF FORGETTING

Thus far we have been speaking of nothing more than the facts. Retroactive and proactive inhibition do occur, and they are powerful. They are strongly affected by such factors as intertask similarity. We now turn to the problem of trying to explain these facts. Why do PI and RI occur at all? What factors or mechanisms contribute to their particular forms? How much knowledge do we have about the processes that underlie and cause these undeniably powerful interference effects? We now step into the world of theory.

An Overview

For many years the *two-factor theory of forgetting* (Melton & Irwin, 1940) stood as the uncontested framework within which psychologists attempted to understand forgetting. Although the two-factor formulation has come into sharp conflict with more recent conceptions of memory, it still stands as one of the major explanatory developments within the field. This section outlines the basic elements of the system and some of the recent challenges to it.

The original formulation of the theory proposes that a given retention loss, or interference effect, can be determined by at least two important factors, *competition* and *unlearning*. Let us first consider competition. Suppose that we have just learned an A–B, A–D sequence. We then attempt to recall the B responses when the A stimuli are presented. We find that we cannot recall all the correct B responses. Some portion of this retention loss may result from *response competition at the time of recall*. When A is presented during the recall phase and we are asked for B, our ability to produce B will sometimes be blocked by D. We mistakenly recall D instead of B. Incompatible responses have been connected to the same stimulus. The recall of one temporarily blocks recall of the other. The incompatible responses compete with each other, cause confusion, and lead to errors in recall. The concept of response competition will be elaborated on shortly. For now, realize that, if we attempt to recall the first-list responses, unwanted recall of the second-list responses may disrupt first-list recall (this would be an RI effect). Similarly, if we attempt to recall the second-list responses, unwanted recall of the first-list items may interfere with recall (this is a PI effect).

The second of the two interference factors is commonly known as *unlearning*, which is, perhaps, not the best choice of labels, but it will have to do. The idea behind the concept of unlearning is that the acquisition of new materials (for example, the A–D list) can bring about losses of the old materials (the A–B list). As subjects learn the A–D list, they suffer a concomitant loss in the strength of the first-list associations. During the learning of the A–D list, the A–B materials are somehow unlearned, weakened, or made less available. First-list associations are lost during second-list learning. Exactly how this unlearning occurs will be the topic of an upcoming section.

For now, several points should be kept in mind. First, either or both of these factors (competition and unlearning) can contribute to an observed interference effect. Second, competition is presumed to be operating *at the time of recall*, whereas unlearning operates *during second-list learning*. The two factors have their impact at different points within the experimental sequence. The third and final point is that response competition is presumed to contribute to *both* PI and RI, whereas unlearning contributes to RI *alone*. Let us first take up the notion that competition contributes to both RI and PI. Unwanted recall of the second list can compete with recall of the first list (RI). Similarly, unwanted recall of the first list can compete with attempts to recall the second list (PI). Now let us turn to the notion that unlearning contributes to RI but *not* PI. As we have noted, unlearning refers to the fact that first-list associations are somehow made unavailable during second-list learning. Hence, first-list retention is clearly affected by unlearning (RI). But second-list, or A–D, materials do not undergo unlearning in our experiment. Hence, losses in second-list retention, or PI, are presumed to be *totally* determined by competition at the time of recall, whereas those of RI are presumed to be determined by *both* competition and unlearning.

The Separation of Competition and Unlearning

In view of the fact that both unlearning and competition can affect retention, how might we go about separating the effects of these two factors in an experimental fashion? For years no one knew quite how to do it. For example, RI experiments would be run in which the subjects would be given the usual two seconds to recall each of the B responses following A–B and A–D learning. A–B losses would be observed, but no one knew whether they resulted from competition at the time of recall or from unlearning or both. Attempts were finally made to eliminate the effects of competition from these experiments. When this was done, whatever retention loss was left could be safely attributed to the unlearning factor. Competition effects were eliminated in a very simple manner. The subjects were asked to recall *both* the B and D responses and were given *unlimited time* to do so. The idea was that, if the subjects were not pressed for time and were free to spend as much time as they wished in searching for, and sorting out, the B and D responses, then the competition effect would be minimized. The obvious assumption here is that competition effects are dependent on time pressure. If we remove the requirement of recalling the critical item within a few seconds, then the confusion, blocking, and momentary competition between B and D responses are eliminated. This line of reasoning led to the development of what is commonly called the MMFR (modified, modified free-recall) test (Barnes & Underwood, 1959). In this type of recall test the subjects are not pressed for time at all and are asked to recall the B and D responses in any order in which they come to mind. When this unpaced recall task is used, any remaining retention losses can be attributed to the unlearning factor alone and are presumed to be free from the effect of the momentary competition factor.

As we have seen, classical two-factor theory states that PI is determined completely by response competition at the time of recall. It has also been commonly assumed that the MMFR task effectively eliminates the effects of competition. Hence, it follows that *no* PI should appear when the MMFR task is employed. After learning an A–B, A–D sequence, subjects should have no trouble recalling the D responses if they are given plenty of time to do so and are not subjected to the confusion produced by paced or limited recall time. This seems to be a reasonable prediction. Unfortunately, PI effects *have* been consistently observed with the MMFR task (Ceraso & Henderson, 1965; Postman, Stark, & Fraser, 1968). Possibly the MMFR task does not effectively eliminate competition effects after all. Or PI might result from something beyond the competition factor. Whatever the final outcome, this contradiction, or unpredicted result, typifies the problems facing the development and refinement of the two-factor theory. The interested reader is referred to Anderson (1983), Bowles and Glanzer (1983), Postman, Stark, and Burns (1974), Postman and Keppel (1977), and Underwood (1983) for discussions of the nature of PI.

Unlearning as Extinction

Is human forgetting anything like animal "forgetting"? Does human "unlearning" resemble an extinctionlike process? We have already discussed the phenomenon of experimental extinction, which has its origins in the animal literature. Animals "forget," or lose responses, through a process of extinction. The rat, after learning to press a lever for food, will stop the pressing response if food, or reinforcement, no longer follows the occurrence of that response. If the animal does not undergo this active unreinforced responding, the response will be maintained for long periods. Thus, for the rat to stop its response, it must undergo an active process in which the previously reinforced response occurs repeatedly without reinforcement.

Do humans lose such things as verbal responses in a similar manner? Do we forget because we undergo extinction? On an intuitive level it does not seem likely. When we forget someone's name, the title of a book, or a section of a text, it does not *seem* as though we have undergone extinction. Where and when did we make the response and suffer a state of nonreinforcement?

Interestingly, although the mechanism is not obvious, some human forgetting has been thought of as analogous to experimental extinction (Keppel, 1968; Postman, 1971; Postman & Underwood, 1973). Specifically, the *unlearning factor just outlined has been conceived of as an instance of experimental extinction.* The analogy is as follows. Consider the A–B, A–D situation. During A–D learning, the subjects sometimes mistakenly respond with B rather than D. The subjects have just learned the A–B list, and it is "on their mind." These errors may be either overt or covert. Each time the B response occurs as an error, it is *not* reinforced. (The computer or the experimenter does not confirm the B response as correct.) *The occurrence of the B response during A–D learning constitutes an instance of unreinforced responding, or experimental extinction of the A–B association.* The greater the number of overt or covert B responses occurring during A–D learning, the greater is the extinction or unlearning of the A–B associations. This is an interesting idea. It represents an important point of contact between the animal and human literature and suggests that at least some animal extinction and human forgetting may be comparable.

Unlearning and Spontaneous Recovery

If the unlearning factor is truly analogous to experimental extinction, then human forgetting should display the important properties of the extinction phenomenon. *Spontaneous recovery* is a case in point. If you will recall, a response that has been extinguished will, with rest, recover some of its strength. For example, suppose that a rat's bar-pressing response has been completely extinguished and that the animal has been removed from the Skinner box for, say, 24 hours. We find that, when the animal is returned to the box after the rest interval, the response has spontaneously recovered some of its strength.

If the analogy between unlearning and extinction is to be maintained, then a similar sort of recovery phenomenon must occur with verbal materials. If an A–B list is extinguished during A–D learning, then, as time passes, the A–B list must show some recovery. The unlearning or extinction must be at least partially reversible. Although the results have not been completely consistent, such a recovery phenomenon has been demonstrated (Forrester, 1970; Martin & Mackay, 1970; Shulman & Martin, 1970). It is not an easy effect to obtain, but the fact that it has been observed lends some support to the extinction interpretation of unlearning.

Competition: Specific versus General

In our introductory discussion of response competition we noted that retrieval of one response will sometimes be blocked by the unwanted recall of the other response that has been associated with the same stimulus. This effect is referred to as *specific response competition*. The recall of one specific response blocks the recall of another specific response. But another type of competition also leads to disruption of the retention process. It is referred to as *response-set interference* and has been elaborated by Postman, Stark, and Fraser (1968). (The ideas behind the response-set interference hypothesis were originally put forward by Newton and Wickens in 1956.) The response-set interference analysis goes like this: While subjects are learning a first list, they restrict their responses to those that are appropriate to that list. They inhibit the occurrence of incorrect responses, or responses that do not belong to the set of correct first-list responses. Then, when the subjects are shifted over to a second list, they shift over to the set of correct second-list responses. They inhibit the occurrence of the entire set of first-list responses. They concentrate or focus on the set of correct second-list responses. But the subjects cannot shift from one set of responses to another instantaneously. As Postman and Underwood (1973) put it, the tendency to give responses from a given list is possessed of a certain amount of inertia. The subjects will have a strong tendency to continue to give responses from the most recently learned list. It takes a while for the subjects to shake off this tendency, or to change their orientation. Hence, after the subjects have completed second-list learning, the tendency to give second-list responses persists for a while.

Now suppose that we ask the subjects for the first-list responses immediately following the completion of second-list learning. Presumably, the subjects will be plagued by the persisting tendency to give responses from the more recently learned list. These second-list responses will compete with, and block, retrieval of the first-list responses. Thus, at least part of the subjects' inability to retrieve the first-list responses in an RI situation can be attributed to response-set interference.

Researchers have made many attempts to test the response-set interference hypothesis. The formulation has led to a good number of testable hypotheses and has received considerable support in the literature. See Cofer, Failie, and Horton (1971), Lehr, Frank, and Mattison (1972), and Postman and Stark (1969).

One point should be kept firmly in mind. The notion of response-set interference is not intended to *replace* the other interference mechanisms (that is, unlearning and specific response competition). It is intended to *supplement* them. In any given situation *any* of these interference mechanisms may contribute to overall retention losses. It is the task of the proponents of the two-factor position to delineate clearly when, and to what extent, each of these potential sources of interference determines overall forgetting.

CHALLENGES TO UNLEARNING
Independent Retrieval

The two-factor theory is undergoing revision and refinement. Despite what its detractors say, it does have explanatory power, and it has generated an enormous amount of research. The theory is not without faults. It is not entirely comprehensive, nor can it adequately account for all known interference effects (for example, PI obtained with the MMFR test). We begin our exploration of alternative conceptions of memory by examining some of the challenges to the classical two-factor interpretation of interference effects. Then, in successive sections we shall discuss alternative models of memory and their adequacy in relation to the two-factor position.

According to classical two-factor theory, A–B associations are unlearned during A–D learning. Martin (1971) and a number of other investigators have suggested that some evidence denies this unlearning principle. They reason that, if learning A–D entails unlearning A–B, then the recall of B should be less likely when D is recalled than when D is not recalled. In other words, the recall of B and D should be dependent on each other. As the strength of A–D is built up, the strength of A–B should decrease. Thus, if we test for the recall of both responses, the subjects should be less likely to recall B when D is recalled. The probabilities of recalling B and D should be inversely related.

A number of investigators have obtained results that appear to contradict this expected inverse relationship between B and D recall (Greeno, James, & DaPolito, 1971; Martin, 1971; Martin & Greeno, 1972; Wichawut & Martin, 1971). In general, they found that B and D recall are independent of each other. That is, the recall of B is just as likely given that D is recalled as it is given that D is not recalled. This effect has been labeled the *independent retrieval phenomenon*. Martin (1971) suggests the concept of unlearning is deflated because the unlearning principle requires, or implies, an inverse relationship between B and D recall. Martin suggests that we must look elsewhere for an explanation of RI effects.

The validity and relevance of the independent retrieval phenomenon is not universally accepted (see Hintzman, 1972). Postman and Underwood (1973) have attacked the very logic put forward by Martin (1971). They suggest that Martin is wrong in assuming that the unlearning principle demands an inverse relationship between B and D recall. They argue that the actual acquiring of the D response is not critical in the unlearning of the B response. As we have seen, it is the *occurrence of B as an unreinforced response during A–D learning* that is the critical factor in the unlearning of the A–B association. Second-list, or A–D, learning merely provides the *opportunity* for the B response to occur as an error. Nothing in two-factor theory states that it is the learning of the A–D association that actually causes the A–B loss or that the A–B associations *must* be unlearned before A–D associations can be learned. Thus, two-factor theory, according to Postman and Underwood (1973), does not demand an inverse relationship between B and D recall.

Encoding Variability

In any case, whether or not the independent retrieval phenomenon actually invalidates the unlearning principle, Martin (1971, 1972) has proposed an alternative interpretation of interference effects. His formulation is intended to replace, and not merely supplement, the classical two-factor interpretation. It is based on his concept of *stimulus encoding variability*. If you will recall, a given stimulus is conceived of as possessing many different attributes, or components. During A–B learning the B response is not connected to the entire A stimulus but rather to some selected portion of the overall stimulus. Then, during A–D learning the D response is not connected to this same set of attributes. It is connected to a different, or at least partially different, set of stimulus attributes. Thus, D and B are connected to different *functional* stimuli even though the *nominal* stimulus is identical in A–B and A–D learning. For example, if the A stimulus is ZQKO, then the B response might be connected to Z, whereas D might be connected to Q. Granting that this is true, how does RI occur, and why does the subject have trouble recalling the B responses when presented the total A stimulus after A–B and A–D have been learned? According to Martin, it happens because of a *persisting tendency to sample, select, or attend to those stimulus attributes utilized during A–D learning*. Following A–D learning the subjects continue to "pay attention to" those stimulus attributes that they have most *recently* used in hooking up responses. Hence, because of their continuing attention to these most recently utilized attributes, the D response is cued off rather than the B response.

Let us consider a very simplified example. Suppose that a subject is required to connect *dog* to *norop* during A–B learning. Imagine that this subject once owned a dog named Norton. Hence, she might easily master this particular item by associating *dog* with *nor* and might ignore the remaining letters in the nominal stimulus (*op*). Now, during A–D learning the subject might be required to connect *eye* to the stimulus *norop*. The letters *op* might remind the subject of optical. Thus, she might find it convenient and simple to associate *eye* with *op* and ignore the remaining letters (*nor*). Thus, *dog* is connected to *nor*, and *eye* is connected to *op*. Then, during the retention test following A–D learning the subject is asked to recall *dog* given *norop* as a cue. Martin (1971) argues that the subject will continue to attend to, or sample, the stimulus attributes most recently utilized. She will focus on, or sample, *op*. *Op* leads to *eye* rather than *dog*. Hence, we have a disruption in the subject's ability to recall the first-list response, or an RI effect.

Stimulus versus Response Persistence

Martin's explanation of interference sounds a bit like the Postman, Stark, and Fraser (1968) notion of response-set interference. In both analyses subjects cannot recall the first list because they are still bound up with the second list. The involvement with the second list persists after second-list learning and, in some sense, blocks out recall of the first list. The two analyses do differ in terms of their emphasis. On the one hand, Martin focuses on a persisting tendency to attend to the set of stimulus attributes utilized during second-list learning. On the other hand, Postman, Stark, and Fraser (1968) emphasize a persisting tendency to give second-list responses. Martin focuses on *stimulus persistence*, whereas Postman focuses on *response persistence*. It would seem reasonable to suspect that both might be right. The tendency to continue giving recent responses *and* to continue attending to recently utilized stimulus components might both contribute to RI. Martin's analysis might best be taken as a supplement to, rather than as a replacement for, the more traditional interference mechanisms. Martin's stimulus-encoding-variability hypothesis has received considerable attention in the literature (for example, Ellis, 1973; Goggin & Martin, 1970; Martin, 1972; Mueller, Gautt, & Evans, 1974; Williams & Underwood, 1970).

Accessibility versus Unavailability

Martin's (1971) independent retrieval phenomenon and his encoding variability interpretation of the so-called unlearning effect are not the only factors marshaled against the traditional interpretation of interference effects. A number of authors (see Nelson & Brooks, 1974; Reynolds, 1977; Tulving & Psotka, 1971) begin their attack by distinguishing between item *availability* and item *accessibility*. If an item is stored in our memory, on the one hand, it is available. If it is unavailable, then it is permanently gone from our memory or was never there. Accessibility, on the other hand, refers to our ability to pull available items out of our memory store, or to retrieve them. An item can be available (stored) without being accessible (retrievable). For example, you probably have the name of the president whose picture is on a $10 bill stored or available, but, for any number of reasons, it might be temporarily inaccessible (you cannot recall it at the moment). If an item is unavailable, it can never be accessible, whereas an available item can sometimes be accessible and sometimes not.

The argument here is about whether unlearning is the same as unavailability. According to interference theory, if an item is unlearned, it becomes permanently unavailable, and if it is unavailable, it should also be totally inaccessible. But if an item that has presumably been unlearned can be retrieved, or is accessible, then it must not have been truly unavailable.

The following sort of experiment has been conducted to test these ideas. Subjects learn six successive tasks and are then tested for retention of the first-task responses. It is usually noted that retention of the first-list material is poor. This is an RI effect, and the two-factor theory assumes that the first-list materials could not be recalled because they were unlearned during List 2–6 learning and are thus unavailable. But now something a little different is done. The subjects are tested for first-task recall again. This time they are given some hints, or clues. For example, they might be given the names of categories to which the thus far unrecalled first-task items belong. If the unlearning hypothesis is correct and the items are truly unavailable, this kind of hint should not help the subjects recall more first-task items. But it does. Subjects can recall items during the second test of first-task recall that they did not remember during the first test. The conclusion that some draw from this result is that the items were not really unavailable, or unlearned, after all;

they were merely temporarily inaccessible. The conclusion is that RI does not result from unlearning (unavailability) but rather from inaccessibility. The items are presumed to be "in there" somewhere and not totally lost through unlearning.

This kind of experiment convinces some people that the unlearning principle is incorrect and that RI is a matter of item inaccessibility rather than permanent unavailability. But it will probably take quite a few more clever experiments before the venerable concept of unlearning is finally laid to rest (see Brosgole & Grosso, 1983).

DECAY THEORY

Perhaps the oldest, and perhaps the simplest, interpretation of memory is called *decay theory*, or sometimes *disuse theory*. (Decay theory is the second of the six interpretations of memory we shall discuss, interference theory having been the first.) Quite simply, decay theory suggests that associations somehow *grow weaker, or fade, with the passage of time*. This possibility has intuitive appeal, because our memories do seem to fade with disconcerting regularity. The decay notion suggests that forgetting is a simple, inexorable function of time, as though our memories grow weaker as they grow older. And yet the decay hypothesis has proved to be relatively unfruitful. It has not led to many testable hypotheses. The reason may be that it is impossible to eliminate all sources of interference from a given experimental situation. For example, suppose that we wish to demonstrate that the memory traces of a learned list decay with time. Accordingly, we have our subjects learn a list and then test for retention after a designated interval. To ensure that any loss we observe results from decay, and not RI, we must ensure that the subjects learn *nothing* during the retention interval. If they learn anything at all, then the loss could result from RI. It is difficult to "turn subjects off" during a time interval. We could put them to sleep, but such a procedure does not eliminate the possibility that some kind of learning activity will occur while they are dropping off to sleep, while they are actively dreaming, or while they are awakening. (Interestingly, studies involving such sleep procedures seem to support an interference, rather than a decay, interpretation of forgetting [Ekstrand, 1967].) And even if we were sure that the subjects learned nothing at all during the retention interval, we still could not attribute a retention loss to decay, because of possible PI effects. All the subjects' preexperimental experiences constitute potential sources of proactive interference. (We have to assume that they have learned something before they enter the experimental situation.) In short, the definitive decay experiment is, as far as we know, impossible. To run a good decay experiment we would have to round up subjects before they had learned any potentially interfering material at all. Then, after they had learned the critical materials, we would have to "turn them off" immediately and completely until the time of the retention test. Thus far, no one has been able to establish such a pattern, although attempts to demonstrate decay have been made (Reitman, 1974; Roediger, Knight, & Kantowitz, 1977).

This is not to say that decay does not operate or contribute to observed retention losses. Interference theoreticians are very aware that some portion of our retention losses *may* result from decay. They are merely pointing out that it is currently impossible to isolate the decay effect, or to separate it from interference effects. It is like a constant added to all our interference effects. But we *can* create, predict, and observe enormous variations in retention owing to obvious interference factors (for example, by varying the amount, or type, of interfering activity). Hence, much

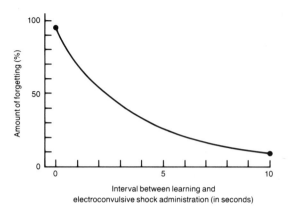

Figure 8.2 A hypothetical animal retrograde amnesia gradient.

more emphasis has been placed on interference effects simply because (1) they are extensive and (2) we can relate them to changes in our independent variables.

Another interesting fact about the decay idea is that, even though it is extremely controversial and has not been demonstrated to everyone's satisfaction, it has been routinely incorporated as a subprocess into many recent memory models. As we shall see in Chapter 9, theoreticians have unhesitatingly assumed that some kinds of stored information decay with the passage of time, even though experimental verification of this fact is lacking.

CONSOLIDATION

The third of our six approaches to the understanding of memory is called the *consolidation hypothesis.*

Retrograde Amnesia

We begin our discussion of consolidation by first looking at an intriguing experimental finding called the *retrograde amnesia effect* (Groves & Rebec, 1988). In a retrograde amnesia study an animal first learns a particular response (an avoidance response, for example). After acquisition of the response the animal is subjected to an amnesic agent, such as electroconvulsive shock, puromycin, or potassium chloride. The animal is then tested for the original response. The animal's memory for the recently learned behavior seems to be impaired. This retrograde amnesic effect appears to increase as the time between the learning and the introduction of the amnesic agent is decreased (see Figure 8.2). In other words, recent memories suffer the most. If you shock the animal immediately, the learning is less likely to become permanent than if you allow time to pass before administering the amnesic agent (Barraco & Stettner, 1976; Kinsbourne & Wood, 1975; McGaugh & Gold, 1976).

The retrograde amnesia procedures are reminiscent of the electroconvulsive shock treatments sometimes used with human patients, particularly those found to be deeply depressed. The general procedure is one in which the patient is first given a muscle relaxant (to prevent damage in the upcoming, electrically induced convulsion). Electric current is then passed through the brain for a brief moment by way of electrodes attached to the patient's temples. Two of the major results of this type of treatment are that (1) patients come out of their depressed state, at least temporarily, and (2) they suffer from some degree of amnesia, with more recent memories suffering more than older memories.

Parenthetically, retrograde amnesia is usually distinguished from *anterograde amnesia.* In the former, the problem lies in remembering materials learned before the trauma. In the latter, the deficit lies in the subject's inability to remember *new* materials, or materials presented *after* the trauma. While our focus here is on retrograde amnesia, we will discuss anterograde amnesia in more detail in Chapter 10 (see Hirst, Johnson, Phelps, & Volpe, 1988; Shimamura & Squire, 1988).

The Consolidation Hypothesis

Given that retrograde amnesia is a phenomenon that can easily be demonstrated with animals and, for that matter, with humans, what accounts for the effect?

Some interpretations (McGaugh, 1966, 1988) emphasize the concept of *consolidation.* The notion here is that the amnesic agent somehow disrupts consolidation of the memory trace. For a memory trace to become permanent, it needs a little time to consolidate. Consolidation interpretations argue that factors such as electroconvulsive shock disrupt and prevent the transfer of information into permanent store. The explanation is that the amnesic agents render the information unavailable on future tests. Think of the stored information as cement. For it to become permanent it must have time to harden. If someone stirs it about before it hardens, its eventual form may be nothing like the form in which it was originally poured (see Squire, 1987).

Reversible Amnesia

The original consolidation hypothesis centered on the idea that amnesic agents such as electroconvulsive shock caused *permanent* memory losses. Shock was supposed to block completely the "laying down," or storage, of memory traces. But a number of experiments (see Quartermain & Botwinick, 1975; Squire, 1987) have shown that retrograde amnesia is *not* permanent. Information that has been "lost" through the introduction of amnesic agents *can* be regained, or "reactivated." Several techniques are used for observing the reversibility of amnesia. They include (1) the introduction of appropriate "reminders," or prompts, and (2) the observance of "spontaneous" recovery of the lost information (Gerson & Henderson, 1978; Lewis, 1979; Squire, 1987).

The reversibility of amnesia suggests that the information is *available* all along (stored) but is not *accessible* (cannot be retrieved) until appropriate reminders, or other critical conditions, are present. In other words, electroconvulsive shock does not prevent storage of information. It merely disrupts the subject's ability to utilize or retrieve whatever information is stored. Suppose that you are listening to an old-time radio program. The heroine suffers a head injury in an automobile accident. She cannot remember a thing. Her family and friends are upset, to say the least. She contemplates ending it all. But with the careful help and prompting of her family physician it all begins to come back. She "regains her memory" and marries Mark after all. The point here is that she never really lost anything. The information was still in storage, but she could not pull it out, or retrieve it, until prompted or reminded. The information was available but temporarily inaccessible.

This view, emphasizing the disruption of retrieval processes, has received considerable support in the literature (Miller, Ott, Berk, & Springer, 1974; Miller & Springer, 1974; Spear, 1973). At the same time, proponents of the storage position have not disappeared (Gold & King, 1974; McGaugh, 1988). A fine healthy controversy exists, with interesting studies appearing in the current literature (see Gold, 1989; Gabriel, Sparenburg, & Stolar, 1986).

In summary, we have looked at three approaches to the understanding of memory in this chapter—interference theory, decay, and consolidation. Each has something to offer, and at present none can be discarded out of hand. In Chapter 9 we discuss three additional approaches to the study of memory—separate-store models, levels of processing, and semantic-network models. It is probably fair to say that the following chapter covers more modern interpretations than those discussed in this chapter; for the most part these newer models are described as being in the *information processing* tradition.

SUMMARY

1. *Proactive inhibition* (PI) refers to losses in our ability to remember a given set of materials that can be attributed to the interfering effects of *previously* learned materials.
2. Negative transfer involves a two-step experiment, whereas a PI design involves three steps.
3. *Retroactive inhibition* (RI) refers to memory losses that can be attributed to the interfering effects of *subsequently* learned materials.
4. Filler tasks are used in the second step of an RI control condition to prevent rehearsal.
5. Retroactive and proactive facilitation occur under certain circumstances.
6. *Intertask similarity* has been recognized as important in determining RI and PI effects. Osgood's transfer and retroaction surface gives us a rough idea of the kinds of RI effect expected under conditions of varying intertask similarity.
7. Interference effects are not limited to arbitrary tasks such as paired-associate learning. For example, they appear with connected discourse, with varying languages, when animals are employed as subjects, and in spatial learning.
8. The classical *two-factor theory of forgetting* proposes that interference effects are determined by *competition* at the time of recall and by the *unlearning* of first-list associations that occurs during second-list learning.
9. Specific competition is presumed to contribute to both RI and PI, whereas unlearning affects RI but not PI.
10. Unlearning effects are presumed to be separated from competition effects through the use of unpaced retention tests. If the subjects are given as much time as they wish to attempt retrieval, their performance will not be affected by competition. This type of unpaced retention test has been labeled MMFR.
11. If the MMFR task eliminates competition and PI is determined completely by competition, then no PI should appear when the MMFR test is used. This

straightforward prediction has not been confirmed. Proactive inhibition does occur with MMFR. This could mean that the theory needs revision or that MMFR does not eliminate competition.

12. Unlearning has been thought of as an extinctionlike process. During A–D learning the subjects sometimes make B responses, either overtly or covertly. The B responses, which are occurring as errors during A–D learning, are unreinforced (uncomfirmed) and are thus thought to be analogous to responses undergoing experimental extinction. This formulation provides a point of contact between human verbal learning and the basic animal literature, wherein the concept of experimental extinction developed.

13. If the extinction interpretation of unlearning is correct, then unlearned first-list associations should recover some of their strength with rest. In support of this interpretation spontaneous recovery of first-list associations has been demonstrated.

14. There are two types of response competition. *Specific response competition* refers to the recall of one specific response blocking the recall of another specific response. *Response-set interference* refers to the blocking of one set of responses (for example, the entire set of first-list responses) by the tendency to continue to give responses from the most recently learned list.

15. Response-set interference is intended as a supplement to, rather than as a replacement for, the other interference mechanisms (that is, specific competition and unlearning).

16. The independent retrieval phenomenon refers to the fact that recall of B is just as likely given that D is recalled as it is given that D is not recalled. It has been suggested that this phenomenon invalidates the unlearning principle. A controversy surrounds the logic of this attack on the two-factor theory.

17. In any case, alternative interpretations of interference effects have been proposed. For example, the *encoding variability interpretation* suggests that subjects connect B and D to different attributes of A in an A–B, A–D situation. Then, when tested for B given A as a cue, the subjects display an RI effect because of a tendency to continue to select, or attend to, those attributes of A that were attended to during the more recent learning task (A–D).

18. The encoding variability interpretation and the response-set interference hypothesis seem similar in that both suggest that RI results from a persisting involvement with the second task. The former emphasizes a persisting tendency to attend to certain stimulus attributes, whereas the latter emphasizes a persisting tendency to give second-list responses. Both tendencies may contribute to overall RI effects. One interpretation need not invalidate the other.

19. The unlearning principle has also been attacked by those who feel RI can be explained in terms of item *inaccessibility* rather than permanent *unavailability*.

20. Evidence for the idea of inaccessibility comes from studies showing that a cued, or prompted, second test can lead to recall of items not recovered during a first test.

21. The *decay hypothesis*, or the notion that memory traces somehow fade with the passage of time, has been proposed as an alternative to the interference mechanisms. The decay hypothesis has proved to be relatively unfruitful, for it is currently impossible to eliminate all sources of interference within a memory experiment.

22. In *retrograde amnesia* studies, animals first learn a particular response. Then, after the administration of some amnesic agent, such as electroconvulsive shock, it is found that the response has been lost. This effect appears to be similar to electroconvulsive shock treatment used with depressed human patients.
23. Anterograde amnesia, to be discussed in Chapter 10, involves the inability to remember new materials, or materials presented after the trauma.
24. Retrograde amnesia has been interpreted as disruption of the encoding and storage processes (the *consolidation hypothesis*).
25. However, the discovery of the reversibility of retrograde amnesia has prompted many to contend that the effect involves a disruption of retrieval processes rather than encoding or storage processes.

CHAPTER

9

MEMORY MODELS II: SEPARATE STORES, LEVELS, AND SEMANTIC NETWORKS

THE COMPONENTS OF MEMORY:
ENCODING, STORAGE, AND RETRIEVAL

Before 1960, the two-factor theory of interference pretty much dominated the field of forgetting and retention. With its foundation in Hullian-type S-R psychology and its emphasis on such basic experimental phenomena as extinction and spontaneous recovery, it stood as the major, relatively uncontested, conception of forgetting. But the last 30 years have seen a spectacular explosion in thinking and theorizing about human memory processes. In contrast to the early years we now have many models of memory, with more appearing all the time. Although the interference, decay, and consolidation approaches discussed in the last chapter are still influential, they appear to be undergoing replacement by the newer approaches described in this chapter.

Our purpose now is to examine the most important of these models, including *separate-store models* developed during the 1960s, the *levels-of-processing* approach appearing in the early 1970s, and *semantic-network models* that enjoyed a wave of popularity in the 1980s.

But before we move to consider specific memory models, we should spend a moment with the three aspects of memory: *encoding, storage,* and *retrieval.* The distinctions among these three elements, or components, of the overall memory process seem to permeate most models of memory. In fact, researchers loyal to the older interference approach to memory use these labels and think about memory in terms of them. Thus, the distinctions among encoding, storage, and retrieval *do not belong to, or characterize, a single theoretical orientation, or model.*

It has become commonplace to speak of encoding, storage, and retrieval as the essential components of the overall memory system. The distinctions among these components have been enormously helpful in stimulating and clarifying our thinking about some very complicated mental events. At the same time you should be aware that these components have not been separated or, for that matter, even defined to everyone's satisfaction. Whether these three components truly represent distinct, independent components of the overall memory system remains to be seen.

Murdock (1974) has characterized the three components about as well as anyone could. *Encoding* refers to the process by which the nervous system develops a representation of an external stimulus. The stimulus is a physical object or event that acts on, or has an effect on, the nervous system. This relatively lasting effect is referred to as the internal code for the external object or event. The nervous system now contains an encoded representation of the stimulus. *Storage* refers to the persistence of encoded material over time. Murdock draws a parallel between the storage process and the tape recording of a musical composition. For all practical purposes the information stored on the tape does not change. Human memory rarely possesses the same degree of fidelity, but it does involve the storage of information over time. *Retrieval,* according to Murdock, refers to the utilization of this stored information. Such information may be *available* (stored) but not *accessible* (easily located and used). For example, we may know (have stored) the names of all of the United States, but at any given moment we may not be able to retrieve all of them. Hence, the information is available but not accessible. It is stored, but we may have trouble retrieving it. Figure 9.1 is a pictorial representation of the relationships among encoding, storage, and retrieval.

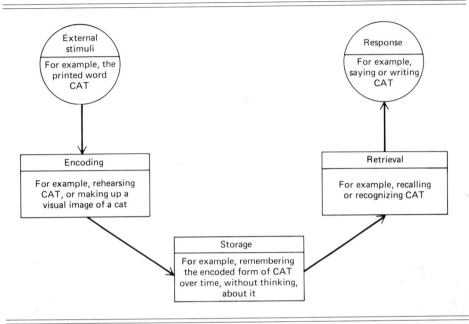

Figure 9.1 General form of encoding, storage, and retrieval in memory.

THE INFORMATION–PROCESSING APPROACHES

New ways of thinking about memory were stimulated by the advent of the computer age. Whereas theorizing about memory before 1960 was pretty much restricted to talking about stimuli, responses, and associations between them, the language of computers has since become commonplace. Mathematical models and computer-simulation models are on the upsurge. Psychologists have begun to try to describe memory in terms of information processing and have conceptualized human memory in terms of elements such as flow charts, outputs, control programs, buffers, instructions, execution, processing, and storage.

A few representative examples of this information-processing approach follow. Many models are available to choose from, and most of them are new. Many of them are vague, and they are often untested. We cannot be sure which ones will stand the test of time and which ones will fade from view. Although many of them appear to account for a good portion of the available experimental data, none of them has emerged as "the" model.

The discussion in this chapter will take the following form. First, we shall consider several *separate-storage* models. It is characteristic of these models to propose two or more separate and distinct memory stores. For instance, many of them distinguish between short-term store (STS) and long-term store (LTS). Second, we shall consider the *levels-of-processing* approach to the understanding of memory. This approach differs from the separate-store approach in that it does not think of the overall memory system as being composed of separate stores, or "boxes," into which and out of which information is processed. Rather, as we have seen, the levels-of-processing approach argues that the durability of a memory trace is determined by the "depth" at which it is processed. The levels-of-processing approach is still an information-processing approach. But it is more of an approach than a theory or model, and it does not postulate separate stores. Third, we shall discuss several varieties of the newest form of model building, which can be labeled the *semantic-network* approach. According to this approach, memory is best thought of in terms of complex structures, or networks, of interrelated information.

SEPARATE–STORE MODELS
Primary and Secondary Memory

Let us begin our discussion of *separate-store* models with a relatively simple conception of memory. The model proposed by Waugh and Norman (1965) is given in Figure 9.2. It represents a relatively early attempt to distinguish between two types of memory and to couch a description of these stores in information-processing language.

According to Waugh and Norman (1965), every item (stimulus) that is perceived enters *primary memory* (PM). Once in PM, an item will be lost, or forgotten, unless it is rehearsed. Rehearsal can be overt or covert, intentional or unintentional, conscious or unconscious. If an item is rehearsed, it remains in PM and may enter *secondary memory* (SM). Secondary memory is considered to be a more permanent store. Once in SM an item need not be rehearsed to be maintained. Waugh and Norman were trying to capture the following kind of event or experience. Suppose that you are presented with a series of digits (say, 87391063). If you read off this series and then *prevent* yourself from saying it over and over, you will forget it quite quickly (probably within a minute). But if you rehearse it, either silently or aloud, you can maintain it, you will not forget it, and you will be able to pronounce it on demand. If you rehearse it long enough, it will enter SM. In contrast to items in PM, items in SM are not lost when they are not rehearsed. If we rehearse the example sequence of digits enough times, it will become a relatively permanent memory, or enter our SM. We will be able to retrieve it even after it has left consciousness.

The capacity of PM is limited. That is, there is a limit to the number of items we can hold in our PM. If we are given a string of dozens of digits, we probably will not be able to hold them all in our working memory. But most people can handle 5, 6, 7, 8, or 9 items without too much difficulty. The exact capacity of primary memory is unknown (Glanzer & Razel, 1974).

New items will "bump out" old ones. Suppose that we have been presented a series of eight words and are having a little trouble rehearsing them without forgetting any of them. Now the experimenter presents additional words. According to Waugh and Norman, something has to go. If we are to take in the new words, then we must drop, or lose, a corresponding number of old items that we have been holding in PM. Old items will be lost as we try to accommodate the new ones. We cannot handle an unlimited number of items in our PM.

An event in PM is thought to be part of the contents of our awareness. PM contents form the contents, of the psychological present (Klatzky, 1984; Stern, 1985). In contrast, an item recalled from SM has been absent from consciousness. Secondary memory represents the psychological past. According to Waugh and

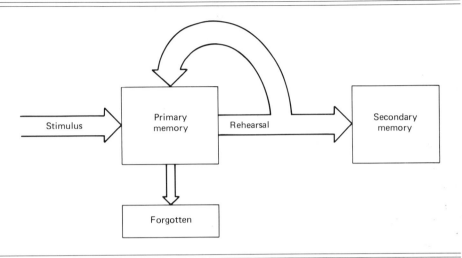

Figure 9.2 The Waugh-Norman memory model. (After Waugh, N. C., and Norman, D. A. Primary memory. *Psychological Review*, 1965, 72, 89–104. Fig. 2, p. 93. Copyright 1965 by the American Psychological Association. Reprinted by permission.)

Norman (1965), PM contains a relatively accurate record of recently perceived events. Material stored in SM may be distorted and full of gaps.

Obviously, this type of model is far from complete. Many questions are left unanswered. For example, how much rehearsal is required for different types of material to pass from PM to SM? Can some information pass directly through PM into SM without being rehearsed at all (for example, traumatic events)? How are materials brought back from SM to PM? Waugh and Norman never intended their model to be complete and perfect. They presented it as a beginning, or approach, to the understanding of human memory. It is more a way of thinking about memory than a detailed statement of all the processes involved in memory.

One aspect of the Waugh and Norman model deserves special attention, because it is characteristic of many of the current information-processing models. The authors postulate two memory stores, one for materials retained for short periods of time and another for materials retained for longer periods of time. This distinction is the essence of the separate-storage model. The dichotomy between *short-term store* (STS) and *long-term store* (LTS) (newer terms for PM and SM) has become one of the focal differences between the information-processing approach and the older two-factor theory of interference. If you will recall, interference theory makes no mention of any distinction between short-term store and long-term store. There is only one memory system. Materials can be learned to different degrees, thereby becoming more or less resistant to interference, but memory over short periods is not conceived of as fundamentally different from memory operating over longer periods.

The proposed dichotomy between LTS and STS suggests that the principles and mechanisms that govern the retention of materials for short periods are fundamentally different from those that govern the retention of materials for longer periods. We shall discuss the validity of this controversial dichotomy in detail in Chapter 10.

The Atkinson-Shiffrin Buffer Model

The Waugh-Norman model serves as a simple introduction to the realm of model building. It possesses the basic dichotomy between PM and SM, which is inherent in so many current separate-store models. But the model developed by Atkinson and Shiffrin (1965, 1968, 1971) provides a more full-blown example of the information-processing trend.

A brief glance at the flow chart in Figure 9.3 will reveal certain characteristics that appear to be similar to those of the Waugh and Norman (1965) model. For example, the model contains a box labeled "short-term store" and a box labeled "long-term store."

Essentially, the concepts of short-term store (STS) and long-term store (LTS) introduced by Atkinson and Shiffrin are the same as the Waugh-Norman concepts of primary and secondary memory. But notice that the Atkinson-Shiffrin model introduces a new store, a third box called the "sensory register." This third component of the overall memory system precedes STS. The model thus expands the number of stores from two to three.

The principal characteristic of the sensory register is that information stored within it decays in a *very* brief period of time. The exact length of this decay interval is not known. It has generally been estimated at about half a second for visual materials and three seconds for hearing, although some investigators have proposed slightly longer or shorter estimates. In contrast to STS, where information is often thought to be lost within, say, 5, 10, 15, or perhaps 30 seconds, unrehearsed information in the sensory register is seldom thought to persist much longer than a few seconds. The evidence leading to the postulation of the sensory register will be reviewed shortly.

Although the Atkinson-Shiffrin concept of STS is very similar to the Waugh-Norman notion of primary memory, Atkinson and Shiffrin have expanded the idea a bit more than did Waugh and Norman (see Atkinson, Brelsford, & Shiffrin, 1967; Murdock, 1972). In addition to adding the sensory register they elaborated on the short-term store by postulating a *rehearsal buffer* (see Figure 9.3). This buffer is composed of a certain number of slots, or bins. These are locations within which item information is stored. The number of these slots is definitely limited (that is, the buffer is composed of r slots). In addition, the bins are ordered. They have a definite sequence to them. The order is conveyed by the notation r, r−1, r−2, . . . 1. Slot r holds the newest information in the buffer, whereas Slot 1 holds the oldest, or the item information that has been in the buffer for the longest period of time.

Because there is a fixed number of slots in the buffer, the inclusion of a new bit of information can be achieved only through the displacement of an old one (given that all the slots are full). New items are assumed to come in at the top, or to fill the r slot. Which item will be lost when a new item enters Slot r? In a very general sense, we can say that the older an item, the more likely it is to be displaced by the inclusion of a new item. Obviously this statement is an oversimplification. Atkinson and his colleagues were well aware that the displacement of an item is a complicated event (see Phillips, Shiffrin, & Atkinson, 1967).

Without going into any great detail we can grasp the complexity of item displacement by imagining a boy picking up pebbles on the beach. His hand will hold just so many stones. Each time he picks up a new one, he must, if he wishes to keep

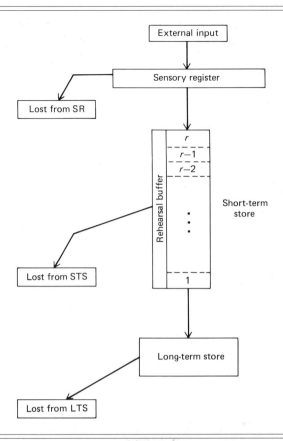

Figure 9.3 A version of the Atkinson-Shiffrin memory model. (After Atkinson, R. C., and Shiffrin, R. M. The control of short-term memory. *Scientific American,* August 1971, pp. 82–90. Copyright © 1971 by Scientific American, Inc. All rights reserved.)

it, drop one of the old ones. Which one will be drop? Just imagine what goes into this "simple" decision. It is true that there may be a tendency to drop the stone that has been held the longest. But the boy will also probably consider which pebbles he likes the most and which ones he has examined closely. In an analogous manner the process of dropping items from STS is probably multiply determined.

Be that as it may, the system does postulate an additional mechanism concerning the displacement effect. Once an item is displaced from, say, a slot near the bottom of the column of slots, what happens to the information in the remaining slots? According to the theory, all items older than the displaced item hold their place. They stay in the same slots. All items newer than the displaced item move down one slot. Obviously this postulation complicates matters, for it requires that older and newer items be given separate consideration.

In summary, the Atkinson-Shiffrin model is similar to the earlier Waugh-Norman model, but it is more complex. Specifically, it adds the third box, the sensory register, and it expands on the functioning of STS, or PM.

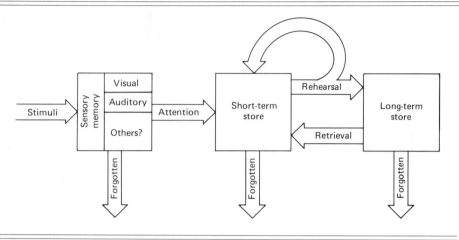

Figure 9.4 A summary separate-store model of memory.

A Summary Separate-Store Models

Having briefly looked at the Waugh-Norman and Atkinson-Shiffrin separate-store models, including some of the similarities and differences between them, it is time to consider a general, summary model of the separate-store variety. Such a model is shown in Figure 9.4.

In the following sections in this chapter we shall look at the major components of this summary model and try to do two things. First, we shall look at the general characteristics of each component as they can be distilled from the literature. Second, we shall look at some of the data and evidence that have been marshaled in support of these components. Beginning at the left of Figure 9.4, we shall consider each of the separate-store components individually.

Sensory Memory: Iconic and Echoic

In this section we discuss what Atkinson and Shiffrin have called the sensory register, or what others have called *sensory memory*. Basically, sensory memory is thought of as a memory store with a very brief duration period, something like half a second to three seconds. It is supposed to contain very basic, unelaborated impressions of the external environment, which decay rapidly unless processed into one of the other stores (that is, STS and LTS).

Most research has focused on *visual* and *auditory* sensory memory, although some sensory-memory systems may be associated with the other senses. A few researchers have investigated sensory memory in the minor senses such as touch, taste, and smell (see Hill & Bliss, 1968), but we shall restrict our attention to visual and verbal sensory memory. If you follow the instructions in Box 9.1 you may get a better idea of what a sensory memory is.

ICONIC MEMORY.   Early evidence for the existence of a visual sensory memory, sometimes called *iconic memory,* came from the work of Averbach and Coriell (1961) and Sperling (1960, 1963). Sperling (1960) showed that when exposed to a

---

Box 9.1 Examples of Sensory Memory

Visual sensory memory. Take a flashlight into a dark room and turn it on. Swing your wrist around in a circular motion, shining the flashlight onto a distant wall. If your motion is quick enough, you will see a complete circle. Your visual sensory memory stores the beginning of the circle while you examine the end of the circle.

Auditory sensory memory. Take your hands and beat a quick rhythm on the desk. Can you still hear the echo after the beating is finished?

Tactile (touch) sensory memory. Take the palms of your hands and quickly rub them along a horizontal edge of your desk, moving your hands so that the heel touches first and the fingertips touch last. Can you still feel the sharp edge, even after your hand is off the desk?

---

visual array for a very brief, single presentation, people can remember a great deal more than was formerly believed to be the case, at least for a brief period. This work led to the postulation of the visual sensory memory, or the memory that takes in a great deal of visual information in a very accurate manner but cannot hold that information for very long.

Sperling used a tachistoscope, which is a piece of equipment that will present visual stimuli for very, very brief periods. He presented rectangular arrangements of letters such as those on the left side of Figure 9.5. These arrays were flashed for 50 milliseconds (1/20th of a second). The subjects then were asked to report what they had seen. Without any special instructions they were able to report no more than four or five letters correctly. Now comes the interesting part. By using a pre-arranged signal, which was presented immediately after presentation of the letter array, Sperling asked the subject to recall a *specific* row. A high-pitched tone meant that the subjects were to recall the top row. Low and intermediate tones indicated to the subjects that they were to recall the bottom or middle row, respectively. The surprising result was that the subjects could recall *any* given row with 100% accuracy. This finding suggests that a very rapidly decaying "visual image," "after-image," or "visual sensation" persists beyond the termination of the actual stimulus. It is as though the subjects "see" the entire array of letters for a moment after the actual physical stimulus has been terminated. It is there for them to read. But this "afterimage" is not there for long. When asked to report the top row, the subjects can do so without error. They merely refer to the "visual image," or whatever you wish to call it, and read off the correct letters. But while they are reading off, or encoding, the top row, the other rows are fading rapidly. By the time they have finished reading off the top row, the lower rows have faded to the point at which the subjects can no longer report them. The Sperling test procedure forces the subjects to attend to some portion of the total array. While they are attending to this selected portion, the entire array is decaying, rendering a report of the remaining items impossible.

This is a rather interesting result. It suggests that incoming visual information is present as a rapidly decaying "visual image." If encoded, or read off from this

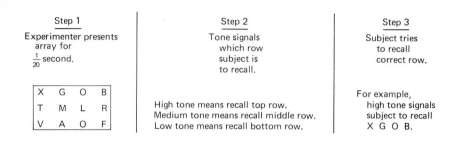

Figure 9.5 Sperling's demonstration of visual sensual memory.

visual sensation, the information moves into STS. If it is not attended to almost immediately, it will be lost. Thus, in the separate-store model it seems to be *attention* that moves information from the sensory register into STS. Those few stimuli that we can *attend to*, before they fade away, will be processed into STS (see Figure 9.4). The rest will be gone, and unless they are presented again, they will never be remembered.

ECHOIC MEMORY: STIMULUS–SUFFIX EFFECT AND PAS.   Given that Sperling's (1960) experiment demonstrates the existence of a visual sensory memory, what evidence is there for auditory sensory memory? This form of very short-term memory is often referred to as *echoic* memory, presumably because like an echo it involves a faithful, but short-lived, trace of auditory stimuli (see Massaro, 1970, 1972; Neisser, 1967).

Much of the evidence for echoic memory comes from the work that has been done on the *stimulus-suffix effect* (Cowan, 1988; Crowder, 1974, 1978; Greenberg & Engle, 1983; Kallman & Massaro, 1983). The stimulus-suffix effect is a curious one. Subjects read a list of words and then try to recall them in order. If the last word in the list is followed by a redundant word, which is a word that follows all lists and need not be recalled, then the last word in the list is difficult to recall. For example, suppose that you are told you will be hearing a list of words and that following the list you will hear the word *jump*. You are told that you do not need to recall *jump* and that *jump* will follow other lists that you will be trying to recall; it will be redundant in the experiment. Somehow the inclusion of the word *jump*, a redundant suffix, disrupts your recall of the last, or the last few, words in the list.

Let us say that you are asked to listen to and recall 20 lists of words. Half of these lists are followed by a redundant suffix such as the word *jump*. The remaining lists are not. Over the entire series of lists your recall of the last word in the lists containing the suffix will be lower than your recall of the last word in the lists containing no suffix. Why? Crowder has suggested that this suffix effect occurs because of the existence of an auditory sensory memory that he calls *precategorical acoustic storage*, or PAS. Precategorical acoustic storage is presumed to be a sound-based store that can retain a few sounds for very brief periods. By adding that last suffix we are overloading PAS, or bumping out the last word(s) in the list. Investigators in this area talk about the redundant suffix "overwriting" or "displacing" the last few items in the serial list that are being held in PAS. Without a suffix the last few words in the list go into PAS and are maintained there long enough to be recalled very well on the serial recall test. But when a suffix is added, *it* takes the place of the last word in the serial list and thereby reduces our ability to recall the bumped, or displaced, last serial word.

Notice that PAS is thought of as a store with a very limited capacity. It can hold only a few items, and the addition of even one more item, such as a redundant suffix, bumps out old items. This finding is in contrast to the current conception of the *visual* sensory memory, which holds that *large* amounts of visual stimulation are held for brief periods of time. Thus, even though iconic and echoic memory are both thought of as sensory memories, they do differ, with the former possessing a larger capacity than the latter. In addition, material in iconic memory is thought to decay much more rapidly than material in echoic memory (half a second versus about three seconds).

Two Phases of Sensory Memory?

The usual description of sensory memory suggests that there is a visual sensory store and an auditory sensory memory, as we have described them. But some authors (Cowan, 1987a, 1987b, 1988) feel that there are really two distinct phases to each of these memory stores.

Specifically, it is postulated that in a first very brief phase sensations are extended for several hundred milliseconds. During this phase the material remains relatively unanalyzed and exists as a kind of afterimage. The second phase holds materials for several seconds, contains partially analyzed material, and is what textbooks usually refer to as sensory memory. The very brief first phase is the new component that these authors are suggesting. In essence, they are suggesting a fourth type of memory, including the first sensory phase, the second sensory phase, short-term store, and long-term store. Whether or not the addition of this distinction between the two phases of sensory memory is necessary remains to be seen. Cowan acknowledges that the proposed second phase may be part of the traditional conception of short-term store (Cowan 1988).

Short-Term Store

For years, the investigation of short-term memory, or short-term store, dominated the information-processing approach to memory. Recently, more and more attention has been devoted to the examination of sensory memory and long-term memory. But a huge quantity of data concerned with short-term memory processes has accumulated. Hence, this section will only serve as an introduction to the area of short-term memory. We shall be referring to short-term memory in connection with many different concerns throughout the remainder of this text. For now, our purpose is to get a rough view of short-term store.

As we have already seen, short-term store, or STS, is characterized as a limited-capacity system, which handles information that is to be stored for relatively short periods. At present the time limit imposed on STS seems to be fairly arbitrary. Many investigators tend to think of STS as a system in which information will be lost within 30 seconds or so unless it is processed further.

Items in STS can be maintained through rehearsal. If items are not rehearsed, they will be lost from STS (Anderson & Craik, 1974). Thus, there may well be two ways in which items are lost from STS. First, old items may be displaced by new, incoming items. Second, items may be lost if they are not rehearsed.

Item rehearsal does something in addition to maintaining information in STS. Namely, rehearsal of information held in STS may contribute to its transfer to LTS. Notice that rehearsal *may* contribute to transfer. It does not *necessarily* lead to transfer to LTS (Jacoby & Bartz, 1972). Items may be rehearsed in STS without being transferred to LTS, but for items to be transferred from STS to LTS they must be rehearsed (Atkinson & Shiffrin, 1971).

In general, then, the longer an item has been maintained in STS by rehearsal, the more *likely* it is to be transferred to LTS. The longer we hold information (for example, the sequence BXGBJKL) in STS by rehearsing it, the more likely it is to become part of our "permanent" memory.

An item can be in both STS and LTS at the same time. For example, think of your mother's name. When you think of it, it will be in both STS and LTS. An item can be in LTS but not STS. For example, all of the things we "know" but are not now thinking of are in LTS but not STS. An item can be in STS but not LTS. For example, NELZIPRELLY is now in your STS. But it probably will not enter your LTS unless, for some peculiar reason, you rehearse it several times (but see Brown & Kulik, 1977).

We shall return to a consideration of STS in the next chapter. At that time we shall consider the validity of the construct. We shall ask whether it is even necessary to distinguish between STS and LTS, and we shall trace some of the experimental data that bear on this issue.

Long-Term Store

Until recently, long-term store, or memory over long periods, did not receive as much attention as short-term store within the information-processing tradition. Although interference theory has been interested in LTS for many years, information-processing theoreticians focused first on short-term memory. But things have changed rapidly and there have been many new and exciting developments in the area of LTS. We shall discuss many of these LTS issues in upcoming chapters, particularly Chapters 10 and 11 (see also Pillemer, Goldsmith, Panter & White, 1988).

For now, our purpose is to look at the general dimensions of what is commonly referred to as LTS and at its relationships to sensory memory and STS. Detailed analyses and new developments will be considered later.

Generally speaking, information is presumed to enter LTS from STS through the process of rehearsal. Once information is in LTS, it is no longer rehearsed (unless it is brought back to STS). Information is often assumed to be lost from LTS through the combined effects of both decay and interference. The decay rate is presumably much slower than that of STS. Although information is often thought to decay from STS in a matter of seconds, estimates of the LTS decay rate range up to years. Once in LTS, information is presumed to be stored quite permanently. (The exact values of the decay rates associated with the sensory register, STS, and LTS are not particularly important at this point in our investigations. In fact, psychologists are not even sure that decay necessarily operates in all of these stores.)

Let us consider the proposition that LTS is affected by interference factors. When information-processing theoreticians speak of interference effects in LTS,

Table 9.1   Commonly Accepted Differences among the Three Stages of Verbal Memory

FEATURE	SENSORY REGISTER	SHORT–TERM STORE	LONG–TERM STORE
Entry of information	Preattentive	Requires attention	Rehearsal
Maintenance of information	Not possible	Continued attention, rehearsal	Repetition, organization
Format of information	Literal copy of input	Phonemic, probably visual, probably semantic	Largely semantic, some auditory and visual
Capacity	Large	Small	No known limit
Information loss	Decay	Displacement, possibly decay	Possibly no loss; loss of accessibility or discriminability by interference
Trace duration	.25–2 seconds	Up to 30 seconds	Minutes to years
Retrieval	Readout	Probably automatic; items in consciousness; temporal/phonemic cues	Retrieval cues, possibly search process

Adapted from Craik, F. I. M., and Lockhart, R. S. Levels of processing: A framework for memory research. *Journal of Verbal Learning and Verbal Behavior*, 1972, *11*, 671–684. Copyright 1972 by Academic Press, Inc. Reprinted by permission.

many are presumably referring to such factors as proactive and retroactive inhibition and the associated concepts of unlearning and response competition. Thus, the information-processing models often acknowledge and attempt to incorporate the interference mechanisms outlined in the last chapter. There has been a tendency to locate these interference effects in LTS and to leave STS and sensory memory relatively free of them. In fact, one of the most controversial distinctions between STS and LTS has been based on the notion that information in STS is not subject to interference effects. Many psychologists have raised questions concerning the validity of this distinction, as we shall learn in the next chapter.

In summary, the separate-store models propose that information is transferred from sensory memory to STS through a process of attention. Otherwise, information decays from sensory memory in a fraction of a second. The short-term store has a limited capacity. Information is transferred from STS to LTS through a process of rehearsal, and unless it is rehearsed, such information may be lost from STS in a matter of seconds. Information may also be lost from STS through a process of displacement. Information stored in LTS, in contrast, is quite permanent. It is subject to a very slow decay process and to interference effects. Thus, not everything that enters the sensory register reaches STS, not everything that enters STS is transferred to LTS, but information that does make it all the way through to LTS is considered to be relatively permanent.

Table 9.1 summarizes the differences among the three memory systems we have been discussing, as envisioned by Craik and Lockhart (1972). Again keep in mind that the values contained in Table 9.1 are *only rough estimates*. Different researchers will assign different values to some of these factors. Not enough is known to be certain of the exact values.

STS as Active LTS

Bower and Hilgard (1981), Cowan (1988), Norman (1968) and others have argued that something is wrong with the way information passes through traditional separate-store models. In these models information typically passes from left to right; it must pass through STS before it can enter LTS. But consider the following example: Suppose someone presented you with the sequence A, O, N, K, H, J, B with instructions to try to remember it. The traditional models suggest that you have to rehearse this sequence before it can enter LTS. But, in fact, in order to remember this sequence you refer to LTS. You search LTS and discover you already know the letters. You search LTS and find you don't know the order of these items. You discover that your task is to learn a new sequence of old items. This process clearly involves reference to LTS, and that is what concerns these authors. The interplay between LTS and STS is more extensive than one would imagine given the traditional linear model.

The solution offered by these authors is to think of STS as an *active* portion of LTS. According to Cowan (1988), "short-term storage consists of the elements within the long-term store that are currently in a heightened state of activation" (1988, pp. 164–165). STS involves prior LTS information; when you learn A, O, N, K, H, J, B you utilize LTS information. According to these authors it is more sensible to think of STS as an activated portion of LTS (see Figure 9.6).

Control Processes and Structural Properties

Atkinson and Shiffrin (1968, 1971) distinguish between the fixed, *structural properties* of the overall memory system and *control processes*. The distinction is an important one. Control processes refer to the fact that the individual can go about *using* the fixed structural properties of the system in many different ways. For example, STS has the *capacity* to hold a certain amount of information. This capacity represents a fixed, structural property of the system. But whether we choose to fill STS is another matter entirely. We do not have to fill it; we can partially fill it or leave it empty. Just because someone flashes a lot of words in front of us does not mean we have to put them in our STS. We do, after all, have some choice in the matter. In addition, we can maintain information in STS or "let it go." We can transfer information to LTS or refrain from doing so. We can pull information back from LTS into STS and so on. The structural properties of the system set limits on what we can do. For example, we cannot hold an unlimited amount of information in STS. But within the limits of its structural properties we can "use our memory." These choices, decisions, and strategies are what Atkinson and Shiffrin call control processes.

It is simple to see that the separate-store model becomes very complicated when we begin to consider control processes: We have a willful, unpredictable *human being* on our hands. We must consider all his or her needs, wants, wishes, and decision processes. At the same time, the introduction of control processes immediately makes the model much more appealing and much more closely related to the world of human experience.

Atkinson and Shiffrin place considerable emphasis on control processes and their relation to the fixed structure of the model (see also Hinrichs & Grunke, 1975). They have many interesting things to say about control proceeses, and you are referred to their work for a full explanation of the concept. For the purpose of

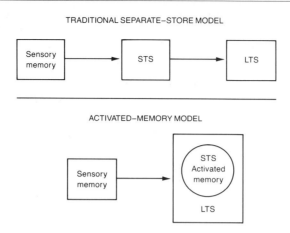

TRADITIONAL SEPARATE–STORE MODEL

ACTIVATED–MEMORY MODEL

Figure 9.6 Alternative separate-store model.

this text we will consider a couple of examples of the effects of human strategies on the use of the system. These examples are merely representative of many investigations and should be understood in that light. (In a sense, most of Chapter 11, in which we discuss organizational strategies in memory, is concerned with control processes. So we will have a great deal more to say about control processes as the text progresses.)

The first example of control processes is a study done by Bellezza and Walker (1974). This interesting experiment is based on the assumption that what we do with information within the memory system depends on what we want to do with it, or feel we need to do with it. Accordingly, one group of subjects was presented with a list of seven words and asked to recall all the words immediately following presentation. The subjects were then presented with another list of words and asked for immediate recall of that list, and so on, until seven different lists had been presented and tested. Before any lists were presented the subjects were told that they would receive "1 point" for every word recalled correctly. These subjects were free to rehearse in such a manner as to maintain each list in STS. They felt no need to try to transfer the information to LTS, for they believed that they would be given only an immediate-recall test. They did not need to store the information permanently, for storage in STS would be more than adequate to maintain the material through the immediate-retention test. However, these subjects were "fooled" by the experimenter. Following the presentation and testing of all seven lists, the experimenter asked the subjects to try to recall all of the words from all seven lists in one final retention test. The subjects were told that they would be given "10 points" for each correct item on this final recall test. Obviously, these subjects were not ready for this development. They had not tried to transfer information from STS to LTS in preparation for this final test. They did very well on the immediate tests but very poorly on the final test. The assumption here is that, by the time the final test arrived, materials had been lost from STS. In addition, they had not been put into LTS, hence the poor performance on the final test.

Another group of subjects was treated in exactly the same manner, except that these subjects were told before being exposed to any of the lists that they would be tested for immediate retention *and* that they would be given the final recall test. Correct items in immediate recall were to receive "1 point," whereas correct items in final recall would receive "10 points." If you were placed in a similar situation, you would probably try to ensure that you would be able to remember as much as possible on that final test, because that is where the larger payoff would be. You would rehearse in such a way as to maximize transfer from STS to LTS. You would not especially care about what stayed in STS so long as you were sure lots of information was going into LTS. The results of this strategy are apparent in Figure 9.7. As you can see, the storage condition (told only about the immediate tests) did well on the immediate tests and poorly in the final test. The coding condition (told about both immediate and final recall) did better than the storage subects on the final test but not so well as that group on the immediate tests. Because of their awareness of the big, 10-point payoff the coding subjects utilized the fixed structural properties of the memory system such that storage in LTS was maximized. The effort that these subjects put into transferring materials to LTS seems to have somehow detracted from their maintenance of information in STS. We can only speculate about the reasons for this poor performance in STS by the coding subjects. For example, they may have merely rehearsed fewer of the presented items a greater number of times to ensure that they would be transferred to LTS.

The study demonstrates that, depending on the needs of the subject, the memory system can be used in different ways to achieve different ends. It also suggests that rehearsal is not a unitary process. That is, certain types of rehearsal appear to maximize storage in STS and other rehearsal strategies maximize storage in LTS (Craik & Watkins, 1973; Jacoby, 1973; Woodward & Bjork, 1973).

If you will recall, we discussed Type I (maintenance) rehearsal and Type II (coding) rehearsal in Chapter 5. Type I rehearsal is the kind used by the subject to keep information "in mind," or in STS. Type II rehearsal is what we use to transfer information from STS to LTS (see Woodward, Bjork & Jongeward, 1973). Although Bellezza and Walker did not use the Type I and Type II labels, the distinction betwen these two forms of rehearsal is the basis of their study.

The distinction between control processes and structural properties of the memory system is becoming ingrained in our ways of thinking about memory, and it forms the impetus for a good deal of research. For example, Peterson, Thomas, and Johnson (1977) point out that for certain retention tests it might be best to try to remember items in terms of visual images, whereas other retention tests might be best attacked through the use of verbal rehearsal (see also Rundus, 1977).

CULTURAL DIFFERENCES IN CONTROL PROCESSES.   Wagner (1978) has done some cross-cultural work and come to the conclusion that the structural properties of the human memory system are universal. That is, all members of the species (for we are, after all, members of the same species) possess the same structural properties. But the control processes used in different countries and cultures probably do vary.

DIRECTED FORGETTING.   Bjork's (1972, 1975) work on directed forgetting represents another good example of the operation of control processes in memory. In one situation he presented four successive paired associates. Color background

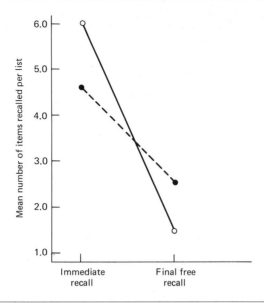

Figure 9.7 Number of words recalled per list in the storage (○) and coding (●) conditions. (Adapted from Bellezza, F. S., and Walker, R. J. Storage-coding trade-off in short-term store. *Journal of Experimental Psychology*, 1974, *102*, 629–633. Copyright 1974 by the American Psychological Association. Reprinted by permission.)

cues instructed the subjects either to forget the first two items or to retain them for possible future testing. Bjork found that retention of the *last* two items was superior when the subjects had been informed that they need not try to maintain the first two. He speculates that the "forget" cues initiate control processes that free rehearsal time for the last two items and that somehow differentiate the to-be-remembered items from the to-be-forgotten items (see also Bjork & Geiselman, 1978).

The distinction between control processes and structural properties need not be limited to the separate-store models that we have been considering, even though the distinction was originally developed in connection with the Atkinson-Shiffrin model. It is a general distinction that can be useful no matter what model is under consideration. We can begin to see the kind of fun that psychologists can have with such a model. Propositions based on the interaction of the structure of the system and the control processes can be tested in the laboratory and related to the world outside the laboratory. The control processes "put the human back" in the system.

THE LEVELS–OF–PROCESSING APPROACH
Introduction

The preceding sections concerned with separate-store models of memory should convey the fact that psychologists do not agree about precisely how many and what kind of stores, or boxes, we should include in our formulation of the memory process. But the controversy is not limited to disagreement among separate-storage modelers. Specifically, the *levels-of-processing approach* challenges the entire notion of separate stores. According to this viewpoint, which was introduced in Chapter 5, the durability of a memory trace is determined by the "depth" to which it is processed. The deeper the processing, the more durable is the trace. As you will recall, if the structural properties of a piece of information (for example, what it looks like) are attended to, then processing will be relatively shallow, and the trace will be weak. But if the acoustic, or phonemic, properties (what it sounds like) are attended to, the memory trace will be more durable. Finally, if the semantic properties (for example, the meaning of a word) are attended to, then processing is at the deepest level, and the memory trace will be most durable. (Some of the tasks that have been used to produce different levels of processing are contained back in Table 5.1).

This approach, which is not really a theory at all, does not postulate separate stores. It argues that we can think of a *continuum* of memory strengths, which is determined by level of processing, from shallow (weak) to deep (strong). It says nothing at all about discrete boxes. In this sense it is closer to the interference approach, in that it conceives of memory as a unitary process in which the strength of a memory trace can be increased through rehearsal. But even though it is similar to interference theory in this one sense, we should keep in mind that the levels-of-processing approach is really an information-processing approach. Thus, it has something in common with both the interference and separate-store conceptions of memory (see Baddeley, 1978; Glanzer & Koppenall, 1977).

The basic experimental design used to study levels of processing is an incidental learning paradigm. As noted, Craik and Tulving (1975) had subjects make judgments about words presented for very, very brief moments. In the shallow processing condition the subjects judged whether the words were typed in capital letters. In a second condition the subjects judged whether the stimulus word rhymed with a designated word. Finally, in the deepest level of processing the subjects judged whether the stimulus word fit into a sentence frame. Then, in a surprise recall test it was found that recall increased as depth of processing increased.

The theme of incidental learning has many variations. A number of experiments supporting the levels-of-processing hypothesis were described in Chapter 5 in detail. Generally speaking, whatever the particular form of processing required by the experimenter, it has been found repeatedly that *retention increases as depth of processing increases* (Cermak & Reale, 1978; Craik & Lockhart, 1972; Hunt & Mitchell, 1978; McDowall, 1979; Moeser, 1983; Smith, Theodor, & Franklin, 1983).

But in spite of its popularity the levels-of-processing approach has been severely criticized. As noted in Chapter 5, foremost among these criticisms has been the assertion that deep processing does not always or necessarily lead to greater trace durability. In addition, information processed on a shallow level can be quite durable (see Morris, Bransford, & Franks, 1977; Nelson, 1977; Nelson & Vining, 1979).

Furthermore, Nelson (1977) argues that there is a *circularity* to the levels approach, because we have no independent measures of what we mean by "depth." First we say that, if processing is deep, retention will be better. Then we say that, if recall was better, processing must have been deep.

Baddeley (1978) feels that the levels approach can be used as a general rule of thumb but that too many exceptions make it impossible to utilize it in any hard and fast manner (see Hunt, Elliott, & Spence, 1979). For example, Eysenck and Eysenck (1979) report some interesting results having to do with the amount of effort required to pull information back into consciousness after it has been processed to different levels. First, they had subjects process words at different depths. Then they had them try to do two things at once: recall the words and press a lever when a sound occurred. They found that the lever-pressing latency went up (it took them longer to press the lever in response to the sound) when subjects were trying to recall deeply processed and heavily elaborated words. Simply put, trying to recall deeply processed words "used up" more of the subjects' capacity to process information than did the retrieval of words processed at a shallow level.

This result is interesting because, whereas most other data indicate that deep processing leads to greater trace durability, these authors report that retrieving deeply processed material requires more attention and effort than does the retrieval of shallow-processed information (see also McDaniel, Friedman, & Bourne, 1978). In other words, many data are consistent with the levels approach, but not all of them.

Evidence for Elaboration and Distinctiveness

In Chapter 5 the concepts of *elaboration* and *distinctiveness* were introduced in connection with efforts to understand *why* deeper processing leads to better retention (see Walker & Jones, 1983). If you will recall, the elaboration hypothesis maintains that semantic processing leads to richer, more elaborate encoding, which in turn facilitates retention. The distinctiveness hypothesis holds that deeper processing helps make the to-be-remembered stimulus more distinct from other stored information and, therefore, more recallable. Although Chapter 5 described the distinctiveness and elaboration hypotheses, it did not actually present any data in support of them. We now turn to that task.

Let's first look at two experiments that support the elaboration hypothesis. Klein and Saltz (1976) ran a typical levels-of-processing experiment in which subjects first made semantic judgments about stimuli and were then tested for recall of those words in a surprise test. But the interesting variation in their experiment was that some subjects made only one judgment about the stimuli (for example, Is this stimulus pleasant or unpleasant?), and other subjects made *two* judgments about the same stimuli (for example, Is this stimulus pleasant or unpleasant, *and* is it big or little?). In agreement with the elaboration hypothesis, words rated on two dimensions were recalled more often than words rated on a single dimension.

Craik and Tulving (1975) developed a second means of increasing semantic elaboration. Subjects were unexpectedly asked to recall words after they had decided whether those words would fit into a sentence frame provided by the experimenters. The crucial aspect of the study was that there were three different levels of sentence-frame complexity, as follows:

Simple: She cooked the _____ .
Medium: The ripe _____ tasted delicious.
Complex: The small lady angrily picked up the red _____ .

The results showed, among other things, that recall of the correct words went up as the degree of sentence-frame complexity went up, especially when subjects were provided the frames as cues, or prompts. These results support the elaboration hypothesis.

Now what about experimental support for the distinctiveness hypothesis? Are more distinctive units recalled more readily than less distinctive ones? The answer seems to be yes. Words that have distinctive unusual *shapes (lymph, khaki, afghan)* are said to be *orthographically distinct.* Hunt and Elliott (1980) have shown that these words are better recalled than more commonly shaped, less orthographically distinct words such as *leaky, kennel,* and *airway.* Without a doubt it is the peculiar shape of these words that leads to their better recall. If the words are presented auditorily, the recall of the two types does not differ. Furthermore, if all words are presented in capital letters, then LYMPH, KHAKI, and AFGHAN are no better recalled than *LEAKY, KENNEL,* and *AIRWAY.* The different heights of lower-case letters presumably create the distinctiveness that leads to better recall (see also Moscovitch & Craik, 1976).

In summary, the original levels-of-processing conception of memory has been modified and expanded by the recent emphasis on elaboration and distinctiveness, and it seems that *both* elaboration and distinctiveness can lead to better recall.

Encoding Specificity

Another development relative to the levels-of-processing approach is best introduced by an experiment. In an *encoding-specificity* experiment (see Thomson & Tulving, 1970) all subjects are shown a list of words that they will later try to recall. Some subjects see only this list, and others see the list *plus* a word related to each of the to-be-recalled words. For example, one subject might see *wood* alone, and another subject might see the to-be-recalled word *wood* plus *tree.* Then, at the time of recall half of each kind of subject was given *tree* and asked to recall *wood*; the remaining subjects were not shown *tree* when attempting to recall *wood.*

The results were these: Subjects who saw *tree both* at the time of learning and at the time of recall did best in recalling *wood.* That was not surprising. But what was surprising was that the group that *never* saw *tree* was better at recalling *wood* than were the groups that saw *tree either* at the time of learning *or* at the time of recall.

This kind of experiment demonstrates what Tulving and his associates call the *encoding-specificity principle: Recall will be best when the cues present at the time of learning and the time of recall are most alike.* If you learn *wood* when *tree* is present, you will best be able to recall *wood* if *tree* is present at the time of recall. But if *tree* is *not* present during the learning of *wood,* then *wood* will best be recalled in the absence of *tree.* To maximize retrieval, cues present at input should also be present at recall.

The levels-of-processing approach emphasizes *encoding* processes in memory; it states that our ability to remember material will be determined by how we encode that material. The encoding-specificity principle extends the analysis to include the idea that our ability to remember material will also be affected by *retrieval* conditions as well as encoding processes. For example, suppose we encode a given item to a certain depth. Recall of that item will not be completely determined by that depth of processing; it will also be affected by what cues are present at the time of recall. If the cues at recall are the *same* as those that were present during learning, *then* recall will be good. If cue conditions during learning and recall differ greatly, recall will suffer.

SEMANTIC–NETWORK MODELS
Common Characteristics

Having considered separate-store models and the levels-of-processing approach we now turn to the third, newest, and last type of memory model to be discussed in this chapter—*semantic-network models*. The phrase refers to quite a wide range of theoretical efforts, but most of these models have at least two attributes in common. First, they deal with the storage of *semantic* (meaningful) material. In preceding sections we have sometimes discussed the retention of relatively meaningless materials (such as nonsense syllables) that have been learned in the laboratory. Now we are going to concentrate on memory for meaningful materials such as words, phrases, sentences, and prose. We are beginning the study of our knowledge about language and the meaningful world around us.

Second, semantic-network models assume that stored knowledge is best thought of in terms of multiple interconnected associations, relationships, or pathways. Instead of thinking of single stimuli being connected to single responses (the old S-R conception) semantic-network models think of a unit of information as being embedded in an organized, structured *network* composed of other units and their functional relationships to one another. As we shall see, the exact nature of these functioning networks varies depending on the type of semantic-network model we are considering.

Our emphasis in this section will be on *lexical memory*, or memory for *words*. A lexicon is a group of ordered words. For example, a dictionary is a lexicon. So when we speak of lexical memory, we are focusing on our store of words (our vocabulary) as distinct from grammar, sentence memories, experiences, or any other kind of stored information. When we study lexical memory, we want to know how words are encoded, stored, and retrieved (see Chambers, 1979; Clark & Gerrig, 1983; Glanzer & Ehrenreich, 1979; Taft, 1979). Later, in Chapter 13, we shall see how semantic-network models also help us understand memory for more complex forms of information such as sentences, prose, and general knowledge. In this chapter we restrict our attention for the most part to the simplest applications of network models by focusing on lexical memory. We now turn to the first of four semantic-network models.

Hierarchies

A number of authors have proposed that the best way to think about the structure of lexical memory is in terms of *hierarchies*. Collins and Quillian (1972) have developed an interesting hierarchical conception of the lexicon (see Figure 9.8). The concept *animal* is broken down into *birds* and *fish*, which, in turn, are broken down further. Characteristics of a given word are stored with that word. But notice also that, if a given word at a given level has a certain characteristic, all other words below that word in the hierarchy also automatically possess that same characteristic. Thus, if we enter the network at *fish* and note that *fish* can swim, we know that all word entries below fish (on the same branch of the network) also can swim (that is, *sharks* and *salmon* can swim).

Notice how efficient this storage system is. If we enter at the bottom of the hierarchy (for example, *ostrich*), we immediately know quite a bit about ostriches. We know not only what is stored at that point (long legs, tall, cannot fly) but many other things as well. By moving up in the hierarchy we find that ostriches have

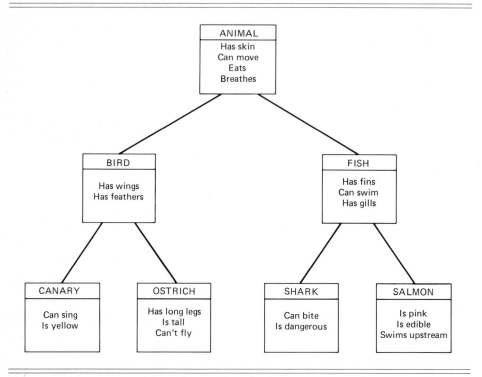

Figure 9.8 A memory model involving a three-level semantic network, or hierarchy. (Adapted from Collins, A. M., and Quillian, M. R. Retrieval time from semantic memory. *Journal of Verbal Learning and Verbal Behavior*, 1969, 8, 240–247. Fig. 1, p. 241.)

wings and feathers. Still further up we find that ostriches eat, breathe, have skin, and can move. This network is efficient because not every attribute of a given word need be stored with that word. For example, the information *has skin* does not have to be repeatedly stored with each of the animals in the network. It is stored only once but is accessible from all points in the network.

The next question is whether this conception of lexical memory predicts observed events. Although far from being completely validated, the hierarchy does seem to be consistent with certain data. For example, it predicts that certain kinds of questions should take longer to answer than others. Consider the following:

1. Do canaries sing?
2. Do canaries have wings?
3. Do canaries have skin?

Which of these questions do you think would be *most quickly* answered? Collins and Quillian predicted that the first question would be most quickly answered, because *sing* is stored directly with *canary*. Next, they predicted that the second question would be answered more slowly than the first question but not so slowly as the third question. These predictions were confirmed experimentally: The idea of *wings* is stored one level higher in the hierarchy than *canary,* whereas *skin* is stored *two* levels above *canary* in the hierarchy. According to the model, it takes time for activation to move from one level to another. The further apart two items are in the hierarchy, the longer it takes for a decision to be made about the relationship between them. Thus, at least some evidence has demonstrated the usefulness of a hierarchical conception of memory.

As a further example of the hierarchical position we will discuss an approach taken by Lindsay and Norman (1972). Be aware that the available models differ considerably and that this example is but one chosen from many. Let us begin with a simple concept, such as *tavern.* We all have this concept stored within us, and it is not stored in isolation. It is related in many ways to many other bits of stored information. How might we characterize the relations between this bit of information (*tavern*) and the rest of the information that is stored within us? In attempting to characterize these relationships, or to define the position held by *tavern* amid an enormous amount of stored information, Lindsay and Norman distinguish among "classes," "examples," and "properties." Thus, *tavern* belongs to a certain *class,* which we can designate as *establishments. Tavern* is one example of an establishment. *Tavern* also has certain *properties.* For example, it holds *beer* and *wine. Beer* and *wine* are *properties* that we have come to associate with *tavern.* Finally, there are certain *examples* of the concept *tavern* (for example, *Luigi's*). A picture, or diagram, of the semantic network that might be associated with the concept *tavern* is given in Figure 9.9. This network defines the relationships among *tavern* and its various classes, properties, and examples. Hilgard and Bower (1975) discuss the network as follows:

> A realistic memory, of course, contains thousands of such concepts, each with very many connections, so that the actual topographical representation would look like a huge "wiring diagram." But a fantastic amount of information is inherently encoded in such graph structures. To see just a hint of this, consider the fragment of a semantic network surrounding the concept of a *tavern* [as shown in Figure 9.9]. This graph implicitly encodes the information that a tavern is a kind of business establishment (as is a drugstore), which has beer and wine, and Luigi's is an example of a tavern. It also gives some properties of beer, wine, and Luigi's. This is only a fragment, of course, and much more information could and would be in a realistic memory. But notice how very many questions one is enabled to answer with just this fragment. For example, it can answer questions that require chains of subset relations, such as that "Luigi's is an establishment" or that "A drugstore is a place." It can also read out the properties or classes that any two concepts have in common. Thus, if we ask the system to compare the similarities and differences of beer and wine, it would quickly find that the similarities are that they are both beverages sold at taverns, but one is made from fermented grain while the other is made from fermented fruit. The number of factual relationships derivable and possible questions that can be answered increases exponentially as the number of encoded predicates or "bits of knowledge" increases. (pp. 594–595)

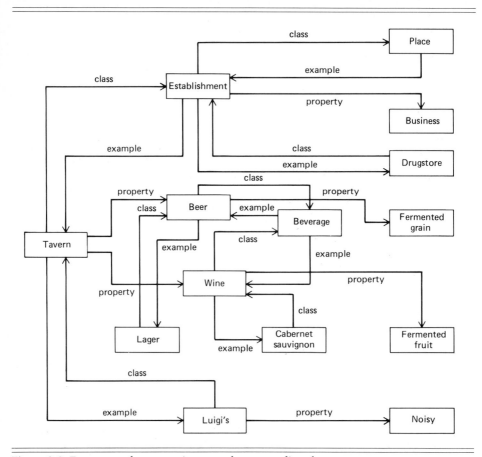

Figure 9.9 Fragment of a semantic network surrounding the concept *tavern*. (Adapted from Lindsay, P. H., and Norman, D. A. *Human information processing: An introduction to psychology.* Academic Press, 1972. Fig. 10.5, p. 389.)

It should be obvious at this point that any attempt to characterize the existing structure, or organization, of memory is difficult. The preceding example seems somewhat complicated. But when we realize that it represents nothing more than a very rough description of a very tiny segment of the total amount of information stored within each of us, then we can begin to grasp the magnitude of the task before us. Modeling of this sort is in its infancy. If they are to be complete, such models must, of necessity, become more and more elaborate. Can you imagine attempting to draw up blueprints, or networks, that capture all of the overlapping and interrelated information stored within but a single individual? Putting a man on the moon was probably simple compared with this task. Perhaps models of this sort will never be complete. Rather, they will probably serve a heuristic purpose, stimulating thinking and suggesting questions.

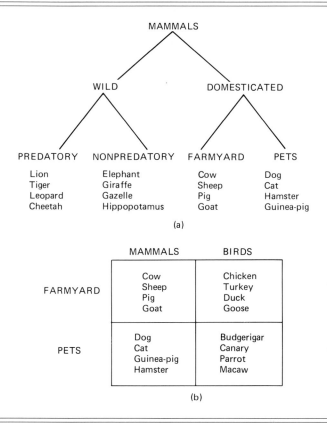

Figure 9.10 Two ways of thinking about lexical memory: (a) hierarchy and (b) matrix. (Adapted from Broadbent, D. E., Cooper, P. J., and Broadbent, M. H. P. A comparison of hierarchical and matrix retrieval schemes in recall. *Journal of Experimental Psychology: Human Learning and Memory*, 1978, 4, 486–497. Fig. 1, p. 487. Copyright 1978 by the American Psychological Association. Reprinted by permission.)

Matrices

Although many investigators think of lexical memory in terms of hierarchies containing categories and instances of those categories, others think of the lexicon in terms of *matrices*. Figure 9.10 contains a sample matrix (and, for comparison, a sample hierarchy).

Broadbent, Cooper, and Broadbent (1978) compared the hierarchical scheme and the matrix scheme. Their basic technique was to present the *same* list of words in either a hierarchy, a matrix, or a random order and then test for recall. They reasoned, that, if we naturally use a hierarchical scheme when we store words, then hierarchical presentation of the 16 words should facilitate recall relative to matrix or random presentation. What they found was that *both* the hierarchy and the matrix facilitated recall relative to the random control but that they did not differ from each other. Words presented in the matrix form were remembered about as well as words presented in the hierarchy form.

Organization helped, but it made little difference which form of organization was used. Broadbent, Cooper, and Broadbent (1978) speculate that the four groups of items were what were important. They suggest that one item in a group stimulating one other item in the group (for example, *dog* and *cat*) may have been more important than the generating structure, or the cue words (printed in capital letters in Figure 9.10).

The question of whether information is stored in hierarchies or matrices remains unanswered. The answer may be somewhat more complicated than a simple choice of one over the other. Some information may best be stored in matrices, whereas hierarchical storage may be more suitable for other kinds of information. Huttenlocher and Lui (1979), for example, suggest that nouns may be stored in hierarchies, whereas verbs tend to be stored in matrices.

Feature Models

The third approach to the understanding of lexical memory is often termed the *feature* (or sometimes the *attribute* or *property*) approach (see Smith, Shoben, & Rips, 1974). In general, this approach is concerned with how we categorize nouns when they are presented to us. For example, if *canary* is presented to us, what determines how long it will take us to decide whether *canary* belongs to the category *bird*? In the hierarchy and matrix approaches just described, the quickness of this decision is determined by such things as how close the target and prime are to each other in some arrangement of words. In the feature approach the emphasis is not on any notion of spatial arrangement. Rather, the emphasis is on the number of features, or attributes, that *canary* and *bird* have in common.

Hampton (1979) distinguishes between *defining features* and *characteristic features*. Defining features, on the one hand, provide necessary and sufficient criteria for making a decision about category membership. Characteristic features, on the other hand, are typical attributes of items belonging to the category, but they are not sufficient in and of themselves for determining category membership. For example, it is characteristic of birds to fly. But animals other than birds can fly, and some birds do not fly. Thus, flying is characteristic of birds, but does not define them. On the other hand, birds are animals with feathers. These are defining characteristics, for if an object is an animal with feathers, it must be a bird.

Hampton says that we reach a decision about whether a noun belongs to a category in two steps. First, we determine how many attributes an item has in common with the category. If there is a very large number of common attributes or a very small number of common attributes, then our decision is made swiftly and can be made on the basis of characteristic attributes. But if the overlap between category and item appears to be intermediate, then we become more careful, and we compare only defining attributes of the category with the attributes of the instance. This takes a little longer, or produces a slower decision process (see also McClosky & Glucksberg, 1979).

To this point we have discussed three ways of thinking about word storage (hierarchies, matrices, feature analyses). Although these approaches do differ, they also

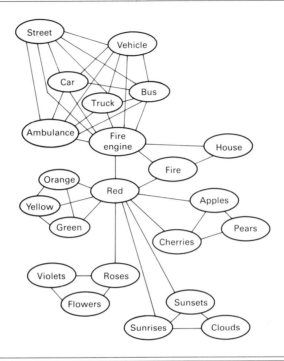

Figure 9.11 Example of a spreading-activation model in which the length of each line (link) represents the degree of association between two concepts. (Adapted from Collins, A. M., and Loftus, E. F. A spreading activation theory of semantic processing. *Psychological Review,* 1975, 82, 407–428. Copyright 1975 by the American Psychological Association. Reprinted by permission.)

have one thing in common: They all assume that organization is crucial in memory. They represent the kinds of efforts that are being made in the structural, or organizational, approach to the study of memory.

Spreading-Activation Models

The fourth kind of semantic-network model is called *spreading-activation theory,* and is extremely popular today. As we shall see, spreading-activation models have a good deal in common with other network models, but they introduce some new ideas as well. For example, these models are more general in that they are not limited to hierarchical relationships. They acknowledge other kinds of semantic relationships, too.

The original spreading-activation model, presented by Collins and Loftus (1975), is characterized in Figure 9.11. Notice first that the words stored in this network are interrelated in many more ways than a simple hierarchical configuration. Semantic storage is seen as being quite tangled and intertwined. Next, notice that the lines, or links between words, vary in length. For example, the link between *red* and *orange* is shorter than the line between *red* and *roses*. The *shorter* the length of the line between two words, the *stronger* the semantic relationships between those two words.

The central assumption of the model is that, when a word is processed (such as when a subject sees the word *red*), *activation* spreads out along the pathways of the network. This spreading activation, going out in all directions, is assumed to weaken as it travels outward. Although it is not defined precisely, activation refers to the idea that an activated unit can be more easily processed (recalled, retrieved, recognized, judged, evaluated) than an unactivated unit.

The model makes two further assumptions. First, activation decreases over time. For example, if you present the word *red*, surrounding elements will be activated for a little while but not forever. Second, intervening activities will decrease activation. Thus, if you present *street* after presenting *red*, the activation emanating from *red* will decrease.

Spreading Activation and Priming

The spreading-activation model has had its greatest success in accounting for the *priming effect* in *lexical decision* experiments. First, the subjects are shown a prime, such as the word *bird*. Then the subjects are shown, for a very brief period, a target item, which may be a related word, such as *canary*, or any other string of letters (for example, *house*, *preef*). The subjects' task is to make, as quickly as possible, some decision about the target item, such as deciding if it is a word, telling what the word is, or deciding if it belongs to a certain category.

In general, it has been found that the speed of these decisions is increased if the prime is related to the target word. The closer the relationship, the faster is the decision. In other words, the time required for processing of the target item is reduced if the subjects are given information about the target item ahead of time in the form of a related prime. The usual interpretation is that the prime activates related material in the semantic network and makes it more readily processed. The longer you present the prime, the greater the spreading activation.

Priming experiments are extremely popular these days (Donnelly, 1988; Hashtroudi, Ferguson, Rappold, & Chrosniak, 1988; Lupker, 1988; McEvoy, 1988; Mitchell & Brown, 1988; Solomon, Haymon, Ohta, Law, & Tulving, 1988; Watkins & Gibson, 1988; Williams, 1988). Most of these studies support and elaborate on the spreading-activation position. Some studies, however, seem to conflict with the model (see Neely, Schmidt, & Roediger, 1983). The model has been criticized for its lack of precision, for the great number of assumptions it makes, and for its inability to make crisp, clean predictions (McCloskey & Glucksberg, 1979). In addition, others have argued that priming effects can be explained without reference to the spreading-activation model (Ratclift & McKoon, 1988).

Essentially, we are going to have to wait for the dust to settle before a reasonable assessment of the spreading-activation position can be made. At present, it is just too controversial to evaluate with any confidence. Some feel that this approach represents the one true path of the future, whereas others believe that it is a remarkably weak endeavor.

Nevertheless, research and theorizing go on. In particular, John Anderson (1983) has presented a spreading-activation theory of memory called ACT. This theory makes many of the same assumptions as Collins and Loftus (1975). But ACT is a much more general, mathematical, wide-ranging, and comprehensive model. Because ACT considers the storage of sentences, connected discourse, and knowledge in general, as well as lexical memory, a consideration of it will be delayed until Chapter 13. For now, it is enough to know that Anderson and others like him are hard at work tinkering with their models in an effort to extend our understanding of memory.

Generation Effects

The generation effect refers to the fact that items generated by the subject will be better remembered than items merely read by that subject. For example, suppose one group of subjects was given cart–d____ and asked to generate a word that rhymes with cart (e.g., dart). A second group of subjects was merely presented with cart-dart and asked to read the pair. Then both groups were asked to recall the generated item (dart). The generation effect refers to the fact that dart will be remembered better by the group that generated it than by the group merely asked to read the item; items that subjects generate are better remembered than items they read.

Many different generation rules have produced the generation effect. For example, the generation condition might involve giving the subject long–_____ and asking the subject to come up with an opposite (e.g., short). Synonyms (sea–ocean) and categories (diamond–ruby) have also been used.

The empirical finding of the generation effect is not in question. Many different authors using many different kinds of materials and tasks have produced the effect (see Gardiner, 1988; Nairne, 1988; Nairne & Widner, 1988). On the other hand, the theoretical interpretation of the generation effect is extremely controversial. Several interpretations are currently available (see Gardiner, Gregg, & Hampton, 1988; Hirshman and Bjork, 1988). Exactly how generation effects tie in with semantic network models remains to be seen. But at the very least the generation method provides us with a tool that can be used to peer into the complex world of lexical memory.

SUMMARY

1. Before the 1960s the two-factor theory of interference dominated the field of forgetting.
2. The last 25 years have witnessed the rapid development of the *information-processing approach* to the understanding of memory.
3. In contrast to earlier years, we now have a large number of available memory models.
4. *Encoding* refers to the processes by which a representation of physical objects and events is developed by the nervous system.
5. *Storage* refers to the persistence of information over time.
6. *Retrieval* refers to the search for, and utilization of, stored information.
7. *Separate-store models* propose two or more separate and distinct memory stores.
8. Levels of processing and semantic-network models provide alternative conceptions of memory.

9. According to the Waugh-Norman model, perceived items enter a limited-capacity *primary memory* (PM). Rehearsal will maintain items in PM and may contribute to their transfer to a more permanent *secondary memory* (SM).

10. The introduction of new items into PM will bump out old ones.

11. An item in PM is part of the contents of our awareness.

12. The distinction between PM (or STS) and SM (or LTS) is characteristic of many current models. This dichotomy is in contrast to the unitary conception of memory suggested by interference theory.

13. The Atkinson-Shiffrin model has three components: *sensory register, short-term store* (STS), and *long-term store* (LTS).

14. Information in sensory memory decays within a few seconds.

15. Information is transferred from sensory memory to STS through a process of *attention*.

16. Visual sensory memory, or *iconic* memory, has been demonstrated by the work of Sperling.

17. Auditory sensory memory, or *echoic* memory, is also thought to exist. The *stimulus-suffix effect* in serial learning is taken as evidence for this form of memory. Echoic memory is often called precategorical acoustic storage (PAS).

18. Sensory memory may be composed of two phases.

19. Short-term store has a limited capacity.

20. Unless rehearsed, information may be lost from STS in a matter of seconds. Information may also be lost from STS through a displacement process.

21. Information is transferred from STS to LTS through rehearsal.

22. Storage in LTS is relatively permanent.

23. Information in LTS is subject to slow decay and interference.

24. STS is sometimes thought of as an active part of LTS.

25. *Control processes* refer to the fact that the individual can go about using the fixed *structural properties* of the memory system in many different ways.

26. As an example of control processes, subjects choose between alternative methods of rehearsing. Certain types of rehearsal maximize storage in STS, whereas other rehearsal strategies maximize storage in LTS.

27. Structural properties may be universal, whereas control processes may vary across cultures.

28. *Directed forgetting* represents an example of the utilization of control processes.

29. The *levels-of-processing approach* argues against the separate-store approach. It maintains that durability of memory trace increases as depth of processing increases.

30. An incidental-learning paradigm is used to study levels. Various forms of orientation toward stimulus materials determine depth of processing.

31. Retrieval of deeply processed information may require more of our processing capacity than retrieval of shallowly processed material.

32. The levels approach has been criticized because shallowly processed information can be well retained and because we have no independent measure of depth.

33. The emphasis in the levels approach has shifted to a study of the *elaboration* hypothesis and the *distinctiveness* hypothesis. These two factors have been assumed by some to account for depth-of-processing effects.

34. Encoding specificity refers to the fact that recall will be best when cues present at the time of recall and at the time of learning are most alike.

35. Semantic-network models assume that the storage of meaningful material is best thought of in terms of multiple, interconnected associations or relationships.

36. Lexical memory refers to that part of semantic memory involving words.

37. Theorizing about lexical memory centers around *hierarchical* models and models based on *matrices, features,* and *spreading activation.*

38. In hierarchical models words are assumed to be interconnected in hierarchies. Most hierarchies are efficient storage models, because not all information about each word has to be stored with that word.

39. Presenting information in a matrix facilitates recall, but no better than hierarchical presentation does.

40. Feature models emphasize the number of attributes that are common to a category and an instance whose membership in the category is to be judged.

41. *Defining features* provide necessary and sufficient criteria for making a decision about category membership. *Characteristic features* are typical attributes but are not sufficient for defining category membership.

42. When the number of common features is high or low, a decision is made quickly, and it can be made on the basis of characteristic features. But when the number of common attributes is intermediate, defining features are referred to, and the decision-making process is slowed.

43. Spreading-activation models assume complex relationships among stored units of information. When a unit is processed, activation spreads out along the pathways of the network.

44. Activation decreases with time and is reduced by intervening activity.

45. Spreading activation accounts for the priming effect in lexical decision experiments.

46. In lexical decision experiments a prime is first presented, and then a target item is presented. The subjects must make some decision about the target item, such as "Is it a word?" or "What is this word?"

47. It has been found that the decision process is accelerated if the prime is related to the target and if the prime is presented for longer periods.

48. The conclusion is that the prime *activates* related material in our lexical structure.

49. ACT, Anderson's spreading-activation model, is a comprehensive theory of the storage and retrieval of knowledge.

50. Generation effects refer to the fact that items generated by the subject are better remembered than items merely read by the subject.

CHAPTER

10

ISSUES IN MEMORY

INTRODUCTION

Many divisions of memory have been proposed. Distinctions among processes and subprocesses can, and do, lead to controversy. The purpose of this chapter is to outline some of these important points of conflict in the study of memory.

1. We shall consider the distinction between short-term and long-term store. Are the principles that govern memory over short intervals truly different from those that govern memory over longer intervals?
2. We shall question the nature of the difference between recognition memory and recall memory.
3. We shall discuss the popular distinction between memory for temporal and spatial events (episodic) and memory for knowledge and facts (semantic).
4. We shall consider the parallels between animal and human memory.
5. We shall examine the distinction that is often made between automatic and controlled processes in memory.
6. We shall explore the effect of context, or state, on memory.
7. We shall review split-brain research, which suggests that the two hemispheres of the brain tend to process different types of information.
8. We shall review some of the diseases that lead to memory abnormalities.

SEPARATE STORES?
RI and PI in STS

We begin by addressing the distinction between long-term store (LTS) and short-term store (STS) that is so characteristic of information-processing models of memory. The postulation of two (or more) memory stores obviously requires that the stores differ in important ways. If we can identify one or more ways in which the principles governing the retention of information over short intervals differ from the principles governing the retention of information over longer periods, we may be able to justify the distinction. If we cannot, then we might as well give up the distinction as an intriguing but irrelevant idea.

Let us begin our story by going back to 1959. At that time Peterson and Peterson developed what has come to be known as the *distractor technique* for the study of short-term memory. Subjects are first shown a stimulus (for example, three consonants) for a brief moment. They are then required to perform some distractor task, such as counting backward by threes for a set number of seconds (for example, 3 or 18 seconds). The subjects are then required to recall the original three-letter stimulus. The distractor task (counting backward by threes) is designed to keep the subjects from rehearsing the stimulus during the retention interval. If the subjects were not distracted in this manner, they would merely repeat the stimulus item over and over, thereby ensuring perfect recall.

The overall Peterson and Peterson task sounds very simple. All we have to do is remember a group of three letters for a few seconds. If we are presented with XKZ, it seems highly unlikely that we would ever forget such a simple item within 18 seconds. And yet the results of these experiments are quite remarkable. Retention of simple three-unit stimulus drops to as little as 10% after 18 seconds. That means we are not able to recall more than 1 out of 10 trigrams that we try to remember for only 18 seconds. A finding like that represents an enormous amount of forgetting over a brief period of time.

We can see how these results tie in with the notion of STS, or primary memory. It seems as though the information is lost or decays within a few seconds because it is not rehearsed enough either to maintain it within STS or transfer it to LTS. (The distractor task prevents the requisite rehearsal.)

RI AND PI.   The question arises as to what accounts for this dramatic and unexpected loss over so short an interval. At the time the effect was first observed, interference theory, with its emphasis on proactive inhibition (PI) and retroactive inhibition (RI), was in full swing. It had been clearly demonstrated that long-term retention losses were heavily determined by PI and RI. But this new short-term memory task represented something unique and unknown. Did PI and RI operate here just as they did in long-term memory? Could interference theory account for some or all of the enormous forgetting observed in this new procedure? At first, it seemed to some as though interference mechanisms could not account for the losses over such short intervals. It did not seem as though the loss could be an RI effect, because it did not appear as if the subjects were learning anything between the presentation of the syllable and its recall test that could cause unlearning of, or competition with, the syllable. In addition, data were presented suggesting recall did not decrease as the number of *prior* syllables that the subjects learned and recalled increased (Peterson, 1963; Peterson & Peterson, 1959). That is, a significant PI effect was not observed. Psychologists began to suspect that interference mechanisms operated in LTS but *not* in STS. Short-term memory was perhaps free from interference effects, whereas long-term memory was heavily influenced by interference mechanisms. (The most common suggestions concerning the determining mechanisms in STS were decay and displacement.)

But the proponents of interference theory were not long in responding to this potential schism. In an excellent study Keppel and Underwood (1962) outlined the problem and pursued a PI effect in the Peterson and Peterson (1959) situation. Using carefully controlled procedures they attempted to avoid methodological problems they identified in the original study. In contrast to the Petersons, they found that subjects' ability to recall successive stimuli *decreased* as the number of previously learned and tested items increased (see Figure 10.1). They demonstrated that PI does, after all, operate in short-term memory. It was a dramatic success for the interference position, for it argued that all retention, whether long or short, is subject to PI. It argued against the necessity of a distinction between long-term and short-term memory.

Since the original Keppel and Underwood (1962) study PI has been found in short-term memory many times (Loess, 1964; Mendell, 1977; Nowaczyk, Shaughnessy, & Zimmerman, 1974; Wickens, 1970). In addition, subsequent research has indicated that RI, as well as PI, operates in short-term memory situations. For reports of RI in short-term memory the interested reader is referred to Posner and Rossman (1965) and to Posner and Konick (1966).

RELEASE FROM PI.   There is one more area of research indicating that interference operates in a similar manner in both STS and LTS. We begin by noting that interference in LTS is heavily affected by similarity of the materials. We have already seen in previous chapters that similar materials often interfere with one another

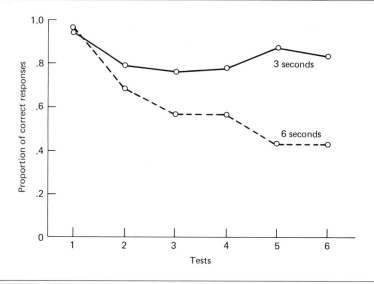

Figure 10.1 Proactive inhibition in the Peterson-Peterson situation. Proportion of correct responses as a function of the number of previous items and length of retention interval. (Adapted from Keppel, G., and Underwood, B. J. Proactive inhibition in short-term retention of single items. *Journal of Verbal Learning and Verbal Behavior,* 1962, *1,* 153–161. Fig. 4, p. 158.)

much more than do strongly dissimilar materials in both transfer and LTS situations. Now the question becomes this: Does similarity affect interference in STS in the same way?

The *release-from-PI* effect indicates that the answer to this question is yes. Release from PI was originally demonstrated by Wickens, Born, and Allen (1963), but it has been demonstrated many times since then (see Bird, 1977; Russ-Eft, 1979). Subjects are first given five trials of the Peterson and Peterson type, with the materials all being drawn from the same form class (for example, all words). As these trials progress, PI builds up. That is, performance on the succeeding trials decreases. Then, on the sixth trial, the Peterson and Peterson procedure is maintained, but the type of material presented is changed. The subjects might be presented a nonsense syllable instead of a word. This shift in the form class of the material produces a "release from PI"; performance on the sixth trial jumps dramatically (see Figure 10.2). The notion here is that interference in STS is affected by similarity in much the same manner that similarity affects interference in LTS; high similarity increases interference.

In conclusion, it can no longer be said that a distinction between short-term memory and long-term memory can be made on the basis of the notion that short-term memory is free from interference effects. Short-term memory is subject to PI and RI. If we are to find a valid basis for the distinction between short-term and long-term memory, we must look elsewhere (see Crowder, 1982).

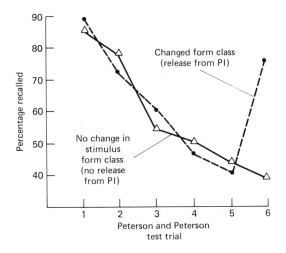

Figure 10.2 Release from PI (hypothetical data).

Acoustic versus Semantic Coding

What else might distinguish short-term memory from long term memory? Early research seemed to indicate that short-term memory might involve *acoustic coding* processes, whereas long-term memory might involve *semantic coding* processes (Conrad, 1964; Wickelgren, 1965). We can store information in short-term memory on the basis of the *sounds* of the items, whereas we can store information in long-term memory on the basis of the *meaning* of the material. If we wish to store information for a short period, we may focus on the sounds of the to-be-remembered material. For example, many of us have had the experience of having been given a phone number (824-2105, say) in a crowded, noisy room. While frantically searching for pencil and paper, we repeat the number over and over, maintaining the sounds of the digits. We in no way attempt to deal with the material on any more complicated level. We do not try to group the digits or to relate them to our past life. We merely maintain the information through sound. But, if we wish to remember the same number for a long period, we may encode it in a more complicated fashion. For example, we might relate the digits to events in our life (8 divided by 2 is 4; 21 plus 5 is my age, and so on). In other words, we may involve meaning in our coding process.

For a time the distinction between long-term memory and short-term memory based on semantic and acoustic coding processes seemed to be gaining wide acceptance (Adams, 1967; Baddeley, 1966a, 1966b; Baddeley & Patterson, 1971; Kintsch & Buschke, 1969). But the semantic-acoustic distinction fell on hard times. Evidence began to accumulate that semantic coding might, after all, be involved in short-term memory (Shulman, 1971, 1972). Similarly, evidence for acoustic effects in long-term memory began to appear (Bruce & Crowley, 1970; Dale & McGlaughlin, 1971; McGlaughlin & Dale, 1971; Nelson & Rothbart,

1972). It may well be that short-term memory *often* involves acoustic coding and that long-term memory *characteristically* involves semantic coding, but neither system is as restricted as Baddeley and others originally suggested. Depending on the demands of the task, we are capable of coding in many different ways. (For further discussion see Forrester, 1972; Glassman, 1972; Jacoby & Goolkasian, 1973; Tell, 1972; Wickelgren, 1973.) Once again we are forced to look elsewhere for support for the distinction between short-term and long-term memory.

Serial-Position Effects

When we are presented with a list of items (a string of words, for example) and asked to recall them immediately in any order we wish, a very interesting pattern of results is obtained. These results are summarized by the curve in Figure 10.3. Notice that items toward the end of the list are recalled better than any of the others. This fact is called the *recency effect*. Items toward the beginning of the list are recalled more often than items in the middle, but not as well as the end items. This fact is called the *primacy effect*. Items in the middle of the list are the most difficult to recall.

THE PRIMACY EFFECT.   Let us first dispense with the primacy effect, which is of minor interest to us in attempting to distinguish short-term from long-term memory. The general assumption concerning the primacy effect is that it reflects a greater amount of rehearsal given to early items in the list. Early items are recalled fairly well because they are rehearsed more than later items (see Rundus, 1971). Put yourself in the position of rehearsing a serial list. One item is exposed at a time. When the first item appears, you rehearse it over and over as many times as you can before the second item appears. When the second item does appear, you probably rehearse from the beginning of the list, repeating items 1 and 2 over and over again. When item 3 appears, you still attempt to rehearse from the beginning of the list, and so on. If this rehearsal strategy is followed, it is clear that early items will be rehearsed more than later items. Hence, they are learned and recalled better than later items (Reynolds & Houston, 1964).

THE RECENCY EFFECT.   Why are the last items recalled best of all? The rehearsal strategy just outlined cannot account for the recency effect. The most common interpretation of the recency effect (see Glanzer, 1972; Kintsch & Polson, 1979; Murdock, 1974) involves the distinction between short-term and long-term memory. During presentation, all items enter short-term memory. As additional items are presented, some of the earlier items are lost. Some items are transferred to long-term memory. Immediately after all the items in the list have been presented, the items toward the end of the list are still in short-term memory. As a result these items have an extremely high probability of being recalled in an immediate retention test. Items further back in the list are no longer in short-term memory. Hence, relative to the end items, they have some lower probability of being recalled. The assumption is made that the recency effect is the result of the end items being *stored in short-term memory at the time of recall*. Lower recall of items further back in the list results from some of them having been lost completely and some having been moved into long-term memory.

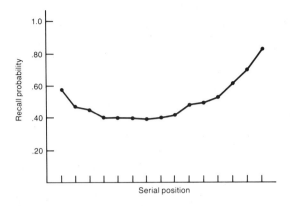

Figure 10.3 Hypothetical serial-position curve for free recall.

This is an interesting explanation, but it is not without its critics (see Brodie & Murdock, 1977). As Wickelgren (1973) points out, there is no real need to postulate two memory systems to account for the recency effect. A single-memory model can account for it just as well as the two-memory model. Assume for the moment that there is only one memory store. Information enters this store and is then lost over time (owing to decay or interference). If we assume, as Wickelgren (1973) does, that this memory trace is lost *rapidly at first and then more slowly,* then the recency effect can be explained by a single memory model. The critical assumption in this explanation is the notion that memory traces decay, or are lost, rapidly at first and then more slowly. It is the idea that forgetting will be most rapid immediately after learning and that the rate of forgetting will then be reduced as time goes on. Applied to the recency effect this position would argue that end items have not yet undergone this initial, substantial loss. Items further back in the list have already suffered the initial, substantial loss in strength. In summary, the recency effect can be understood in terms of a two-memory position *or* in terms of a single-memory position involving a slowing rate of loss. The recency effect does not *prove* that short-term memory is different from long-term memory. To the contrary, the distinction between short-term and long-term memory provides but one interpretation of the recency effect (see Watkins & Peynircioglu, 1983).

NEGATIVE RECENCY.   Wickelgren's interpretation of the recency effect is quite damaging to the notion that two memory stores are necessary to account for recency. Nevertheless, it is instructive to pursue the controversy a step further. The general strategy followed by those who believe in a two-memory interpretation of the recency effect has been to try to find variables that affect only one portion of the serial position curve. It is assumed that, if a variable affects only the end of the curve, it is affecting short-term but not long-term memory. Similarly, if a variable affects only the beginning and intermediate positions or all positions equally, it is assumed that it is affecting long-term memory and not short-term memory (see Watkins, 1972; Whitten, 1978).

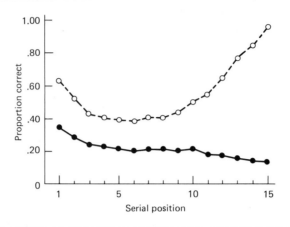

Figure 10.4 Serial-position curves for immediate (○) and final (●) recall. (Adapted from Craik, F. I. M. The fate of primary memory items in free recall. *Journal of Verbal Learning and Verbal Behavior,* 1970, 9, 143–148. Fig. 2, p. 145.)

For our purposes we shall deal with one particular variable, which has received considerable attention. Craik (1970) presented ten successive lists to his subjects. They were tested for recall immediately after the presentation of each list. This immediate-recall test produced the expected kind of serial-position effect, with a pronounced recency effect (see upper curve in Figure 10.4). But then Craik did something a little different. After all ten lists had been presented and tested, he asked the subjects to recall as many of the items as they could from the lists. The results of this final recall test were quite striking (see the lower curve in Figure 10.4). The recency effect disappeared. In fact, recall of the final items in the list dropped below recall of items in earlier positions. This finding has been termed the *negative recency effect.*

The negative recency effect has received a good deal of attention (Bartlett & Tulving, 1974; Cohen, 1970; Jacoby & Bartz, 1972). Many have looked on it as support for the distinction between long-term and short-term memory. The idea is that the end items can be recalled well in an immediate test because they are still in short-term memory. But in the final test the end items are not well recalled because they are no longer in short-term memory. They have either been lost or transferred to long-term memory with a relatively low probability of recovery. It is assumed that final recall of the end items drops below recall of earlier items because the end items have not been rehearsed as much as earlier items and are thus less likely to have been transferred to long-term memory.

But Wickelgren (1973) attacks this interpretation, too. He argues that the negative recency effect can also be handled by a single-memory formulation. He argues that the recency effect disappears in the final recall test because the traces of the end items have undergone the kind of rapid loss, or initial decay, that we described above. His explanation of the fact that end-item recall actually drops below the recall of earlier items is identical to the reasoning proposed by the two-memory proponents. That is, earlier items are rehearsed more, learned better, and recalled more easily. According to Wickelgren, there is no need to postulate two memory systems. Thus, the evidence for two memory system drawn from serial situations is, at best, equivocal.

Clinical Evidence

Another line of potential support for the long-term—short-term distinction comes from studies of human patients who have suffered bilateral damage to, or surgical ablation of, the hippocampus. Many of the surgical treatments were undertaken in an effort to relieve severe epileptic conditions. If you are interested in the exact procedures and the nature of the damage to the brain, good accounts can be found in Baddeley and Warrington (1970), Milner (1966), Squire (1987), and Warrington and Weiskrantz (1968, 1970).

What concerns us is the peculiar effect these events, either accidental or surgical, have on the patients' memories:

1. The ability to retain new information for very short intervals appears to be normal.
2. Memory for events that occurred before the brain damage appears to be normal.
3. The patients are unable to retain any new information for long periods.

In other words, although old long-term memories and the entire short-term memory system appear to be intact, the subjects display an almost complete inability to form new long-term memory traces. It seems that the patients' ability to transfer information from short-term memory to long-term memory has been destroyed. Information already in long-term memory appears to remain intact and can be retrieved, but no new information can be entered into long-term memory. Such patients can carry on conversations (through the use of short-term memory). But they cannot remember a person they met and talked with a few minutes before. (Information has been lost from short-term memory without having been transferred to long-term memory.) They know who they are and what their life was like before the damage (intact old long-term memory). But they have no lasting idea of what has happened to them or the world since their brain trauma (no new long-term memory). Imagine what this condition must be like. The patients have no idea of what has happened since the trauma. In fact, they are even unaware that any time has passed at all since the trauma. For them, regardless of how long they have been there, they just came to the hospital "yesterday." Nothing has happened to them (that they can recall) since they came into the hospital.

This disability, although unfortunate for the individuals involved, has been taken as evidence for the existence of two memory systems. Is it possible to think of these results in terms of a single memory store? Rather than arguing that the brain trauma somehow destroyed the subjects' ability to transfer information from a distinct short-term memory to a distinct long-term memory, could we not argue that the trauma merely limits how well an item can be learned? Materials can be learned to the point at which they can be remembered for a short interval of time, but they cannot be learned to the point at which they will be remembered for very long. If we think of a single memory trace that can increase in strength, then these results can be thought of in terms of a limit having been put on the strength that this memory trace can attain.

Another problem with trying to use these data as evidence for two memory stores is that sometimes the capacity to store new information in LTS is, although severely retarded, not entirely eliminated. For example, Lewis (1979) reports the case of H. M. In spite of losing almost all ability to store new information in LTS, H. M. did know that he had some form of memory impairment. He could retain some visual and tactile maze learning. He was able to learn a simple factory job. He retained, permanently, the information that President John F. Kennedy had been assassinated. In addition, H. M.'s IQ before the operation was 104. Two years after the operation his IQ was 112. And seven years later it was 118. In other words, the loss of the ability to move information into LTS is not, after all, as clear and distinct as the proponents of the two-memory position would need it to be to convince everyone of the validity of their position.

Who knows enough about what ablation and damage do to the brain to conclude that one or another interpretation is correct? It would seem, whatever the final outcome concerning long-term versus short-term memory, that this type of evidence is difficult to accept as conclusive. There are just too many unknowns in the situation and too many alternative explanations to be certain that we have clearly distinguished between long-term memory and short-term memory. For further clinical evidence and argument you are referred to Warrington and Shallice (1969) and Squire (1987).

The distinction between long-term memory and short-term memory will be with us for a long time. It has now marbled much of our thinking about memory, but whether it is a valid distinction remains to be seen. We have examined four areas of study that have been proposed as providing evidence for the distinction, yet none of them seem to provide any *conclusive* evidence for the distinction. We have not exhausted the relevant areas of research (Wickelgren, 1973, and Crowder, 1982, provide fuller reviews). But the sample we have considered suggests that, at the very least, the distinction between long-term and short-term memory should be approached with caution (see Bernbach, 1975; Craik & Lockhart, 1972; Martinez & Kesner, 1986; Mishkin & Appenzeller, 1987).

RECALL VERSUS RECOGNITION

We now move to the second major issue to be considered in this chapter. Is recognition memory fundamentally different from recall memory? When we are asked to *recognize* something, such as the correct answer to a question on a multiple-choice exam, are we doing something fundamentally different from what we do when we try to *recall* the answer to the same question? On an operational level, recall and recognition are clearly distinct. In a recall test we ask, "What is the item?" and in a recognition task we ask, "Is this the item?" (Underwood, 1972). We wish to find out whether this clear-cut operational distinction reflects any important underlying differences in the memory processes.

Before we address that question, let us be sure we understand the difference between recall and recognition tasks. In a typical recall task, the subjects might be presented with a list of words and then asked to recall as many of them as they can.

In a recognition task the subjects might be presented with the same list. But then during the test phase they would be presented with pairs of words. One member of the pair would be an "old" item, or one that they had already seen. The second member of each pair would be a new item, or a lure. The subjects would be required to indicate which of the two items in each pair was the "old" item. This is a typical recognition task, but there are many other varieties (see Hall, 1983; Kausler, 1974). The essence of all the recognition tasks is that the subjects must be able to recognize an item as having been observed before in a certain context (for example, in the list of presented items).

Recognition is generally superior to recall (but not always; see Watkins & Tulving, 1975). Very early in the study of memory it was discovered that we are able to recognize more than we can recall (Hollingworth, 1913; McDougall, 1904; Myers, 1914). In a typical study the subjects are presented with lists of syllables, words, pictures, or colors. They are then tested for recall and recognition. Subjects are typically able to recognize many more stimuli than they can recall. For example, sit down and try to list as many native American tribes or groups as you can. After a while it will seem as though you have exhausted your store of information. But you have not. You will be able to recognize many more, even though you could not recall them (for example, you may not have recalled, but may recognize, Choctaw, Cree, Pueblo, Mohawk, Blackfoot, Eskimo, Yurok, Seminole, Cheyenne, Ojibwa, Chippewa, Mohegan, Seneca, Ute, Zuni, and Arapaho).

Sometimes the gap between recall and recognition is extremely wide. For example, Standing (1973) has shown that thousands of pictures shown to subjects can be recognized later with apparent ease. The title of his article is, in fact, "Learning 10,000 Pictures." But when we turn to our ability to recall pictures, rather than merely recognize them, we find a different story entirely. Nickerson and Adams (1979) gave subjects empty circles and asked them to draw in U.S. pennies. As can be seen in Figure 10.5, the subjects were not very accurate at all. Something like 95% of them either omitted or incorrectly located the word *liberty*. Fifty percent of the subjects located Lincoln's head incorrectly. In other words, although we do seem to be able to recognize thousands of pictures, our ability to recall even such a simple, common object as a penny is severely limited. A gap like this between recall and recognition certainly deserves our attention (see also Rubin & Kontis, 1983).

Hypothesis 1: Unitary Strength

Does this difference between recall and recognition reflect significant differences in memory processes? There are three major interpretations of the situation. The first, usually labeled the unitary-strength interpretation, maintains that the difference is not particularly important. It has been assumed that the two tasks merely differ in terms of their sensitivity. Memorized items are assumed to differ in strength; the recognition test picks up, or reveals, weaker items than does the recall test. Some items seem to be strong enough to be recognized but not quite strong enough to be recalled. According to this traditional view, the difference between recognition and recall does not imply anything at all about underlying process differences. Memory is viewed as a unitary process in which items vary from weak to strong. The threshold for recognition is lower than it is for recall. Although this view is a traditional one and some psychologists feel it is outmoded, it does have its adherents (see Rabinowitz & Mandler, 1977; Tulving & Thomson, 1971).

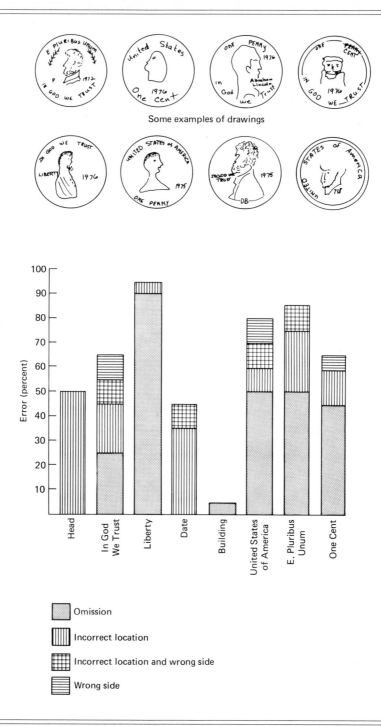

Figure 10.5 Errors produced during recall of a penny. (Adapted from Nickerson, R. S., and Adams, M. J. Long-term memory for a common object. *Cognitive Psychology*, 1979, *11*, 287–307. Figs. 1 and 2, p. 289.)

Hypothesis 2: Generation–Recognition

Suppose that we present subjects with a list of 500 words. Half of the words are common (for example, *child, office, supply*). Half are uncommon (for example, *ferule, julep, wattled*). Then we test for recognition of these words. It has been found that *uncommon words are more easily recognized than common words* (McCormack & Swenson, 1972; Shepard, 1967). If recall and recognition involve similar processes, we would expect the same sort of effect to appear when we tested for recall of common and uncommon words. But just the opposite effect has appeared. *Common words appear to be better recalled than uncommon words* (Kinsbourne & George, 1974; Murdock, 1960). The same variable (common versus uncommon) thus has opposite effects on recall and recognition. This disparity has led many investigators to suggest that recognition and recall may well involve different underlying processes (see Bower & Bostrom, 1968; Kintsch, 1970).

Identifying these differences is another matter. One common interpretation has been that recall involves retrieval processes, whereas recognition does not. In a sense recall is seen as involving all the processes of recognition, and then some. Recall and recognition are often viewed as being different not so much in the nature of the underlying processes but in terms of the *number* of processes involved. In order to recognize a bit of information, on the one hand, the subjects must have somehow encoded and stored it, but they need not search for it during the recognition test. To recall an item, on the other hand, the subjects must encode, store, *and* retrieve.

Putting it another way, subjects asked to recall an item must first *generate* that item, or dredge it (and presumably many others) up out of storage, and then *recognize* it as the correct item. When subjects are asked to recognize an item, the generating is done by the experimenter, and the subjects need only recognize the provided item.

Hypothesis 3: Control Process

Another way to think about the differences between recall and recognition is in terms of variations in control processes. If you will recall, Atkinson and Shiffrin (1971) refer to the fact that we use the fixed structural properties of the memory system in many different ways. Differences between recall and recognition might be traced to differences in control processes rather than to fundamentally different memory systems. In attempting to memorize materials for future recall, individuals may use the fixed structural properties of the memory system in one way. In attempting to memorize for future recognition, they may change their rehearsal strategy and utilize the fixed properties of the system in another way (see Griffith, 1975).

Subjects do, in fact, code material differently, depending on whether they expect a recall test or a recognition test (Leonard & Whitten, 1983). For example, Carey and Lockhart (1973) had subjects learn a list with the expectation that they would be tested for recall. In a surprise move the subjects were actually tested for recognition. Their recognition performance was much poorer when they had been expecting a recall test than when they had been expecting a recognition test. Of course, the situation would become complicated if the individuals were unaware of the nature of the upcoming retention test (recall or recognition). In this case the subjects' strategy would be to maximize their chances of success in the light of their *best guess* about the nature of the upcoming test.

As a further example of the ways in which we might differ in our preparation for recall and recognition tests, consider what we might do with an item such as XKLMJG. If we are to try to recall XKLMJG, we must be sure the entire item is encoded. But if we encode the item for recognition, we might attend to some portion of the stimulus rather than to the whole thing (for example, encoding the fact that an item with L and M in the middle is an "old" item).

Pursuing this notion that recall and recognition may involve differences in control processes, we may ask what *kinds* of differences there are between the two. Schmidt (1983) has provided some information concerning memory for prose. He found that people expecting a multiple-choice test (recognition) remembered a great deal of detail. In contrast, people expecting an essay test (recall) remembered higher-order units, trends, and themes. In other words, our expectations about how we will have to use information can have quite complex effects on how we process that material.

Recognition Failure

Thus far we have been talking as though recognition were *always* better than recall. But such is not the case. The *recognition-failure phenomenon* has been demonstrated repeatedly (see Flexser & Tulving, 1978; Jones, 1978; Muter, 1978; Nilsson, Law, & Tulving, 1988). The basic experimental demonstration of recognition failure goes like this: The subjects study A–B pairs. They are first tested for recognition of the B elements alone. Then they are tested for recall of B, given A as a cue. In this situation researchers often find that subjects can recall B items that they were unable to recognize. This very controversial but robust effect adds to the complexity of the distinction between recall and recognition. Later in this chapter, in a section on the role of contextual cues in memory, we shall consider the current interpretations of the recognition-failure effect. But for now, we need to point out that the recognition-failure effect is not predicted by two of our major interpretations of the recall-recognition difference. The unitary-strength theory does not predict it, and the generation-recognition position does not predict it, either. Both of these theories, or hypotheses, predict that recognition will be better than recall. Thus, we are left with two interpretations of the recall-recognition difference that conflict with the recognition-failure effect. Perhaps the third interpretation of the recall-recognition difference, the one having to do with differences in control processes, will prove to be the one that can account for the recognition-failure effect.

Priming and Recognition Failure

Another phenomenon resembles recognition failure. It occurs in priming experiments. As you will recall, priming is demonstrated by first presenting a prime and then a target item that varies in its relationship to the prime. When the prime and the target items are related, then perception of the target is facilitated. As we have seen, this effect has been demonstrated many times; perception of the target item is primed by the presentation of the first item.

The effect we wish to discuss here is a little different. Watkins and Gibson (1988) ran a typical priming experiment but, in addition, tested for *recognition of the primes* as well as for perception of the target items. In a kind of recognition failure they found that subjects would sometimes be unable to recognize the prime items even though the beneficial target-perception effect was still observed. In other words, subjects failed to recognize primes even when they actually helped enhance perception of the target items. Exactly what this means in terms of the relationship between recognition and recall remains to be seen. At the very least it points out that recognition is not as simple a matter as was once supposed (see also Donnelly, 1988).

In summary, recall and recognition do differ on an operational level. Certain variables do affect the two differentially. And yet there is little agreement over what these differences mean. We have seen that the differences have been interpreted in terms of a unitary-strength hypothesis, a generation-recognition hypothesis, and differences in control processes, including organizational differences. If this all seems a bit confusing, you should understand that it is the field of psychology presenting various interpretations and not you that is confused. There simply is no general agreement about the relationship between recall and recognition.

EPISODIC VERSUS SEMANTIC MEMORY

Thus far we have asked whether short-term memory is different from long-term memory and whether recognition memory is different from recall memory. These distinctions exemplify the tendency to split, or divide, memory. Another example of this trend is found in the suggestion that different *types* of information will require different memory models. Thus, we might need one sort of model to account for our ability to remember words and another model to account for our ability to remember sentences or paragraphs. We might need one model to account for the encoding, storage, and retrieval of visual information, another to account for auditory information, and so on.

Typical of this tendency to suggest that different principles will govern memory for different types of information is Tulving's (1972, 1985) distinction between *episodic* and *semantic* memory. Episodic memory, on the one hand, is assumed to store information about temporally arranged or dated events and episodes. Personal experiences are stored in episodic memory. Semantic memory, on the other hand, refers to memory for the meaning of words, concepts, and facts. Information stored in semantic memory is not temporally ordered, or related to time.

Examples of the kind of information stored in episodic memory would be:

1. I remember spending the early years of my life in Utica.
2. I must be at school tomorrow before 8:30 A.M.
3. I met a very uninteresting person on the bus yesterday.

Most laboratory experiments involve episodic memory. For example, remembering that LXG was paired with KPY *in a particular laboratory experiment* would be an episodic memory.

Examples of the kind of nontemporal information stored in semantic memory would be:

1. 2 + 2 = 4.
2. Whales nurse their young.
3. Almost everyone has a nose.

These bits of information are not temporally ordered—they are not remembered in temporal relation to other experiences.

In describing the distinction Tulving (1972) does point out that the two systems often interact with each other. But he feels that they can function independently and that they may well differ from each other in terms of encoding, storage, and retrieval processes. For example, Neely and Payne (1983) report some findings suggesting that recognition failure, described in the preceding section, may occur in episodic but not semantic memory.

The Tip-of-the-Tongue Phenomenon

We have all had the experience of feeling confident that we know a particular word but being unable to recall it. We know we know the word, but we can't quite retrieve it. This experience has been called the *tip-of-the-tongue* (TOT) phenomenon by Brown and McNeil (1966).

The material in Box 10.1 may help you experience TOT. Try to supply the correct word for each of these definitions. Sometimes you will know the word right away. Sometimes you will be sure you don't know the word. But sometimes you will have the feeling that the word is "on the tip of your tongue." (The correct words are contained in the box on page 302.)

What does TOT have to do with the distinction between semantic and episodic memory? Generally speaking TOT has been thought of as involving semantic and not episodic memory; it involves retrieval of materials (usually words) that are not temporally ordered. But some research (Schachter, 1983) suggests that TOT can be demonstrated in episodic as well as in semantic memory. Hence, even though the distinction between episodic and semantic memory is logically clear, it is not so easy to demonstrate that difference experimentally.

Flashbulb Memories

Whether the distinction between episodic and semantic memory will prove to be a lasting distinction remains to be seen (see McKoon & Ratcliff, 1979). The two types of memory have not been compared experimentally very many times. One reason is that the vast majority of experimental studies involves information of the episodic variety. Most experiments put subjects through an "episode," which they have to remember. Fewer studies have been concerned with preexperimental semantic information existing in long-term store. This situation is changing, however. More and more efforts to study "natural" versus "laboratory" memory are appearing (see Wilkinson & Koestler, 1983). One kind of natural episodic memory that has been studied is called *flashbulb memory* (Bohannon, 1988; Winograd & Killinger, 1983). Flashbulb memories involve a situation in which we first learned of a very surprising, arousing, or emotional event. For example, think about when you first learned that the Challenger had exploded, or that John Lennon had been shot. You will probably be able to recall quite a bit about some or all of the following aspects of these situations:

1. Where were you?
2. What was going on when you heard the news?
3. Who gave you the news?

Box 10.1   The Tip-of-the-Tongue Phenomenon

Look at each of the definitions below. Supply the appropriate word for the definitions, if you know it. Indicate "Don't know" for those that you are certain you don't know. Mark TOT next to those for which you are reasonably certain you know the word, though you can't recall it now. For these words, supply at least one word that sounds similar to the target word. The answers appear on the following page.

1. An absolute ruler, a tyrant.
2. A stone having a cavity lined with crystals.
3. A great circle of the earth passing through the geographic poles and any given point on the earth's surface.
4. Worthy of respect or reverence by reason of age and dignity.
5. Shedding leaves each year, as opposed to evergreen.
6. A person appointed to act as a substitute for another.
7. Five offspring born at a single birth.
8. A special quality of leadership that captures the popular imagination and inspires unswerving allegiance.
9. The red coloring matter of the red blood corpuscles.
10. Flying reptiles that were extinct at the end of the Mesozoic Era.
11. A spring from which hot water, steam, or mud gushes out at intervals, found in Yellowstone National Park.
12. The second stomach of a bird, which has thick, muscular walls.
13. The green coloring matter found in plants.
14. The long-haired wild ox of central Asia, often domesticated as a beast of burden.
15. The art of speaking in such a way that the voice seems to come from another place.

From *Cognition*, 2nd ed., by Margaret Matlin. Copyright © 1989 by Holt, Rinehart and Winston, Inc., reprinted by permission of the publisher.

---

4. What were your immediate feelings?
5. What did those around you feel?
6. What happened immediately after you received the news?

Your episodic memory for this event will be quite detailed when compared with your memory for less surprising, less emotional events. For example, what do you remember about the situation in which you first learned that George Bush was going to run for president? Probably nothing at all. Surprising, emotional events tend to be elaborated more heavily than ordinary events, and they tend to be tied to the temporal aspect of the situation. Flashbulb memories can best be described as extreme episodic memories.

Unfortunately, not everyone agrees that flashbulb memories warrant a special memory mechanism. Some investigators feel that the distraction may be a straw man and that we need not postulate any special process to account for it (see Cohen, McClosky, & Wible, 1988; Schmidt & Bohannon, 1988).

Answers to Definitions in Box 10.1

1. despot	**6.** surrogate	**11.** geyser
2. geode	**7.** quintuplets	**12.** gizzard
3. meridian	**8.** charisma	**13.** chlorophyll
4. venerable	**9.** hemoglobin	**14.** yak
5. deciduous	**10.** pterodactyl	**15.** ventriloquism

Mixed Memories

One of the basic problems with the semantic-episodic distinction is that many memories may involve episodic, semantic, or *both* episodic and semantic aspects, and we are not very good at demonstrating which one. For example, we know that the naming of a flashed word is facilitated by a single prior presentation of that word in a long list of words. But as Feustel, Shiffrin, and Salasoo (1983) point out, we don't really know whether this facilitation involves semantic memory, episodic memory, or both. What was stored during that first exposure—memory for the event, memory of the word, or both? At this point we simply don't know.

Studying "natural" verses "laboratory" memory doesn't solve all our problems, either. Our memory for "real life" events is probably the result of some complex process involving repeated attempts to recall, rehearse, and elaborate the stored information (see Wilkinson & Koestler, 1983). For example, your memories of your childhood are probably the result of many conversations (rehearsals) you have had with your parents and others through the years. Any given memory you have may be a complex mix of semantic and episodic elements.

In any case, the distinction between episodic and semantic memory does provide us with an example of the tendency to propose different models for different types of information (see Hintzman, 1984; Klatsky, 1984; Wolters, 1984; and Yantis & Meyer, 1988).

ANIMAL MEMORY

Let us return to a familiar question: Do we need one theory or set of theories to account for human behavior and another to account for animal behavior? More specifically, do animals and humans forget in essentially the same manner, or are they such different creatures that we will be forced to develop distinct models for each?

We have seen that a large number of species have been used in the study of learning and memory. Rats, cats, monkeys, guinea pigs, pigeons, *Planaria*, and even the octopus have all been used in the laboratory. We can only assume that the investigators using these animals wanted to discover laws and principles that would eventually help them understand human behavior.

Until recently, memory per se did not receive a great deal of attention in the field of animal behavior. But the recent upsurge of interest in human memory has been paralleled by a similar swell of interest in animal memory. Demonstrations of animal-memory phenomena have ranged all the way from bowed serial-position curves (Wagner & Pfautz, 1978) and memory for discrimination (Smith & Spear,

1979) to demonstrations of PI and RI in classical conditioning situations (Wickens, Tuber, Nield, & Wickens, 1977), observational learning in rats (Denny, Bell, & Clos, 1983), and paired-associate learning in animals (Kesner & DeSpain, 1988).

The position taken in this text is that, in spite of an enormous gap between the animal and human literatures, there are important points of contact. These points of contact will be emphasized. You should be aware that this is a biased position. Many authors argue that theories of animal and human memory will have to be different and that a single, unified theory of memory encompassing animal and human behavior is highly unlikely (Grant, 1964).

If you think about it for a moment, you will realize that we began to discuss similarities between animal and human memory systems in Chapter 8, where consolidation theory was outlined. Consolidation theory, although based for the most part on animal experimentation, is a system designed to describe memory events not only for animal populations but also for humans. There are many other points of contact between animal and human memory. For example, in Chapter 12 we shall learn how animals solve problems and form concepts in ways that parallel the methods used by humans. And in Chapter 13 we shall discuss the fascinating controversy surrounding apes and language.

For now, we want to consider four major areas of contact between animal and human memory—*interference effects, short-term memory, spatial memory*, and *memory for serial patterns*.

Interference and Animal Memory

If we want to argue that animal and human memory processes are similar, and we know (see Chapter 8) that interference operates in human memory, then interference should also operate in animal memory. Do animals suffer losses in retention that can be attributed to the effects of prior learning (PI) and subsequent learning (RI)? The answer appears to be yes. Poor retention of an acquired response system in animals does appear to be related to previous and subsequent learning. As Spear (1971) puts it, interference phenomena such as PI and RI are common types of retention lapse in animals, although they are often not recognized as such. A number of studies specifically designed to demonstrate PI and RI in animals have been successful (Edhouse & White, 1988a, 1988b; Jitsumori, Wright, & Cook, 1988; Roitblat & Harley, 1988). It is difficult to conclude with any certainty that the PI and RI effects in animal and human designs are strictly comparable (see Gleitman, 1971; Revusky, 1971). But the rough correspondence between animal and human experiments and results does suggest that we must take seriously the possibility of similar cross-species interference effects.

When considering interference phenomena and the predominantly human verbal research associated with them we must keep in mind that many interference concepts are found in the early animal literature. We have already seen that the unlearning factor in the two-factor theory of interference has been viewed as analogous to the experimental extinction phenomenon. In addition, demonstrations of spontaneous recovery in human verbal behavior provide another point of contact between human learning and animal conditioning.

How one interprets these points of contact is another matter. Some authors (for example, Winograd, 1971) argue that, although some interference concepts have their roots in the animal laboratory, the meanings of the concepts change as the

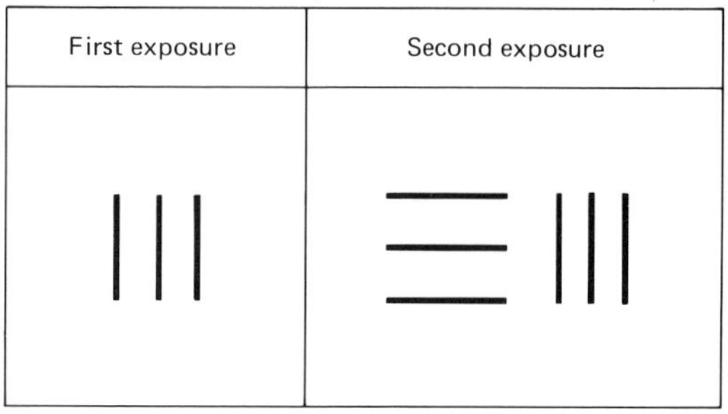

First exposure	Second exposure

Figure 10.6 The DMTS procedure. The animal is first exposed to a particular stimulus configuration (vertical lines). Then, after a delay the animal is exposed to the old stimulus paired with a new stimulus, and choice behavior is observed.

concepts are applied to human situations. The labels may be the same (*extinction, spontaneous recovery*, and so on), but the processes to which they are applied differ in the animal and human verbal situations. Many other authors feel, however, that interference effects are pervasive in the animal kingdom. For them, the traditional emphasis on human research in the area of memory does not necessarily imply that human and animal memory systems are qualitatively different.

DMTS and Animal STS

Investigators in the field of animal memory have developed a technique to study STS in animals. As we know, the Peterson-Peterson distractor technique is one of the major paradigms in the study of human STS. So as we review this new animal paradigm, which is known as the *delayed-matching-to-sample* procedure, or DMTS, we should ask ourselves how comparable the two techniques are. Can we compare data obtained from animals in DMTS situations with human data gathered in distractor situations? The best answer is that we should be very cautious about making too much of the similarities between the animal and human procedures, but we can proceed hopefully.

The basic DMTS procedure is this: An animal (for example, a pigeon) is shown a stimulus such as the one in the left side of Figure 10.6. Then a short delay, or retention interval, is introduced. Then the two stimuli on the right side of Figure 10.6 are presented. If the animal responds to the "correct" stimulus, the one it had seen previously, it is rewarded.

In the last ten years, we have witnessed an enormous growth in the use of this paradigm (see Downing, Okanoya, & Dooling, 1988; Forestell & Herman, 1988; Roitblat & Harley, 1988; Spetch & Wilkie, 1983). Correct DMTS performance drops off very rapidly and steeply as the time between the two stimulus presentations increases. If the animal in a DMTS situation is delayed for as little as a few seconds, correct matching deteriorates rapidly. As we learned in Chapter 9, this is also what appears in studies of human short-term memory; performance drops off rapidly in a few seconds. Similarly, just as interference effects have been found in

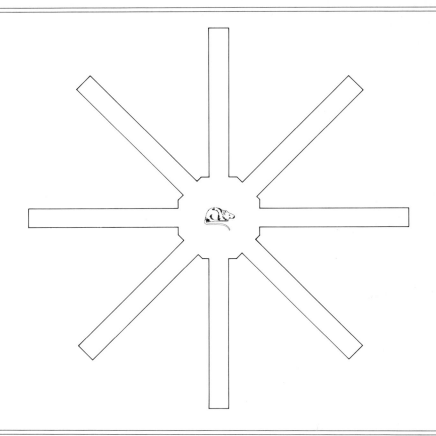

Figure 10.7 A radial maze. (Adapted from Olton, D. S., and Samuelson, R. J. Remembrance of places passed: Spatial memory in rats. *Journal of Experimental Psychology*, 1976, 2, 97–116. Copyright 1976 by the American Psychological Association. Reprinted by permission.)

have been demonstrated, suggesting that animal and human short-term memory processes are similar (see Edhouse & White, 1988a, 1988b).

There are some obvious differences, however, between DMTS and the Peterson and Peterson method. In the human situation, for instance, the retention interval is always filled with a distractor task, such as counting backward by threes. In the DMTS situation the animal is often left alone. And the Peterson and Peterson experiment is a recall situation, whereas DMTS involves recognition. These differences need not lead us to conclude that the effects obtained in the two situations are totally incomparable. But they do suggest that we be cautious.

Animal Spatial Memory

What else about animal performance leads us to suspect that humans are not all that different from animals in their memory processes? One area of research that is often mentioned has to do with the rat's behavior in a *radial maze* (see Figure 10.7).

It is obvious that humans can remember and utilize information about the spatial configuration of their environment. For example, when you search for a clean pair of socks in the morning, you tend to look in every reasonable spot without repeating yourself. You don't look in the same drawer twice (at least not until you have exhausted other possibilities), because you can remember that you just looked there. Our spatial memory is good but not perfect. For example, we tend to remember a given distance with many turns as being longer than the same distance with fewer turns (Moar & Bower, 1983). But can animals engage in similar behavior? It would be to their advantage in terms of such things as food gathering if they could. If a hummingbird feeds on the nectar of a certain flower, it would be advantageous if the bird could remember *not* to visit that particular flower again for a while until the plant had had time to replenish the nectar supply.

This kind of beneficial memory for location in space has been demonstrated using rats in a radial maze like that in Figure 10.7 (Olton, 1978; Olton & Samuelson, 1976). The maze had eight arms radiating out from a central area. A piece of food was put in the end of each arm. The rat was placed in the central area and allowed to choose and go into any arm. Once it ate the food in a particular arm, that arm remained without food, even though the rat could go back into that arm at any time.

The question was what the hungry rat would do given the opportunity to roam this maze freely. Quite simply, the rat very quickly learned to enter only arms that it had not previously entered. If we define a correct choice as entering a previously unentered arm, we find that within a few trials the mean number of correct choices was above seven. The rat almost never entered a previously visited arm, thereby rendering its food gathering very efficient.

This behavior seems to be consistent with the idea that the rat has a good memory for spatial locations. But some alternative interpretations must be considered. For example, it is possible that the rats were "marking" the arms they visited with, say, a drop of urine (see Travis, Ludvigson, & Eslinger, 1988). In this way they could use odor as a cue not to revisit a particular arm. This possibility has been discounted by several kinds of experiments. Olton and Samuelson (1976) soaked the maze with after-shave lotion to hide any possible odor trails the rats might be leaving. And Zoladek and Roberts (1978) surgically disrupted the rats' ability to smell. In both these studies the rats still performed well in the maze, suggesting that it is spatial memory and not odor that accounts for the effects.

Another possibility is that the rats are merely learning a chain of responses, such as always going into the next arm to the right. This interpretation is denied by the fact that the rats do *not* always make their choices in some fixed sequence, such as moving counterclockwise around the maze. Despite some regularity in their choice patterning, it is not enough to account for their performance. These and other studies lead us to the conclusion that rats do possess spatial memory and that, in this sense, their memory apparatus is similar to that of the human (see Brown, Wheeler, & Riley, 1989; Ilersich, Mazmanian, & Roberts, 1988; Jacobs, Zaborowski, & Whishaw, 1989; Spetch & Honig, 1988).

However, other species may be even better than rats when it comes to using spatial memory. Field work (see Balda & Kamil, 1988) indicates that Clark's nutcrackers (*Nucitraga Columbiana*) spend their fall seasons storing pine seeds in about 7,500 different subterranean caches. These caches, containing up to 33,000 seeds, constitute the birds' total diet during the winter. Although the exact mechanisms are not understood, Balda and Kamil report that the birds have memory for up to 30 cache sites in experimental settings, many more locations than can be remembered by rats. They also report accurate memory in birds for cache locations for up to 6 months.

In other words, even though spatial memory is a point of contact between humans and animals, tremendous species differences do exist, suggesting that animal and human memory systems are not identical.

Serial-Pattern Learning in Animals

Obviously many of the tasks we deal with in everyday life involve serial patterns. We often have to learn "what follows what." For example, written and spoken language involve complex serial patterns. Similarly, music involves the organization of successive sounds. Humans are very good at analyzing, perceiving, and remembering serial patterns. For example, consider the sequence:

1234234534564567 _____

What goes in the blanks? The answer (5678) is even more obvious when we group the numbers as:

1234 2345 3456 4567 _____

The question we want to address here is whether animals also respond to, and learn about, the serial patterns inherent in the stimuli they perceive. Hulse (1978; Hulse & Dorsky, 1979) put the question to experimental test. Two groups of hungry rats were allowed to run down a runway to a goal box, where they received different numbers of food pellets. One group of animals received 14 pellets on the first run, 7 pellets on the second run, 3 on the third, then 1, and finally 0 on the fifth run. Thus, this group experienced a 14-7-3-1-0 sequence, with each run producing a smaller reward than the preceding run. This was called the *monotonic* group. The second, or *nonmonotonic*, group received rewards in a 14-1-3-7-0 sequence. The assumption was that, for a rat, the 14-7-3-1-0 sequence would be much simpler than the 14-1-3-7-0 sequence.

As both groups gained more experience through repeated runs through their assigned sequence, it was assumed that they would learn about the serial patterning of the rewards. Specifically, it was predicted that both groups would learn to run fast on the first trail of each sequence, when both were rewarded with 14 pellets. It was also assumed that they would both learn to slow down on the fifth run of each series, because no reward was given on this run. Figure 10.8 shows that this is what happened; both groups ran fast on the 14-pellet run and slow on the 0-pellet run.

But now comes the crucial prediction. If rats really do pay attention to serial patterns, and the 14-7-3-1-0 sequence is simpler than the 14-1-3-7-0 pattern, then the monotonic group should be more likely to learn that the fifth run produced no food and should thus run slower than the nonmonotonic group on the 0-pellet run.

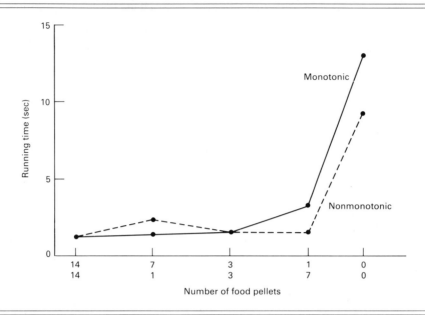

Figure 10.8 Asymptotic running times on five successive runs reinforced by different numbers of food pellets. One group of rats received a monotonic, decreasing series of food quantities (14-7-3-1-0 pellets). The other group received a nonmonotonic series of food quantities (14-1-3-7-0 pellets). [From Hulse, S. H. Cognitive structure and serial pattern learning by animals. In Hulse, S. H., Fowler, H., and Honig, W. K. (Eds.), *Cognitive processes in animal behavior.* Hillsdale, NJ: Lawrence Erlbaum Associates, 1978.]

As you can see in Figure 10.8, that was the case. These kinds of experiments have been taken as evidence for the idea that rats do process and utilize serial stimulus patterns. They may not be as good at it as humans are, but they learn patterns (see also Self & Gaffan, 1983).

In summary, theories about animal and human memory have much in common. *Many of the principles and mechanisms found in the study of human memory are also found in the animal literature.* Whether the investigations of animal memory and human memory will eventually converge or diverge remains to be seen. At present, the best that can be said is that the two fields, although somewhat isolated, do seem to be feeding into and benefitting from each other.

AUTOMATIC VERSUS CONTROLLED PROCESSING

The distinction between automatic and controlled processing was introduced in Chapter 5, but it bears mentioning again because it is an important dichotomy in the current study of memory. Controlled processing of information is effortful, slow, serial, and limited in capacity. Automatic processing is faster, is parallel, and includes unlimited capacity without attention on the part of the subject being required (see Fisk & Schneider, 1984; Reiner & Morrison, 1983; Rosinski, Golinkoff, & Kukish, 1975; Salmaso, Baroni, Job, & Peron, 1983; Schneider & Shiff-rin, 1977).

The ultimate usefulness of this distinction remains to be seen. Some feel it is important, but others doubt that the two systems can be clearly separated.

CONTEXTUAL CUES AND STATE–DEPENDENT MEMORY

The situation, or context, in which we learn something is very important when it comes to remembering what we have learned. If we learn a task in Situation A and are then tested for recall of that task, we will do better if we are tested in the original Situation A than we will if the situation is changed to B.

A number of diverse experiments demonstrate the truth of this generalization. For example, Smith (1979) had subjects learn some material in Room A and then tested for recall either in Room A or Room B. He found superior recall in Room A. In a second experiment he encouraged the subjects to try to remember and imagine Room A even though they were being tested in Room B. In this case he found less of a decrement in recall when subjects were tested in Room B. *State-dependent memory* is a term often used to describe these sorts of effects, because memory seems to be dependent on the state, or situation, that existed during original learning.

State-dependent effects are not limited to rooms. Similar effects can be obtained with chemical states (Eich, Weingartner, Stillman, & Gillin, 1975). In these studies subjects learn a task either under the influence of a particular drug (for example, alcohol, caffeine) or drug free and are then tested either with or without the drug. If retention is better under unchanged conditions (that is, drug–drug or no drug–no drug) than under changed conditions, we say state-dependent memory has been demonstrated.

Context effects are not limited to rooms or drugs, either. The verbal context in which a word is learned can be important, too (Baker & Santa, 1977; Smith, Glenberg, & Bjork, 1978; Tweedy, Lapinski, & Schvaneveldt, 1977). If a word is learned while embedded in a particular semantic context (for example, between two other words), free recall of that word will be better if the surrounding words are presented during recall efforts.

Stanovich and West (1983a, 1983b) have extended the analysis of the importance of the verbal context by showing that the processing of the last word in a sentence is better if the preceding sentence is congruous. Visual contexts can be important, too. For example, Biederman, Glass, and Stacy (1973) had subjects search for particular objects either in a whole, normal picture or in that same picture when it had been cut into six pieces and rearranged. Search was much more effective in the whole condition, presumably because the context of the objects in their proper relationships served as effective cues in the search process (see also Winograd & Lynn, 1979).

Bower (1981) has demonstrated what he calls *mood-dependent learning*. He found that happy subjects remembered words that they had learned in another happy situation more easily than words learned in a sad condition. In general, the similarity of emotions during learning and recall can facilitate correct recall. If you learn under sad conditions you will recall better under sad conditions. If you learn while happy, then you will recall better when happy (Isen, 1984; Gilligan & Bower, 1984).

State-dependent-memory effects and the general importance of context in memory have become important as the study of memory grows. Interested readers are referred to Fernandez and Glenberg (1985), Fiske and Taylor (1984), and Hastie (1983) for more detailed accounts and analyses of context effects.

One Brain or Two?

As a final example of the kinds of distinctions that are being made in the study of memory and information processing we shall address some very intriguing suggestions concerning brain functions that come from what have been called "split-brain" experiments (Sperry, 1961). The vertebrate brain is surprisingly symmetrical. The structures of the left side of the brain seem to be duplicated perfectly on the right side. This symmetry poses some very interesting questions concerning the location of memory "traces." Is all information processed equally on both sides of the brain? If the structures on both sides of the brain are identical, is the information processed within them identical?

Interestingly, the answer seems to be no. Gazzaniga (1972, 1984) and Gazzaniga and Sperry (1967) investigated a number of humans whose two halves of the brain had been separated surgically. Very simply, the two halves, or hemispheres, of the brain are normally connected, or bridged, by an extensive bundle of fibers known as the *corpus callosum*. In order to alleviate severe epilepsy, some patients undergo an operation in which almost all of their corpus callosum is removed. In other words, the two halves of the brain are essentially "disconnected" as in Figure 10.9. As it turns out, it is possible to deal with these disconnected halves independently. Entry into one or the other half can be accomplished by restricting visual stimuli to one half of the visual field. A stimulus flashed to the left half of the visual field will be relayed to the right side of the brain. A visual stimulus flashed to the right side of the visual field will be relayed to the left side of the brain. By restricting input to half of the visual field investigators can be sure that they are dealing with but half of the brain in a "split-brain" patient (see Figure 10.9).

In testing split-brain subjects Gazzaniga and his colleagues found that the left half of the brain tends to be relatively specialized for active speech events, such as talking and writing. The left side of the brain can read words and initiate speech. When a printed word is presented to the left side of the brain, the split-brain subjects can read it and say it aloud. The right side of the brain seems to be more involved with nonverbal information and spatial reasoning. It does not do too well with verbal production. For example, if a word is flashed on the left half of the visual field (right hemisphere of the brain), subjects appear unable to say the word aloud. But if they are asked to recognize the word rather than recall it, they can do so. The right half of the brain apparently has the ability to recognize verbal units but not to initiate verbal responses. The notion that the left and right halves of the brain are specialized for verbal and nonverbal factors, respectively, gains support from the work of other investigators (see Galin & Ornstein, 1972; Milner, 1968).

This line of research does not suggest that the two hemispheres of the brain can handle *only* certain types of information, nor does it imply that the hemispheres do not "communicate" with each other. To the contrary, in normal individuals half of the brain seems capable of "taking over" the functions of the other half if the other has been damaged or incapacitated. In addition, the corpus callosum appar-

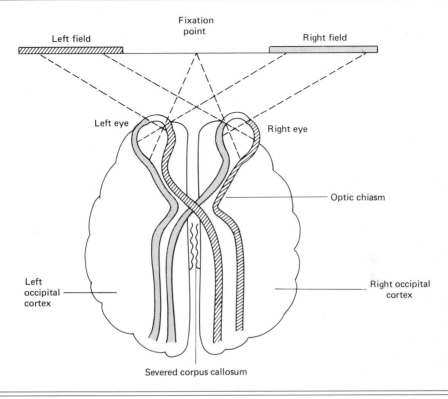

Figure 10.9 Split-brain experiment. The corpus callosum is severed. When a stimulus is presented in the left field only, all messages are conducted to the right hemisphere. When a stimulus is presented to the right field only, all neural messages go to the left hemisphere.

ently provides a means of transferring information processed on one side of the brain into the other. But it does appear that the two sides are specialized for distinct functions (see also Bleier, Houston, & Byne, 1986; Hellige & Wong, 1983; McKeever & Hoff, 1983; and Sperry, 1983).

Split-brain research represents an attempt to understand learning and memory on a physiological level. Research of this sort may one day help us understand and remedy diseases, such as those described in Box 10.2, which blot out our memory abilities.

SUMMARY

1. Many divisions of memory have been proposed. This chapter considers several important distinctions.
2. The first widely discussed distinction is between *short-term memory* and *long-term memory*. Several areas of research bear on this issue.

Box 10.2 Memory Diseases

Understanding the biology and psychology of memory doesn't allay an age-old terror: of losing the capacity to remember. We shudder when we read about how Rita Hayworth slid into the abyss of Alzheimer's disease when she was in her early 60s—and how she [was] unable . . . at the age of 67, to remember the title of even one of her more than 60 films. We want, above all, to be reassured that it won't happen to *us*. And the good news is—it probably won't. While most older people experience some degree of "benign forgetfulness," only a minority develop Alzheimer's, and other diseases of memory, including amnesia and a severe form of memory loss that can accompany chronic alcoholism, are relatively uncommon. But for those afflicted, and their families, they can be devastating.

Alzheimer's Disease

A degenerative brain disorder of unknown origin, Alzheimer's is irreversible and incurable, but it is definitely not a normal or inevitable part of the aging process, affecting only about 7 percent of Americans over 65. Although Alzheimer's patients eventually suffer deterioration of all cognitive functions, often the earliest sign—and the disease's hallmark in the popular imagination—is loss of memory.

At the beginning, the patient may forget things like appointments, anniversaries and recent experiences; usually he will belittle or deny the problem. As the disease progresses, he will have trouble with language and such familiar tasks as brushing his teeth. Eventually, he will be unable to remember where he lives, how old he is or even the name of his spouse. In the most advanced stage, the Alzheimer's victim will be unable to talk at all, and the disease will ravage his body as well as his mind.

In their search for the causes of Alzheimer's, researchers are looking for viruses, toxins and aberrant genes (heredity plays a distinct role in 10 to 15 percent of Alzheimer's cases; their offspring have a 50 percent higher than normal risk of being afflicted). They do know that at autopsy, the brains of Alzheimer's patients exhibit abnormal tangles and patches of dying nerve cells, and some show lesions in the area adjacent to the hippocampus, the seat of memory. Alzheimer's sufferers also have been found to have abnormally low levels of certain neurotransmitters, notably acetylcholine. But simply giving patients supplemental choline does not work, explains Katherine L. Bick, deputy director of the National Institute of Neurological and Communicative Disorders and Strokes, because other neuro-transmitters also seem to be involved in memory deficits.

Bick believes that some current animal research shows promise for victims of Alzheimer's. A Swedish team has implanted youthful cortical cells in the brains of aging rats, enabling them to find a route out of a milky swimming pool that previously had stymied them. In another study, rats placed in an "enriched" envi-ronment—one full of perceptual stimuli—grew new neural connections, which
(continued on page 313)

3. At one time it was suggested that interference effects (PI and RI) operate in long-term memory but not short-term memory. This proposal has been dis-proved. Both PI and RI operate in short-term memory.
4. *Release from PI* demonstrates that similarity effects operate in STS as well as LTS interference situations.

(continued from page 312)
suggests to Bick that new cell populations might be trained to take over for those that die in Alzheimer's patients.

Although no magic potion has yet been found to annihilate the scourge of Alzheimer's, much can be done to help patients cope, particularly in the early stages. "Environmental cues," like signs reminding them to turn off the stove or to flush the toilet, can make their daily lives safer and more dignified.

Amnesia
Pure memory loss without damage to other mental functions can accompany almost any injury to or disease of the brain. It usually involves both the left and right sides of the brain and may be temporary or permanent; it often occurs with Parkinson's disease, Huntington's disease, strokes, encephalitis and the latter stages of AIDS. A blow to the head is the best-known cause of amnesia, but the condition can also develop when the brain is deprived of oxygen—through a blood clot, for example, or improperly administered anesthesia.

In what is called anterograde amnesia, victims can't remember anything that happened to them after the onset of the memory loss, including a conversation of five minutes ago. In retrograde amnesia, the victim can remember *only* what has happened since he lost his memory; everything before that is irretrievable. Retrograde amnesiacs turn up with some frequency on television soap operas, but in real life this form of memory loss is rare.

Alcoholic Korsakoff's Syndrome
Some cases of chronic amnesia occur in alcoholics who have not only been drinking heavily for many years, but also eating inappropriately, resulting in a thiamine deficiency. Their other intellectual faculties may be intact, but they sometimes have hallucinations and recite imaginary experiences to fill in the memory gaps. Autopsies of Korsakoff's patients, who are usually 50 to 70 years old when the syndrome begins, reveal a total degeneration of the mamillary bodies, structures connected to the hippocampus that are critical to the intake and retention of information. The early phase of Korsakoff's, which is sometimes reversible, is called Wernicke's encephalopathy.

For those of us with a relatively intact memory, life without it seems unthinkable. But consider the case of a Michigan woman who developed amnesia after an aneurysm operation. Retaining her IQ of 145, she keeps a detailed schedule of what she's going to do every 15 minutes, crossing off each event as it happens so she will know she has done it. Lunch is on the schedule because she doesn't want to miss it—or eat it twice. When she takes trips she writes herself 20 postcards each day, so that she can "remember" the journey when she gets home. "Most people's lives are an accumulation of the past," she says. "Mine no longer is. I decided to optimize the present."

5. Early research suggested that short-term memory might involve *acoustic coding processes*, whereas long-term memory might involve *semantic coding processes*. This conclusion was drawn from studies that seemed to indicate that subjects would confuse acoustically similar materials in short-term memory and confuse semantically similar materials in long-term memory.

6. But the acoustic-semantic distinction has been rejected. It now appears that short-term and long-term memory are flexible in terms of coding. Depending on the demands of the task and the desires of the subject, short-term and long-term memory may involve acoustic coding, semantic coding, or both.

7. The *recency effect* in the free recall of a serial list refers to the fact that the items toward the end of the list are recalled better than earlier ones.

8. This recency effect has been interpreted in terms of the two-memory position. Items toward the end of the list are presumed to be in short-term memory at the time of recall and, thus, easily recalled. Earlier items are no longer in short-term memory (lost or transferred to long-term memory) and are less likely to be recalled.

9. Wickelgren argues that the recency effect can also be interpreted in terms of a single-memory position. If we assume that memory traces are lost rapidly at first and then more slowly, we do not need to postulate two memory stores.

10. *Negative recency* refers to the fact that recall of the end items will drop below recall of earlier items if the recall test is delayed.

11. Negative recency has also been interpreted as evidence for two memory stores. But alternative interpretations are available.

12. Patients who have suffered bilateral damage of the hippocampus have sometimes been unable to form new long-term memories. Old long-term memories remain intact, as does the entire short-term memory system. The loss of the ability to transfer information from short-term store to long-term store has been taken as evidence for the two-memory position. But alternative interpretations are available.

13. *Amnesic effects* do not appear to be as total or permanent as the separate-store position would suggest.

14. The distinction between short-term memory and long-term memory has not been conclusively substantiated.

15. The second major distinction of the chapter is between *recall* and *recognition.* In a recall task we ask, "What is the item?" In a recognition test we ask, "Is this the item?" Recognition tends to be superior to recall, and sometimes it is far superior.

16. *The unitary-strength hypothesis* holds that recognition and recall do not involve fundamentally different processes. Recognition is merely seen as a more sensitive indicator of memory traces within a single-memory framework.

17. But some variables (for example, common versus uncommon items) affect recall and recognition in opposite ways. This fact has led many to suggest that the two are truly different.

18. The *generation-recognition hypothesis* holds that recall involves encoding, storage, *and* retrieval, whereas recognition involves only encoding and storage.

19. The *control hypothesis* argues that we differ in how we use our single-memory system when we are encoding for recall or encoding for recognition.

20. We may organize more when coding for recall than when we code for recognition.

21. *Recognition failure* refers to the fact that we can sometimes recall material that we have been unable to recognize. This phenomenon is not predicted by either the unitary-strength hypothesis or the generation-recognition hypothesis.

22. A type of recognition failure can appear in priming experiments, too.
23. *Episodic memory* versus *semantic memory* refers to the idea that one model may be required for the storage of temporally ordered personal experiences (episodic) and another for nontemporal facts (semantic).
24. The tip-of-the-tongue phenomenon bears upon the semantic-episodic distinction.
25. Flashbulb memories, while interesting, may not require special memory processes.
26. Many memories may have both episodic and semantic characteristics.
27. Some have suggested that we shall need different models to account for human and animal memory.
28. Yet animal and human memory systems appear to have much in common. For example, PI and RI have been observed in animal situations. Extinction, spontaneous recovery, and paired-associate learning have also been implicated in human as well as animal situations.
29. The *delayed-matching-to-sample* procedure is used to study short-term memory in animals. Although not identical to the distractor technique, it is similar.
30. Spatial memory has been shown to be roughly equivalent in humans and animals.
31. Species show remarkable differences in their abilities to remember spatial material. These differences suggest that animal and human memory systems may be less alike than is often supposed.
32. Both animals and humans engage in serial-pattern learning.
33. Some information may be processed automatically and some in a controlled manner.
34. If we learn a task in one situation, we will do better on a retention test if we are tested in the same rather than a different situation. Such state-dependent memory emphasizes the importance of context in memory and can be demonstrated when the context involved is geographical, chemical, verbal, or visual.
35. Mood (happy, sad) may constitute a context that can affect learning and memory.
36. Split-brain research suggests that the two hemispheres of the brain tend to process different types of information.
37. Alzheimer's disease, amnesia, and Korsakoff's Syndrome all represent memory disorders currently under investigation.

CHAPTER

11

IMPROVING MEMORY THROUGH ORGANIZATION, ELABORATION, AND IMAGERY

INTRODUCTION

The psychology of memory is awash with studies of "organization in memory," "structure in memory," and "elaboration in memory." The meaning of these phrases varies from investigation to investigation. At present, investigators have no firm consensus concerning the definition of organizational processes within the overall memory process. And yet common elements do appear among the various uses of the phrases. Usually, these phrases can be used interchangeably. The purpose of this chapter is to introduce the complexities of the "organizational," "elaborative," or "structural" approach to memory.

This approach is not completely distinct from alternative ways of looking at memory. In fact, it has much in common with other interpretations, particularly information-processing theory. In the structural approach, however, the *emphasis* is on organizational processes within the overall memory system. The structural approach is not bound up with any one theory, as is the interference approach. Rather, it is an orientation toward the question of memory that stresses the fact that we do not passively store information exactly as it is delivered to us. Instead, we structure, interrelate, elaborate, and organize it. We try to systematize information so that both storage and retrieval will be efficient. As Cofer (1975) puts it, we operate as though our memory system resembles an *encyclopedia*, a *dictionary*, or a *library*.

Let us begin our discussion with an example. Consider a game that children play when they are trying to fight off boredom on long car trips. The first player begins by saying, "I went to the store and bought an apple." The second player says, "I went to the store and bought an apple and a knife." The third says, "I went to the store and bought an apple, a knife, and a shirt," and so on, until someone makes an error in recalling the building chain of items. Each player must recall all the previous items and add one new one. How might you go about remembering the growing list of items? One technique might involve the simple rehearsal, or repetition, of the items over and over in the correct order. But there are other possibilities. Some people find it convenient to build mental "images" with the items. Thus, one player might imagine a green apple impaled on a golden knife and wrapped in a blue shirt. When recall is required, she merely summons up the "picture," or image, and reads off the necessary items. These images (whatever they are) can vary tremendously. They may be simple or complex, active or passive, ordinary or unusual, and so on. This process of relating items to one another in a visual image is one example of an organizational, or structural, strategy. The player is doing more than rehearsing items. She is structuring the items and relating them to one another through the use of a mental image.

Another player might remember the same items by constructing a sentence. The words in the sentence might begin with the first letters of the to-be-remembered items. Thus, "Another king said . . ." might provide a vivid means for remembering *apple, knife, shirt*. The player relates the items to one another, or organizes the materials, by imbedding them within a sentence. Another individual might use a sentence construction technique of a different sort. This player might make up a sentence using the items themselves rather than their first letters—for example, "The old man picked up the *apple* and looked for his *knife* in his *shirt* pocket."

Each of these players is organizing, imagining, structuring, elaborating, ordering, systematizing, or relating the to-be-remembered items in a different manner.

The number of possible organizational schemes, or strategies, is almost unlimited. We can categorize and group items. We can string them in series. We can relate them to one another and to information we bring into the situation. We refer to this vast array of mental activities as organization in memory.

In attempting to characterize the evolving organizational approach we shall discuss several areas of research that have been subsumed by the heading. We shall discuss experimental demonstrations of the individual's ability to *improve retention through the use of organizational processes*. For a more complete review on organizational research you are referred to Reynolds and Flagg (1983).

Before we turn to our review of specific areas of research, we should note that an interest in organization in memory is not new. In fact, current interest in such processes really represents a *return* to areas that have long been of interest to psychologists. We are witnessing a swing of the pendulum, so to speak. As Postman (1972) and others have pointed out, one of the basic tenets of Gestalt psychology was that memory is governed by principles of organization and perceptual grouping. In the early days methods for measuring organizational activities were lacking. As a result the concepts of Gestalt psychology never obtained firm experimental support. Lack of adequate experimental techniques forced psychologists to lay the questions aside. But interest in the issues the Gestalt psychologists raised never completely disappeared. The past three decades have seen a renewal of interest in organization in memory. This explosion of activity was made possible by the development of some new techniques for measuring and quantifying the elusive organizational activities. Some of these new techniques and the data they have yielded will be discussed in the sections that follow.

Actually, we have already begun our study of organization. For example, our discussion of semantic-network models in Chapter 9 represents an instance of concern for structure in memory. So keep in mind that the topics and issues we discuss here are inherent in many of the topics we have already discussed.

EARLY WORK: WORD ASSOCIATIONS

Some very early, relatively unsophisticated evidence for the existence of organization in memory was revealed by the development of the *word-association test* (Kent & Rosanoff, 1910). The test consists of 100 common words. The subject's task is to "give the first word that comes to mind" in response to each of the 100 words. It is an interesting test, and one that most individuals do not mind at all. As it turns out, there are some extremely common responses to many of these words. Thus, *mother* often evokes *father*, and *black* elicits *white* with consistently high probabilities. Yet not everyone gives these common responses. Some people have come up with unique responses, to say the least (see Table 11.1). But a great number of individuals from various groups over the years have given the same responses (Fox, 1970; Jenkins & Russell, 1960). Mackenzie (1972) and Rubin (1983) provide reviews of much of the research done with word associations.

For our purposes the important point is that these consistent patterns of word associations suggest that words are organized, or structured, within each of us. They are not merely lumped, or piled randomly, within us somewhere. They are related to one another in a distinct manner. In a very rough way the word association test reveals some of this structure.

Table 11.1   Word-Association Responses Given by 100 Subjects to Some Selected
Stimulus Words

STIMULUS	RESPONSE FREQUENCY	RESPONSE
Woman	59	Man
	10	Child, girl
	4	Sex
	2	Love, mother
	1	Friend, world, clean, thin, hair, old, soft, pretty, female, baby, home, lady, fold
Chair	55	Table
	15	Sit
	4	Seat, desk
	2	Legs, couch, bed
	1	Study, home, blue, soft, foot, arm, plastic, yellow, wood, rest, hard, window, floor, comfortable, professor, house
Blossom	74	Flower
	7	Apple
	4	Rose
	2	Springtime
	1	Cut, pretty, bud, bouquet, Pasadena, sniff, smell, blooms, red, tree, plant, sweet, orange

Unpublished data obtained by the author.

It should come as no surprise to learn that this structure can change as we grow and develop. Petrey (1977) gave a word-association test to kindergarten children and to first-, third-, and fifth-graders. He found a dramatic shift in the associations these children gave as they grew older (see Table 11.2). When they were very young, the children tended to give *episodic* responses. If you will recall, episodic memory is memory for temporally related events or episodes. The young children's associations showed a distinct autobiographical quality (for example, *go to bed* in response to *dark*), whereas older children gave more semantic responses to the same stimuli (for example, *light* to *dark*). (A semantic response is one that has to do with *meaning* rather than episode.)

The word-association test has been used in clinical situations. Some psychotherapists believe that they can learn something about individuals by examining their responses on a word-association test. The responses may provide the therapist with insights into the patient's personality or mental state. If in response to *mother* the patient says *father, home,* or *love,* the therapist may be led to one set of conclusions. But if the patient's response to *mother* is *blood vein, rape,* or *horror,* the therapist might begin to think along different lines. Though it does not provide us with a great deal of information about mental organization, the word-association test does represent an early, and ongoing, technique for tapping into existing memory structures.

CHUNKING: 7 ± 2

Suppose that we are presented with the following letters, one at a time: F, L, S, M, P, U, J, E. We are then asked to recall them immediately in any order. We might be able to accomplish this feat, but we would certainly be hard pressed to handle any more information. But it is possible to organize this material in such a way that our

Table 11.2   Children's Word-Association Responses, Showing the Shift from Episodic to Semantic Associations as the Children Grow Older

		GRADE LEVEL			
STIMULUS	RESPONSE	KINDER-GARTEN	1ST	3RD	5TH
Examine	*Doctor,* or *eye*	23	46	49	27
Examine	*Look at, check up,* or *test*	1	7	51	120
Dark	*Moon, stars, go to bed,* or *go to sleep*	23	25	3	1
Dark	*Light*	25	85	185	180
Long	*Grass*	16	11	7	5
Long	*Short*	9	56	177	164
Give	*A present*	24	18	4	5
Give	*Take*	2	6	56	99

Adapted from Petrey, S. Word associations and the development of lexical memory. *Cognition,* 1977, *5,* 57–71. Table 1, p. 64. Used by permission of Elsevier Science Publishers B. V.

memory would hardly be taxed at all. For example, we can rearrange the letters to spell JUMPS and ELF. By doing this we can remember all eight letters easily and have plenty of memory capacity left over. We could easily handle a lot more letters, especially if they could also be arranged as words. By organizing the information we have greatly expanded the capacity of our immediate memory.

The concept of the memory *chunk* was introduced by Miller (1956). Miller argues that our *immediate memory is limited by the number of chunks of information that it can handle but that the amount of information contained in each chunk may vary.* As long as the information can be expressed as a single response, then it represents one chunk. Thus, JUMPS and ELF each represent one chunk, but each chunk contains several units of information (letters). In a sense the process of increasing the size of a chunk seems to involve our ability to characterize many different units of information with fewer and fewer responses. Thus, instead of having to say F, L, S, M, P, U, J, E (eight responses, or eight chunks), we say JUMPS and ELF (two responses, or two chunks). By transforming eight responses into two responses we are freeing ourselves to handle additional information. Miller's best guess was that we can handle *seven plus or minus two* chunks of information. Each chunk may vary in terms of the amount of information it contains. Thus, O is one chunk, SO is one chunk, SOP is one chunk, and STOP is one chunk. It is just as easy to remember one of these as another, even though they vary in terms of number of letters. If we can increase the amount of information contained in each chunk, we can greatly expand our memory capacity, even though it is limited to approximately seven chunks.

Experimental Evidence

There are experimental data supporting Miller's contention that our capacity to process information is limited. Consider Figure 11.1. This figure contains data obtained by Graesser and Mandler (1978). They gave subjects sets of nouns ranging in number from 1 to 12. On receiving a group of nouns the subjects' task was to find a dimension, feature, or attribute that linked the set members together. For example, if a particular set contained *dog* and *goat,* the subjects might say that they

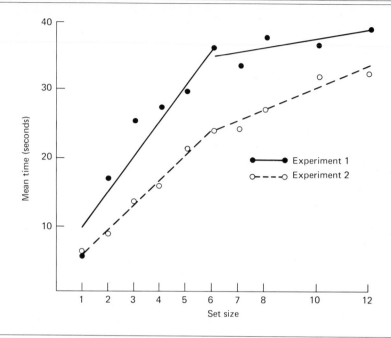

Figure 11.1 Mean response times for the production of responses relating the members of sets to one another as a function of set size. (From Graesser, A., and Mandler, G. Limited processing capacity constrains the storage of unrelated sets of words and retrieval from natural categories. *Journal of Experimental Psychology: Human Learning and Memory*, 1978, 4, 86–100. Fig. 1, p. 88. Copyright 1978 by the American Psychological Association. Reprinted by permission.)

were both animals or that they both had a *g* in them. Graesser and Mandler measured the latencies of these responses. If you will notice, the number of seconds that it took subjects to find some linking dimension or feature increased in a linear fashion up to about 6 nouns per set. Then a distinct break occurred, and after that (from about 6 items to about 12 items per set) the rate of increase in the number of seconds required to find a response was lower than the increase observed up to 6 nouns per set. The authors argue that this break, or change in slope, is evidence for the notion of a limited processing capacity.

They explain the decreased slope this way: With up to 6 nouns per set the subjects are trying to find a dimension or feature that will link *all* items in the set. But when the subjects are given more than 6 nouns per set, they cannot handle them all at once; the task exceeds their limited capacity. So what do they do? They begin to find dimensions, or features, that will link up to 6 nouns but will not cover the extra nouns that the experimenter has piled on. The slope decreases after 6 nouns per set because the subjects can *select* from among the provided nouns and deal with nouns that are easily related to one another; with 6 or fewer nouns the subjects try to deal with everything the experimenter presents, regardless of how difficult it is to respond to.

The authors, in fact, report that the responses that subjects gave to sets containing up to 6 nouns tended to cover all 6 nouns, whereas the responses they gave to sets containing more than 6 nouns did not cover, or link, all of the nouns in these larger sets. Their conclusion is that subjects can handle, or process, only about 6 items at one time in this kind of task.

Rewriting

Here is another example of the way in which we can increase the amount of information contained in each of our seven plus or minus two chunks. Suppose that we are presented the following binary digits and asked to recall the sequence: 101000100111001110. See if you can read the sequence once and then recall it correctly. Now, as it stands, that is a rather difficult task. The sequence contains 18 bits of information, and it probably exceeds our memory capacity. But suppose that before reading off the sequence we had learned the following: 0 means 00, 1 means 01, 2 means 10, and 3 means 11. In other words, we have given *new names* to all possible sequences of two binary digits. Having learned this new language we are now ready to tackle the original sequence. As the sequence is being presented, we can recode it in terms of our new language. Thus:

Original   10 10 00 10 01 11 00 11 10

Recoded   2   2   0   2   1   3   0   3   2

To remember the original sequence of 18 binary digits all we have to do is remember 220213032. This may *still* exceed our memory span, but it certainly represents an improvement. We have cut the number of units we must remember in half. When asked to recall the original sequence, we merely recall as much of 220213032 as we can and decode it as we go along. In other words, by organizing the to-be-remembered information (through rewriting) we have vastly improved retention.

RECALL BY CATEGORY
Clustering

If you have a pencil and paper handy, you might want to try the following experiment. Read the list of words contained in Table 11.3, and then immediately write down as many as you can recall *in any order you wish*. Now, having exhausted your ability to recall the items, look over your responses. Notice that you have probably grouped the items according to categories. Thus, you may have recalled two or more trees together or several animals together. Similarly, you may have recalled colors or cities together. This grouping phenomenon is called *clustering in recall*. It refers to the fact that items drawn from various categories, and presented *randomly*, will be recalled *together*. In other words, there is not a one-to-one relationship between order of input and order of output. We seem to do some organizing in there somewhere.

The concept of clustering has a very long history. Its emergence as an important phenomenon began with the work of Bousfield (1953; Bousfield & Sedgewick, 1944). Since then many interesting questions have been asked. For example, does *total* recall of items from the list go up as clustering goes up? In other words, does

Table 11.3   Free-Recall List Used in Clustering Demonstration

HEMLOCK
CARROT
PARIS
BLACK
LETTUCE
ELM
ZEBRA
PEAS
NEW YORK
RED
SEATTLE
MOOSE
BROCCOLI
WOLF
BLUE
COW
PINE
TOMATO
BROWN
SYCAMORE
MOSCOW
CROW
REDWOOD
MAPLE
SQUASH
TOLEDO
ORANGE
YELLOW
AMSTERDAM
SNAKE

any evidence suggest that organizing according to categories goes hand in hand with improved retention? The answer to this question is a qualified yes. The relationship between clustering and overall recall has not been as strong as one might have expected. But several studies do seem to suggest a positive relationship between clustering and recall. You are referred to Cofer (1967), Forrester and King (1971), Puff (1970), Thompson, Hamlin, and Roenker (1972), and Weist (1972) for a full exposition of this issue.

Exhaustive Categories

Another example of the kind of research done in connection with category clustering deals with the difference between *exhaustive and nonexhaustive categories*. When a list involves nonexhaustive categories, the list does not contain *all* of the members of the categories. For example, if our list includes 15 vegetables, we have not exhausted the category of vegetables. Exhaustive categories usually involve very few members, all of which are included in our list. For example, a category of seasons may be exhaustive (summer, fall, winter, spring). The planets of our solar system could be an exhaustive category. Psychologists have asked which of these two types of category produces (1) the best overall recall and (2) the greatest amount of clustering. Cohen (1963, 1966) presents data suggesting that both total recall and clustering are greater for exhaustive than for nonexhaustive categories. It seems that we are more able to work with exhaustive categories, perhaps because we know when we are done with a category. Our organizational efforts seem to yield better retention in this instance. These examples should provide the flavor of the research that has been done in connection with category clustering (see also Buschke, 1977; D'Agostino, 1969; Hubert & Levin, 1977; Segal, 1969).

Subjective Organization

Tulving (1962) is the person responsible for the concept of *subjective organization* and for the associated technique for assessing organization in memory. In a typical subjective organization (SO) experiment the subjects receive a long list of randomly presented items, one at a time. The items do not belong to any obvious, experimenter-imposed categories. The subjects are then asked to recall as many of the items as they can, in any order. Following recall the list is again presented, usually in a new random order. A series of recall and presentation phases follow in this fashion. Tulving and others have found that the order in which the subjects recall these items begins to assume some consistency from recall trial to recall trial. The subjects begin to recall certain words together even though they are not presented together. The subjects are somehow ordering, or structuring, the material. Their output becomes consistent despite random input. Clearly, the subjects are free to use any organizational strategy they wish. They might build a visual image, construct a story, relate items that sound or look alike, or use some other unique, individual scheme. In any case the constant order in which the subjects recall the items reveals that they are imposing some sort of structure on the materials.

At the same time it should be noted that the SO technique does not tell us exactly *what* this developing organization is (see Mandler, Worden, & Graesser, 1974). All we know is that *something* is happening. This fact underlines an important difference between the clustering technique and the SO procedure. In the clustering method, on the one hand, we *do* have some idea of the type of organizational activity that is occurring. As experimenters we define the categories and impose them on the subjects. In SO studies, on the other hand, we can observe the development of idiosyncratic organizational strategies unhindered by any experimenter-imposed constraints.

Does increasing SO lead to greater recall? This question is critical. Unfortunately, the available data are equivocal. Several studies have reported a positive relationship between overall recall and subjective organization (Allen, 1968; Mayhew, 1967; Tulving, 1962, 1964). Others have failed to find the expected relationship (Carterette & Coleman, 1963; Postman, 1970). There are at least two ways to view the problem (Wood, 1972). First, these results may mean that SO does not facilitate retention. Second, a true and strong relationship between this type of organization and overall recall may so far have been obscured by methodological problems.

In any case, whether or not Tulving's original formulation of SO stands the test of time, the concept has had considerable impact on our thinking and research. It is only reasonable to assume that it will be modified and supplemented by newer techniques. In a sense, Tulving's SO helped open the floodgates and allowed the current emphasis on organization, structure, and elaboration to become widespread.

ATTENTIONAL STRATEGIES: STIMULUS SELECTION

Organizational activities take many additional forms, and information can be treated in many different ways. One interesting process involves not the elaboration or transformation of information but the selection of specific, usable stimulus information from within an array of available stimulus information. What we are talking about here is the fact that individuals do not always use the entire stimulus presented to them. They may select some portion or element of the overall stimulus and associate the response with that selected portion. This process is termed *stimulus selection*, and it is particularly interesting because it appears quite consistently in both animal and human learning situations. Stimulus selection (or *cue selection*, as it is sometimes called) provides us with one more example of the way in which animal and human capacities run parallel to each other.

Humans

Let us begin with an example involving human selection. In a paired-associate situation the subjects first learn a list in which the responses (for example, digits) are paired with different compound stimuli (for example, nonsense syllables surrounded by different colors). An example of a stimulus would be XGK surrounded by a blue rectangle. After learning the list the subjects are given each component of the stimuli individually (for example, a color by itself or a nonsense syllable by itself) and tested for recall of the responses. If one component is more likely to elicit the response in the recall test, we begin to suspect that some sort of selection process has been going on during the original learning phase. Using this procedure Underwood, Ham, and Ekstrand (1962) found that subjects *selected the colors over the syllables* (see Figure 11.2). This suggests that the colors are somehow more easily utilized than nonsense syllables in building associations.

The investigation of stimulus selection in paired-associate learning has led to all sorts of concerns. For example, what determines which component of a compound stimulus will be selected? As it turns out, many different variables affect the selection process. Postman and Greenbloom (1967) found that, if the stimuli are difficult-to-pronounce trigrams (for example, XZC or QKX), the subjects tend to select the first letter in the syllable (X or Q). Thus, ordinal position seems to be important in stimulus selection. Other things being equal, we will select the component in the left position, presumably because we read from left to right. Additional variables have been investigated and discussed by Houston (1967), Merryman and Merryman (1971), Richardson (1971, 1972), and Richardson and Chisholm (1969). In a very general sense it seems that the component that becomes most effective is the one that is most easily utilized as a cue. In other words, subjects follow the path of least resistance and utilize whatever they perceive to be the most convenient cue in a given situation. Since subjects and situations differ enormously, it is easy to see why the selection process may vary so much.

Animals

Animals display stimulus selection, too (Kamin, 1969a; Wagner, 1969; Wagner, Logan, Haberlundt, & Price, 1968). It appears that they process information in ways roughly parallel to those of the human. For example, Kamin (1969a) demonstrated a form of stimulus selection in a classical conditioning situation. Animals experienced a series of pairings of shock (UCS) with a particular CS, which we shall designate as A. This procedure resulted in an emotional response's becoming conditioned to the previously neutral CS (A). After these initial pairings an *additional* CS (X) was added to the situation. The CS became AX. AX was then paired with the shock (UCS) for a series of trials. The question was whether the emotional

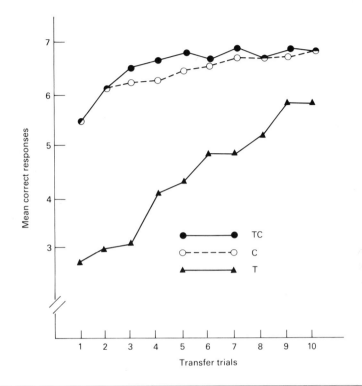

Figure 11.2 Acquisition curves on ten test trials. During these trials the TC group received both the colors and the syllables as stimuli, the C group received only the colors, and the T group received only the syllables. (Adapted from Underwood, B. J., Ham, M., and Ekstrand, B. R. Cue selection in paired-associate learning. *Journal of Experimental Psychology*, 1962, 64, 405–409. Copyright 1962 by the American Psychological Association. Reprinted by permission.)

response would become associated with the new stimulus component (X). Relative to an appropriate control condition, it did not. The A component had already been associated with the emotional response produced by the shock. The introduction of an additional cue (X) was redundant.

This effect represents an organizational effort on the part of the animal. It seems to correspond to the sort of effects that are obtained with humans. In both cases (animal and human) a response is associated with some portion of a total stimulus array. Performance is facilitated by an efficient distribution of attention and effort.

DO MENTAL IMAGES EXIST?

Think of a giraffe. . . . Take your time. . . . Make it a small one. About three feet tall. Pink toenails. Now put the giraffe in a fire engine. More than likely what you have been experiencing (if you have been willing to engage in this sort of nonsense) are what psychologists call visual images. These images interest psychologists because they are such vivid, subjective experiences and because they seem to be an important aspect of our mental activity. They have interested psychologists for a long time, but they also have been troublesome because they are so difficult to quantify or to measure. For example, how would you go about comparing your image of a giraffe with someone else's image of a giraffe? We cannot observe images directly. We cannot lay them out on the table and measure or weigh them. They are such fleeting, subjective experiences that we have some trouble talking about them at all. And yet they do seem to be important components of thought. In this section we shall discuss some of the current efforts to deal with these elusive, important experiences. Specifically, we shall concern ourselves with the role that these images play in the memory process. As we shall see, retention can be heavily affected by vivid mental imagery. The formation and use of images is a complex and important process (see Kosslyn, Reiser, Farah, & Fliegel, 1983).

Before we turn to the nature of the impact of images on memory, we should ask a very basic question: Is there any *experimental* evidence for the existence of mental images above and beyond the subjective experiences we all have? In this section we review three different kinds of experimental evidence that some have taken to mean that visual imagery is a perceptual experience analogous to "pictures in the head." It is difficult to account for these findings if one tries to insist that all encoding is verbal.

Scanning Experiments

Scanning experiments, which have been taken as evidence for the existence of visual images, are based on the assumption that the time it takes to scan between two objects will increase as the distance between those two objects is increased. Let us simplify the situation by describing an experiment. Kosslyn, Ball, and Reiser (1978) had subjects study the map contained in Figure 11.3. The subjects were asked to learn the locations of the objects marked with an X on the map. The map was then removed. Subjects were asked to form an image of the whole map and to focus on one of the objects named by the experimenter. When the experimenter named a second object, the subject's task was to imagine a black dot moving in a straight line from the first object to the second object. When the black dot reached the second object, the subjects stopped a timer by pushing a button. In agreement with the idea that the subjects were somehow scanning a mental visual image, the time it took to press the button increased as the distance between the two objects increased. It is difficult to imagine how this effect would have appeared if the subjects had verbally rather than visually encoded the spatial information.

Blind Subjects and Scanning

The interpretation of this kind of scanning effect is complicated, however, by results reported by Kerr (1983). He used a flat board with raised objects attached to it (see Figure 11.4). As in the Kosslyn, Ball, and Reiser study, subjects were asked to learn the positions of the objects and then asked to scan mentally from one to another. But the unique and crucial aspect of the Kerr study was that the subjects were congenitally blind. They learned the positions of the raised objects by touch. Then they were asked to form an image of the whole board (without using words like *look* or *see*) and to scan from one object to another. The author's argument

Figure 11.3 A fictional map used to study the effect of distances on mental scanning time. (From Kosslyn, S. M., Ball, T. M., and Reiser, B. J. Visual images preserve metric spatial information: Evidence from studies of image scanning. *Journal of Experimental Psychology: Human Perception and Performance*, 1978, 4, 47–60. Copyright 1978 by the American Psychological Association. Reprinted by permission.)

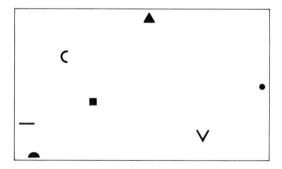

Figure 11.4 The board and figures used in a scanning experiment with the congenitally blind. (Adapted from Kerr, N. H. The role of vision in visual imagery experiments: Evidence from the congenitally blind. *Journal of Experimental Psychology*, 1983, 265–277. Fig. 1, p. 267. Copyright 1983 by the American Psychological Association. Reprinted by permission.)

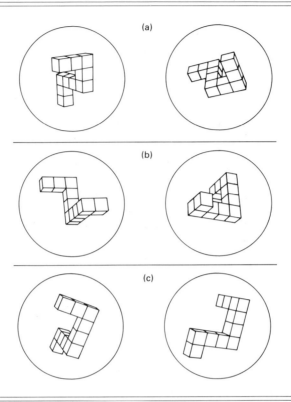

Figure 11.5 Examples of pairs of patterns differing in orientation. (From Shepard, R. N., and Metzler, J. Mental rotation of three-dimensional objects. *Science*, 1971, *171*, 701–703. Copyright 1971 by the American Association for the Advancement of Science. Reprinted by permission.)

here is that, if the scanning effect is essentially a visionlike experience, it should not appear with congenitally blind subjects. But it did; the time it took blind subjects to scan from one object to another increased as the distance between those objects increased. Kerr suggests that images of spatial relationships are therefore not *necessarily* like pictures in the head. His results do not prove that visual images do not exist. They do suggest, however, that other, perhaps nonvisual, images may also be utilizable by humans (see also DeBeni & Cornoldi, 1988; Halpern, 1988).

Mental Rotation: Three Dimensional

A second kind of support for the existence of mental images comes from mental rotation studies. Consider the objects in Figure 11.5. Your task is to decide if the two members of each pair are the same or different. Shepard and Metzler (1971) asked subjects to judge 1,600 such pairs of objects. The subjects pulled one lever with their right hand if they believed the two objects in a given pair were the same and a different lever with their left hand if they concluded that the two objects were not the same. The experimenters carefully measured how long it took the subjects to make these decisions.

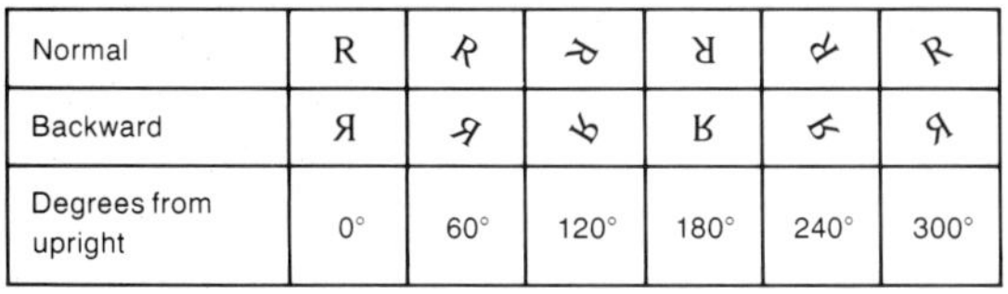

Normal	R	*R*	⊰	Я	⇙	ℛ
Backward	Я	⅁	⅋	Ʀ	⅃	⅄
Degrees from upright	0°	60°	120°	180°	240°	300°

Figure 11.6 Example of reversed and rotated letter stimuli. [From Cooper, L. A., and Shepard, R. N. Chronometric studies of the rotation of mental images. In W. G. Chase (Ed.), *Visual information processing*. Academic Press, 1973.]

The crucial aspect of the experiment was that members of each pair differed in orientation from 0° to 180°. It was found that the more the two members of a given pair differed in terms of orientation, the longer it took the subjects to make a decision about them. This finding is consistent with the idea that subjects imagined one object rotating until it either matched or failed to match the other object. The farther they had to rotate the object, the longer the decision took. When the subjects were asked how they had performed this task, they indicated that they had rotated a visual image of one of the objects until it had the same orientation as the other.

Although the exact significance of these findings is not entirely clear (see Carpenter & Eisenberg, 1978), many feel that they demonstrate our ability to, at least part of the time, store and use visual mental imagery.

Mental Rotation: Two Dimensional

The rotation effect described above involved three-dimensional figures. Rotation effects can be demonstrated using simpler two-dimensional figures. Cooper and Shepard (1973) first presented subjects with a letter (for example, R). Then they presented a second letter that was either the same as the first letter (R) or its mirror image (Я). The subjects' task was to decide as quickly as possible whether the second letter was normal or reversed. In addition the second letters were not always presented in the upright position. Sometimes they were rotated a particular number of degrees from the upright position. Figure 11.6 provides examples of the rotations used. The idea was that the subjects first had to rotate the letter to the upright position and then decide whether or not it was reversed. Thus the further the rotation from the upright position the longer the decision process should take. Figure 11.7 indicates that the further a letter was rotated from the upright position the longer it took the subjects to come to a decision about whether or not the item was normal or reversed. As you can see, 180°, which represents the maximum rotation from the upright position, resulted in the slowest reaction time.

Imagery and Interference

One other kind of effect supports the idea that we really do experience and use visual mental imagery. Matlin (1983) suggests that you try to imagine a good friend's face with your eyes closed. That is not too difficult, is it? But now try to

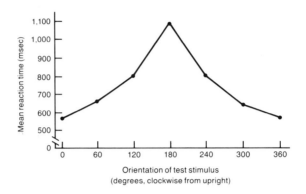

Figure 11.7 Reaction times required to decide whether or not an item was normal or reversed as a function of number of degrees rotated from the upright. [From Cooper, L. A., and Shepard, R. N. Chronometric studies of the rotation of mental images. In W. G. Chase (Ed.), *Visual information processing*. Academic Press, 1973.]

imagine the same face while your eyes wander over the words on this page. You will probably have trouble "looking" at the face and the words at the same time.

This kind of *interference effect* has been brought into the laboratory by Brooks (1968). Consider the material in Figure 11.8. Subjects first saw a block letter such as the C in the figure. The letter was then removed, and the subjects had to decide from memory whether each corner of the block letter was either at the very top or the very bottom of that letter. For example, beginning with the star in Figure 11.8 and moving clockwise the correct answers are yes, yes, no, no, no, no, yes, yes.

Among other things, Brooks had subjects answer in two different ways. Some merely said yes and no verbally. Others had to respond by pointing to Ys and Ns in a complex spatial array of letters such as that on the right side of Figure 11.8. Brooks felt that pointing would involve a lot of interfering visual processing whereas vocalizing would not. In other words, trying to keep the visual image of a C in mind while also looking for Ys and Ns would be difficult. Answering with a verbal yes or no should not interfere. Hence, Brooks predicted that performance in the pointing condition would be poorer than in the speaking condition, and that is what he found. A visual mode of responding interfered with a visual task, whereas a verbal mode of responding did not.

Brooks also turned the situation around and had additional subjects perform a verbal task (such as making judgments about words in remembered sentences). In this case verbal responding produced interference, whereas pointing did not.

In summary, Brooks' work suggests that we do, at least sometimes, store and use visual images and not just verbal material. Thus, at least three kinds of evidence (scanning, rotation, interference) suggest we take very seriously the idea of visionlike pictures in the head. These images need not be whole or complete representations of what we see, but they do seem to contain a good bit of detail, and we seem to be able to form, store, and use them when the need arises.

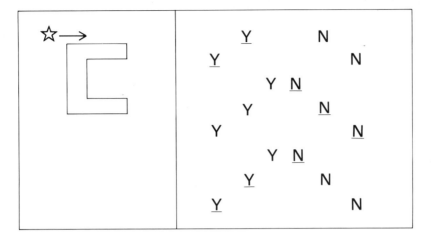

Figure 11.8 An example of the materials used by Brooks (1968) and described in the text.

IMAGERY AND LEARNING

Imagery can apparently enhance learning. One technique used to demonstrate this assertion involves the manipulation of the imagery value of verbal materials. The idea is that items high in imagery value should be easier to learn than items low in imagery value. In one early experiment, Paivio, Smythe, and Yuille (1968) defined imagery value in terms of ratings previous subjects had given. High value items were those that were rated as easy to imagine while low value items were those rated difficult to imagine. Using these imagery values, the investigators developed four kinds of paired associates. In one type of pair, both the stimulus and the response were high in imagery value. In a second type of pair, both the stimuli and responses were low in imagery value. Some items had high value stimuli and low value responses. Finally others were composed of low value stimuli and high value responses. Then new subjects were asked to learn all four types of pairs. As can be seen in Figure 11.9, imagery values had a significant impact on learning. The easiest pairs to recall were those high in both stimulus and response imagery value while the most difficult were those low in both stimulus and response imagery value. Mixed pairs produced intermediate levels of recall. Clearly, these results demonstrate that items that are easy to imagine are also easy to learn and remember.

WHAT ARE IMAGES? TWO HYPOTHESES

What exactly are these elusive images that we all experience? Currently, there are two major ways of thinking about images. First, the *perceptual-experience* interpretation, that proposes, although we may not actually have pictures in our head, we do experience something similar to what happens when we look at a real object. In other words, an image is a perceptual experience that has something in common with the experience of actually seeing something. The problem with this

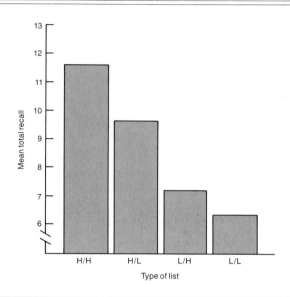

Figure 11.9 The recall of paired associates as a function of the imagery value of the stimulus and the response terms: H = high imagery value and L = low imagery value. (From Paivio, A., Smythe, P. C., and Yuille, J. C. Imagery versus meaningfulness of nouns in paired-associate learning. *Canadian Journal of Psychology*, 1968, 22, 427–441.)

formulation is its vagueness. No one seems to be able to pin down the nature of this proposed perceptual experience (see Farah, 1988).

The second hypothesis, called the *propositional interpretation*, argues that the best way to think about images is in terms of abstract propositions (Anderson, 1978, 1979; Anderson & Paulson, 1978; Hampson & Morris, 1978.) According to this view, images are best thought of in terms of rules and words rather than pictures. For example, consider the stimulus "a circle is over a square." According to the perceptual-experience hypothesis, we might store this as ○▫ ; that is, we might construct some form of visual image of the relationship. The propositional interpretation, in contrast, would argue that we store something like (*above, circle, square*), which, in the language of logic, is the way that we designate the proposition that a circle is above a square.

Many investigators, including Anderson (1978), argue that it is impossible to distinguish between the perceptual-experience hypothesis and the propositional hypothesis. These investigators feel that, given the difficulty in trying to articulate the perceptual-experience position, the propositional interpretation is to be preferred.

As we have seen, however, a number of investigators argue that an image is definitely more than an abstract proposition (see Hayes-Roth, 1979; Farah, 1988). Neisser (1978), for example, points to the following sort of demonstration as support for the perceptual-experience hypothesis. If asked to describe a hawk's beak, people will report evoking an image of an entire hawk and then "inspecting" that image, or searching for the beak. The argument is that something really like a picture in the head can be evoked in its entirety and then scanned for detail. At present we have no clear way to decide which of these two hypotheses concerning the nature of images is better.

DUAL–TRACE THEORY: VERBAL AND VISUAL CODING

All this talk about visual imagery should not cause us to lose sight of one important fact. We do not *always* encode information in terms of visual images, whatever they are. We do not *have* to use visual imagery. We can, after all, encode information verbally as well as visually. If you are trying to remember the word *horse*, you do not have to cook up an image of a horse. You can obviously process this item as a word possessing auditory and semantic attributes rather than visual attributes. For example, if you wish to, you can probably encode *horse* both visually *and* verbally (see Schwanenflugel and Shoben, 1983).

Paivio (1975, 1978) has proposed what has become known as the *dual-trace hypothesis*. According to this hypothesis, any given stimulus (verbal or visual) can be encoded verbally or visually (or both). We have the capacity to encode a given bit of information either visually or verbally. Exactly which type of coding we use depends on the nature of the information to be coded and the demands of the task. Paivio distinguishes between *concrete items (horse, boat, apple)* and *abstract items (justice, even, obtuse)*. He argues that both concrete and abstract items are easily coded verbally. But concrete items are much more likely to be coded visually than are abstract items. It is easier to come up with a visual image for *horse* than for *obtuse*. Concrete items are also much more likely to be encoded *both* verbally and visually. An abstract item is much more likely to be coded *only* in a verbal sense. The reader interested in pursuing this line of reasoning is referred to the large body of research (Berrian, Metzler, Kroll, & Clark-Meyers, 1979; Harris, Morris, & Bassett, 1977; Kulhavy & Heinen, 1974; Lutz & Scheirer, 1974; Mondani & Battig, 1973; Nilsson, 1975; Pellegrino, Rosinsky, Cheisi, & Siegel, 1977; Pellegrino, Siegel, & Dhawan, 1975; Wortman & Sparling, 1974).

Although Paivio's hypothesis has received considerable attention, it would be premature to conclude that the relationship between verbal and visual encoding has been clearly delineated.

Mixed Coding

One final note concerning verbal and visual encoding: On the one hand, several authors (for example, Hilgard & Bower, 1975) have suggested that verbal encoding is particularly useful for information that is of a sequential nature, or distributed in time. On the other hand, the visual mode is often seen as a specialized means of encoding information that is presented simultaneously and is distributed in space. Whether this intriguing possibility will prove to be valid remains to be seen. It is already clear that the distinction is not indisputable. For example, sequential information *can* be stored visually. We can encode sequentially presented items by placing them in ordered positions within an overall visual image (for example, put the early items on the left and later items on the right, or put first items on the first floor of a tall building and later items on higher floors). Similarly, it seems reasonable to assume that we can encode spatially distributed items in a verbal manner. For example, we might encode the information on a map by storing "San Francisco is above Los Angeles." The point here is that the mind is flexible enough to utilize both means of coding for both types of information.

Table 11.4   Examples of Visual and Verbal Mediators Used by Subjects in Acquiring Trigram–Word Pairs

STIMULUS	RESPONSE	MEDIATING EVENT
CYF	– KID	C and K similar in sound.
XBN	– GAT	Gat is odd word. X is odd letter.
DSU	– CAT	D to Dog to CAT.
CFY	– DOG	C to Cat to DOG.
XBN	– RAT	X suggested poison, and poison, RAT.
TPM	– AND	T associated with symbol (&) for AND.
RZL	– SAT	R to Rump to SAT.
RZL	– SAT	R and S in alphabetical order.
DSU	– BAN	U-BAN (brand of coffee).
RZL	– KID	RZL suggested Russell; Russell is a KID.
CFY	– THE	Remembered because first one in list.
KHQ	– FAN	KHQ to radio to radio FAN.
IGW	– MAN	W inverted looks likes M, hence MAN.
IGW	– MAN	IG to IGnorant to IGnorant Man.
RZL	– BOY	RZL looks like lazy: hence, lazy BOY.
RZL	– CAT	Z is hissing sound of CAT.

Adapted from Underwood, B. J., and Schulz, R. W. *Meaningfulness and verbal learning.* Philadelphia: Lippincott, 1960, p. 299. Copyright © 1960 by J. B. Lippincott. Reprinted by permission of Harper and Row, Publishers, Inc.

In fact, it seems reasonable to assume that much of our natural encoding efforts involve *both* verbal and visual processes. We may seldom use *pure* visual or *pure* verbal codes. For example, Underwood and Schulz (1960) had subjects learn lists of nonsense syllables paired with words. After learning the lists the subjects were asked how they had managed the task. Many of them reported some sort of activity involving images. Some of their results are contained in Table 11.4. From the subjects' responses it seems clear that their efforts could easily have involved *both verbal and visual* components. Assuming that we can trust subject reports, we would be forced to conclude that the verbal and visual modes of encoding often go hand in hand.

People differ in how much elaborating they do, whether it be verbal, visual, or combined elaboration. For example, Wang (1983) compared the amounts of elaborating that slow learners did with the amounts fast learners displayed. The fast learners showed a marked superiority in how much elaborating they did. Even more intriguing is the fact that, when Wang gave the elaborations developed by slow learners and those developed by fast learners to new subjects, the new subjects receiving the fast learners' elaborations learned the material more easily than did the new subjects receiving the slow learners' elaborations. In other words, people differ in terms of the quality as well as the quantity of the elaborations they develop.

MEMORY FOR PICTURES

Generally speaking, although there are exceptions (see Postman, 1978), memory for pictures is better than memory for the verbal names of those pictures (see Intraub, 1979; Loftus & Kallman, 1979). For example, if you are shown a series of words including *dog, cloud, branch, pencil,* and *car* and asked to remember them, you will find it a little harder to do than if you had been shown a series of *pictures* including a dog, a cloud, a branch, a pencil, and a car.

This difference has stimulated an enormous amount of research and thought (see Kosslyn & Schwartz, 1977; MacLeod, 1988; Nelson & McEvoy, 1979; Pezdek, Maki, Valencia-Laver, Wetstone, Stoeckert, & Dougherty, 1988). The basic question underlying much of this work is this: Do we process and store picture stimuli in a manner that is different from the way in which we process and store verbal stimuli?

As you might expect, some say yes and some say no. The dual-code hypothesis discussed previously (Paivio, 1978) argues that pictures are better remembered than words because they are more likely than words to be coded both verbally and in terms of some kind of visual image. Thus, this position argues that we do process pictures differently from words; we are more likely to encode them in two ways.

Other investigators are not convinced that pictures are really handled in any way that is dramatically different from the way we process words (see Bajo, 1988; Durso & Johnson, 1979; Hogaboam & Pellegrino, 1978; Loftus & Kallman, 1979).

INTERACTING IMAGES

Given this large and growing body of research concerning images and mental processing, can it be applied practically? Some areas do seem relevant to the problem of improving retention. For example, a number of investigators have shown that paired associates are retained better if the stimuli and responses of each pair are related to each other through the use of some visual image (Corbett, 1977). These images can be developed by the subject (Bower, 1972; Dempster & Rohwer, 1974; Paivio, 1971), or they can be given to the subject by the experimenter (Wollen & Lowry, 1974).

What kinds of images are best? Some evidence suggests that *interactive images* are better than *noninteractive images*. For example, if you are attempting to remember the pair *horse–orange*, it is probably better to imagine a horse eating an orange than it is to imagine a horse standing in one place and an orange lying in another spot (Bower, 1970; Robbins, Bray, Irvin, & Wise, 1974). Apparently interactive imagery is better than separation imagery, although *both* of these seem to be better than no imagery at all.

However, some researchers (for example, Begg, 1978) have found that interactive imagery is not *always* superior to separate imagery. Furthermore, Nelson, Greene, Ronk, Hatchett, and Igl (1978) found that any interactive imagery was better than no interactive imagery but that increasing the *number* of interactive images did not further increase recall. They had one group of subjects make up a noninteractive image such as the one in Figure 11.10a. A second group developed one single interactive image such as that in Figure 11.10b. Two additional groups developed multiple interactive images such as those in Figure 11.10c and 11.10d. It was found that all three interactive-imagery groups did better in a retention test but that they did not differ from one another. In other words, there appears to be a limit to how useful interactive imagery can be to us. One good interactive image seems to help us just as much as various kinds of multiple interactive image (see also Day & Bellezza, 1983).

It is often asserted that making up strange, unusual, bizarre interactions will lead to better retention than will devising ordinary interactions. Although some

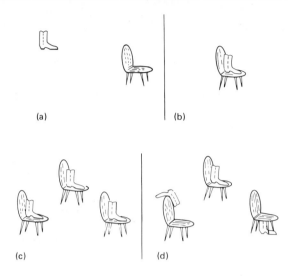

Figure 11.10 Examples of the kinds of images that could be formed for the word pair *boot–chair* in each of the four conditions: (a) noninteractive image, (b) single interactive image, (c) homogeneous multiple interactive image, (d) heterogeneous multiple interactive image. (Adapted from Nelson, T. O., Greene, G., Ronk, B., Hatchett, G., and Igl, V. Effect of multiple images on associative learning. *Memory and Cognition*, 1978, 6, 337–341. Fig. 1, p. 338.)

evidence supports this idea (see Lesgold & Goldman, 1973; Webber & Marshall, 1978), the available data are not completely convincing. For example, Wollen, Weber, and Lowery (1972) showed subjects pictures like those in Figure 11.11. The authors found that interaction was important but that bizarreness was not. That is, interacting pairs were recalled better than noninteracting pairs regardless of their degree of bizarreness. Bizarreness had no effect on recall, so the conclusion we must draw is that bizarreness may sometimes be helpful but is not always a critical variable.

IMAGERY AND THERAPY

Traditionally, emotional factors such as anxiety have been measured by self-reports or physiological measures. These methods have been fairly effective in identifying emotional turmoil. But recent research has suggested that a more sensitive assessment of anxiety may be available through the use of imagery. For example, Suler and Katkin (1988) ran the following study. Snake-fearful and non-snake-fearful subjects were first shown the drawing in Figure 11.12 for six seconds. Then they were asked to imagine the figure and, starting with the lower left corner and moving in a clockwise direction, indicate whether or not the rope entwined around the letter obscured each successive corner. Thus, the correct answers in Figure 11.12 would be no, no, no, no, no, yes, no, and so on, until all corners had been

Noninteracting, nonbizarre

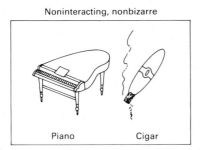

Noninteracting, bizarre

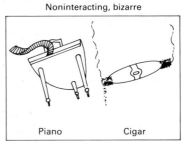

Interacting, nonbizarre

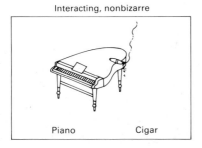

Interacting, bizarre

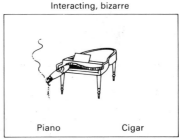

Figure 11.11 Sample materials for the four conditions in an experiment on the bizarreness of imagery. (Adapted from Wollen, K. A., Weber, A., and Lowry, D. H. Bizarreness versus interaction of mental images as determinants of learning. *Cognitive Psychology*, 1972, 2, 518–523.)

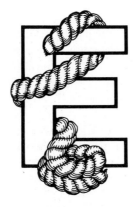

Figure 11.12 Example of a rope letter. (From Suler, J. R., and Katkin, E. S. Mental imagery of fear-related stimuli. *Journal of Mental Imagery*, 1988, *12*, 115–124. Fig. 3, p. 112, care of Brandon House, P.O. Box 240, Bronx, NY 10471.)

Figure 11.13 Example of a snake letter. (From Suler, J. R., and Katkin, E. S. Mental imagery of fear-related stimuli. *Journal of Mental Imagery*, 1988, *12*, 115–124. Fig. 2, p. 118, care of Brandon House, P.O. Box 240, Bronx, NY 10471.)

judged. Other subjects were shown the snake-enwrapped letter in Figure 11.13 and asked to perform the same sort of judgment task. They were asked to refer to their mental image of the stimulus and indicate whether or not the body of the snake concealed each corner.

The results indicated that snake-fearful and non-snake-fearful subjects made the same number of errors on the nonemotional (rope) stimulus. But on the snake stimulus the snake-fearful subjects made many more errors than the non-snake-fearful subjects did. The authors point out that this imagery-related method of distinguishing between fearful and non-snake-fearful subjects may well be more sensitive than the traditional methods involving self-reports and physiological measures.

The use of imagery is not restricted to attempts to assess anxiety as described above. More and more serious attempts to use imagery in therapy situations are appearing. For example, through the use of positive rather than negative mental imagery about their bodies and its capabilities, cancer patients can experience lessened stress and discomfort (Fiore, 1988). Similarly, Achterberg, Kenner, and Lawlis (1988) have found that positive mental imagery can help alleviate the anguish that severe burn patients experience.

MNEMONICS

Mnemonics are organizational or elaborative techniques that we can use to improve retention. Generally, mnemonics help us remember a new set of materials by relating it to some old, well-learned set of materials.

Rhyming

Many mnemonics involve visual images. Let us consider an example of the way in which a mnemonic technique involving visual imagery can facilitate retention. We begin with a little game, or mnemonic, for remembering lists of unrelated words (Miller, Galanter, & Pribram, 1960). First, we must refresh ourselves with respect

Table 11.5 Rhyme Used in Mnemonic Memory Plan

One is a bun.
Two is a shoe.
Three is a tree.
Four is a door.
Five is a hive.
Six is a stick.
Seven is heaven.
Eight is a gate.
Nine is wine.
Ten is a hen.

to an old children's rhyme. Rehearse the rhyme contained in Table 11.5 a couple of times. Once you have this rhyme firmly in mind, you are ready to move to the next step, which is to learn a list of 10 unrelated words. The first word in the list is to be associated with "one is a bun." The second word is to be associated with "two is a shoe," and so on through the list. The first word is to be associated with "one is a bun" through the creation of some vivid visual image containing both a *bun* and the first word. For example, if the first word were *house*, you might imagine a house made of steaming hot-cross buns or a row of tiny green and red houses tucked neatly into a sliced bun. Each of the successive words in the list is to be involved with the appropriate rhyme element through the creation of some vivid image. Try this plan with the list of words contained in Table 11.6. run through the list, one at at time. Give yourself enough time to establish a firm image for each word.

Assuming that you have completed the task, we shall test the effectiveness of the mnemonic by asking a series of questions. Cover the list of words. What is the seventh word? What goes with *door*? What goes with *wine*? What is the third word? What is the fifth word? In a subjective way you can probably sense what is occurring. The test words are so bound into your visual images that it is a simple matter to recall them. This plan for remembering has been tested experimentally. Bugelski (1968) had an experimental group learn lists of words using this plan and had control subjects learn the same lists without the plan. The experimental subjects recalled significantly more items than did the controls. In all likelihood, if you had not first learned the rhyme and been instructed in how to create images, your recall of the list would have been reduced.

Table 11.6 List of Words to be Used in Mnemonic Memory Plan

CAR
FLAG
CLOCK
BOOK
KNIFE
SHIRT
DRUM
SCISSORS
PEN
SKI

Table 11.7   A List of Words Will Be Easier to Remember If You Make up a Story That Includes All of the To-Be-Remembered Words

WORD LISTS	STORIES
Bird Costume Mailbox Head River Nurse Theater Wax Eyelid Furnace	A man dressed in a *Bird Costume* and wearing a *Mailbox* on his *Head* was seen leaping into the *River*. A *Nurse* ran out of a nearby *Theater* and applied *Wax* to his *Eyelids*, but her efforts were in vain. He died and was tossed into the *Furnace*.
Rustler Penthouse Mountain Sloth Tavern Fuzz Gland Antler Pencil Vitamin	A *Rustler* lived in a *Penthouse* on top of a *Mountain*. His specialty was the three-toed *Sloth*. He would take his captive animals to a *Tavern*, where he would remove *Fuzz* from their *Glands*. Unfortunately, all this exposure to sloth fuzz caused him to grow *Antlers*. So he gave up his profession and went to work in a *Pencil* factory. As a precaution he also took a lot of *Vitamin* E.

Adapted from Houston, J. P., Hammen, C., Padilla, A., and Bee, H. *Invitation to Psychology*, 3rd ed. San Diego: Harcourt Brace Jovanovich, 1989, Table 8.3, p. 331. Reprinted by permission of the publisher.

Inventing Stories

Another type of mnemonic technique involves making up stories using the to-be-remembered words (Bower & Clark, 1969). Consider the word lists in Table 11.7. One of the easiest ways to learn these lists is to invent a story containing all of the words in the target list. The stories on the right side of Table 11.7 enable us to remember not only the target words but the *order* of the words as well. The stories containing the words are easier to remember than the words alone.

The Method of Loci

There are many additional mnemonic techiques. One of them is called the *method of loci* and is described below by Houston, Hammen, Padilla, and Bee (1989, pp. 330–332).

The *method of loci* works by placing mental images of what we are trying to remember in *ordered mental locations*. This method was invented by the ancient Greeks, who used it to help them remember topics and issues during long public speeches. The first step in using the method of loci is to establish an ordered series of known locations. For example, you might take a "mental walk" through a very familiar building such as your home. A walk outside will do just as well, as long as it involves a series of known locations. At distinct points along your mental walk, you "place" vivid images of what you are trying to remember—the first item in the first location, the second in the second, and so on.

For example, suppose you are trying to remember a list of items to be purchased at a hardware store. The items include *nails*, a *hammer*, a *pair of pliers*, a *chisel*, and a *measuring tape*. Now suppose you have chosen a "mental walk" through your house as a means of supplying convenient, well-known "locations," or "hooks," on which to place the images of the objects to be remembered. It has been suggested that this system works best if the images are vivid. Thus, if your walk begins at the front door, you might visualize the front door nailed shut with hundreds of green and maroon nails. Approaching the stairway, you might imagine a huge hammer with legs sliding down the bannister. In the kitchen you might have an enormous pair of pink pliers pinching the refrigerator in half. In the dining room you could visualize hundreds of little blue chisels buzzing about the food like flies. In the backyard, you might imagine a snakelike measuring tape devouring apples.

Try this method for yourself using the words below. First, establish your mental walk. Then fill the locations with vivid images of the items. Then test the system by "taking a walk" through your locations, and see how simple it is to recall not only the items but their correct order as well.

Forest
Mayor
Pillar
Rooster
Tablespoon
Gymnast
Infant
Shack
Textbook
Warplane

The Keyword Method

As a final example of mnemonic methods consider the technique described here by Houston, Hammen, Padilla, and Bee (1989, p. 333).

> The *keyword method* is a technique for remembering the English meaning of foreign words (Atkinson, 1975; Pressley & Levin, 1981). Suppose you want to remember that the Spanish word "carta" means "letter." The first step is to think of an English word that sounds like "carta," such as "cart." This is the keyword. Next, form a visual image of the keyword and the English translation, such as a mail carrier pulling a kiddy-cart full of letters. Later, when you are given "carta" and asked for the English meaning, "carta" will remind you of "cart" which will, in turn, key off the visual image containing the "letter" you are after. (See also Carney, Levin, & Morrison, 1988.)

ORGANIZATION AND ASSOCIATIONS

This chapter about organization, elaboration, and imagery closes with a question that contrasts earlier stimulus-response conceptions of memory with more recent cognitive approaches. Does a more cognitive approach that emphasizes organization, elaboration, and imagery preclude a consideration of S-R associations? In one sense an organizational approach does seem to be concerned with elements that are not easily described in terms of S-R associations (images, structures, and the like). The organizational approach seems to be concerned with "cognitive" events that might better be described in terms of some new, nonassociative language. And yet, as Postman (1972) suggests, there is no necessary disagreement between associative and organizational conceptions of memory (see also Voss, 1972). The two approaches clearly refer to two different ways of thinking and speaking about the same events. As Postman puts it, the differences between the two approaches appear to be a matter of language more than anything else. In a sense it seems that the organizational approach focuses on the complexity and the structure of the processes and events that intervene between input and output. The organizational psychologist speaks of these intervening mental events using a certain kind of language (for example, one that emphasizes such components as chunks, networks, and higher-order units). But these same mental events could probably be translated into S-R language. It would merely be a matter of trying to *identify extremely complex, interacting S-R relationships.*

SUMMARY

1. Organization, structure, elaboration, and imagery are important concepts in the modern study of memory.
2. Organizational activities refer to what we do to information between input and output. Although there is little agreement concerning an exact definition or organization, most conceptions refer to the fact that we often systematize, relate, structure, order, select, elaborate, and transform information.
3. An interest in organization is not new. The issues of organization were raised by Gestalt psychologists many years ago. New methods of assessing organization have renewed interest in their issues.
4. In a *word-association test* the subjects' task is to give the first word that comes to mind in response to a set of stimulus words. Some stimulus words tend to elicit common responses (for example, *black–white*). The patterns of obtained word associations suggest that words are somehow structured, or organized, within us.
5. As children grow older, their word associations become more semantic and less episodic.
6. Word-association tests have been used in clinical settings in attempts to reveal the patients' emotional and cognitive states.
7. The capacity of immediate memory is probably limited by the number of *chunks* of information it can hold (7 ± 2).
8. A chunk may vary in terms of the amount of information that it contains.
9. In general, as long as information can be expressed as a single response, it represents a single chunk.
10. We can increase the capacity of our immediate memory by increasing the amount of information contained in our chunks of information.
11. Response times for the production of responses relating the members of sets to one another show a definite break at about six items.
12. We can increase the amount of information in a chunk by a process of rewriting.
13. *Category clustering in recall* refers to the fact that items drawn from various categories and presented randomly will often be recalled together.

14. Although the issue is not completely resolved, some evidence suggests that overall recall increases as clustering increases.

15. Total recall and clustering both seem to be greater for *exhaustive* than for *nonexhaustive* categories.

16. In *subjective organization* experiments, lists of items are randomly presented and recalled over and over. It is found that the order of recall takes on consistency despite random input.

17. Subjective organization experiments do not provide us with much information concerning the *nature* of the evolving organization.

18. The relationship between subjective organization and overall recall has not been clearly determined.

19. *Stimulus selection* refers to the fact that the organism does not always use the entire stimulus presented to it. Sometimes we select some portion of the presented stimulus and associate the response with that portion.

20. Many factors, including ordinal position, have been shown to influence stimulus selection.

21. Animals as well as humans display stimulus selection. This represents another similarity between animal and human learning processes.

22. *Mental images* are the subject of much current investigation. Imagery can be shown to improve retention.

23. The results of many scanning experiments support the idea that we do encode, store, and use visionlike mental images.

24. However, the fact that congenitally blind subjects can also display typical scanning-experiment results requires that we be cautious in our interpretation of scanning results.

25. Mental-rotation experiments, also taken as support for visual imagery, show that the speed of matching two objects decreases as the difference in orientation of the two objects increases.

26. Mental rotation can be demonstrated with either two-dimensional or three-dimensional stimuli.

27. Interference effects in imagery also support the idea of a pictures-in-the-head interpretation of imagery.

28. Imagery can enhance learning and retention.

29. Imagery has been interpreted according to a *perceptual-experience* hypothesis and a *propositional interpretation*.

30. According to the *dual-trace hypothesis*, both concrete and abstract items are likely to be coded verbally. But concrete items are more likely to be coded visually than are abstract items.

31. Although the distinction does not always hold true, some investigators have suggested that spatially distributed information is often encoded visually, whereas temporally distributed information is often encoded verbally.

32. It seems likely that our *natural* encoding efforts probably involve both verbal and visual components.

33. It has been found that better learners elaborate more than slow learners. In addition the elaborations developed by fast learners help new learners more than do the elaborations of slow learners.

34. Memory for pictures is usually better than memory for the names of those pictures. Some feel that pictures are processed and stored in a manner that is

fundamentally different from the way in which we store verbal stimuli; others do not.

35. Paired associates are retained better when the stimuli and responses are related to each other through the creation of some visual image.
36. *Interactive images* appear to be more effective than *noninteractive images*.
37. Bizarreness of image may sometimes be helpful, but not always.
38. There is a limit to how helpful interactive imagery can be.
39. Imagery can be used to assess anxiety.
40. Imagery may prove to be useful in therapeutic situations involving such things as cancer and burns.
41. *Mnemonics* are techniques we use to improve retention. Rhyming and the composition of stories using to-be-remembered items can be helpful.
42. Other mnemonic techniques include the *method of loci* and the *keyword method*.
43. The organizational approach does not necessarily preclude a consideration of S-R associations.

SELECTED
COGNITIVE
PROCESSES

Recent years have witnessed a sharp resurgence of interest in *cognitive processes*. Essentially, cognitive psychologists are interested in studying and understanding *complex mental events*. They are not afraid to talk about ideas, images, thoughts, symbols, knowledge, and reasoning. In fact, it is just these elusive, complex mental events that intrigue cognitive psychologists. They do not want to be limited to a consideration of strictly observable events; they want to "look inside the head" and understand our mental tools and manipulations. Whereas Hull, some decades ago, argued that to maintain rigor we must avoid a consideration of "mentalistic" events, modern cognitive psychologists argue that we can, after all, understand complex mental events even though they cannot be observed directly. They feel that, although Hull and the behaviorists may have been right in their time, our new experimental techniques and our ever-increasing store of analytical tools now enable us to return to many interesting questions about thought and thinking that have been neglected for some time.

Because cognitive psychology is now reborn, or at least in the ascendance, it should not be surprising to learn that there is a good deal of disagreement over what is meant by cognition. Houston, Hammer, Padilla, and Bee (1989) point out that there are at least five popular ways of looking at cognition:

1. *Cognition as information processing.* Many psychologists think of cognition as the overall processing of information. According to Neisser (1967), *cognition* is an inclusive term that refers to all the processes by which sensory input is transformed, reduced, elaborated, stored, retrieved, and used. Although very broad and general, this definition does have value, because it underlines the fact that many cognitive psychologists think about thinking in terms of information processing. They use the language of computers. In fact, some have attempted to construct computer programs that will *simulate* human thinking. These efforts usually fall under the heading of *artificial intelligence* (AI).

2. *Cognition as manipulation of mental symbols.* Some psychologists prefer to think of cognitive events as the manipulation of mental symbols. As we have seen, a symbol is anything that stands for, or represents, something else. Therefore, when you think of a dog, whatever it is that you are thinking of is a symbol for *dog*. Symbols free us from being trapped in the present. They allow us to make excursions into the past and future. For example, when you think of the Boston Tea Party, you are visiting the past through the use of symbols. When you think about the next presidential election, you are moving into the future in a way that would not be possible without symbols.

3. *Cognition as problem solving.* As you will recall, we mentioned problem solving back in Chapter 1. A problem exists when a motivated organism is blocked from attaining a goal by an obstacle or obstacles. Some cognitive psychologists like to think of problem solving as the essence of cognition. They feel that cognition refers to the ways in which we gather and use information in the pursuit of the solution to problems. Obviously, some cognitive events, such as finding the answer to a mathematical question, involve problem solving. But the real question is whether *all* cognitive events are of the problem-solving variety. For example, suppose that the name or face of an old friend "pops into your mind." Was this a case of problem solving? It may well be some subtle form of problem solving, such as satisfying a fantasy wish or avoiding boredom. But it seems more likely that problem solving may be one form of cognitive event, rather than the other way around. Still, some hold to the position that all cognition is problem solving.

4. *Cognition as thinking.* Most cognitive psychologists would agree that one of their primary interests is in the area of *thinking*. A firm definition of thinking is currently unavailable in the field of psychology. Stating that cognition is thinking does not get us very far. For heuristic purposes, however, drawing a parallel between thinking and cognition can be helpful. The term *thinking* certainly covers an enormous range of very complex events, and most of them seem to be described equally well as cognitive events.

5. *Cognition as knowing, remembering, perceiving, thinking, judging, problem solving, reasoning, learning, imagining, conceptualizing, and using language.* According to this approach, the best way to think about cognition is to list every kind of event that might possibly be considered cognition and let the matter go at that. No attempt is made to be more precise. At this early stage in the investigation of cognition, this approach has merit.

These five approaches are not isolated and distinct ways of viewing cognition. Rather, each seems to *emphasize* some salient quality of the overall concept of cognition. When thinking about cognition, it is a good idea to keep them all in mind, for each has something to offer.

It should also be clear by now that we have already begun our study of cognition in many of the preceding chapters. We have already looked at topics such as memory, organization, information processing, and so on, all of which clearly represent issues that are of interest to the cognitive psychologist. We have been considering cognition all along. You cannot really think about learning and memory without thinking about cognition.

In the next two chapters we will consider some selected topics that are often mentioned as being of *special* concern to the cognitive psychologist. Thus, in Chapter 12 we shall discuss *concept formation* and *problem solving*. In Chapter 13 we shall address the wonderful area of *language usage*. Remember that these are selected topics; they do not exhaust the concerns of the cognitive psychologist. But they are representative of the cognitive approach.

CHAPTER

12

CONCEPTS

AND

PROBLEMS

WHAT IS CONCEPT FORMATION?
Defining Concepts

In Chapter 1 we noted that a concept is a symbol or group of symbols that stands for a class, or group, of objects or events that possess common properties. Thus, *house* is a concept because it is a symbol that stands for a large group of objects, all of which possess common characteristics. Most words with the exception of proper nouns, which refer to only a single object, are concepts. Concepts need not involve language. For example, babies can have a concept of *mother* long before they have acquired language. Concepts help us to think efficiently, because they free us from having to give a unique label to each new instance of a concept. For example, if we see a new car, we do not have to give it a unique label. We just label it as one more car. Concepts are so ingrained in our thought processes that it is difficult to imagine what life would be like without them.

Concepts are related to one another in complicated ways. For example, a concept can be an instance of another, broader concept. Thus, *bee* is a concept, but it is also an instance of the concept *insect*, which, in turn, is an instance of the concept *animal*.

Defining Concept Formation

Concept formation, which is of particular concern to learning psychologists, refers to how we go about learning or acquiring concepts. Specifically, psychologists are interested in understanding how we learn to identify objects or events as examples of particular concepts. When we see a baby that we have never seen before, we readily identify it as an example of the concept *baby*. When, where, and how did we learn this complex ability to categorize correctly so many objects and events? These questions intrigue the cognitive psychologist and lead to the experiments that we will consider in this chapter.

Concepts and Problems

In a sense concept formation can be thought of as an example of problem solving. The problem is to learn the concept, or to acquire the ability to identify correctly examples of the concept. So we are dealing essentially with a simple form of problem solving when we discuss concept formation. Later in this chapter we shall turn to more complicated problems.

A Sample Experiment

Let us begin our study of concepts by considering a "typical" experimental design.

1. Reed (1972) taught subjects concepts based on schematic faces similar to those in Figure 12.1; the attributes of these faces are face shape (narrow or wide), eye position (high or low), and mouth shape (smile or frown). The stimuli for the experiment are defined by selecting some number of attributes—ways in which the stimuli can differ—and constructing all the possible stimuli from selected values of these attributes.

2. The experimenter defines the concept to be learned by choosing one or more of the attribute values—perhaps a wide face. All stimuli that have wide faces are then instances of the concept to be learned. The other attribute values—eye position and mouth shape—do not affect category membership and are called irrelevant attributes. (Note that the experimenter could also define as a concept a com-

Figure 12.1 Face stimuli similar to those used by Reed (1972) in studying concept formation. The faces vary on the dimensions of face shape (wide or narrow), eye position (high or low), and mouth shape (smile or frown).

plex combination of the attributes—perhaps a narrow face with both a smile and high eyes.)

3. Subjects are shown the stimuli in some order, usually random, and classify each stimulus either as being or not being an instance of the concept. Feedback is generally given after each trial. Stimuli are shown to the subjects until some criterion of performance is met, usually some number of consecutive correct responses. By classifying many stimuli correctly, the subjects are assumed to have learned the concept.

This simple experimental design can be very useful in exploring many different aspects of concept formation. For example, we might be interested in knowing how the number of attributes affects concept learning. So we would have one group of subjects learn the concept *wide face* while we simultaneously varied only one other attribute (for example, eye position); another group would learn the same *wide face* concept while we varied two or more other attributes (for example, eye position and mouth shape). Presumably we would find that the concept would be easier to learn when fewer irrelevant attributes were varied; the situation would be simpler and easier to "figure out."

DISCOVERING ATTRIBUTES AND RULES

Concept-formation tasks often require us to make two kinds of discoveries. First, we must decide which attributes are relevant, and second, we must discover the rules that tell us how to combine these attributes. As we have seen, *attributes* are ways that stimuli can *differ* from one another, such as size, shape, and color. *Rules* tell us how these attributes are *related* to one another. For example, suppose you found that smiling, wide faces and frowning, narrow faces were correct stimuli in Figure 12.1. By coming to realize that these stimuli were correct you would have

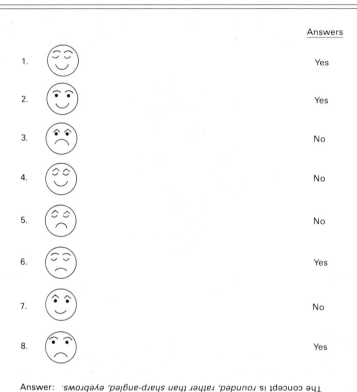

Answer: ˙sʍoɹqǝʎǝ 'pǝʃƃuɐ-dɹɐɥs uɐɥʇ ɹǝɥʇɐɹ 'pǝpunoɹ sı ʇdǝɔuoɔ ǝɥꞱ

Figure 12.2 An attribute discovery task. Before you begin, place a piece of paper so that it hides the correct answers on the right-hand side of the page. Looking only at the figures on the left-hand side, say yes if you believe that the figure is an example of the concept and no if you believe that it is not. Only one attribute is relevant in this task. After judging each pair move the paper down to see the answer. Continue until you think you know what the concept is, and then check below to see whether you are correct. (From *Cognition* by Margaret Matlin. Copyright © 1983. Reprinted by permission of Holt, Rinehart and Winston.)

discovered that face shape and mouth shape were the relevant attributes, whereas eye position was irrelevant. But you would also have learned a *rule* telling you how to combine the attributes to identify instances: "Only frowning narrow faces and smiling wide faces are correct."

Interestingly, any given experiment can involve attribute discovery alone, rule learning alone, or both. Let us look at each of these subprocesses individually.

Attribute Learning

Matlin (1983) provides a nice example of an attribute-discovery task where no rule learning is required. Try the demonstration in Figure 12.2 before reading any further. As you will realize, eyebrow shape is the relevant attribute (rounded rather

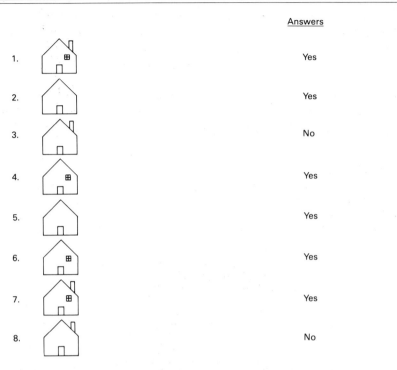

Answers

1.   Yes

2.   Yes

3.   No

4.   Yes

5.   Yes

6.   Yes

7.   Yes

8.   No

Answer: Conditional rule: If a figure has a chimney, then it must have a window to be an example. All figures without chimneys are also examples.

Figure 12.3 A rule-discovery task. Before you begin, place a piece of paper so that it hides the correct answers on the right-hand side of the page. Looking only at the figures on the left-hand side, say yes if you believe that the figure is an example of the concept and no if you believe that it is not. The attributes *presence or absence of chimney* and *presence or absence of window* are relevant. Your task is to figure out the rule for combining these attributes so that you can decide which figures are examples of the concept. After judging each item, move the paper to see the answer. Continue until you think you know what the concept is, and then check to see whether you are correct. (From *Cognition* by Margaret Matlin. Copyright © 1983. Reprinted by permission of Holt, Rinehart and Winston.)

than peaked eyebrows are instances of the concept). At the same time you will realize that this task did not require you to learn a rule relating the attributes to one another.

Rule Learning

Matlin (1983) also provides a good example of a concept-formation task that requires you to learn a rule when the relevant attributes are provided. Try the demonstration in Figure 12.3 before reading further. You will experience what we mean by rule learning in the absence of attribute discovery.

Combined Learning

Obviously, many, perhaps most, concept-formation tasks require us to discover relevant attributes *and* rules relating those attributes. Go back to the task in Figure 12.3, for example, and imagine trying to solve it if you had not first been told that chimneys and windows were the relevant attributes. The task would have been much more difficult.

Rule Complexity

Thinking about concepts in terms of rules seems to have helped psychologists (see Anglin, 1977; McCloskey & Glucksberg, 1978; Rosch, 1978). They feel comfortable with this kind of language. One of the obvious things that they have considered is the fact that concept-defining rules can vary enormously in terms of their complexity. Psychologists want to know whether this is important. Are concepts that are defined by simple rules any easier to learn than concepts defined by more complex rules? To answer this question imagine that you are a subject in an experiment. You are shown a series of cards, each of which contains one circle and one square. The circles and squares may be either red or green. For each card you must choose the item that is "correct," or belongs to the category that the psychologist has in mind. Now the psychologist may have a very simple concept in mind, such as *anything that is red*. In this case you will quickly learn the concept and always choose red items, whether circles or squares.

But the psychologist can make the task more difficult. For instance, she might define the concept you are after as *all green circles*. In this situation you would have to learn to pick only green circles and to refrain from choosing green squares, red squares, and red circles. Finally, the psychologist could complicate the situation even more by defining the concept as *red and not square*, or *square and not red*. This rule demands that you choose only red circles and green squares.

Attempting to determine whether concepts defined by complex rules are harder to master than concepts defined by simple rules, Haygood and Bourne (1965) developed a series of rules that increase in logical complexity (see also Bruner, Goodnow, & Austin, 1956; Neisser & Weene, 1962). These concept-defining rules are listed in Table 12.1. Complexity increases as one moves down the table from the top (on either the left or right side—take your pick). The researchers predicted, reasonably enough, that concept learning would become more difficult as rule complexity increased, and, in fact, this is essentially what they found. Concepts defined by the rules at the bottom of Table 12.1 were more difficult to master than concepts higher up in the table.

THE EARLY S–R INTERPRETATION

Psychologists have always been interested in *how* concept learning occurs. In this chapter we shall touch on several distinct interpretations of concept formation. For the moment we want to focus upon one of the very earliest interpretations. Specifically, the behaviorists, including Hull, felt that concept learning could be best understood as an instance of *discrimination* learning. Hull and others noticed a similarity between the concept-learning situation and the discrimination-learning situation. In a discrimination-learning task, if you will recall, a pigeon might have to learn to discriminate among various colored lights, learning to respond to only

Table 12.1   Rule-Defining Concepts of Increasing Logical Complexity*

BASIC RULES			COMPLEMENTARY RULES		
NAME	SYMBOLIC DESCRIP- TION	VERBAL DESCRIPTION	NAME	SYMBOLIC DESCRIP- TION	VERBAL DESCRIPTION
Affirmation	R	Anything that is red is an example.	Negation	$\bar{R}$	Anything not red is an example.
Conjunction	$R \cap S$	All red squares.	Alternative denial	$\bar{R} \cup \bar{S}$	All items either not red or not square.
Inclusive disjunction	$R \cup S$	All items either red or square or both.	Joint denial	$\bar{R} \cap \bar{S}$	All items neither red nor square.
Conditional	$R \rightarrow S$	Everything green; also, if red, item must be square.	Exclusion	$R \cap \bar{S}$	All items red and not square.
Biconditional	$R \leftrightarrow S$	Red items, if they are square; square items if red.	Exclusive disjunction	$R \bar{\cup} S$	All items are either red or square but not both.

*As one moves down the table (on either the left or right side), the rules become more complex. In general, the concepts defined by these rules are more difficult to master.

Adapted from Haygood, R. C., and Bourne, L. E. Attribute- and rule-learning aspects of conceptual behavior. *Psychological Review*, 1965, 72, 175–195. Fig. 1, p. 178. Copyright 1965 by the American Psychological Association. Reprinted by permission.

one of them. Similarly, in the concept-learning situation the human must learn to discriminate among a number of different stimulus values, learning to respond to only one of them.

This behaviorist, or stimulus-response (S-R), view was supported by one of the classic experiments in concept learning, carried out by Hull (1920). In this experiment subjects were trained to classify Chinese alphabet characters into different categories, depending on the presence of a certain "radical," or line segment, used in the construction of the character (Figure 12.4). Although many of Hull's subjects were able to learn the task, they were unable to explain *how* they were classifying the characters. Hull was very impressed by this inability of subjects to describe their performance, and he stressed the importance of analyzing the subjects' behavior and *not* their introspections.

Hull's experiment fit quite nicely into the behaviorist view that was developing at the time; not only was introspection unscientific, but the subjects could not even do it! This kind of result reinforced the behaviorists' notion that we should look only at observable behavior and avoid speculations about what goes on "inside the head."

THE HYPOTHESIS–TESTING INTERPRETATION

Beginning in the 1950s, however, psychologists began to depart from the strict behaviorist position. They began asking questions about what complex mental processes are involved in concept formation. This movement toward modern cognitive psychology brought with it a resurgence of interest in introspection, tempered by the careful evaluation of these introspections against experimental data. Out of this movement arose the idea that concept formation involves hypothesis

Figure 12.4 Some of the materials used by Hull in demonstrating concept formation. Each of the six different "radicals," or concepts, is imbedded in all of the characters in its row. The subjects first were given the characters in List 1 and asked to associate a different nonsense syllable with each one. Then they were given the second list and asked to again associate the same nonsense syllables with these new characters. In the second list the nonsense syllable was paired with the second-list character, which contained the same radical that appeared in the first-list character paired with that syllable. Then they learned the third list, again being required to associate the nonsense syllables with the characters that contained the "correct" radicals. By the time the sixth list was reached, the subjects were very good at giving the correct nonsense syllables on the very first presentation of the characters, even though they had little idea of how they could do it. (Adapted from Hull, C. L. Quantitative aspects of the evolution of concepts. *Psychological Monographs*, Whole No. 123, 1920. Copyright 1920 by the American Psychological Association.)

testing, something that Hull would never have considered because it involves thinking about what goes on in the mind. The hypothesis-testing interpretation has pretty well supplanted the older discrimination-learning interpretation, and it remains very influential today.

Instead of viewing concept learning as a somewhat more advanced case of discrimination learning, many psychologists see concept learning as a process of testing hypotheses—guesses about what the true classification rule might be. The subject is assumed to select one of the hypotheses and use it to classify the stimuli. For example, consider the stimuli in Figure 12.1. There are six simple hypotheses: *wide face, narrow face, high eyes, low eyes, smiling,* and *frowning.* Subjects might begin

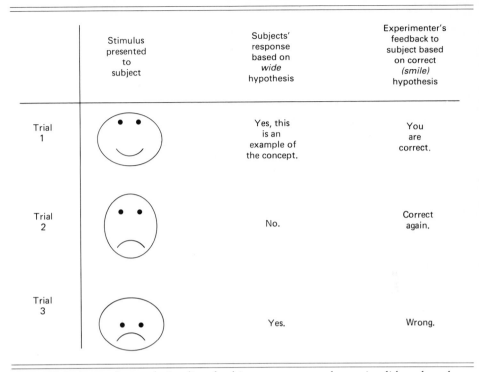

Stimulus presented to subject	Subjects' response based on *wide* hypothesis	Experimenter's feedback to subject based on correct *(smile)* hypothesis
Trial 1	Yes, this is an example of the concept.	You are correct.
Trial 2	No.	Correct again.
Trial 3	Yes.	Wrong.

Figure 12.5 A sample set of stimuli and subject responses to those stimuli based on the hypothesis that *wide* is the concept and feedback given to the subject on each of three trials. The correct hypothesis is *smile*, not *wide*.

an experiment by guessing that the hypothesis *wide face* will correctly classify the stimuli. If the rule that correctly defines the concept is *smile*, they would respond to the stimuli as shown in Figure 12.5.

On Trials 1 and 2 *wide face* seems to work. This, however, is only because thus far *wide face* has appeared only with *smile* and has not appeared without *smile*. In Trial 3, when *wide face* and *frown* appear together, the subject's hypothesis leads to an incorrect response. After Trial 3 the subject knows that *wide face* is not the correct hypothesis and selects a new hypothesis to replace the old, incorrect one. This, too, may be incorrect, and yet another hypothesis will have to be tried. This process will continue until the subject finally selects the proper hypothesis (*smile*) and makes a long string of correct responses, terminating the experiment.

Conservative Focusing

In a classic paper Bruner, Goodnow, and Austin (1956) reported a series of experiments that described hypothesis-testing procedures in great detail. Although no specific theory was presented to account for the results, Bruner and his co-workers isolated many of the critical questions that any theory of concept learning must confront, and they described many methods used by their subjects to test hypotheses (see also Johnson, 1978). One of these methods is particularly interesting, because it represents the optimal strategy for concept learning. Bruner, Goodnow, and Austin used a slightly different technique from the one described earlier. Rather than being shown the stimuli in random order, the subjects *told* the experimenter which stimulus they wanted to have classified: "Is the wide, low-eye, smiling face an instance of the concept?" With this ability to select stimuli for classification, the subjects used a strategy called *conservative focusing*. In conservative focusing the subject takes a very simple, direct approach and focuses on a single attribute at a time, checking it out completely before moving on to another dimension—hence, the label.

For instance, consider the example cited above involving faces. Suppose that the correct hypothesis is *smile*. A subject begins his task by selecting and focusing on one guess, or hypothesis. Let us say that he guesses that *wide face* is correct. He begins by asking whether *wide face–low eyes–smile* is an instance of the correct category. He will be told that it is. Then, because he is guessing that *wide face* is correct, he changes *wide face* to *narrow face*, leaving the other two attributes alone. Specifically, he asks about *narrow face–low eyes–smile*. Again he is told that he is correct. So much for his first guess that *wide face* is the concept. He now knows that *wide face* cannot be the concept, because if it were, *narrow face–low eyes–smile* would not belong to the correct category. So he changes his focus. Having eliminated the *wide–narrow* attribute, he turns to one of the two remaining attributes. Let us say that he guesses that *smile* is correct. To test this guess he varies that single attribute, holding the other two constant, and asks about *narrow face–low eyes–frown*. He is told that this is not an instance of the category, and he has the answer! *Smile* must be the concept, because instances with it included are correct and instances without it are incorrect. He has found the concept by focusing on and eliminating one attribute at a time.

If the subject adopts this strategy in an experiment such as Bruner, Goodnow, and Austin's, very good performance is guaranteed. These conditions, however, are not typical of much of the work in concept learning. If category membership depends on two attribute values—say, a wide, smiling face—conservative focusing will not work. In addition, most experiments use random presentation of stimuli, so some time may pass before a stimulus is presented that will allow the use of conservative focusing. By that time the subject may have forgotten the stimulus that was originally selected or, perhaps, which of the attributes had been shown to be irrelevant to category membership. Performance on most concept-learning experiments is therefore almost always well below the ideal specified by conservative focusing. Conservative focusing is an optimal strategy only when the subject can select the stimuli to be evaluated and when a single dimension is involved.

"Watching" People Use Hypotheses: Blank Trials

Levine (1966, 1975) devised an ingenious experimental method that enables us to do what all previous research had failed to do. Specifically, Levine's design enables us not only to tell *whether* a subject is using a hypothesis but also to determine exactly *what* that hypothesis is and *when* the subject changes from that hypothesis to a new one.

Subjects were shown a series of cards, each of which contained two letters. The subjects' task was to choose one of the two letters on each card. The letters differed in color (black or white), letter (X or T), size (large or small), and position (left or right side of card) (see Figure 12.6). The correct hypothesis was one of the eight

Blank trial	Stimulus presented to subject	Eight possible hypotheses controlling subjects choices:							
		X	T	Black	White	Left	Right	Large	Small
		Response expected according to above hypotheses							
1	**X** T	X	T	X	T	X	T	X	T
2	X **T**	X	T	T	X	X	T	T	X
3	**T** X	X	T	T	X	T	X	X	T
4	T **X**	X	T	X	T	T	X	T	X

Figure 12.6 The eight response patterns in Levine's (1966) experiment and the hypotheses indicated by those patterns. (Adapted from Levine, M. Hypothesis behavior by humans during discrimination learning. *Journal of Experimental Psychology*, 1966, *71*, 331–338. Fig. 1, p. 331. Copyright 1966 by the American Psychological Association. Reprinted by permission.)

simple possibilities (small, large, black, white, T, X, left, right). On the first trial the subjects were shown a card and told which of the two letters was correct. But then Levine did something a little different. Subjects were given a series of four "blank trials" during which they had to choose one of the letters, but *no feedback* was given during these blank trials. The assumption was that, although subjects might change their hypothesis following a trial with feedback, they would not change during the blank trials because no information about the correctness of their responses was given. Furthermore, these blank trials were specially designed so that, if the subject was using a specific hypothesis, that hypothesis could be accurately detected by the pattern of responses that he or she gave over the four blank trials.

The specially selected stimuli that were presented during the four blank trials are shown in Figure 12.6. Notice that the patterns of responses for the eight different hypotheses are all different. By matching the subject's actual responses against these patterns we can determine which of the eight hypotheses the subject was actually using. For example, if a subject gave T T T T over the four trials, we can be sure that he was guessing that *T* was the correct hypothesis. Similarly, if a subject responded with X T X T, we can be sure she was using the hypothesis *large*. In addition, if a subject gave a pattern of responses other than those in Figure 12.6, we can be sure that none of the eight simple hypotheses was being used consistently in all four blank trials. This is an ingenious and very clever way to determine what people are guessing without having to ask them.

What did Levine learn using the "blank trial" method? First, he found that in over 90% of the blank trial series one or another of the eight hypotheses was being used. In other words, people did not just skip around trying any old thing on any given trial. They did, after all, pick one hypothesis and stick to it through the four blank trials. They did not switch from one hypothesis to another during the blank series. Second, Levine found that subjects almost always stuck with that same hypothesis on the feedback trial following the four blank trials. They held to their "game plan" and used the same hypothesis that they had been using during the blank trials on the feedback trial following the blank trials. Third, by looking at performance on *successive* series of four blank trials, interspersed among feedback trials, it was possible to note *when* subjects changed hypotheses and *what* new hypotheses they changed to. For example, if a subject gave T T T T on one set of four blank trials and then, after another feedback trial, gave T X T X on another series of four blank trials, it can be inferred that the subject shifted from testing the hypothesis that *T* was correct to testing the hypothesis that *small* was correct. Fourth, Levine was able to show that, as the experiment progressed, subjects eliminated incorrect hypotheses and no longer considered them. When they tried a hypothesis and found it not to work, they did not put it back in the "pool" of available hypotheses and did not test it again later. Although they were not perfect at doing this, they did not, for the most part, waste time in testing them again. In summary, Levine's work suggests very strongly that hypothesis testing plays an important part in concept learning and that humans are fairly methodical and careful in their hypothesis-testing efforts.

On the other hand, Levine's position has been challenged. Kellogg, Robbins, and Bourne (1978), for example, have shown that if subjects are asked to recall the hypotheses they utilized in concept formation, they recall early hypotheses as well as they do later hypotheses. This result has been taken as evidence against the idea that successful hypotheses are retained while unsuccessful ones are deleted (see also Rebe & Allen, 1978).

NATURAL CATEGORIES

Many psychologists have argued that the typical concept-formation tasks used in our laboratories are very artificial and quite unrelated to the concepts we develop and utilize outside the confines of the laboratory. Eleanor Rosch, at the University of California, Berkeley, was one of the first to raise and explore this criticism leveled at laboratory concept tasks (Rosch, 1973). She and others point out that by studying such artificial concepts as *red squares* or *wide frowns* we are learning very little about the complex concepts we actually encounter in everyday life.

There are two main criticisms of the laboratory approach. First, natural categories are hierarchical in the sense that larger categories often contain smaller categories. For instance, *bees* are *insects*, which are, in turn, *animals*. Most early laboratory experiments did not take these critical hierarchical relationships into account. Second, laboratory work failed to account for the fact that some instances of certain categories are more representative of that category than are other instances (Medin, Dewey, & Murphy, 1983; Roth & Mervis, 1983). For example, *robin* is more representative of the category *bird* than is *penguin*. In traditional laboratory tasks this important fact was not taken into account. The experimenter arranged the materials and tasks without regard for these variations in representativeness.

Table 12.2   Examples of Subordinate, Basic, and Superordinate Categories

SUPERORDINATE	BASIC LEVEL	SUBORDINATES	
Musical instrument	Guitar	Folk guitar	Classical guitar
	Piano	Grand piano	Upright piano
	Drum	Kettle drum	Bass drum
Fruit	Apple	Delicious apple	Mackintosh apple
	Peach	Freestone peach	Cling peach
	Grapes	Concord grapes	Green seedless grapes
Tool	Hammer	Ball-peen hammer	Claw hammer
	Saw	Hack hand saw	Cross-cutting hand saw
	Screwdriver	Phillips screwdriver	Regular screwdriver
Clothing	Pants	Levi's	Double-knit pants
	Socks	Knee socks	Ankle socks
	Shirt	Dress shirt	Knit shirt
Furniture	Table	Kitchen table	Dining-room table
	Lamp	Floor lamp	Desk lamp
	Chair	Kitchen chair	Living-room chair
Vehicle	Car	Sports car	Four-door sedan car
	Bus	City bus	Cross-country bus
	Truck	Pickup truck	Tractor-trailer truck

From Rosch, E. H., Mervis, C. B., Gray, W. D., Johnson, D. M., and Boyes-Braem, P. Basic objects in natural categories. *Cognitive Psychology*, 1976, *8*, 382–440. Copyright 1976 by Academic Press, Inc. Reprinted by permission.

There are other criticisms of the traditional lab approach. Barsalou (1983) points out that to understand concepts we must acknowledge such facts as that certain categories like *things to sell at a garage sale* are useful and functional but that they are not as well established in memory as a concept like *fruit*. But the two criticisms we have mentioned, hierarchical structure and variations in the representativeness of instances, deserve further comment individually.

Hierarchical Organization

Rosch, Mervis, Gray, Johnson, and Boyes-Braem (1976) argued that the hierarchical nature of naturally occurring categories can best be understood by referring to the three levels depicted in Table 12.2. These levels reflect the fact that any given object can belong to several different but related categories. For example, you can refer to what you play as your *musical instrument*, your *guitar*, or your *folk guitar*. Or you can refer to what you drive as your *vehicle*, your *truck*, or your *pickup truck*.

Superordinate category levels are the most general. *Fruit, tools,* and *clothing* are examples of superordinate categories. *Subordinate* category levels are the most specific, including examples such as *Delicious apples, ball-peen hammer,* and *Levi's*. But notice that the *intermediate* category levels, containing examples such as *apple, hammer,* and *pants* are called *basic-level* categories by Rosch and her colleagues. They feel that this category level is the most important of the three— hence, the label *basic level*. They believe that categories at this level carry the most information and are the most different from one another. This is the first of the three types of categories we learn and is the most important in language (Reed, 1982).

Rosch, Mervis, Gray, Johnson, and Boyes-Braem (1976) identified some of the characteristics that make *basic-level categories* important:

1. *Common attributes.* Members of a given basic-level category have many attributes in common. For example, consider the basic-level category *pants.* You can think of a lot of attributes that all pants have in common, including legs, belt loops, waist, cloth, pockets, and so on. But now try to think of attributes that *all* instances of the corresponding *superordinate* category *clothing* have in common. It's not so easy, is it? And finally, try to think of attributes that all instances of the subordinate category *Levi's* have in common, above and beyond what is already included in the basic-level category *pants.* The point here is that most of the information is contained in the basic level.

2. *Common motor movements.* Instances of basic-level categories seem to have many motor movements in common. For example, we all put our pants on the same way, regardless of what kind of pants they are. Instances of superordinate categories have few movements in common. Specifically, can you think of any movements that are common to all examples of clothing? And adding a subordinate category doesn't add much new information about motor movements that is not already contained in the basic-level category (that is, we put on *Levi's* the same way we put on our *double-knits*). The point is that the increase in common motor movements is great as we move from superordinate to basic but very small, if at all, as we move from basic to subordinate.

3. *Common shapes.* All instances of superordinate categories don't have similar shapes. For example, all kinds of clothing do not look alike. But at the basic level, the shapes of most samples are similar. For instance, most pants look quite a bit alike. Examples at the subordinate level also show considerable overlap in shape, but not much more than at the basic level. Once again, the common shape increases greatly when we move from superordinate (*clothing*) to basic (*pants*) but not much further as we move to subordinate (*Levi's*).

4. *Object identification.* What do you call what you are sitting on right now? You call it a *chair.* You don't call it a *piece of furniture*, and you don't call it a *library chair* or a *wingback chair.* Rosch and her co-workers found that people prefer to identify an object by its basic-level name.

In summary, basic-level categories seem to be the most important of the three levels because examples at this level have many common attributes, have common associated motor movements, have common shapes, and tend to be used in identifying objects. Rosch's analyses of the complexity of the hierarchical relationships of categories is all part and parcel of the new look in concept research, which emphasizes natural rather than artificially defined concepts.

Family Resemblances

If you will recall, the second difference between the old laboratory approach and the new "natural" approach to the study of concepts has to do with the fact that the former approach does not account for the fact that instances of a given category may be more or less representative of that category. For example, the concept *vehicle* is well represented by *car* but not well represented by *elevator*. Rosch and Mervis (1975) use the phrase *family resemblance* to refer to how well instances of a category represent that category. Table 12.3 contains twenty members of six categories that have been ranked by subjects for their typicality, with Item 1 being the

Table 12.3   Typicality of Members in Six Superordinate Categories

			CATEGORY			
ITEM	FURNITURE	VEHICLE	FRUIT	WEAPON	VEGETABLE	CLOTHING
1	Chair	Car	Orange	Gun	Peas	Pants
2	Sofa	Truck	Apple	Knife	Carrots	Shirt
3	Table	Bus	Banana	Sword	String beans	Dress
4	Dresser	Motorcycle	Peach	Bomb	Spinach	Skirt
5	Desk	Train	Pear	Hand grenade	Broccoli	Jacket
6	Bed	Trolley car	Apricot	Spear	Asparagus	Coat
7	Bookcase	Bicycle	Plum	Cannon	Corn	Sweater
8	Footstool	Airplane	Grapes	Bow and arrow	Cauliflower	Underpants
9	Lamp	Boat	Strawberry	Club	Brussels sprouts	Socks
10	Piano	Tractor	Grapefruit	Tank	Lettuce	Pajamas
11	Cushion	Cart	Pineapple	Teargas	Beets	Bathing suit
12	Mirror	Wheelchair	Blueberry	Whip	Tomato	Shoes
13	Rug	Tank	Lemon	Icepick	Lima beans	Vest
14	Radio	Raft	Watermelon	Fists	Eggplant	Tie
15	Stove	Sled	Honeydew	Rocket	Onion	Mittens
16	Clock	Horse	Pomegranate	Poison	Potato	Hat
17	Picture	Blimp	Date	Scissors	Yam	Apron
18	Closet	Skates	Coconut	Words	Mushroom	Purse
19	Vase	Wheelbarrow	Tomato	Foot	Pumpkin	Wristwatch
20	Telephone	Elevator	Olive	Screwdriver	Rice	Necklace

From Rosch, E. H., and Mervis, C. B. Family resemblances: Studies in the internal structure of categories. *Cognitive Psychology*, 1975, 7 573–605. Copyright 1975 by Academic Press, Inc. Reprinted by permission.

most typical. The existence of these differences isn't so surprising; in fact, the rankings in Table 12.3 are much as we might expect. The interesting question is *why* these differences exist. Why is *knife* more typical of the category *weapon* than is *scissors*? By asking subjects to list attributes of the items in Table 12.3 and by then comparing attributes, Rosch and Mervis were able to find support for the following hypotheses:

1. Good members of a category share many attributes with other members of that category. For example, *car* has more in common with the other nineteen instances of *vehicle* than does *elevator*.
2. Good members of a category share few attributes with members of other categories. For example, *rocket* (a poor example of *weapon*) is more likely to have attributes in common with *vehicle* than is *gun* (a good example of *weapon*).

PROTOTYPES

How do we go about recognizing novel objects as members of categories? For example, how does a young child decide that a newly encountered animal is a *cat* rather than a *bird*? Two general classes of models are designed to answer this question: *prototype models* and *feature-frequency models*. This section describes prototype models, with feature-frequency models to follow. The prototype model suggests that we develop a prototype, or a *best example*, of the category and then compare novel patterns with that prototype in order to decide whether that novel stimulus belongs to that category (Armstrong, Gleitman, & Gleitman, 1983).

Consider the object in Figure 12.7. Is this object more like a rectangle or a triangle? Think carefully about what you do as you try to reach a decision. In some

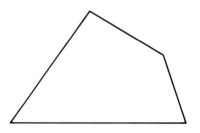

Figure 12.7 An ambiguous concept. Is this figure more like a triangle or a rectangle?

sense you compare Figure 12.7 with an ideal model, or pattern, of a rectangle, don't you? You do the same sort of thing with a pattern of an ideal triangle, too. These internal patterns of perfect triangles and rectangles are what psychologists call prototypes.

Some concepts seem to be more perceptual than logical in nature. In these cases learning a concept may be more like developing an idealized, internal "picture," or prototype, than like learning some logical rule that can be stated verbally. Once the pattern, or prototype, that defines a given concept is developed (for example, an internal picture of an ideal triangle), we can use that prototype to make decisions about any stimulus that is given to us. We can take a presented stimulus and "hold it up against" the prototype. We decide if a given stimulus is a member of the category (for example, *triangle*) by comparing the presented stimulus with the prototype. If it is similar enough, we include it. If it is too different, we reject it (see Figure 12.8).

Many concepts are defined better by prototypes than by logical rules. For example, consider the concept *chicken*. If someone showed you a bird that you had never seen before and asked you if it was a chicken, how would you go about making a decision? Would you start thinking about logical rules that define "chickenness"? Or would you somehow compare the overall appearance of the animal with your internal picture of an ideal chicken? You would probably use the prototype approach. In fact, you probably cannot even *think* of a logical rule that defines "chickenness," much less use such a rule to make a decision about category membership. But we all do have some internal prototype of *chicken* that we can use as a standard against which to judge new gallinaceous individuals.

A good deal of work has been done in connection with the prototype approach (see Franks & Bransford, 1971; Lasky & Kallio, 1978; Palmer, 1978; Peterson, Meagher, Chail, & Gillie, 1973; Posner, 1970, 1973; Posner, Goldsmith, & Welton, 1967; Posner & Keele, 1968; Rosch, 1977). This research suggests that we probably do form prototypes in connection with a great many concepts, especially when these concepts are of a perceptual rather than a logical nature. At the same time, however, we may develop and utilize logical rules that describe *how class members can differ from the prototype but still be members of the category* (see Lasky & Kallio, 1978). For example, we may have a *chicken* prototype within us

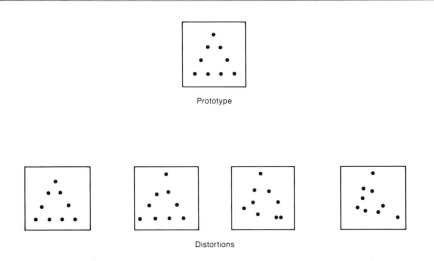

Prototype

Distortions

Figure 12.8 An example of one prototype and distortions of that prototype used by Posner and Keele to study prototype formation. Think about how you decide whether or not each of the distortions is a triangle. In some sense, you compare each of the distortions with the "best example" prototype. (From Posner, M. I., Goldsmith, R., and Welton, K. E., Jr. Perceived distance and the classification of distorted patterns. *Journal of Experimental Psychology*, 1967, 73, 28–38. American Psychological Association. Reprinted by permission.)

somewhere, but at the same time we may also have rules, such as "chickens usually have red wattles, but not always," that we use to reconcile differences between the ideal prototype and the new bird that we are considering.

In other words, and this should not surprise anyone, we probably use *both* prototypes and logical rules in deciding category membership. In fact, as noted, some feel that there may not be very much difference between rule learning and prototype formation. We are clever, and we use a number of strategies and techniques to accomplish this task.

FEATURE–FREQUENCY MODELS

Although comparing a novel stimulus with a prototype is one way to think about how we make decisions concerning category membership, there are other interpretations of the process. According to feature-frequency theory, we *count up* the number of features, or attributes, that our novel stimulus has in common with various categories and assign it to the category with which it has the most feature matches (see Kellogg, 1983; Toppino & Bucher, 1983).

It appears that both prototype and feature-frequency models can help us understand the process of classifying novel stimuli. But, as Reed (1982) points out, the situation is fairly complicated. He suggests that one type of model may be best with certain kinds of stimuli, whereas other stimuli may be best dealt with in terms of the alternative type of model.

ANIMALS AND CONCEPTS

Thus far we have been discussing concepts as though they were the property of humans alone. This is probably not true. Animals can form and use some concepts, too. They can distinguish between members of their own species and members of other species. This ability seems to involve concept formation, perhaps of the prototype variety. Cats have a very clear idea of what is, and what is not, a human. Many dogs seem to have a *mail carrier* concept. Most animals can discriminate easily between edible and inedible foods. Apes can apparently utilize language to a degree; this must involve the development and use of concepts. Wolves have been known to toss pieces of dried caribou skin, bark, and sticks about in a Frisbee-like fashion, suggesting the concept *toy*. Animals have enormously complicated communication systems, many of which probably involve the learning of concepts. For general reviews of concept formation, see Donahoe and Wessells (1980), Hulse, Fowler, and Honig (1978), and Pepperwood (1983).

Four-Choice Concept Learning

On a more experimental level, Bhatt, Wasserman, Reynolds, and Knauss (1988) and Wasserman, Kiedinger, and Bhatt (1988) demonstrated that pigeons can learn to classify stimuli from at least four different categories. The stimuli were color slides of objects such as cats, people, flowers, and cars. The pigeons were faced with four keys, each associated with one of the categories. Thus if a person appeared, a peck to one particular key would produce a reinforcement. If a flower appeared, a peck to another specific key would yield the desired reinforcement, and so on, with each key being associated with a particular class of objects. The authors found that the pigeons could master this task. Most important was the fact that, after some training, *new* stimuli, never before seen, could be categorized correctly, suggesting that conceptual behavior was involved.

The Oddity Concept

In spite of available demonstrations of animal concept formation, there is considerable controversy about exactly how well animals form concepts. The *oddity* concept is a case in point. In an oddity study the animal is required to indicate whether a presented stimulus is the same or different from a preceding stimulus. An example of a typical oddity study follows: A pigeon is faced with three keys. The center key lights up either red or green. A peck on this key lights up the side keys, one red and one green. Reinforcement then depends on which side key is pecked. If the experimenter is studying the formation of an oddity concept, then a peck to the side key that is different from the center key will be reinforced. The idea is that the pigeon is using an oddity concept; the "correct" key is the one that is different from the center key.

Of course, as the experiment has been outlined so far the pigeon may not be learning an oddity concept at all. It may merely be learning "If red, then green" and "If green, then red." To avoid this problem, after training on red and green has progressed, experimenters present two *novel* stimuli (blue and yellow, for example). If the animal masters this immediately then the evidence supports the involvement of an oddity concept. If performance in the blue and yellow situation is poor then there is little evidence for the use of the oddity concept. The available data are contradictory. It is probably fair to say that mastery of the oddity concept is limited to humans and chimpanzees. In other words, animals do use concepts, but not nearly as successfully as humans, particularly when the concepts are of an abstract nature (see Blough, 1989; D'Amato & Van Sant, 1988; Roberts & Mazmanian, 1988; Thomas & Noble, 1988; and Wright, Cook, Rivera, Sands, & Delius, 1988).

PROBLEM SOLVING

We now turn away from the topic of concept formation and direct our attention to what psychologists have learned about *problem solving*. Back in Chapter 1 we defined a problem as something that exists *when a motivated organism is trying to reach a goal but is blocked from doing so by an obstacle or obstacles*. Problems come in many shapes and forms, but they all involve the blockage of motive satisfaction. For example, problems can be rather simple, involving memory search (for example, "What is the longest word you can think of that spells the same thing forward and backward?"). Or problems can be very complex (for example, "How do we go about maintaining a worldwide balance of power?"). It is clear that each of us faces many different kinds of problems every day. Hence, it is also clear that a firm understanding of the processes involved in problem solving would be to our advantage.

It is not easy to distinguish among problems, concepts, and cognitive activity. We have already seen that some people think of all cognitive activity in terms of problem solving. We have also discovered that concept formation can be thought of as one type, or form, of problem solving, where the problem is to discover the correct concept.

For our purposes let us make the following distinctions. Cognitive activity is a more general term than problem solving, covering a wider range of activities. *Problem solving is one form of cognitive activity, but not the only one*. Many types of cognition, such as perceiving, imagining, and remembering, are not easily thought of as problem solving.

Although this may be an oversimplification, we have also seen that it is helpful to think of concept formation as one form of simple problem solving. Basically, the kinds of situations that have been studied under the label of problem solving tend to be more *complex* than those studied under the heading of concept formation (but see our section on natural categories).

For example, problem-solving tasks typically involve more possible solutions than concept-formation tasks. In a concept-formation task, on the one hand, often only a limited number of hypotheses are possible (for example, *red, black, circle, square*), and these are all provided by the experimenter. In problem solving, on the other hand, the number of possible answers can be almost unlimited, and none is provided by the experimenter (for example, *words that spell the same thing forward and backward*).

Furthermore, solving problems often (but not always) requires considerable *world knowledge* that is not explicitly stated in the problem. This is different from the typical concept-formation task, in which most of the required information is supplied by the experimenter. For example, finding the correct concept among *red, black, circle*, and *square* does not require the large vocabulary that is essential to finding long words that spell the same thing in both directions.

(a)

(b)

(c)

Figure 12.9 Insightful problem solving. A chimpanzee was faced with the problem of getting a bunch of bananas that was suspended out of reach (a). The chimp first stacked the boxes on top one another (b) and then climbed up them to reach the fruit (c). (Photos from The Three Lines.)

Given that we know that problem solving is one form of cognitive activity and that concept formation is one form of problem solving, we can turn to the important interpretations of problem solving, both classical and modern.

Gestalt Interpretations of Problem Solving

INSIGHT AND TRIAL AND ERROR.   One of the classic controversies in the field of problem solving concerns the issue of insight versus trial and error. Gestalt psychologists (see Wertheimer, 1945) argued that the solution to a problem is achieved in a "flash of insight." One minute you do not have the answer, and the next

Figure 12.10 Maier's (1931) string problem. The strings are to be tied together, but the subject cannot reach the two of them at the same time.

moment you do. It is something like a lightbulb being snapped on inside your head. The solution to the problem is assumed to be perceived in an all-or-none fashion. It is the, "Aha! I have it!" experience.

In contrast to this insight process, one can think of problem solving as a process of trial and error in which subjects plod along in a somewhat blind fashion, trying out different solutions until they stumble on the correct one. There is no "flash of insight" in this process; rather, the subjects do not even perceive the solution until after it has been discovered through trial-and-error activities.

In support of their insight interpretation Gestalt psychologists pointed out that problems are often solved *suddenly* and *permanently*. For example, suppose that a banana is suspended just beyond the reach of a chimpanzee in a cage containing several scattered boxes. The Gestalt psychologists observed that after several futile attempts to acquire the banana by reaching, some apes would become quiet for a moment and then, all of a sudden, stack the boxes, climb on top of them, and reach the banana, as if they had experienced a flash of insight. Once this solution was perceived, it tended not to be forgotten; it was permanent. Figure 12.9 depicts a chimpanzee solving the problem by stacking boxes on top of one another in the manner the Gestalt psychologists observed.

Another problem that is relevant to the question of insight versus trial and error (Maier, 1931) is shown in Figure 12.10. Two strings are hung from the ceiling of a room, and a subject is told to tie the ends of the strings together. The problem here is that the strings are too short for the subject to pick up one, walk over to the other, and tie them together; some other way to grasp both strings at once must be found. To help the subject, a number of objects are also in the room, including a hammer and a pair of pliers. (Stop here and try to solve the problem before going on.)

This problem can be solved quite simply by tying the hammer (or the pair of pliers) to one of the strings, swinging it like a pendulum, grasping the other string, catching the "pendulum," and then tying the strings together. To find this solution, however, the subject must stop thinking of the hammer as a tool and instead think of it as an object with mass that is capable of acting like a pendulum.

Gestalt psychologists observed that solutions in situations such as this one often have all the characteristics of the insight experience. The subjects, in fact, will often say, "I've got it," and proceed to solve the problem.

But does this kind of evidence really eliminate trial-and-error processes? Probably not. For example, it is entirely possible that the so-called insight experience is really nothing more than *mental trial and error*. As the subjects stand there holding one string and looking at the other, they may be "trying out" alternatives on a mental level. They will "try" various alternatives on a mental level without actually performing them on a physical level. Eventually, they will hit on the correct alternative and immediately recognize it as the right one. "Aha!" So even though we all do experience the flash of insight that the Gestalt psychologists were talking about, mental trial and error may be at the basis of this subjective experience. At present, there is no good way to resolve this controversy completely. It may well turn out that *both* trial and error and true insight operate in problem solving.

FUNCTIONAL FIXEDNESS.   Gestalt psychologists also introduced the interesting idea of *functional fixedness*. This refers to the fact that an object is defined by its uses. Consider the problem developed by Duncker (1945) (see also Weisberg, DiCamillo, & Phillips, 1978; Weisberg & Suls, 1973). A subject was given a candle, a book of matches, and a box of tacks and was told to "get the candle up on the wall so it will burn properly." (Again, stop reading and try to solve the problem.)

A solution to this problem that is frequently missed is to use the box containing the tacks as a "candleholder": Take the tacks out of the box, tack the box to the wall, and put the candle in the box. People tend not to think of using the box as part of the solution to the problem because they think of it as a container and not a "shelf"; the nature of the box is "functionally fixed." To solve the problem the subjects must overcome this tendency to think of the box as nothing more than a box; they must be able to think of using it in a new and unusual way. (See Box 12.1 for another example of avoiding functional fixedness in problem solving.)

Interestingly, Duncker presented his candle problem to subjects with the tacks either inside or outside the box. When the tacks were outside the box, more subjects were able to solve the problem, as the perception of the box as a container for the tacks was presumably lessened.

The Maier (1931) string problem mentioned above also contains the element of functional fixedness. To solve that problem the subject must overcome the tendency to think of the hammer or pair of pliers as tools and to break away into thinking about using them as pendulums.

The initial use of boxes as containers inhibits their later use as a shelf. The initial use of pliers as tools inhibits their use as a pendulum. In both cases the first experience inhibits the second. We will learn more about transfer effecs in problem solving, both positive and negative, in an upcoming section of this chapter.

Box 12.1 "Breaking Out" of Functional Fixedness

DEAR ABBY: With all the publicity you gave panty hose, I have a true story for you.

When Mt. St. Helens erupted in May of 1980, blowing the top 2,500 feet into the air, the volcanic ash was so heavy that in Spokane at 3 o'clock in the afternoon, it looked like midnight! In Yakima, Washington, breathing was difficult.

Automobiles sucked the ash into their air filters and the abrasion ruined the engines. When one family was stranded when their air filter became plugged, the husband removed the plugged filter, borrowed his wife's panty hose, wrapped them around the air intake as a filter, and they continued their trip in safety.

They were stopped by a highway patrolman near Moses Lake, Washington, where there was up to 7 inches of the volcanic stuff on the ground. (You can still see it.) The patrolman asked how they could keep going. They explained that they shook the ashes from the panty hose each time the engine quit.

The Highway Patrol then purchased panty hose for their cars and continued to help stranded motorists in that area. Panty hose saved many engines until proper filters could be installed.

KEN THELANDER, Seattle

DEAR KEN: Thank you for sharing your unusual story.

The experiments of the Gestalt psychologists are revealing demonstrations of problem solving, but they do not really tell us anything about *how* people solve problems. Great importance was placed on the role of insight, but the Gestalt experiments offer no clues about how or why someone suddenly interprets a string as the arm of a pendulum or a box as a candleholder. As in perception and memory, the vagueness of the Gestalt theories keeps them from being of significant use to us in truly understanding problem solving.

Subgoals

As the information-processing approach to psychology developed, however, theories better able to describe problem solving became available. Many of these theories suggest that the overall problem should *be broken down into a set of secondary goals, or subgoals, each more easily solved than the original.* Thus, the essence of making a plan is the definition of subgoals. Similarly, these subgoals might themselves need to be broken down into subgoals, and so on. Once the problem has been reduced to a set of directly solvable tasks, they can be carried out, and the problem can be solved.

For example, consider the problem of writing a book. It is tough to sit down and begin writing from page one. So we break the problem down into subgoals. We might set as a subgoal the development of a list of chapters. Then within each chapter we might address several issues. Writing about one issue within one chapter of the overall book is a subgoal that is not so difficult. Once that subgoal is reached, another can be tackled without having to panic over the somewhat overwhelming task of "writing a book." By dealing with smaller, more easily handled subgoals, we can solve the overall problem. A difficult, complex problem can be managed if it can be broken down into a set of smaller, simpler problems (see Miller, Galanter, & Pribram, 1960).

Algorithms

It is easy to say that the best strategy is to break complex problems down into simple ones, but deciding how to do that may be difficult. There may be several ways to divide up a problem, but only a few of these may actually increase the likelihood of reaching a solution. Sometimes the substeps we should take are quite clear and distinct, but sometimes they are not.

Let us consider first the case in which the subgoals are clear and obvious. Take, for example, a simple arithmetic problem, such as multiplying two numbers. There is a very specific set of actions that can be taken in this problem—defined by the laws of mathematics—and these actions can be applied to the multiplication problem in a very direct way to obtain an answer. In fact, these actions are so specific and well defined that, if they are properly applied in the proper order, a correct answer to the problem will *always* be obtained. As such, these actions represent what psychologists call an *algorithm* for multiplication. An algorithm is a procedure that, if correctly applied, will *always* result in success.

Heuristics

Unfortunately, we cannot always tell ahead of time how a problem should be broken down. We do not always have clear, simple rules that will always lead to a solution. We do not always have an algorithm for our problem. In these cases, we must turn to *heuristic* problem solving rather than algorithmic problem solving. In heuristic problem solving we try to make good *guesses* about what might be the best way to handle the problem.

Consider the game of chess, for example: No simple set of actions exists for chess—the game is simply too complex. We cannot win a chess game in the same way that we solve a multiplication problem; we do not have a set of clear, simple actions to follow. But there are general "hints" that, if observed, will greatly increase our chance of winning. These are the kinds of suggestions that we can find in a chess book: "Keep your knights off the edges of the board." "Protect your queen above all else." And so on. These rules are the *heuristics* of chess. They are based on a sound understanding of what is needed to win, and, although they will not *guarantee* success, they greatly improve our chances. Observing these and other heuristics will sometimes prevent us from finding a winning solution (for instance, in a game in which we have to sacrifice our queen in order to win), but, more often than not, they will help us find a solution to the problem.

Thus, heuristic problem solving, which is probably very common in our everyday life, involves making educated guesses about what would be the best way to solve a problem. For example, suppose that you wish to become the friend of an attractive person. You do not quite know how to do it. That is, you do not have a clear algorithm for the problem. So you make some educated guesses. You know that the person is shy, so you do not just jump all over him. You adopt a cautious, casual approach. You know that he likes the out-of-doors, so you try talking about nature. You do your best to break the problem down into simpler subproblems, based on your best guess about what will work. You search through all of the possible things that you might do and try to find a sequence of actions that will lead to success (see also Nisbett, Krantz, Jepson, & Kunda, 1983).

Strategies: Working Backward

Thus far we have noted that problem solution can be facilitated by defining sub-goals and by making educated guesses about what to do to solve the problem. In addition, psychologists have noted that there are overall strategies that can be adopted in our attempts to apply heuristics and generate subgoals.

For example, Newell and Simon (1972) discuss the strategy of *working backward*. In a very complex problem it is easy to work on the problem without knowing whether you are really making any progress. Something is being done, but it may not be taking you any closer to the solution. This is especially true when the problem has only one solution (as opposed to games such as chess, which have many winning positions). In such problems working backward can be a very useful strategy. The idea is to reverse the problem so that you start with the goal and try to reach the given information. Solving a problem in this way still requires effort, but because your work is always in direct contact with the goal, many "blind alleys" can be avoided.

Suppose that you want to trace a route from New York to San Francisco on a road map. You could start in New York and work your way west. But because you will not be able to predict what is ahead, you may end up on a detour to Des Moines. If you start in San Francisco and work backward toward New York, however, you may be able to avoid some of these "dead ends."

Many other strategies can be adopted in problem solving. As Sweller (1983) points out, exactly which strategy you follow will depend on the nature of the problem and your understanding of that problem. With one type of problem, for example, you might decide that your best strategy is to take your past moves into account each time you consider a new move, whereas in another situation you might deem past moves irrelevant.

Protocol Analysis

Thus far it has been suggested that, when solving problems, people do the following:

1. They break large problems down into simpler, smaller problems.
2. They make guesses about what would be best to do to solve the problem.
3. They follow overall strategies in their efforts to find a solution.

You might reasonably ask what kinds of data lead psychologists to conclude that these three principles of problem solving are valid. Some of the work on problem solving involves *protocol analysis*, or the study of the verbal reports that subjects give while they are solving a problem. In essence, the subjects "think out loud" while solving the problem, and the psychologist then examines these reports.

Needless to say, many investigators through the years have objected to the use of this sort of self-reporting. They have argued that self-reports are generally unreliable and that subjects do not really know or cannot really tell you what they are doing. Nonetheless, it appears that, even though these data are unacceptable to some, the careful analysis of subjects' protocols, combined with more objective measures when possible, has significantly advanced our understanding of problem solving. Let's look at the kind of problem-solving situation in which subjects' verbal reports have been recorded.

One type of problem that has been studied extensively by protocol analysis is the "cryptarithmetic" problem. A set of letters is arranged in the form of an arithmetic problem, such as:

$$
\begin{array}{r}
\text{DONALD} \\
+ \ \text{GERALD} \\
\hline
\text{ROBERT}
\end{array}
$$

Each letter stands for a different digit from 0 to 9, and the value of one of the letters is given (here, D = 5). The subject's goal is to figure out the values of the other letters. (Again, you might stop and try solving this problem. This is a tough one.)

Logically speaking, the information that D is equal to 5 is all that is needed to solve the problem. As a start, it is clear that, because D = 5, the T in the right-hand column must be 0. This is because D (5) plus D (5) must equal (10). The values of the other letters can be deduced in similar ways. The general procedure is to ask the subjects to talk out loud as they work. (The solution is T = 0, G = 1, O = 2, B = 3, A = 4, D = 5, N = 6, R = 7, L = 8, E = 9.) Then, by looking at what subjects have said, the investigator can determine if subgoals were established, if heuristics were employed, and if strategies were followed.

Both Bartlett (1958) and Newell and Simon (1972) have studied this particular problem. What they found was that the steps reported by subjects generally conformed to the three principles of problem solving that we have been discussing. Subjects do break down the overall problem into smaller problems, they do make "best guesses" about what to do, and they can and do follow strategies (such as working backward).

Transfer in Problem Solving

What transfer effects result from solving a series of related problems? We have already seen that both positive and negative transfer effects can sometimes occur. Sometimes solving one or more problems will *help* you to solve subsequent problems, and sometimes it will *hinder* your solution of those subsequent problems.

As an example of positive transfer, we can note that monkeys required to solve successive discrimination problems become better and better at it until, after several hundred similar problems, they are able to solve additional problems in one trial. And you certainly remember that practice on successive math problems helped you to quickly solve similar problems.

The functional-fixedness effect described earlier represents an instance of negative transfer in problem solving. Perhaps an even clearer example is provided by Luchins's (1942) "water jug" problem. Subjects were asked, "Given three jugs that contain 21, 127, and 3 quarts, how would you measure 100 quarts?" Nearly all of Luchins's subjects reported filling the largest jar and then removing 27 quarts with

Table 12.4   Jar Problems

	JAR CAPACITIES			AMOUNT OF WATER TO
PROBLEM	JAR A	JAR B	JAR C	BE OBTAINED
1	21	127	3	100
2	14	163	25	99
3	18	43	10	5
4	9	42	6	21
5	20	59	4	31
6	23	49	3	20
7	10	27	7	3

In each case, use a water tap and the jars to obtain the amount of water in the right-hand column.

the help of the other two jars. Subjects then went on to solve a second problem: "How would you measure 20 quarts with 23, 49, and 3 quart jars?" Surprisingly, 81% of Luchins's subjects solved this problem by a method identical to the first problem, one that involved all three jars; control subjects uniformly solved it the simple way, by filling the 23-quart jar and taking out 3 quarts (see Table 12.4 for additional examples). Thus, previous experience with a particular kind of problem can both help and hurt our subsequent efforts to solve additional problems (see also Table 12.5).

But even though positive and negative transfer effects in problem solving have been identified, the situation is far from clear. Positive transfer effects are often weak or nonexistent. One theme that does seem to appear repeatedly is the idea that the occurrence of positive transfer seems to depend on *how* the initial problem was solved. For example, Mayer (1974) found that subjects who were initially taught to solve problems by algorithm (rule) did best when transferred to nearly identical problems. Subjects taught to solve problems by a heuristic method (discovery), in turn, did better on subsequent problems that required significant understanding of the problem's concepts (see also Jeffries, 1979; Perfetto, Bransford, & Franks, 1983).

Table 12.5   Another Example of Negative Transfer

Read the words *aloud* from top to bottom.

MACARTHUR
MACINTOSH
MACCARTHY
MACBETH
MACDOWELL
MACKENZIE
MACDONALD
MACHINES
MACDILLON

Now look at the next-to-last word.
You may have mispronounced it.

Knowledge and Problem Solving

Closely related to the question of transfer in problem solving is the issue of how important knowledge about the general domain of a problem is in the solution of a problem. Specifically, if you know more about a problem area, are you more likely to be able to solve problems in that area? Can biologists, with training and knowledge in the field of biology, solve problems related to biology faster and more easily than people without knowledge of biology? Can lawyers solve legal problems faster than nonlawyers?

The intuitive answer is yes, and the data support that hunch. Generally speaking, knowledge about a given area can facilitate problem solution within that area. Prior knowledge "transfers" to the current problem.

Let us look at a couple of examples of the way in which knowledge aids problem solving. DeGroot (1946, 1965) assembled a group of chess experts and a group of novices. He compared these two groups in terms of general memory ability and found that they were equivalent; the chess experts did not have better memory abilities than novices. Next, both groups were shown two arrangements of chess pieces on a board, forming either a meaningful board arrangement (taken from the middle of an actual chess game) or simply a random arrangement of the pieces on the board. Each board was exposed for a few seconds, and the subjects were then asked to reconstruct the placement of the pieces to the best of their ability. De-Groot found that the experts were better than the novices at reproducing the meaningful board positions but were no better than the novices when it came to recalling the random positions. This suggests that the experts somehow were better able to use their past, intensive experience with the game to recognize and encode board positions into a set of meaningful chunks, such as "the castled black king is forked by a knight." They did not have to remember the locations of many isolated individual pieces. This ability to chunk, or recognize and remember, *patterns* of two or more pieces, rather than isolated locations, naturally led to superior recall by the experts on the meaningful positions.

Thus, it can be argued that experts' ability to win games (solve problems) is facilitated by knowledge about common (and not so common) patterns of pieces that occur in the game. Their task in planning future moves is greatly simplified. They can think about alternative changes of simple patterns, or chunks, each involving two or more pieces, rather than having to remember and consider alternative placements of each and every piece (see also Anderson, 1985).

The fact that knowledge about a field can aid problem solving has been demonstrated in other areas, too. For example, Reitman (1976) has found similar effects when comparing Go masters with novices at the game of Go. The importance of knowledge in solving computer-programming problems has been described by Reitman, McKeithen, Rueter, and Hirtle (1980). Finally, Bhaskar and Simon (1977) report findings suggesting that general knowledge about chemical engineering can facilitate the solution of chemical-engineering problems.

But before we all go running off convinced that prior knowledge *always* helps problem solving, we should note that there are exceptions. For example, Weisberg, DiCamillo, and Phillips (1978) had subjects first learn a paired associate composed of the word *candle* and *box* embedded in a list of similar paired associates. The subjects then tried to solve the candle-on-the-wall problem described earlier

(Duncker, 1945). That was the problem in which subjects were given a candle, matches, and a box of tacks and asked to mount the lighted candle on the wall.

If prior information always helped problem solution, you would expect these subjects to do well on the problem. After all, they had almost been given the answer in the form of the *candle–box* paired associate. But these authors found a facilitative effect only under certain circumstances. Specifically, if before trying to solve the problem the subjects were told that one of the just-learned paired associates could help them solve the problem, then it did. But if the subjects were told nothing about the relevance of the paired associates, their performance was not improved. Thus, simple knowledge about a problem, without a realization of the relevance of that knowledge, is not enough to aid problem solution.

Planning and Problem Solving

Planning a sequence of steps appears to be important in problem solving. Although planning may not be all that crucial in some simple, artificial laboratory problems, real-life problems do seem to benefit from some planning. More complex problems often need more planning. For example, Hayes-Roth and Hayes-Roth (1979) studied how people go about a series of errands in a given day. In solving this sort of problem subjects go to great extremes in planning where to go, when, and in what order. We all are familiar with this experience, so we do not need to go into detail. The point is that a little planning saves backtracking and wasted effort (see also Hanley & Levine, 1983).

Ill-Defined Problems

Ill-defined problems are *problems for which we have no clear way of judging whether a solution is correct.* When we are faced with building a house, selecting a course, or composing a musical composition, we are certainly faced with important problems. But even when we have "solved" them, we are not sure that our solution is the best one. People can disagree about any solution at which we arrive. Some people will feel that their new house is "just perfect," and others might conclude that they could never live with those "funny windows."

Ill-defined problems are troublesome because (1) they may actually be more common in our everyday life than well-defined problems and (2) they lead to continued uncertainty: "Should I have gone to medical school?" "Should we have painted the walls blue?" With well-defined problems (for example, How much is 2 + 2?) there is no disagreement and uncertainty about the solution. But with ill-defined problems there always is.

Still, life must go on, and we must solve ill-defined problems. How do we do it? Matlin (1983) has outlined several strategies we use, as follows:

1. We break the problem down into several subproblems. We might say, "Look, let's just worry about the design of the kitchen today and leave the rest for later."
2. We can add structure to the situation that limits possibilities. "So we agree it will be a modern design with lots of redwood. Now, what can we do within those constraints?"

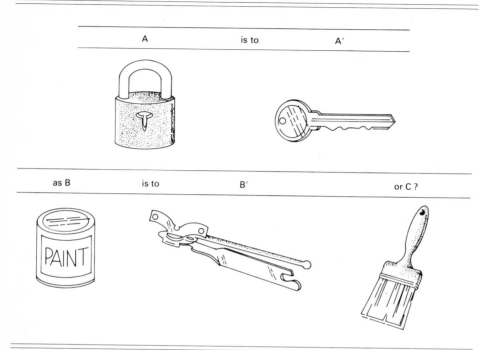

Figure 12.11 Materials used in demonstrating that chimps can solve problems using analogical reasoning. (Adapted from Gillan, D. J., Premack, D., and Woodruff, G. Reasoning in the chimpanzee I. Analogical reasoning. *Journal of Experimental Psychology,* 1981, 7, 1–17. Copyright 1981 by the American Psychological Association. Reprinted by permission.)

3. We can start work on the problem before we fully understand it. "Let's just go ahead and put in the bathroom there. Later we'll see how everything else will fit."

4. We can stop before the "perfect" solution is reached. "It's good enough. I like it. Let's quit."

ANIMALS AND PROBLEMS

As we have seen, animals are capable of solving many problems. And in Chapter 13 we will address the fascinating subject of language use by apes. But to close this chapter we will describe an example of animal problem solving that underlines the fact that animals are capable of very complex cognitive activity. Gillan, Premack, and Woodruff (1981) wanted to find out if chimps could solve problems involving analogical reasoning. The materials they used are shown in Figure 12.11. The general form of the problem was, "A is to A′ as B is to which of two alternatives, B′ or C?" A lock (A) is to a key (A′) as a closed paint can (B) is to which of the two alternatives, a can opener (B′) or a paint brush (C)? The chimps were able to handle this problem; they chose B′, indicating that they understood that a lock is to a key as a closed can is to a can opener. This seems to demonstrate considerable reasoning power on the part of the animal.

SUMMARY

1. Cognition may be defined in at least five ways: as information processing, as manipulation of mental symbols, as problem solving, as thinking, and as a collection of mental processes.
2. A concept is a symbol that stands for a class of objects or events that possess common attributes.
3. Concepts can be verbal or nonverbal, can be simple or complex, and are related to one another in complicated ways. They help us think.
4. Concept formation can be thought of as a special kind of problem solving.
5. In a typical experiment subjects are asked to judge whether successive stimuli, which vary along a number of dimensions, are members of the concept the experimenter has in mind.
6. Concept learning may involve attribute discovery, rule discovery, or both.
7. Concept-learning difficulty increases as rule complexity increases.
8. The old *S-R interpretation* of concept learning argues that concept formation is similar to stimulus discrimination. This interpretation avoids having to think about what goes on "in the mind."
9. But the *hypothesis-testing* approach has pretty well replaced the older S-R conception. According to this view, subjects test successive guesses, or hypotheses, about what the correct hypothesis is. Hypotheses are tested and rejected until the correct one is discovered.
10. In *conservative-focusing* experiments the subject can demand to have any stimulus classified, rather than having to wait until that stimulus appears in a random order, as is the case in most concept experiments. In conservative focusing the subject focuses on one dimension at a time and investigates it thoroughly before moving on to another dimension.
11. Conservative focusing is an excellent strategy, but only when the subject is free to call for certain stimuli and only when the concept involves a single dimension.
12. Levine's work with response patterns during *blank trials* allows us to determine what hypothesis, if any, people are using and when, and to what hypothesis they change.
13. Levine's work has been challenged on a number of fronts.
14. Natural categories, as distinct from experimenter-defined laboratory categories, are hierarchical.
15. Superordinate, basic-level, and subordinate categories have been defined.
16. Basic-level categories have common attributes, motor movements, and shapes. Members of these categories are also used to identify objects.
17. Instances of a category may be more or less representative of that category.
18. Complex concept formation has been thought of as prototype formation.
19. Feature-frequency models of concept formation have also been developed.
20. In prototype formation an ideal pattern, or image, of the concept (such as *triangle*) is developed and used as a standard against which to judge any given stimulus that is to be categorized.
21. However, it also appears that, even when a prototype is used, rules are developed that indicate just how much a stimulus can differ from the prototype and still be called a member of the category. Thus, both rules and prototypes are probably used simultaneously.

22. Animals form and use concepts, including the mastery of four-choice concept learning.
23. Nevertheless, there is no doubt that humans can learn more abstract concepts than other animals. For example, animals other than humans and chimpanzees probably cannot learn an oddity concept.
24. *Problems* exist when a motivated organism is blocked from reaching a goal.
25. Problem solving is one form of cognitive activity.
26. Gestalt psychologists emphasize the *flash of insight* in problem solving. They note that problem solving is often sudden and permanent.
27. But the insight experience may be nothing more than the result of *mental trial and error*.
28. *Functional fixedness* refers to a failure to solve a problem because one or more of the available elements is perceived as being usable only in a limited, prescribed, unhelpful manner.
29. People can solve problems by breaking them down into simpler problems, or *subgoals*, each of which is easier to solve than the overall problem.
30. *Algorithmic* problem solving is said to occur when a procedure that will always lead to a correct solution is followed.
31. *Heuristic* problem solving occurs when we make reasoned guesses about what might be the best thing to do. This process helps problem solving but does not guarantee a correct solution.
32. Organisms follow overall strategies while solving problems, such as working backward.
33. In protocol analysis the subjects' self-reports of what they are doing during problem solving are examined.
34. Positive and negative transfer effects can sometimes, but not always, be demonstrated in problem solving.
35. Knowledge about the general domain of a problem can facilitate problem solution.
36. Planning helps problem solving, particularly with complex problems.
37. Ill-defined problems are those for which we have no clear way of judging whether a solution is correct.
38. There are several strategies for solving ill-defined problems.
39. Animals can solve complex problems.

CHAPTER

13

LANGUAGE

THE IMPORTANCE OF LANGUAGE

Did you ever stop to consider the fact that, by spending a few days in your local library, you can know more about physics than Galileo ever knew, more about psychology than Freud ever dreamed of, and more about natural selection than Darwin was aware of? Language contributes to this ability. It ensures, through written and spoken records, that knowledge is cumulative and that we will not have to rediscover everything that our ancestors discovered. Language enables us to stockpile information. It allows us to build on previous information. It certainly allows us to store information in excess of the capacity of our immediate memory.

In addition, language allows us to communicate with one another in highly so-phisticated ways. It is true that animals of many species communicate with one another. They do have their own interesting languages. Bees can communicate the location of a food source by varying their bodily movements (von Frisch, 1974). Their famous "waggle dance" can convey information not only about direction but distance as well (Gould, 1982). Birds, too, have complex forms of communication. Birds' songs can and do convey courtship rituals, territorial claims, mate location, and alarm signals (Gould, 1982; Marler & Peters, 1981). And, as we shall see in the last section of this chapter, apes appear capable of using the rudiments of language as we know it. But in general, animal communication is limited when compared with that of the human being. We are the true masters of language, and our use of language seems to set us apart from the rest of the animal kingdom.

The use of language is such an everyday activity for us that we take it for granted. Even the simplest studies of language show, however, that language comprehen-sion and use is incredibly complex. Language is so intertwined with our thought processes that it is difficult to imagine what thinking would be like without it.

Hence, if we are to understand the so-called higher, or cognitive, mental proc-esses, we must also comprehend language processes. Even though some cognitive events may not involve language, so much of our thinking does involve language that the two can hardly be understood in isolation from each other. Table 13.1 lists

Table 13.1   Some Common Ways Humans Use Language

Solving problems
Describing events
Describing objects
Telling others what to do
Acting
Teaching
Guessing or answering
Telling stories
Asking questions
Expressing emotions
Greeting and thanking people
Singing
Reading
Speculating
Predicting and reporting
Daydreaming
Translating
Learning and storing information
Creating

some of the ways in which we use language. You can probably think of some additional examples.

In summary, language helps us in at least three important ways:

1. It helps us communicate effectively.
2. It allows us to store enormous amounts of information.
3. It aids our thought processes by providing a system of symbolic representation.

The study of language use and language learning is a wide-ranging field, touching on many of the issues that we have already discussed in this text. In this chapter we shall first consider language development. Then, in increasing order of complexity, we shall explore the nature and storage of *words*, the construction, comprehension, and retention of *sentences*, and memory for *prose*. Finally, in keeping with our concern about the relationship between animal and human learning, we shall discuss language in apes.

LANGUAGE DEVELOPMENT

In this section on language development we describe briefly the steps that humans follow in their initial acquisition of language. We do not intend to theorize about mechanisms underlying language (that is saved for later sections) but, rather, to outline some of the interesting regularities that appear in our early life.

Aside from crying, coughing, sneezing, and hiccuping, the sounds that newborn babies make are quite limited. But it is not too many months before most babies begin to put out an impressive array of verbal sounds, usually called *babbling*. This babbling, which often seems to be done with great enthusiasm, contains many of the basic sounds of full-blown adult speech. It seems as if the very basic verbal units, or sounds, are almost innate. At the very least they occur spontaneously and do not need to be "learned" in the sense that they must be practiced before they are perfected. It almost seems that the acquisition of language refers to the ordering and organizing of units of sound that are given, or innate.

Evidence shows that *all* human babies, regardless of where they live or under what conditions, engage in comparable amounts and types of babbling (see Atkinson, MacWhinney, & Stoel, 1970; Lenneberg, 1967). The environment does not seem to have much of an initial impact on this babbling. As we grow and interact with the environment, however, we begin to restrict our vocalizations to those that compose the elements of the language spoken in our environment. Chinese children begin to concentrate on the sounds that make up the Chinese language. French children begin to make "French" sounds. By the time we are adults, we find it difficult to produce the sounds necessary for another language, even though we could do it as infants.

At about 1 year of age (the time varies from child to child), children begin to acquire a few words. They are on their way to building a vocabulary. Although it starts slowly, the acquisition of a vocabulary soon accelerates. By the time they are 5 years old, children may have a vocabulary of several thousand words. Growth of the vocabulary can continue throughout life. For example, you will now add to your vocabulary by learning that *holophrastic speech* (McNeil, 1970) refers to the fact that young children often use a single word to express an entire idea. For instance, a child may say, "No," but mean, "No, I don't want to be put down. Hold me and tell me wonderful things." Children apparently understand much more than they are able to verbalize.

The first sentences children produce, at somewhere around the age of 18 months, tend to be composed of two words. The child will say, "More juice," or "No bed," or "See baby." Again, starting slowly, the child soon accelerates in the acquisition of two-word sentences, using several thousand different ones by the age of 2 to 2½.

Telegraphic speech refers to the tendency of children at this age to maintain the correct order of words but to leave out many of the less important ones. For example, a child might say, "Doggie baby," meaning "The doggie licked the baby." The understanding is there, but the technical language ability is not.

Between 2 and 3, children begin to produce longer sentences. More complex grammatical forms appear. Children vary widely in how quickly they acquire language. Some are amazingly quick about it, whereas others learn more slowly. Still, it is fair to say that almost all children show quite rapid development in this area. We are "born to talk," and we waste little time getting to it.

Interestingly, even though some children acquire grammar faster than others, the *order* in which that grammar is learned seems to be constant from child to child. They learn the rules of grammar in the same sequence even though the rate of acquisition may differ. For example, adding the suffix *-ing* appears early, whereas adding *'s* to indicate possession usually occurs later (see Table 13.2). Finally, children seem to try out, or test, various guesses, or hypotheses, about what is correct grammar. Through feedback from the adult world they appear to alter and correct their hypotheses. They do not just jump right in with a complete copy of adult speech.

THEORIES OF LANGUAGE ACQUISITION
The Conditioning Approach

Language acquisition has been interpreted in a number of ways. For example, the acquisition of word meaning has been thought of in terms of classical conditioning. The spoken word *doggie* is repeatedly paired with a real dog and its actions. The spoken word *doggie* is a CS, whereas the actual dog is the UCS. Whatever reaction the child has to the real dog will become classically conditioned to the word *doggie* and will constitute its meaning.

Similarly, language acquisition has been thought of in terms of instrumental conditioning. Each time a young child says a word or uses a little sentence, he or she is praised and rewarded by adults. Just as a rat learns to press a bar for food reinforcement, the child learns to speak and use language in return for social rewards (see Bloom, 1975; Bloom & Esposito, 1975).

Shaping is probably important in the instrumental conditioning of languages. For example, if a 2-year-old says, "See my 'flection?" she will be rewarded, because to say *'flection* at that age represents a pretty close approximation of *reflection*. But as the child grows older, adults will demand closer and closer approximations to the word *reflection* before a reward will be delivered.

These conditioning interpretations of language acquisition have been severely criticized. Specifically, it has been argued that language acquisition is too complex

Table 13.2   The Approximate Order in Which Children Acquire Some Selected Grammatical Rules*

ITEM	EXAMPLE
1. Present progressive: *ing*	He is sitt*ing* down.
2. Preposition: *in*	The mouse is *in* the box.
3. Preposition: *on*	The book is *on* the table.
4. Plural: *-s*	The dog*s* ran away.
5. Past irregular: e.g., *went*	The boy *went* home.
6. Possessive: *-'s*	The girl'*s* dog is big.
7. Uncontractible copula *be*: e.g., *are, was*	*Are* they boys or girls? *Was* that a dog?
8. Articles: *the, a, an*	He has *a* book.
9. Past regular: *-ed*	He jump*ed* the stream.
10. Third person regular: *-s*	She run*s* fast.
11. Third person irregular: e.g., *has, does*	*Does* the dog bark?
12. Uncontractible auxiliary *be*: e.g., *is, were*	*Is* he running? *Were* they at home?
13. Contractible copula *be*: e.g., *'s, -re*	That'*s* a spaniel. They'*re* pretty.
14. Contractible auxiliary *be*: e.g., *-'s, -'re*	He'*s* doing it. They'*re* running slowly.

*Although some children may acquire these elements faster than others, all children tend to follow the same order of acquisition.

Adapted from Clark, H. H., and Clark, E. V. *Psychology and Language.* New York: Harcourt Brace Jovanovich, 1977, after Brown, R. A. *First language: The early stages.* Cambridge, MA: Harvard University Press, 1973. Reprinted by permission of the publisher.

to be interpreted in terms of a simple S-R framework. It has been pointed out that language use has a *generative, creative* aspect, which is difficult to reconcile with simple S-R notions. Children use language in new and novel ways, as though they are testing hypotheses. They generate new language patterns that they have never heard before.

The Psycholinguistic Approach

All of these criticisms, coupled with other developments, have led to what is generally known as the *psycholinguistic* approach to language acquisition. There are two important aspects of the psycholinguistic approach. First, humans are seen as genetically prepared to acquire and use language. We are ready and willing, in a biological sense, to acquire language. Box 13.1 contains some of the reasons why many people emphasize a biological component of human language use. Second, proponents of the psycholinguistic approach argue that we learn to use rules and test hypotheses when we acquire language, rather than learning specific S-R connections. Although the psycholinguistic approach does not necessarily disprove the S-R approach, it has become the favored way of thinking about language acquisition. In the following sections we shall be using the language of the *psycholinguistic approach*. At the same time you should keep in mind that the older S-R conditioning approach, although out of vogue, has not been completely discredited. For

---

Box 13.1 Is Language Innate?

Some of the reasons why investigators have argued that language has an innate biological quality are listed below.

1. Humans possess many anatomical specializations related to language use from the shape and placement of the larynx to specialization of language functions in the left hemisphere of the brain.
2. Damage to certain parts of the brain (in the left hemisphere only) lead to damaged or lost linguistic abilities. Moreover, time of damage during childhood is related to clinical outcome. Damage to the left hemisphere during the first few years of life can be overcome; after puberty it cannot be.
3. Language cannot be suppressed. Studies of completely untutored deaf children found that they spontaneously invent sign language to use with each other.
4. The time of onset and early steps of language learning are universal around the world.
5. The early sequence of language acquisition is closely correlated with motor development, which is known to be due entirely to maturation. Just as children kept swaddled begin to walk at the same time as unswaddled children, Lenneberg reports a baby at the babbling stage who was tracheostomized for six months, and who picked up babbling not where she left off but where she should have been when the tracheostomy was reversed.
6. Language cannot be taught to any other species. Although this claim is controversial, it is not clearly false.
7. Linguistic universals do exist.
8. Certain forms of aphasia (disordered language) are inheritable.
9. Timing of speech onset and onset of speech deficits (if any) are more similar between identical than between fraternal twins.
10. So-called wolf-children denied access to speech until adolescence cannot learn language despite intensive tutoring, while similar children discovered at an earlier age can learn language.
11. Language is present in all cultures.

According to Lenneberg (1969) as summarized by Leahey, T. H., and Harris, R. J. *Human learning*, second ed., © 1989, pp. 355–356. Adapted by permission of Prentice Hall, Inc., Englewood Cliffs, N.J.

---

example, to note that we learn rules when we learn language is not to deny the validity of the conditioning approach. The use of the rule is reinforced just as more discrete, identifiable responses are reinforced.

WORDS: STRUCTURE AND STORAGE

Having briefly looked at the development of language in the human infant, let us turn our attention to what psychologists have learned about the nature of language. The rest of this chapter will be devoted to increasingly complex levels of language. Specifically, a consideration of the structure and storage of *words* will be followed by a discussion of how words are combined into meaningful *sentences*. Finally, the grouping of these sentences into meaningful *prose* will be considered.

Phonemes and Morphemes

All spoken languages are composed of between 15 and 85 basic sounds. English consists of something like 45 sounds rearranged in many ways. These basic sounds, or building blocks, are called *phonemes* by linguists and psychologists. Many of the English phonemes correspond to the sounds of the letters of the alphabet, although some of them involve combinations of letter sounds. Thus the *t* sound at the beginning of *tack* is a phoneme, and so is the *sh* sound at the beginning of *should*.

Phonemes alone generally have no meaning. They must be combined with one another to form meaningful units. These combinations of phonemes are called *morphemes*. Morphemes are the smallest meaningful units in a language. A morpheme is most often, but not always, composed of two or more phonemes. For example, the words *a* and *I* are morphemes composed of single phonemes.

Many, but not all, morphemes are words. For example, *run* and *tap* are morphemes that are also words. But prefixes and suffixes such as *pre-* and *-ness* are also morphemes even though they are not words. They are morphemes because they have meaning, as in *pre*judged and happi*ness*, even though they are not words by themselves. Many words are composed of single morphemes, such as *run* and *tap*. But many other words are composed of more than one morpheme. Thus, *helpful* is a word composed of two meaningful morphemes (*help* and *-ful*).

Languages have rules about the ways in which phonemes and morphemes can be combined into "legal," or acceptable, words. For example, certain phoneme combinations are not acceptable in English. How many English words can you think of that begin with *hp*? None, because this combination is not acceptable under the rules of English. For that matter, an initial *h* is never followed by b, c, d, f, g, h, j, k, l, m, n, p, q, r, s, t, v, w, x, or z, unless somebody has slipped in a new one. Thus, of the 26 letters of the alphabet only 6 (a, e, i, o, u, y) are allowed to occur after *h* at the beginning of a word. These rules, shared by a population, make communication possible. If a group of people agrees on a set of rules for the construction of legal words and abides by these understood rules, then communication occurs without the problems that would happen if everyone had different rules about word construction.

Lexical Memory: Semantic Networks

Before turning to the study of the arrangement of words into sentences and sentences into prose, brief mention should be made of word storage, or lexical memory and meaning. Psychologists have long been interested in the meanings of words and in the storage of those meanings.

Perhaps the most noticeable property of words is that they are associated with other words. The notion of associations among words is not new and dates back at least as far as Aristotle, whose ideas were a starting point for psychology to begin its study of word meaning. According to this early approach, the meaning of a word is, in some sense, defined by its association with other words. Some have argued that the meaning of a word *is* the constellation of words that are associated with it. We have already had a chance to look at some word-association experiments in Chapter 11 (see also Deese, 1962; Garskof & Houston, 1963).

While fruitful, the word-association approach was short lived. However, several different approaches to the understanding of lexical storage and word meaning grew out of the realization that the word-association approach was an oversimplification of a very complex situation.

In Chapter 9 we outlined some of the other available conceptions of word storage, most of which can be subsumed under the heading of semantic-network models. Hence, all we need do here is refresh our memory with respect to these newer models and point out that they serve as, among other things, conceptions of lexical memory. If you will recall, these models included *hierarchies* (Collins & Quillian, 1972), *matrices* (Broadbent, Cooper, & Broadbent, 1978), *feature models* (Smith, Shoben, & Rips, 1974), and *spreading-activation* conceptions (Collins & Loftus, 1975).

These approaches to the understanding of word storage substantially advanced our knowledge of language processes and provided better ways of thinking about how the information we have in our head is organized (see also Anderson, 1983; Hayes-Roth & Hayes-Roth, 1975; McClosky & Glucksberg, 1979; Yantis & Meyer, 1988). This work also foreshadowed much of the recent attention given to sentences and prose, to which we now turn.

SENTENCES

Having looked at lexical memory, or memory for words, in Chapters 9 and 11 and having reviewed this topic in the preceding section, we are ready to move on to the next major division in the study of language—the study of sentences (see Dubois & Denis, 1988; Schwanenflugel & LaCount, 1988; Williams, 1988).

Phrase-Structure Grammar

The study of sentences properly begins with the study of *grammar* (see Berwick & Weinberg, 1983). A grammar is a set of rules defining legal and illegal sentences. Just as there are rules that govern how phonemes and morphemes can be combined to make words, so, too, are there rules that dictate how words can be grouped into complete or acceptable sentences. The purpose of a grammar is to specify what strings of words do and do not correspond to legal sentences: "Bob kissed Mary" is a legal sentence, but "Alphabet purple run" is not. A sentence must have certain kinds of words in certain orders to pass the test of a true sentence.

Many grammars are hierarchical. In them a sentence is first broken up into several *phrases*, or small groups of words centered on nouns or verbs. These phrases, in turn, are broken down further (see Figure 13.1). Grammars that work in this manner are called *phrase-structure grammars*. Figure 13.1 shows how the sentence "The dog chased the cat" is *parsed* into a tree structure, or is analyzed for its constituent components.

Actually, the grammar itself is not the tree structure in the upper portion of Figure 13.1; rather, it is the list of *rewrite rules* at the bottom of the figure. These rules describe how parts of the sentence can be rewritten as being composed of even smaller parts. For example, Rule 1 states that a sentence can be rewritten as a noun phrase followed by a verb phrase. This corresponds to the top-level breakdown in the tree structure. Similarly, Rule 2 states that a noun phrase can be rewritten as, or is composed of, a determiner (*a* or *the*) followed by a noun. Rule 3 states that a verb phrase can be rewritten, or is composed of, a verb followed by a noun phrase. This noun phrase, contained within the verb phrase, can also be broken down into a determiner and a noun, just like any noun phrase.

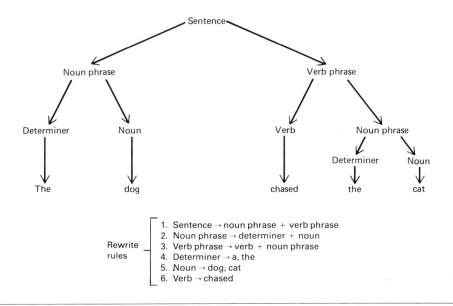

Figure 13.1 A simple phrase-structure grammar.

Rules 4–6 essentially specify the vocabulary of this very limited grammar that we are considering. (A "real-life" grammar would obviously have much more substance than this example.) Legal determiners in this limited grammar are *a* and *the*, legal nouns are *dog* and *cat*, and the only legal verb in this grammar is *chased*. The combination of the structure rules (1–3) and the vocabulary rules (4–6) allow for a considerable number of legal sentences (for example, "A dog chased a cat," "The cat chased a dog," and so on). Strings of words that do not follow these rules (for example, "A cat followed a dog," "Chased cat dog a the") are not legal, according to this limited grammar.

The task of the linguist is to develop a grammar, or list of rules, that is capable of generating all legal sentences in a given language while not generating any illegal ones—quite a task, to say the least.

Psychological Reality of Phrase-Structure Grammar

What kind of evidence supports the idea that a phrase-structure analysis of the sentence is reasonable and correct? In other words, even though we can break sentences down into phrases on a logical level, how do we know that phrases are psychologically important to language users? Maybe the whole phrase analysis is little more than a logical exercise, and perhaps it has little to do with how we go about generating and understanding sentences.

CLICK MIGRATION.   At least two kinds of experiments provide evidence to suggest that phrases are important and significant to us when we construct and try to understand sentences. In the first type of experiment (click migration), Fodor and

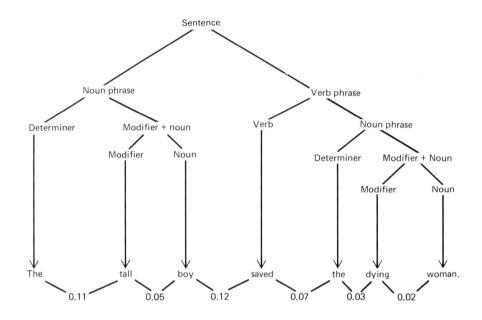

Figure 13.2 The phrase structure of a sentence and the corresponding transitional error probabilities obtained by Johnson. (Adapted from Johnson, N. F. The psychological reality of phrase-structure rules. *Journal of Verbal Learning and Verbal Behavior*, 1965, 4, 469–475. Fig. 1, p. 471, and Table 2, p. 472.)

Bever (1965) superimposed auditory clicks over a tape recording of a sentence. Sometimes the clicks were placed in the middle of a phrase, and sometimes at the beginning or end of a phrase. Both the clicks and the sentence could be heard clearly. Subjects listened to the recording and were asked to indicate at what points in the sentence the clicks had occurred. Many of the clicks that were placed in the middle of a phrase were erroneously reported as having occurred at the end of the phrase; the clicks "migrated." Whereas it is difficult to tell exactly what this effect means, it seems to suggest that the subjects were, in fact, processing the sentence in terms of phrases. Comprehending a given phrase took precedence over the click-perception task, so that perception of the click was in some sense delayed until the subject had finished processing that phrase. In a sense, the subject was too busy nailing down that phrase to pay attention to the click (see also Garrett, Bever, & Fodor, 1966).

The extent of click migration is somewhat limited. For instance, Seitz and Weber (1974) found that the effect can be reduced if subjects are allowed to read the sentence along with its auditory presentation (see also Reber, 1973). The major point to be made, however, is that during ordinary sentence comprehension special attention does seem to be paid to major phrases. Trying to understand language processing in terms of phrases does seem to make some sense.

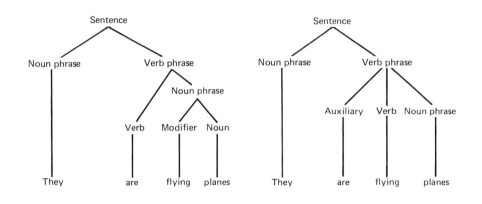

Figure 13.3 The two different structures for "They are flying planes."

ERROR PROBABILITIES.   The second kind of experiment that supports the phrase analysis of sentences has to do with *transitional error probabilities*. Johnson (1965) had subjects memorize and later recall sentences such as that in Figure 13.2. He then compared the phrase structure of the sentence with the probabilities of incorrectly recalling the words from the sentence. The numbers below the sentence show the transitional error probabilities. For instance, given that *tall* was recalled, the probability of making an error in recalling *boy* was .05. It is clear that high error rates are found when moving from the recall of one phrase to the next; the average error rate *within* the noun and verb phrases is .06, compared with the rate of .12 when crossing from the noun phrase to the verb phrase. The click-migration and transitional-error-probability studies argue strongly for the psychological validity of phrases.

Problems with Phrase-Structure Grammars

Phrase-structure grammars provide useful, convenient ways to think about sentences. And yet there is far more to language than can be accounted for by these grammars. They are fine as far as they go, but they do not go far enough. Phrase grammars have at least two significant flaws.

FLAW 1.   The first flaw has to do with the fact that some sentences can have two different meanings. Consider the sentence "They are flying planes." The two possible structures for this sentence are shown in Figure 13.3. This statement is called an *ambiguous* sentence (see Reardon & Katz, 1983). The ambiguity in the meaning of the sentence comes from the fact that *they* can refer either to the planes or to the people who might be flying them. Thus, one version states that there are people who are in the process of flying planes, whereas the other version refers to planes that are meant for flying as opposed to, say, model planes. "They are eating pears" is another ambiguous sentence (see Box 13.2 for some examples of humorous ambiguous statements).

Box 13.2 Some Examples of Ambiguous Statements

Headlines: "Man Eating Fish Mistakenly Sold as Pet"
"Group Studies Changing Hospital to Jail"
"UFO Talks at University"
"All Ohio Condemned to Face Death"
"Deer Kill 100,000"
"Police Kill Man with Club"
"Professor Gives Talk on Mars"
"Criticisms about Council Members Growing Ugly"
Sign in gym: "I will be taking people out of lockers who haven't paid their rental
fee."
Report in newspaper: "She saw sexual intercourse taking place between two trees
in the park."
Sign at bank: "Drive through window"
Signs: "SLOW MEN WORKING"
"SLOW CHILDREN CROSSING"
"FOR BATHROOM USE STAIRS"

From Leahey, T. H., and Harris, R. J. *Human learning*, second ed. © 1989, p. 174. Adapted by permission of Prentice Hall, Inc., Englewood Cliffs, N.J.

The correct parsing of these sentences clearly depends on which meaning is intended. Since phrase-structure grammars deal only with the words in the sentence and not at all with what the speaker *intended* or *meant* by the sentence, they do not adequately handle these sentences. We need to know more about what the language user means, or intends to convey, before we can completely understand language.

FLAW 2.   The second flaw in phrase-structure grammars is that many sentences with different structures express the same idea. For example, consider the active–passive distinction. Read the following sentences:

1. The dog chased the cat.
2. The cat was chased by the dog.
3. The cat chased the dog.

Now let's simply look at the surface structure, or the word orders, in these sentences, as does phrase-structure grammar. Sentences 1 and 3 are quite similar physically. In fact, they are much more similar physically than are Sentences 1 and 2. And yet 1 and 2 mean the same thing, whereas 1 and 3 do not. If we restricted our attention to these superficial, surface characteristics, such as word order, we would make errors in our understanding of the nature of sentences. Phrase-structure grammar, with its emphasis on superficial physical characteristics, is not enough to understand complex language usage.

Surface and Deep Structure

In attempting to overcome the inability of phrase-structure grammar to account for these problems, Noam Chomsky (1957, 1965) introduced the important distinction between *deep* and *surface* structure. He argued that a sound theory of sentence structure must be based not on superficial, surface characteristics, such as word order, but on the underlying idea intended by the user of the sentence. Although this theory is somewhat of an oversimplification, the difference between *surface* and *deep* structure is the difference between wording and the basic meaning underlying that particular wording. The same deep structure (the basic structure of the idea) can be expressed in different ways, or involve different surface structures.

Verbatim versus Meaning Memory

One obvious question related to this distinction between surface and deep structure, or wording and basic idea, is this: Which is more easily remembered, the wording or the basic idea of a sentence? Sachs (1967, 1974) has done some interesting experiments that suggest an answer here. Sachs' subjects read short paragraphs that contained "target sentences." For example, a paragraph concerning the discovery of the telescope might contain the sentence "He sent a letter about it to Galileo, the great Italian scientist." The subjects were then shown a set of sentences and asked to choose the one that was the same as the embedded one. They were given the following choices:

1. He sent a letter about it to Galileo, the great Italian scientist. (same wording)
2. He sent Galileo, the great Italian scientist, a letter about it. (different word order, same meaning)
3. A letter about it was sent to Galileo, the great Italian scientist. (passive transformation, same meaning)
4. Galileo, the great Italian scientist, sent him a letter about it. (different meaning)

Notice that Sentences 1, 2, and 3 all have roughly the same meaning. Sentence 4, however, has a very different meaning from the other three. The results of the experiment were quite clear. When the target sentence was embedded in the middle of the paragraph, the subjects could identify the correct sentence at a rate only slightly better than chance. They were very likely to pick one of the paraphrases (2 or 3). But the subjects were almost always able to reject the sentence with the different meaning (4). In other words, although they were not very good at remembering the exact wording of the sentence, they were very good at remembering the basic idea.

It is not so much that we *cannot* remember the wording. We choose, or prefer, to remember the basic idea. This was demonstrated by Wanner (1974), who showed that, when subjects are instructed to concentrate on the wording of a sentence, wording identification can be quite accurate (see also Keenan, MacWhinney, & Mayhew, 1977).

Transformational Grammar

Chomsky, in pursuing this distinction, introduced the idea of *transformational grammar*. According to this notion, deep-structure ideas that people have can be expressed as sentences by applying various transformations to the deep-structure content. In other words, by applying some different transformations to the deep-structure content we can develop different surface structures (different orders of words) that express the same idea.

EXAMPLES OF TRANSFORMATION.   Consider the sentence "The dog chased the cat." This sentence is a direct expression of the underlying idea, or deep structure; it is the idea we have in mind and is expressed in the active tense. If we wished to express this underlying idea in a passive form, we could apply a transformation, as follows:

1. Exchange the position of the two noun phrases.
2. Replace the verb with the phrase "was chased by."

If we do this, we have transformed the active "The dog chased the cat" to the passive "The cat was chased by the dog." In performing this transformation (steps 1 and 2 above) we have altered the surface structure (the order of the words and the exact words we used), but we have not changed the deep structure, or the underlying idea: "The dog chased the cat."

Several transformations can be performed in succession, leading to a wide variety of sentences all expressing pretty much the same underlying deep structure:

1. "The cat was not chased by the dog."
   (passive negation)
2. "Was the cat chased by the dog?"
   (passive question)
3. "Was the cat not chased by the dog?"
   (passive negative question)

All of these sentences are derived from the same basic, underlying idea.

The problems posed by ambiguous sentences, such as "They are flying planes," can be handled by transformational grammars, because these grammars do take deep structure into account, as phrase-structure grammars do not. Transformational grammars do consider the two different deep structures underlying the two interpretations of the ambiguous sentence. The two different deep structures are expressed by a common surface structure only because the application of transformations to their different deep structures happens to lead to the same sentence.

MIXED LABORATORY RESULTS.   Chomsky's idea about transformational grammar led to a prediction that was testable in the laboratory. Specifically, as the number of transformations required to convert a deep structure into a particular surface structure increases, that surface structure should be more difficult to comprehend and remember. The more transformations required, the greater the complexity of the surface structure and the more difficult the tasks of comprehension and memory. For example, "The cheese was eaten by the mouse" should be more easily remembered than "Was the cheese not eaten by the mouse?" because the first sentence involves fewer transformations from the deep structure ("The mouse ate the cheese") than does the second sentence.

One technique that can be used to study this hypothesis is called the *sentence-verification technique* (see Carpenter & Just, 1975; Clark & Chase, 1972; Trabasso, Rollins, & Shaughnessy, 1971). In this method subjects are shown a simple picture, such as a set of red dots, and a sentence that might describe the picture, such as "The dots are red" or "Red is the color of the dots." The subjects' task is to judge whether the sentence is an accurate description of the picture and to push a yes or no button as quickly as possible. The sentences presented to the subjects varied in derivational complexity and in whether they accurately described the pictures. By varying the complexity of the sentences one can determine whether complexity affects comprehension as revealed by reaction time.

The early results looked very promising. A number of investigators reported results suggesting that memory for surface structures involving more transformations would be poor (see Savin & Perchonock, 1965; Wason, 1961). This rosy state of affairs did not last long, however. Since those early studies, a number of investigators have reported findings that contradict the idea that number of transformations should be correlated with difficulty in memory (see Fodor, Bever, & Garrett, 1974).

Consider, for example, the following sentences: (1) "John is happier than Mary" and (2) "John is happier than Mary is happy." Sentence 1 is easier to understand and remember than Sentence 2. And yet Sentence 1 is derived from Sentence 2 by a deletion transformation. In other words, these sentences contradict the idea that greater numbers of transformation lead to greater complexity and more difficult comprehension.

Thus, Chomsky's ideas about transformational grammar, although revolutionizing the field of linguistics, did not provide all the answers. Psychologists, while maintaining many of Chomsky's notions, moved on to additional concerns. We now turn to some of these other developments.

HAM and ACT

Many theories and computer models have dealt with the representation of meaning in memory (see Anderson & Bower, 1973; Cowan, 1988; Cullingford, 1978; Hayes-Roth & Hayes-Roth, 1977; Hayes-Roth & Thorndyke, 1979; Schank & Abelson, 1977). Because these models and experiments are complex and perhaps better suited for study in a graduate-level course, we will concentrate on one of the better-known examples. The model we have chosen is called HAM, for *human associative memory*. A newer version of HAM has been called ACT (see Anderson, 1976, 1983). If you will recall, we discussed Anderson's ACT theory, which is a mathematically oriented, all-encompassing spreading-activation theory of memory, in Chapter 9. For our purposes here a discussion of the simpler HAM version will be sufficient to provide the flavor of this type of theorizing.

PROPOSITIONS.　HAM is a model of how information is encoded, stored, and retrieved. Specifically, HAM stores information about the world as *propositions*. A proposition is the meaning behind words. For example, "Leaves are green" is not a proposition. The proposition is the abstract idea expressed by these three words;

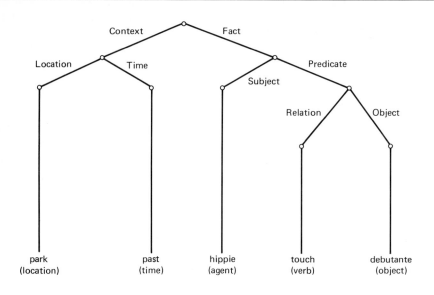

Figure 13.4 Input tree representing the way that the sentence "In the park the hippie touched the debutante" is stored according to HAM. (Adapted from Anderson, J. R., and Bower, G. H. *Human associative memory*. Washington, D.C.: Winston, 1973. Figure on p. 145.)

the same proposition could also be expressed by a picture of a green leaf. A proposition is an abstract idea or assertion about the world that can be expressed in different ways. In a sense a proposition is an assertion about the world that may be true or false. For example, a picture of a red, white, and blue leaf or the statement "Leaves are red, white, and blue" both express the same underlying (and incorrect) proposition. It is difficult to grasp the nature of a proposition, but for our purposes it is best thought of as the meaning behind an expression or assertion, regardless of the form of that expression. HAM uses propositions, rather than words or pictures, as the units that are stored.

INPUT TREES.   Let us consider how HAM stores complex propositions in memory. Consider the sentence "In the park the hippie touched the debutante." There is a complex meaning, or proposition, behind this string of words. HAM stores this proposition in what is called an *input tree* (see Figure 13.4). The contents of Figure 13.4 represent how HAM stores a complex proposition. Let us look at this stored input tree in detail. Begin at the top. Notice that the first branching refers to a distinction between *context* and *fact*. In our proposition something happened (the hippie touched the debutante) in a certain *context* (in the park and in the past). The context of the event is broken down further into *location* (the park) and *time* (the past). The fact (the hippie touched the debutante) is also further broken down, into *subject* (the hippie) and *predicate* (touched the debutante). Finally, the predicate is broken down into a *relation* (touched) and an *object* (the debutante). The authors of HAM argue that a representation of this *complex input tree is what is stored in memory*. Notice that the sentence "In the park the hippie touched the debutante" is *not* stored. The abstract meaning of this sentence is stored, and it is stored as a structure of elements that bear particular relationships to one another. HAM provides a way to think about what we store in our memory when someone reads us the sentence "In the park the hippie touched the debutante." We hear the sentence and store its meaning as an abstract proposition expressed by the input tree, rather than in terms of the actual words contained in the sentence.

INCREMENTAL CUING.   Now, given that the HAM authors believe that this is a good way to think about how a sentence is stored, what evidence is there for or against such a conception? Most of Anderson and Bower's (1973) experiments are very complex and require mathematical sophistication. But some of them can be described here. In one experiment, for example, subjects first studied 72 sentences. Each sentence contained four elements: a location (such as *park*), an agent (such as *hippie*), a verb (such as *touched*), and an object (such as *debutante*). The subjects were then tested for their ability to remember these four elements in each of the 72 sentences by an *incremental cuing* method. In this method the subjects first were given *one* of the four critical elements in a given sentence and asked to recall the remaining three. Then they were given two of the four critical words, including the one first presented, and asked to recall the remaining two. Finally, the subjects were given three of the critical words and asked to recall the remaining word.

For example, on the first test the subjects might be given "In the ____ the *hippie* ____ the ____." On the second test they might be given "In the ____ the *hippie touched* the ____." And so on.

By using this incremental-cuing technique we can test some predictions made by the input tree in Figure 13.4. To retrieve information from the stored tree it is assumed by HAM that the subjects start at the bottom with what is given to them (for example, the word *park* or some other word or set of words) and search back up from the bottom of the tree, following all the links that have been firmly stored. The subjects follow along all existing links, recalling and reporting the words found there, until a dead end (a broken or nonestablished link) is encountered, or the total set of words is recalled correctly.

For example, assume that a subject is given *park* and can recall only *hippie*. This result means that all the links between *park* and *hippie* must be intact. Now, why could the subject not recall *touched* and *debutante*? Several things could account for these failures. For instance, the *predicate* link might be broken or weak, whereas the *relation* and *object* links are strong, as depicted in Figure 13.5. If a weak *predicate* link is causing the absence of *touched* and *debutante*, then a second cuing, where both *park* and *touched* are presented, should reveal this fact. In this case, recall of *debutante* should occur along with recall of *hippie*. However, if the *predicate* link is strong and the *relation* and *object* links are absent, then second-level cuing, where both *park* and *touched* are presented, would not lead to recall of *debutante* (see Figure 13.6).

Without going into any greater detail it can be seen how intricate predictions and tests of these predictions can be made with HAM. In general, Anderson and Bower (1973) are able to present quite a number of data consistent with their model. As is so often true in psychological theorizing, however, some data seem to

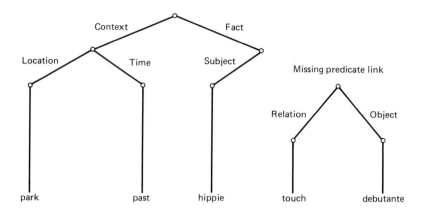

Figure 13.5 HAM input tree assuming that predicate link is missing. In this case the presentation of *park* alone will not elicit *debutante*, but the presentation of *touch* along with *park* should elicit *debutante*.

contradict the theory (see Foss & Harwood, 1975). Regardless of what eventually happens to it, HAM characterizes the kind of complex model building that is considered in this area (see also Anderson, 1983).

PROSE

Thus far we have discussed research and theorizing that is centered on words and sentences. But obviously language consists of more than these elements. This section describes some of the thinking that has been done about prose, or textual material (see Waters, 1983; Oakhill, 1988).

Context Sentences

Let us begin on a simple level, where we consider only a couple of sentences at a time. One of the first things investigators in this area found was that *our understanding of a given sentence can be strongly affected by the sentences that surround it* in a piece of prose. In other words, sentences do not occur in a vacuum. They exist in a *context*, and that influential context is composed of the sentences that surround them.

DIFFICULTY IN COMPREHENSION: THE GIVEN–NEW PRINCIPLE.   The sentence context surrounding a given sentence can affect (1) the ease with which we understand that target sentence and (2) the actual nature of our understanding of that sentence. Let us first look at some examples of how the difficulty of understanding a given sentence can be affected by surrounding sentences.

Haviland and Clark (1974) and Clark and Haviland (1977) found that the second of the following sentences was easily understood: "John took the beer out of the truck. The beer was warm." But Haviland and Clark also demonstrated that, by making a very simple change in the first sentence, the time it took subjects to

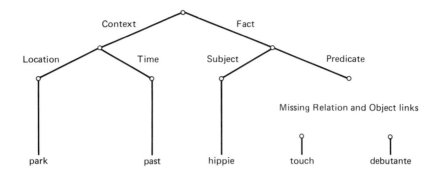

Figure 13.6 HAM input tree assuming that relation and object are missing. In this case the presentation of *park* alone will not elicit *debutante*, but neither will the presentation of *park* and *touch* together.

understand the second sentence could be increased dramatically: "John took the picnic supplies out of the truck. The beer was warm." In both instances the sentence to be understood ("The beer was warm") was the same, but depending on the context it was easy or difficult to understand.

The cause of the increased comprehension time is clear. When reading the latter pair of sentences, it is necessary to infer that beer refers to the picnic supplies mentioned in the first sentence. The reader's store of knowledge must be searched to verify the fact that beer is a reasonable example of picnic supplies, and this extra processing slows the subject up and delays the response.

Haviland and Clark have demonstrated that the key to this phenomenon is the assumption that a reference to beer has already been made in the first sentence. This has been referred to as the *Given-New* principle. The Given-New principle states that in connected discourse each sentence refers to something in a previous sentence (beer) and also adds something new (warm). When the connection between the sentences is explicit, as in the first pair of sentences, comprehension is easy. But when an obvious connection cannot be found, as in the second pair of sentences, the subject must work to find the connection.

Here is another example of how comprehension can be affected by surrounding sentences: "John liked Mary's bike. He took it." In this pair the second sentence is easily understood. But consider "John liked Bill's bike. He took it." Here the second sentence is difficult to understand. By changing one word in the first sentence the second sentence can be made quite ambiguous (see also Baker, 1988; Baker & Wagner, 1987; Gerrig & Healy, 1983; Keenan & Kintsch, 1974).

NATURE OF COMPREHENSION.   Not only can the sentences surrounding a given sentence affect how rapidly that target sentence is understood, but the contextual sentence can influence what is actually understood as well. For example, Thorndyke (1976) had subjects read, "The hamburger chain owner was afraid his love of French fries would ruin his marriage." On the surface, the sentence does not make sense. However, if this sentence is accompanied by "The hamburger chain owner decided to join Weight-Watchers in order to save his marriage," our understanding of the sentence will change dramatically.

SEMANTIC INTEGRATION.   Another phenomenon that has been discovered is that of *semantic integration*. This refers to the fact that, when we read two or more sentences, we are likely to combine them, or integrate them, in such a way that our understanding of the situation draws on both sentences. For example, Hayes-Roth and Thorndyke (1979) had subjects read two separate stories. One story contained the sentence "King Egbert was a dictator." The second story contained "Albert hated all dictators." Hayes-Roth and Thorndyke found that the subjects would integrate these two sentences and draw the inference that "Albert hated King Egbert." In other words, they filled out their understanding of the situation by putting the information from two separate sentences together (see also Bransford & Franks, 1971).

Longer Strings: Verbal Context

Most of the studies cited above are concerned with one or two sentences. In a continuing effort to study phenomena that more and more closely approximate the real world, however, psychologists have studied longer and longer segments of connected discourse. Context effects appear in longer texts as well as in the case of pairs of sentences. In other words, in a narrative, or story, the meaning that we derive from any given sentence and from the narrative as a whole is strongly affected by the nature of all of the sentences in the narrative. Consider the following passage. What is it about?

> The procedure is actually quite simple. First, you arrange things into different groups. Of course, one pile may be sufficient depending on how much there is to do. If you have to go somewhere else due to lack of facilities, that is the next step, otherwise, you are pretty well set. It is important not to overdo things. That is, it is better to do a few things at once than too many. In the short run this may not seem too important but complications can easily arise. A mistake can be expensive as well. At first the whole process will seem complicated. Soon, however, it will become just another facet of life. It is difficult to foresee any end to the necessity for this task in the immediate future, but then one never can tell. After the procedure is completed one arranges the materials into different groups again. Then they can be put in their appropriate places. Eventually they will be used once more and the whole cycle will then have to be repeated. However, this is part of life. (Bransford & Johnson, 1972, p. 322)

It is difficult to say what this passage is all about, because the sentences are so vague and ambiguous that they give you little help in your efforts to understand the other sentences. In other words, the context provided by all of these sentences is weak and unhelpful. Now substitute the words *pile of clothing* for *pile* and the words *washing machine* for *facilities*, and read through the passage again. The sentences will make sense this time, because we have enriched the context a bit. Now sentences within the passage will help you to understand the other sentences.

Visual Context

Our understanding of narrative material is strongly affected by the verbal context in which it is located, as the example above illustrates. But our comprehension of a passage of verbal material can be strongly affected by *visual* contextual factors as well. Bransford and Johnson (1972) had three groups of subjects read the following passage and then attempt to recall as many of the ideas in it as they could. Before proceeding, read through the passage and attempt to recall as much of it as you can.

> If the balloons popped, the sound wouldn't be able to carry, since everything would be too far away from the correct floor. A closed window would also prevent the sound from carrying, since most buildings tend to be well insulated. Since the whole operation depends on a steady flow of electricity, a break in the middle of the wire would also cause problems. Of course, the fellow could shout, but the human voice is not loud enough to carry that far. An additional problem is that a string could break on the instrument. Then there could be no accompaniment to the message. It is clear that the best situation would involve less distance. Then there would be fewer potential problems. With face to face contact, the least number of things could go wrong. (p. 392)

It's not easy is it? In fact, one of the three groups in the experiment did what you just did and was able to recall an average of only 3.6 ideas from a maximum of 14. The other two groups were treated differently. One group was shown the picture in Figure 13.7 before it read the passage. The other group was shown the picture immediately after it read the passage. In essence, this picture provides a visual context in which to try to understand the passage.

The group that saw the picture before reading the passage benefited greatly; it recalled an average of 8 ideas. But, interestingly, the people who saw the picture after reading the passage did not benefit; their mean recall was the same as the group not seeing the picture at all (3.6). The picture did not just provide helpful hints or reminders about what was in the passage. If it had, the group seeing the picture after reading the passage would have been helped. This suggests that the picture actually improved comprehension in the group seeing it first, which in turn, improved recall.

The situation is not a simple one, because additional research (Anderson & Pickert, 1978) has shown that under some circumstances contextual information presented following the reading of a passage can improve recall. In other words, it is clear that contextual information, both verbal and visual, can have a strong impact on our comprehension of passages, but the intricate details of the effect are not yet clear (see also Brewer & Dupree, 1983).

The Structure of Stories

Just as psychologists have tried to understand the structure of sentences by building grammars and trees, they have also tried to analyze simple stories. For example, Kintsch, Kozminsky, Streby, McKoon, and Keenan (1975) developed short stories, or texts, similar to the following: "The Greeks loved beautiful art. When the Romans

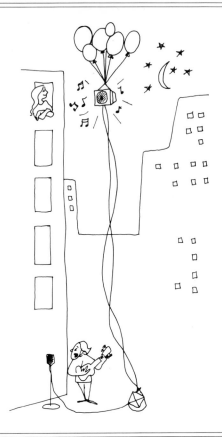

Figure 13.7 Appropriate context for the balloon passage. [From Bransford, J. D., and Johnson, M. K. Considerations of some problems of comprehension. In W. G. Chase (Ed.), *Visual information processing*. Copyright 1973 by Academic Press, Inc. Reprinted by permission.]

conquered the Greeks, they copied them, and, thus, learned to create beautiful art."

One way to think about the structure of this story is to break it down into a list of propositions, as follows:

1. (love, Greek, art)
2. (beautiful, art)
3. (conquer, Roman, Greek)
4. (copy, Roman, Greek)
5. (when, 3, 4)
6. (learn, Roman, 8)
7. (consequence, 3, 6)
8. (create, Roman, 2)

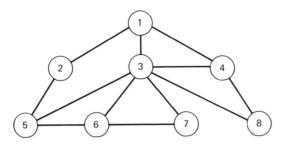

Figure 13.8 Hierarchical text structure of the Greek passage. Propositions that are related to one another, in that they contain one or more common elements, are connected by a line. (Adapted from Kintsch, W. *Memory and cognition.* New York: Wiley, 1977. Figure 6.9, p. 359. Copyright © 1977.)

Remember that propositions are shorthand ways of noting abstract ideas. Thus, (*conquer, Roman, Greek*) refers to the abstract idea, in all its complexity, that the Romans conquered the Greeks.

Kintsch (1974) points out that to describe this story as a list of propositions is all well and good, but it is not enough because it does not give us a very good idea about which propositions are interconnected, or which propositions are related to one another. To grasp the overall organization of a coherent story, we must have some way of expressing how these listed propositions are related to one another. To do this, Kintsch (1977) developed the *hierarchical text structure* contained in Figure 13.8. The basis for this hierarchy is that two propositions are related if they contain the same element, or elements. Thus, Proposition 2 is related to Proposition 1 because both propositions contain the element *art*. Similarly, Proposition 4 is related to Proposition 1 because both contain the element *Greek*. The lines drawn between two circles in Figure 13.8 indicate that the connected propositions contain common elements. Sometimes one proposition contains all of the elements contained in another proposition (for example, Proposition 7 contains all of Proposition 2).

The hierarchical text structure in Figure 13.8 is supposed to give us an overall picture of the structure of our little story. It contains all of the propositions that make up the story, and it shows how all of these propositions are related to one another. High-level propositions, or important propositions, are at the top of the figure, whereas low-level, or less important, propositions are at the bottom.

This kind of analysis of the structure of a story has led to a number of predictions, which have been experimentally confirmed:

1. When people recall a paragraph like this, their recall is correlated with level of proposition. That is, more high-level propositions (like Proposition 1) are recalled than low-level propositions (like Proposition 8). People remember the important facts and tend to forget the details. People are more likely to

remember that Greeks loved art than they are to remember that the Romans copied them, and so on (Kintsch et al., 1975; Mandler & Johnson, 1977; Meyer, 1975; Thorndyke, 1977).

2. When the number of words in a story is kept constant, the reading time for the text increases as the number of propositions in the story increases (Kintsch & Keene, 1973). In other words, it takes longer to read stories that are jam-packed with assertions.

3. Using a large number of words or elements (*Greek, Roman, art, beautiful,* and so on), as opposed to referring to the same few things over and over, also leads to increased reading time and decreased recall (Kintsch et al., 1975).

4. The ability of a word to act as a recall cue increases as the number of propositions in which it appears increases (Wanner, 1974).

Thus, the idea of describing the structure of a story as a list of propositions and in terms of a hierarchy relating those propositions to one another seems to be a good start. This is not the end of the line, however. A number of investigators have expanded this interpretation of prose structure, and the interested reader is referred to Kintsch and van Dijk (1978), Miller and Kintsch (1980), and Spilich, Vesonder, Chiesi, and Voss (1979).

One interesting alternative approach has been adopted by Thorndyke (1977). He also proposes that the general structure of a story is very important in terms of how well we can remember it. But the structure he developed contained the following elements:

1. the *setting*, describing characters, location, and time
2. the *themes*, providing focus and goals
3. the *plot*, involving steps to achieve the goals
4. the *resolution*, or final outcome

The following story contains each of these four elements:

[1] Circle Island is located in the middle of the Atlantic Ocean [2] north of Ronald Island. [3] The main occupations on the island are farming and ranching. [4] Circle Island has good soil but [5] few rivers and [6] hence a shortage of water. [7] The island is run democratically. [8] All issues are decided by a majority vote of the islanders. [9] The governing body is a senate [10] whose job is to carry out the will of the majority. [11] Recently, an island scientist discovered a cheap method [12] of converting salt water into fresh water. [13] As a result, the island farmers wanted [14] to build a canal across the island, [15] so that they could use water from the canal [16] to cultivate the island's central region. [17] Therefore, the farmers formed a procanal association [18] and persuaded a few senators [19] to join. [20] The procanal association brought the construction idea to a vote. [21] All the islanders voted. [22] The majority voted in favor of construction. [23] The senate, however, decided that [24] the farmers' proposed canal was ecologically unsound. [25] The senators agreed [26] to build a smaller canal [27] that was 2 feet wide and 1 foot deep. [28] After starting construction on the smaller canal, [29] the islanders discovered that

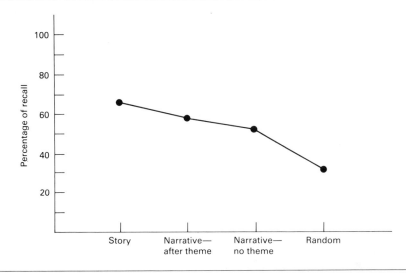

Figure 13.9 Recall of the Circle Island passage for the different experimental conditions. (From Thorndyke, P. W. Cognitive structures in comprehension and memory of narrative discourse. *Cognitive Psychology*, 1977, 9, 77–110. Copyright 1977 by Academic Press, Inc. Reprinted by permission.)

[30] no water would flow into it. [31] Thus the project was abandoned. [32] The farmers were angry [33] because of the failure of the canal project. [34] Civil war appeared inevitable. (Thorndyke, 1977, p. 80)

The statements have been numbered for our discussion and were not numbered when the subjects read the story. The first ten statements describe the setting, the next six statements outline the theme, the plot is contained in statements 17–31, and the resolution is contained in the last three statements.

To show how very important the arrangement of these four elements is in determining how well we recall the story, Thorndyke set up four conditions. In one condition subjects read the story just as you see it above. In a second condition the theme came at the end of the story. In a third condition the statement of the theme was omitted entirely. In the fourth and most extreme condition the sentences were presented randomly. After they read their version of the story, all subjects tried to recall the ideas in the story.

Figure 13.9 contains the recall data. Clearly, recall was strongly influenced by the organization. Recall was best when setting, theme, plot, and resolution followed one another in an orderly fashion; random presentation of the sentences led to poor comprehension and recall.

Knowledge Distorts Memory

It is ironic but true that our general knowledge, or what we know about the world, will often introduce distortions into our attempts to remember prose material. What we are talking about here is a major context effect. When we are presented prose material, it is not presented in a vacuum; it occurs in the context of everything else that we have stored in our memory systems. And the content of those memory systems colors, or influences, our retention of the newly presented material.

Bartlett's (1932) early work represents a famous and prime example of the distorting effects of our previous knowledge on our attempts to remember new materials. Bartlett had subjects read an Indian folktale called *The War of the Ghosts*. He then had them attempt to reproduce the material after intervals of time ranging from very brief to up to 10 years. In some cases he had subjects try to recall the same story repeatedly over time. What he found was that the subjects' recall was characterized by deletion, simplification, extrapolation, and invention. The subjects took a lot out of the original prose and put a lot of new material into it. Bartlett and others have suggested that recall of the material is heavily affected by what the subject already knows, or has stored. The subjects left out parts that seemed strange or unfamiliar to them. The story was shortened. It became more coherent. Less-familiar elements, such as *canoe* and *hunting seals*, became the more familiar *boat* and *fishing*. Subjects added elements entirely absent in the original story, such as *dark forests* and *totems*. Although some investigators (see Cofer, 1973; Spiro, 1977; Zangwell, 1972) have failed to find the same degree of distortion reported by Bartlett, most investigators agree that distortion does occur and that it is related to what the subject already knows and has stored.

Construction versus Reconstruction

One of the questions that has intrigued investigators in this general area has to do with *when* the distortions described by Bartlett occur. Do they occur at the time the material is originally being presented? Or do they occur when the subject is attempting to recall the material? Changes occurring during initial presentation of the material are usually called *constructive* changes, whereas changes occurring during recall are called *reconstructive* changes. In all likelihood *both* constructive and reconstructive changes occur. It would be an oversimplification to assume that all the observed distortions are either constructive or reconstructive. The available evidence suggests that both occur (see Hanawalt & Demarest, 1939; Keenan & Kintsch, 1974; McKoon & Keenan, 1974).

Here is an example of the way psychologists have established that some distortions occur at the time of recall. In an early study Carmichael, Hogan, and Walter (1932) presented materials such as those contained in Figure 13.10 to subjects. Before each picture was presented, the experimenter said, "The next figure resembles . . ." and then gave one of the two descriptions listed in Figure 13.10. One group of subjects received one description, whereas another group received the other. Subjects then tried to reproduce the figure they were shown. As can be seen in Figure 13.10, the subjects' drawings were strongly influenced by the verbal labels that had been provided. In a sense these results demonstrate a context effect, in which the subjects' knowledge influenced what they remembered.

The results do indicate that distortion occurs and that it is influenced by a subject's knowledge, but they do not clearly establish when the distortion occurs. It could occur constructively (when the material is presented) or reconstructively (when the drawing is recalled). So Hanawalt and Demarest (1939) did the experiment over again with the added condition that the verbal descriptions were not

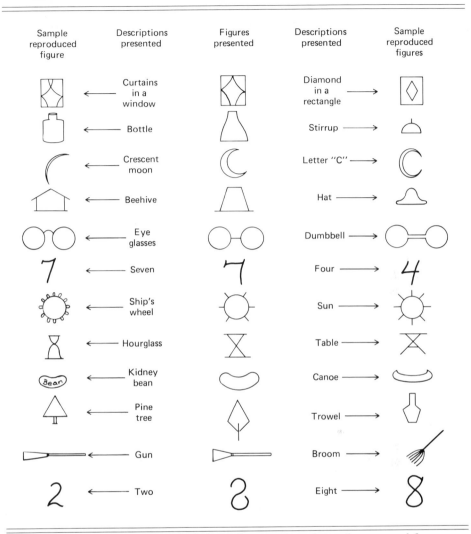

Sample reproduced figure	Descriptions presented	Figures presented	Descriptions presented	Sample reproduced figures
	← Curtains in a window		Diamond in a rectangle →	
	← Bottle		Stirrup →	
	← Crescent moon		Letter "C" →	
	← Beehive		Hat →	
	← Eye glasses		Dumbbell →	
	← Seven		Four →	
	← Ship's wheel		Sun →	
	← Hourglass		Table →	
	← Kidney bean		Canoe →	
	← Pine tree		Trowel →	
	← Gun		Broom →	
	← Two		Eight →	

Figure 13.10 The effects of verbal labels on the retention of visually presented figures. Subjects received either one or the other of the alternative descriptions and then attempted to reproduce the figures in the middle column. Sample reproductions in the extreme left and right columns illustrate the impact of verbal labels on retention. (Adapted from Carmichael, L. C., Hogan, H. P., and Walter, A. A. An experimental study of the effects of language on the reproduction of visually perceived forms. *Journal of Experimental Psychology*, 1932, 15, 73–86. Figure 27, p. 80. Copyright 1932 by the American Psychological Association.)

given during the learning phase of the experiment. They were given only at the time of recall. The researchers still found distortions occurring. Although this experiment does not completely clear up the issue, it does indicate that at least *some* reconstructive distortion occurs; distortion is not all of the constructive type (see also Bahrick, 1984; Johnson, 1986; Neisser, 1984).

Schemata

To account for these distortions and changes that people introduce into prose material that they are trying to remember, Bartlett introduced the idea of schemata (plural of schema). A *schema*, or a *frame*, as it is called by some modern investigators, refers to the organized body of information an individual has about some action, concept, event, or other segment of knowledge. For instance, a reader might have a schema that organizes everything that reader knows about *war*—it requires weapons, people are killed in battles, and so on. People can have schemata representing knowledge about *real estate, psychology, bathing suits*, and *justice*. In other words, *any* body of knowledge, organized around a central core concept, represents a schema.

According to Bartlett, distortions in memory occur because people interpret the incoming story in terms of existing schemata. In a sense the schema is the context in which the story occurs, and the subject's memory of that story is influenced not only by the story material itself but also by the schema.

When people read *The War of the Ghosts*, they were likely to leave out details that sounded strange to them and to alter the story so that it conformed to stories they had already heard. They made the story conform to existing schemata. They were likely to add elements of war with which they were familiar and to delete elements of war that were unfamiliar to them, or did not occur in their existing war schema. Everything not in their existing war schema would be likely to be dropped out. Everything in their war schema not in the story would be likely to be added. The longer the delay between presentation and recall, the more likely the subject is to put in these details from existing schemata (see Sulin & Dooling, 1974).

Stories tend to be constructed differently in different cultures. Thus, we have a *story* schema that contains our ideas about what a story is. But native Americans had a different story schema. Hence, when we try to recall an old "Indian" story, we distort it so that it is brought more into line with our ideas about what constitutes a story. This cultural aspect of story telling was demonstrated by Kintsch and van Dijk (1975). They gave subjects either stories from Boccaccio's *Decameron*, whose structures are not unusual to American subjects, and native American folktales, which are written with a very different and unfamiliar structure. These authors found that the subjects' summaries of the *Decameron* stories were much more accurate than their summaries of the native American tales. The lack of appropriate schemata for the native American stories made their accurate retention difficult.

Anderson and Pickert (1978) provide another interesting example of the importance of schemata in prose memory. Subjects read a rather neutral description of a house from either of two different viewpoints; they pretended they were either a potential house buyer or a burglar. Then they attempted to recall the description of the house. Once they got to the point where they could recall nothing more, they were asked to recall whatever they could given the alternative viewpoint. The subjects who had first recalled from the home buyer's viewpoint then tried to recall from a burglar's viewpoint. Similarly, the burglar became a home buyer. Recall went up. When the subjects shifted perspective, they were able to recall more details that were unavailable when they were operating from the first perspective. The newly made burglar suddenly remembered that the door was hidden by tall bushes, while the newly made home buyer suddenly remembered that the living room was large. Using a new schema (adopting a new viewpoint) allowed access to information that was not easily available under the original schema.

A "Common Cents" Schema

Rubin and Kontis (1983) have presented some data that indicate that people have a very general schema for U.S. coins (penny, nickel, dime, quarter) that is different from each of the individual coins. They gave subjects some empty circles and asked them to fill in the details of the four U.S. coins. The subjects were told that the experimenters were more interested in their knowledge of the coins than in artistic ability and that they should fill in as much detail as possible. Once this was done, the experimenters determined which inscriptions, placements, and orientations had been provided *most often* by the subjects. A pictorial representation of these results is contained in Figure 13.11. The actual U.S. coins are presented on the right side of the figure for comparison. But look at the coins on the left. These are the modal coins drawn up by the authors. There are two important things to notice. First, none of the modal coins based on subjects' recall corresponds accurately with the actual coins. Second, all four modal coins have a great deal in common. All profiles face to the left. "In God we trust" is at the upper edge. The date is always in the lower right quadrant. The value of the coin is at the bottom. In other words, we seem to have a general conception, or schema, of U.S. coins that strongly affects what we will do when we try to reproduce the coins. Once again, distortions in memory occur because we interpret incoming information (the request to draw a coin) in terms of our "coin schema."

The reader interested in pursuing schemata is referred to Ahn, Mooney, Brewer, and De Jong, 1987; Alba and Hasher, 1983; Brewer and Nakamura, 1984; Casson, 1983; Pohl, Colonius, and Thuring, 1985; Rumelhart, 1980; Thorndike, 1984; Vosniadou and Brewer, 1987; Wittig and Williams, 1984.

Eyewitness Reporting: Courtroom Testimony

Loftus and Palmer (1974) report another interesting example of how our understanding of a situation can be affected by context. They showed subjects a film of a traffic accident and then asked them one of two questions: "How fast were the cars going when they *bumped*?" or "How fast were the cars going when they *smashed*?" (emphasis added). Then the subjects were dismissed with instructions to return in one week. At this second session it was found that the subjects who had been asked the *smashed* question during the first session were very likely (and incorrectly) to say that they had seen broken glass in the film. In other words, the context sentence influenced their understanding of the situation (see Bekerian & Bowers, 1983; Weinberg, Wadsworth, & Baron, 1983).

Obviously, this kind of result has important implications for courtroom testimony. It suggests that leading questions can strongly affect what an eyewitness will report having seen. False reports may occur, depending upon how questions are asked. The problem is not easily resolved. As Reed (1982) puts it:

A judge can immediately rule leading questions out of order, but not before the members of the jury have heard the question. Instructions from the

Figure 13.11 Modal and actual coins. (From Rubin, D. C., and Kontis, T. C. A schema for common cents. *Memory and Cognition*, 1983, *11*, 335–341. Fig. 1, p. 336, and Fig. 2, p. 338.)

judge to disregard certain evidence may not prevent the jury from considering that evidence when making their decision. More subtle uses of language, such as use of the word *crash* rather than the word *hit*, may not even be identified as potentially misleading. (p. 250)

Eyewitnesses are asked repeatedly by police, lawyers, and others to remember what they have seen and experienced. At times this form of repeated questioning seems to border on harassment. Going over and over the same ground drains the witnesses and seems to go nowhere. In an interesting study Scrivner and Safer (1988) set out to determine the effects of repeated questioning on recall. They had 90 undergraduates watch a two-minute videotape that showed a robber breaking into a house and shooting three innocent victims. The subjects were then asked repeatedly to recall the details of the film, even as long as 48 hours after having viewed it. The data suggest that subjects were able to recall increasing numbers of details on successive recall trials. The grilling and repeated questioning of witnesses does seem to be a reasonable and helpful approach after all. For additional research on eyewitness reporting see Kassin, 1984; Loftus and Messo, 1987; Yuille and Cutshall, 1986.

APES AND LANGUAGE

We have come a long way in our investigation of language. Starting with language development, we have worked our way through what is known about words, sentences, and stories. But one intriguing area of investigation remains—that of language in apes. Clearly, when we study ape language we are not going to get to the point where we read stories to them and then investigate the schemata they use in trying to recall the material. But because our concern throughout this book has been the continuity of human and animal research, we do want to ask the most basic question: Can apes use language at all?

Although the topic is controversial, with some arguing that apes do not develop true language (see Ristau & Robbins, 1982; Terrace, 1979; Ward, 1983), the accumulating evidence is fairly convincing: It appears that apes may be able to use at least the rudiments of language. They do not use it as ingeniously and as creatively as humans, but they do seem capable of using language on a level roughly equivalent to that displayed by humans in their earliest stages of language development (see Rumbaugh, McDonald, Sevcik, Hopkins, & Rubert, 1986).

In early studies of language and apes (see Hayes & Hayes, 1952) an effort was made to teach chimpanzees to speak. Unfortunately, this approach was very frustrating because the animals could learn to produce only a very few words, such as *cup* and *up,* and these only with great difficulty. As it finally turned out, the problem was not so much that this was all the language the animals could learn but that they had trouble vocalizing. It was trying to speak that was the problem. (But see Box 13.3.)

Gardner and Gardner (1971, 1975a, 1975b, 1978) hit on a new idea. If the chimpanzee could not speak, perhaps it could use *sign language.* Sure enough, their now famous chimpanzee, named Washoe, was able to learn and use about 150 signs of the American Sign Language. She was able to master simple sentences, such as "Hurry gimme toothbrush" and "You me go out hurry." When she was late, she sometimes signed "hurry" to herself. She used to swear at other animals and once called a rhesus monkey a "dirty monkey" (Linden, 1975). Clearly, Washoe never did, and never will, acquire the ability to use language in the manner that adult humans do. But she was not entirely *without* language, either. She did display some creative language use. For example, once she had learned *more* to request more tickling, she would use it in other situations, such as "More food" or "More juice." In fact, she actually invented a few signs, such as one for *bib,* that she had never seen before! Many chimps have now been taught sign language, and many of them seem to display a degree of inventiveness (see Fouts & Couch, 1976; Linden, 1975; Patterson, 1978).

An alternative to the use of sign language has been developed by Premack (1970, 1976), who used pieces of colored plastic of different shapes to represent the

---

Box 13.3 Study Suggests That Monkeys Can "Talk"

Anyone who has ever owned a pet has wondered if animals can "talk."

Monkeys can, according to Dr. Peter Marler, a zoologist.

Marler bases his belief on seven years of experiments on monkey communities in East Africa. He has determined that the warning cry emitted by a monkey when attacked by a leopard differs from the cry given when an eagle attacks.

"A monkey will never give an eagle alarm when, say, an elephant walks by," he said. "It will give an elephant alarm cry."

Marler's findings suggest that a primitive form of language exists in a nonhuman society. He believes that when the monkeys cry out, "they are expressing their thoughts, as well as their feelings." This challenges widely held beliefs that animal noises merely express emotions such as fear and passion.

Marler, of Rockefeller University, spoke recently at the American Society of Primatologists meeting at Michigan State University.

"It seems as if, when an animal makes an eagle alarm call, it evokes the image of an eagle in the minds of the other monkeys," Marler said. "When you play back a recording of an eagle alarm call, they look up into the sky."

If a leopard is encountered and an alarm sounded, he explained, "the monkeys escape to the tops of the trees. This is the right thing to do because the leopard hunts down below in the dense bush. But if the eagle is the predator, the monkeys flee into the dense bush."

Marler and two doctoral assistants began observing colonies of vervet monkeys near Nairobi, Kenya, in 1976. They made audio and video recordings and established that the monkeys had specific warning cries for different predators.

"We had lots of experiences with animals in nature that didn't jibe with the traditional view," he said. "It seems they are using the alarm calls as if they were the names of animals. When we played the tapes back and the predators were not around, they evoked their escape mechanisms.

"Clearly there is an objective relationship between the predator call and the predator."

Now Marler is studying rhesus monkeys. He has found that they also have sounds for specific dangers encountered within a monkey colony.

From Hugh McCann, *Los Angeles Times*, November 30, 1983, Part IA, p. 6. Copyright, 1985 *The Detroit News*.

---

components of language rather than hand movements. A chimp named Sarah would place these symbols on a board to correspond roughly with the word order in a sentence. She was able to master and use a set of plastic symbols well over 100 in number.

Roger Fouts (Fouts, Hirsch, & Fouts, 1982) has reported some intriguing results. He has found that two chimps proficient in sign language will sign messages to each other. He also reports that not only will a young chimp imitate an older chimp's use of sign language but also the older chimp will actively *teach* sign language to the younger animal.

In summary, even though serious reservations exist (see Pate & Rumbaugh, 1983) and we will have to await further research, it appears at present that chimps can use language on a level with the least experienced human being. Thus, the gap between the illustrious human and the lowly animal may be smaller than has long been believed (see also Miles, 1983; Fouts, 1983; Stokoe, 1983).

SUMMARY

1. Even though animals can communicate with one another in complex ways, humans are truly set apart from the other animals in terms of their use of language.
2. *Language* enables us to communicate and to stockpile information. It may facilitate thinking, as well.
3. All human babies display spontaneous *babbling* early in life. This babbling appears to include all of the sounds necessary to speak any language, even though the child quickly begins to concentrate on the sounds contained in the language of his or her environment.
4. True words and *holophrastic* speech tend to be picked up quickly in the first few years of life. *Two-word sentences* and *telegraphic speech* follow.
5. Although children vary in terms of how quickly they acquire language, they all appear to acquire grammar in the same order.
6. Early theories of language acquisition based on *conditioning principles* have been replaced by the *psycholinguistic approach*, which argues that language usage is genetically based and involves hypothesis testing as well as creative thinking.
7. Spoken languages are composed of basic sound units called *phonemes*. These basic sounds are combined to form *morphemes*, the smallest meaningful unit in language. Morphemes are combined to form words.
8. Early efforts to study word storage focused on word-association tasks. More recently, word storage has been thought of in terms of *hierarchies, matrices, feature comparisons*, and *spreading activation*.
9. *Phrase-structure grammar* analyzes sentences in terms of phrases, or groups of words centered on nouns or verbs.
10. Phrase-structure grammar can be depicted in terms of *tree structures* and *re-write rules*.
11. In *click-migration* studies, clicks superimposed over sentences are perceived as occurring at the end of a phrase even though they actually may have occurred in the middle of the phrase. This effect has been taken as evidence for the psychological reality of phrases. *Transitional error analyses* offer further support for phrase-structure grammar.
12. Phrase grammars are limited, because they do not account for such things as ambiguous sentences and do not capture the fact that many different sentences express the same idea.
13. *Surface structure* refers to the wording of a sentence, whereas *deep structure* refers roughly to the idea behind the sentence.
14. The meaning of a sentence tends to be remembered better than its exact wording.
15. According to *transformational grammar*, different surface structures can be developed from the same deep structures through the application of various transformations. Several transformations can be performed in succession, leading to a wide variety of sentences.

16. Sentences that are the result of greater numbers of transformations are sometimes, but not always, more difficult to comprehend and remember.
17. The sentence-verification technique is used to study this hypothesis.
18. *HAM* and *ACT* are computer-based models of how information is encoded, stored, and retrieved. HAM stores propositions, not sentences.
19. *Input trees* describe the manner in which HAM stores propositions. Using the methods of *incremental cuing*, various tests of HAM can be made. These tests have sometimes, but not always, been successful.
20. The meaning we derive from a sentence is affected by the surrounding sentences, or *context*. Context sentences affect not only the difficulty of understanding a given sentence but the actual meaning of the target sentence as well.
21. The Given-New principle states that in prose each sentence reflects something in a previous sentence and also adds something new.
22. *Semantic integration* refers to the fact that we combine, or integrate, separate sentences so that our understanding is affected by both sentences.
23. Context effects, both verbal and visual, can occur in longer pieces of prose as well as in the case of two or three sentences.
24. The *structure of stories* can be described in terms of a list of propositions and a hierarchical text structure relating those propositions to one another. Stories can also be thought of in terms of setting, theme, plot, and resolution.
25. Bartlett's early work indicates that what we know about the world can affect our efforts to remember any given piece of material. We tend to delete, simplify, extrapolate, and invent when we try to recall prose material.
26. Some errors are *constructive*, in that they occur at the time the material is originally presented. Other errors, occurring at the time of recall, are called *reconstructive* errors.
27. The organized body of knowledge an individual has about a given topic, which influences and distorts recall of prose material, is called a *schema*, or frame.
28. Everything in the schema is likely to be added to the story, and everything in the story but not the schema is likely to be dropped. Cultural differences in schemata exist, and they affect recall.
29. Using a new schema (adopting a new viewpoint) can improve recall.
30. Context effects may have important implications for courtroom testimony.
31. Repeated reuse tests, as embodied by the process of questioning eyewitnesses repeatedly, can improve recall.
32. Apes appear to be able to use the rudiments of language. Although they have great difficulty in speaking, they can use sign language and plastic symbols in place of speech. When they do so, they appear to be able to use language about as well as a human who is just beginning to develop language use.

REFERENCES

Abramson, L. Y., Seligman, M. E. P., & Teasdale, J. D. Learned helplessness in humans: Critique and reformulation. *Journal of Abnormal Psychology*, 1978, *87*, 49–74.

Achterberg, J., Kenner, C., & Lawlis, G. F. Severe burn injury: A comparison of relaxation, imagery and biofeedback for pain management. *Journal of Mental Imagery*, 1988, *12(1)*, 71–88.

Adams, J. A. *Human memory*. New York: McGraw-Hill, 1967.

Ader, R. Conditioned taste aversions and immunopharmacology. *Annals of the New York Academy of Sciences*, 1985, *63*, 247–251.

Ahn, W.-K., Mooney, R. J., Brewer, W. F., & DeJong, G. F. Schema acquistion from one example: Psychological evidence for explanation-based learning. In *Proceedings of the Ninth Annual Conference of the Cognitive Science Society*. Hillsdale, N. J.: Lawrence Erlbaum Associates, 1987, 50–57.

Ainsworth, M. D. S. The development of infant-mother attachment. In B. M. Caldwell and H. R. Ricciuti (Eds.), *Review of Child Development Research* (Vol. 3). Chicago: University of Chicago Press, 1973.

Alba, J. W., & Hasher, L. Is memory schematic? *Psychological Bulletin*, 1983, *93*, 203–231.

Allen, K. E., Henke, L. B., Harris, F. R., Baer, D. M., & Reynolds, N. J. Control of hyperactivity by social reinforcement of attending behavior. *Journal of Educational Psychology*, 1967, *58*, 231–237.

Allen, M. M. Rehearsal strategies and response cueing as determinants of organization in free recall. *Journal of Verbal Learning and Verbal Behavior*, 1968, *7*, 58–63.

Alloy, L. B., & Bersh, P. J. Partial control and learned helplessness in rats: Control over shock intensity prevents interference with subsequent escape. *Animal Learning and Behavior*, 1979, *7*, 157–164.

Amsel, A. The role of frustrative nonreward in noncontinuous reward situations. *Psychological Bulletin*, 1958, *55*, 102–119.

Anderson, C. M. B., & Craik, F. I. M. The effect of a concurrent task on recall from primary memory. *Journal of Verbal Learning and Verbal Behavior*, 1974, *13*, 107–113.

Anderson, D. C., Crowell, C. R., Cunningham, C. L., & Lupo, J. V. Behavior during shock exposure as a determinant of subsequent interference with shuttle box escape—Avoidance learning in the rat. *Journal of Experimental Psychology: Animal Behavior Processes*, 1979, *5*, 243–257.

Anderson, J. R. A spreading activation theory of memory. *Journal of Verbal Learning and Verbal Memory*, 1983, *22*, 261–295.

Anderson, J. R. Arguments concerning representations for mental imagery. *Psychological Review*, 1978, *85*, 249–277.

Anderson, J. R. *Cognitive psychology and its implications* (2nd ed.). New York: W. H. Freeman, 1985.

Anderson, J. R. Further arguments concerning representations for mental imagery: A reply to Hayes-Roth and Pylyshyn. *Psychological Review*, 1979, *86*, 395–406.

Anderson, J. R. *Language, memory, and thought*. Hillsdale, N. J.: Lawrence Erlbaum Associates, 1976.

Anderson, J. R., & Bower, G. H. *Human associative memory*. New York: Wiley, 1973.

Anderson, J. R., & Paulson, R. Interference in memory for pictorial information. *Cognitive Psychology*, 1978, *10*, 178–202.

Anderson, R. C., & Pickert, J. W. Recall of previously unrecallable information following a shift in perspective. *Journal of Verbal Learning and Verbal Behavior*, 1978, *17*, 1–12.

Anglin, J. M. *Word, object, and conceptual development*. New York: Norton, 1977.

Anisman, H. Neurochemical changes elicited by stress: Behavioral correlates. In H. Anisman & G. Bignami (Eds.), *Psychopharmacology of aversively motivated behavior*. New York: Plenum, 1978.

Anisman, H., de Catanzaro, D., & Remington, G. Escape performance following exposure to inescapable shock: Deficits in motor response maintenance. *Journal of Experimental Psychology: Animal Behavior Processes*, 1978, *4*, 197–218.

Anisman, H., Grimmer, L., Irwin, J., Remington, G., & Sklar, L. S. Escape performance after inescapable shock in selectively bred lines of mice: Response maintenance and catecholamine activity. *Journal of Comparative and Physiological Psychology*, 1979, 93, 229–241.

Anrep, G. V. Pitch discrimination in the dog. *Journal of Physiology*, 1920, 53, 367–385.

Archer, E. J. Postrest performance in motor learning as a function of prerest degree of distribution of practice. *Journal of Experimental Psychology*, 1954, 47, 47–51.

Armstrong, S. L., Gleitman, L. R., & Gleitman, H. What some concepts might not be. *Cognition*, 1983, 13, 263–308.

Armus, H. L., & Garlich, M. M. Secondary reinforcement strength as a function of schedule of primary reinforcement. *Journal of Comparative and Physiological Psychology*, 1961, 54, 56–58.

Atkinson, K., MacWhinney, B., & Stoel, C. An experiment on recognition of babbling. *Papers and reports on child language development*. Stanford, Calif.: Stanford University Press, 1970.

Atkinson, R. C. Mnemotechnics in second-language learning. *American Psychologist*, 1975, 30, 821–828.

Atkinson, R. C., Bower, G. H., & Crothers, E. J. *Introduction to mathematical learning theory*. New York: Wiley, 1965.

Atkinson, R. C., Brelsford, J. W., & Shiffrin, R. M. Multiprocess models for memory with applications to a continuous presentation task. *Journal of Mathematical Psychology*, 1967, 4, 277–300.

Atkinson, R. C., & Estes, W. K. Stimulus sampling theory. In R. D. Luce, R. R. Bush, & E. Galanter (Eds.), *Handbook of mathematical psychology* (Vol. 2). New York: Wiley, 1963.

Atkinson, R. C., & Shiffrin, R. M. Mathematical models for memory and learning. Technical Report Number 79, Institute for Mathematical Studies in the Social Sciences, Stanford University, 1965.

Atkinson, R. C., & Shiffrin, R. M. Human memory: A proposed system and its control processes. In K. W. Spence & J. T. Spence (Eds.), *The psychology of learning and motivation: Advances in research and theory* (Vol. 2). New York: Academic Press, 1968.

Atkinson, R. C., & Shiffrin, R. M. The control of short-term memory. *Scientific American*, August 1971, 82–90.

Atthowe, J. M., & Krasner, L. Preliminary report on the application of contingent reinforcement procedures (token economy) on a "chronic" psychiatric ward. *Journal of Abnormal Psychology*, 1968, 73, 37–43.

Atwood, M. E., Masson, M. E. J., & Polson, P. G. Further explorations with a process model for water jug problems. *Memory and Cognition*, 1980, 8, 182–192.

Atwood, M. E., & Polson, P. G. A process model for water jug problems. *Cognitive Psychology*, 1976, 8, 191–216.

Averbach, E., & Coriell, A. S. Short-term memory in vision. *Bell System Technical Journal*, 1961, 40, 309–328.

Ayers, T. J., Jonides, J., Reitman, J. S., Egan, J. C., & Howard, D. A. Differing suffix effects for the same physical stimulus. *Journal of Experimental Psychology*, 1979, 5, 315–321.

Azrin, N., Hontos, P. T., & Besalel-Azrin, V. Elimination of enuresis without a conditioning apparatus: An extension of office instruction of the child and parents. *Behavior Therapy*, 1979, 10, 14–15.

Baddeley, A. D. Short-term memory for word sequences as a function of acoustic, semantic, and formal similarity. *Quarterly Journal of Experimental Psychology*, 1966, 18, 362–365. (a)

Baddeley, A. D. The influence of acoustic and semantic similarity on long-term memory for word sequences. *Quarterly Journal of Experimental Psychology*, 1966, 18, 302–309. (b)

Baddeley, A. D. The trouble with levels: A reexamination of Craik and Lockhart's framework for memory research. *Psychological Review*, 1978, 85, 139–152.

Baddeley, A., & Hull, A. Prefix and suffix effects. Do they have a common basis? *Journal of Verbal Learning and Verbal Behavior*, 1979, 18, 129–140.

Baddeley, A. D., & Patterson, K. E. The relation between long-term and short-term memory. *British Medical Bulletin*, 1971, 27, 237–242.

Baddeley, A. D., & Warrington, E. K. Amnesia and the distinction between long- and short-term memory. *Journal of Verbal Learning and Verbal Behavior*, 1970, 9, 176–189.

Baer, D. M., & Gray, P. H. Imprinting to a different species without overt following. *Perceptual and Motor Skills*, 1960, 10, 171–174.

Baer, L., Minichiello, W. E., Jenike, M. A., & Holland, A. Use of a portable computer program to assist behavioral treatment in a case of obsessive compulsive disorder. *Journal of Behavior Therapy and Psychiatry*, 1988, 19(3), 237–240.

Bahrick, H. P. Long-term memories: How durable, and how enduring? *Physiological Psychology*, 1984, 12, 53–58.

Bajo, M. T. Semantic facilitation with pictures and words. *Journal of Experimental Psychology: Learning, Memory, and Cognition*, 1988, 14(4), 579–589.

Baker, L. Differences in the standards used by college students for evaluating their comprehension of expository prose. *Reading Research Quarterly*, 1985, 20, 297–313.

Baker, L., & Santa, J. L. Semantic integration and context. *Memory and Cognition*, 1977, 5, 151–154.

Baker, L., & Wagner, J. L. Evaluating information for truthfulness: The effects of logical subordination. *Memory and Cognition*, 1987, 15, 247–255.

Balda, R. P., & Kamil, A. C. The spatial memory of Clark's nutcrackers (*Nucifraga columbiana*) in an analogue of the radial arm maze. *Animal Learning and Behavior*, 1988, 16(2), 116–122.

Balsam, P. D. The functions of context in learning and performance. In P. D. Balsam & A. Tomie (Eds.), *Context and learning*. Hillsdale, N. J.: Lawrence Erlbaum Associates, 1985.

Barber, T. X. *LSD, marijuana, yoga, and hypnosis*. Chicago: Aldine, 1970.

Barnes, J. M., & Underwood, B. J. "Fate" of first-list associations in transfer theory. *Journal of Experimental Psychology*, 1959, 58, 97–105.

Barraco, R. A., & Stettner, L. J. Antibiotics and memory. *Psychological Bulletin*, 1976, 83, 242–302.

Barrett, J. E., Hoffman, H. S., Stratton, J. W., & Newby, V. Aversive control of following in imprinted ducklings. *Learning and Motivation*, 1971, 2, 202–213.

Barrios, B. A., & Shigetomi, C. C. Coping skills training for the management of anxiety: A critical review. *Behavior Therapy*, 1979, 10, 491–522.

Barsalou, L. W. Ad hoc categories. *Memory and Cognition*, 1983, 11, 211–227.

Bartlett, F. C. *Remembering*. Cambridge, England: Cambridge University Press, 1932.

Bartlett, F. C. *Thinking*. New York: Basic Books, 1958.

Bartlett, J. C., & Tulving, E. Effects of temporal and semantic encoding in immediate recall upon subsequent retrieval. *Journal of Verbal Learning and Verbal Behavior*, 1974, 13, 297–309.

Bartling, C. A., & Thompson, C. P. Encoding specificity: Retrieval asymmetry in the recognition failure paradigm. *Journal of Experimental Psychology: Human Learning and Memory*, 1977, 3, 690–700.

Barton, E. J., & Ascione, F. R. Sharing in preschool children: Facilitation, stimulus generalization, response generalization, and maintenance. *Journal of Applied Behavior Analysis*, 1979, 12, 417–430.

Bartram, D. J. Post-iconic visual storage: Chunking in the reproduction of briefly displayed visual patterns. *Cognitive Psychology*, 1978, 10, 324–355.

Bateson, P. P. G. Effect of similarity between rearing and testing conditions on chick's following and avoidance responses. *Journal of Comparative and Physiological Psychology*, 1964, 57, 100–103.

Bateson, P. P. G. The characteristics and contexts of imprinting. *Biological Reviews of the Cambridge Philosophical Society*, 1966, 41, 177–220.

Bateson, P. P. G. Imprinting and the development of preferences. In A. Ambrose (Ed.), *Stimulation in early infancy*. New York: Academic Press, 1969.

Batson, J. D. Effects of repeated lithium injections on temperature, activity, and flavor conditioning in rats. *Animal Learning and Behavior*, 1983, 11, 199–204.

Battig, W. F. Paired-associate learning. In T. R. Dixon & D. L. Horton (Eds.), *Verbal behavior and general behavior theory*. Englewood Cliffs, N. J.: Prentice-Hall, 1968.

Baum, M. Dissociation of respondent and operant processes in avoidance learning. *Journal of Comparative and Physiological Psychology*, 1969, 67, 83–88.

Beatty, W. W., & Shavalia, D. A. Spatial memory in rats: Time course of working memory and effects of anesthetics. *Behavioral and Neural Biology*, 1980, 28, 454–462.

Beck, C. H. M., Huh, T. J. S., Mumby, D. G., & Fundytus, M. E. Schedule-induced behavior in rats: Pellets versus powder. *Animal Learning and Behavior*, 1989, 17, 49–62.

Bedford, J., & Anger, D. Flight as an avoidance response in pigeons. Paper presented at Psychonomic Society meeting, St. Louis, October 1968.

Begg, I. Imagery and organization in memory: Instructional effects. *Memory and Cognition*, 1978, 6, 174–183.

Bekerian, D. A., & Bowers, J. M. Eyewitness testimony: Were we misled? *Journal of Experimental Psychology*, 1983, 9, 139–145.

Bellezza, F. S., Cheesman, F. L., & Reddy, B. G. Organization and semantic elaboration in free recall. *Journal of Experimental Psychology: Human Learning and Memory*, 1977, 3, 539–550.

Bellezza, F. S., & Walker, R. J. Storage coding trade-off in short-term store. *Journal of Experimental Psychology*, 1974, 102, 629–633.

Berlyne, D. E. The reward-value of indifferent stimulation. In J. T. Tapp (Ed.), *Reinforcement and behavior*. New York: Academic Press, 1969.

Bernbach, H. A. Replication processes in human memory and learning. In G. H. Bower & J. T. Spence (Eds.), *The psychology of learning and motivation: Advances in research and theory* (Vol.3). New York: Academic Press, 1969.

Bernbach, H. A. Rate of presentation in free recall: A problem of two-stage memory theories. *Journal of Experimental Psychology: Human Learning and Memory*, 1975, 104, 18–22.

Bernstein, I. L. Learned taste aversion in children receiving chemotherapy. *Science*, 1968, 200, 1302.

Berrian, R. W., Metzler, D. P., Kroll,N. E. A., & Clark-Meyers, G. M. Estimates of imagery, ease of definition, and animateness for 328 adjectives. *Journal of Experimental Psychology: Human Learning and Memory*, 1979, 5, 435–447.

Bersh, P. J. The influence of two variables upon the establishment of a secondary reinforcer for operant responses. *Journal of Experimental Psychology*, 1951, 41, 62–73.

Berwick. R. C., & Weinberg, A. S. The role of grammars in models of language use. *Cognition*, 1983, 13, 1–61.

Best, M. R., Gemberling, G. A., & Johnson, P. E. Disrupting the conditioned stimulus preexposure effect in flavor-aversion learning: Effects of interoceptive distractor manipulations. *Journal of Experimental Psychology: Animal Behavior Processes*, 1979, 5, 321–334.

Best, P. J., Best, M. R., & Mickley, G. A. Conditioned aversion to distinct environmental stimuli resulting from gastrointestinal distress. *Journal of Comparative and Physiological Psychology*, 1973, 85, 250–257.

Bhaskar, R., & Simon, H. A. Problem solving in semantically rich domains: An example from engineering thermodynamics. *Cognitive Science*, 1977, 1, 193–215.

Bhatt, R. S., Wasserman, E. A., Reynolds, W. F., Jr., & Knauss, K. S. Conceptual behavior in pigeons: Categorization of both familiar and novel examples from four classes of natural and artificial stimuli. *Journal of Experimental Psychology: Animal Behavior Processes*, 1988, 14(3), 219–234.

Biederman, I., Glass, A. L., & Stacy, W. Searching for objects in realworld scenes. *Journal of Experimental Psychology*, 1973, 97, 22–27.

Bijou, S. W. Methodology for the experimental analysis of child behavior. *Psychological Reports*, 1957, 3, 243–250. (a)

Bijou, S. W. Patterns of reinforcement and resistance to extinction in young children. *Child Development*, 1957, 28, 47–54. (b)

Bilodeau, E. A., & Howell, D. C. Free association norms by discrete and continued methods. ONR Technical Report No. 1, 1965, Tulane University, Contract Nonr475 (10).

Bilodeau, I. M. Information feedback. In E. A. Bilodeau (Ed.), *Acquisition of skill*. New York: Academic Press, 1966.

Bindra, D. A unified account of classical conditioning and operant training. In A. H. Black & W. F. Prokasy (Eds.), *Classical conditioning II: Current research and theory*. New York: Appleton, 1972.

Bindra, D. A motivational view of learning, performance and behavior modification. *Psychological Review*, 1974, 81, 199–213.

Bird, B. L., Cataldo, M. F., & Parker, L. Behavioral medicine for muscular disorders. In S. M. Turner, K. S. Calhoun, & H. E. Adams (Eds.), *Handbook of clinical behavior therapy*. New York: Wiley, 1981.

Bird, C. P. Proactive inhibition as a function of orienting task characteristics. *Memory and Cognition*, 1977, 5, 27–31.

Birnbaum, I. Long-term retention of first-list associations in the A–B, A–C paradigm. *Journal of Verbal Learning and Verbal Behavior*, 1965, 4, 515–520.

Bitterman, M. E., Menzel, R., Fietz, A., & Schafer, S. Classical conditioning of proboscis extension in honeybees (*Apis mellifera*). *Journal of Comparative Psychology*, 1983, *97*, 107–119.

Bjork, R. A. Positive forgetting: The noninterference of items intentionally forgotten. *Journal of Verbal Learning and Verbal Behavior*, 1970, *9*, 255–268.

Bjork, R. A. Short-term storage: The ordered output of a central processor. In F. Restle, R. M. Shiffrin, N. J. Castellad, H. R. Lindman, & D. B. Pisoni (Eds.), *Cognitive Theory*, (Vol. 1). Hillsdale, N. J.: Lawrence Erlbaum Associates, 1975.

Bjork, R. A. Theoretical implications of directed forgetting. In A. W. Melton & E. Martin (Eds.), *Coding processes in human memory*. Washington D. C.: V. H. Winston, 1972.

Bjork, R. A., & Geiselman, R. E. Constituent processes in the differentiation of items in memory. *Journal of Experimental Psychology: Human Learning and Memory*, 1978, *4*, 347–361.

Black, A. H., & Prokasy, W. F. (Eds.), *Classical conditioning II: Current theory and research*. New York: Appleton, 1972.

Black, D. A., & Friesen, J. G. Deposit money: A component in a self-directed minimal intervention program for weight control. *Behavior Therapy*, 1983, *14*, 333–340.

Blanchard, E. B., & Young, L. D. Of promises and evidence: A reply to Engel. *Psychological Bulletin*, 1974, *81*, 44–46.

Blanchard, R. J., Mast, M., & Blanchard, D. C. Stimulus control of defensive reactions in the albino rat. *Journal of Comparative and Physiological Psychology*, 1975, *88*, 81–88.

Bleier, R., Houston, L., & Byne, W. Can the corpus callosum predict gender, age, handiness, or cognitive differences? *Trends in the Neurosciences*, 1986, *99*, 391–394.

Bloom, K. Social elicitation of infant vocal behavior. *Journal of Experimental Child Psychology*, 1975, *20*, 51–58.

Bloom, K., & Esposito, A. Social conditioning and its proper control procedures. *Journal of Experimental Child Psychology*, 1975, *20*, 51–58.

Blough, D. S. Odd-item search in pigeons: Display size and transfer effects. *Journal of Experimental Psychology: Animal Behavior Processes*, 1989, *15*, 14–22.

Blough, D. S. Steady state data and a quantitative model of operant generalization and discrimination. *Journal of Experimental Psychology: Animal Behavior Processes*, 1975, *104*, 3–21.

Blough, D., & Blough, P. Animal psychophysics. In W. K. Harris & J. E. R. Staddon (Eds.), *Handbook of operant behavior*. Englewood Cliffs, N. J.: Prentice-Hall, 1977.

Blough, D. S., & Lipsitt, L. P. The discriminative control of behavior. In J. W. Kling & L. A. Riggs (Eds.), *Woodworth and Scholsberg's experimental psychology*. New York: Holt, Rinehart & Winston, 1971.

Blough, P. M. Overall and local contrast in multiple schedules. *Animal Learning & Behavior*, 1988, *16*, 395–403.

Bobrow, D. G., & Norman, D. A. Some principles of memory schemata. In D. G. Bobrow & A. M. Collins (Eds.), *Representation and understanding*. New York: Academic Press, 1975.

Bohannon, J. N. Flashbulb memories for the space shuttle disaster: A tale of two theories. *Cognition*, 1988, *29*, 179–196.

Bolles, R. C. Species-specific defense reactions and avoidance learning. *Psychological Review*, 1970, *77*, 32–48.

Bolles, R., & Seelbach, S. Punishing and reinforcing effects of noise onset and termination for different responses. *Journal of Comparative and Physiological Psychology*, 1964, *58*, 127–132.

Bourne, L. E., Dominowski, R. L., & Loftus, E. F. *Cognitive processes*. Englewood Cliffs, N. J.: Prentice-Hall, 1979.

Bousfield, W. A. The occurrence of clustering in the recall of randomly arranged associates. *Journal of General Psychology*, 1953, *49*, 229–240.

Bousfield. W. A., & Sedgewick, C. H. An analysis of sequences of retricted associative responses. *Journal of General Psychology*, 1944, *30*, 149–165.

Bower, G. H. Imagery as a relational organizer in associative learning. *Journal of Verbal Learning and Verbal Behavior*, 1970, *9*, 529–533.

Bower, G.H. Mental imagery and associative learning. In L. W. Gregg (Ed.), *Cognition in learning and memory*. New York: Wiley, 1972.

Bower, G. H. Mood and memory. *American Psychologist*, 1981, *36*, 129–148.

Bower, G. H., Black, J. B., & Turner, T. J. Scripts in memory for text. *Cognitive Psychology*, 1979, *11*, 177–220.

Bower, G. H., & Bostrom, A. Absence of within-list PI and RI in short-term recognition memory. *Psychonomic Science*, 1968, *10*, 211–212.

Bower, G. H., & Clark, M. C. Narrative stories as mediators for serial learning. *Psychonomic Science*, 1969, *14*, 181–182.

Bower, G. H., & Hilgard, E. R. *Theories of learning* (5th ed.). Englewood Cliffs, N. J.: Prentice-Hall, 1981.

Bower, G. H., & Theios, J. A learning model for discrete performance levels. In R. C. Atkinson, (Ed.), *Studies in mathematical psychology*. Stanford, Calif.: Stanford University Press, 1964.

Bowlby, J. *Attachment and loss* (Vol. 1: *Attachment*). New York: Basic Books, 1969.

Bowles, N. L., & Glanzer, M. An analysis of interference in recognition memory. *Memory and Cognition*, 1983, *11*, 307–315.

Bowyer, P. A., & Humphreys, M. S. Effect of recognition test on a subsequent cued-recall test. *Journal of Experimental Psychology: Human Learning and Memory*, 1979, *5*, 348–359.

Boyle, M. E., & Greer, R. D. Operant procedures and the comatose patient. *Journal of Applied Behavior Analysis*, 1983, *16*, 3–12.

Bracewell, R. J., & Black, A. H. The effects of restraint and noncontingent preshock on subsequent escape learning in the rat. *Learning and Motivation*, 1974, *5*, 53–69.

Brackbill, Y. Extinction of the smiling response in infants as a function of reinforcement schedules. *Child Development*, 1958, *29*, 115–124.

Brackbill, Y., Adams, G., & Reaney, T. P. A parametric study of the delay-retention effect. *Psychological Reports*, 1967, *20*, 433–434.

Bracker, B. S. *Learned voluntary control of systolic blood pressure by spinal cord injury patients*. Ph.D dissertation, New York University, New York, 1977.

Brandon, S. E., & Bitterman, M. E. Analysis of autoshaping in goldfish. *Animal Learning and Behavior*, 1979, *7*, 57–62.

Bransford, J. D., & Franks, J. J. The abstraction of linguistic ideas. *Cognitive Psychology*, 1971, *2*, 331–350.

Bransford, J. D., & Johnson, M. K. Contextual prerequisites for understanding: Some investigations of comprehension and recall. *Journal of Verbal Learning and Verbal Behavior*, 1972, *11*, 717–720.

Bransford, J. D., & Johnson, M. K. Considerations of some problems of comprehension. In W. G. Chase (Ed.), *Visual information processing*. New York: Academic Press, 1973.

Breland, K., & Breland, M. The misbehavior of organisms. *American Psychologist*, 1961, *16*, 681–684.

Breland, K., & Breland, M. *Animal behavior*. New York: Macmillan, 1966.

Brewer, W. F., & Dupree, D. A. Use of plan schemata in the recall and recognition of goal-directed actions. *Journal of Experimental Psychology*, 1983, *9*, 117–129.

Brewer, W. F., & Nakamura, G. V. The nature and functions of schemas. In R. S. Wyer & T. K. Srull (Eds.), *Handbook of social cognition*. Hillsdale, N. J.: Lawrence Erlbaum Associates, 1984.

Broadbent, D. E., Cooper, P. J., & Broadbent, M. H. P. A comparison of hierarchical and matrix retrieval schemes in recall. *Journal of Experimental Psychology: Human Learning and Memory*, 1978, *4*, 486–497.

Brodie, D. A., & Murdock, B. B. Effects of presentation time on nominal and functional serial position curves of free recall. *Journal of Verbal Learning and Verbal Behavior*, 1977, *16*, 185–200.

Brogden. W. J., Lipman, E. A., & Culler, E. The role of incentive in conditioning and extinction. *American Journal of Psychology*, 1938, *51*, 109–117.

Brooks, L. R. Spatial and verbal components of the act of recall. *Canadian Journal of Psychology*, 1968, *22*, 349–368.

Brosgole, L., & Grosso, J. J. The phenomenal determination of retroaction and proaction: III. Contextual vs. temporal organization of two lists. *Bulletin of the Psychonomic Society*, 1983, *21*, 15–18.

Brown, A. L., & Kane, M. J. Preschool children can learn to transfer: Learning to learn and learning from example. *Cognitive Psychology*, 1988, *20*, 493–523.

Brown, G. E., & Dixon, P. A. Learned helplessness in the gerbil? *Journal of Comparative Psychology*, 1983, *97*, 90–92.

Brown, J. L. The effect of drive on learning with secondary reinforcement. *Journal of Comparative and Physiological Psychology*, 1956, *51*, 254–260.

Brown, J. S. Factors determining conflict reactions in different discriminations. *Journal of Experimental Psychology*, 1942, *31*, 272–292.

Brown, M. F., Wheeler, E. A., & Riley, D. Evidence for a shift in the choice criterion of rats in a 12-arm radial maze. *Animal Learning and Behavior*, 1987, 17, 12–30.

Brown, P., & Jenkins, H. M. Autoshaping of the pigeon's key-peck. *Journal of the Experimental Analysis of Behavior*, 1968, 11, 1–8.

Brown, R. *A first language: The early stages.* Cambridge, Mass.: Harvard University Press, 1973.

Brown, R., & Kulik, J. Flashbulb memories. *Cognition*, 1977, 5, 73–99.

Brown, R., & McNeill, D. The "tip-of-the-tongue" phenomenon. *Journal of Verbal Learning and Verbal Behavior*, 1966, 5, 325–377.

Brown, R. T., & Hamilton, A. S. Imprinting: Effects of discrepancy from rearing conditions on approach to a familiar imprinting object in a novel situation. *Journal of Comparative and Physiological Psychology*, 1977, 91, 784–793.

Bruce, D., & Crowley, J. J. Acoustic similarity effects on retrieval from secondary memory. *Journal of Verbal Learning and Verbal Behavior*, 1970, 9, 190–196.

Bruner, J. S., Goodnow, J. J., & Austin, G. A. *A study of thinking.* New York: Wiley, 1956.

Buchanan, G. M., & Bitterman, M. E. Learning in honeybees as a function of amount and frequency of reward. *Animal Learning & Behavior*, 1988, 16(3), 247–255.

Bugelski, B. R. Extinction with and without subgoal reinforcement. *Journal of Comparative Psychology*, 1938, 26, 121–133.

Bugelski, B. R. Presentation time, total time, and mediation in paired-associate learning. *Journal of Experimental Psychology*, 1962, 63, 409–412.

Bugelski, B. R. Images as mediators in one-trial paired-associate learning. II: Self-timing in successive lists. *Journal of Experimental Psychology*, 1968, 77, 328–334.

Bugelski, B. R., & Cadwallader, T. C. A reappraisal of the transfer and retroaction surface. *Journal of Experimental Psychology*, 1956, 52, 360–366.

Burgio, L. D., Whitman, T. L., & Reid, D. H. A participative management approach for improving direct-care staff performance in an institutional setting. *Journal of Applied Behavior Analysis*, 1983, 16, 37–53.

Buschke, H. Two-dimensional recall: Immediate identification of clusters in episodic and semantic memory. *Journal of Verbal Learning and Verbal Behavior*, 1977, 16, 201–215.

Bushnell, M. C., & Weiss, S. J. Microanalysis of variable-interval performance during stimulus compounding. *Animal Learning and Behavior*, 1978, 6, 66–71.

Butler, R. A. Discrimination by rhesus monkeys to visual-exploration motivation. *Journal of Comparative and Physiological Psychology*, 1953, 46, 95–98.

Butler, R. A. Investigative behavior. In A. M. Schrier, H. F. Harlow, & F. Stollnitz (Eds.), *Behavior of nonhuman primates*, Vol. II. New York: Academic Press, 1965.

Capaldi, E. D., Viveiros, D. M., & Campbell, D. H. Food as a contextual cue in counterconditioning experiments: Is there a counterconditioning process? *Animal Learning and Behavior*, 1983, 11, 213–222.

Capaldi, E. J. Memory and learning: A sequential viewpoint. In W. K. Honig & R. H. James (Eds.), *Animal memory.* New York: Academic Press, 1971.

Capaldi, E. J. Effects of schedule and delay of reinforcement on acquisition speed. *Animal Learning and Behavior*, 1978, 6, 330–334.

Capaldi, E. J., Miller, D. J., & Alptekin, S. Multiple-food-unit-incentive effect: Nonconservation of weight of food reward by rats. *Journal of Experimental Psychology: Animal Behavior Processes*, 1989, 15(1), 75–80.

Carey, S. T., & Lockhart, R. S. Encoding differences in recognition and recall. *Memory and Cognition*, 1973, 1, 297–300.

Carmichael, L., Hogan, H. P., & Walter, A. A. An experimental study of the effect of language on the reproduction of visually perceived forms. *Journal of Experimental Psychology*, 1932, 15, 73–86.

Carney, R. N., Levin, J. R., & Morrison, C. R. Mnemonic learning of artists and their paintings. *American Educational Research Journal*, Spring 1988, 25(1), 107–125.

Carpenter, P. A., & Eisenberg, P. Mental rotation and the frame of reference in blind and sighted individuals. *Perception and Psychophysics*, 1978, 23, 117–124.

Carpenter, P. A., & Just, M. A. Sentence comprehension: A psycholinguistic processing model of verification. *Psychological Review*, 1975, *82*, 45–73.

Carr, E. G., & Kologinsky, E. Acquisition of sign language by autistic children II: Spontaneity and generalization effects. *Journal of Applied Behavior Analysis*, 1983, *16*, 297–314.

Carterette, E. C., & Coleman, E. A. Organization in free recall. Paper presented at meeting of Psychonomic Society, Bryn Mawr, Pa., August 1963.

Casson, R. W. Schemata in cognitive anthropology. *Annual Review of Anthropology*, 1983, *12*, 429–462.

Ceraso, J., & Henderson, A. Unavailability and associative loss in RI and PI. *Journal of Experimental Psychology*, 1965, *70*, 300–303.

Cermak, L. S., & Reale, L. Depth of processing and retention of words by alcoholic Korsakoff patients. *Journal of Experimental Psychology*, 1978, *4*, 165–174.

Chambers, S. M. Letter and order information in lexical access. *Journal of Verbal Learning and Verbal Behavior*, 1979, *18*, 225–241.

Channell, S., & Hall, G. Contextual effects in latent inhibition with an appetitive conditioning procedure. *Animal Learning and Behavior*, 1983, *11*, 67–74.

Charlton, S. G. Differential conditionability: Reinforcing grooming in golden hamsters. *Animal Learning and Behavior*, 1983, *11*, 27–34.

Chase, W. G., & Simon, H. A. Perception in chess. *Cognitive Psychology*, 1973, *4*, 55–81.

Cheafle, M. D., & Rudy, J. W. Analysis of second-order odor-aversion conditioning in neonatal rats: Implications for Kamin's blocking effect. *Journal of Experimental Psychology: Animal Behavior Processes*, 1978, *4*, 237–249.

Chizar, D. A., & Spear, N. E. Proactive interference in a T-maze brightness discrimination task. *Psychonomic Science*, 1968, *11*, 107–108.

Chomsky, N. *Syntactic structures*. The Hague: Mouton, 1957.

Chomsky, N. *Aspects of the theory of syntax*. Cambridge, Mass.: MIT Press, 1965.

Clark H. H., & Chase, W. G. On the process of comparing sentences against pictures. *Cognitive Psychology*, 1972, *3*, 472–517.

Clark, H. H., & Clark, E. V. *Psychology and language*. New York: Harcourt Brace Jovanovich, 1977.

Clark, H. H., & Gerrig, R. J. Understanding old words with new meanings. *Journal of Verbal Learning and Verbal Behavior*, 1983, *22*, 591–608.

Clark, H. H., & Haviland, S. E. Comprehension and the given–new contract. In R. O. Freedle (Ed.), *Discourse processes: Advances in research and theory* (Vol. 1). Norwood, N. J.: Ablex, 1977.

Claxton, G. Special review feature: Memory research. *British Journal of Research*, 1978, *69*, 513–520.

Cofer, C. N. Does conceptual organization influence the amount retained in immediate free recall? In B. Kleinmuntz (Ed.), *Concepts and the structure of memory*. New York: Wiley, 1967.

Cofer, C. N. Constructive processes in memory. *American Scientist*, 1973, *61*, 537–543.

Cofer, C. N. *The structure of human memory*. San Francisco: W. H. Freeman, 1975.

Cofer, C. N., & Appley, M. H. *Motivation: Theory and research*. New York: Wiley, 1964.

Cofer, C. N., Failie, N. F., & Horton, D. L. Retroactive inhibition following reinstatement or maintenance of first-list responses by means of free recall. *Journal of Experimental Psychology*, 1971, *90*, 197–205.

Cohen, B. H. An investigation of recoding in free recall. *Journal of Experimental Psychology*, 1963, *65*, 368–376.

Cohen, B. H. Some-or-none characteristics of coding behavior. *Journal of Verbal Learning and Verbal Behavior*, 1966, *5*, 182–187.

Cohen, C. The case for the use of animals in biomedical research. *The New England Journal of Medicine*, 1986, *315*, 865–870.

Cohen, N. J., McCloskey, M., & Wible, C. G. There is still no case for a flashbulb-memory mechanism: Reply to Schmidt and Bohannon. *Journal of Experimental Psychology: General*, 1988, *117(3)*, 336–338.

Cohen, P. S., & Campagnoni, F. R. The nature and determinants of spatial retreat in the pigeon between periodic grain presentation. *Animal Learning and Behavior*, 1989, *17*, 39–48.

Cohen, R. L. Recency effects in long-term recall and recognition. *Journal of Verbal Learning and Verbal Behavior*, 1970, 9, 672–678.

Coleman, R. S., Whitman, T. L., & Johnson, M. R. Suppression of self-stimulatory behavior of a profoundly retarded boy across staff and settings: An assessment of situational generalization. *Behavior Therapy*, 1979, 10, 266–280.

Coleman, S. R. Consequences of response-contingent change in unconditioned stimulus intensity upon the rabbit (*Oryctolagus cuniculus*) nictitating membrane response. *Journal of Comparative and Physiological Psychology*, 1975, 88, 591–595.

Collier, G. Life in a closed economy: The ecology of learning and motivation. In M. D. Zeiler & P. Harzem (Eds.), *Advances in analysis of behavior: Biological factors in learning.* (Vol. 3). New York: Wiley, 1983.

Collier, G. Some properties of saccharin as a reinforcer. *Journal of Experimental Psychology*, 1962, 64, 184–191.

Collier, G., & Marx, M. H. Changes in performance as a function of shifts in the magnitude of reinforcement. *Journal of Experimental Psychology*, 1959, 57, 305–309.

Collins, A. M., & Loftus, E. F. A spreading activation theory of semantic processing. *Psychological Review*, 1975, 82, 407–428.

Collins, A. M., & Quillian, M. R. Retrieval time from semantic memory. *Journal of Verbal Learning and Verbal Behavior*, 1969, 8, 240–247.

Collins, A. M., & Quillian, M. R. How to make a language user. In E. Tulving & W. Donaldson (Eds.), *Organization and memory.* New York: Academic Press, 1972.

Commons, M. L., Kacelnik, A., & Shettleworth, S. J. *Quantitative analyses of behavior: Foraging (Vol. 6).* Hillsdale, N. J.: Lawrence Erlbaum Associates, 1987.

Conger, R., & Killeen, P. Use of concurrent operants in small group research. *Pacific Sociological Review*, 1974, 17, 399–416.

Conrad, R. Acoustic confusions in immediate memory. *British Journal of Psychology*, 1964, 55, 75–84.

Cooper, E. H., & Pantle, A. J. The total-time hypothesis in verbal learning. *Psychological Bulletin*, 1967, 68, 221–234.

Cooper, L. A., & Shepard, R. N. Chronometric studies of the rotation of mental images. In W. G. Chase (Ed.), *Visual information processing.* New York: Academic Press, 1973.

Corbett, A. T. Retrieval dynamics for rote and visual image mnemonics. *Journal of Verbal Learning and Verbal Behavior*, 1977, 16, 233–246.

Cotman, C. W., & McGaugh, J. L. *Behavioral neuroscience.* New York: Academic Press, 1980.

Couvillon, P. A., Klosterhalfen, S., & Bitterman, M. F. Analysis of overshadowing in honeybees. *Journal of Comparative Psychology*, 1983, 97, 154–166.

Cowan, N. Auditory memory: Procedures to examine two phases. In W. A. Yost & C. S. Watson (Eds.), *Auditory processing of complex sounds.* Hillsdale, N. J.: Lawrence Erlbaum Associates, 1987, 289–298. (a)

Cowan, N. Auditory sensory storage in relation to the growth of sensation and acoustic information extraction. *Journal of Experimental Psychology*, 1987, 13, 43–50. (b)

Cowan, N. Evolving conceptions of memory storage, selective attention, and their mutual constraints within the human information-processing system. *Psychological Bulletin*, 1988, 104, 163–191.

Craik, F. I. M. The fate of primary memory items in free recall. *Journal of Verbal Learning and Verbal Behavior*, 1970, 9, 143–148.

Craik, F. I. M. Levels of processing: Overview and closing comments. In L. S. Cermak & F. I. M. Craik (Eds.), *Levels of processing in human memory.* Hillsdale, N. J.: Lawrence Erlbaum Associates, 1979.

Craik, F. I. M., & Lockhart, R. S. Levels of processing: A framework for memory research. *Journal of Verbal Learning and Verbal Behavior*, 1972, 11, 671–684.

Craik, F. I. M., & Tulving, E. Depth of processing and the retention of words in episodic memory. *Journal of Experimental Psychology: General*, 1975, 104, 268–294.

Craik, F. I. M. & Watkins, M. J. The role of rehearsal in short-term memory. *Journal of Verbal Learning and Verbal Behavior*, 1973, 12, 599–607.

Crawford, M., Masterson, F., & Wilson, D. Species-specific defense reactions in escape-from-fear situations. *Animal Learning and Behavior*, 1977, *5*, 63–72.

Crespi, L. P. Quantitative variation of incentive and performance in the white rat. *American Journal of Psychology*, 1942, *55*, 467–517.

Crider, A. B., Goethals, G. R., Kavanaugh, R. D., & Solomon, P. R. *Psychology*. Glenview, Ill.: Scott, Foresman, 1989.

Crowder, R. G. Proactive and retroactive inhibition in the retention of a T-maze habit in rats. *Journal of Experimental Psychology*, 1967, *74*, 167–171.

Crowder, R. G. Inferential problems in echoic memory. In P. M. A. Rabbitt & S. Dornic (Eds.), *Attention and performance* (Vol. 5). London: Academic Press, 1974.

Crowder, R. G. Mechanisms of auditory backward masking in the stimulus suffix effect. *Psychological Review*, 1978, *85*, 502–524.

Crowder, R. G. The demise of short-term memory. *Acta Psychologica*, 1982, 291–323.

Crowell, C. R., & Bernhardt, T. P. The feature-positive effect and sign-tracking behavior during discrimination learning in the rat. *Animal Learning and Behavior*, 1979, *7*, 313–317.

Culbertson, J. L. Effects of brief reinforcement delays on acquisition and extinction of brightness discriminations in rats. *Journal of Comparative and Physiological Psychology*, 1970, *70*, 317–325.

Cullingford, R. Script application: Computer understanding of newspaper stories. Unpublished doctoral dissertation, Department of Computer Science, Yale University, 1978.

D'Agostino, P. R. The blocked-random effect in recall and recognition. *Journal of Verbal Learning and Verbal Behavior*, 1969, *8*, 815–820.

D'Agostino, P. R., & DeRemer, P. Repetition effects as a function of rehearsal and encoding variability. *Journal of Verbal Learning and Verbal Behavior*, 1973, *12*, 108–113.

Dale, H. C. A., & McGlaughlin, A. Evidence for acoustic coding in long-term memory. *Quarterly Journal of Experimental Psychology*, 1971, *23*, 1–7.

Dallett, K. M. The transfer surface reexamined. *Journal of Verbal Learning and Verbal Behavior*, 1962, *1*, 91–94.

Dalton, A. J., Rubino, C. A., & Hislop, M. W. Some effects of token rewards on school achievement of children with Down's syndrome. *Journal of Applied Behavior Analysis*, 1973, *6*, 251–259.

D'Amato, M. R. Secondary reinforcement and magnitude of primary reinforcement. *Journal of Comparative and Physiological Psychology*, 1955, *48*, 378–380.

D'Amato, M. R., & Fazzaro, J. Discriminated lever-press avoidance learning as a function of type and intensity of shock. *Journal of Comparative and Physiological Psychology*, 1966, *61*, 313–315.

D'Amato, M. R., & Van Sant, P. The person concept in monkeys (*Cebus Apella*). *Journal of Experimental Psychology: Animal Behavior Processes*, 1988, *14(1)*, 43–55.

D'Amato, M. R., Fazzaro, J., & Etkins, M. Anticipatory responding and avoidance discrimination as factors in avoidance conditioning. *Journal of Experimental Psychology*, 1968, *77*, 41–47.

Davidson, M. C. A functional analysis of chained fixed-interval schedule performance. *Journal of the Experimental Analysis of Behavior*, 1974, *21*, 323–330.

Davidson, N. A., & Grayson Osborne, J. Fixed-ratio and fixed-interval schedule control of matching-to-sample errors by children. *Journal of the Experimental Analysis of Behavior*, 1974, *21*, 27–36.

Davis, H., & Perusse, R. Human-based social interaction can reward a rat's behavior. *Animal Learning and Behavior*, 1988, *16(1)*, 89–92.

Davison, M. C. Preference for mixed-interval versus fixed-interval schedules: Number of component intervals. *Journal of the Experimental Analysis of Behavior*, 1972, *17*, 169–176.

Dawley, J. M. Generalization of the CS-preexposure effect transfers to taste-aversion learning. *Animal Learning and Behavior*, 1979, *7*, 23–24.

Day, J. C., & Bellezza, F. S. The relation between visual imagery mediators and recall. *Memory and Cognition*, 1983, *11*, 251–257.

Dean, M. G., & Kausler, D. H. Degree of first-list learning and stimulus meaningfulness as related to transfer in the A–B, C–B paradigm. *Journal of Verbal Learning and Verbal Behavior*. 1964, *3*, 330–334.

De Beni, R., & Cornoldi, C. Imagery limitations in totally congenitally blind subjects. *Journal of Experimental Psychology: Learning, Memory, and Cognition*, 1988, *14(4)*, 650–655.

Deese, J. On the structure of associative meaning. *Psychological Review*, 1962, 69, 161–175.

deGroot, A. D. *Het denken van den Schaker*. Amsterdam: North-Holland, 1946.

deGroot, A. D. *Thought and chance in chess*. The Hague: Moulton, 1965.

Dempster, F. N. Retroactive interference in the retention of prose: A reconsideration and new evidence. *Applied Cognitive Psychology*, 1988, 2, 97–113.

Dempser, F. N., & Rohwer, W. D. Component analysis of the elaborative encoding effect in paired-associate learning. *Journal of Experimental Psychology*, 1974, *103*, 400–408.

den Heyer, K., Briand, K., & Dannenberg, G. L. Strategic factors in lexical-decision tasks: Evidence for automatic and attention-driven processes. *Memory and Cognition*, 1983, *11*, 374–381.

Denny, M. R., Bell, R. C., & Clos, C. Two-choice, observational learning and reversal in the rat: S–S versus S–R effects. *Animal Learning and Behavior*, 1983, *11*, 223–228.

Derry, P. A., & Stone, G. L. Effects of cognitive-adjunct treatment on assertiveness. *Cognitive Theory and Research*, 1979, 3, 213–221.

Dess, N. K., & Overmier, J. B. General learned irrelevance: Proactive effects on Pavlovian conditioning in dogs. *Learning and Motivation*, 1989, 20, 1–14.

Deutsch, J. A. The neural basis of memory. *Psychology Today*, 1968, 1, 56–61.

Deutsch, J. A. The cholinergic synapse and the site of memory. *Science*, 1971, *174*, 788–794.

Deutsch, J. A., & Deutsch, D. *Physiological psychology*. Homewood, Ill.: Dorsey, 1973.

Dickinson, A., & Mackintosh, N. J. Classical conditioning in animals. In M. R. Rosensweig & L. W. Porter (Eds.), *Annual review of psychology* (Vol. 29). Palo Alto, Calif.: Annual Reviews, 1978.

Dinsmoor, J. A. A quantitative comparison of the discriminative and reinforcing functions of a stimulus. *Journal of Experimental Psychology*, 1950, 40, 458–472.

Dixon, M. J., Helsel, W. J., Rojahn, J., Cipollone, R., & Lubetsky, M. J. Aversive conditioning of visual screening with aromatic ammonia for treating aggressive and disruptive behavior in a developmentally disabled child. *Behavior Modification*, January 1989, *13(1)*, 91–107.

Dobrzecka, C., & Konorski, J. Qualitative versus directional cues in differential conditioning. I. Left leg–right leg differentiation to cues of a mixed character. *Acta Biologiae Experimentale*, 1967, 27, 163–168.

Dobrzecka, C., & Konorski, J. Qualitative versus directional cues in differential conditioning. *Acta Biologiae Experimentale*, 1968, *28*, 61–69.

Doke, L., Wolery, M., & Sumberg, C. Effects and side effects of response-contingent ammonia spirits. *Behavior Modification*, 1983, 7, 531–556.

Domjan, M. Ingestional aversion learning: Unique and general processes. In J. S. Rosenblatt, R. A. Hinde, C. Beer, & M. Busnel (Eds.), *Advances in the study of behavior* (Vol. 11). New York: Academic Press, 1980.

Domjan, M., & Buckhard, B. *The principles of learning and behavior*. Monterey, Calif.: Brooks/Cole, 1982.

Domjan, M., & Galef, B. G. Biological constraints on instrumental and classical conditioning. Retrospect and prospect. *Animal Learning and Behavior*, 1983, *11*, 151–161.

Domjan, M., Greene, P., & North, N. C. Contextual conditioning and the control of copulatory behavior by species-specific sign stimuli in male Japanese quail. *Journal of Experimental Psychology: Animal Behavior Processes*, 1989, *15(2)*, 147–153.

Donahoe, J. W., & Wessells, M. G. *Learning, language, and memory*. New York: Harper & Row, 1980.

Donnelly, R. E. Priming effects in successive episodic tests. *Journal of Experimental Psychology: Learning, Memory, and Cognition*, 1988, *14(2)*, 256–265.

Donovan, T. R., & Gershman, L. Experimental anxiety reduction: Systematic desensitization versus a false-feedback expectancy manipulation. *Journal of Behavior Therapy and Experimental Psychiatry*, 1979, *10*, 173–179.

Dooling, D. J., & Christiaansen, R. E. Episodic and semantic aspects of memory for prose. *Journal of Experimental Psychology: Human Learning and Memory*, 1977, 3, 428–436.

Dooling, J. L., & Lachman, R. Effects of comprehension on retention of prose. *Journal of Experimental Psychology*, 1971, *88*, 216–222.

Doran, J., & Holland, J. G. Control by stimulus features during fading. *Journal of the Experimental Analysis of Behavior*, 1979, *31*, 177–187.

Downing, J. D., Okanoya, K., & Dooling, R. J. Auditory short-term memory in the budgerigar (*Melopsittacus undulatus*). *Animal Learning and Behavior*, 1988, *16(2)*, 153–156.

Drachman, D. A., & Arbit, J. Memory and the hippocampal complex. *Archives of Neurology*, 1966, *15*, 52–61.

Dubois, D., & Denis, M. Knowledge organization and instantiation of general terms in sentence comprehension. *Journal of Experimental Psychology: Learning, Memory, and Cognition*, 1988, *14(4)*, 604–611.

Duncker, K. On problem-solving. *Psychological Monographs*, 1945, *58(5, Whole No. 270)*.

Dunham, P. J. Contrasted conditions of reinforcement: A selective critique. *Psychological Bulletin*, 1968, *69*, 295–315.

Dunham, P. J. Changes in unpunished responding during response-contingent punishment. *Animal Learning and Behavior*, 1978, *6*, 174–180.

Dunham, P. J., & Kilps, B. Shifts in magnitude of reinforcement: Confounded factors or contrast effects? *Journal of Experimental Psychology*, 1969, *79*, 373–374.

Durlach, P. J. Effect of signaling intertrial unconditioned stimuli in autoshaping. *Journal of Experimental Psychology*, 1983, *9*, 374–389.

Durso, F. T., & Johnson, M. K. Facilitation in naming and categorizing repeated pictures and words. *Journal of Experimental Psychology*, 1979, *5*, 449–459.

Dworkin, B. R., & Miller, N. E. Failure to replicate visceral learning in the acute curarized rat preparation. *Behavioral Neuroscience*, 1986, *100*, 299–314.

Edhouse, W. V., & White, K. G. Cumulative proactive interference in animal memory. *Animal Learning and Behavior*, 1988, *16(4)*, 461–467. (a)

Edhouse, W. V., & White, K. G. Sources of proactive interference in animal memory. *Journal of Experimental Psychology: Animal Behavior Processes*, 1988, *14(1)*, 56–70. (b)

Egan, D. E., & Greeno, J. G. Theory of rule induction: Knowledge acquired in concept learning, serial pattern learning, and problem solving. In L. W. Gregg (Ed.), *Knowledge and cognition*. Hillsdale, N. J.: Lawrence Erlbaum Associates, 1974

Egger, M. D., & Miller, N. E. Secondary reinforcement in rats as a function of information value and reliability of the stimulus. *Journal of Experimental Psychology*, 1962, *64*, 97–104.

Egger, M. D., & Miller, N. E. When is a reward reinforcing? An experimental study of the information hypothesis. *Journal of Comparative and Physiological Psychology*, 1963, *56*, 132–137.

Eibl-Eibesfeldt, I. *Love and hate: The natural history of behavior patterns*. New York: Holt, Rinehart & Winston, 1972.

Eich, J. E., Weingartner, H., Stillman, R. C., & Gillin, J. C. State-dependent accessibility of retrieval cues in the retention of a categorized list. *Journal of Verbal Learning and Verbal Behavior*, 1975, *14*, 408–417.

Ekstrand, B. R. Effect of sleep on memory. *Journal of Experimental Psychology*, 1967, *75*, 64–72.

Ekstrand, B. R., Wallace, W. P., & Underwood, B. J. A frequency theory of verbal-discrimination learning. *Psychological Review*, 1966, *73*, 566–578.

Ellis, H. C. *Fundamentals of human learning and cognition*. Dubuque, Iowa: William C. Brown, 1972.

Ellis, H. C. Stimulus encoding processes in human learning and memory. In G. H. Bower (Ed.), *The psychology of learning and motivation* (Vol. 7). New York: Academic Press, 1973.

Elmes, D. G. Interference in spatial memory. *Journal of Experimental Psychology: Learning, Memory, and Cognition*, 1988, *14(4)*, 668–675.

Elmes, D. G., Greener, W. I., & Wilkinson, W. C. Free recall of items presented after massed- and distributed-practice items. *American Journal of Psychology*, 1972, *85*, 237–240.

Elmes, D. G., Dye, G. S., & Herdian, N. J. What is the role of affect in the spacing effect? *Memory and Cognition*, 1983, *11*, 144–151.

Emmelkamp, P. M. G. The behavioral study of clinical phobias. In M. Hersen, R. M. Eisler, & P. M. Miller (Eds.), *Progress in behavior modification* (Vol. 8). New York: Academic Press, 1979.

Entwisle, D. R. *Word associations of young children*. Baltimore: Johns Hopkins Press, 1966.

Ernst, G. W., & Newell, A. *GPS: A case study in generality and problem solving*. New York: Academic Press, 1969.

Essock-Vitale, S. M. Comparison of ape and monkey modes of problem solution. *Journal of Comparative and Physiological Psychology*, 1978, 92, 942–957.

Estes, W. K. The statistical approach to learning theory. In S. Koch (Ed.), *Psychology: A study of a science* (Vol. 2). New York: McGraw-Hill, 1959.

Estes, W. K. Learning theory and the new "mental chemistry." *Psychological Review*, 1960, 67, 207–223.

Estes, W. K. New perspectives on some old issue in association theory. In N. J. Mackintosh & W. K. Honig (Eds.), *Fundamental issues in associative learning*. Halifax: Dalhousie University Press, 1969.

Estes, W. K., & Suppes, P. Foundations of linear models. In R. R. Bush & W. K. Estes (Eds.), *Studies in mathematical learning theory*. Stanford, Calif.: Stanford University Press, 1959.

Eysenck, M. W., & Eysenck, M. C. Processing depth, elaboration of coding, memory-stores, and expended processing capacity. *Journal of Experimental Psychology: Human Learning and Memory*, 1979, 5, 472–484.

Fabricius, E. Zur Ethologie junger Anatiden. *Acta Zoologica Fennica*, 1951, 68, 1–175.

Fabricius, E. Experiments on the following response of Mallard ducklings. *British Journal of Animal Behavior*, 1955, 3, 122.

Fabricius, E. Some aspects of imprinting in birds. *Symposium of the Zoological Society of London*, 1962, 8, 139–148.

Fabricius, E., & Boyd, H. Experiments on the following reactions of ducklings. *Wildfowl Trust Annual Report*, 1954, 6, 84–89.

Falk, J. L. The nature and determinants of adjunctive behavior. *Physiology and Behavior*, 1971, 6, 577–588.

Fanselow, M. S., & Tighe, T. J. Contextual conditioning with massed versus distributed unconditional stimuli in the absence of explicit conditional stimuli. *Journal of Experimental Psychology: Animal Behavior Processes*, 1988, 14(2), 187–199.

Fantino, E. Aversive control. In J. A. Nevin & G. S. Reynolds (Eds.), *The study of behavior: Learning, motivation, emotion, and instinct*. Glenview, Ill.: Scott, Foresman, 1973.

Fantino, E. Conditioned reinforcement: Choice and information. In W. K. Honig & J. E. R. Staddon (Eds.), *Handbook of operant behavior*. Englewood Cliffs, N. J.: Prentice-Hall, 1977.

Fantino, E., & Herrnstein, R. J. Secondary reinforcement and number of primary reinforcements. *Journal of the Experimental Analysis of Behavior*, 1968, 11, 9–14.

Fantino, E., & Logan, C. A. *The experimental analysis of behavior: A biological perspective*. San Francisco: W. H. Freeman, 1979.

Fantino, E., Sharp, D., & Cole, M. Factors facilitating lever press avoidance. *Journal of Comparative and Physiological Psychology*, 1966, 63, 214–217.

Farah, M. J. Is visual imagery really visual? Overlooked evidence from neuropsychology. *Psychological Review*, 1988, 95(3), 307–317.

Fenton, F., Calof, A., & Katzev, R. The effect of controllable and uncontrollable neonatal preshocks on adult escape/avoidance behavior in guinea pigs (*Cavia porcellus*). *Animal Learning and Behavior*, 1979, 7, 372–376.

Fernandez, A., & Glenberg, A. M. Changing environmental context does not reliably affect memory. *Memory and Cognition*, 1985, 13, 333–345.

Feustel, T. C., Shiffrin, R. M., & Salasoo, A. Episodic and lexical contributions to the repetition effect in word identification. *Journal of Experimental Psychology*, 1983, 112, 309–346.

Fields, L. Acquisition of stimulus control while introducing new stimuli in learning. *Journal of the Experimental Analysis of Behavior*, 1979, 32, 121–127.

Findley, J. D., & Brady, J. V. Facilitation of large ratio performances by use of a conditioned reinforcement. *Journal of the Experimental Analysis of Behavior*, 1965, 8, 125–129.

Finney, J. W., Rapoff, M. A., Hall, C. L., & Christophersen, E. R. Replication and social validation of habit reversed treatment for tics. *Behavior Therapy*, 1983, 14, 116–126.

Fiore, N. A. The inner healer: Imagery for coping with cancer and its therapy. *Journal of Mental Imagery*, 1988, 12(2), 79–82.

Fisk, A. D., & Schneider, W. Memory as a function of attention, level of processing, and automatization. *Journal of Experimental Psychology*, 1984, *10*, 181–197.

Fiske, D. W., & Maddi, S. R. *Functions of varied experience.* Homewood, Ill.: Dorsey, 1961.

Fiske, S., & Taylor, S. E. *Social cognition.* Reading, Mass.: Addison-Wesley, 1984.

Fitts, P. M., & Posner, M. I. *Human performance.* Monterey, Calif.: Brooks/Cole, 1967.

Flexser, A. J., & Tulving, E. Retrieval independence in recognition and recall. *Psychological Review*, 1978, *85*, 153–171.

Fodor, J. A. *The language of thought.* New York: Crowell, 1975.

Fodor, J. A., & Bever, T. G. The psychological reality of linguistic segments. *Journal of Verbal Learning and Verbal Behavior*, 1965, *4*, 414–420.

Fodor, J. A., Bever, T. G., & Garrett, M. F. *The psychology of language.* New York: McGraw-Hill, 1974.

Forestell, P. H., & Herman, L. M. Delayed matching of visual materials by a bottlenosed dolphin aided by auditory symbols. *Animal Learning and Behavior*, 1988, *16(2)*, 137–146.

Forrester, W. E. Retroactive inhibition and spontaneous recovery in the A–B, D–C paradigm. *Journal of Verbal Learning and Verbal Behavior*, 1970, *9*, 525–528.

Forrester, W. E. Effects of semantic and acoustic relatedness on free recall in a between-subjects design. *Psychological Reports*, 1972, *30*, 637–638.

Forrester, W. E., & King, D. J. Effects of semantic and acoustic relatedness of free recall and clustering. *Journal of Experimental Psychology*, 1971, *88*, 16–19.

Foss, D. J., & Harwood, D. A. Memory for sentences: Implication for human associative memory. *Journal of Verbal Learning and Verbal Behavior*, 1975, *14*, 1–16.

Fouts, R. S. Chimpanzee language and elephant tails: A theoretical synthesis. In J. de Luce & H. T. Wilder (Eds.), *Language in primates: Perspectives and implications.* New York: Springer-Verlag, 1983.

Fouts, R. S., & Couch, J. B. Cultural evolution of learned language in chimpanzees. In M. E. Hahn & E. C. Simmel (Eds.), *Communicative behavior and evolution.* New York: Academic Press, 1976.

Fouts, R. S., Hirsch, A. D., & Fouts, D. H. Cultural transmission of a human language in a chimpanzee mother/infant relationship. In H. E. Fitzgerald, J. A. Mullins, & P. Page (Eds.), *Psychological perspectives: Child nurturance series* (Vol. 4). New York: Plenum, 1982.

Fowler, H. *Curiosity and exploratory behavior.* New York: Macmillan, 1965.

Fox, P. W. Patterns of stability and change in behaviors of free associations. *Journal of Verbal Learning and Verbal Behavior*, 1970, *9*, 30–36.

Frankel, A., & Snyder, M. L. Poor performance following unsolvable problems: Learned helplessness or egotism? *Journal of Personality and Social Psychology*, 1978, *38*, 1425–1428.

Franks, J. J., & Bransford, J. D. Abstraction of visual patterns. *Journal of Experimental Psychology*, 1971, *90*, 65–74.

Frey, P. W., & Sears, R. J. Model of conditioning incorporating the Rescorla-Wagner associative axiom, a dynamic attention process, and a catastrophe rule. *Psychological Review*, 1978, *85*, 321–340.

Friman, P. C. Eliminating chronic thumb sucking by preventing a covarying response. *Journal of Behavior Therapy & Experimental Psychiatry*, 1988, *19(4)*, 301–304.

Fudim, O. K. Sensory preconditioning of flavors with a formalin-produced sodium need. *Journal of Experimental Psychology: Animal Behavior Processes*, 1978, *4*, 276–285.

Gabriel, M., Sparenburg, S. P., & Stolar, N. *The neurobiology of memory:* Ledoux & Hirst, 1986.

Gaioni, S. J., Hoffman, H. S., DePaulo, P., & Stratton, V. N. Imprinting in older ducklings. *Animal Learning and Behavior*, 1978, *6*, 19–26.

Galin, D., & Ornstein, R. Lateral specialization of cognitive mode: An EEG study. *Psychophysiology*, 1972, *9*, 412–418.

Gallagher, J. S. Sexual imprinting: A sensitive period in Japanese quail. (*Coturnix japonica*). *Journal of Comparative and Physiological Psychology*, 1977, *91*, 72–78.

Gallistel, C. R. Self-stimulation in the rat: Quantitative characteristics of the reward pathway. *Journal of Comparative and Physiological Psychology*, 1978, *92*, 977–998.

Gamzu, E., & Schwam, E. Autoshaping and automaintenance of a key-press response in squirrel monkeys. *Journal of the Experimental Analysis of Behavior*, 1974, 21, 361–371.

Ganz, L. Hue generalization and hue discriminability in *Macaca mulatta*. *Journal of Experimental Psychology*, 1962, 64, 142–150.

Ganz, L., & Riesen, A. H. Stimulus generalization to hue in the dark-reared macaque. *Journal of Comparative and Physiological Psychology*, 1962, 55, 92–99.

Garcia, J., Ervin, F., & Koelling, R. Learning with prolonged delay of reinforcement. *Psychonomic Science*, 1966, 5, 121–122.

Garcia, J., Ervin, F., Yorke, C., & Koelling, R. Conditioning with delayed vitamin injections. *Science*, 1967, 155, 716–718.

Garcia, J., Hankins, W. G., & Rusiniak, K. W. Behavioral regulation of the milieu interne in man and rat. *Science*, 1974, 185, 824–831.

Garcia, J., & Koelling, R. Relation of cue to consequence in avoidance learning. *Psychonomic Science*, 1966, 4, 123–124.

Garcia, J., McGowan, B. K., & Green, K. F. Biological constraints on conditioning. In A. H. Black & W. F. Prokasy (Eds.), *Classical conditioning II: Current theory and research*. New York: Appleton, 1972.

Garcia, J., & Rusiniak, K. W. What the nose learns from the mouth. Paper presented at the Symposium on Chemical Signals in Vertebrate and Aquatic Mammals, Syracuse University, 1979.

Garcia, J., Rusiniak, K. W., & Brett, L. P. Conditioning food-illness aversions in wild animals: Caveant Cononici. In H. Davis & H. M. B. Hurwitz (Eds.), *Operant-Pavlovian interactions*. Hillsdale, N. J.: Lawrence Erlbaum Associates, 1977.

Gardiner, J. M. Generation and priming effects in word-fragment completion. *Journal of Experimental Psychology: Learning, Memory, and Cognition*, 1988, 14(3), 495–501.

Gardiner, J. M., Gregg, V. H., & Hampton, J. A. Word frequency and generation effects. *Journal of Experimental Psychology: Learning, Memory, and Cognition*, 1988, 14(4), 687–693.

Gardner, B. T., & Gardner, R. A. Two-way communication with an infant chimpanzee. In A. Schrier & F. Stollnitz (Eds.), *Behavior of nonhuman primates* (Vol. 4). New York: Academic Press, 1971.

Gardner, B.T., & Gardner, R. A. Evidence for sentence constituents in the early utterances of child and chimpanzee. *Journal of Experimental Psychology: General*, 1975, 104, 244–267. (a)

Gardner, R. A., & Gardner, B. T. Early signs of language in child and chimpanzee. *Science*, 1975, 187, 752–753. (b)

Gardner, R. A., & Gardner, B. T. Comparative psychology and language acquisition. *Annals of the New York Academy of Science*, 1978, 309, 37–76.

Garfinkel, P. E., Kline, S. A., & Stancer, H. C. Treatment of anorexia nervosa using operant conditioning techniques. *Journal of Nervous and Mental Disease*, 1973, 157, 428–433.

Garrett, M., Bever, T., & Fodor, J. The active use of grammar in speech perception. *Perception and Psychophysics*, 1966, 1, 30–32.

Garskof, B. E., & Houston, J. P. Measurement of verbal relatedness: An idiographic approach. *Psychological Review*, 1963, 70, 277–288.

Gartman, L. M., & Johnson, N. F. Massed versus distributed repetition of homographs: A test of the differential-encoding hypothesis. *Journal of Verbal Learning and Verbal Behavior*, 1972, 11, 801–808.

Gazzaniga, M. S. One brain—two minds? *American Science*, 1972, 60, 311–317.

Gazzaniga, M. S. *The bisected brain*. New York: Appleton, 1970.

Gazzaniga, M. S. Right hemisphere language: Remaining problems. *American Psychologist*, 1984, 39, 1494–1495.

Gazzaniga, M. S., & Sperry, R. W. Language after section of the cerebral commisures. *Brain*, 1967, 90, 131–148.

Geller, E. S. Rewarding safety belt usage at an industrial setting: Tests of treatment generality and response maintenance. *Journal of Applied Behavior Analysis*, 1983, 16, 189–202.

Gerall, A. A., Sampson, P. B., & Boslov, G. L. Classical conditioning of human pupillary dilation. *Journal of Experimental Psychology*, 1957, 54, 457–474.

Gerrig, R. S., & Healy, A. T. Dual process in metaphor understanding: Comprehension and appreciation. *Journal of Experimental Psychology*, 1983, 9, 667–675.

Gerson, R., & Henderson, R.W. Conditions that potentiate the effects of electroconvulsive shock administered 24 hours after aversive training. *Animal Learning and Behavior*, 1978, *6*, 346–351.

Ghatala, E. S., Levin, J. R., Bell, J. A., Truman, D. L., & Lodico, M. G. The effects of semantic and nonsemantic factors in the integration of verbal units in recognition memory. *Journal of Experimental Psychology: Human Learning and Memory*, 1978, *4*, 647–655.

Gibbons, J., Baldock, M. D., Locurto, C., Gold, L., & Terrace, H. S. Trial and intertrial durations in autoshaping. *Journal of Experimental Psychology: Animal Behavior Processes*, 1977, *3*, 264–268.

Gibbs, C. M., Latham, S. B., & Gormezano, I. Classical conditioning of the rabbit membrane response: Effects of reinforcement schedule on response maintenance and resistance to extinction. *Animal Learning and Behavior*, 1978, *6*, 209–215.

Gibson, E. J. A systematic application of the concepts of generalization and differentiation to verbal learning. *Psychological Review*, 1940, *47*, 196–229.

Gibson, E. J. Retroactive inhibition as a function of degree of generalization between tasks. *Journal of Experimental Psychology*, 1941, *28*, 93–115.

Gillan, D. J., Premack, D., & Woodruff, G. Reasoning in the chimpanzee: I. Analogical reasoning. *Journal of Experimental Psychology*, 1981, *7*, 1–17.

Gilligan, S. G., & Bower, G. H. Cognitive consequences of emotional arousal. In C. E. Izard, J. Kagan, & R. B. Zajonc (Eds.), *Emotions, cognition, & behavior*. Cambridge, England: Cambridge University Press, 1984.

Glanzer, M. Storage mechanisms in recall. In G. H. Bower (Ed.), *The psychology of learning and motivation* (Vol. 5). New York: Academic Press, 1972.

Glanzer, M., & Ehrenreich, S. L. Structure and search of the internal lexicon. *Journal of Verbal Learning and Verbal Behavior*, 1979, *18*, 381–398.

Glanzer, M., & Koppenall, L. The effect of encoding tasks on free recall: Stages and levels. *Journal of Verbal Learning and Verbal Behavior*, 1977, *16*, 21–28.

Glanzer, M., & Razel, M. The size of the unit in short-term storage. *Journal of Verbal Learning and Verbal Behavior*, 1974, *13*, 114–131.

Glanzer, M., & Schwartz, A. Mnemonic structure in free recall: Differential effects on STS and LTS. *Journal of Verbal Learning and Verbal Behavior*, 1971, *10*, 194–198.

Glassman, E. Macromolecules and behavior: A commentary. In F. O. Schmitt & F. G. Worden (Eds.), *The neurosciences: Third study program*. Cambridge, Mass.: MIT Press, 1974.

Glassman, W. E. Subvocal activity and acoustic confusions in short-term memory. *Journal of Experimental Psychology*, 1972, *96*, 164–169.

Glazer, H. I., & Weiss, J. M. Long-term and transitory interference effects. *Journal of Experimental Psychology: Animal Behavior Processes*, 1976, *2*, 191–201.

Gleitman, H. Forgetting of long-term memories in animals. In W. K. Honig & P. H. R. James (Eds.), *Animal memory*. New York: Academic Press, 1971.

Gleitman, H., & Jung, L. Retention in rats: The effect of proactive interference. *Science*, 1963, *142*, 1683–1684.

Glenberg, A. M. Influences of retrieval processes on the spacing effect in free recall. *Journal of Experimental Psychology: Human Learning and Memory*, 1977, *3*, 282–294.

Glenberg, A. M. Component-levels theory of the effects of spacing of repetitions on recall and recognition. *Memory and Cognition*, 1979, *7*, 95–112.

Glenberg, A. M., & Adams, F. Type I rehearsal and recognition. *Journal of Verbal Learning and Verbal Behavior*, 1978, *17*, 455–463.

Glenberg, A. M., & Bradley, M. M. Mental contiguity. *Journal of Experimental Psychology: Human Learning and Memory*, 1979, *5*, 88–97.

Glenberg, A. M., Smith, S. M., & Green, C. Type I rehearsal: Maintenance and more. *Journal of Verbal Learning and Verbal Behavior*, 1977, *16*, 339–352.

Glickman, S. E., & Schiff, B. B. A biological theory of reinforcement. *Psychological Review*, 1967, *74*, 81–109.

Glow, P. H., & Winefield, A. H. Response contingent sensory change in a causally structured environment. *Animal Learning and Behavior*, 1978, *6*, 1–18.

Goggin, J., & Martin, E. Forced stimulus encoding and retroactive interference. *Journal of Experimental Psychology*, 1970, *84*, 131–136.

Gold, P. Neurobiological features common to memory modulation by many treatments. *Animal Learning and Behavior*, 1989, *17*, 94–100.

Gold, P. E., & King, R. A. Retrograde amnesia: Storage failure versus retrieval failure. *Psychological Review*, 1974, *81*, 465–469.

Goldiamond, I. Stuttering and fluency as manipulatable operant response classes. In L. Krasner & L. P. Ullman (Eds.), *Research in behavior modification*. New York: Holt, Rinehart & Winston, 1965.

Goldstein, D. S. Instrumental cardiovascular conditioning: A review. *The Pavlovian Journal of Biological Science*. 1979, *14*, 108–127.

Goldwater, B. C. Psychological significance of pupillary movement. *Psychological Bulletin*, 1972, 77, 340–355.

Gollub, L. R. Conditioned reinforcement: Schedules effect. In W. K. Honig & J. E. R. Staddon (Eds.), *Handbook of operant behavior*. Englewood Cliffs, N. J.: Prentice-Hall, 1977.

Gordon, W. C. *Learning and memory*. Belmont, Calif.: Wadsworth, 1989.

Gormezano, I., Kehoe, E. J., & Marshall, B. S. Twenty years of classical conditioning research with the rabbit. *Progress in Psychobiology and Physiological Psychology*, 1983, *10*, 197–275.

Gormezano, I., Prokasy, W. F., & Thompson, R. F. *Classical conditioning*. Hillsdale, N. J.: Lawrence Erlbaum Associates, 1987.

Gould, J. L. *Ethology*. New York: Norton, 1982.

Graesser, A., & Mandler, G. Limited processing capacity constrains the storage of unrelated sets of words and retrieval from natural categories. *Journal of Experimental Psychology: Human Learning and Memory*, 1978, *4*, 86–100.

Grant, D. A. Classical and operant conditioning. In A. W. Melton (Ed.), *Categories of human learning*. New York: Academic Press, 1964.

Grant, D. S. Proactive interference in pigeon short-term memory. *Journal of Experimental Psychology: Animal Behavior Processes*, 1975, *1*, 207–220.

Grant, D. S. Effect of sample presentation time on long-delay matching in the pigeon. *Learning and Motivation*, 1976, *7*, 580–590.

Grant, D. S., Brewster, R. G., & Stierhoff, K. A. "Surprisingness" and short-term retention in pigeons. *Journal of Experimental Psycholgy*, 1983, *9*, 63–79.

Gray, J. J. Positive reinforcement and punishment in the treatment of childhood trichotillomania. *Journal of Behavior Therapy and Experimental Psychiatry*, 1979, *10*, 125–129.

Green, E. Biofeedback for mind–body self-regulation: Healing and creativity. In D. Shapiro, T. X. Barber, L. V. DiCara, J. Kamiya, N. E. Miller, & J. Stoyva (Eds.), *Biofeedback and self-control 1972*. Chicago: Aldine, 1973.

Green, L., & Rachlin, H. Economic and biological influences on a pigeon's key peck. *Journal of the Experimental Analysis of Behavior*, 1975, *23*, 55–62.

Green, L., Rachlin, H., & Hanson, J. Matching and maximizing concurrent ratio-interval schedules. *Journal of the Experimental Analysis of Behavior*, 1983, *40*, 217–224.

Greenberg, S. N., & Engle, R. W. Voice change in the stimulus suffix effect: Are the effects structural or strategic? *Memory and Cognition*, 1983, *11*, 551–556.

Greeno, J. G. Conservation of information-processing capacity in paired-associate memorizing. *Journal of Verbal Learning and Verbal Behavior*, 1970, *9*, 581–586.

Greeno, J. G. Hobbits and orcs: Acquisition of a sequential concept. *Cognitive Psychology*, 1974, *6*, 270–292.

Greeno, J. G., James, C. T., & DaPolito, F. J. A cognitive interpretation of negative transfer and forgetting of paired associates. *Journal of Verbal Learning and Verbal Behavior*, 1971, *10*, 331–345.

Greeno, J. G., Magone, M. E., & Chaiklin, S. Theory of constructions and set in problem solving. *Memory and Cognition*, 1979, *7*, 445–461.

Greenspoon, J. The reinforcing effect of two spoken sounds on the frequency of two responses. *American Journal of Psychology*, 1955, *68*, 409–416.

Grice, G. R. The relation of secondary reinforcement to delayed reward in visual discrimination learning. *Journal of Experimental Psychology*, 1948, *38*, 1–16.

Grice, G. R., & Hunter, J. J. Stimulus intensity effects depend on the type of experimental design. *Psychological Review*, 1964, 71, 247–256.

Griffith, D. Comparison of control processes for recognition and recall. *Journal of Experimental Psychology: Human Learning and Memory*, 1975, 104, 223–228.

Groves, P. M., & Rebec, G. V. *Introduction to biological psychology* (3rd ed.). Dubuque, Iowa: Wm. C. Brown, 1988.

Gustavson, C. R., Garcia, J., Hankins, W. G., & Rusiniak, K. W. Coyote predation control by aversive conditioning. *Science*, 1974, 184, 581–583.

Guthrie, E. R. Association as a function of time interval. *Psychological Review*, 1933, 40, 355–367.

Guthrie, E. R. *The psychology of learning*. New York: Harper, 1935.

Guthrie, E. R. *The psychology of learning* (rev. ed.). New York: Harper, 1952.

Guttman, N., & Kalish, H. I. Discriminability and stimulus generalization. *Journal of Experimental Psychology*, 1956, 51, 79–88.

Gynther, M. D. Differential eyelid conditioning as a function of stimulus similarity and strength of response to the CS. *Journal of Experimental Psychology*, 1957, 53, 408–416.

Haggbloom, S. J. Blocking and partial reinforcement: Effects of N–R transitions early vs. late in training on resistance to extinction. *Bulletin of the Psychonomic Society*, 1983, 21, 153–156.

Haig, K. A., Rawlins, J. N. P., Olton, D. S., Mead, A., & Taylor, B. Food searching strategies of rats: Variables affecting the relative strength of stay and shift strategies. *Journal of Experimental Psychology*, 1983, 9, 337–348.

Hall, J. F. *Learning and memory*. Boston: Allyn & Bacon, 1989.

Hall, G., & Pearce, J. M. Latent inhibition of a CS during CS–US pairing. *Journal of Experimental Psychology*, 1979, 5, 31–42.

Hall, J. F. Studies in secondary reinforcement: II. Secondary reinforcement as a function of the strength of the drive during primary reinforcement. *Journal of Comparative and Physiological Psychology*, 1951, 44, 462–466.

Hall, J. F. *Classical conditioning and instrumental learning: A contemporary approach*. Philadelphia: Lippincott, 1976.

Hall, J. F. *An invitation to learning and memory*. Boston: Allyn & Bacon, 1982.

Hall, J. F. Recall versus recognition: A methodological note. *Journal of Experimental Psychology*, 1983, 9, 346–349.

Hall, R. D., & Kling, J. W. Amount of consumatory activity and performance in a modified T maze. *Journal of Comparative and Physiological Psychology*, 1960, 53, 165–168.

Halle, J. W., Marshall, A. M., & Spradlin, J. E. Time delay: A technique to increase language use and facilitate generalization in retarded children. *Journal of Applied Behavior Analysis*, 1979, 12, 431–439.

Halpern, A. R. Mental scanning in auditory imagery for songs. *Journal of Experimental Psychology: Learning, Memory and Cognition*, 1988, 14(3), 434–443.

Hamilton, R. J. Retroactive facilitation as a function of degree of generalization between tasks. *Journal of Experimental Psychology*, 1943, 32, 363–376.

Hampson, P. J., & Morris, P. E. Unfulfilled expectations: A criticism of Neisser's theory of imagery. *Cognition*, 1978, 6, 79–85.

Hampton, J. A. Polymorphous concepts in semantic memory. *Journal of Verbal Learning and Verbal Behavior*, 1979, 18, 441–461.

Hanawalt, N. G., & Demarest, I. H. The effect of verbal suggestion in the recall period upon the reproduction of visually perceived forms. *Journal of Experimental Psychology*, 1939, 25, 159–174.

Hankins, W. G., Rusiniak, K. W., & Garcia, J. Dissociation of odor and taste in shock-avoidance learning. *Behavioral Biology*, 1976, 18, 345.

Hanley, G. L., & Levine, M. Spatial problem solving: The integration of independently learned cognitive maps. *Memory and Cognition*, 1983, 11, 415–422.

Hansen, G., Tomie, A., Thomas, D. R., & Thomas, D. H. Effect of test stimulus range on stimulus generalization in human subjects. *Journal of Experimental Psychology*, 1974, 102, 634–639.

Harlow, H. F. Forward conditioning, backward conditioning and pseudoconditioning in the goldfish. *Journal of Genetic Psychology*, 1939, 55, 49–58.

Harlow, H. F. Learning by rhesus monkeys on the basis of manipulation–exploration motives. *Science*, 1953, 117, 466–467.

Harlow, H. F., Harlow, M. C., & Meyer, D. R. Learning motivated by a manipulation drive. *Journal of Experimental Psychology*, 1950, 40, 228–234.

Harlow, H. F., & Toltzein, F. Formation of pseudoconditioned responses in cats. *Journal of General Psychology*, 1940, 23, 367–375.

Harris, P. L., Morris, P. E., & Bassett, E. Classifying pictures and words: Implications for the dual-coding hypothesis. *Memory and Cognition*, 1977, 5, 242–246.

Hasher, L., & Chromiak, W. The processing of frequency information: An automatic mechanism? *Journal of Verbal Learning and Verbal Behavior*, 1977, 16, 173–184.

Hashtroudi, S., Ferguson, S. A., Rappold, V. A., & Chrosniak, L. D. Data-driven and conceptually driven processes in partial-word identification and recognition. *Journal of Experimental Psychology: Learning, Memory, and Cognition*, 1988, 14(4), 749–757.

Hastie, R. Social inference. *Annual Review of Psychology*, 1983, 34, 511–542.

Hatch, J. P., & Gatchel, R. J. Development of physiological response patterns concomitant with the learning of voluntary heart rate control. *Journal of Comparative and Physiological Psychology*, 1979, 93, 306–313.

Haviland, S. E., & Clark, H. H. What's new? Acquiring new information as a process in comprehension. *Journal of Verbal Learning and Verbal Behavior*, 1974, 13, 515–521.

Hayes, J. R., & Simon, H. A. Understanding written problem instructions. In L. W. Gregg (Ed.), *Knowledge and cognition*. Hillsdale, N. J.: Lawrence Erlbaum Associates, 1974.

Hayes, K. J., & Hayes, C. Imitation in a home-raised chimpanzee. *Journal of Comparative and Physiological Psychology*, 1952, 45, 450–459.

Hayes-Roth, B., & Hayes-Roth, F. Plasticity in memorial networks. *Journal of Verbal Learning and Verbal Behavior*, 1975, 14, 506–522.

Hayes-Roth, B., & Hayes-Roth, F. The prominence of lexical information in memory: Representations of meaning. *Journal of Verbal Learning and Verbal Behavior*, 1977, 16, 119–136.

Hayes-Roth, B., & Hayes-Roth, F. A cognitive model of planning. *Cognitive Science*, 1979, 3, 275–310.

Hayes-Roth, B., & Thorndyke, P. W. Integration of knowledge from text. *Journal of Verbal Learning and Verbal Behavior*, 1979, 18, 91–108.

Hayes-Roth, F. Distinguishing theories of representation: A critique of Anderson's "Argument concerning mental imagery." *Psychological Review*, 1979, 86, 376–382.

Haygood, R. C., & Bourne, L. E. Attribute and rule-learning aspects of conceptual behavior. *Psychological Review*, 1965, 72, 175–195.

Hearst, E., & Koresko, M. B. Stimulus generalization and the amount of prior training on variable-interval reinforcement. *Journal of Comparative and Physiological Psychology*, 1968, 66, 133–138.

Hearst, E., Koresko, M. B., & Poppen, R. Stimulus generalization and the response reinforcement contingency. *Journal of the Experimental Analysis of Behavior*, 1964, 7, 369–380.

Heath, R. G., & Mickle, W. A. Evaluation of seven years' experience with depth electrode studies in human patients. In E. R. Ramey & D. S. O'Doherty (Eds.), *Electrical studies on the unanesthetized brain*. New York: Harper & Row, 1960.

Hebb, D. O. *The organization of behavior*. New York: Wiley, 1949.

Hebert, J. A., Bullock, M., Levitt, L., Woodward, K.G., & McGuirk, F. D. Context and frequency effects in the generalization of a human voluntary response. *Journal of Experimental Psychology*, 1974, 102, 456–462.

Heinroth, O. Beiträge zur Biologie, namentlich Ethologie und Physiologie der Anatiden. *Verhandlungen 5 Internationalen Ornitholegisch Kongress*, 1911, 589–702.

Hellige, J. B., Cox, P. J., & Litvac, L. Information processing in the cerebral hemispheres: Selective hemispheric activation and capacity limitations. *Journal of Experimental Psychology: General*, 1979, 108, 251–279.

Hellige, J. B., & Grant, D. A. Eyelid conditioning performance when the mode of reinforcement is changed from classical to instrumental avoidance and vice versa. *Journal of Experimental Psychology*, 1974, 102, 710–719. (a)

Hellige, J. B., & Grant, D. A. Response rate and development of response topography in eyelid conditioning under different conditions of reinforcement. *Journal of Experimental Psychology*, 1974, 103, 574–582. (b)

Hellige, S. B., & Wong, T. M. Hemispheric-specific interference in dichotic listening: Task variables and individual differences. *Journal of Experimental Psychology*, 1983, *112*, 218–239.

Henik, A., Friedrich, F. J., & Kellogg, W. A. The dependence of semantic relatedness effects upon prime processing. *Memory and Cognition*, 1983, *11*, 366–373.

Herrnstein, R. J. On the law of effect. *Journal of the Experimental Analysis of Behavior*, 1970, *13*, 243–266.

Herrnstein, R. J. Acquisition, generalization, and discrimination reversal of a natural concept. *Journal of Experimental Psychology: Animal Behavior Processes*, 1979, *5*, 116–129.

Hess, E. H. "Imprinting" in animals. *Scientific American*, 1958, *199*, 81–90.

Hess, E. H. Imprinting. *Science*, 1959, *130*, 133–141.

Hess, E. H. Imprinting in birds. *Science*, 1964, *146*, 1128–1139.

Hess, E. H. Ethology and developmental psychology. In P. Mussen (Ed.), *Carmichael's manual of child psychology*. New York: Wiley, 1970.

Hess, E. H. "Imprinting" in a natural laboratory. *Scientific American*, 1972, *227*, 24–31.

Hess, E. H. *Imprinting*. Princeton, N. J.: Van Nostrand-Reinhold, 1973.

Hess, E. H., & Schaefer, H. H. Innate behavior patterns as indications of the "critical period." *Zeitschrift für Tierpsychologie*, 1959, *16*, 155–160.

Hewett, F. M. Teaching speech to an autistic child through operant conditioning. *American Journal of Orthopsychiatry*, 1965, *35*, 927–936.

Hilgard, E. R., & Bower, G. H. *Theories of learning* (4th ed.). Englewood Cliffs, N. J.: Prentice-Hall, 1975.

Hilgard, E. R., & Marquis, D. G. *Conditioning and learning*. New York: Appleton, 1940.

Hill, F. A., & Wickens, D. D. The effect of stimulus compounding in paired-associate learning. *Journal of Verbal Learning and Verbal Behavior*, 1962, *1*, 144–151.

Hill, J. W., & Bliss, J. C. Modeling a tactile sensory register. *Perception and Psychophysics*, 1968, *4*, 91–101.

Hill, W. F. Activity as an autonomous drive. *Journal of Comparative and Physiological Psychology*, 1965, *49*, 15–19.

Hill, W. F. *Learning: A survey of psychological interpretations*. Scranton, Pa.: Chandler, 1971.

Hinrichs, J. V., & Grunke, M. E. Control processes in short-term memory: Use of retention interval information. *Journal of Experimental Psychology: Human Learning and Memory*, 1975, *104*, 229–237.

Hinson, J. M., & Staddon, J. E. R. Matching, maximizing, and hill-climbing. *Journal of the Experimental Analysis of Behavior*, 1983, *40*, 321–331.

Hintzman, D. L. On testing the independence of associations. *Psychological Review*, 1972, *79*, 261–264.

Hintzman, D. L. Repetition and memory. In G. H. Bower (Ed.), *The psychology of learning and motivation* (Vol. 10). New York: Academic Press, 1976.

Hintzman, D. L. *The psychology of learning and memory*. San Francisco: W. H. Freeman, 1978.

Hintzman, D. L. Episodic versus semantic memory: A distinction whose time has come—and gone? *Behavioral and Brain Sciences*, 1984, *7*, 240–241.

Hintzman, D. L., & Block, R. A. Repetition and memory: Evidence for a multiple trace hypothesis. *Journal of Experimental Psychology*, 1971, *88*, 297–306.

Hintzman, D. L., Block, R. A., & Summers, J. J. Modality tags and memory for repetitions: Locus of the spacing effect. *Journal of Verbal Learning and Verbal Behavior*, 1973, *12*, 229–239.

Hintzman, D. L., & Stern, D. Contextual variability and memory for frequency. *Journal of Experimental Psychology: Human Learning and Memory*, 1978, *4*, 539–549.

Hirshman, E., & Bjork, R. A. The generation effect: Support for a two-factor theory. *Journal of Experimental Psychology: Learning, Memory, and Cognition*, 1988, *14(3)*, 484–494.

Hirst, W., Phelps, E. A., Johnson, M. K., & Volpe, B. T. More on recognition and recall in amnesics. *Journal of Experimental Psychology: Learning, Memory, and Cognition*, 1988, *14(4)*, 758–762.

Hobbs, S. H., & Elkins, R. L. Operant performance of rats selectively bred for strong and weak acquisition of conditioned taste aversion. *Bulletin of the Psychonomic Society*, 1983, *21*, 303–306.

Hobson, S. L. Discriminability of fixed ratio schedules for pigeons: Effects of absolute ratio size. *Journal of the Experimental Analysis of Behavior*, 1975, *23*, 25–35.

Hoffman, H., & Spear, N. E. Facilitation and impairment of conditioning in the preweanling rat after prior exposure to the conditioned stimulus. *Animal Learning and Behavior*, 1989, *17*, 63–69.

Hoffman, H. S., & Ratner, A. M. A reinforcement model of imprinting: Implications for socialization in monkeys and men. *Psychological Review*, 1973, *80*, 527–544.

Hoffman, H. S., Ratner, A. M., & Eisener, L. A. Role of visual imprinting in the emergence of specific filial attachments in ducklings. *Journal of Comparative and Physiological Psychology*, 1972, *81*, 399–409.

Hogaboam, T. W., & Pellegrino, J. W. Hunting for individual differences in cognitive processes: Verbal ability and semantic processing of pictures and words. *Memory and Cognition*, 1978, *6*, 189–193.

Holden, A. E., O'Brien, G. T., Barlow, D. H., & Stetson, D. Self-help manual for agoraphobia: A preliminary report. *Behavior Therapy*, 1983, *14*, 545–556.

Holland, M. K., & Tarlow, G. *Using psychology* (2nd ed.). Boston: Little, Brown, 1980.

Holland, P. C. Conditioned stimulus as a determinant of the form of the Pavlovian conditioned response. *Journal of Experimental Psychology: Animal Behavior Processes*, 1977, *3*, 77–104.

Holland, P. C. Differential effects of omission contingencies on various components of Pavlovian appetitive conditioned responding in rats. *Journal of Experimental Psychology*, 1979, *5*, 178–193.

Holland, P. C., & Rescorla, R. A. Second-order conditioning with food unconditioned stimulus. *Journal of Comparative and Physiological Psychology*, 1975, *88*, 459–467.

Hollandsworth, J. G., Glazeski, R. C., Kirkland, K., Jones, G. E., & Van Norman, L. R. An analysis of the nature and effects of test anxiety: Cognitive, behavioral, and physiological components. *Cognitive Therapy and Research*, 1979, *3*, 165–180.

Hollingworth, H. C. Characteristic differences between recall and recognition. *American Journal of Psychology*, 1913, *24*, 533–544.

Honig, W. K. Discrimination, generalization, and transfer on the basis of stimulus differences. In D. I. Mostofsky (Ed.), *Stimulus generalization*. Stanford, Calif.: Stanford University Press, 1965.

Honig, W. K., & James, P. H. R. (Eds.), *Animal memory*. New York: Academic Press, 1971.

Houston, J. P. Verbal transfer and interlist similarities. *Psychological Review*, 1964, *71*, 412–414.

Houston, J. P. Verbal transfer as a function of S_1–R_2 and S_2–R_1 interlist similarity. *Journal of Experimental Psychology*, 1966, *71*, 232–235. (a)

Houston, J. P. First-list retention and time and method of recall. *Journal of Experimental Psychology*, 1966, *71*, 839–843. (b)

Houston, J. P. Stimulus selection as influenced by degrees of learning, attention, prior associations, and experience with the stimulus components. *Journal of Experimental Psychology*, 1967, *73*, 509–516.

Houston, J. P. *Motivation*. New York: Macmillan, 1985.

Houston, J. P., Bee, H., & Rimm, D. C. *Invitation to psychology* (2nd ed.). New York: Academic Press, 1983.

Houston, J. P., Hammen, C., Padilla, A., & Bee, H. *Invitation to psychology* (3rd ed.). San Diego: Harcourt Brace Jovanovich, 1989.

Hovland, C. I. The generalization of conditioned responses: IV. The effects of varying amounts of reinforcement upon the degree of generalization of conditioned responses. *Journal of Experimental Psychology*, 1937, *21*, 261–276.

Hubert, L. J., & Levin, J. R. Inference models for categorical clustering. *Psychological Bulletin*, 1977, *84*, 878–887.

Hull, C. L. Quantitative aspects of the evolution of concepts. *Psychological Monographs*, Whole No. 123, 1920.

Hull, C. L. *Principles of behavior*. New York: Appleton, 1943.

Hull, C. L. *Essentials of behavior*. New Haven, Conn.: Yale University Press, 1951.

Hull, C. L. *A behavior system*. New Haven, Conn.: Yale University Press, 1952.

Hulse, S. H. A precision liquid feeding system controlled by licking behavior. *Journal of the Experimental Analysis of Behavior*, 1960, *3*, 1.

Hulse, S. H. Reinforcement contrast effects in rats following experimental definition of a dimension of reinforcement magnitude. *Journal of Comparative and Physiological Psychology*, 1973, *85*, 160–170.

Hulse, S. H. Cognitive structure and serial pattern learning by animals. In S. H. Hulse, H. Fowler, & W. K. Honig (Eds.), *Cognitive processes in animal behavior*, Hillsdale, N. J.: Lawrence Erlbaum Associates, 1978.

Hulse, S. H., & Dorsky, N. P. Serial pattern learning by rats: Transfer of a formally defined stimulus relationship and the significance of nonreinforcement. *Animal Learning and Behavior*, 1979, *7*, 211–220.

Hulse, S. H., Egeth, H., & Deese, J. *The psychology of learning*. New York: McGraw-Hill, 1980.

Hulse, S. H., Fowler, H., & Honig, W. K. *Cognitive processes in animal behavior*. Hillsdale, N. J.: Lawrence Erlbaum Associates, 1978.

Humphreys, L. G. Generalization as a function of method of reinforcement. *Journal of Experimental Psychology*, 1939, *25*, 361–372.

Hunt, E. L. Establishment of conditioned responses in chick embryos. *Journal of Comparative and Physiological Psychology*, 1949, *42*, 107–117.

Hunt, R. R., & Elliot, J. M. The role of nonsemantic information in memory: Orthographic distinctiveness effects on retention. *Journal of Experimental Psychology*, 1980, *109*, 49–74.

Hunt, R. R., Elliott, J. M., & Spence, M. J. Independent effects of process and structure on encoding. *Journal of Experimental Psychology: Human Learning and Memory*, 1979, *5*, 339–347.

Hunt, R. R., & Mitchell, D. B. Specificity in nonsemantic orienting tasks and distinctive memory traces. *Journal of Experimental Psychology: Human Learning and Memory*, 1978, *4*, 121–135.

Hursh, S. R., & Fantino, E. Relative delay of reinforcement and choice. *Journal of the Experimental Analysis of Behavior*, 1973, *19*, 437–450.

Hutt, P. J. Rate of bar press as a function of quality and quantity of food reward. *Journal of Comparative and Physiological Psychology*, 1954, *47*, 235–239.

Huttenlocher, J., & Kubieck, L. F. The source of relatedness effects on naming latency. *Journal of Experimental Psychology*, 1983, *9*, 486–496.

Huttenlocher, J., & Lui, F. The semantic organization of some simple nouns and verbs. *Journal of Verbal Learning and Verbal Behavior*, 1979, *18*, 141–162.

Ilersich, T. J., Mazmanian, D. S., & Roberts, W. A. Foraging for covered and uncovered food on a radial maze. *Animal Learning and Behavior*, 1988, *16(4)*, 388–394.

Innis, N. K. Stimulus control of behavior during postreinforcement pause of FI schedules. *Animal Learning and Behavior*, 1979, *7*, 203–210.

Intraub, H. The role of implicit naming in pictorial encoding. *Journal of Experimental Psychology: Human Learning and Memory*, 1979, *5*, 78–87.

Isen, A. M. Toward understanding the role of affect in cognition. In R. S. Wyer & T. K. Krull (Eds.), *Handbook of social cognition* (Vol. 3). Hillsdale, N. J.: Lawrence Erlbaum Associates, 1984.

Jackson, R. L., & Fritsche, M. B. Potentiation and overshadowing in pigeons. *Learning and Motivation*, 1989, *20*, 15–35.

Jackson, R. L., & Minor, T. R. Effects of signaling inescapable shock on subsequent escape learning: Implications for theories of coping and "learned helplessness." *Journal of Experimental Psychology: Animal Behavior Processes*, 1988, *14(4)*, 390–400.

Jacob, R. G., Turner, S. M., Szekely, B. C., & Eidelman, B. H. Predicting outcome of relaxation therapy in headaches: The role of depression. *Behavior Therapy*, 1983, *14*, 457–465.

Jacobs, W. J., Zaborowski, J. A., & Whishaw, I. Q. Rats repeatedly placed on a hidden platform learn but quickly forget its location. *Journal of Experimental Psychology: Animal Behavior Processes*, 1989, *15(1)*, 36–42.

Jacoby, L. L. Encoding processes, rehearsal, and recall requirements. *Journal of Verbal Learning and Verbal Behavior*, 1973, *12*, 302–312.

Jacoby, L. L., & Bartz, W. H. Rehearsal and transfer to LTS. *Journal of Verbal Learning and Verbal Behavior*, 1972, *11*, 561–565.

Jacoby, L. L., & Goolkasian, P. Semantic versus acoustic coding: Retention and conditions of organization. *Journal of Verbal Learning and Verbal Behavior*, 1973, *12*, 324–333.

James, H. Flicker: An unconditioned stimulus for imprinting. *Canadian Journal of Psychology*, 1959, *13*, 59–67.

James, H. Imprinting with visual flicker: Evidence for a critical period. *Canadian Journal of Psychology*, 1960, *14*, 13–20.

James, W. *Principles of psychology.* New York: Holt, Rinehart & Winston, 1890.

Jeffrey, W. E. The effects of verbal and nonverbal responses in mediating an instrumental act. *Journal of Experimental Psychology*, 1953, *45*, 327–333.

Jeffries, R. The acquisition of expertise on simple puzzles. Paper presented at the meeting of the American Educational Research Association, San Francisco, 1979.

Jeffries, R., Polson, P. G., Razran, L., & Atwood, M. E. A process model for missionaries—cannibals and other river-crossing problems. *Cognitive Psychology*, 1977, *9*, 412–440.

Jenkins, H. M., & Harrison, R. H. Effect of discrimination training on auditory generalization. *Journal of Experimental Psychology*, 1960, *59*, 246–253.

Jenkins, H. M., & Moore, B. R. The form of the auto-shaped response with food or water reinforcers. *Journal of the Experimental Analysis of Behavior*, 1973, *20*, 163–181.

Jenkins, J. J., & Russell, W. A. Systematic changes in word association norms, 1910–1952. *Journal of Abnormal and Social Psychology*, 1960, *60*, 293–303.

Jitsumori, M., Wright, A. A., & Cook, R. G. Long-term proactive interference and novelty enhancement effects in monkey list memory. *Journal of Experimental Psychology: Animal Behavior Processes*, 1988, *14(2)*, 146–154.

Johnson, E. S. Validation of concept-learning strategies. *Journal of Experimental Psychology: General*, 1978, *107*, 237–265.

Johnson, N. F. The psychological reality of phrase-structure rules. *Journal of Verbal Learning and Verbal Behavior*, 1965, *4*, 469–475.

Johnson, R. E. Remembering of prose: Holistic or piecemeal losses. *Journal of Memory and Language*, 1986, *25*, 525–538.

Johnston, M. K., Kelley, C. S., Harris, F. R., & Wolf, M. M. An application of reinforcement principles to development of motor skills of a young child. *Child Development*, 1966, *37*, 379–387.

Jones, G. V. Recognition failure and dual mechanisms in recall. *Psychological Review*, 1978, *85*, 464–469.

Jones, J. E. All-or-none versus incremental learning. *Psychological Review*, 1962, 69, 156–160.

Jung, J. Effects of response meaningfulness (*m*) on transfer of training under two different paradigms. *Journal of Experimental Psychology*, 1963, *65*, 377–384.

Jung, J., & Bailey, J. *Contemporary psychology experiments: Adaptations for laboratory.* New York: Wiley, 1966.

Kallman, H. J., & Massaro, D. W. Backward masking, the suffix effect and pre-perceptual storage. *Journal of Experimental Psychology*, 1983, *9*, 312–327.

Kallman, W. M., & Gilmore, J. D. Vascular disorders. In S. M. Turner, K. S. Calhoun, & H. E. Adams (Eds.), *Handbook of clinical behavior therapy*. New York: Wiley, 1981.

Kamil, A. C., Krebs, J. R., & Pulliam, H. R. (Eds.), *Foraging behavior.* New York: Plenum, 1987.

Kamin, L. J. Predictability, surprise, attention, and conditioning. In R. Church & B. Campbell (Eds.), *Punishment and aversive behavior.* New York: Appleton, 1969. (a)

Kamin, L. J. Selective association and conditioning. In N. J. Mackintosh & W. K. Honig (Eds.), *Fundamental issues in associative learning.* Halifax: Dalhousie University Press, 1969. (b)

Kamin, L. J., & Brimer, C. J. The effects of intensity of conditioned and unconditioned stimuli on a conditioned emotional response. *Canadian Journal of Psychology*, 1963, *17*, 194–198.

Kamiya, J., Barber, T. X., Miller, N. E., Shapiro, D., & Stoyva, J. (Eds.), *Biofeedback and self-control.* Chicago: Aldine, 1977.

Kanungo, R. Meaning mediation in verbal transfer. *British Journal of Psychology*, 1967, *58*, 205–212.

Karen, R. L. *An introduction to behavior theory and its applications.* New York: Harper & Row, 1974.

Kassin, S. M. Eyewitness identification: Victims vs. bystanders. *Journal of Applied Psychology*, 1984, *14*, 519–529.

Katz, J. J., & Fodor, J. A. The structure of a semantic theory. *Language*, 1963, *39*, 170–210.

Kausler, D. H. *The psychology of verbal learning and memory.* New York: Academic Press, 1974.

Kausler, D. H., & Yadrick, R. M. Item identifications following varying study trials on a multiple-item recognition learning task. *Journal of Experimental Psychology: Human Learning and Memory*, 1977, *3*, 203–210.

Keefe, F. M., Surwitt, R., & Pilon, R. N. Biofeedback, autogenic training, and progressive relaxation in the treatment of Raynaud's disease: A comparative study. *Journal of Applied Behavior Analysis*, 1980, *13*, 3–11.

Keenan, J. M., & Kintsch, W. The identification of explicitly and implicitly presented information. In W. Kintsch (Ed.), *The representation of meaning in memory*. Hillsdale, N. J.: Lawrence Erlbaum Associates, 1974.

Keenan, J, M., & Moore, R. E. Memory for images of concealed objects: A reexamination of Neisser and Kerr. *Journal of Experimental Psychology: Human Learning and Memory*, 1979, *5*, 374–385.

Keenan, J. M., MacWhinney, B., & Mayhew, D. Pragmatics in memory: A study of natural conversation. *Journal of Verbal Learning and Verbal Behavior*, 1977, *16*, 549–560.

Kehoe, E. J. CS–UCS contiguity and CS intensity in conditioning of the rabbit's nictitating membrane response to serial compound stimuli. *Journal of Experimental Psychology*, 1983, *9*, 307–319.

Kehoe, E. J., Gibbs, C. M., Garcia, E., & Gormezano, I. Associative transfer and stimulus selection in classical conditioning of the rabbit's nictitating membrane response to serial compound CSs. *Journal of Experimental Psychology: Animal Behavior Processes*, 1979, *5*, 1–18.

Keith-Lucas, T., & Guttman, N. Robust single-trial delayed backward conditioning. *Journal of Comparative and Physiological Psychology*, 1975, *88*, 468–476.

Keller, K. The role of elicited responding in behavior control. *Journal of the Experimental Analysis of Behavior*, 1974, *21*, 237–248.

Kellogg, R. T. Age differences in hypothesis testing and frequency processing in concept learning. *Bulletin of the Psychonomic Society*, 1983, *21*, 101–104.

Kellogg, R. T., Robbins, D. W., & Bourne, L. E. Memory for intratrial events in feature identification. *Journal of Experimental Psychology: Human Learning and Memory*, 1978, *4*, 256–265.

Kendall, S. B. Preference for intermittent reinforcement. *Journal of the Experimental Analysis of Behavior*, 1974, *21*, 463–473.

Kennedy, T. D. Reinforcement frequency, task characteristics, and interval of awareness assessment as factors in verbal conditioning without awareness. *Journal of Experimental Psychology*, 1971, *88*, 103–112.

Kent, G. H., & Rosanoff, A. J. A study of association in insanity. *American Journal of Insanity*, 1910, *67*, 37–96, 317–390.

Keppel, G. Retroactive and proactive inhibition. In T. R. Dixon & D. Horton (Eds.), *Verbal behavior and general behavior theory*. Englewood Cliffs, N. J.: Prentice-Hall, 1968.

Keppel, G., Postman, L., & Zavortink, B. Studies of learning to learn: VIII. The influence of massive amounts of training upon the learning and retention of paired-associate lists. *Journal of Verbal Learning and Verbal Behavior*, 1968, *7*, 790–796.

Keppel, G., & Underwood, B. J. Proactive inhibition in short-term retention of single items. *Journal of Verbal Learning and Verbal Behavior*, 1962, *1*, 153–161.

Keppel, G., Zavortink, B., & Shiff, B. B. Unlearning in the A–B, A–C paradigm as a function of percentage occurrence of response members. *Journal of Experimental Psychology*, 1967, *74*, 172–177.

Kerr, N., Myerson, L., & Michael, J. A procedure for shaping vocalizations in a mute child. In L. P. Ullman & L. Krasner (Eds.), *Case studies in behavior modification*. New York: Holt, Rinehart & Winston, 1965.

Kerr, N. H. The role of vision in "visual imagery" experiments: Evidence from the congenitally blind. *Journal of Experimental Psychology*, 1983, *112*, 265–277.

Kesner, R. P., & DeSpain, M. J. Correspondence between rats and humans in the utilization of retrospective and prospective codes. *Animal Learning and Behavior*, 1988, *16(3)*, 299–302.

Kiger, J. I., & Glass, A. L. The facilitation of lexical decisions by a prime occurring after the target. *Memory and Cognition*, 1983, *11*, 356–365.

Kimble, G. A. Performance and reminiscence in motor learning as a function of the degree of distribution of practice. *Journal of Experimental Psychology*, 1949, *39*, 500–510.

Kimble, G. A. *Hilgard and Marquis' conditioning and learning.* New York: Appleton, 1961.

Kimble, G. A. *Foundations of conditioning and learning.* New York: Appleton, 1967.

Kimble, G. A., & Reynolds, B. Eyelid conditioning as a function of the interval between conditioned and unconditioned stimuli. In G. A. Kimble (Ed.), *Foundations of conditioning and learning.* New York: Appleton, 1967.

Kimmel, H. D. Instrumental inhibitory factors in classical conditioning. In W. F. Prokasy (Ed.), *Classical conditioning: A symposium.* New York: Appleton, 1965.

Kinsbourne, M., & George, J. The mechanism of the word-frequency effect on recognition memory. *Journal of Verbal Learning and Verbal Behavior,* 1974, *13,* 63–69.

Kinsbourne, M., & Wood, F. Short-term memory processes and the amnesic syndrome. In D. Deutsch & J. A. Deutsch (Eds.), *Short-term memory.* New York: Academic Press, 1975.

Kintsch, W. *Learning, memory, and conceptual processes.* New York: Wiley, 1970.

Kintsch, W. *The representation of meaning in memory.* Hillsdale, N. J.: Lawrence Erlbaum Associates, 1974.

Kintsch, W. *Memory and cognition.* New York: Wiley, 1977.

Kintsch, W., & Buschke, H. Homophones and synonyms in short-term memory. *Journal of Experimental Psychology,* 1969, *80,* 403–407.

Kintsch, W., & Keenan, J. M. Reading rate and retention as a function of the number of propositions in the base structure of sentences. *Cognitive Psychology,* 1973, *5,* 257–274.

Kintsch, W., Kozminsky, E., Streby, W. J., McKoon, G., & Keenan, J. M. Comprehension and recall of text as a function of content variables. *Journal of Verbal Learning and Verbal Behavior,* 1975, *14,* 196–214.

Kintsch, W., & Polson, P. G. On nominal and functional serial position curves: Implications for short-term memory curves? *Psychological Review,* 1979, *86,* 407–413.

Kintsch, W., & van Dijk, T. A. Comment on se rapelle et on résume des histoires. *Languages,* 1975, *40,* 98–116.

Kintsch, W., & van Dijk, T. A. Toward a model of text comprehension and production. *Psychological Review,* 1978, *85,* 363–394.

Klatzky, R. L. Armchair theorists have more fun. *Behavioral and Brain Sciences,* 1984, *7,* 244.

Klatzky, R. L. *Memory and awareness.* San Francisco: W. H. Freeman, 1984.

Klein, K., & Saltz, E. Specifying the mechanisms in a level-of-processing approach to memory. *Journal of Experimental Psychology,* 1976, *2,* 671–679.

Klein, R. D. Modifying academic performance in the grade school classroom. In M. Hersen, R. M. Eisler, & P. M. Miller (Eds.), *Progress in behavior modification* (Vol. 8). New York: Academic Press, 1979.

Kleitsch, E. C., Whitman, T. L., & Santos, J. Increasing verbal interaction among elderly socially isolated mentally retarded adults: A group language training procedure. *Journal of Applied Behavior Analysis,* 1983, *16,* 217–233.

Kling, J. W. Learning: An introductory survey. In J. W. Kling & L. A. Riggs (Eds.), *Woodworth and Schlosberg's experimental psychology.* New York: Holt, Rinehart & Winston, 1971.

Kling, J. W., & Schrier, A. M. Positive reinforcement. In J. W. Kling & L. A. Riggs, (Eds.), *Woodworth and Schlosberg's experimental psychology.* New York: Holt, Rinehart & Winston, 1971.

Klinger, E. Consequences of commitment to and disengagement from incentives. *Psychological Review,* 1975, *82,* 1–25.

Klunder, C. S., & O'Boyle, M. Suppression of predatory behavior in laboratory mice following lithium chloride injections or electric shock. *Animal Learning and Behavior,* 1979, *7,* 13–16.

Knight, M. F., & McKenzie, H. S. Elimination of bedtime thumbsucking in home setting through contingent reading. *Journal of Applied Behavior Analysis.* 1974, *7,* 33–38.

Kohler, E. A., & Ayres, J. J. B. The Kamin blocking effect with variable-duration CSs. *Animal Learning and Behavior,* 1979, *7,* 347–350.

Kohler, W. Simple structural functions in the chimpanzee and in the chicken. In W. D. Ellis (Ed.), *A source book on Gestalt psychology.* London: Routledge & Kegan Paul, 1955.

Kolers, P. A. Reading a year later. *Journal of Experimental Psychology: Human Learning and Memory,* 1976, *2,* 554–565.

Konorski, J. *Integrative activity of the brain.* Chicago: University of Chicago Press, 1967.

Koppenaal, R. J., & Jagoda, E. Proactive inhibition of a maze position habit. *Journal of Experimental Psychology,* 1968, 76, 664–668.

Kosslyn, S. M., Ball, T. M., & Reiser, B. J. Visual images preserve metric spatial information: Evidence from studies of image scanning. *Journal of Experimental Psychology,* 1978, 4, 47–60.

Kosslyn, S. M., Reiser, B. J., Farah, M. J., & Fliegel, S. L. Generating visual images: Units and relations. *Journal of Experimental Psychology,* 1983, 112, 278–303.

Kosslyn, S. M., & Schwartz, S. P. A simulation of visual imagery. *Cognitive Science,* 1977, 1, 265–295.

Kovach, J. K., & Hess, E. H. Imprinting: Effects of painful stimulation upon the following response. *Journal of Comparative and Physiological Psychology,* 1963, 56, 461–464.

Kozminsky, E. Altering comprehension: The effect of biasing titles on text comprehension. *Memory and Cognition,* 1977, 5, 482–490.

Kraemer, P. J., Hoffman, H., & Spear, N. E. Attenuation of the CS-preexposure effect after a retention interval in preweanling rats. *Animal Learning and Behavior,* 1988, 16, 185–190.

Kraemer, P. J., Lariviere, N. A., & Spear, N. E. Expression of a taste aversion conditioned with an odor-taste compound: Overshadowing is relatively weak in weanlings and decreases over a retention interval in adults. *Animal Learning and Behavior,* 1988, 16(2), 164–168.

Krechevsky, I. "Hypotheses" in rats. *Psychological Review,* 1932, 39, 516–532.

Kubie, J. L., & Halpern, M. Chemical senses involved in garter snake prey training. *Journal of Comparative and Physiological Psychology,* 1979, 93, 648–667.

Kulhavy, R. W., & Heinen, J. R. K. Mnemonic transformations and verbal coding processes. *Journal of Experimental Psychology,* 1974, 102, 173–175.

Kurz, E. M., & Levitsky, D. A. Lithium chloride and avoidance of novel places. *Behavioral Neuroscience,* 1983, 97, 445–451.

Lacey, J. I., & Smith, R. L. Conditioning and generalization of unconscious anxiety. *Science,* 1954, 120, 1045–1052.

Lacey, J. I., Smith, R. L., & Green, A. Use of conditioned autonomic responses in the study of anxiety. *Psychosomatic Medicine, XVII,* 1955, 208–217.

Landauer, T. K. Reinforcement as consolidation. *Psychological Review,* 1969, 76, 82–96.

Landauer, T. K. Consolidation in human memory: Retrograde amnesia effects of confusable items in paired-associate learning. *Journal of Verbal Learning and Verbal Behavior,* 1974, 13, 45–53.

Lang, P. J., Geer, J., & Hnatiow, M. Semantic generalization of conditioned autonomic responses. *Journal of Experimental Psychology,* 1963, 65, 552–558.

Lashley, K. S., & Wade, M. The Pavlovian theory of generalization. *Psychological Review,* 1946, 53, 72–87.

Lasky, R. E., & Kallio, K. D. Transformation rules in concept learning. *Memory and Cognition,* 1978, 6, 491–495.

Lawicka, W. The role of stimulus modality in successive discrimination and differentiation learning. *Bulletin of the Polish Academy of Sciences,* 1964, 12, 35–38.

Lazarus, A. A. The elimination of children's phobias by deconditioning. In H. J. Eysenck (Ed.), *Behaviour therapy and the neuroses.* London: Pergamon, 1960.

Lea, G. Chronometric analysis of the method of loci. *Journal of Experimental Psychology: Human Perception and Performance,* 1975, 104, 95–104.

Leahey, T. H., & Harris, R. J. *Human learning.* Englewood Cliffs, N. J.: Prentice-Hall, 1989.

Ledwidge, B. Cognitive behavior modification: A step in the wrong direction? *Psychological Bulletin,* 1978, 85, 353–375.

Ledwidge, B. Cognitive behavior modification or new ways to change minds: Reply to Mahoney and Kazdin. *Psychological Bulletin,* 1979, 86, 1050–1053.

Lee, R. K., & Maier, S. F. Inescapable shock and attention to internal versus external cues in a water discrimination escape task. *Journal of Experimental Psychology: Animal Behavior Processes,* 1988, 14(3), 302–310.

Leeming, F. C., & Little, G. L. Escape learning in houseflies (*Musca domestica*). *Journal of Comparative and Physiological Psychology,* 1977, 91, 260–269.

Lehr, D. J., Frank, R. C., & Mattison, D. W. Retroactive inhibition, spontaneous recovery, and type of interpolated learning. *Journal of Experimental Psychology*, 1972, *92*, 232–236.

Leibeskind, J. C., Lewis, J. W., Shavit, Y., Terman, G. W., & Melnechuk, T. Our natural capacities for pain suppression. *Advances*, 1983, *1*, 8–11.

Lenneberg, E. H. *The biological foundations of language.* New York: Wiley, 1967.

Lenneberg, E. H. On explaining language. *Science*, 1969, *164*, 635–643.

Leonard, J. M., & Whitten, W. B. Information stored when expecting recall or recognition. *Journal of Experimental Psychology*, 1983, *9*, 440–455.

Lesgold. A. M., & Goldman, S. R. Encoding uniqueness and the imagery mnemonic in associative learning. *Journal of Verbal Learning and Verbal Behavior*, 1973, *12*, 193–202.

Lett, B. T. Delayed reward learning: Disproof of the traditional theory. *Learning and Motivation*, 1973, *4*, 237–246.

Levenson, R. W. Feedback effects and respiratory involvement in voluntary control of heart rate. *Psychophysiology*, 1976, *13*, 108–114.

Levin, J. R., Ghatala, E. S., & Wilder, L. Picture-word differences in discrimination learning: I. Apparent frequency manipulations. *Journal of Experimental Psychology*, 1974, *102*, 691–695.

Levine, M. Hypothesis behavior by humans during discrimination learning. *Journal of Experimental Psychology*, 1966, *71*, 331–338.

Levine, M. *A cognitive theory of learning.* Hillsdale, N. J.: Lawrence Erlbaum Associates, 1975.

Lewis, D. J. Acquisition, extinction, and spontaneous recovery as a function of percentage of reinforcement and intertrial intervals. *Journal of Experimental Psychology*, 1956, *51*, 45–53.

Lewis, D. J. Partial reinforcement: A selective review of the literature since 1950. *Psychological Bulletin*, 1960, *57*, 1–28.

Lewis, D. J. Psychobiology of active and inactive memory. *Psychological Bulletin*, 1979, *86*, 1054–1083.

Lewis, J. W., & Leibeskind, J. C. Pain suppressive systems of the brain. *Trends in Pharmacological Sciences*, 1983, *4*, 73–75.

Ley, R. Encoding specificity and unidirectional associates in cued recall. *Memory and Cognition*, 1977, *5*, 523–528.

Lieberman, D. A., McIntosh, D. C., & Thomas, G. V. Learning when reward is delayed: A marking hypothesis. *Journal of Experimental Psychology: Animal Behavior Processes*, 1979, *5*, 224–242.

Light, L. L., Kimble, G. A., & Pellegrino, J. W. Comments on *Episodic memory: When recognition fails,* by Watkins and Tulving. *Journal of Experimental Psychology*, 1975, *104*, 30–36.

Linden, E. *Apes, men and language.* New York: Dutton, 1975.

Lindsay, P. H., & Norman, D. A. *Human information processing: An introduction to psychology.* New York: Academic Press, 1972.

Livesey, P. J., & Rankine-Wilson, J. Delayed alternation learning under electrical (blocking) stimulation of the caudate nucleus in the cat. *Journal of Comparative and Physiological Psychology*, 1975, *88*, 342–354.

Locke, E. A. Behavior modification is not cognitive—and other myths: A reply to Ledwidge. *Cognitive Therapy and Research*, 1979, *3*, 119–125.

Lockhard, R. B. Several tests of stimulus-change and preference theory in relation to light-controlled behavior in rats. *Journal of Comparative and Physiological Psychology*, 1966, *62*, 415–426.

Loess, H. Proactive inhibition in short-term memory. *Journal of Verbal Learning and Verbal Behavior*, 1964, *3*, 362–368.

Loftus, E. F. Category dominance, instance dominance, and categorization time. *Journal of Experimental Psychology*, 1973, *97*, 70–74.

Loftus, E. F., & Messo, J. Some facts about "weapon focus." *Law and Human Behavior*, 1987, *11*, 55–62.

Loftus, E. F., Miller, D. G., & Burns, H. J. Semantic integration of verbal information into a visual memory. *Journal of Experimental Psychology*, 1978, *4*, 19–31.

Loftus, E. F., & Palmer, J. C. Reconstruction of automobile destruction: An example of the interaction between language and memory. *Journal of Verbal Learning and Verbal Behavior*, 1974, *13*, 585–589.

Loftus, G. R. A comparison of recognition and recall in a continuous memory task. *Journal of Experimental Psychology*, 1971, *91*, 220–226.

Loftus, G. R., & Kallman, H. J. Encoding and use of detail information in picture recognition. *Journal of Experimental Psychology: Human Learning and Memory*, 1979, *5*, 197–211.

Logan, F. A. A comparison of avoidance and nonavoidance eyelid conditioning. *Journal of Experimental Psychology*, 1951, *42*, 390–393.

Logan, F. A. *Fundamentals of learning and motivation*. Dubuque, Iowa: Wm. C. Brown, 1970.

Logue, A. W. Taste aversion and the generality of the laws of learning. *Psychological Bulletin*, 1979, *86*, 276–296.

Logue, A. W., Chavarro, A., Rachlin, H., & Reeder, R. W. Impulsiveness in pigeons living in the experimental chamber. *Animal Learning and Behavior*, 1988, *16(1)*, 31–39.

Lombardi, B. R., & Flaherty, C. F. Apparent disinhibition of successive but not of simultaneous negative contrast. *Animal Learning and Behavior*, 1978, *6*, 30–42.

Lopez, M., Hicks, R. E., & Young, R. K. Retroactive inhibition in a bilingual A–B, A–B' paradigm. *Journal of Experimental Psychology*, 1974, *103*, 85–90.

Lorenz, K. Der Kumpan in der Umwelt des Vogels. *Journal of Ornithology*, 1935, *83*, 137–213, 289–413.

Lorenz, K. The companion in the bird's world. *Auk*, 1937, *54*, 245–273.

Lorenz, K. The comparative method of studying innate behavior patterns. In *Society for Experimental Biology, Symposium No. 4, Physiological mechanisms in animal behavior*. New York: Academic Press, 1950.

Lorenz, K. Innate bases of learning. In K. H. Pribram (Ed.), *On the biology of learning*. New York: Harcourt, Brace, & World, 1969.

Lovaas, O. I. A behavior therapy approach to the treatment of childhood schizophrenia. In J. P. Hill (Ed.), *Minnesota symposia on child psychology* (Vol. 1). Minneapolis: University of Minnesota Press, 1967.

Lovaas, O. I., Berberich, J. P., Perdoff, B. F., & Schaeffer, B. Acquisition of imitative speech by schizophrenic children. *Science*, 1966, *151*, 705–706.

Lovibond, P. F. Facilitation of instrumental behavior by a Pavlovian appetitive conditioned stimulus. *Journal of Experimental Psychology*, 1983, *9*, 225–247.

Luchins, A. S. Mechanization in problem solving: The effect of Einstellung. *Psychological Monographs*, 1942, *54* (Whole No. 248).

Lundin, R. W. *Personality: A behavioral analysis*. New York: Macmillan, 1974.

Lupker, S. J. Picture naming: An investigation of the nature of categorical priming. *Journal of Experimental Psychology: Learning, Memory, and Cognition*, 1988, *14(3)*, 444–455.

Lutz, W. J., & Scheirer, C. J. Coding processes for pictures and words. *Journal of Verbal Learning and Verbal Behavior*, 1974, *13*, 316–320.

Lutzker, J. R., & Sherman, J. A. Producing generative sentence usage by imitation and reinforcement procedures. *Journal of Applied Behavior Analysis*, 1974, *7*, 447–460.

Macht, M. L. & Spear, N. E. Priming effects in episodic memory. *Journal of Experimental Psychology: Human Learning and Memory*, 1977, *3*, 733–741.

Mackenzie, B. D. Measuring the strength, structure and reliability of free associations. *Psychological Bulletin*, 1972, *77*, 438–445.

Mackintosh, N. J. *The psychology of animal learning*. London: Academic Press, 1974.

Mackintosh, N. J. A theory of attention: Variations of the associability of stimulus with reinforcement. *Psychological Review*, 1975, *82*, 276–298.

Mackintosh, N. J. Stimulus control: Attentional factors. In W. K. Honig & J. E. R. Staddon (Eds.), *Handbook of operant behavior*. Englewood Cliffs, N. J.: Prentice-Hall, 1977.

Mackintosh, N. J. *Conditioning and associative learning*. New York: Oxford University Press, 1983.

MacLeod, C. M. Forgotten but not gone: Savings for pictures and words in long-term memory. *Journal of Experimental Psychology: Learning, Memory, and Cognition*, 1988, *14(2)*, 195–212.

Madden, D. J., & Bastian, J. Probing echoic memory with different voices. *Memory and Cognition*, 1977, *5*, 331–334.

Madigan, R. J. Reinforcement contexts effects on fixed-interval responding. *Animal Learning and Behavior*, 1978, *6*, 193–197.

Madigan, S. W. Intraserial repetition and coding processes in free recall. *Journal of Verbal Learning and Verbal Behavior*, 1969, *8*, 828–835.

Maggio, J. C., & Harder, D. B. Genotype and environment interactively determine the magnitude, directionality, and abolition of defensive burying in mice. *Animal Learning and Behavior*, 1983, *11*, 162–172.

Mahoney, M. J. Cognitive and noncognitive views in behavior modification. In P. Sjödén, S. Bates, & W. S. Dockens (Eds.), *Trends in behavior therapy*. New York: Academic Press, 1979.

Mahoney, M. J., & Kazdin, A. E. Cognitive behavior modification: Misconceptions and premature evaluation. *Psychological Bulletin*, 1979, *86*, 1044–1049.

Maier, N. R. F. Reasoning in humans: II. The solution of a problem and its appearance in consciousness. *Journal of Comparative Psychology*, 1931, *12*, 181–194.

Maier, N. R. F., Glazer, N. M., & Klee, J. B. Studies of abnormal behavior in the rat: III. The development of behavior fixations through frustration. *Journal of Experimental Psychology*, 1940, *26*, 521–546.

Maier, N. R. F., & Klee, J. B. Studies of abnormal behavior in the rat: XVII. Guidance versus trial and error in the alteration of habits and fixations. *Journal of Psychology*, 1945, *19*, 133–163.

Maier, S. F. Failure to escape traumatic electric shock: Incompatible skeletal-motor responses or learned helplessness? *Learning and Motivation*, 1970, *1*, 157–169.

Maier, S. F., Allaway, T. A., & Gleitman, H. Proactive inhibition in rats after prior partial reversal: A critique of the spontaneous recovery hypothesis. *Psychonomic Science*, 1967, *9*, 63–64.

Maier, S. F., Seligman, M. E., & Solomon, R. L. Pavlovian fear conditioning and learned helplessness. In B. A. Campbell & R. M. Church (Eds.), *Punishment and aversive behavior*. New York: Appleton, 1969.

Maier, S. F., Sherman, J. E., Lewis, J. W., Terman, G. W., & Leibeskind, J. C. The opoid/monopoid nature of stress induced analgesia and learned helplessness. *Journal of Experimental Psychology*, 1983, *9*, 80–90.

Maier, S. F., & Warren, D. A. Controllability and safety signals exert dissimilar proactive effects on nociception and escape performance. *Journal of Experimental Psychology: Animal Behavior Processes*, 1988, *14(1)*, 18–25.

Malloy, T. E., & Ellis, H. C. Attention and cue-producing responses in response-mediated stimulus generalization. *Journal of Experimental Psychology*, 1970, *83*, 191–200.

Maltzman, I. Orienting in classical conditioning and generalization of the galvanic skin response to words: An overview. *Journal of Experimental Psycholgy*, 1977, *106*, 111–119.

Mandler, G., Worden, P. E., & Graesser, A. C. Subjective disorganization: Search for the locus of list organization. *Journal of Verbal Learning and Verbal Behavior*, 1974, *13*, 220–235.

Mandler, J. M., & Johnson, N. J. Remembrance of things passed: Story structure and recall. *Cognitive Psychology*, 1977, *9*, 111–151.

Manning, B. H. Application of cognitive behavior modification: First and third graders' self-management of classroom behaviors. *American Educational Research Journal*, Summer 1988, *25(2)*, 193–212.

Margolius, G. Stimulus generalization of an instrumental response as a function of the number of reinforced trials. *Journal of Experimental Psychology*, 1955, *49*, 105–111.

Marler, P., & Peters, S. Sparrows learn adult song and more from memory. *Science*, 1981, *213*, 780–782.

Martin, E. Stimulus pronunciability in aural paired-associate learning. *Journal of Verbal Learning and Verbal Behavior*, 1966, *5*, 18–22.

Martin, E. Verbal learning theory and independent retrieval phenomena. *Psychological Review*, 1971, *78*, 314–332.

Martin, E. Stimulus encoding in learning and transfer. In A. W. Melton & E. Martin (Eds.), *Coding processes in human memory*. New York: Wiley, 1972.

Martin, E., & Greeno, J. G. Independence of associations tested: A reply to D. L. Hintzman. *Psychological Reivew*, 1972, *79*, 265–267.

Martin, E., & Mackay, S. A test of the list-differentiation hypothesis. *American Journal of Psychology*, 1970, *83*, 311–321.

Martin, E., & Schultz, R. W. Aural paired-associate learning: Pronunciability and the interval between stimulus and response. *Journal of Verbal Learning and Verbal Behavior*, 1963, *1*, 389–391.

Martinez, J. L., & Kesner, R. P. (Eds.), *Learning and memory: A biological view*. Orlando, FL: Academic Press, 1986.

Marx, M. H., & Knarr, F. A. Long-term development of reinforcing properties of a stimulus as a function of temporal relationship to food reinforcement. *Journal of Comparative and Physiological Psychology*, 1963, *56*, 546–550.

Masek, B. J., Epstein, L. H., & Russo, D. C. Behavioral perspectives in preventive medicine. In S. M. Turner, S. Calhoun, & E. H. Adams (Eds.), *Handbook of clinical behavior therapy*. New York: Wiley, 1981.

Massaro, D. W. Preperceptual auditory images. *Journal of Experimental Psychology*, 1970, *85*, 411–417.

Massaro, D. W. Preperceptual images, processing time, and perceptual units in auditory perception. *Psychological Review*, 1972, *79*, 124–145.

Massaro, D. W., Jones, R. D., Lipscomb, C., & Scholz, R. Role of prior knowledge on naming and lexical decisions with good and poor stimulus information. *Journal of Experimental Psychology: Human Learning and Memory*, 1978, *4*, 498–512.

Matlin, M. *Cognition*. New York: Holt, Rinehart & Winston, 1983.

Matzel, L. D., Held, F. P., & Miller, R. R. Information and expression of simultaneous and backward associations: Implications for contiguity theory. *Learning and Motivation*, 1988, *19*, 317–344.

Matzel, L. D., Schachtman, T. R., & Miller, R. R. Learned irrelevance exceeds the sum of CS-preexposure and US-preexposure deficits. *Journal of Experimental Psychology*, 1988, *14*, 311–319.

Mayhew, A. J. Interlist changes in subjective organization during free-recall learning. *Journal of Experimental Psychology*, 1967, *74*, 425–430.

McCain, G., & Garrett, B. L. Generalization to stimuli of different brightness in three straight alley studies. *Psychological Reports*, 1964, *15*, 368–370.

McCall, R. B. Initial-consequent-change surface in light contingent bar pressing. *Journal of Comparative and Physiological Psychology*, 1966, *62*, 35–42.

McCarthy, M. A., & Houston, J. P. *Fundamentals of early childhood education*. Cambridge, Mass.: Winthrop, 1980.

McCloskey, M., & Glucksberg, S. Natural categories: Well-defined or fuzzy sets? *Memory and Cognition*, 1978, *6*, 462–472.

McCloskey, M., & Glucksberg, S. Decision processes in verifying category membership statements: Implications for models of semantic memory. *Cognitive Psychology*, 1979, *11*, 1–37.

McConnell, J. V. *Understanding human behavior: An introduction to psychology*. New York: Holt, Rinehart & Winston, 1974.

McCormack, P. D., & Swenson, A. L. Recognition memory for common and rare words. *Journal of Experimental Psychology*, 1972, *95*, 72–77.

McDaniel, M. A., Friedman, A., & Bourne, L. Remembering levels of information in words. *Memory and Cognition*, 1978, *6*, 146–154.

McDougall, R. Recognition and recall. *Journal of Philosophical Psychology and Scientific Methods*, 1904, *1*, 229–233.

McDowall, J. Effects of encoding instructions and retrieval cuing on recall in Korsakoff patients. *Memory and Cognition*, 1979, *7*, 232–239.

McEvoy, C. L. Automatic and strategic processes in picture naming. *Journal of Experimental Psychology: Learning, Memory, and Cognition*, 1988, *14(4)*, 618–626.

McGaugh, J. L. Modulation of memory storage processes. In P. R. Solomon, G. R. Goethals, C. M. Kelley, & B. Stephens (Eds.), *Memory: Interdisciplinary approaches*. New York: Springer-Verlag, 1988.

McGaugh, J. L. Time-dependent processes in memory storage. *Science*, 1966, *153*, 1351–1358.

McGaugh, J. L., & Dawson, R. G. Modification of memory storage processes. In W. K. Honig & P. H. R. James (Eds.), *Animal memory*. New York: Academic Press, 1971.

McGaugh, J. L., & Gold, P. E. Modulation of memory by electrical stimulation of the brain. In M. R. Rosenzweig & E. L. Bennett (Eds.), *Neural mechanisms in learning and memory*. Cambridge, Mass.: MIT Press, 1976.

McGeoch, J. A., & Irion, A. L. *The psychology of human learning.* New York: Longmans, Green, 1952.

McGlaughlin, A., & Dale, H. C. A. Stimulus similarity and transfer in long-term paired-associate learning. *British Journal of Psychology,* 1971, *62,* 37–40.

McKeever, W. F., & Hoff, A. L. Further evidence of the absence of measurable interhemispheric transfer time in left-handers who employ an inverted handwriting posture. *Bulletin of the Psychonomic Society,* 1983, *21,* 255–258.

McKoon, G., & Keenan, J. M. Response latencies to explicit and implicit statements as a function of the delay between reading and test. In W. Kintsch (Ed.), *The representation of meaning in memory.* Hillsdale, N. J.: Lawrence Erlbaum Associates, 1974.

McKoon, G., & Ratcliff, R. Priming in episodic and semantic memory. *Journal of Verbal Learning and Verbal Behavior,* 1979, *18,* 463–480.

McNally, R. J., Calamari, J. E., Hansen, P. M., & Kaliher, C. Behavioral treatment of psychogenic polydipsia. *Journal of Behavior Therapy and Experimental Psychiatry,* 1988, *19(1),* 57–61.

McNeil, D. *The acquisition of language: The study of developmental psycholinguistics.* New York: Harper & Row, 1970.

Medin, D. L., Dewey, G. I., & Murphy, T. D. Relationship between item and category naming: Evidence that abstraction is not automatic. *Journal of Experimental Psychology,* 1983, *9,* 607–625.

Mehiel, R., & Bolles, R. C. Learned flavor preferences based on calories are independent of initial hedonic value. *Animal Learning and Behavior,* 1988, *16,* 383–387.

Meichenbaum, D. Cognitive-behavior modification: Future directions. In P. Sjödén, S. Bates, & W. S. Dockens (Eds.), *Trends in behavior therapy.* New York: Academic Press, 1979. (a)

Meichenbaum, D. Cognition behavior modification: The need for a fairer assessment. *Cognitive Therapy and Research,* 1979, *3,* 127–132. (b)

Melching, W. H. The acquired value of an intermittently presented neutral stimulus. *Journal of Comparative and Physiological Psychology,* 1954, *47,* 370–374.

Melton, A. W. The end-spurt in memorization curves as an artifact of the averaging of individual curves. *Psychological Monographs,* 1936, *47,* 119–134.

Melton, A. W. Implications of short-term for a general theory of memory. *Journal of Verbal Learning and Verbal Behavior,* 1963, *2,* 1–21.

Melton, A. W. The situation with respect to the spacing of repetitions and memory. *Journal of Verbal Learning and Verbal Behavior,* 1970, *9,* 596–606.

Melton, A. W., & Irwin, J. M. The influence of degree of interpolated learning on retroactive inhibition and the overt transfer of specific responses. *American Journal of Psychology,* 1940, *53,* 173–203.

Melton, A. W., & Martin, E. (Eds.), *Coding processes in human memory.* New York: Wiley, 1972.

Melvin, K. B., Cloar, F. T., & Massingill, L. S. Imprinting of bobwhite quail to a hawk. *Psychological Record,* 1967, *17,* 235–238.

Memmott, J., & Reberg, D. Differential conditioned suppression in the Konorski–Lawicka paradigm. *Animal Learning and Behavior,* 1977, *5,* 124–128.

Mendell, P. R. Effects of length of retention interval on proactive inhibition in short-term visual memory. *Journal of Experimental Psychology: Human Learning and Memory,* 1977, *3,* 264–269.

Merryman, C. T., & Merryman, S. S. Stimulus encoding in the A–B′, Ax–B and the A–B′ᵣ, Ax–B paradigms. *Journal of Verbal Learning and Verbal Behavior,* 1971, *10,* 681–685.

Meyer, B. *The organization of prose and its effects upon memory.* Amsterdam: North-Holland, 1975.

Michael, R. P., Bonsall, R. W., & Zumpe, D. Consort bonding and operant behavior by female rhesus monkeys. *Journal of Comparative and Physiological Psychology,* 1978, *92,* 837–845.

Mikulincer, M. A case study of three theories of learned helplessness: The role of test importance. *Motivation and Emotion,* 1988, *12(4).*

Miles, H. L. Apes and language: The search for communicative competence. In J. de Luce & H. T. Wilder (Eds.), *Language in primates: Perspectives and implications.* New York: Springer-Verlag, 1983.

Miles, R. C. The relative effectiveness of secondary reinforcers throughout deprivation and habit-strength parameters. *Journal of Comparative and Physiological Psychology,* 1956, *49,* 126–130.

Miller, A. J., & Kratochwill, T. R. Reduction of frequent stomach complaints by time out. *Behavior Therapy*, 1979, *10*, 211–218.

Miller, G. A. The magical number seven plus or minus two: Some limits on our capacity for processing information. *Psychological Review*, 1956, *63*, 81–97.

Miller, G. A., Galanter, E., & Pribram, K. H. *Plans and the structure of behavior*. New York: Holt, Rinehart & Winston, 1960.

Miller, I. W., & Norman, W. H. Learned helplessness in humans: A review and attribution-theory model. *Psychological Bulletin*, 1979, *86*, 93–118.

Miller, J. R., & Kintsch, W. Readability and recall of short prose passages: A theoretical analysis. *Journal of Experimental Psychology: Human Learning and Memory*, 1980, *6*, 335–354.

Miller, L. Compounding of discriminative stimuli correlated with chained and multiple schedules. *Journal of the Experimental Analysis of Behavior*, 1975, *23*, 95–102.

Miller, N. E. Learnable drives and rewards. In S. S. Stevens (Ed.), *Handbook of experimental psychology*. New York: Wiley, 1951.

Miller, N. E. Liberalization of basic S–R concepts: Extensions to conflict behavior, motivation, and social learning. In S. Koch (Ed.), *Psychology: A study of a science* (Vol. 2). New York: McGraw-Hill, 1959.

Miller, N. E. Interactions between learned and physical factors in mental illness. *Seminars in Psychiatry*, 1972, *4*, 239–254.

Miller, N. E. Interactions between learned and physical factors in mental illness. In D. Shapiro, T. X. Barber, L. V. DiCara, J. Kamiya, N. E. Miller, & J. Stoyva (Eds.), *Biofeedback and self-control: 1972*. Chicago: Aldine, 1973.

Miller, N. E. Behavioral medicine as a new frontier: Opportunities and dangers. In S. Weiss (Ed.), *Proceedings of the National Heart Lung Institute Work Conference Health Behavior*. Washington D. C.: DHEW, Pub. No. (NIH) 76–868, 1976.

Miller, N. E. Biofeedback and visceral learning. In M. R. Rosensweig & L. W. Porter (Eds.), *Annual Review of Psychology* (Vol. 29). Palo Alto, Calif.: Annual Reviews, 1978.

Miller, N. E. The morality and humaneness of animal research on stress and pain. In D. D. Kelly (Ed.), *Stress-induced analgesia. Annals of the New York Academy of Science*, 1986, *467*, 502–504.

Miller, N. E., & Banuazizi, A. Instrumental learning by curarized rats of a specific visceral response, intestinal or cardiac. *Journal of Comparative and Physiological Psychology*, 1968, *65*, 1–17.

Miller, R. R., Greco, C., Vigorite, M., & Marlin, N. A. Signaled tailshock is perceived as similar to a stronger unsignaled tailshock: Implications for a functional analysis of classical conditioning. *Journal of Experimental Psychology*, 1983, *9*, 105–131.

Miller, R. R., Ott, C. A., Berk, A. M., & Springer, A. D. Appetitive memory restoration after electroconvulsive shock in the rat. *Journal of Comparative and Physiological Psychology*, 1974, *87*, 717–723.

Miller, R. R., & Springer, A. D. Induced recovery of memory in rats following electroconvulsive shock. *Physiology and Behavior*, 1972, *8*, 645–651.

Miller, R. R., & Springer, A. D. Amnesia, consolidation, and retrieval. *Psychological Review*, 1973, *80*, 69–79.

Miller, R. R., & Springer, A. D. Implications of recovery from experimental amnesia. *Psychological Review*, 1974, *81*, 470–473.

Millward, R. B. Theoretical and experimental approaches to human learning. In J. W. Kling & L. A. Riggs (Eds.), *Woodworth and Schlosberg's experimental psychology*. New York: Holt, Rinehart & Winston, 1971.

Milner, B. R. Amnesia following operation on temporal lobes. In C. W. N. Whitty & O. L. Zangwill (Eds.), *Amnesia*. London: Butterworths, 1966.

Milner, B. R. Visual recognition and recall after right temporal-lobe excision in man. *Neuropsychologia*, 1968, *6*, 191–209.

Milner, B. R. Memory and the medial temporal region of the brain. In K. Pribram & D. Broadbent (Eds.), *Biology of memory*. New York: Academic Press, 1970.

Mineka, S. The role of fear in theories of avoidance learning, flooding, and extinction. *Psychological Bulletin*, 1979, *86*, 985–1010.

Mineka, S., & Gino, A. Dissociative effects of different types and amounts of nonreinforced CS exposure on avoidance extinction and the CER. *Learning and Motivation*, 1979, *10*, 141–160.

Minsky, M. A. A framework for representing knowledge. In P. Winston (Ed.), *The psychology of computer vision*. New York: McGraw-Hill, 1975.

Mishkin, M., & Appenzeller, T. The anatomy of memory. *Scientific American*, June 1987, 80–89.

Mitchell, D., Kirschbaum, E. H., & Perry, R. L. Effects of nephobia and habituation on the poison-induced avoidance of exteroceptive stimuli in the rat. *Journal of Experimental Psychology: Animal Behavior Processes*, 1975, *104*, 47–55.

Mitchell, D. B., & Brown, A. S. Persistent repetition priming in picture naming and its dissociation from recognition memory. *Journal of Experimental Psychology: Learning, Memory, and Cognition*, 1988, *14(2)*, 213–222.

Moar, I., & Bower, G. H. Inconsistency in spatial knowledge. *Memory and Cognition*, 1983, *11*, 107–113.

Modaresi, H. A. Reinforcement versus species-specific defense reactions as determinants of avoidance barpressing. *Journal of Experimental Psychology: Animal Behavior Processes*, 1989, *15(1)*, 65–74.

Moeser, S. D. Levels of processing: Qualitative differences or task–demand differences. *Memory and Cognition*, 1983, *11*, 316–323.

Moltz, H. Imprinting: Empirical basis and theoretical significance. *Psychological Bulletin*, 1960, *57*, 291–314.

Moltz, H. Imprinting: An epigenetic approach. *Psychological Review*, 1963, *70*, 123–138.

Mondani, M. S., & Battig, W. F. Imaginal and verbal mnemonics as related to paired-associate learning and directionality of associations. *Journal of Verbal Learning and Verbal Behavior*, 1973, *12*, 401–408.

Monroe, B., & Barker, L. M. A contingency analysis of taste aversion conditioning. *Animal Learning and Behavior*, 1979, *7*, 141–143.

Montgomery, K. C. The relations between fear induced by novel stimuli and exploratory behavior. *Journal of Comparative and Physiological Psychology*, 1955, *48*, 254–260.

Mook, D. G. Oral and postingestional determinants of the intake of various solutions in rats with esophogeal fistulas. *Journal of Comparative and Physiological Psychology*, 1963, *56*, 645–659.

Moon, J. R., & Eisler, R. M. Anger control: An experimental comparison of three behavioral treatments. *Behavior Therapy*, 1983, *14*, 493–505.

Moore, J. W. Stimulus control: Studies of auditory generalization in rabbits. In A. H. Black & W. F. Prokasy (Eds.), *Classical conditioning II: Current theory and research*. New York: Appleton, 1972.

Morgan, M. J., & Nicholas, D. J. Discrimination between reinforced action patterns in the rat. *Learning and Motivation*, 1979, *10*, 1–22.

Morosko, T. E., & Baer, P. E. Avoidance conditioning of alcoholics. In R. Ulrich, T. Stachnik, & J. Mabry (Eds.), *Control of human behavior* (Vol. 2). Glenview, Ill.: Scott, Foresman, 1970.

Morris, C. D., Bransford, J. D., & Franks, J. J. Levels of processing versus transfer appropriate processing. *Journal of Verbal Learning and Verbal Behavior*, 1977, *16*, 519–533.

Moscovitch, M., & Craik, F. I. M. Depth of processing, retrieval cues, and uniqueness of encoding as factors in recall. *Journal of Verbal Learning and Verbal Behavior*, 1976, *15*, 447–458.

Mowrer, O. H. *Learning theory and behavior*. New York: Wiley, 1960.

Mowrer, O. H., & Jones, H. M. Habit strength as a function of the pattern of reinforcement. *Journal of Experimental Psychology*, 1945, *35*, 293–311.

Mowrer, O. H., & Lamoreaux, R. R. Avoidance conditioning and signal duration—a study of secondary motivation and reward. *Psychological Monographs*, 1942, *54*, No. 247.

Mowrer, O. H., & Lamoreaux, R. R. Fear as an intervening variable in avoidance conditioning. *Journal of Comparative Psychology*, 1946, *39*, 29–50.

Mueller, J. H., Gautt, P., Evans, J. H. Stimulus encoding in A–Br transfer. *Journal of Experimental Psychology*, 1974, *103*, 54–61.

Mueller, P. G., Crow, R. E., & Cheney, C. D. Schedule-induced locomotor activity in humans. *Journal of the Experimental Analysis of Behavior*, 1979, *31*, 83–90.

Murdock, B. B., Jr. Short-term memory. In G. H. Bower (Ed.), *The psychology of learning and motivation: Advances in research and therapy* (Vol. 5). New York: Academic Press, 1972.

Murdock, B. B. *Human memory: Theory and data*. New York: Wiley, 1974.

Muter, P. Recognition failure of recallable words in semantic memory. *Memory and Cognition*, 1978, 6, 9–12.

Myers, G. C. A. A comparative study of recognition and recall. *Psychological Review*, 1914, 21, 442–456.

Naire, J. S. Associative processing during rote rehearsal. *Journal of Experimental Psychology*, 1983, 9, 3–20.

Nairne, J. S., & Widner, R. L., Jr. Familiarity and lexicality as determinants of the generation effect. *Journal of Experimental Psychology: Learning, Memory, and Cognition*, 1988, 14(4), 694–699.

Nairne, J. S. The mnemonic value of perceptual identification. *Journal of Experimental Psychology: Learning, Memory, and Cognition*, 1988, 14(2), 248–255.

Nation, J. R., & Massad, P. Persistence training: A partial reinforcement procedure for reversing learned helplessness and depression. *Journal of Experimental Psychology*, 1978, 107, 436–451.

Naveh-Benjamin, M., & Jonides, J. Cognitive load and maintenance rehearsal. *Journal of Verbal Learning and Verbal Behavior*, 1984, 23, 494–507. (a)

Naveh-Benjamin, M., & Jonides, J. Maintenance rehearsal: A two-component analysis. *Journal of Experimental Psychology: Learning, Memory, and Cognition*, 1984, 10, 369–385. (b)

Munford, P. R., & Pally, R. Outpatient contingency management of operant vomiting. *Journal of Behavior Therapy and Experimental Psychiatry*, 1979, 10, 135–137.

Munn, N. L. *Handbook of psychological research on the rat.* Boston: Houghton Mifflin, 1950.

Murdock, B. B., Jr. The immediate retention of unrelated words. *Journal of Experimental Psychology*, 1960, 60, 222–234.

Neely, J. H. Semantic priming and retrieval from lexical memory: Rules of inhibitionless spreading activation and limited-capacity attention. *Journal of Experimental Psychology: General*, 1977, 106, 226–254.

Neely, J. H., & Payne, D. G. A direct comparison of recognition failure rates for recallable names in episodic and semantic memory tests. *Memory and Cognition*, 1983, 11, 161–171.

Neely, J. H., Schmidt, S. R., & Roediger, H. L. Inhibition from related primes in recognition memory. *Journal of Experimental Psychology*, 1983, 9, 196–211.

Neisser, U. *Cognitive psychology.* New York: Appleton, 1967.

Neisser, U. Anticipations, images, and introspection. *Cognition*, 1978, 6, 169–174.

Neisser, U. Interpreting Harry Bahrick's discovery: What confers immunity against forgetting? *Journal of Experimental Psychology: General*, 1984, 113, 32–35.

Neisser, U., & Weene, P. Hierarchies in concept attainment. *Journal of Experimental Psychology*, 1962, 64, 640–645.

Nelson, D. L., & Brooks, D. H. Retroactive inhibition of rhyme categories in free recall: Inaccessibility and unavailability of information. *Journal of Experimental Psychology*, 1974, 102, 277–283.

Nelson, D. L., & McEvoy, C. L. Effects of retention interval and modality on sensory and semantic trace information. *Memory and Cognition*, 1979, 7, 557–562.

Nelson, D. L., Reed, V. S., & McEvoy, C. L. Learning to order pictures and words: A model of sensory and semantic encoding. *Journal of Experimental Psychology: Human Learning and Memory*, 1977, 3, 485–497.

Nelson, G. L., & Cone, J. D. Multiple-baseline analysis of a token economy for psychiatric inpatients. *Journal of Applied Behavior Analysis*, 1979, 12, 255–271.

Nelson, T. O. Repetition and depth of processing. *Journal of Verbal Learning and Verbal Behavior*, 1977, 16, 151–171.

Nelson, T. O., Greene, G., Ronk, B., Hatchett, G., & Igl, V. Effect of multiple images on associative learning. *Memory and Cognition*, 1978, 6, 337–341.

Nelson, T. O., & Rothbart, R. Acoustic savings for items forgotten from long-term memory. *Journal of Experimental Psychology*, 1972, 93, 357–360.

Nelson, T. O., & Vining, S. K. Effect of semantic versus structural processing on long-term retention. *Journal of Experimental Psychology: Human Memory and Learning*, 1979, 4, 198–209.

Neumann, K. F., Critelli, J. W., Tang, C. S. K., & Schneider, L. J. Placebo effects in the treatment of male dating anxiety. *Journal of Behavior Therapy and Experimental Psychiatry*, 1988, 19(2), 135–141.

Nevin, J. A. On the form of the relation between response rates in a multiple schedule. *Journal of the Experimental Analysis of Behavior*, 1974, 21, 237–248. (a)

Nevin, J. A. Response strength in multiple schedules. *Journal of the Experimental Analysis of Behavior*, 1974, *21*, 389–408. (b)

Newell, A., Shaw, J. C., & Simon, H. A. Elements of a theory of human problem solving. *Psychological Review*, 1958, *65*, 151–166.

Newell, A., & Simon, H. A. *Human problem solving*. Englewood Cliffs, N. J.: Prentice-Hall, 1972.

Newton, J. M., & Wickens, D. D. Retroactive inhibition as a function of the temporal position of interpolated learning. *Journal of Experimental Psychology*, 1956, *51*, 149–154.

Nickerson, R. S., & Adams, M. J. Long-term memory for a common object. *Cognitive Psychology*, 1979, *11*, 287–307.

Nilsson, L.-G., Law, J., & Tulving, E. Recognition failure of recallable unique names: Evidence for an empirical law of memory and learning. *Journal of Experimental Psychology: Learning, Memory, and Cognition*, 1988, *14(2)*, 266–277.

Nilsson, L.-G. Locus of the modality effect in free recall: A reply to Watkins. *Journal of Experimental Psychology: Human Learning and Memory*, 1975, *104*, 13–17.

Nisbett, R. E., Krantz, D. H., Jepson, C., & Kunda, Z. The use of statistical heuristics in everyday inductive reasoning. *Psychological Review*, 1983, *90*, 339–364.

Nodine, C. F. Temporal variables in paired-associate learning: The law of contiguity revisited. *Psychological Review*, 1969, *76*, 351–362.

Norborg, J., Osborne, S., & Fanting, E. Duration of components and response rates on multiple fixed-ratio schedules. *Animal Learning and Behavior*, 1983, *11*, 51–59.

Norman, D. A. Toward a theory of memory and attention. *Psychological Review*, 1968, *75(6)*, 522–536.

Norman, D. A. (Ed.), *Models of human memory*. New York: Academic Press, 1970.

Norman, D. A., & Rumelhart, D. E. *Explorations in cognition*. San Francisco: W. H. Freeman, 1975.

Nowaczyk, R. H., Shaughnessy, J. J., & Zimmerman, J. Proactive interference in short-term retention and the measurement of degree of learning: A new technique. *Journal of Experimental Psychology*, 1974, *103*, 45–53.

Oakhill, J. Text memory and integration at different times of day. *Applied Cognitive Psychology*, Vol. 2, 1988, 203–212.

O'Brien, T. P., Riner, L. S., & Budd, K. S. The effects of a child's self-evaluation program on compliance with parental instructions in the home. *Journal of Applied Behavior Analysis*, 1983, *16*, 69–79.

O'Connell, D. N., Shore, R. E., & Orne, M. T. Hypnotic age regression: An empirical and methodological analysis. *Journal of Abnormal Psychology*, 1970, *76*, 32.

Oden, D. L., Thompson, R. K. R., & Premack, D. Spontaneous transfer of matching by infant chimpanzees (*pan troglodytes*). *Journal of Experimental Psychology: Animal Behavior Processes*, 1988, *14(2)*, 140–145.

Odling-Smee, F. J. The overshadowing of background stimuli by an informative CS in aversive Pavlovian conditioning with rats. *Animal Learning and Behavior*, 1978, *6*, 43–51.

Öhman, A. Fear relevance, autonomic conditioning, and phobias: A laboratory model. In P. Sjödén, S. Bates, & W. S. Dockens (Eds.), *Trends in behavior therapy*. New York: Academic Press, 1979.

Olds, J., & Milner, P. Positive reinforcement produced by electrical stimulation of septal area and other regions of rat brain. *Journal of Comparative and Physiological Psychology*, 1954, *47*, 419–427.

Olton, D. S. Characteristics of spatial memory. In S. H. Hulse, H. Fowler, & W. K. Honig (Eds.), *Cognitive processes in animal behavior*. Hillsdale, N. J.: Lawrence Erlbaum Associates, 1978.

Olton, D. S., & Samuelson, R. J. Remembrance of places passed: Spatial memory in rats. *Journal of Experimental Psychology*, 1976, *2*, 97–116.

Orlando, R., & Bijou, S. W. Single and multiple schedules of reinforcement in developmentally retarded children. *Journal of the Experimental Analysis of Behavior*, 1960, *3*, 339–348.

Orne, M. T. Hypnosis, motivation, and the ecological validity of the psychological experiment. In W. S. Arnold & M. M. Page (Eds.), *Nebraska symposium on motivation*. Lincoln, NE: University of Nebraska Press, 1970.

Osborne, S. R. The free food (contrafreeloading) phenomenon: A review and analysis. *Animal Learning and Behavior*, 1977, *5*, 221–235.

Osborne, S. R. A quantitative analysis of the effects of amount of reinforcement on two response classes. *Journal of Experimental Psychology: Animal Behavior Processes*, 1978, 4, 297–317.

Osgood, C. E. Meaningful similarity and interference in learning. *Journal of Experimental Psychology*, 1946, 36, 277–301.

Osgood, C. E. The similarity paradox in human learning: A resolution. *Psychological Review*, 1949, 56, 132–143.

Osgood, C. E. *Method and theory in experimental psychology*. London and New York: Oxford University Press, 1953.

Packman, J. L., & Battig, W. F. Effects of different kinds of semantic processing on memory for words. *Memory and Cognition*, 1978, 6, 502–508.

Paivio, A. *Imagery and verbal processes*. New York: Holt, Rinehart & Winston, 1971.

Paivio, A. Coding distinctions and repetition effects in memory. In G. H. Bower (Ed.), *The psychology of learning and motivation* (Vol. 9). New York: Academic Press, 1975.

Paivio, A. Mental comparisons involving abstract attributes. *Memory and Cognition*, 1978, 6, 199–208.

Paivio, A., & Foth, D. Imaginal and verbal mediators and noun concreteness in paired-associate learning: The elusive interaction. *Journal of Verbal Learning and Verbal Behavior*, 1970, 9, 384–390.

Paivio, A., Smythe, P. C., & Yuille, J. C. Imagery versus meaningfulness of nouns in paired-associate learning. *Canadian Journal of Psychology*, 1968, 22, 427–441.

Palmer, S. E. Fundamental aspects of cognitive representation. In E. Rosch & B. B. Lloyds (Eds.), *Cognition and categorization*. Hillsdale, N. J.: Lawrence Erlbaum Associates, 1978.

Papini, M. R., Mustaca, A. E., & Bitterman, M. E. Successive negative contrast in the consummatory responding of didelphid marsupials. *Animal Learning and Behavior*, 1988, 16(1), 53–57.

Parkinson, J. K., & Medin, D. L. Emerging attributes in monkey short-term memory. *Journal of Experimental Psychology*, 1983, 9, 31–40.

Parkinson, S. R. An alternative interpretation of the stimulus suffix effect. *Journal of Experimental Psychology: Human Learning and Memory*, 1978, 4, 362–369.

Pate, J. L., & Rumbaugh, D. M. The language-like behavior of Lana chimpanzee: Is it merely discrimination and paired-associate learning? *Animal Learning and Behavior*, 1983, 11, 134–138.

Patterson, F. G. The gestures of a gorilla: Language acquisition in another Pongid. *Brain and Language*, 1978, 5, 72–97.

Pavlov, I. P. *Conditioned reflexes* (translated by G. V. Anrep). London and New York: Oxford University Press, 1927.

Pavlov, I. P. *Lectures on conditioned reflexes*. New York: International Publishers, 1928.

Pearce, J. M., & Hall, G. Loss of associability by a compound stimulus comprising excitatory and inhibitory elements. *Journal of Experimental Psychology: Animal Behavior Processes*, 1979, 5, 19–30.

Pelchat, M. L., Grill, H. J., Rozin, P., & Jacobs, J. Quality of acquired responses to tastes by *Rattus norregicas* depends upon type of associated discomfort. *Journal of Comparative Psychology*, 1983, 2, 140–153.

Pellegrino, J. W., Rosinski, R. R., Chiesi, H. L., & Siegel, A. Picture–word differences in decision latency: An analysis of single and dual memory models. *Memory and Cognition*, 1977, 5, 383–396.

Pellegrino, J. W., Siegel, A. W., & Dhawan, M. Short-term retention of pictures and words: Evidence for dual coding systems. *Journal of Experimental Psychology: Human Learning and Memory*, 1975, 104, 95–102.

Penfield, W. Consciousness, memory, and man's conditioned reflexes. In K. Pribram (Ed.), *On the biology of learning*. New York: Harcourt Brace Jovanovich, 1969.

Peniston, E. G. Evaluation of long-term therapeutic efficacy of behavior modification program with chronic male psychiatric inpatients. *Journal of Behavior Therapy and Experimental Psychiatry*, 1988, 19(2), 95–101.

Penney, C. G. Interactions of suffix effects with suffix delay and recall modality in serial recall. *Journal of Experimental Psychology: Human Learning and Memory*, 1979, 5, 507–521.

Pepperwood, I. M. Cognition in the African grey parrot: Preliminary evidence for auditory/vocal comprehension of the class concept. *Animal Learning and Behavior,* 1983, *11,* 179–185.

Perfetto, G. A., Bransford, J. D., & Franks, J. J. Constraints on access in a problem solving context. *Memory and Cognition,* 1983, *11,* 24–31.

Perin, C. T. A quantitative investigation of the delay-of-reinforcement gradient. *Journal of Experimental Psychology,* 1943, *32,* 37–51.

Perkins, C. C. The relation of secondary reward to gradients of reinforcement. *Journal of Experimental Psychology,* 1947, *37,* 377–392.

Peters, D. P., & McHose, J. H. Effects of varied preshift reward magnitude on successive negative contrast effects in rats. *Journal of Comparative and Physiological Psychology,* 1974, *86,* 85–95.

Peters, R. H. Learned aversions to copulatory behaviors in male rats. *Behavioral Neuroscience,* 1983, *97,* 140–145.

Peterson, L. R. Immediate memory: Data and theory. In C. N. Cofer & B. S. Musgrave (Eds.), *Verbal behavior and learning.* New York: McGraw-Hill, 1963.

Peterson, L. R., & Peterson, M. J. Short-term retention of individual verbal items. *Journal of Experimental Psychology,* 1959, *58,* 193–198.

Peterson, M. J., Meagher, R. B., Chail, H., & Gillie, S. The abstraction and generalization of dot patterns. *Cognitive Psychology,* 1973, *4,* 378–398.

Peterson, M. J., Thomas, J. E., & Johnson, H. Imagery, rehearsal, and the compatibility of input–output tasks. *Memory and Cognition,* 1977, *5,* 415–422.

Peterson, N. Effect of monochromatic rearing on the control of responding by wavelength. *Science,* 1962, *136,* 774–775.

Petrey, S. Word associations and the development of lexical memory. *Cognition,* 1977, *5,* 57–71.

Pezdek, K., Maki, R., Valencia-Laver, D., Whetstone, T., Stoeckert, J., & Doughterty, T. Picture memory: Recognizing added and deleted details. *Journal of Experimental Psychology: Learning, Memory, and Cognition,* 1988, *14(3),* 468–476.

Pfaffmann, C. Taste preference and reinforcement. In J. T. Tapp (Ed.), *Reinforcement and behavior.* New York: Academic Press, 1969.

Pfautz, P. L., Donegan, N. H., & Wagner, A. R. Sensory preconditioning versus protection from habituation. *Journal of Experimental Psychology: Animal Behavior Processes,* 1978, *4,* 286–295.

Phillips, J. L., Shiffrin, R. M., & Atkinson, R. C. The effects of list length on short-term memory. *Journal of Verbal Learning and Verbal Behavior,* 1967, *6,* 303–311.

Pierce, C. H., & Risley, T. R. Recreation as a reinforcer: Increasing membership and decreasing disruptions in an urban recreation center. *Journal of Applied Behavior Analysis,* 1974, *7,* 403–411.

Pillemer, D. B., Goldsmith, L. R., Panter, A. T., & White, S. H. Very long-term memories of the first year in college. *Journal of Experimental Psychology: Learning, Memory, and Cognition,* 1988, *14(4),* 709–715.

Pisacreta, R., Redwood, E., & Witt, K. Autoshaping with several concurrently available conditioned stimuli. *Bulletin of the Psychonomic Society,* 1983, *21,* 65–68.

Pittenger, D. J., & Pavlik, W. B. Resistance to extinction in humans: Analysis of the generalized partial reinforcement effect. *Learning and Motivation,* 1989, *20,* 60–72.

Pittenger, D. J., Pavlik, W. B., Flora, S. R., & Kontos, J. M. The persistence of learned behaviors in humans as a function of changes in reinforcement schedule and response. *Learning and Motivation,* 1988, *19,* 300–316.

Platt, J. R., & Day, R. B. A hierarchical response-unit analysis of resistance to extinction following fixed-number and fixed-consecutive-number reinforcement. *Journal of Experimental Psychology: Animal Behavior Processes,* 1979, *5,* 307–320.

Plotkin, W. B. The alpha experience revisited: Biofeedback in the transformation of psychological state. *Psychological Bulletin,* 1979, *86,* 1132–1148.

Pohl, R., Colonius, H., & Thuring, M. Recognition of script-based inferences. *Psychological Review,* 1985, *87,* 532–552.

Polya, G. *How to solve it.* Garden City, N. Y.: Doubleday-Anchor, 1957.

Popik, R. S., Stern, S. D., & Frey, P. W. Second-order conditioning: Different outcomes in fear and eyelid conditioning. *Animal Behavior and Learning*, 1979, 7, 355–359.

Posner, M. I. Retention of abstract ideas. *Journal of Experimental Psychology*, 1970, 83, 304–308.

Posner, M. I. *Cognition: An introduction.* Glenview, Ill.: Scott, Foresman, 1973.

Posner, M. I., Goldsmith, R., & Welton, K. E. Perceived distance and the classification of distorted patterns. *Journal of Experimental Psychology*, 1967, 73, 28–38.

Posner, M. I., & Keele, S. On the genesis of abstract ideas. *Journal of Experimental Psychology*, 1968, 77, 353–363.

Posner, M. I., & Konick, A. On the role of interference in short-term retention. *Journal of Experimental Psychology*, 1966, 72, 221–231.

Posner, M. I., & Rossman, E. Effect of size and location of informational transforms upon short-term retention. *Journal of Experimental Psychology*, 1965, 70, 496–505.

Posner, M. I., & Snyder, C. R. R. Attention and cognitive control. In R. L. Solso (Ed.), *Information processing and cognition: The Loyola Symposium.* Hillsdale, N. J.: Lawrence Erlbaum Associates, 1975.

Posobiec, K., & Renfrew, J. W. Successful self-management of severe bulimia: A case study. *Journal of Behavior Therapy and Experimental Psychiatry*, 1988, 19(1), 63–68.

Postman, L. Repetition and paired-associate learning. *American Journal of Psychology*, 1962, 75, 372–389. (a)

Postman, L. Transfer of training as a function of experimental paradigm and degree of first-list learning. *Journal of Verbal Learning and Verbal Behavior*, 1962, 1, 109–118. (b)

Postman, L. Experimental analysis of learning to learn. In G. H. Bower & J. T. Spence (Eds.), *The psychology of learning and motivation* (Vol. 3). New York: Academic Press, 1969.

Postman, L. Effects of word frequency on acquisition and retention under conditions of free-recall learning. *Quarterly Journal of Experimental Psychology*, 1970, 22, 185–195.

Postman, L. Transfer, interference and forgetting. In J. W. Kling & L. A. Riggs (Eds.), *Woodworth and Schlosberg's experimental psychology.* New York: Holt, Rinehart & Winston, 1971.

Postman, L. A pragmatic view of organization theory. In E. Tulving & W. Donaldson (Eds.), *Organization of memory.* New York: Academic Press, 1972.

Postman, L. Picture–word differences in the acquisition and retention of paired-associates. *Journal of Experimental Psychology: Human Learning and Memory*, 1978, 4, 146–157.

Postman, L., & Gray, W. Maintenance of prior associations and proactive inhibition. *Journal of Experimental Psychology: Human Learning and Memory*, 1977, 3, 255–263.

Postman, L., & Greenbloom, R. Conditions of cue selection in the acquisition of paired-associate lists. *Journal of Experimental Psychology*, 1967, 73, 91–100.

Postman, L., & Keppel, G. Conditions of cumulative proactive inhibition. *Journal of Experimental Psychology: General*, 1977, 106, 376–403.

Postman, L., & Schwartz, M. Studies of learning to learn: I. Transfer as a function of method of practice and class of verbal materials. *Journal of Verbal Learning and Verbal Behavior*, 1964, 3, 37–49.

Postman, L., & Stark, K. Role of response availability in transfer and interference. *Journal of Experimental Psychology*, 1969, 79, 168–177.

Postman, L., Stark, K., & Burns, S. Sources of proactive inhibition on unpaced tests of retention. *American Journal of Psychology*, 1974, 87, 33–56.

Postman, L., Stark, K., & Fraser, J. Temporal changes in interference. *Journal of Verbal Learning and Verbal Behavior*, 1968, 7, 672–694.

Postman, L., & Underwood, B. J. Critical issues in interference theory. *Memory and Cognition*, 1973, 1, 19–40.

Potter, M. C., & Faulconer, B. A. Time to understand pictures and words. *Nature*, 1975, 253, 437–438.

Poulson, C. L. Operant conditioning of vocalization rate of infants with Down syndrome. *American Journal on Mental Retardation*, 1988, 93(1), 57–63.

Powell, L., Felce, D., Jenkins, J., & Lunt, B. Increasing engagement in a home for the elderly by providing an indoor gardening activity. *Behavior Research and Therapy*, 1979, *17*, 127–135.

Premack, D. Toward empirical behavioral laws: I. Positive reinforcement. *Psychological Review*, 1959, *66*, 219–233.

Premack, D. Reinforcement theory. In D. Levin (Ed.), *Nebraska symposium on motivation*. Lincoln, NE: University of Nebraska Press, 1965.

Premack, D. A functional analysis of language. *Journal of the Experimental Analysis of Behavior*, 1970, *14*, 107–125.

Premack, D. Catching up with common sense or two sides of a generalization: Reinforcement and punishment. In R. Glasser (Ed.), *The nature of reinforcement*. New York: Academic Press, 1971.

Premack, D. Language in chimpanzees? *Science*, 1971, *172*, 808–822.

Premack, D. *Intelligence in ape and man*. Hillsdale, N. J.: Lawrence Erlbaum Associates, 1976.

Pressley, M., & Levine, J. R. The keyword method and recall of vocabulary words from definitions. *Journal of Experimental Psychology*, 1981, *7*, 72–76.

Prokasy, W. F., Hall, J. F., & Fawcett, J. T. Adaptation, sensitization, forward and backward conditioning, and pseudo-conditioning of the GSR. *Psychological Reports*, 1962, *10*, 103–106.

Puff, C. R. Role of clustering in free recall. *Journal of Experimental Psychology*, 1970, *86*, 384–386.

Pullen, M. R., & Turney, T. H. Response modes in simultaneous and successive visual discriminations. *Animal Learning and Behavior*, 1977, *5*, 73–77.

Purtle, R. B. Peak shift: A review. *Psychological Bulletin*, 1973, *80*, 408–421.

Pylyshyn, Z. W. What the mind's eye tells the mind's brain: A critique of mental imagery. *Psychological Bulletin*, 1973, *80*, 1–24.

Quartermain, D., & Botwinick, C. Y. Role of the biogenic amines in the reversal of cycloheximide-induced amnesia. *Journal of Comparative and Physiological Psychology*, 1975, *88*, 386–401.

Rabiner, D. L., Kling, J. W., & Spraguer, P. M. Modulation of taste-induced drinking. The effects of concentration shifts and drinking interruptions. *Animal Behavior and Learning*, 1988, *16*, 365–376.

Rabinowitz, J. C., Mandler, G., & Barsalou, L. W. Recognition failure: Another case of retrieval failure. *Journal of Verbal Learning and Verbal Behavior*, 1977, *16*, 639–643.

Rabinowitz, J. C., Mandler, G., & Patterson, K. E. Determinants of recognition and recall: Accessibility and generation. *Journal of Experimental Psychology: General*, 1977, *106*, 302–329.

Rabinowitz, M., & Mandler, J. M. Organization and information retrieval. *Journal of Experimental Psychology*, 1983, *9*, 430–439.

Rachlin, H. *Behavior and learning*. San Francisco: W. H. Freeman, 1976.

Rachlin, H., & Burkhard, B. The temporal triangle: Response substitution in instrumental conditioning. *Psychological Review*, 1978, *85*, 22–47.

Rachlin, H. C., & Hineline, P. N. Training and maintenance of key pecking in the pigeon by negative reinforcement. *Science*, 1967, *157*, 954–955.

Rajecki, D. W. Imprinting in precocial birds: Interpretation, evidence, and evaluation. *Psychological Review*, 1973, *79*, 48–58.

Ramsay, A. O. Familial recognition in domestic birds. *Auk*, 1951, *68*, 1–16.

Ramsay, R. W. Bereavement: A behavioral treatment of pathological grief. In P. Sjödén, S. Bates, & W. S. Dockens (Eds.), *Trends in behavior therapy*. New York: Academic Press, 1979.

Randich, A., & Haggard, D. Exposure to the unconditioned stimulus alone: Effects on retention and acquisition of conditioned suppression. *Journal of Experimental Psychology*, 1983, *9*, 147–159.

Raser, G. A. Recording of semantic and acoustic information in short-term memory. *Journal of Verbal Learning and Verbal Behavior*, 1969, *8*, 567–574.

Ratcliff, R., & McKoon, G. A retrieval theory of priming in memory. *Psychological Review*, 1988, *95(3)*, 385–408.

Rayner, K., & Posnansky, C. Stages of processing in word identification. *Journal of Experimental Psychology: General*, 1978, *107*, 64–80.

Razran, G. Stimulus generalization of conditioned responses. *Psychological Bulletin*, 1949, *46*, 337–365.

Razran, G. *Mind in evolution: An East/West synthesis of learned behavior and cognition*. Boston: Houghton Mifflin, 1971.

Real, P. G., & Hobson, S. L. Noncontingent and contingent no-choice intervals and concurrent performance. *Animal Learning and Behavior*, 1983, *11*, 44–50.

Reardon, R., & Katz, S. Comprehending ambiguity in the sentence-verification paradigm: Basic process or problem solving? *Bulletin of the Psychonomic Society*, 1983, *21*, 373–376.

Reber, A. A., & Allen, R. Analogical and abstraction strategies in synthetic grammar learning: A functionalist interpretation. *Cognition*, 1978, *6*, 189–221.

Reber, A. S. What clicks may tell us about speech perception. *Journal of Psycholinguistic Research*, 1973, *2*, 286–287.

Reder, L. M., & Ross, B. H. Integrated knowledge in different tasks: The role of retrieval strategy on fan effects. *Journal of Experimental Psychology*, 1983, *9*, 55–72.

Redford, M. E., & Perkins, C. C. The role of autopecking in behavioral contrast. *Journal of the Experimental Analysis of Behavior*, 1974, *21*, 145–150.

Reed, S. K. Pattern recognition and categorization. *Cognitive Psychology*, 1972, *3*, 383–407.

Reed, S. K., Ernst, G. W., & Banerji, R. The role of analogy in transfer between similar problem states. *Cognitive Psychology*, 1974, *6*, 435–450.

Reed, S. K. *Cognition: Theory and applications*. Monterey, Calif.: Brooks/Cole, 1982.

Reese, H. W. *The perception of stimulus relations*, New York: Academic Press, 1968.

Reiner, M. E., & Morrison, F. J. Is semantic interference really automatic? *Bulletin of the Psychonomic Society*, 1983, *21*, 271–274.

Reitman, J. S. Without surreptitious rehearsal, information in short-term memory decays. *Journal of Verbal Learning and Verbal Behavior*, 1974, *13*, 365–377.

Reitman, J. S. Skilled perception in Go: Deducing memory structures from inter-response times. *Cognitive Psychology*, 1976, *8*, 336–356.

Reitman, J. S., McKeithen, K. B., Rueter, H. R., & Hirtle, S. Knowledge organization of expert and novice programmers. *Cognitive Psychology*, 1980, *12*, 273–280.

Rekers, G. A., & Lovaas, O. I. Behavioral treatment of deviant sex-role behaviors in a male child. *Journal of Applied Behavior Analysis*, 1974, *7*, 173–190.

Rescorla, R. A. Aspects of the reinforcer learned in second-order Pavlovian conditioning. *Journal of Experimental Psychology*, 1979, *5*, 79–95.

Rescorla, R. A. Associative learning: Some consequences of contiguity. In N. M. Weinberger, J. L. McGaugh, & G. Lynch (Eds.), *Memory systems of the brain*. New York: Guildford Press, 1985.

Rescorla, R. A. Pavlovian conditioning: It's not what you think it is. *American Psychologist*, 1988, *43*, 151–160.

Rescorla, R. A., & Colwill, R. M. Within-compound associations in unblocking. *Journal of Experimental Psychology*, 1983, *9*, 390–400.

Rescorla, R. A., & Cunningham, C. L. Spatial contiguity facilitates Pavlovian second-order conditioning. *Journal of Experimental Psychology: Animal Behavior Processes*, 1979, *5*, 152–161.

Rescorla, R. A., & Holland, P. C. Associations in Pavlovian conditioned inhibition. *Learning and Motivation*, 1977, *8*, 429–447.

Rescorla, R. A., & Solomon, R. L. Two-process learning theory: Relationships between Pavlovian conditioning and instrumental learning. *Psychological Review*, 1967, *74*, 151–182.

Rescorla, R. A., & Wagner, A. R. A theory of Pavlovian conditioning: Variations in the effectiveness of reinforcement and nonreinforcement. In A. Black & W. F. Prokasy (Eds.), *Classical conditioning: II. Current research and theory*. New York: Appleton, 1972.

Revusky, S. H. Aversion to sucrose produced by contingent X-irradiation—temporal and dosage parameters. *Journal of Comparative and Physiological Psychology*, 1968, *65*, 17–22.

Revusky, S. H. The role of interference in association over a delay. In W. K. Honig & H. James (Eds.), *Animal memory*. New York: Academic Press, 1971.

Revusky, S. H., & Garcia, J. Learned associations over long delays. In G. H. Bower (Ed.), *The psychology of learning and motivation: Advances in theory and research* (Vol. 4). New York: Academic Press, 1970.

Reynolds, A. G., & Flagg, P. W. *Cognitive psychology*. Boston: Little, Brown, 1983.

Reynolds, G. S. Behavioral contrast. *Journal of the Experimental Analysis of Behavior*, 1961, *4*, 57–61. (a)

Reynolds, G. S. Relativity of response rate and reinforcement in a multiple schedule. *Journal of the Experimental Analysis of Behavior*, 1961, *4*, 179–184. (b)

Reynolds, J. H. Unavailable and inaccessible information in retroactive inhibition of paired associates. *Journal of Experimental Psychology: Human Learning and Memory*, 1977, *3*, 68–77.

Reynolds, J. H., & Houston, J. P. Rehearsal strategies and the primacy effect in serial learning. *Psychonomic Science*, 1964, *1*, 279–280.

Reynolds, W. F., Pavlik, W. B., & Goldstein, E. Secondary reinforcement effects as a function of reward magnitude training methods. *Psychological Reports*, 1964, *15*, 7–10.

Richards, R. W. Inhibitory stimulus control and the magnitude of delayed reinforcement. *Journal of the Experimental Analysis of Behavior*, 1974, *21*, 501–509.

Richards, R. W., & Marcattilo, A. J. Stimulus control and delayed reinforcement. *Learning and Motivation*, 1978, *9*, 54–68.

Richardson, J. Cue effectiveness and abstraction in paired-associate learning. *Psychological Bulletin*, 1971, *75*, 73–91.

Richardson, J. Encoding and stimulus selection in paired-associate verbal learning. In A. W. Melton & E. Martin (Eds.), *Coding processes in human memory*. New York: Wiley, 1972.

Richard, J., & Chisholm. D. C. Transfer of cue selection based on letter position. *Journal of Experimental Psychology*, 1969, *80*, 299–303.

Richardson, J. T. E. Precategorical acoustic storage and postcategorical lexical storage. *Cognitive Psychology*, 1979, *11*, 265–286.

Rider, D. P. Concurrent ratio schedules: Fixed vs. variable response requirements. *Journal of the Experimental Analysis of Behavior*, 1979, *31*, 225–237.

Riley, A. L., Jacobs, W. J., & Mastropaolo, J. P. The effects of extensive taste preexposure on the acquisition of conditioned taste aversion. *Bulletin of the Psychonomic Society*, 1983, *21*, 221–224.

Riley, D. A. *Discrimination learning*. Boston: Allyn & Bacon, 1968.

Riley, D. A., & Levin, T. C. Stimulus-generalization gradients in chickens reared in monochromatic light and tested with a single wavelength value. *Journal of Comparative and Physiological Psychology*, 1971, *75*, 399–402.

Rilling, M., & Caplan, H. J. Frequency of reinforcement as a determinant of extinction-induced aggression during errorless discrimination learning. *Journal of the Experimental Analysis of Behavior*, 1975, *23*, 121–129.

Ristau, C. A., & Robbins, D. Language in the great apes: A critical review. In J. S. Rosenblatt, R. A. Hinde, C. Beer, & M. C. Busnel (Eds.), *Advances in the study of behavior* (Vol. 12). New York: Academic Press, 1982.

Robbins, D., Bray, J. F., Irvin, J. R., & Wise, P. S. Memorial strategy and imagery: An interaction between instructions and rated imagery. *Journal of Experimental Psychology*, 1974, *102*, 706–709.

Robbins, S. J. Role of context in performance on a random schedule in autoshaping. *Journal of Experimental Psychology: Animal Behavior Processes*, 1988, *14(4)*, 413–424.

Roberts, M. W. Enforcing chair timeouts with room timeouts. *Behavior Modification*, 1988, *12(3)*, 353–370.

Roberts, W. A., & Grant D. S. An analysis of light-induced retroactive inhibition in pigeon short-term memory. *Journal of Experimental Psychology: Animal Behavior Processes*, 1978, *4*, 219–236.

Roberts, W. A., Mazmanian, D. S. Concept learning at different levels of abstraction by pigeons, monkeys, and people. *Journal of Experimental Psychology: Animal Behavior Processes*, 1988, *14(3)*, 247–260.

Rock, I. The role of repetition in associative learning. *American Journal of Psychology*, 1957, *70*, 186–193.

Roediger, H. L., Knight, J. L., & Kantowitz, B. H. Inferring decay in short-term memory: The issue of capacity. *Memory and Cognition*, 1977, *5*, 167–176.

Roediger, H. L., Neeley, J. H., & Blaxton, T. A. Inhibition from related primes in semantic memory retrieval: A reappraisal of Brown's (1979) paradigm. *Journal of Experimental Psychology*, 1983, *9*, 478–485.

Roediger, H. L., Stellon, C. C., & Tulving, E. Inhibition from part-list cues and rate of recall. *Journal of Experimental Psychology: Human Learning and Memory*, 1977, *3*, 174–188.

Rogers, T. B., Kuiper, N. A., & Kirker, W. S. Self-reference and the encoding of personal information. *Journal of Personality and Social Psychology*, 1977, *35*, 677–688.

Roitblat, H. L., & Harley, H. E. Spatial delayed matching-to-sample performance by rats: Learning, memory, and proactive interference. *Journal of Experimental Psychology: Animal Behavior Processes*, 1988, *14(1)*, 71–82.

Roitblat, H. L., & Scopatz, R. A. Sequential effects in pigeon delayed matching-to-sample performance. *Journal of Experimental Psychology*, 1983, *9*, 202–221.

Rosch, E. Principles of categorization. In E. Rosch & B. B. Lloyd (Eds.), *Cognition and categorization*. Hillsdale, N. J.: Lawrence Erlbaum Associates, 1978.

Rosch, E. H. Natural categories. *Cognitive Psychology*, 1973, *4*, 328–350.

Rosch, E. H. Human categorization. In N. Warren (Ed.), *Advances in cross-cultural psychology* (Vol. 1). London: Academic Press, 1977.

Rosch, E. H., & Mervis, C. B. Family resemblances: Studies in the internal structure of categories. *Cognitive Psychology*, 1975, *7*, 573–605.

Rosch, E. H., Mervis, C. B., Gray, W. D., Johnson, D. M., & Boyes-Braem, P. Basic objects in natural categories. *Cognitive Psychology*, 1976, *8*, 382–439.

Rose, J. E., & Fantino, E. Conditioned reinforcement and discrimination in second-order schedules. *Journal of the Experimental Analysis of Behavior*, 1978, *29*, 393–418.

Rosenfeld, H. M., & Baer, D. M. Unnoticed verbal conditioning of an aware experimenter by a more aware subject: The double-agent effect. *Psychological Review*, 1969, *76*, 425–432.

Rosinski, R. R., Golinkoff, R. M., & Kukish, K. S. Automatic semantic processing in a picture-word interference task. *Child Development*, 1975, *46*, 247–253.

Ross, L. E., & Ross, S. M. Conditioned stimulus parameters and the interstimulus interval: The processing of CS information in differential conditioning. In A. H. Black & W. F. Prokasy (Eds.), *Classical conditioning II: Current theory and research*. New York: Appleton, 1972.

Roth, E. M., & Mervis, C. B. Fuzzy set theory and class inclusion relations in semantic categories. *Journal of Verbal Learning and Verbal Behavior*, 1983, *22*, 509–525.

Routtenberg, A. The two arousal hypothesis: Reticular formation and limbic system. *Psychological Review*, 1968, *75*, 51–80.

Rovee-Collier, C. K., & Capatides, J. B. Positive behavioral contrast in 3-month-old infants on multiple conjugate reinforcement schedules. *Journal of the Experimental Analysis of Behavior*, 1979, *32*, 15–27.

Rowe, E. Discrimination learning of pictures and words: A replication of picture superiority. *Journal of Experimental Child Psychology*, 1972, *14*, 303–312.

Rowland, K. F. Environmental events predicting death for the elderly. *Psychological Bulletin*, 1977, *84*, 349–372.

Rozin, P. Specific aversions as a component in specific hungers. *Journal of Comparative and Physiological Psychology*, 1967, *63*, 421–428.

Rozin, P. Specific aversions and neophobia resulting from vitamin deficiency or poisoning in half wild and domestic rats. *Journal of Comparative and Physiological Psychology*, 1968, *66*, 82–88.

Rozin, P. Central or peripheral mediation of learning with long CS–UCS intervals in the feeding system. *Journal of Comparative and Physiological Psychology*, 1969, *67*, 421–429.

Rozin, P., & Kalat, J. W. Specific hungers and poison avoidance as adaptive specializations of learning. *Psychological Review*, 1971, *78*, 459–486.

Rubin, D. C. Associative asymmetry, availability, and retrieval. *Memory and Cognition*, 1983, *11*, 83–92.

Rubin, D. C., & Kontis, T. C. A schema for common cents. *Memory and Cognition*, 1983, *11*, 335–341.

Rudolph, R. L., & Honig, W. K. Effects of monochromatic rearing on spectral discrimination learning and the peak shift in chicks. *Journal of the Experimental Analysis of Behavior*, 1972, *17*, 107–111.

Rumelhart, D. E. Schemata: The building blocks of cognition. In R. Spiro, B. C. Bruce, & W. F. Brewer (Eds.), *Theoretical issues in reading comprehension*. Hillsdale, N. J.: Lawrence Erlbaum Associates, 1980.

Rumelhart, D. E., & Ortony, A. The representation of knowledge in memory. In R. C. Anderson, R. J. Spiro, & W. E. Montague (Eds.), *Schooling and the acquisition of knowledge.* Hillsdale, N. J.: Lawrence Erlbaum Associates, 1977.

Rundus, D. Analysis of rehearsal processes in free recall. *Journal of Experimental Psychology,* 1971, 89, 63–77.

Rundus, D. Maintenance rehearsal and single-level processing. *Journal of Verbal Learning and Verbal Behavior,* 1977, 16, 665–681.

Russ-Eft, D. Proactive interference: Buildup and release for individual words. *Journal of Experimental Psychology,* 1979, 5, 422–434.

Sachs, J. D. S. Recognition memory for syntactic and semantic aspects of connected discourse. *Perception and Psychophysics,* 1967, 2, 437–442.

Sachs, J. D. S. Memory in reading and listening to discourse. *Memory and Cognition,* 1974, 2, 95–100.

Sakitt, B., & Appleman, I. B. The effects of memory load and the contrast of the rod signal on partial report superiority in a Sperling task. *Memory and Cognition,* 1978, 6, 562–567.

Salmaso, P., Baroni, M. R., Job, R., & Peron, E. M. Schematic information, attention, and memory for places. *Journal of Experimental Psychology,* 1983, 9, 263–268.

Saltz, E. Spontaneous recovery of letter-sequence habits. *Journal of Experimental Psychology,* 1965, 69, 304–307.

Saltz, E. *The cognitive bases of human learning.* Homewood, Ill.: Dorsey, 1971.

Saltzman, I. J. Maze learning in the absence of primary reinforcement: A study of secondary reinforcement. *Journal of Comparative and Physiological Psychology,* 1949, 42, 161–173.

Salzen, E. A., & Sluckin, W. The incidence of the following response and the duration of responsiveness in domestic fowl. *Animal Behavior,* 1959, 7, 172–179.

Sanchez, V. Behavioral treatment of chronic hair pulling in a two year old. *Journal of Behavior Therapy and Experimental Psychiatry,* 1979, 10, 241–245.

Sargent, J., Walters, D., & Green, E. Psychosomatic self-regulation of migraine headaches. *Seminar in Psychiatry,* 1973, 5, 415–428.

Savage-Rumbaugh, S., McDonald, K., Sevcik, R., Hopkins, W., & Rubert, E. Spontaneous symbol acquisition and communicative use by pygmy chimpanzee. *Journal of Experimental Psychology: General,* 1986, 115, 211–235.

Savin, H. B., & Perchonock, E. Grammatical structure and the immediate recall of English sentences. *Journal of Verbal Learning and Verbal Behavior,* 1965, 4, 348–353.

Schachter, D. L. Feeling of knowing in episodic memory. *Journal of Experimental Psychology,* 1983, 9, 39–54.

Schaefer, H. H., & Martin, P. L. Behavioral therapy for "apathy" of hospitalized schizophrenics. *Psychological Reports,* 1966, 19, 1147–1158.

Schank, R. C. SAM—A story understander. Technical Report No. 43, Department of Computer Science, Yale University, 1975.

Schank, R. C., & Abelson, R. P. *Scripts, plans, goals, and understanding: An inquiry into human knowledge structures.* Hillsdale, N. J.: Lawrence Erlbaum Associates, 1977.

Schmidt, S. R. The effects of recall and recognition test expectancies on the retention of prose. *Memory and Cognition,* 1983, 11, 172–180.

Schmidt, S. R., & Bohannon, J. N. In defense of the flashbulb-memory hypothesis: A comment on McCloskey, Wible, and Cohen (1988). *Journal of Experimental Psychology: General,* 1988, 117(3), 332–335.

Schmitt, D. R. Effects of reinforcement rate and reinforcer magnitude on choice behavior in humans. *Journal of the Experimental Analysis of Behavior,* 1974, 21, 409–419.

Schneider, W., & Fisk, A. D. Automatic category search and its transfer. *Journal of Experimental Psychology,* 1974, 10, 1–15.

Schneider, W., & Shiffrin, R. M. Controlled and automatic human information processing: I. Detection, search and attention. *Psychological Review,* 1977, 84, 1–66.

Schoenfeld, W. N., Antonitis, J. J., & Bersh, P. J. A preliminary study of training conditions necessary for secondary reinforcement. *Journal of Experimental Psychology,* 1950, 40, 40–45.

Schreibman, L., O'Neill, R. E., & Koegel, R. L. Behavioral training for siblings of autistic children. *Journal of Applied Behavior Analysis,* 1983, 16, 129–138.

Schwanenflugel, P. J., & LaCount, K. L. Semantic relatedness and the scope of facilitation for upcoming words in sentences. *Journal of Experimental Psychology: Learning, Memory, and Cognition*, 1988, *14(2)*, 344–354.

Schwanenflugel, P. J., & Shoben, E. J. Differential context effects in the comprehension of abstract and concrete verbal materials. *Journal of Experimental Psychology*, 1983, 9, 82–102.

Schwartz, B. *Psychology of learning and behavior*. New York: Norton, 1989.

Scrivner, E., & Safer, M. A. Eyewitnesses show hypermnesia for details about a violent event. *Journal of Applied Psychology*, 1988, *73(3)*, 371–377.

Searleman, A. A review of right hemisphere linguistic capabilities. *Psychological Bulletin*, 1977, 84, 503–528.

Seaver, W. B., & Patterson, A. H. Decreasing fuel-oil consumption through feedback and social commendation. *Journal of Applied Behavior Analysis*, 1976, 9, 147–152.

Segal, E. M. Hierarchical structure in free recall. *Journal of Experimental Psychology*, 1969, 80, 59–63.

Seidenberg, M. S., & Petitto, L. A. Signing behavior in apes: A critical review. *Cognition*, 1979, 7, 177–215.

Seitz, M. R., & Weber, B. A. Effects of response requirements on the location of clicks superimposed on sentences. *Memory and Cognition*, 1974, 2, 43–46.

Self, R., & Gaffan, E. A. An analysis of serial pattern learning by rats. *Animal Learning and Behavior*, 1983, 11, 10–18.

Seligmann, J., Hager, M., & Springen, K. The fear of forgetting. *Newsweek*, Sept. 29, 1986, 51.

Seligman, M. E. P. On the generality of the laws of learning. *Psychological Review*, 1970, 77, 406–418.

Seligman, M. E. P. *Helplessness. On depression, development, and death*. San Francisco: W. H. Freeman, 1975.

Seybert, J. A., Baer, L. P., Harvey, R. J., Ludwig, K., & Gerard, I. C. Resistance to extinction as a function of percentage of reward: A reinforcement-level interpretation. *Animal Learning and Behavior*, 1979, 7, 233–238.

Shallice, T., & Warrington, E. K. Independent functioning of verbal memory stores: A neuro-psychological study. *Quarterly Journal of Experimental Psychology*, 1970, 22, 261–273.

Shapiro, D., Barber, T. X., DiCara, L. V., Kamiya, J., Miller, N. E., & Stoyva, J. (Eds.), *Biofeedback and self-control 1972*. Chicago: Aldine, 1973.

Shapiro, D., & Schwartz, G. E. Biofeedback and visceral learning: Clinical applications. *Seminars in Psychiatry*, 1972, 4, 171–184.

Shaughnessy, J. J. Persistence of the spacing effect in free recall under varying incidental learning conditions. *Memory and Cognition*, 1976, 4, 369–377.

Sheffield, F. D. A drive induction theory of reinforcement. In R. N. Haber (Ed.), *Current research in motivation*. New York: Holt, Rinehart & Winston, 1966.

Shepard, R. N. Recognition memory for words, sentences, and pictures. *Journal of Verbal Learning and Verbal Behavior*, 1967, 6, 156–163.

Shepard, R. N., & Metzler, J. Mental rotation of three-dimensional objects. *Science*, 1971, *171*, 701–703.

Sherman, J. E. US inflation with trace and simultaneous fear conditioning. *Animal Learning and Behavior*, 1978, 6, 463–468.

Sherman, R. A. *Behavior modification: Theory and practice*. Monterey, Calif.: Brooks/Cole, 1973.

Shettleworth, S. J. Reinforcement and the organization of behavior in golden hamsters: Punishment of three action patterns. *Learning and Motivation*, 1978, 9, 99–123.

Shettleworth, S. J. Animals foraging in the lab: Problems and promises. *Journal of Experimental Psychology: Animal Behavior Processes*, 1989, *15(1)*, 81–87.

Shimamura, A. P., & Squire, L. R. Long-term memory in amnesia: Cued recall, recognition memory, and confidence ratings. *Journal of Experimental Psychology: Learning, Memory, and Cognition*, 1988, *14(4)*, 763–770.

Shuell, T. J. Clustering and organization in free recall. *Psychological Bulletin*, 1969, 72, 353–374.

Shulman, H. G. Similarity effects in short-term memory. *Psychological Bulletin*, 1971, 75, 399–415.

Shulman, H. G. Semantic confusion errors in short-term memory. *Journal of Verbal Learning and Verbal Behavior*, 1972, 11, 221–227.

Shulman, H. G., & Martin, E. Effects of response set similarity on unlearning and spontaneous recovery. *Journal of Experimental Psychology*, 1970, 86, 230–235.

Sidman, M. A note on functional relations obtained from group data. *Psychological Bulletin*, 1952, *49*, 263–269.

Silverstein, A. Unlearning, spontaneous recovery, and the partial reinforcement effect in paired-associate learning. *Journal of Experimental Psychology*, 1967, *73*, 15–21.

Simon, H. A., & Hayes, J. R. The understanding process: Problem isomorphs. *Cognitive Psychology*, 1976, *8*, 165–190.

Simon, H. A., & Reed, S. K. Modeling strategy shifts in a problem-solving task. *Cognitive Psychology*, 1976, *8*, 86–97.

Singh, N. N. Aversive control of breath holding. *Journal of Behavior Therapy and Experimental Psychiatry*, 1979, *10*, 147–149.

Sisqueland, E. R. Basic learning processes: Instrumental conditioning in infants. In H. W. Reese & L. P. Lipsitt (Eds.), *Experimental child psychology: The scientific study of child behavior and development*. New York: Academic Press, 1970.

Skinner, B. F. *The behavior of organisms: An experimental analysis*. New York: Appleton, 1938.

Skinner, B. F. Superstition in the pigeon. *Journal of Experimental Psychology*, 1948, *38*, 168–172.

Skinner, B. F. *Science and human behavior*. New York: Macmillan, 1953.

Slamecka, N. J. Retroactive inhibition of connected discourse as a function of practice level. *Journal of Experimental Psychology*, 1960, *59*, 104–108.

Slamecka, N. J. Proactive inhibition of connected discourse. *Journal of Experimental Psychology*, 1961, *62*, 295–301.

Slamecka, N. J. Supplementary report: A search for spontaneous recovery of verbal associations. *Journal of Verbal Learning and Verbal Behavior*, 1966, *5*, 205–207.

Sloman, S. A., Gordan-Hayman, C. A., Ohta, N., Law, J., & Tulving, E. Forgetting in primed fragment completion. *Journal of Experimental Psychology*, 1988, *14*, 223–239.

Sloman, S. A., Hayman, C. A. G., Ohta, N., Law, J., & Tulving, E. Forgetting in primed fragment completion. *Journal of Experimental Psychology: Learning, Memory, and Cognition*, 1988, *14(2)*, 223–239.

Sluckin, W. *Imprinting and early learning*. Chicago: Aldine, 1965.

Sluckin, W., & Salzen, E. A. Imprinting and perceptual learning. *Quarterly Journal of Experimental Psychology*, 1961, *13*, 65–77.

Smith, E. E., Shoben, E. J., & Rips, L. J. Structure and process in semantic memory: A feature model for semantic decisions. *Psychological Review*, 1974, *81*, 214–241.

Smith, F. V., & Hoyes, P. A. Properties of the visual stimuli for the approach response in the domestic chick. *Animal Behavior*, 1961, *9*, 159–166.

Smith, G. J., & Spear, N. E. Reactivation of an appetitive discrimination memory following retroactive interference. *Animal Learning and Behavior*, 1979, *7*, 289–293.

Smith, J. C., & Roll, D. L. Trace conditioning with X-rays as the aversive stimulus. *Psychonomic Science*, 1967, *9*, 11–12.

Smith, M. C., Theodor, L., & Franklin, P. E. The relationship between contextual facilitation and depth of processing. *Journal of Experimental Psychology*, 1983, *9*, 697–712.

Smith, S. M. Remembering in and out of context. *Journal of Experimental Psychology: Human Learning and Memory*, 1979, *5*, 460–471.

Smith, S. M., Glenberg, A. M., & Bjork, R. A. Environmental context and human memory. *Memory and Cognition*, 1978, *6*, 342–353.

Solomon, R. L. Punishment. *American Psychologist*, 1964, *19*, 239–253.

Solomon, R. L., & Corbit, J. P. An opponent-process theory of motivation. *Psychological Review*, 1974, *81*, 119–145.

Spalding, D. A. Instinct, with original observations on young animals. *MacMillan's Magazine*, 1873, *27*, 283–293. [Reprinted; *British Journal of Animal Behavior*, 1954, *2*, 2–11.]

Spear, N. E. Forgetting as retrieval failure. In W. K. Honig & P. H. R. James (Eds.), *Animal memory*. New York: Academic Press, 1971.

Spear, N. E. Retrieval of memory in animals. *Psychological Review*, 1973, *80*, 163–194.

Spelt, D. K. The conditioning of the human fetus *in utero*. *Journal of Experimental Psychology*, 1948, *38*, 338–346.

Spence, K. W. The nature of discrimination learning in animals. *Psychological Review*, 1936, *43*, 427–449.

Spence, K. W. The differential response in animals to stimuli varying within a single dimension. *Psychological Review*, 1937, *44*, 430–444.

Spence, K. W. The role of secondary reinforcement in delayed reward learning. *Psychological Review*, 1947, *54*, 1–8.

Spence, K. W. *Behavior theory and conditioning*. New Haven, Conn.: Yale University Press, 1956.

Spence, K. W. *Behavior theory and learning: Selected papers*. Englewood Cliffs, N. J.: Prentice-Hall, 1960.

Spence, K. W., Haggard, D. F., & Ross, L. UCS intensity and the associative (habit) strength of the eyelid CR. *Journal of Experimental Psychology*, 1955, *25*, 323–332.

Sperber, R. D., McCauley, C., Ragain, R. D., & Weil, C. M. Semantic priming effects on picture and word processing. *Memory and Cognition*, 1979, *7*, 339–345.

Sperling, G. The information available in brief visual presentations. *Psychological Monographs*, 1960, *74*, (11, Whole No. 498).

Sperling, G. A model for visual memory tasks. *Human Factors*, 1963, *5*, 19–31.

Sperry, R. W. Cerebral organization and behavior. *Science*, 1961, *133*, 1749–1757.

Sperry, R. W. Some effects of disconnecting the cerebral hemispheres. *Science*, 1982, *217*, 1223–1226.

Spetch, M. L., & Honig, W. K. Characteristics of pigeons' spatial working memory in an open-field task. *Animal Learning & Behavior*, 1988, *16(2)*, 123–131.

Spetch, M. L., & Wilkie, D. M. Subjective shortening: A model of pigeons' memory for event duration. *Journal of Experimental Psychology*, 1983, *9*, 14–30.

Spielberger, C. D. Theoretical and epistemological issues in verbal conditioning. In S. Rosenberg (Ed.), *Directions in psycholinguistics*. New York: Macmillan, 1965.

Spilich, G. J., Vesonder, G. T., Chiesi, H. L., & Voss J. F. Text processing of domain-related information for individuals with high and low domain knowledge. *Journal of Verbal Learning and Verbal Behavior*, 1979, *18*, 275–290.

Spiro, R. J. Remembering information from text: The state of schema approach. In R. C. Anderson, R. J. Spiro, & W. E. Montague (Eds.), *Schooling and the acquisition of knowledge*. Hillsdale, N. J.: Lawrence Erlbaum Associates, 1977.

Spooner, A., & Kellogg, W. N. The backward conditioning curve. *American Journal of Psychology*, 1947, *60*, 321–334.

Squire, L. R. *Memory and brain*. New York: Oxford University Press, 1987.

Squires, N., Norborg, J., & Fantino, E. Second-order schedules: Discrimination of components. *Journal of the Experimental Analysis of Behavior*, 1975, *24*, 157–171.

Staddon, J. E. R., & Ettinger, R. N. *Learning: An introduction to the principles of adaption behavior*. San Diego: Harcourt Brace Jovanovich, 1989.

Standing, L. Learning 10,000 pictures. *Quarterly Journal of Experimental Psychology*, 1973, *25*, 207–222.

Stanovich, K. E., & West, R. F. The generalizability of context effects on word recognition: A reconsideration of the roles of parafoveal priming and sentence context. *Memory and Cognition*, 1983, *11*, 49–58. (a)

Stanovich, K. E., & West, R. F. On priming by a sentence context. *Journal of Experimental Psychology*, 1983, *12*, 1–40. (b)

Stein, L. Reward transmitters: Catecholamines and opoid peptides. In M. A. Lipton, A. DiMascio, & K. R. Killam (Eds.), *Psychopharmacology: A generation of progress*. New York: Raven Press, 1978.

Steinhauer, G. D., Davol, G. H., & Lee, A. A procedure for autoshaping the pigeon's key peck to an auditory stimulus. *Journal of the Experimental Analysis of Behavior*, 1977, *28*, 97–98.

Stephens, C. E., Pear, J. J., Wray, L. D., & Jackson, G. C. Some effects of reinforcement schedules in teaching picture names to retarded children. *Journal of Applied Behavior Analysis*, 1975, *8*, 435–447.

Stern, L. *The structures and strategies of human memory*. Homewood, Ill.: Dorsey Press, 1985.

Stevens-Long, J., & Rasmussen, M. The acquisition of simple and compound sentence structure in an autistic child. *Journal of Applied Behavior Analysis*, 1974, *7*, 473–479.

Stickney, K. J., & Donahoe, J. W. Attenuation of blocking by a change in US location. *Animal Learning and Behavior*, 1983, *11*, 60–66.

Stokoe, W. C. Apes who sign and critics who don't. In J. de Luce & H. T. Wilder (Eds.), *Language in primates: Perspectives and implications*. New York: Springer-Verlag, 1983.

Strassman, H. D., Thaler, M. D., & Schein, E. H. A prisoner of war syndrome: Apathy as a reaction to severe stress. *American Journal of Psychiatry*, 1956, *112*, 998–1003.

Straw, L., & Terre, L. An evaluation of individualized behavioral obesity treatment and maintenance strategies. *Behavior Therapy*, 1983, *14*, 225–266.

Suler, J. R., & Katkin, E. S. Mental imagery of fear-related stimuli. *Journal of Mental Imagery*, 1988, *12(1)*, 115–124.

Sulin, R. A., & Dooling, D. J. Intrusion of a thematic idea in retention of prose. *Journal of Experimental Psychology*, 1974, *103*, 255–262.

Sumby, W. H. Word frequency and serial position effects. *Journal of Verbal Learning and Verbal Behavior*, 1963, *1*, 443–450.

Sutherland, N. S., & Mackintosh, N. J. *Mechanisms of animal discrimination learning.* New York: Academic Press, 1971.

Sweller, J. Control mechanisms in problem solving. *Memory and Cognition*, 1983, *11*, 32–40.

Szakmary, G. A. Second-order conditioning of the conditioned emotional response: Some methodological considerations. *Animal Learning and Behavior*, 1979, *7*, 181–184.

Szwejkowska, G. Qualitative versus directional cues in differential conditioning: II. Go–no go differentiation to cues of a mixed character. *Acta Biologiae Experimentale*, 1967, *27*, 169–175.

Taffel, C. Anxiety and the conditioning of verbal behavior. *Journal of Abnormal and Social Psychology*, 1955, *51*, 496–501.

Taft, M. Lexical access via an orthographic code: The basic orthographic syllabic structure (BOSS). *Journal of Verbal Learning and Verbal Behavior*, 1979, *18*, 21–39.

Tallad, G. A. *Deranged memory: A psychonomic study of the amnesic syndrome.* New York: Academic Press, 1965.

Tapp, J. T. Current status and future directions. In J. T. Tapp (Ed.), *Reinforcement and behavior.* New York: Academic Press, 1969.

Tarler-Benlolo, L. The role of relaxation in biofeedback training: A critical review of the literature. *Psychological Bulletin*, 1978, *85*, 727–755.

Tarpy, R. M. *Basic principles of learning.* Glenview, Ill.: Scott, Foresman, 1975.

Tell, P. M. The role of certain acoustic and semantic factors at short and long retention intervals. *Journal of Verbal Learning and Verbal Behavior*, 1972, *11*, 455–464.

Terrace, H. S. Discrimination learning with and without "errors." Unpublished doctoral dissertation, Harvard University, 1961.

Terrace, H. S. Discrimination learning with and without "errors." *Journal of the Experimental Analysis of Behavior*, 1963, *6*, 1–27. (a)

Terrace, H. S. Errorless transfer of a discrimination across two continua. *Journal of the Experimental Analysis of Behavior*, 1963, *6*, 223–232. (b)

Terrace, H. S. Wavelength generalization after discrimination learning with and without errors. *Science*, 1964, *144*, 78–80.

Terrace, H. S. By-products of discrimination learning. In G. H. Bower (Ed.), *The psychology of learning and motivation* (Vol. 5). New York: Academic Press, 1972.

Terrace, H. S. Is problem-solving language? *Journal of the Experimental Analysis of Behavior*, 1979, *31*, 161–175.

Theios, T. The partial reinforcement effect sustained through blocks of continuous reinforcement. *Journal of Experimental Psychology*, 1962, *64*, 1–6.

Thomas, D. R., Mariner, R. W., & Sherry, G. Role of pre-experimental experience in the development of stimulus control. *Journal of Experimental Psychology*, 1969, *79*, 375–376.

Thomas, D. R., & Mitchell, K. Instructions and stimulus categorizing in a measure of stimulus generalization. *Journal of the Experimental Analysis of Behavior*, 1962, *5*, 375–381.

Thomas, D. R., Svinicki, M. D., & Vogt, J. Adaptation level as a factor in human discrimination learning and stimulus generalization. *Journal of Experimental Psychology*, 1973, *97*, 210–219.

Thomas, G. V., Leiberman, D. A., McIntosh, D. C., & Ronaldson, P. The role of marking when reward is delayed. *Journal of Experimental Psychology*, 1983, *9*, 401–411.

Thomas, J. C. An analysis of behavior in the hobbits–orcs problem. *Cognitive Psychology*, 1974, *6*, 257–269.

Thomas, R. K., & Noble, L. M. Visual and olfactory oddity learning in rats: What evidence is necessary to show conceptual behavior? *Animal Learning and Behavior*, 1988, *16(2)*, 157–163.

Thompson, C. P., Hamlin, V. J., & Roenker, D. L. A comment on the role of clustering in free recall. *Journal of Experimental Psychology*, 1972, 94, 108–109.

Thompson, R., & McConnell, J. Classical conditioning in the planarian, *Dugesia dorotocephala*. *Journal of Comparative and Physiological Psychology*, 1955, 48, 65–68.

Thomson, D. M., & Tulving, E. Associative encoding and retrieval: Weak and strong cues. *Journal of Experimental Psychology*, 1970, 86, 255–262.

Thorndike, E. L. *The psychology of learning*. New York: Teachers College, 1913.

Thorndyke, P. W. The role of inferences in discourse comprehension. *Journal of Verbal Learning and Verbal Behavior*, 1976, 15, 437–446.

Thorndyke, P. W. Cognitive structures in comprehension and memory of narrative discourse. *Cognitive Psychology*, 1977, 9, 77–110.

Thorndyke, P. W. Applications of schema theory in cognitive research. In J. R. Anderson & S. M. Kosslyn (Eds.), *Tutorials in learning and memory*. San Francisco: W. H. Freeman, 1984, 167–191.

Thorndyke, P. W., & Bower, G. H. Storage and retrieval processes in sentence memory. *Cognitive Psychology*, 1974, 6, 515–543.

Thorpe, W. H. *Learning and instinct in animals*. Cambridge, Mass.: Harvard University Press, 1956.

Thorpe, W. H. *Learning and instinct in animals* (2nd ed.). Cambridge, Mass.: Harvard University Press, 1963.

Thune, L. E. Warm-up effect as a function of level of practice in verbal learning. *Journal of Experimental Psychology*, 1951, 42, 250–256.

Timberlake, W. A molar equilibrium theory of learned performance. In G. H. Bower (Ed.), *The psychology of learning and motivation* (Vol. 14). New York: Academic Press, 1980.

Timberlake, W., & Allison, J. Response deprivation: An empirical approach to instrumental performance. *Psychological Review*, 1974, 81, 146–164.

Timberlake, W., & Washburne, D. A. Feeding ecology and laboratory predatory behavior toward live and artificial moving prey in seven rodent species. *Animal Learning & Behavior*, 1989, 17, 2–11.

Tinbergen, N. *The study of instinct*. Oxford: Oxford University Press, 1951.

Tinbergen, N. The curious behavior of the stickleback. *Scientific American*, 1952, 187, 22–26.

Toppino, T. C., & Bucher, N. M. Acquiring conjunctive concepts: When and why does feature frequency affect feature identification? *Memory and Cognition*, 1983, 11, 407–414.

Tortora, D. F. Safety training: The elimination of avoidance-motivated aggression in dogs. *Journal of Experimental Psychology*, 1983, 112, 176–214.

Trabasso, T. R., Rollins, H., & Shaughnessy, E. Storage and verification stages in processing concepts. *Cognitive Psychology*, 1971, 2, 239–289.

Tracey, D. A., Briddell, D. W., & Wilson, G. T. Generalization of verbal conditioning to verbal and nonverbal behaviors: Group therapy with chronic psychiatric patients. *Journal of Applied Behavior Analysis*, 1974, 7, 391–402.

Tracy, W. K. Wavelength generalization and preference in monochromatically reared ducklings. *Journal of the Experimental Analysis of Behavior*, 1970, 13, 163–178.

Trapold, M. A., & Overmeir, J. B. The second learning process in instrumental learning. In A. H. Black & W. F. Prokasy (Eds.), *Classical conditioning II: Current theory and research*. New York: Appleton, 1972.

Travis, M. N., Ludvigson, H. W., & Eslinger, P. J. A reexamination of the effects of motivational state on utilization of conspecific odors in the rat. *Animal Learning and Behavior*, 1988, 16(3), 318–323.

Treisman, A. M. Contextual cues in selective listening. *Quarterly Journal of Experimental Psychology*, 1960, 12, 242–248.

Tulving, E. Subjective organization in free recall of "unrelated" words. *Psychological Review*, 1962, 69, 344–354.

Tulving, E. Intratrial and intertrial retention: Notes towards a theory of free recall verbal learning. *Psychological Review*, 1964, 71, 219–237.

Tulving, E. Subjective organization and effects of repetition in multitrial free-recall learning. *Journal of Verbal Learning and Verbal Behavior*, 1966, 5, 193–197.

Tulving, E. Retrograde amnesia in free recall. *Science*, 1969, 164, 88–90.

Tulving, E. Episodic and semantic memory. In E. Tulving & W. Donaldson (Eds.), *Organization of memory*. New York: Academic Press, 1972.

Tulving, E. How many memory systems are there? *American Psychologist*, 1985, *40*, 385–398.

Tulving, E., & Psotka, J. Retroactive inhibition in free recall: Inaccessibility of information available in the memory store. *Journal of Experimental Psychology*, 1971, *87*, 1–8.

Tulving, E., & Thomson, D. M. Retrieval processes in recognition memory: Effects of associative context. *Journal of Experimental Psychology*, 1971, *87*, 116–124.

Turner, S. M., Holzman, A., & Jacob, R. G. Treatment of compulsive looking by imaginal thought-stopping. *Behavior Modification*, 1983, *7*, 576–582.

Tweedy, J.R., Lapinski, R. H., & Schvaneveldt, R. W. Semantic-context effects on word recognition: Influence of varying the proportion of items presented in an appropriate context. *Memory and Cognition*, 1977, *5*, 84–89.

Tyron, G. S. A review and critique of thought stopping research. *Journal of Behavior Therapy and Experimental Psychiatry*, 1979, *10*, 189–192.

Tyron, G. S., & Palladino, J. J. Thought stopping: A case study and observations. *Journal of Behavior Therapy and Experimental Psychiatry*, 1979, *10*, 151–154.

Underwood, B. J. Interference and forgetting. *Psychological Review*, 1957, *64*, 49–60.

Underwood, B. J. Ten years of massed practice on distributed practice. *Psychological Review*, 1961, *68*, 229–247.

Underwood, B. J. A breakdown of the Total-Time Law in free-recall learning. *Journal of Verbal Learning and Verbal Behavior*, 1970, *9*, 573–580.

Underwood, B. J. Are we overloading memory? In A. W. Melton & E. Martin (Eds.), *Coding processes in human memory*. New York: Wiley, 1972.

Underwood, B. J. "Conceptual" similarity and cumulative proactive inhibition. *Journal of Experimental Psychology*, 1983, *9*, 456–461.

Underwood, B. J., Boruch, R. F., & Malmi, R. A. Composition of episodic memory. *Journal of Experimental Psychology: General*, 1978, *107*, 393–419.

Underwood, B. J., & Freund, J. S. Relative frequency judgements and verbal discrimination learning. *Journal of Experimental Psychology*, 1970, *83*, 279–285.

Underwood, B. J., Ham, M., & Ekstrand, B. Cue selection in paired-associate learning. *Journal of Experimental Psychology*, 1962, *64*, 405–409.

Underwood, B. J., Jesse, F., & Ekstrand, B. R. Knowledge of rights and wrongs in verbal discrimination. *Journal of Verbal Learning and Verbal Behavior*, 1964, *3*, 183–186.

Underwood, B. J., & Keppel, G. One trial learning? *Journal of Verbal Learning and Verbal Behavior*, 1962, *1*, 1–13.

Underwood, B. J., & Schulz, R. W. *Meaningfulness and verbal learning*. Philadelphia: Lippincott, 1960.

Urcuioli, P. J., & Kasprow, W. J. Long-delay learning in the T-maze: Effects of marking and delay-interval location. *Learning and Motivation*, 1988, *19*, 66–86.

Valenstein, E. S. *Brain stimulation and motivation: Research and commentary*. Glenview, Ill.: Scott, Foresman, 1973.

Van Buskirk, S. S. A two-phase perspective on the treatment of anorexia nervosa. *Psychological Bulletin*, 1977, *84*, 529–538.

Van Houten, R., & Rudolph, R. The development of stimulus control with and without a lighted key. *Journal of the Experimental Analysis of Behavior*, 1972, *18*, 217–222.

Vasta, R., & Wortman, H. A. Nocturnal bruxism treated by massed negative practice. *Behavior Modification*, 1988, *12(4)*, 618–626.

Verplanck, W. S. The operant conditioning of human motor behavior. *Psychological Bulletin*, 1956, *53*, 70–83.

Vincent, S. B. The function of the vibrissae in the behavior of the white rat. *Behavioral Monographs*, 1912, *5*.

Voeks, V. W. Acquisition of S–R connections: A test of Hull's and Guthrie's theories. *Journal of Experimental Psychology*, 1954, *47*, 137–147.

Vosniadou, S., & Brewer, W. F. Theories of knowledge restructuring in development. *Review of Educational Research*, 1987, *57*, 51–67.

Voss, J. F. On the relationship of associative and organizational processes. In E. Tulving & W. Donaldson (Eds.), *Organization of memory*. New York: Academic Press, 1972.

Wagner, A. R. Stimulus selection and a "modified continuity theory." In G. H. Bower & J. T. Spence (Eds.), *The psychology of learning and motivation* (Vol. 3). New York: Academic Press, 1969.

Wagner, A. R., Logan, R. A., Haberlundt, K., & Price, T. Stimulus selection in animal discrimination learning. *Journal of Experimental Psychology*, 1968, 76, 171–180.

Wagner, A. R., & Pfautz, P. L. A bowed serial-position function in habituation of sequential stimuli. *Animal Learning and Behavior*, 1978, 6, 395–400.

Wagner, D. A. Memories of Morocco: The influence of age, schooling, and environment on memory. *Cognitive Psychology*, 1978, 10, 1–28.

Wahlsten, D. L., & Cole, M. Classical and avoidance training of leg flexion in the dog. In A. H. Black & W. F. Prokasy (Eds.), *Classical conditioning II: Current theory and research*. New York: Appleton, 1972.

Walk, R. D., & Walters, C. P. Effect of visual deprivation on depth discrimination of hooded rats. *Journal of Comparative and Physiological Psychology*, 1973, 85, 559–563.

Walker, N., & Jones, P. Encoding processes and the recall of text. *Memory and Cognition*, 1983, 11, 275–282.

Wallace, R. K., & Benson, H. The physiology of meditation. *Scientific American*, 1972, 226, 84–90.

Wallace, W. P. Consistency of emission order in free recall. *Journal of Verbal Learning and Verbal Behavior*, 1970, 9, 58–68.

Wallace, W. P. Recognition failure of recallable words and recognizable words. *Journal of Experimental Psychology: Human Learning and Memory*, 1978, 4, 441–452.

Wang, A. Y. Individual differences in learning speed. *Journal of Experimental Psychology*, 1983, 9, 300–311.

Wanner, E. *On remembering, forgetting and understanding sentences*. The Hague: Mouton, 1974.

Ward, E. F. Teaching sign language to a chimpanzee: Some historical references. *Journal of the Experimental Analysis of Behavior*, 1983, 40, 341–342.

Ward, L. B. Reminiscence and rote learning. *Psychological Monographs*, 1937, 49 (220).

Warren, R. E. Time and spread of activation in memory. *Journal of Experimental Psychology: Human Learning and Memory*, 1977, 3, 458–466.

Warrington, E. K., & Shallice, T. The selective impairment of auditory verbal short-term memory. *Brain*, 1969, 92, 885–896.

Warrington, E. K., & Weiskrantz, L. New method of testing long-term retention with special reference to amnesic patients. *Nature*, 1968, 217, 972–974.

Warrington, E. K., & Weiskrantz, L. Amnesic syndrome: Consolidation or retrieval? *Nature*, 1970, 228, 628–630.

Wason, P. C. Response to affirmative and negative binary statements. *British Journal of Psychology*, 1961, 52, 133–142.

Wasserman, E. A., Kiedinger, R. E., & Bhatt, R. S. Conceptual behavior in pigeons: Categories, subcategories, and pseudocategories. *Journal of Experimental Psychology: Animal Behavior Processes*, 1988, 14(3), 235–246.

Wasserman, E. A., & Molina, E. J. Explicitly unpaired key light and food-presentations: Interference with subsequent auto-shaped key pecking in pigeons. *Journal of Experimental Psychology: Animal Behavior Processes*, 1975, 104, 30–38.

Waters, H. S. Superordinate–subordinate structure in prose passages and the importance of propositions. *Journal of Experimental Psychology*, 1983, 9, 294–299.

Watkins, M. J. Locus of the modality effect in free recall. *Journal of Verbal Learning and Verbal Behavior*, 1972, 11, 644–648.

Watkins, M. J., & Gibson, J. M. On the relation between perceptual priming and recognition memory. *Journal of Experimental Psychology: Learning, Memory, and Cognition*, 1988, 14(3), 477–483.

Watkins, M. J., & Peynircioglu, Z. F. Three recency effects at the same time. *Journal of Verbal Learning and Verbal Behavior*, 1983, 22, 375–384.

Watkins, M. J., & Todres, A. K. Stimulus suffix effect and the item–position distinction. *Journal of Experimental Psychology*, 1979, 5, 322–325.

Watkins, M. J., & Tulving, E. Episodic memory: When recognition fails. *Journal of Experimental Psychology: General*, 1975, 104, 5–29.

Watson, J. B. The effect of delayed feeding upon learning. *Psychobiology*, 1917, 1, 51–60.

Watson-Perczel, M., Lutzker, J. R., Greene, B. F., & McGimpsey, B. J. Assessment and modification of home cleanliness among families adjudicated for child neglect. *Behavior Modification*, January 1988, 12(1), 57–81.

Waugh, N. C. Presentation time and free recall. *Journal of Experimental Psychology*, 1967, 73, 39–44.

Waugh, N. C. On the effective duration of a repeated word. *Journal of Verbal Learning and Verbal Behavior*, 1970, 9, 587–595.

Waugh, N. C., & Norman, D. A. Primary memory. *Psychological Review*, 1965, 72, 89–104.

Weaver, G. E., & Stanny C. J. Short-term retention of pictorial stimuli as assessed by a probe recognition technique. *Journal of Experimental Psychology: Human Learning and Memory*, 1978, 4, 55–65.

Webber, S. M, & Marshall, P. H. Bizarreness effects in imagery as a function of processing level and delay. *Journal of Mental Imagery*, 1978, 2, 291–300.

Weiner, B. Motivation and memory. *Psychological Monographs*, 1966, 80 (18 Whole No. 626).

Weinberg, H. I., Wadsworth, J., & Baron, R. S. Demand and the impact of leading questions on eyewitness testimony. *Memory and Cognition*, 1983, 11, 101–104.

Weisberg, P., & Waldrop, P. B. Fixed-interval work habits of Congress. *Journal of Applied Behavior Analysis*, 1972, 5, 93–97.

Weisberg, R., DiCamillo, M., & Phillips, D. Transferring old associations to new situations: A nonautomatic process. *Journal of Verbal Learning and Verbal Behavior*, 1978, 17, 219–228.

Weisberg, R., & Suls, J. M. An information processing model of Duncker's candle problem. *Cognitive Psychology*, 1973, 4, 255–277.

Weisman, R. G., & Davis, E. R. Response-dependent shock in second-order fixed-ratio schedules of food presentation. *Journal of the Experimental Analysis of Behavior*, 1975, 23, 103–109.

Weist, R. M. Associative structure and free recall. *Journal of Experimental Psychology*, 1972, 94, 110–112.

Wertheimer, M. *Productive thinking.* New York: Harper & Row, 1945.

Wessells, M. G. The effects of reinforcement upon the prepecking behaviors of pigeons in the autoshaping experiment. *Journal of the Experimental Analysis of Behavior*, 1974, 21, 125–144.

Wexler, K. A. A review of John R. Anderson's *Language, Memory and Thought. Cognition*, 1978, 7, 327–351.

White, J. M. Changeover ratio effect on concurrent variable-interval performance. *Journal of the Experimental Analysis of Behavior*, 1979, 31, 239–252.

Whitehead, W. E., Lurie, E., & Blackwell, B. Classical conditioning of decreases in human systolic blood pressure. *Journal of Applied Behavior Analysis*, 1976, 9, 153–157.

Whitlow, J. W., & Estes, W. K. Judgements of relative frequency in relation to shifts of event frequencies: Evidence for a limited-capacity model. *Journal of Experimental Psychology: Human Learning and Memory*, 1979, 5, 395–408.

Whitlow, J. W., & Skaar, E. The role of numerosity in judgements of overall frequency. *Journal of Experimental Psychology*, 1979, 5, 409–421.

Whitten, W. B. Initial-retrieval "depth" and the negative recency effect. *Memory and Cognition*, 1978, 6, 590–598.

Wichawut, C., & Martin, E. Independence of A–B and A–C associations in retroaction. *Journal of Verbal Learning and Verbal Behavior*, 1971, 10, 316–321.

Wickelgren, W. A. Acoustic similarity and intrusions in short-term memory. *Journal of Experimental Psychology*, 1965, 70, 102–108.

Wickelgren, W. A. The long and the short of memory. *Psychological Bulletin*, 1973, 80, 425–438.

Wickens, C., Tuber, D. S., & Wickens, D. D. Memory for the conditioned response: The proactive effect of preexposure to potential conditioning stimuli and context change. *Journal of Experimental Psychology: General*, 1983, 112, 41–57.

Wickens, D. D. Encoding categories of words: An empirical approach to meaning. *Psychological Review*, 1970, 77, 1–15.

Wickens, D. D. Classical conditioning. In *Encyclopedia of psychology.* New York: Wiley, 1984.

Wickens, D. D., Born, D. G., & Allen, C. K. Proactive inhibition and item similarity in short-term memory. *Journal of Verbal Learning and Verbal Behavior*, 1963, 2, 440–445.

Wickens, D. D., Schroder, H. M., & Snide, J. D. Primary stimulus generalization of the GSR under two conditions. *Journal of Experimental Psychology*, 1954, 47, 52–56.

Wickens, D. D., Tuber, D. S., Nield, A. F., & Wickens, C. Memory for the conditioned response: The effects of potential interference introduced before and after original conditioning. *Journal of Experimental Psychology: General*, 1977, *106*, 47–70.

Wickens, D. D., & Wickens, C. D. Some factors related to pseudo-conditioning. *Journal of Experimental Psychology*, 1942, *31*, 518–526.

Wielkiewicz, R. M. Effects of CSs for food and water upon rats bar-pressing for different magnitudes of food reinforcement. *Animal Learning and Behavior*, 1979, *7*, 246–250.

Wike, E. L. *Secondary reinforcement*. New York: Harper, 1966.

Wilder, L., & Levin, J. R. A developmental study of pronouncing responses in the discrimination learning of words and pictures. *Journal of Experimental Child Psychology*, 1973, *15*, 278–286.

Wilkinson, A. C., & Koestler, R. Repeated recall: A new model and tests of its generality from childhood to old age. *Journal of Experimental Psychology*, 1983, *112*, 423–451.

William, R., & Gentry, D. *Behavioral approaches to medical treatment*. Cambridge, Mass.: Balinger, 1977.

Williams, B. A. Contrast effects in simultaneous discrimination learning. *Animal Learning and Behavior*, 1977, *5*, 47–50.

Williams, B. A. The effects of stimulus similarity on different types of behavioral contrast. *Animal Learning and Behavior*, 1988, *16(2)*, 206–216.

Williams, B. A., & Royalty, P. A test of the melioration theory of matching. *Journal of Experimental Psychology: Animal Behavior Processes*, 1989, *15(2)*, 99–113.

Williams, C. D. The elimination of tantrum behavior by extinction procedures. *Journal of Abnormal and Social Psychology*, 1959, *59*, 269.

Williams, J. L. Effects of the duration of a secondary reinforcer on subsequent instrumental responses. *Journal of Experimental Psychology*, 1970, *83*, 348–351.

Williams, J. L. *Operant learning: Procedures for changing behavior*. Monterey, Calif.: Brooks/Cole, 1973.

Williams, J. N. Constraints upon semantic activation during sentence comprehension. *Language and Cognitive Processes*, 1988, *3(3)*, 165–206.

Williams, R. F., & Underwood, B. J. Encoding variability: Tests of the Martin hypothesis. *Journal of Experimental Psychology*, 1970, *86*, 317–324.

Wilson, C. The effects of sensory stimulation in inducing or intensifying the "transport response" in white rats. *Animal Learning and Behavior*, 1988, *16(1)*, 83–88.

Wilson, G. T. Behavioral treatment of obesity: Maintenance strategies and long-term efficacy. In P. Sjödén, S. Bates, & W. S. Docken (Eds.), *Trends in behavior therapy*. New York: Academic Press, 1979.

Wilson, G. T., Leaf, R. C., & Nathan, P. E. The aversive control of excessive alcohol consumption by chronic alcoholics in the laboratory setting. *Journal of Applied Behavior Analysis*, 1975, *8*, 13–16.

Wingfield, A. *Human learning and memory: An introduction*. New York: Harper & Row, 1979.

Winnick, W. A., & Hunt, J. M. The effect of an extra stimulus upon strength of response during acquisition and extinction. *Journal of Experimental Psychology*, 1951, *41*, 205–215.

Winograd, E. Some issues relating animal memory to human memory. In W. K. Honig & P. H. R. James (Eds.), *Animal memory*. New York: Academic Press, 1971.

Winograd, E., & Killinger, W. A. Relating age at encoding in early childhood to adult recall: Development of flashbulb memories. *Journal of Experimental Psychology*, 1983, *12*, 413–422.

Winograd, E., & Lynn, D. S. Role of contextual imagery in associative recall. *Memory and Cognition*, 1979, *7*, 29–34.

Witting, A. F., & Williams, G. *Psychology: An introduction*. New York: McGraw-Hill, 1984.

Wolfe, D. A., Mendes, M. G., & Factor, D. A parent-administered program to reduce children's television viewing. *Journal of Applied Behavior Analysis*, 1984, *17*, 267–272.

Wolfe, J. B. The effect of delayed reward upon learning in the white rat. *Journal of Comparative Psychology*, 1934, *17*, 1–21.

Wolfe, J. B. Effectiveness of token-rewards for chimpanzees. *Comparative Psychology Monograph*, 1936, No. 60, 12.

Wolfle, H. M. Time factors in conditioned finger-withdrawal. *Journal of General Psychology*, 1930, 4, 372–378.

Wolfle, H. M. Conditioning as a function of the interval between the conditioned and original stimulus. *Journal of General Psychology*, 1931, 7, 80–103.

Wollen, K. A., & Lowry, D. H. Conditions that determine effectiveness of picture-mediated paired-associate learning. *Journal of Experimental Psychology*, 1974, 102, 181–183.

Wollen, K. A., Weber, A., & Lowry, D. H. Bizarreness versus interaction of mental images as determinants of learning. *Cognitive Psychology*, 1972, 2, 518–523.

Wolpe, J. *Psychotherapy by reciprocal inhibition*. Stanford, Calif.: Stanford University Press, 1958.

Wolpe, J. *The practice of behavior therapy*. New York: Pergamon, 1969.

Wolpe, J., & Lazarus, A. A. *Behavior therapy techniques: A guide to the treatment of neuroses*. New York: Pergamon, 1966.

Wolters, G. Memory: Two systems or one system with many subsystems? *Behavioral and Brain Sciences*, 1984, 7, 256–257.

Wood, G. Organizational processes and free recall. In E. Tulving & W. Donaldson (Eds.), *Organization of memory*. New York: Academic Press, 1972.

Wood, G. *Cognitive psychology: A skills approach*. Monterey, Calif.: Brooks/Cole, 1983.

Woodruff, G. Behavioral contrast and type of reward: Role of elicited response topography. *Animal Learning and Behavior*, 1979, 7, 339–346.

Woodward, A. E., Bjork, R. A., & Jongeward, R. H. Recall and recognition as a function of primary rehearsal. *Journal of Verbal Learning and Verbal Behavior*, 1973, 12, 608–617.

Wortman, P. M., Sparling, P. B. Acquisition and retention of mnemonic information in long-term memory. *Journal of Experimental Psychology*, 1974, 102, 22–26.

Wright, A. A., Cook, R. G., Rivera, J. J., Sands, S. F., & Delius, J. D. Concept learning by pigeons: Matching-to-sample with trial-unique video picture stimuli. *Animal Learning and Behavior*, 1988, 16(4), 436–444.

Yantis, S., & Meyer, D. E. Dynamics of activation in semantic and episodic memory. *Journal of Experimental Psychology: General*, 1988, 117(2), 130–147.

Yoburn, B. C., & Cohen, P. Assessment of attack and drinking in White King pigeons on response-independent food schedules. *Journal of the Experimental Analysis of Behavior*, 1979, 31, 91–101.

Young, P. T. Hedonic organization and regulation of behavior. *Psychological Review*, 1966, 73, 59–86.

Yuille, J. C., & Cutshall, J. L. A case study of eyewitness memory of a crime. *Journal of Applied Psychology*, 1986, 71, 291–301.

Yuki, G., Wexley, K. N., & Seymore, J. Effectiveness of pay incentives under variable ratio and continuous reinforcement schedules. *Journal of Applied Psychology*, 1972, 56, 10–13.

Zangwell, O. L. Remembering revisited. *Quarterly Journal of Experimental Psychology*, 1972, 24, 123–138.

Zastrow, C. How to become more assertive. In C. Zastrow & D. H. Chang (Eds.), *The personal problem solver*. Englewood Cliffs, N. J.: Prentice-Hall, 1977.

Zeaman, D. Response latency as a function of the amount of reinforcement. *Journal of Experimental Psychology*, 1949, 39, 466–483.

Zeiler, M. D. Stimulus definition and choice. In L. P. Lipsitt & C. C. Spiker (Eds.), *Advances in child development and behavior* (Vol. 3). New York: Academic Press, 1967.

Zeiler, M. D., & Buchman, I. B. Response requirements as constraints on responding. *Journal of the Experimental Analysis of Behavior*, 1979, 32, 29–49.

Zentall, T. R., & Hogan, D. E. Short-term proactive inhibition in the pigeon. *Learning and Motivation*, 1977, 8, 367–386.

Zoladek, L., & Roberts, W. A. The sensory basis of spatial memory in the rat. *Animal Learning and Behavior*, 1978, 6, 77–81.

NAME INDEX

SUBJECT INDEX

A

Acoustic coding, semantic coding versus, 289–290

Acoustic storage, precategorical, 262–263

Acquisition, 73, *73, 74, 75*, 121–123
  contiguity and, 122–123
  extinction as, 76
  of language, 386–388
  practice and, 123
  reinforcement and, 123

ACT, 397–400

Afterimage, 128

Age regression, hypnotic, 144

Alcoholic(s), stimulus generalization and, 82

Alcoholic Korsakoff's syndrome, 312–313

Algebraic summation, discrimination learning and, 208–210, *209*

Algorithms, problem solving and, 374

All-or-none learning, 134–135
  gradual learning versus, 140–148
  Guthrie's and Estes' approaches to, 143, *145*, 145–146

Alpha response, 30

Alzheimer's disease, 312–313

Ambiguity, phrase-structure grammar and, *393*, 393–394

Amnesia, 312–313
  in alcoholic Korsakoff's syndrome, 312–313
  anterograde, 248
  retrograde, *247*, 247–248
  reversible, 248–249

Amount of reinforcement, 164, 178–182
  components of, 178–179
  impulsive behavior and, 182
  insects and, 179–180, *180*
  reinforcement contrast and, 180–181, *181*

Animal(s)
  concept learning and, 368–369
  problem solving and, 380, *380*

Animal memory, 302–308
  delayed-matching-to-sample procedure and, *304*, 304–305
  interference and, 303–304
  recall by category and, 326–327
  serial-pattern learning and, 307–308, *308*
  spatial, *305*, 305–307

Anorexia nervosa, reward training and, 41

Anterograde amnesia, consolidation and, 248

Anxiety, imagery and, 338, *339*, 340, *340*

Apes, language and, 413–415

Approach behavior, imprinting and, 114

Arousal, optimal-arousal-level theories of reinforcement and, 189–190

Artificial intelligence (AI), 348

Assertion training, 53, *54–55*

Associative learning, discrimination and, 217

Associative memory. *See* Human associative memory

Atkinson-Shiffrin buffer model, *258–259, 259*

Attention, 127
  iconic memory and, 262
  stimulus selection and, 325–327

Attributes, 353–355
  learning, *354*, 354–355, *355, 356*

Attributions, learned helplessness and, 45–46

Auditory sensory memory, 261

Automatic processing, controlled processing versus, 155, *156*, 308–309

Autoshaping
  classical conditioning and, 66
  reinforcement schedules and, 172

Averaging, 137–140
  of group versus individual data, 137–139, *138*
  types of, *139*, 139–140, *141*

Aversion therapy. *See also* Taste aversion
  avoidance training and, 44–47, *45*
  bait shyness and, 98–99

Avoidance during imprinting, 115

Avoidance training, 42–47
  aversion therapy and, 44–47, *45*
  bait shyness and, 96
  classical conditioning in, 66
  example of, 42, *43*
  flooding and, 42
  learned helplessness and, 43–44
  relationship to escape training, 48
  relationship to punishment training, 50
  two-factor theory of, 42–43

B

Babbling, 385

Backward conditioning, 28, *29*, 133
  all-or-none position and, 135

Bait shyness, 33, 95–99
  aversion therapy and, 98–99
  avoidance conditioning and, 96
  control of predation and, 98
  preparedness and, 96–97

Basic-level categories, concept learning and, 364